T0212489

# Lecture Notes of the Institute for Computer Sciences, Social Informatics and Telecommunications Engineering 209

More information about this series at http://www.springer.com/series/8197

Qianbin Chen · Weixiao Meng
Liqiang Zhao (Eds.)

# Communications and Networking

11th EAI International Conference, ChinaCom 2016
Chongqing, China, September 24–26, 2016
Proceedings, Part I

 Springer

*Editors*

Qianbin Chen
Post and Telecommunications
Chongqing University
Chongqing
China

Liqiang Zhao
Xidian University
Xi'an
China

Weixiao Meng
Harbin Institute of Technology (HIT)
Harbin
China

ISSN 1867-8211          ISSN 1867-822X  (electronic)
Lecture Notes of the Institute for Computer Sciences, Social Informatics
and Telecommunications Engineering
ISBN 978-3-319-66624-2          ISBN 978-3-319-66625-9  (eBook)
DOI 10.1007/978-3-319-66625-9

Library of Congress Control Number: 2017953406

Printed on acid-free paper

This Springer imprint is published by Springer Nature
The registered company is Springer International Publishing AG
The registered company address is: Gewerbestrasse 11, 6330 Cham, Switzerland

# Preface

On behalf of the Organizing Committee of the 11th EAI International Conference on Communications and Networking in China (ChinaCom 2016), we would like to welcome you to the proceedings of this conference. ChinaCom aims to bring together international researchers and practitioners in networking and communications under one roof, building a showcase of these fields in China. The conference is being positioned as the premier international annual event for the presentation of original and fundamental research advances in the field of communications and networks.

ChinaCom 2016 was jointly hosted by Chongqing University of Posts and Telecommunications and Xidian University during September 24–26, 2016. The conference received 181 paper submissions. Based on peer reviewing, 107 papers were accepted and presented at the conference. We thank all the Technical Program Committee (TPC) members and reviewers for their dedicated efforts.

ChinaCom 2016 featured six keynote speeches, four invited talks, and a comprehensive technical program offering numerous sessions in wireless, networks, and security, etc. About 150 experts and scholars from more than 10 countries and regions including China, the USA, Canada, Singapore, etc., attend this year's conference in Chongqing.

As the youngest municipality of China, Chongqing has become the largest industrial and economic center of the upper Yangtze area. Renowned as the Mountain City and famous for its beautiful and unique spots, Chongqing is a popular destination for travelers from all over the world.

We hope you find reading the papers in this volume a rewarding experience.

August 2017

Yanbin Liu
Yunjie Liu

# Organization

## Steering Committee

| | |
|---|---|
| Imrich Chlamtac | CREATE-NET (Chair) |
| Hsiao-Hwa Chen | National Cheng Kung University, Taiwan |
| Ya-Bin Ye | Huawei Europe Research Cente |
| Zheng Zhou | Beijing University of Posts and Telecommunications, China |
| Bo Li | Hong Kong University of Science and Technology, SAR China |
| Andreas F. Molisch | University of Southern California, USA |
| Jun Zheng | Southeast University |
| Zhi-Feng Zhao | Zhejiang University, China |

## Organizing Committee

### General Chairs

| | |
|---|---|
| Yunjie Liu | Academician of Chinese Academy of Engineering, China Unicom |
| Yanbin Liu | Vice-president, Chongqing University of Posts and Telecommunications, China |

### TPC Chairs

| | |
|---|---|
| Weixiao Meng | Harbin Institute of Technology, China |
| Liqiang Zhao | Xidian University, China |
| Qianbin Chen | Chongqing University of Posts and Telecommunications, China |

### Local Chairs

| | |
|---|---|
| Zufan Zhang | Chongqing University of Posts and Telecommunications, China |
| Jiangtao Luo | Chongqing University of Posts and Telecommunications, China |
| Hongxin Tian | Xidian University, China |
| Zhiyuan Ren | Xidian University, China |

### Sponsorship and Exhibits Chair

| | |
|---|---|
| Qiong Huang | Chongqing University of Posts and Telecommunications, China |

**Publicity and Social Media Chair**

Yang Wang                    Chongqing University of Posts and Telecommunications,
                             China

**Web Chair**

Ting Zhang                   Chongqing University of Posts and Telecommunications,
                             China

**Publication Chair**

Rong Chai                    Chongqing University of Posts and Telecommunications,
                             China

## Conference Manager

Barbara Fertalova (EAI, European Alliance for Innovation)

## TPC Chairs of Chinacom 2016

**TPC Chairs**

Weixiao Meng                 Harbin Institute of Technology, China
Qianbin Chen                 Chongqing University of Posts and Telecommunications,
                             China
Liqiang Zhao                 Xidian University, China

**Symposium Chairs**

**Future Internet and Networks Symposium**

Huaglory Tianfield           Glasgow Caledonian University, UK
Guofeng Zhao                 Chongqing University of Posts and Telecommunications,
                             China

**Mobile and Wireless Communications Symposium**

Lin Dai                      City University of Hong Kong, SAR China
Yunjian Jia                  Chongqing University, China

**Optical Networks and Systems Symposium**

Xingwen Yi                   University of Electronic Science and Technology of China,
                             China
Huanlin Liu                  Chongqing University of Posts and Telecommunications,
                             China

## IoT, Smart Cities, and Big Data Symposium

| | |
|---|---|
| Shensheng Tang | Missouri Western State University, USA |
| Wee Peng Tay | Nanyang Technological University, Singapore |
| Rong Yu | Guangdong University of Technology, China |

## Security Symposium

| | |
|---|---|
| Qing Yang | Montana State University, USA |
| Yi Qian | University of Nebraska Lincoln, USA |
| Jun Huang | Chongqing University of Posts and Telecommunications, China |

# Technical Program Committee

| | |
|---|---|
| Rong Chai | Chongqing University of Posts and Telecommunications, China |
| Hongbin Chen | Guilin University of Electronic Technology, China |
| Zhi Chen | University of Electronic Science and Technology of China |
| Peter Chong | Nanyang Technological University, Singapore |
| Dezun Dong | National University of Defense Technology, China |
| Wei Dong | Zhejiang University, China |
| Jun Fang | University of Electronic Science and Technology of China |
| Zesong Fei | Beijing Institute of Technology, China |
| Feifei Gao | Tsinghua University, China |
| Ping Guo | Chongqing University, China |
| Guoqiang Hu | Nanyang Technological University, Singapore |
| Tao Huang | Beijing University of Posts and Telecommunications, China |
| Xiaoge Huang | Chongqing University of Posts and Telecommunications, China |
| Fan Li | Beijing Institute of Technology, China |
| Zhenyu Li | Institute of Computing Technology, Chinese Academy of Sciences, China |
| Hongbo Liu | Indiana University-Purdue University Indianapolis, USA |
| Hongqing Liu | Chongqing University of Posts and Telecommunications, China |
| Jiang Liu | Beijing University of Posts and Telecommunications, China |
| Qiang Liu | University of Electronic Science and Technology of China, China |
| Wenping Liu | Hubei University of Economic, China |
| Rongxing Lu | Nanyang Technological University, Singapore |
| Yilin Mo | Nanyang Technological University, Singapore |
| Jianquan Ouyang | Xiangtan University, China |
| Tian Pan | Beijing University of Posts and Telecommunications, China |

# Contents – Part I

**Signal Detection and Estimation**

# Contents – Part II

**Network Architecture and SDN**

**Signal Detection and Estimation (2)**

## Heterogeneous Networks

## Internet of Things

## Hardware Design and Implementation

## Mobility Management

## SDN and Clouds

## Navigation, Tracking and Localization

## FMN

# Technical Sessions

# Transceiver Optimization in Full Duplex SWIPT Systems with Physical Layer Security

Ruijin Sun, Ying Wang$^{(\boxtimes)}$, and Xinshui Wang

State Key Laboratory of Networking and Switching Technology,
Beijing University of Posts and Telecommunications,
Beijing 100876, People's Republic of China
wangying@bupt.edu.cn

**Abstract.** To meet the requirements of energy saving, high security and high speed for the next generation wireless networks, this paper investigates simultaneous wireless information and power transfer (SWIPT) in full duplex systems taking the physical layer security into account. Specifically, we consider a full duplex wireless system where a full duplex base station (FD-BS) communicates with one downlink user and one uplink user simultaneously, and one idle user also scavenges the radio-frequency (RF) energy broadcasted during the communication for future use. Since the idle user has great potential to intercept the downlink information, we assume that FD-BS exploits the artificial noise (AN), which is another energy source to idle user, to prevent it. The imperfect self-interference cancellation at the FD-BS is considered and the zero forcing (ZF) receiver is adopted to cancel the residual self-interference. Then, the optimal transmitter design at FD-BS are derived to maximize the weighted sum rate of downlink secure and uplink transmission, subject to constraints that the transmission power at FD-BS is restricted and the minimal amount of harvested energy at idle user is guaranteed. The perfect full duplex and half duplex schemes are also introduced for comparison. Extensive simulation results are given to verify the superiority of our proposed full duplex scheme.

**Keywords:** Full duplex system · SWIPT · Physical layer security · Semidefinite program · Convex optimization

## 1 Introduction

Recently, with the exponential surge of energy consumption in wireless communication, green communications have received much attention from both industry and academic. As a promising technology towards green communications, harvesting the ambient radio-frequency (RF) energy can prolong the lifetime of energy-constrained wireless networks. More importantly, scavenging energy from the far-field RF signal transmission enables simultaneous wireless information and power transfer (SWIPT) [1]. Typically, there exist fundamental tradeoffs between harvested energy and received information rate. Many works focused

© ICST Institute for Computer Sciences, Social Informatics and Telecommunications Engineering 2018
Q. Chen et al. (Eds.): ChinaCom 2016, Part I, LNICST 209, pp. 3–13, 2018.
DOI: 10.1007/978-3-319-66625-9_1

on downlink SWIPT systems where a transmitter serves two kinds of receivers, i.e., information decoding receivers (IRs) and energy harvesting receivers (ERs). Based on this scenario, joint information beamforming for IRs and energy beamforming for ERs were investigated [2,3]. In particular, to meet the different power sensitivity requirements of energy harvesting (EH) and information decoding (ID) (e.g., −10 dBm for EH versus −60 dBm for ID), a location-based receiver scheduling scheme was proposed in [3], where ERs need to be closer to the transmitter than IRs. This scheme indeed facilitates the energy harvesting at ERs since they always have better channels due to distance-dependent attenuation.

However, this receiver scheduling scheme may also increase the susceptibility to eavesdropping, because that ERs, the potential eavesdroppers, can more easily overhear the information sent to IRs. In traditional communication networks without energy harvesting, this security issue can be addressed from the physical layer perspective, by transmitting additional artificial noise (AN) to degrade the channel of eavesdroppers [4]. When it comes to downlink SWIPT systems, the power stream for energy supply can naturally serve as AN to prevent eavesdropping. Thus, secure communication in downlink systems with SWIPT was studied [5]. In [5], Liu et al. presented a system secrecy rate maximization problem and a weighted sum-harvested-energy maximization problem via the joint design of information and energy beamforming.

Apart from energy saving and high information security, high information speed is also a main objective of next generation wireless communications. To this end, full duplex, which has the potential to double the system spectral efficiency, has aroused researchers' wide concern. The benefits are intuitively brought by allowing signal transmission and reception at the same time and the same frequency. Recently, the strong self-interference (SI) that full duplex systems suffer from can been greatly suppressed via the effective self-interference cancellation (SIC) techniques, such as antenna separation, analog domain suppression and digital domain suppression [6]. Consequently, a majority of researches on full duplex systems have been investigated, including the re-designed SIC [7] and spectral efficiency analysis [8].

In order to meet the requirements of energy saving, high security as well as high speed for the next generation wireless networks, in this paper, we study full duplex SWIPT systems with the physical layer security. Specifically, we consider a full duplex wireless system where the full duplex base station (FD-BS) communicates with one downlink user and one uplink user simultaneously, and one idle user scavenges the RF energy broadcasted during the communication for future use. Since the idle user has the great potential to intercept the downlink information, we assume that FD-BS exploits the artificial noise (AN), which is another energy source to idle user, to prevent it. Similar to full duplex communication systems [8], the proposed secrecy SWIPT full duplex scenario is also subject to the practical issue of imperfect SIC at the FD-BS. To reduce the computational complexity, the optimal transmitter design with the fixed zero forcing (ZF) receiver at FD-BS are derived to maximize the weighted sum rate of downlink secure and uplink transmission, subject to constraints that the transmission power at FD-BS is restricted and the minimal amount of harvested energy at idle user is guaranteed. The objective function of original non-convex optimization is transformed into a linear fractional form by introducing an non-negative parameter. Then, by applying Charnes-Cooper transformation, semi-definite programming (SDP) and the bi-search method, the optimal parameter as well as optimal transmitter design is achieved. Simulation results are given to verify the superiority of our proposed full duplex scheme.

The remainder of the paper is organized as follows. In Sect. 2, system model and problem formulation are introduced. In Sect. 3 we state the ZF receiver based optimal transmitter optimization. Finally, the simulation results are presented in Sect. 4 before Sect. 5 concludes the paper.

*Notation:* Bold lower and upper case letters are used to denote column vectors and matrices, respectively. The superscripts $\mathbf{H}^T$, $\mathbf{H}^H$, $\mathbf{H}^{-1}$ are standard transpose, (Hermitian) conjugate transpose and inverse of $\mathbf{H}$, respectively. $\text{rank}(\mathbf{S})$ and $\text{Tr}(\mathbf{S})$ denote the rank and trace of matrix $\mathbf{S}$, respectively. $\mathbf{S} \succeq \mathbf{0}(\succ \mathbf{0})$ means that matrix $\mathbf{S}$ is positive semidefinite (positive definite).

## 2    System Model and Problem Formulation

Considering a full-duplex system where one FD-BS, one uplink user $(U_U)$, one downlink user $(U_D)$ and one idle user $(U_I)$ are included, as illustrated in Fig. 1. The FD-BS concurrently communicates with $U_D$ in the downlink and $U_U$ in the uplink . Meanwhile, the idle user scavenges the RF energy broadcasted during the communication. Assume that FD-BS has $N = N_T + N_R$ antennas, of which $N_T$ are used for downlink transmission and $N_R$ are used for uplink receiving. Other users in the system all have a single antenna due to the hardware limitation. Suppose that FD-BS knows all the channel state information (CSI). The idle user also feedbacks its CSI to FD-BS for the purpose of harvesting more energy.

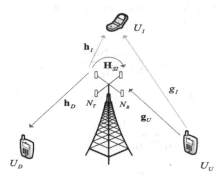

**Fig. 1.** System Model

In order to facilitate energy harvesting, the idle user is assumed to be deployed in more proximity to the FD-BS than the downlink and uplink user.

Thus, signals transmitted by FD-BS is a dominant part of the signals received at idle user. It becomes more easier for the vicious idle user to eavesdrop the information sent by FD-BS. Consequently, in this paper, we mainly prevent the eavesdropping in the downlink channel.

To prevent the eavesdropping, AN is adopted at FD-BS. The transmit message broadcasted by FD-BS is then given as

$$\mathbf{x}_D = \mathbf{s}_D + \mathbf{v}, \tag{1}$$

where $\mathbf{s}_D \in \mathbb{C}^{N_T \times 1}$ is the useful signal vector for $U_D$ and $\mathbf{s}_D \sim \mathcal{CN}(\mathbf{0}, \mathbf{S})$ with the covariance matrix $\mathbf{S} \succeq \mathbf{0}$. $\mathbf{v} \in \mathbb{C}^{N_T \times 1}$ is the AN vector with $\mathbf{v} \sim \mathcal{CN}(\mathbf{0}, \mathbf{V})$ and $\mathbf{V} \succeq \mathbf{0}$. Note that AN also provides another energy source for the idle user.

The data symbol sent by $U_U$ is $s_U \sim \mathcal{CN}(0, 1)$ and its transmission power is $P_U$. Hence, denote the message sent by $U_U$ as

$$x_U = \sqrt{P_U} s_U. \tag{2}$$

The observations at $U_D$ and $U_I$ are respectively represented as

$$y_D = \mathbf{h}_D^H \mathbf{s}_D + \mathbf{h}_D^H \mathbf{v} + z_D \tag{3}$$

and

$$y_I = \mathbf{h}_I^H \mathbf{s}_D + \mathbf{h}_I^H \mathbf{v} + \underbrace{g_I x_U}_{UN} + z_I, \tag{4}$$

where $\mathbf{h}_D \in \mathbb{C}^{N_T \times 1}$ and $\mathbf{h}_I \in \mathbb{C}^{N_T \times 1}$ denote the channel vector from FD-BS to $U_D$ and $U_I$, respectively. $g_I$ represents the complex channel coefficient from $U_U$ to $U_I$. $z_D \sim \mathcal{CN}(0, \sigma_Z^2)$ and $z_I \sim \mathcal{CN}(0, \sigma_Z^2)$ are the corresponding background noise at $U_D$ and $U_I$, respectively. In this paper, we assume that the scheduled $U_D$ and $U_U$ are far from each other and thus ignore the co-channel interference (CCI) from $U_U$ to $U_D$. Note that the third term in (4) also plays as noise to avoid malicious eavesdropping and thus we call it as uplink noise (UN).

The received signal to interference plus noise ratio (SINR) at $U_D$ is given by

$$\gamma_D = \frac{\mathbf{h}_D^H \mathbf{S} \mathbf{h}_D}{\mathbf{h}_D^H \mathbf{V} \mathbf{h}_D + \sigma_Z^2}. \tag{5}$$

The SINR at vicious idle user $U_I$ is given by

$$\gamma_I = \frac{\mathbf{h}_I^H \mathbf{S} \mathbf{h}_I}{\mathbf{h}_I^H \mathbf{V} \mathbf{h}_I + P_U |g_I|^2 + \sigma_Z^2}. \tag{6}$$

Thus, the achievable secrecy rate at downlink user $U_D$ is represented as

$$R_D^{\text{sec}}(\mathbf{S}, \mathbf{V}) = \log_2(1 + \gamma_D) - \log_2(1 + \gamma_I)$$
$$= \log_2\left(1 + \frac{\mathbf{h}_D^H \mathbf{S} \mathbf{h}_D}{\mathbf{h}_D^H \mathbf{V} \mathbf{h}_D + \sigma_Z^2}\right) - \log_2\left(1 + \frac{\mathbf{h}_I^H \mathbf{S} \mathbf{h}_I}{\mathbf{h}_I^H \mathbf{V} \mathbf{h}_I + P_U |g_I|^2 + \sigma_Z^2}\right). \tag{7}$$

Meanwhile, the amount of harvested energy at $U_I$ is expressed as

$$E = \zeta \left( \mathbf{h}_I^H \mathbf{S} \mathbf{h}_I + \mathbf{h}_I^H \mathbf{V} \mathbf{h}_I + P_U |g_I|^2 \right), \tag{8}$$

where $0 < \zeta \leqslant 1$ is the RF energy conversion efficiency.

Next, for the uplink channel, we denote the received signal vector at FD-BS as

$$y_U = \mathbf{w}_R^H \mathbf{g}_U \sqrt{P_U} s_U + \underbrace{\mathbf{w}_R^H \mathbf{H}_{SI} (\mathbf{s}_D + \mathbf{v})}_{SI} + \mathbf{w}_R^H \mathbf{z}_U, \tag{9}$$

where $\mathbf{g}_U \in \mathbb{C}^{N_R \times 1}$ is the complex channel vector from the FD-BS to $U_U$ and $z_U \sim \mathcal{CN}(0, \sigma_Z^2 \mathbf{I}_{N_R})$ is the noise vector. $\mathbf{w}_R \in \mathbb{C}^{N_R \times 1}$ is the receive beamforming at FD-BS and the matrix $\mathbf{H}_{SI} \in \mathbb{C}^{N_R \times N_T}$ is the self-interference (SI) channel from the transmit antennas to the receive antennas at FD-BS.

Thus, the uplink channel information rate and SINR can be respectively given by

$$R_U(\mathbf{S}, \mathbf{V}, \mathbf{w}_R) = \log_2 (1 + \gamma_U) \tag{10}$$

and

$$\gamma_U = \frac{P_U \left| \mathbf{w}_R^H \mathbf{g}_U \right|^2}{\mathbf{w}_R^H \mathbf{H}_{SI} \mathbf{S} \mathbf{H}_{SI}^H \mathbf{w}_R + \mathbf{w}_R^H \mathbf{H}_{SI} \mathbf{V} \mathbf{H}_{SI}^H \mathbf{w}_R + \sigma_z^2 \|\mathbf{w}_R\|_2^2}. \tag{11}$$

From (3), (4) and (9), we observe that the secure downlink and uplink transmission are coupled by the SI and the UN. Since we assume that $U_I$ is interested in the information of FD-BS, the downlink secrecy rate and the uplink rate are two main objectives we desire to optimize. In order to achieve a tradeoff between them, the weighted sum rate of the secure downlink and uplink transmission, which is a very common and useful method to address the multi-objective optimization problem, are maximized in this paper. In particular, the problem is expressed as

$$\mathcal{P}1: \quad \max_{\mathbf{S}, \mathbf{V}, \|\mathbf{w}_R\|^2 = 1} \quad w_D R_D^{\text{sec}}(\mathbf{S}, \mathbf{V}) + w_U R_U(\mathbf{S}, \mathbf{V}, \mathbf{w}_R) \tag{12a}$$

$$\text{s. t.} \quad \text{Tr}(\mathbf{S}) + \text{Tr}(\mathbf{V}) \leqslant P_{BS}, \tag{12b}$$

$$\zeta \left( \mathbf{h}_I^H \mathbf{S} \mathbf{h}_I + \mathbf{h}_I^H \mathbf{V} \mathbf{h}_I + P_U |g_I|^2 \right) \geqslant e^2, \tag{12c}$$

where $P_{BS}$ is the allowable transmission power at the FD-BS and $e^2$ is the minimal amount of energy harvested by idle user $U_I$. $w_D$ and $w_U$ are the positive downlink and uplink weighted factors, respectively. (12b) and (12c) are the power constraint at FD-BS and harvested energy constraint at $U_I$, respectively.

According to [2], the feasible condition of problem $\mathcal{P}1$ is $e^2 \leqslant \zeta(P_{BS} \|\mathbf{h}_I\|_2^2 + P_U |g_I|^2)$. Throughout this paper, we consider the non-trivial case where the positive downlink secrecy rate is achievable.

## 3    Optimal Transmitter Design with ZF Receiver

Under the assumption of $N_R > N_T$, ZF receiver is designed to cancel the SI at the FD-BS perfectly, i.e., $\mathbf{w}_R^H \mathbf{H}_{SI} \mathbf{S} \mathbf{H}_{SI}^H \mathbf{w}_R + \mathbf{w}_R^H \mathbf{H}_{SI} \mathbf{V} \mathbf{H}_{SI}^H \mathbf{w}_R = 0$. It also means that $\mathbf{H}_{SI}^H \mathbf{w}_R = \mathbf{0}$. Via the singular value decomposition (SVD) method, $\mathbf{H}_{SI}^H$ can be expressed as

$$\mathbf{H}_{SI}^H = \mathbf{U} \boldsymbol{\Lambda} \mathbf{V}'^H = \mathbf{U} \boldsymbol{\Lambda} [\hat{\mathbf{V}} \ \tilde{\mathbf{V}}]^H, \tag{13}$$

where $\mathbf{U} \in \mathbb{C}^{N_T \times N_T}$ and $\mathbf{V}' \in \mathbb{C}^{N_R \times N_R}$ are unitary matrices, $\boldsymbol{\Lambda}$ is a $N_T \times N_R$ rectangular diagonal matrix. In addition, $\hat{\mathbf{V}} \in \mathbb{C}^{N_R \times N_T}$ and $\tilde{\mathbf{V}} \in \mathbb{C}^{N_R \times (N_R - N_T)}$ is made up of the first $N_T$ and the last $N_R - N_T$ right singular vectors of $\mathbf{H}_{SI}^H$, respectively. Note that $\tilde{\mathbf{V}}$ with $\tilde{\mathbf{V}}^H \tilde{\mathbf{V}} = \mathbf{I}$ forms an orthogonal basis for the null space of $\mathbf{H}_{SI}^H$. Hence, to satisfy $\mathbf{H}_{SI}^H \mathbf{w}_R = \mathbf{0}$, $\mathbf{w}_R$ is expressed as:

$$\mathbf{w}_R = \tilde{\mathbf{V}} \tilde{\mathbf{w}}_R. \tag{14}$$

Notice that design of $\tilde{\mathbf{w}}_R$ is only related to uplink transmission after SI cancellation. It can be shown that to maximize the uplink rate, $\tilde{\mathbf{w}}_R$ should be aligned to the same direction as the equivalent channel $\tilde{\mathbf{V}}^H \mathbf{g}_U$, i.e., $\tilde{\mathbf{w}}_R^* = \frac{\tilde{\mathbf{V}}^H \mathbf{g}_U}{\|\tilde{\mathbf{V}}^H \mathbf{g}_U\|}$. Then the achievable uplink rate is expressed as

$$R_U^{ZF} = \log_2 \left( 1 + \frac{P_U \left\| \tilde{\mathbf{V}}^H \mathbf{g}_U \right\|^2}{\sigma_z^2} \right). \tag{15}$$

It is observed that the uplink channel rate, $R_U^{ZF}$, is independent of transmitter design with the ZF receiver, which simplifies the problem $\mathcal{P}1$.

Next, we only focus on the maximization of secrecy downlink rate. According to [14], the original problem $\mathcal{P}1$ without uplink rate is equivalent to following $\mathcal{P}2$ with the optimal SINR constraint $\gamma_i$.

$$\mathcal{P}2: \quad \max_{\mathbf{S}, \mathbf{V}} \quad \frac{\mathrm{Tr}(\mathbf{H}_D \mathbf{S})}{\mathrm{Tr}(\mathbf{H}_D \mathbf{V}) + \sigma_Z^2} \tag{16a}$$

$$\text{s. t.} \quad \mathrm{Tr}(\mathbf{H}_I \mathbf{S}) \leqslant \gamma_i \left[ \mathrm{Tr}(\mathbf{H}_I \mathbf{V}) + P_U |g_I|^2 + \sigma_Z^2 \right], \tag{16b}$$

$$\mathrm{Tr}(\mathbf{S}) + \mathrm{Tr}(\mathbf{V}) \leqslant P_{BS}, \tag{16c}$$

$$\mathrm{Tr}(\mathbf{H}_I \mathbf{S}) + \mathrm{Tr}(\mathbf{H}_I \mathbf{V}) + P_U |g_I|^2 \geqslant e^2 / \varsigma, \tag{16d}$$

where $\mathbf{H}_D = \mathbf{h}_D \mathbf{h}_D^H$, $\mathbf{H}_I = \mathbf{h}_I \mathbf{h}_I^H$, and $\gamma_i$ is an introducing positive variable. However, it is still a non-convex optimization problem due to the linear fractional objective function.

From Charnes-Cooper transformation [10], we define $\bar{\mathbf{S}} = \rho\mathbf{S}$, $\bar{\mathbf{V}} = \rho\mathbf{V}$ and rewrite the problem $\mathcal{P}2$ in terms of $\bar{\mathbf{S}}$ and $\bar{\mathbf{V}}$.

$$\mathcal{P}2.1: \quad \max_{\bar{\mathbf{S}},\bar{\mathbf{V}},\rho} \quad \mathrm{Tr}(\mathbf{H}_D\bar{\mathbf{S}}) \tag{17a}$$

$$\text{s. t.} \quad \mathrm{Tr}(\mathbf{H}_D\bar{\mathbf{V}}) + \rho\sigma_Z^2 = 1, \tag{17b}$$

$$\mathrm{Tr}(\mathbf{H}_I\bar{\mathbf{S}}) - \gamma_i\,\mathrm{Tr}(\mathbf{H}_I\bar{\mathbf{V}}) - \rho\gamma_i\left(P_U|g_I|^2 + \sigma_Z^2\right) \leqslant 0, \tag{17c}$$

$$\mathrm{Tr}(\bar{\mathbf{S}}) + \mathrm{Tr}(\bar{\mathbf{V}}) - \rho P_{BS} \leqslant 0, \tag{17d}$$

$$\mathrm{Tr}(\mathbf{H}_I\bar{\mathbf{S}}) + \mathrm{Tr}(\mathbf{H}_I\bar{\mathbf{V}}) + \rho P_U|g_I|^2 - \rho e^2/\zeta \geqslant 0, \tag{17e}$$

$$\rho > 0. \tag{17f}$$

This is a convex SDP problem[1] and hence can be solved by CVX [11].

By denoting its objective value as $h(\gamma_i)$, the original problem $\mathcal{P}1$ without uplink rate becomes $\max_{\gamma_i \geqslant 0} w_D \log_2\left(\frac{1+h(\gamma_i)}{1+\gamma_i}\right)$. Clearly, it is the same as $\max_{\gamma_i \geqslant 0} f(\gamma_i) = \frac{1+h(\gamma_i)}{1+\gamma_i}$.

**Proposition 1:** $f(\gamma_i)$ is quasi-concave in $\gamma_i$ and its maximum can be found through a one-dimensional search.

**Proof:** We first prove that $h(\gamma_i)$ is concave in $\gamma_i$. Let $\lambda$, $\mu$, $\nu$, $\theta$ denote the dual variables of the corresponding constraints in problem $\mathcal{P}2.1$, respectively. Then the Lagrangian function of problem $\mathcal{P}2.1$ is given by

$$L(\bar{\mathbf{S}}, \bar{\mathbf{V}}, \rho, \lambda, \mu, \nu, \theta, \gamma_i) = \mathrm{Tr}(\mathbf{A}\bar{\mathbf{S}}) + \mathrm{Tr}(\mathbf{B}\bar{\mathbf{V}}) + \eta\rho + \lambda \tag{18}$$

where

$$\mathbf{A} = \mathbf{H}_D - \mu\mathbf{H}_I + \nu\mathbf{I} + \theta\mathbf{H}_I, \tag{19}$$

$$\mathbf{B} = -\lambda\mathbf{H}_D + \mu\gamma_i\mathbf{H}_I - \nu\mathbf{I} + \theta\mathbf{H}_I \tag{20}$$

and

$$\eta = -\lambda\sigma_Z^2 + \mu\gamma_i\left(P_U|g_I|^2 + \sigma_Z^2\right) + \nu P_{BS} + \theta\left(P_U|g_I|^2 - e^2/\zeta\right). \tag{21}$$

The Lagrangian dual function is given by

$$g(\lambda, \mu, \nu, \theta, \gamma_i) = \max_{\bar{\mathbf{S}}\succ\mathbf{0},\bar{\mathbf{V}}\succ\mathbf{0},\rho>0} L(\bar{\mathbf{S}}, \bar{\mathbf{V}}, \rho, \lambda, \mu, \nu, \theta, \gamma_i). \tag{22}$$

Since $\mathcal{P}2.1$ is a convex problem and satisfies the slater's condition, the strong duality holds. Thus, $h(\gamma_i) = \min_{\lambda,\mu,\nu,\theta} g(\lambda, \mu, \nu, \theta, \gamma_i)$. It is easily verified that $h(\gamma_i)$ is a point-wise minimum of a family of affine function and hence concave for $\gamma_i > 0$ [12].

---

[1]  It has been proved in [5] that, there exist $\bar{\mathbf{S}}^*$ and $\bar{\mathbf{V}}^*$ which satisfy $\mathrm{rank}(\bar{\mathbf{S}}^*) = 1$ and $\mathrm{rank}(\bar{\mathbf{V}}^*) = 1$.

Then, we use the definition of quasi-concave to prove that $f(\gamma_i)$ is quasi-concave. The superlevel set of function $f(\gamma_i)$ is $\{\gamma_i | 1 + h(\gamma_i) \geqslant \alpha(1 + \gamma_i)\}$ which is a convex set due to the concavity of $h(\gamma_i)$. So $f(\gamma_i)$ is a quasi-concave function in $\gamma_i$ and its maximum can be found through a one-dimensional search. This completes the proposition.                                                              □

In order to find the optimal $\gamma_i$, we take the gradient of $f(\gamma_i)$, i.e.,

$$\frac{df(\gamma_i)}{d\gamma_i} = \frac{(1 + \gamma_i)h'(\gamma_i) - (1 + h(\gamma_i))}{(1 + \gamma_i)^2}. \tag{23}$$

As analyzed before, we have $h(\gamma_i) = L(\bar{\mathbf{S}}^*, \bar{\mathbf{V}}^*, \rho^*, \lambda^*, \mu^*, \nu^*, \theta^*, \gamma_i)$, where $\bar{\mathbf{S}}^*, \bar{\mathbf{V}}^*, \rho^*$ are the optimal primary variables and $\lambda^*, \mu^*, \nu^*, \theta^*$ are the optimal dual variables for a given $\gamma_i$, respectively. With (18), the gradient of $h(\gamma_i)$ can be expressed as

$$\frac{dh(\gamma_i)}{d\gamma_i} = \mathrm{Tr}(\mu^* \mathbf{H}_I \bar{\mathbf{V}}^*) + \mu^*(P_U |g_I|^2 + \sigma_Z^2)\rho^*. \tag{24}$$

Above all, problem $\mathcal{P}2$ can be solved in two steps: (i) Given any $\gamma_i > 0$, we first solve the Problem $\mathcal{P}2.1$ to obtain $h(\gamma_i)$ and $f(\gamma_i)$; (ii) Then, we use the bisection method to find optimal $\gamma_i$ by using the gradient of $f(\gamma_i)$. Repeat these two procedures until problem converges. Detailed steps of proposed algorithm are outlined in Algorithm 1. Different from Algorithm 1, the global optimization solution to the problem $\mathcal{P}2$ can be achieved by Algorithm 1.

---

**Algorithm 1.** SDP based bisection method for problem $\mathcal{P}2$

---

1: Initialize $\gamma_i^{\min}$, $\gamma_i^{\max}$ and tolerance $\varepsilon$;
2: **while** $\gamma_i^{\max} - \gamma_i^{\min} > \varepsilon$ **do**
3:     $\gamma_i := (\gamma_i^{\min} + \gamma_i^{\max})/2$;
4:     solve problem $\mathcal{P}2.1$ by CVX to obtain $\bar{\mathbf{S}}^*$, $\bar{\mathbf{V}}^*$, $\rho^*$, $\lambda^*$, $\mu^*$, $\nu^*$ and $\theta^*$;
5:     Calculate $\frac{df(\gamma_i)}{d\gamma_i}$ according to (23) and (24);
6:     **if** $\frac{df(\gamma_i)}{d\gamma_i} \geqslant 0$ **then**
7:         $\gamma_i^{\min} := \gamma_i$;
8:     **else**
9:         $\gamma_i^{\max} := \gamma_i$;
10:    **end if**
11: **end while**
12: **return** $\mathbf{S}^* = \bar{\mathbf{S}}^*/\rho^*$, $\mathbf{V}^* = \bar{\mathbf{V}}^*/\rho^*$.

---

## 4   Simulation Results

In this section, computer simulation results are presented. Throughout the simulations, the transmission power of FD-BS is set as $P_{BS} = 10\,\mathrm{W}$. The number of antennas at FD-BS is $N = 6$. We set $N_T = 2$, $N_R = 4$. The uplink user transmission power is set as 1 W. The energy harvesting efficiency is set as 50% and the weighted factors of downlink and uplink transmission are equal to 1 for simplicity. We assume that the noise power is the same and equals to $-80\,\mathrm{dB}$. The channel attenuation from FD-BS to downlink user and uplink user is both $70\,\mathrm{dB}$, and the channel attenuation from FD-BS to idle user is $50\,\mathrm{dB}$. These channel entries are independently generated from i.i.d Rayleigh fading with the respective average power values. Moreover, the elements of $\mathbf{H}_{SI}$ is assumed to be $\mathcal{CN}(0, \sigma_{SI}^2)$, where $\sigma_{SI}^2$ is decided by the capability of the SIC techniques and is also equivalent to the negative value of self-interference channel attenuation.

In addition to the proposed full duplex scheme, the perfect full duplex scheme and the half duplex scheme are also introduced for comparison. The perfect full duplex scheme means that the SI is perfectly canceled by SIC techniques. In the half duplex scheme, all $N = 6$ antennas are used for data transmission/reception in 1/2 time slot. All results in this section are obtained by averaging over 100 independent channel realizations. Note that whenever a channel realization or a parameter setting makes the problem infeasible, the achievable sum rate is set to zero.

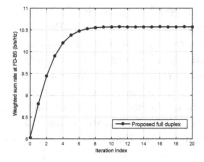

**Fig. 2.** Convergence rate with $N_T = 2$, $N_R = 4$ and $\sigma_{SI}^2 = -90\,\mathrm{dB}$, $e^2 = -20\,\mathrm{dBm}$

At first, we illustrate the convergence of proposed Algorithm 1 in Fig. 2 with $\sigma_{SI}^2 = -90\,\mathrm{dB}$, $e^2 = -20\,\mathrm{dBm}$. Each point on the curves of Fig. 2 records the optimal sum rate achieved at each iteration. It is shown that the Algorithm 1 converges to the optimal value within several iterations.

The impact of the minimum energy requirement on the weighted sum rate for different schemes are shown in Fig. 3 with $\sigma_{SI}^2 = -90\,\mathrm{dB}$ . Note that the achieved weighted sum rate of FD-BS decreases with the increasing of the energy demand. What is more, both the proposed full duplex scheme and the perfect full duplex scheme greatly outperform half duplex scheme when $e^2 < -13\,\mathrm{dBm}$. However, their performances are slightly worse than that of half duplex when $e^2 > -12\,\mathrm{dBm}$. The reason is that it is easier for the half duplex scheme with $N = 6$ downlink antennas in 1/2 time slot than the full duplex schemes with

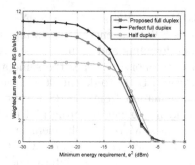

**Fig. 3.** The impact of the minimum energy requirement on the weighted sum rate for different schemes with $N_T = 4$, $N_R = 2$ and $\sigma_{SI}^2 = -90\,\text{dB}$

$N_T = 2$ downlink antennas in one time slot to satisfy the minimum energy requirement.

## 5   Conclusion

In this paper, we have designed a transceiver scheme for full duplex SWIPT with physical layer security. In the system, FD-BS is able to receive date from one uplink user and concurrently transmit data to one downlink user, and one idle user scavenges the RF signals energy. Since the idle user has great potential to intercept the downlink information, we have assumed that FD-BS exploits the artificial noise (AN), which is another energy source to idle user, to prevent it. The weighted sum rate of the secure downlink and uplink transmission has been maximized given the maximal allowable transmission power and the minimal harvested energy requirement. Extensive numerical experiments have been carried out to evaluate the sum rate performance of our proposed schemes.

**Acknowledgment.** This work was supported by National Natural Science Foundation of China (Project 61431003, 61421061) and National 863 Project 2014AA01A705.

## References

1. Varshney, L.R.: Transporting information and energy simultaneously. In: IEEE Information Theory (ISIT), pp. 1612–1616 (2008)
2. Zhang, R., Ho, C.K.: MIMO broadcasting for simultaneous wireless information and power transfer. IEEE Trans. Wirel. Commun. **12**(5), 1989–2001 (2013)
3. Xu, J., Liu, L., Zhang, R.: Multiuser MISO beamforming for simultaneous wireless information and power transfer. IEEE Trans. Signal Process. **62**(18), 4798–4810 (2014)
4. Goel, S., Negi, R.: Guaranteeing secrecy using artificial noise. IEEE Trans. Wirel. Commun. **7**(6), 2180–2189 (2008)
5. Liu, L., Zhang, R., Chua, K.-C.: Secrecy wireless information and power transfer with MISO beamforming. IEEE Trans. Signal Process. **62**(7), 1850–1863 (2014)

6. Duarte, M., Sabharwal, A.: Full-duplex wireless communications using off-the-shelf: feasibility and first results. In: IEEE Signals, Systems and Computers (ASILO-MAR), pp. 1558–1562 (2010)

7. Ahmed, E., Eltawil, A.M., Sabharwal, A.: Self-interference cancellation with phase noise induced ICI suppression for full-duplex systems. In: IEEE Global Communications Conference (GLOBECOM), pp. 3384–3388 (2013)

8. Wang, Y., Sun, R., Wang, X.: Transceiver design to maximize the weighted sum secrecy rate in full-duplex SWIPT systems. IEEE Signal Process. Lett. 23(6), 883–887 (2016)

9. Zhang, L., Zhang, R., Liang, Y.-C., Xin, Y., Cui, S.: On the relationship between the multi-antenna secrecy communications and cognitive radio communications. IEEE Trans. Commun. 58(6), 1877–1886 (2010)

10. Charnes, A., Cooper, W.W.: Programming with linear fractional functionals. Nav. Res. Logist. Q. 9(3), 181–186 (1962). quarterly

11. Grant, M., Boyd, S.: CVX: Matlab software for disciplined convex programming, Version 1.22. http://cvxr.com/cvx

12. Boyd, S., Vandenberghe, L.: Convex Optimization. Cambridge University Press, Cambridge (2004)

# Robust Secure Transmission Scheme in MISO Interference Channel with Simultaneous Wireless Information and Power Transfer

Chong Xue[1(✉)], Jian Xiao[1], Sai Zhao[2], Jingrong Zhou[3], and Maoxin Tian[1]

[1] School of Electronics and Information Technology, Sun Yat-sen University,
Guangzhou 510006, Guangdong, China
`xuech6@mail2.sysu.edu.cn`
[2] School of Mechanical and Electrical Engineering, Guangzhou University,
Guangzhou 510006, Guangdong, China
[3] Huawei Technologies Co. Ltd., Shenzhen 518129, Guangdong, China

**Abstract.** Considering simultaneous wireless information and power transfer (SWIPT), we investigate robust secure transmission scheme in two-user multiple-input-single-output interference channels, where channel uncertainties are modeled by worst-case model. Our objective is to maximize the worst-case sum secrecy rate under individual transmit power constraints and worst-case energy harvest (EH) constraints. We propose an alternative optimization (AO) based algorithm to solve the robust secure transmission problem, and we can obtain a closed form solution in the process of AO algorithm. Simulation results demonstrate that our proposed robust secure transmission scheme has significant performance gain over the non-robust one.

**Keywords:** Simultaneous wireless information and power transfer (SWIPT) · Energy harvest (EH) · Security · Interference channel (IFC) · Multiple-input-single-output (MISO)

## 1 Introduction

Recently, a unified study on simultaneous wireless information and power transfer (SWIPT) has drawn significant attention, which is not only theoretically intricate but also practically valuable for enabling both the wireless data and wireless energy access to mobile terminals at the same time. For two-user single-input-single-output (SISO), MISO, and multiple-input-multiple-output (MIMO) interference channels (IFCs), SWIPT schemes were invested in [1,2].

Due to the openness of wireless transmission medium and the inherent randomness of wireless channel, radio transmission is vulnerable to attacks from unexpected eavesdroppers [3,4]. Secure communications in MISO SWIPT systems were derived in [4,5] where perfect channel state information (CSI) was considered. In practice, it is difficult to obtain perfect CSI because of channel

© ICST Institute for Computer Sciences, Social Informatics and Telecommunications Engineering 2018
Q. Chen et al. (Eds.): ChinaCom 2016, Part I, LNICST 209, pp. 14–23, 2018.
DOI: 10.1007/978-3-319-66625-9_2

estimation and quantization errors. Considering the worst-case channel uncertainties, the robust secure beamforming scheme with SWIPT in MISO channels was proposed in [6].

In this paper, we investigate robust secure transmission scheme in two-user multiple-input-single-output (MISO) interference channels, where channel uncertainties are modeled by worst-case model. Our objective is to maximize the worst-case sum secrecy rate under individual transmit power constraints and worst-case energy harvest (EH) constraints. The formulated optimization problem is nonconvex and we propose an alternative optimization (AO) based algorithm to solve the robust secure transmission problem, and we can obtain a closed form solution in the process of AO algorithm.

## 2    System Model and Problem Formulation

**A**. *System Model*
Consider a two-user MISO IFC system with SWIPT which consists of two transmitters, two ID receivers, a eavesdropper and K EH receivers. Each transmitter is equipped with $N$ antennas. Each energy receiver and the eavesdropper are equipped with single antenna. Each ID receiver decodes the information sent from its correspondence transmitter whereas each EH receiver harvests energy from both transmitters. The eavesdropper decodes the information sent from the two transmitters. Denote the channel responses from transmitter $i$ to ID receiver $j$, energy receiver $k$ and eavesdropper $e$ as $\mathbf{h}_{ij} \in \mathbb{C}^N \times 1$, $\mathbf{g}_{ik} \in \mathbb{C}^N \times 1$ and $\mathbf{h}_{ie} \in \mathbb{C}^N \times 1$.

Denote the confidential signal sent by transmitter $i$ as $\mathbf{x}_i \in \mathbb{C}^{N \times 1}$, $i \in \{1,2\}$, where $\mathbb{E}[\mathbf{x}_i \mathbf{x}_i^\dagger] = \mathbf{I}$ and $\mathbb{E}[\mathbf{x}_i \mathbf{x}_j^\dagger] = \mathbf{I}$ for $i \neq j$. Thus, the received signals at the ID receiver $j$ and the eavesdropper $e$, denoted as $y_j$ and $y_e$, respectively, are

$$y_j = \sum_{i=1}^{2} \mathbf{h}_{ji}^\dagger \mathbf{x}_i + n_j \text{ and } y_e = \sum_{i=1}^{2} \mathbf{h}_{ie}^\dagger \mathbf{x}_i + n_e \tag{1}$$

where $n_j \sim \mathcal{CN}(\mathbf{0}, \sigma^2 \mathbf{I})$ and $n_e \sim \mathcal{CN}(\mathbf{0}, \sigma^2 \mathbf{I})$ are the additive Gaussian noises at the ID receiver $j$ and the eavesdropper $e$, respectively. Without loss of generality, we assume that the noise variance is $\sigma^2 = 1$ in this paper. Therefore, the achievable rate of the ID receiver 1, 2 can be expressed as

$$I_1(\mathbf{x}_1, \mathbf{x}_2) = \log_2(1 + \frac{\mathbf{h}_{11}^\dagger \mathbf{x}_1 \mathbf{x}_1^\dagger \mathbf{h}_{11}}{\mathbf{h}_{21}^\dagger \mathbf{x}_2 \mathbf{x}_2^\dagger \mathbf{h}_{21} + 1}), \tag{2}$$

$$I_2(\mathbf{x}_1, \mathbf{x}_2) = \log_2(1 + \frac{\mathbf{h}_{22}^\dagger \mathbf{x}_2 \mathbf{x}_2^\dagger \mathbf{h}_{22}}{\mathbf{h}_{12}^\dagger \mathbf{x}_1 \mathbf{x}_1^\dagger \mathbf{h}_{12} + 1}) \tag{3}$$

The upper bound of the eavesdropper information rate is

$$I_e(\mathbf{x}_1, \mathbf{x}_2) = \log_2(1 + \mathbf{h}_{1e}^\dagger \mathbf{x}_1 \mathbf{x}_1^\dagger \mathbf{h}_{1e} + \mathbf{h}_{2e}^\dagger \mathbf{x}_2 \mathbf{x}_2^\dagger \mathbf{h}_{2e}) \tag{4}$$

According to [7], the worst-case sum secrecy rate of the system can be expressed as

$$I_S = I_1(\mathbf{x}_1, \mathbf{x}_2) + I_2(\mathbf{x}_1, \mathbf{x}_2) - I_e(\mathbf{x}_1, \mathbf{x}_2) \tag{5}$$

The transmit power constraint at the transmitter $i$ is

$$\|\mathbf{x}_i\|^2 \leq P_i, \ \forall \, i \in \{1, 2\} \tag{6}$$

The harvested energy at energy receiver $k$ should be constrained as

$$\rho(\mathbf{g}_{1k}^\dagger \mathbf{x}_1 \mathbf{x}_1^\dagger \mathbf{g}_{1k} + \mathbf{g}_{2k}^\dagger \mathbf{x}_2 \mathbf{x}_2^\dagger \mathbf{g}_{2k}) \geq Q_k \tag{7}$$

where $\rho$ is the EH efficiency that accounts for the loss in energy transducer and $Q_k$ is the threshold of the harvested energy at EH receiver $k$. Without loss of generality, the EH efficiency is assumed to be $\rho = 1$ in this paper.

**B.** *Problem Formulation*

We assume that the two transmitters know the imperfect CSI on $\mathbf{h}_{ij}$, $\mathbf{g}_{ik}$ and $\mathbf{h}_{ie}$. This assumption is valid because of channel estimation and quantization errors. In this paper, we model the channel uncertainties by worst-case model as in [6] which can be expressed as

$$\mathcal{H}_{ij} = \{\mathbf{h}_{ij} | \mathbf{h}_{ij} = \hat{\mathbf{h}}_{ij} + \Delta\mathbf{h}_{ij}, \Delta\mathbf{h}_{ij}^\dagger \mathbf{V}_{ij} \Delta\mathbf{h}_{ij} \leq 1\}, \tag{8}$$

$$\mathcal{G}_{ik} = \{\mathbf{g}_{ik} | \mathbf{g}_{ik} = \hat{\mathbf{g}}_{ik} + \Delta\mathbf{g}_{ik}, \Delta\mathbf{g}_{ik}^\dagger \mathbf{V}_{ik} \Delta\mathbf{g}_{ik} \leq 1\}, \tag{9}$$

$$\mathcal{H}_{ie} = \{\mathbf{h}_{ie} | \mathbf{h}_{ie} = \hat{\mathbf{h}}_{ie} + \Delta\mathbf{h}_{ie}, \Delta\mathbf{h}_{ie}^\dagger \mathbf{V}_{ie} \Delta\mathbf{h}_{ie} \leq 1\} \tag{10}$$

where $\hat{\mathbf{h}}_{ij}$, $\hat{\mathbf{g}}_{ik}$ and $\hat{\mathbf{h}}_{ie}$ denote the estimates of channels $\mathbf{h}_{ij}$, $\mathbf{g}_{ik}$ and $\mathbf{h}_{ie}$, respectively; $\Delta\mathbf{h}_{ij}$, $\Delta\mathbf{g}_{ik}$ and $\Delta\mathbf{h}_{ie}$ denote the channel uncertainties; $\mathbf{V}_{ij} \succ 0$, $\mathbf{V}_{ik} \succ 0$ and $\mathbf{V}_{ie} \succ 0$ determine the qualities of CSI.

Considering worst-case channel uncertainties, our objective is to maximize worst-case sum secrecy rate subject to individual transmit power constraints at two transmitters and worst-case EH constraints at EH receivers. Thus, the optimization problem is formulated as

$$\max_{\mathbf{x}_1, \mathbf{x}_2} \ \min_{\Delta\mathbf{h}_{ij} \in \mathcal{H}_{ij}, \Delta\mathbf{h}_{ie} \in \mathcal{H}_{ie}} \ I_S \tag{11a}$$

$$\text{s.t.} \ \|\mathbf{x}_i\|^2 \leq P_i, \ \forall \, i \in \{1, 2\}, \tag{11b}$$

$$\sum_{i=1}^{2} \mathbf{g}_{ik}^\dagger \mathbf{x}_i \mathbf{x}_i^\dagger \mathbf{g}_{ik} \geq Q_k, \ \forall \, \Delta\mathbf{g}_{ik} \in \mathcal{G}_{ik}, \forall \, k \in \mathcal{K} \tag{11c}$$

where $\mathcal{K} = \{1, 2, \ldots, K\}$. The robust problem (11) is non-convex which is difficult to solve. Thus, we propose an alternative iteration (AO) algorithm to solve the worst-case sum secrecy rate maximization problem.

## 3 Robust Secure Transmission Scheme

It is observed that the optimization problem (11) is a fractional quadratically constrained quadratic (QCQP) problem, which is non-convex and difficult to solve. Employing the semidefinite relaxation method [8], the problem (11) is equivalently rewritten as

$$\max_{\mathbf{X}_1,\mathbf{X}_2} \min_{\Delta\mathbf{h}_{ij}\in\mathcal{H}_{ij},\Delta\mathbf{h}_{ie}\in\mathcal{H}_{ie}} \eta_1 + \eta_2 + \eta_3 + \eta_4 + \eta_5 \tag{12a}$$

$$\text{s.t. } \operatorname{tr}(\mathbf{X}_i) \leq P_i, \ \forall i \in \{1,2\} \tag{12b}$$

$$\operatorname{rank}(\mathbf{X}_i) = 1, \ \forall i \in \{1,2\} \tag{12c}$$

$$\sum_{i=1}^{2} \operatorname{tr}\left(\mathbf{g}_{ik}\mathbf{X}_i\mathbf{g}_{ik}^\dagger\right) \geq Q_k, \ \forall\Delta\mathbf{g}_{ik} \in \mathcal{G}_{ik}, \forall k \in \mathcal{K} \tag{12d}$$

where

$$\eta_1 = \log_2(1 + \mathbf{h}_{11}^\dagger\mathbf{X}_1\mathbf{h}_{11} + \mathbf{h}_{21}^\dagger\mathbf{X}_2\mathbf{h}_{21}), \tag{13}$$

$$\eta_2 = -\log_2(1 + \mathbf{h}_{21}^\dagger\mathbf{X}_2\mathbf{h}_{21}), \tag{14}$$

$$\eta_3 = \log_2(1 + \mathbf{h}_{12}^\dagger\mathbf{X}_1\mathbf{h}_{12} + \mathbf{h}_{22}^\dagger\mathbf{X}_2\mathbf{h}_{22}), \tag{15}$$

$$\eta_4 = -\log_2(1 + \mathbf{h}_{12}^\dagger\mathbf{X}_1\mathbf{h}_{12}), \tag{16}$$

$$\eta_5 = -\log_2(1 + \mathbf{h}_{1e}^\dagger\mathbf{X}_1\mathbf{h}_{1e} + \mathbf{h}_{2e}^\dagger\mathbf{X}_2\mathbf{h}_{2e}), \tag{17}$$

$$\mathbf{X}_1 = \mathbf{x}_1\mathbf{x}_1^\dagger \text{ and } \mathbf{X}_2 = \mathbf{x}_2\mathbf{x}_2^\dagger \tag{18}$$

In (12a), since $\eta_1, \eta_3$ are concave and $\eta_2, \eta_4, \eta_5$ are convex, (12a) is non-convex. In order to deal with (12a), we have the following proposition.

**Proposition 1.** *Let $a \in \mathcal{R}^{1\times1}$ be a positive scalar and $f(a) = \frac{-ab}{\ln 2} + \log_2 a + \frac{1}{\ln 2}$. We have*

$$-\log_2 b = \max_{a\in\mathcal{R}^{1\times1},a\geq0} f(a) \tag{19}$$

*and the optimal solution to the right-hand side of (19) is $a = \frac{1}{b}$.*

*Proof.* Since $f(a)$ is concave, the partial derivative of $f(a)$ with respect to $a$ is

$$\frac{\partial f(a)}{\partial a} = -\frac{b}{\ln 2} + \frac{1}{a \ln 2} \tag{20}$$

In order to maximize $f(a)$, let $\frac{\partial f(a)}{\partial a} = 0$, we can obtain $b = \frac{1}{a}$. Substituting $b$ into $f(a)$, (19) can be obtained. $\qquad\square$

Using Proposition 1, we transform $\eta_2, \eta_4, \eta_5$ into convex optimization problems

$$\eta_2 = \max_{a_1\in\mathcal{R}^{1\times1},a_1\geq0} \zeta_1(a_1), \tag{21}$$

$$\eta_4 = \max_{a_2\in\mathcal{R}^{1\times1},a_2\geq0} \zeta_2(a_2), \tag{22}$$

$$\eta_5 = \max_{a_3\in\mathcal{R}^{1\times1},a_3\geq0} \zeta_3(a_3) \tag{23}$$

where

$$\zeta_1(a_1) = -\frac{a_1}{\ln 2}(\mathbf{h}_{21}^\dagger \mathbf{X}_2 \mathbf{h}_{21} + 1) + \log_2 a_1 + \frac{1}{\ln 2}, \tag{24}$$

$$\zeta_2(a_2) = -\frac{a_2}{\ln 2}(\mathbf{h}_{12}^\dagger \mathbf{X}_1 \mathbf{h}_{12} + 1) + \log_2 a_2 + \frac{1}{\ln 2}, \tag{25}$$

$$\zeta_1(a_3) = -\frac{a_3}{\ln 2}(\mathbf{h}_{1e}^\dagger \mathbf{X}_1 \mathbf{h}_{1e} + \mathbf{h}_{2e}^\dagger \mathbf{X}_2 \mathbf{h}_{2e} + 1) + \log_2 a_3 + \frac{1}{\ln 2} \tag{26}$$

In the following, we propose to decouple (12) into four optimization problems and employ AO algorithm to iteratively optimize $a_1, a_2, a_3, \mathbf{X}_1$ and $\mathbf{X}_2$. Our design concept is based on the fact that for fixed $\mathbf{X}_1$ and $\mathbf{X}_2$ the optimal solution of $a_1, a_2, a_3$ can be derived, and vice versa.

Given $\mathbf{X}_1^{(n-1)}$ and $\mathbf{X}_2^{(n-1)}$ which are optimal in the $(n-1)$th iteration, we solve

$$a_1^{(n)} = \arg\max_{a_1 \geq 0} -\frac{a_1}{\ln 2}(\max_{\Delta\mathbf{h}_{21}} \mathbf{h}_{21}^\dagger \mathbf{X}_2^{(n-1)} \mathbf{h}_{21} + 1) + \log_2 a_1 + \frac{1}{\ln 2}, \tag{27}$$

$$a_2^{(n)} = \arg\max_{a_2 \geq 0} -\frac{a_2}{\ln 2}(\max_{\Delta\mathbf{h}_{12}} \mathbf{h}_{12}^\dagger \mathbf{X}_1^{(n-1)} \mathbf{h}_{12} + 1) + \log_2 a_2 + \frac{1}{\ln 2}, \tag{28}$$

$$a_3^{(n)} = \arg\max_{a_3 \geq 0} -\frac{a_3}{\ln 2}(\max_{\Delta\mathbf{h}_{ie}} \sum_{i=1}^{2} \mathbf{h}_{ie}^\dagger \mathbf{X}_i^{(n-1)} \mathbf{h}_{ie} + 1) + \log_2 a_3 + \frac{1}{\ln 2} \tag{29}$$

We first solve the problem (27). It is noted that the problem (27) is convex with respect to $a_1$ and $\Delta\mathbf{h}_{21}$, respectively. They are also decoupled. Therefore, we can optimize them respectively. Before solving the problem (27), we first solve the following problem

$$\mathbf{F}_1 = \max_{\Delta\mathbf{h}_{21} \in \mathcal{H}_{21}} (\hat{\mathbf{h}}_{21} + \Delta\mathbf{h}_{21})^\dagger \mathbf{X}_2^{(n-1)} (\hat{\mathbf{h}}_{21} + \Delta\mathbf{h}_{21}) \tag{30a}$$

$$\text{s.t. } \Delta\mathbf{h}_{21}^\dagger \mathbf{V}_{21} \Delta\mathbf{h}_{21} \leq 1 \tag{30b}$$

The Lagrange function of the problem (30) is

$$\varsigma_1 = (\hat{\mathbf{h}}_{21} + \Delta\mathbf{h}_{21})^\dagger \mathbf{X}_2^{(n-1)} (\hat{\mathbf{h}}_{21} + \Delta\mathbf{h}_{21}) + \lambda_1 (\Delta\mathbf{h}_{21}^\dagger \mathbf{V}_{21} \Delta\mathbf{h}_{21} - 1) \tag{31}$$

where $\varsigma_1$ is non-negative Lagrangian multiplier. Obviously, $\varsigma_1$ is convex with respect to $\Delta\mathbf{h}_{21}$. Thus, the KKT condition is satisfied when we solve the problem (27). Therefore, we have

$$\mathbf{F}_1 = \text{tr}\left[(\mathbf{X}_2^{(n-1)} \hat{\mathbf{h}}_{21} \hat{\mathbf{h}}_{21}^\dagger + \mathbf{V}_{21}^{-1} + 2\sqrt{\kappa_1} \mathbf{V}_{21}^{-1})\right] \tag{32}$$

where

$$\kappa_1 = \frac{\text{tr}(\hat{\mathbf{h}}_{21} \hat{\mathbf{h}}_{21}^\dagger \mathbf{X}_2^{(n-1)})}{\text{tr}(\mathbf{X}_2^{(n-1)} \mathbf{V}_{21}^{-1})} \tag{33}$$

According to the Proposition 1 and (30)–(33), the closed form of the problem (27) is

$$a_1^{(n)} = (\mathbf{F}_1 + 1)^{-1} \tag{34}$$

Then, we can use the similar method to solve (28) and (29). Thus, the closed form of $a_2^{(n)}, a_3^{(n)}$ are

$$a_2^{(n)} = (\mathbf{F}_2 + 1)^{-1} \text{ and } a_3^{(n)} = (\mathbf{F}_3 + 1)^{-1} \tag{35}$$

where

$$\mathbf{F}_2 = \mathrm{tr}\left[(\mathbf{X}_1^{(n-1)}\hat{\mathbf{h}}_{12}\hat{\mathbf{h}}_{12}^\dagger + \mathbf{V}_{12}^{-1} + 2\sqrt{\kappa_2}\mathbf{V}_{12}^{-1})\right], \tag{36}$$

$$\mathbf{F}_3 = \sum_{i=1}^{2}\mathrm{tr}\left[(\mathbf{X}_i^{(n-1)}\hat{\mathbf{h}}_{ie}\hat{\mathbf{h}}_{ie}^\dagger + \mathbf{V}_{ie}^{-1} + 2\sqrt{\varpi_i}\mathbf{V}_{ie}^{-1})\right], \tag{37}$$

$$\kappa_2 = \frac{\mathrm{tr}(\hat{\mathbf{h}}_{12}\hat{\mathbf{h}}_{12}^\dagger\mathbf{X}_1^{(n-1)})}{\mathrm{tr}(\mathbf{X}_1^{(n-1)}\mathbf{V}_{12}^{-1})}, \ \varpi_i = \frac{\mathrm{tr}(\hat{\mathbf{h}}_{ie}\hat{\mathbf{h}}_{ie}^\dagger\mathbf{X}_i^{(n-1)})}{\mathrm{tr}(\mathbf{X}_i^{(n-1)}\mathbf{V}_{ie}^{-1})}, \forall i \in \{1,2\} \tag{38}$$

After obtaining $a_1^{(n)}, a_2^{(n)}, a_3^{(n)}$, we solve

$$\max_{\mathbf{X}_1 \succeq 0, \mathbf{X}_2 \succeq 0} \omega \tag{39a}$$

$$\text{s.t.} \quad \mathrm{tr}(\mathbf{X}_i) \le P_i, \ \mathrm{rank}(\mathbf{X}_i) = 1, \ i \in \{1,2\} \tag{39b}$$

$$\mathrm{tr}(\mathbf{h}_{21}\mathbf{h}_{21}^\dagger\mathbf{X}_2) \le \tau_1, \ \forall \Delta\mathbf{h}_{21} \in \mathcal{H}_{21} \tag{39c}$$

$$\mathrm{tr}(\mathbf{h}_{11}\mathbf{h}_{11}^\dagger\mathbf{X}_1) \ge \tau_2, \ \forall \Delta\mathbf{h}_{11} \in \mathcal{H}_{11} \tag{39d}$$

$$\mathrm{tr}(\mathbf{h}_{12}\mathbf{h}_{12}^\dagger\mathbf{X}_1) \le \tau_3, \ \forall \Delta\mathbf{h}_{12} \in \mathcal{H}_{12} \tag{39e}$$

$$\mathrm{tr}(\mathbf{h}_{22}\mathbf{h}_{22}^\dagger\mathbf{X}_2) \ge \tau_4, \ \forall \Delta\mathbf{h}_{22} \in \mathcal{H}_{22} \tag{39f}$$

$$\mathrm{tr}(\mathbf{h}_{1e}\mathbf{h}_{1e}^\dagger\mathbf{X}_1) \le \tau_5, \ \forall \Delta\mathbf{h}_{1e} \in \mathcal{H}_{1e} \tag{39g}$$

$$\mathrm{tr}(\mathbf{h}_{2e}\mathbf{h}_{2e}^\dagger\mathbf{X}_2) \le \tau_6, \ \forall \Delta\mathbf{h}_{2e} \in \mathcal{H}_{2e} \tag{39h}$$

$$\sum_{i=1}^{2}\mathrm{tr}(\mathbf{g}_{ik}\mathbf{g}_{ik}^\dagger\mathbf{X}_i) \ge Q_k, \ \forall \Delta\mathbf{g}_{ik} \in \mathcal{G}_{ik}, i \in \{1,2\} \tag{39i}$$

where

$$\omega = \log_2(\tau_1 + \tau_2 + 1) - \frac{a_1^{(n)}(\tau_1 + 1)}{\ln 2} + \log_2 a_1^{(n)} + \log_2(\tau_3 + \tau_4 + 1)$$

$$- \frac{a_2^{(n)}(\tau_3 + 1)}{\ln 2} + \log_2 a_2^{(n)} - \frac{a_3^{(n)}(\tau_5 + \tau_6 + 1)}{\ln 2} + \log_2 3 + \frac{3}{\ln 2} \tag{40}$$

The problem (39) is a semidefinite programming (SDP). However, the problem has semi-infinite constraints (39c)–(39i) and the rank-one constraint $\mathrm{rank}(\mathbf{X}_i) = 1, \ i \in \{1,2\}$, which are difficult to solve. To make the problem tractable, we convert the constraints (39c)–(39i) into linear matrix inequalities (LMIs) [9] equivalently, using $\mathcal{S}$-Procedure [10].

Applying $\mathcal{S}$-Procedure, and introducing slack variables $\mu_1, \mu_2, \mu_3, \mu_4, \mu_5, \mu_6$ and $\mu_7$, the constraints (39c)–(39i) can be equivalently transformed into the following LMIs

$$\mathbf{W}_1 \triangleq \begin{bmatrix} \mu_1 \mathbf{V}_{21} - \mathbf{X}_2 & -\mathbf{X}_2 \hat{\mathbf{h}}_{21} \\ -\hat{\mathbf{h}}_{21}^\dagger \mathbf{X}_2 & -\mu_1 - \hat{\mathbf{h}}_{21}^\dagger \mathbf{X}_2 \hat{\mathbf{h}}_{21} + \tau_1 \end{bmatrix} \succeq 0 \tag{41}$$

$$\mathbf{W}_2 \triangleq \begin{bmatrix} \mu_2 \mathbf{V}_{11} + \mathbf{X}_1 & \mathbf{X}_1 \hat{\mathbf{h}}_{11} \\ \hat{\mathbf{h}}_{11}^\dagger \mathbf{X}_1 & -\mu_2 + \hat{\mathbf{h}}_{11}^\dagger \mathbf{X}_1 \hat{\mathbf{h}}_{11} - \tau_2 \end{bmatrix} \succeq 0 \tag{42}$$

$$\mathbf{W}_3 \triangleq \begin{bmatrix} \mu_3 \mathbf{V}_{12} - \mathbf{X}_1 & -\mathbf{X}_1 \hat{\mathbf{h}}_{12} \\ -\hat{\mathbf{h}}_{12}^\dagger \mathbf{X}_1 & -\mu_3 - \hat{\mathbf{h}}_{12}^\dagger \mathbf{X}_1 \hat{\mathbf{h}}_{12} + \tau_3 \end{bmatrix} \succeq 0 \tag{43}$$

$$\mathbf{W}_4 \triangleq \begin{bmatrix} \mu_4 \mathbf{V}_{22} + \mathbf{X}_2 & \mathbf{X}_2 \hat{\mathbf{h}}_{22} \\ \hat{\mathbf{h}}_{22}^\dagger \mathbf{X}_2 & -\mu_4 + \hat{\mathbf{h}}_{22}^\dagger \mathbf{X}_2 \hat{\mathbf{h}}_{22} - \tau_4 \end{bmatrix} \succeq 0 \tag{44}$$

$$\mathbf{W}_5 \triangleq \begin{bmatrix} \mu_5 \mathbf{V}_{1e} - \mathbf{X}_1 & -\mathbf{X}_1 \hat{\mathbf{h}}_{1e} \\ -\hat{\mathbf{h}}_{1e}^\dagger \mathbf{X}_1 & -\mu_5 - \hat{\mathbf{h}}_{1e}^\dagger \mathbf{X}_1 \hat{\mathbf{h}}_{1e} + \tau_5 \end{bmatrix} \succeq 0 \tag{45}$$

$$\mathbf{W}_6 \triangleq \begin{bmatrix} \mu_6 \mathbf{V}_{2e} - \mathbf{X}_2 & -\mathbf{X}_2 \hat{\mathbf{h}}_{2e} \\ -\hat{\mathbf{h}}_{2e}^\dagger \mathbf{X}_2 & -\mu_6 - \hat{\mathbf{h}}_{2e}^\dagger \mathbf{X}_2 \hat{\mathbf{h}}_{2e} + \tau_6 \end{bmatrix} \succeq 0 \tag{46}$$

$$\mathbf{W}_7 \triangleq \begin{bmatrix} \mu_7 \mathbf{V}_{1k} + \mathbf{X}_1 & \mathbf{X}_1 \hat{\mathbf{g}}_{1k} \\ \hat{\mathbf{g}}_{1k}^\dagger \mathbf{X}_1 & -\mu_7 - Q_k + \hat{\mathbf{g}}_{1k}^\dagger \mathbf{X}_1 \hat{\mathbf{g}}_{1k} + \mathbf{g}_{2k}^\dagger \mathbf{X}_2 \mathbf{g}_{2k} \end{bmatrix} \succeq 0 \tag{47}$$

We need the extensions of $\mathcal{S}$-Procedure [11] to convert (47) into an LMI. Introducing slack variables $\mu_8$, we equivalently transformed (47) into

$$\mathbf{W}_8 \triangleq \begin{bmatrix} \mu_7 \mathbf{V}_{1k} + \mathbf{X}_1 & \mathbf{X}_1 \hat{\mathbf{g}}_{1k} & \mathbf{0} \\ \hat{\mathbf{g}}_{2k}^\dagger \mathbf{X}_1 & \hat{\varphi} & \hat{\mathbf{g}}_{2k}^\dagger \mathbf{X}_2 \\ \mathbf{0} & \mathbf{X}_2 \hat{\mathbf{g}}_{2k} & \mathbf{X}_2 + \mu_8 \mathbf{V}_{2k} \end{bmatrix} \succeq 0 \tag{48}$$

where

$$\hat{\varphi} = \hat{\mathbf{g}}_{1k}^\dagger \mathbf{X}_1 \hat{\mathbf{g}}_{1k} + \hat{\mathbf{g}}_{2k}^\dagger \mathbf{X}_2 \hat{\mathbf{g}}_{2k} - \mu_7 - \mu_8 - Q_k \tag{49}$$

Combing (41)–(46) and (48) and omitting the rank-one constraint, the optimization problem (39) can be recast as

$$\max_{\mathbf{X}_1 \succeq 0, \mathbf{X}_2 \succeq 0, \mu_j} \omega \tag{50a}$$

$$\text{s.t. } \operatorname{tr}(\mathbf{X}_i) \leq P_i, i \in \{1, 2\} \tag{50b}$$

$$\mathbf{W}_l \succeq 0, \mu_j \geq 0, l \in \{1, \dots, 8\}/7, j \in \{1, \dots, 8\} \tag{50c}$$

Obviously, (50) is a convex SDP problem which can be solved by existing software, e.g., CVX. It is noted that (50) is a rank-one relaxation of the original problem (39). If the optimal solution of (50) is rank-one, it is also the optimal solution of the original problem (39). If the rank of the optimal solution of (50) is greater than 1, we employ the Gaussian randomization (GR) method to generate the suboptimal rank-one solution.

## 4   Simulation Results

In this section, we evaluate the performance of our proposed robust secure transmission scheme through computer simulations. We assume that two-user MISO IFC system consists of two transmitters, two ID receivers, $K = 1$ EH receiver and a eavesdropper. The entries in the channel estimates $\mathbf{h}_{ii}$, $\mathbf{h}_{\bar{i}\bar{i}}$, $\mathbf{h}_{ie}$, $\mathbf{g}_{ik}$, $i \in \{1,2\}$, $\bar{i} \in \{1,2\} - i$, are independent and identically distributed complex Gaussian random variables whose variances are 1, 0.1, 1 and 1 respectively. We assume that the maximum allowable transmit powers of two transmitters are $P_1 = P_2$. The worst-case EH constraint is $Q_k = 0.3P_1$. We produce 500 randomly generated channel realizations and compute the worst-case sum secrecy rate.

The channel uncertainty regions are assumed to be norm-bounded, i.e.,

$$\mathbf{V}_{ij} = \frac{1}{(\tilde{\delta}_{ij}^h)^2}\mathbf{I}, \ \mathbf{V}_{ik} = \frac{1}{(\tilde{\delta}_{ik}^g)^2}\mathbf{I}, \ \text{and} \ \mathbf{V}_{ie} = \frac{1}{(\tilde{\delta}_{ie}^h)^2}\mathbf{I} \tag{51}$$

where $(\tilde{\delta}_{ij}^h)^2$, $(\tilde{\delta}_{ik}^g)^2$ and $(\tilde{\delta}_{ie}^h)^2$ are normalized radii of the uncertainty regions which can be expressed as

$$(\tilde{\delta}_{ij}^h)^2 = \frac{N(\delta_{ij}^h)^2}{\mathbb{E}\left[\|\hat{\mathbf{h}}_{ij}\|_F^2\right]}, \ (\tilde{\delta}_{ik}^g)^2 = \frac{N(\delta_{ik}^g)^2}{\mathbb{E}\left[\|\hat{\mathbf{g}}_{ik}\|_F^2\right]}, \ \text{and} \ (\tilde{\delta}_{ie}^h)^2 = \frac{N(\delta_{ie}^h)^2}{\mathbb{E}\left[\|\hat{\mathbf{h}}_{ie}\|_F^2\right]} \tag{52}$$

We assume that $\delta = (\tilde{\delta}_{ij}^h)^2 = (\tilde{\delta}_{ik}^g)^2 = (\tilde{\delta}_{ie}^h)^2$ in this paper.

For our proposed robust secure transmission scheme, the optimal solution to the rank-relaxed problem of (12) serves as a performance upper bound. In Fig. 1, we present the worst-case sum secrecy rate comparison of the proposed robust secure transmission scheme after GR (denoted as "Robust-GR" in the legend), the performance upper bound (denoted as "Robust") and the non-robust secure transmission scheme (denoted as "Non-Robust" in the legend) for different maximum allowable transmit power to noise power ratios, i.e., $P_i/\sigma^2, i \in \{1,2\}$ and different channel uncertainty of the radius, i.e., $\delta^2$. Each transmitter is equipped with $N = 4$ antennas. The non-robust secure transmission scheme is obtained by solving (12) where $\Delta \mathbf{h}_{ij} = 0, \Delta \mathbf{g}_{ik} = 0$ and $\Delta \mathbf{h}_{ie} = 0, i \in \{1,2\}, j \in \{1,2\}$ and $k \in \mathcal{K}$. After obtaining $\mathbf{X}_1$ and $\mathbf{X}_2$, if the worst-case EH constraint at each EH receiver is not satisfied, an outage occurs and the worst-case sum secrecy rate is 0. If otherwise, the worst-case sum secrecy rate is computed by using the similar method proposed in Sect. 2. From Fig. 1, we can conclude that the performance of the "Robust" secure transmission scheme outperform the performance of the "Non-Robust" secure transmission scheme. It is also found that with the increase of $\delta^2$, the performance gaps between the "Robust" secure transmission scheme and the "Non-Robust" secure transmission scheme become larger, especially at the high $P_i/\sigma^2, i \in \{1,2\}$. This is because when the channel uncertainty of the radius is larger, the "Non-Robust" secure transmission scheme is difficult to steer its antenna beam towards the direction which increases the sum secrecy rate. From Fig. 1, it is observed that the performance of the "Robust-GR" close to

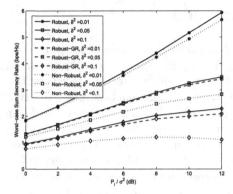

**Fig. 1.** Worst-case sum secrecy rate versus $P_i/\sigma^2, i \in \{1,2\}$; performance comparison of proposed robust secure transmission scheme and the non-robust one, $N = 4$, $K = 1$, $\alpha = 0.3$

the upper bound, and the performance of the "Robust-GR" is better than the "Non-Robust" secure transmission scheme.

In Fig. 2, we compare the outage probability of the proposed robust secure transmission scheme (denoted as "Robust" in the legend) and the non-robust secure transmission scheme (denoted as "Non-Robust" in the legend) for different maximum allowable transmit power to noise power ratios, i.e., $P_i/\sigma^2, i \in \{1,2\}$ and different channel uncertainty of the radius, i.e., $\delta^2$. Each transmitter is equipped with $N = 4$ antennas. From Fig. 2, it is observed that the outage in the proposed "Robust" secure transmission scheme doesn't occur. However, the outage probability of the "Non-Robust" secure transmission scheme becomes larger with the increase of the channel uncertainty of the radius $\delta^2$.

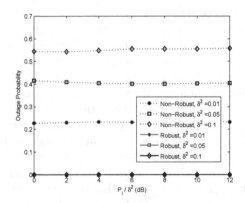

**Fig. 2.** Outage probability versus $P_i/\sigma^2, i \in \{1,2\}$; performance comparison of proposed robust secure transmission scheme and the non-robust one, $N = 4$, $K = 1$, $\alpha = 0.3$

## 5   Conclusion

In this paper, we have invested robust secure transmission scheme for two-user MISO IFC system with SWIPT. Considering the worst-case channel uncertainty model, we propose alternative iteration algorithm to design the transmit convariance matrix. Simulation results demonstrate that our proposed robust secure transmission scheme has significant performance gain over the non-robust one.

## References

1. Shen, C., Li, W-C., Chang, T-H.: Simultaneous information and energy transfer: a two-user MISO interference channel case. In: Proceedings of GLOBECOM, pp. 3862–3867 (2012)
2. Park, J., Clerckx, B.: Joint wireless information and energy transfer in a two-user MIMO interference channel. IEEE Trans. Wirel. Commun. **12**(8), 4210–4221 (2013)
3. Ng, D.W.K., Schober, R.: Resource allocation for secure communication in systems with wireless information and power transfer. In: Proceedings of IEEE Globecom, pp. 1251–1257 (2013)
4. Ng, D.W.K., Xiang, L., Schober, R.: Multi-objective beamforming for secure communication in systems with wireless information and power transfer. In: Proceedings of IEEE PIMRC, pp. 7–12 (2013)
5. Liu, L., Zhang, R., Chua, K.C.: Secrecy wireless information and power transfer with MISO beamforming. IEEE Trans. Signal Process. **62**(7), 1850–1863 (2014)
6. Ng, D.W.K., Lo, E.S., Schober, R.: Robust beamforming for secure communication in systems with wireless information and power transfer. IEEE Trans. Wirel. Commun. **13**(8), 4599–4615 (2014)
7. Somekh-Baruch, A.: On the secure interference channel. In: Proceedings of 51st Annual Allerton Conference on Communication, Control, and Computing, pp. 770–773 (2013)
8. Luo, Z.-Q., Ma, W.-K., So, A.M.-C., Ye, Y., Zhang, S.: Semidefinite relaxation of quadratic optimization problems. IEEE Sig. Process. Mag. **27**(3), 20–34 (2010)
9. Boyd, S., Vandenberghe, L.: Convex Optimization. Cambridge University Press, Cambridge (2004)
10. Beck, A., Eldar, Y.: Strong duality in nonconvex quadratic optimization with two quadratic constraints. SIAM J. Optim. **17**(3), 844–860 (2006)
11. Luo, Z.-Q., Sturm, J.F., Zhang, S.: Multivariate nonnegative quadratic mapping. SIAM J. Optim. **14**(4), 1140–1162 (2004)

# An Effective Limited Feedback Scheme for FD-MIMO Based on Noncoherent Detection and Kronecker Product Codebook

Lisi Jiang[1] and Juling Zeng[2($\boxtimes$)]

[1] Beijing University of Posts and Telecommunications, Beijing, China
[2] China Three Gorges University, Yichang, China
`julingzeng@ctgu.edu.cn`

**Abstract.** The low complexity quantization of channel state information (CSI) and the utilization of vertical freedom of three dimension (3D) channels are two critical issues in the limited feedback design of the *full dimension multi-input-multi-output* (FD-MIMO) systems. In this paper, we propose an effective limited feedback scheme. We first employ Kronecker product based codebook (KPC) to explore the vertical freedom of 3D channels, extending the limited feedback from two dimension (2D) to 3D. Furthermore, we use noncoherent sequence detection (NCSD) to quantify the CSI which includes both the vertical and horizontal channel information. This quantization method exploits the duality between codebook searching and NCSD to transform the CSI quntization on KPC to two parallel NCSD. The complexity is reduced from exponential to linear with the number of antennas. Monte Carlo simulation results show that the proposed scheme provides at least 1.2 dB coding gain compared with traditional 2D limited feedback schemes. Moreover, the proposed scheme outperforms other FD/3D CSI quantization schemes by 0.8 dB coding gain with moderate complexity when the channel is highly spatially correlated.

## 1 Introduction

As a key candidate technology for the fifth-generation (5G) mobile communications system, full dimension multi-input-multi-output (FD-MIMO) has attracted significant attention in the wireless industry and academia in the past few years [1]. Utilizing a large number of antennas in a two-dimension (2D) antenna array panel (AAS), FD-MIMO has two main advantages compared with traditional MIMO. On one hand, the 2D panel allows the extension of spatial separation, providing an extra vertical freedom to improve vertical coverage and overall system capacity. On the other hand, it supports up to at least 64 antennas and increases the range of transmission for improving power efficiency.

The limited feedback system is critical in the realization of FD-MIMO. There are two key challenges need to be solved in the implementation of limited feedback. *First*, the current codebooks which are predominantly designed and optimized for 2D MIMO channels should be extended to 3D channels to entirely

© ICST Institute for Computer Sciences, Social Informatics and Telecommunications Engineering 2018
Q. Chen et al. (Eds.): ChinaCom 2016, Part I, LNICST 209, pp. 24–33, 2018.
DOI: 10.1007/978-3-319-66625-9_3

explore the freedom of vertical dimension of the 3D channels. *Second*, low complexity channel state information (CSI) quantization method should be designed for the limited feedback system to overcome the high quantization complexity caused by the large AAS in FD-MIMO.

To make use of the vertical freedom of 3D channels, Kronecker product based codebook (KPC) is usually employed in FD-MIMO systems [2,3]. [4] demonstrated that the codewords distribution of KPC matches the distribution of optimal beamforming vector of 3D channels, showing the effectiveness of KPC. [2] has adopted a KPC constructed by two Discrete Fourier Transform (DFT) codebooks which is easy to implement. However, the noncoherent sequence detection (NCSD) which can reduce the quantization complexity cannot be used on this DFT based KPC. [5] has proposed a Phase-Shift Keying (PSK) codebook and used the NCSD to reduce quantization complexity. But the PSK codebook is designed for 2D channels. In this paper, we employ a codebook defined as the Kronecker product of two PSK codebooks, in which NCSD can be used by decomposing the codebook and channel.

Conventional codebook searching based CSI quantization method feedback a binary index of the codeword chosen in a common vector quantized (VQ) codebook with the number of codewords exponential to the number of antennas, which leads to a exponential complexity of CSI quantization. In FD-MIMO systems where hundreds of antennas are deployed such complexity is too high to implement [6]. [5,6] has found the duality between the problems of finding the optimal beamforming vector in the codebook and the noncoherent sequence detection (NCSD) which detects the channel vector with linear complexity. Utilizing the duality, CSI quantization can be transformed to NCSD where storage is not needed. However, such duality can only be utilized for PSK codebook but not for KPC. By vestigating the characteristics of 3D channels and KPC, we first decomposite the channel vector into two sub-vectors representing horizontal and vertical channels respectively according to the channel phase information of 3D channels. Then, we transform the CSI quntization to two parallel NCSD by respectively using the duality on the two PSK codebooks which construct the KPC.

## 2   System Model

### 2.1   Beamforming Model with Feedback

We consider a multi-input single-output (MISO) communication system. The transmitter is equipped with $M_t$ transmit antennas and the receiver is equipped with 1 antenna. As shown in Fig. 1, for channel $\mathbf{H} \in \mathbb{C}^{M_t}$, the received signal $y \in \mathbb{C}$ can be written as

$$y = \mathbf{H}\mathbf{w}x + n, \tag{1}$$

where $\mathbf{w} \in \mathbb{C}^{M_t}$ is the beamforming vector with $\|\mathbf{w}\|_2^2 = 1$, $x \in \mathbb{C}$ is the message signal with $E[x] = 0$ and $E[|x|^2] = P$, and $n \in \mathbb{C}$ is additive complex Gaussian noise. For equal gain transmission (EGT), the beamforming vector has the property that $|w_t| = 1/\sqrt{M_t}$ for all $t$. Equal gain transmission is mainly considered in this paper because of its low peak to average power ratio (PAPR). We assume that $\mathbf{H}$ is memoryless MIMO fading channels. The receiver sends the quantification of $\mathbf{H}$ over a limited rate feedback channel. After receiving the feedback, the transmitter will construct a beamforming vector $\mathbf{w}$ according to the quantified $\mathbf{H}$. Aiming to focus on channel quantization design, we assumed that there are no channel estimation errors at the receiver or errors over the feedback channel, which means the perfect CSI.

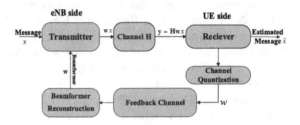

**Fig. 1.** MISO beamforming model with feedback.

## 2.2    3D Channel Model

Uniformed Planar Arrays (UPA) is the most typical antenna array in FD-MIMO. As shown in Fig. 2, antennas are uniformly spaced across the planar. The departure and arrival angles are modeled by using the azimuth angle in X-Y plane and the elevation angle respected to the Z axis [7] in 3D channel modeling. The 3D channel impulse response (CIR) $h(t)$ can be expressed as Eq. (2).

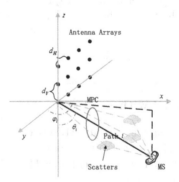

**Fig. 2.** 3D Channel under UPA, $M_{tV}$ vertical antennas with $d_V$ wavelength spacing, and $M_{tH}$ horizontal antennas with $d_H$ wavelength spacing, $M_{tH} M_{tV} = M_t$. $\varphi_i$ and $\theta_i$ are the azimuth angle and the elevation angle for path $i$, respectively.

$$h(t) = \sum_{i=1}^{I_{MPC}} \alpha_i(t)\partial(\Theta_i), \tag{2}$$

where $\alpha_i(t)$ is a zero-mean complex i.i.d. random variable, $\partial(\Theta_i)$ is normalized impulse response to a single path with an Angle of Departure (AoD) $\Theta_i$ modeled in 3D. $I_{MPC}$ is the total number of multi-paths. The AoD of $i$-th multi-path component is given as $\Theta_i = [\theta_i, \varphi_i]^T$. $0 \leq \varphi_i \leq 2\pi$ and $0 \leq \theta_i \leq \pi$ are the azimuth and elevation angles defined with respect to the positive y- and negative z-axis, respectively. Assuming that the antenna elements are vertically polarized, $\Theta_i$ only depends on $\varphi_i$ and $\theta_i$. The $\partial(\Theta_i)$ for a size $M_{tH} \times M_{tV}$ UPA is given by

$$\partial(\Theta_i) = vec(\partial_H(\mu)\partial^T{}_V(\upsilon)), \tag{3}$$

where $\partial_H(\mu) = [1, e^{-j\mu}, ..., e^{-j(M_{tH}-1)\mu}]^T$, $\mu = \frac{2\pi}{\lambda}d_H \cos(\varphi_i)\sin(\theta_i)$, $\partial_V(\upsilon) = [1, e^{-j\upsilon}, ..., e^{-j(M_{tV}-1)\upsilon}]^T$, $\upsilon = \frac{2\pi}{\lambda}d_V \cos(\theta_i)$. $\lambda$ is the wavelength of carriers and operator $vec()$ represents the operation of vectorization. $d_H$ and $d_V$ represent the distance between the antenna elements horizontal and vertical respectively. In common case, $d_H = d_V = 0.5\lambda$. The $\Theta_i$ of each AoD has a Gaussian distribution with a mean value of $\Theta$ and an angular spreading variance of $\sigma$. Particularly, when the channel exhibits full spatial correlation, the channel model can be expressed as Eq. (4).

$$h(t) = \alpha(t)\partial(\Theta), \tag{4}$$

where $\alpha(t)$ is zero-mean complex i.i.d. random variable and $\partial(\Theta)$ is the NIR-SRP for AoD $\Theta$. The channel spatial correlation will increase as the number of multi-paths and the angular spreading variance decrease. It worth noting that the channels are highly correlated in FD-MIMO systems, since the BSs deploys a large scale antenna array in a limited space. In addition, Eq. (4) is very important because the channel can be decomposed, which we will mention in Sect. 4.

## 3   Kronecker Product Codebook Construction

To make use of the vertical freedom of 3D channels, Kronecker product based codebook (KPC) is usually employed in FD-MIMO systems [2,3]. [4] demonstrated that the codewords distribution of KPC matches the distribution of optimal beamforming vector of 3D channels, showing the effectiveness of KPC. [2] has adopted a KPC constructed by two Discrete Fourier Transform (DFT) codebooks which is easy to implement. However, the noncoherent sequence detection (NCSD) which can reduce the quantization complexity cannot be used on this DFT based KPC. [5] has proposed a Phase-Shift Keying (PSK) codebook and used the NCSD to reduce quantization complexity. But the PSK codebook is designed for 2D channels. In this paper, we employ a codebook defined as the Kronecker product of two PSK codebooks, in which NCSD can be used by decomposing the codebook and channel. The Kronecker product based codebook $W_K$ can be generated as follows:

$$W_K = W_V \otimes W_H, \tag{5}$$

where operator $\otimes$ represents the Kronecker product. $W_H$ and $W_V$ represent the horizontal and vertical traditional PSK codebook respectively. We assume $M_{tV}$ and $M_{tH}$ represent the number of vertical antennas and horizontal antennas in UPA, respectively. $W_V$ is a PSK codebook with all possible sequences of PSK symbols with a constellation size of $N_V$. The length of $W_V$ is $M_{tV}$. Similarly, $W_H$ is allpossible sequences of PSK symbols of length $M_{tH}$ with constellation size $N_H$. The codebooks parameters are summarized in Table 1.

**Table 1.** parameters of codebooks

| Codebook name | Codewords vector length | Constellation size |
|---|---|---|
| $W_H$ | $M_{tH}$ | $N_H$ |
| $W_V$ | $M_{tV}$ | $N_V$ |
| $W_K$ | $M_t = M_{tH} M_{tV}$ | *Not PSK symbols* |

We assume that $w_V^1 = 1/M_{tV}$ and $w_H^1 = 1/M_{tH}$.

# 4    Channel Quantization Scheme

This section shows how the optimal codebook search over the proposed PSK-KPC can achieved with linear complexity.

## 4.1    Duality Between Codebook Searching and Non-coherent Sequence Detection

For codebook searching, to maximize the SNR, the receiver chooses the beamforming vector from the codebook according to

$$\mathbf{w}_{opt} = \arg\max_{\mathbf{v} \in C} \frac{\|\mathbf{H}\mathbf{v}\|^2}{\|\mathbf{v}\|^2}, \tag{6}$$

where $\mathbf{H}$ denotes for the channel vector in Sect. 2, $C$ is the codebook, and $\mathbf{v}$ represents the codewords.

Then, for NCSD, we consider a single antenna noncoherent, block fading, additive white Gaussian noise (AWGN) channel. The received vector can be expressed as

$$\mathbf{y} = \beta \mathbf{x} + n, \tag{7}$$

where $\mathbf{x} \in \mathbb{C}^N$ is a vector of $N$ transmitted symbols, $n \in \mathbb{C}^N$ is a vector of i.i.d. AWGN, $\beta \in \mathbb{C}$ is an unknown deterministic channel which is assumed constant for a period of $N$ symbols. $\mathbf{y} \in \mathbb{C}^N$ is the received signal. According to [6], the GLRT-optimal data estimate $\hat{\mathbf{x}}^{GLRT}$ is by solving

$$\hat{\mathbf{x}}^{GLRT} = \arg \min_{\hat{\mathbf{x}} \in \mathbb{C}^N} \min_{\hat{\beta}} \left\| \mathbf{y} - \hat{\beta}\hat{\mathbf{x}} \right\|^2$$

$$= \arg \min_{\hat{\mathbf{x}} \in \mathbb{C}^N} \min_{\alpha \in R^+} \min_{\theta \in [0, 2\pi)} \|\mathbf{y}\|^2 + \alpha^2 \|\hat{\mathbf{x}}\|^2 - 2\alpha \mathrm{Re}(e^{j\theta} \mathbf{y}^H \hat{\mathbf{x}})$$

$$= \arg \min_{\hat{\mathbf{x}} \in \mathbb{C}^N} \min_{\alpha \in R^+} \|\mathbf{y}\|^2 + \alpha^2 \|\hat{\mathbf{x}}\|^2 - 2\alpha \left| \mathbf{y}^H \mathbf{x} \right| \tag{8}$$

$$= \arg \max_{\hat{\mathbf{x}} \in \mathbb{C}^N} \frac{\left| \mathbf{y}^H \mathbf{x} \right|^2}{\|\mathbf{x}\|^2},$$

where $\beta = \alpha e^{j\theta}$, $\alpha \in R^+$ and $\theta \in [0, 2\pi)$.

Noting that in our MISO system $\|\mathbf{Hv}\|^2 = |\mathbf{Hv}|^2$, it can be easily checked from (6) and (8) that finding the optimal codeword and the NCSD problems are equivalent, i.e.,

$$\mathbf{w}_{opt} = \mathbf{v}^{GLRT} = \arg \min_{\mathbf{v} \in C} \min_{\beta} \left\| \mathbf{H}^T - \beta \mathbf{v} \right\|^2, \tag{9}$$

where $C$ denotes the codebook. Therefore, we can find the $\mathbf{w}_{opt}$ using noncoherent block demodulator.

## 4.2 Low Complexity Quantization for CSI

Based on the equivalence between codebook searching and NCSD, low complexity algorithms can be used for CSI quantization. Maximum likelihood (ML) noncoherent PSK sequence detection can be performed using an algorithm in [8]. For $N$ symbols, the complexity is $O(N \log N)$. However, the channel vector to be quantified contains both horizontal and vertical channel phase information. Sequences of only PSK symbols cannot precisely present the 3D characteristic of the channel vectors. Therefore, noncoherent PSK sequence detection cannot be directly applied for KPC CSI quantization. Nevertheless, if we can separate the vertical channel phase information and the horizontal information to construct two sub-channel vectors, the noncoherent PSK sequence detection can then be applied to quantify the two sub-channel vectors. And the final quantization vector can be the Kronecker product of the two sub-channel quantization vectors.

***Step 1: Decomposition of the channel vector.*** Investigating the structure of channel vector in Sect. 2, we find that some specific elements only contain the vertical channel phase information. Therefore, we can decompose the channel vector $\mathbf{H}$ by

$$\hat{\mathbf{H}}_V = \{ \hat{h}_V^n \mid \hat{h}_V^n = h^{nM_{tH}}, n = 0, ..., M_{tV} - 1 \}, \tag{10}$$

$$\hat{\mathbf{H}}_H = \{ \hat{h}_H^m \mid \hat{h}_H^m = h^m, m = 0, ..., M_{tH} - 1 \}, \tag{11}$$

where $h^k$ denotes the $k$-th element of vector $\mathbf{H}$, $\hat{h}_H^m$ denotes the $m$-th element of vector $\hat{\mathbf{H}}_H$ and $\hat{h}_V^n$ denotes the $n$-th element of vector $\hat{\mathbf{H}}_V$. $M_{tH}$ and $M_{tV}$ are the number of antennas in the UPA horizontally and vertically, respectively. We denote the first element of a vector to be 0-th.

After decomposition, $\hat{\mathbf{H}}_V$ only contains the vertical channel information. $\hat{\mathbf{H}}_H$ contains the least vertical channel information, which make itself present most horizontal channel information. In particular, when the channel is fully correlated, the NIR-SRP of the channel is a Kronecker product of two PSK sequences. Therefore, after decomposition, $\hat{\mathbf{H}}_V$ and $\hat{\mathbf{H}}_H$ are two PSK sequences, which completely represent the vertical channel information and horizontal channel information respectively.

***Step 2: Quantization using noncoherent PSK sequence detection.*** Once $\hat{\mathbf{H}}_H$ and $\hat{\mathbf{H}}_V$ are obtained, we can use the noncoherent PSK sequence detection to quantify them. In this case, the cost function (9) has the form as follows

$$
\mathbf{w}_H^{opt} = \arg \min_{\hat{\mathbf{v}}_H \in W_H} \min_{\theta \in [0,2\pi)} \left\| \hat{\mathbf{H}}_H^T - e^{j\theta} \hat{\mathbf{v}}_H \right\|^2 , \tag{12}
$$

$$
\mathbf{w}_V^{opt} = \arg \min_{\hat{\mathbf{v}}_V \in W_V} \min_{\theta \in [0,2\pi)} \left\| \hat{\mathbf{H}}_V^T - e^{j\theta} \hat{\mathbf{v}}_V \right\|^2 , \tag{13}
$$

where $W_H$ and $W_V$ refer to the horizontal and vertical PSK codebooks in Sect. 3, respectively. $\hat{\mathbf{v}}_H$ and $\hat{\mathbf{v}}_V$ denote the codewords in $W_H$ and $W_V$. They are sequences of PSK symbols.

(12) and (13) reduce the search space from $\mathcal{R} = \mathbb{C}$ to $\mathcal{R} = e^{j[0,2\pi)}$ due to constant-modulus property of the codewords. The magnitude of $\beta$ does not influence the corresponding best codeword estimate. A corresponding best codeword estimate exists for each phase $\theta$. Therefore $[0, 2\pi)$ can be partitioned into intervals correspond to obtaining the same codeword estimate. Based on the rotational symmetry of PSK symbols, the search space can be further reduced to $[0, 2\pi/M)$. $M$ denotes the constellation size. In our case, the search space of $\mathbf{w}_H^{opt}$ can be reduced to $[0, 2\pi/N_H)$ and $\mathbf{w}_V^{opt}$ can be reduced to $[0, 2\pi/N_V)$.

The algorithm in [8] first effectively calculates the cross over angles, indicating the nearest neighbor boundaries of $[0, 2\pi/M)$. The cross over angle is defined as the value for $\theta$ in $[0, 2\pi/N_H)$ or $[0, 2\pi/N_H)$ where the cross over happens. The definition of crossing over can refer to [8]. Then the algorithm sorts the angels in order of phase, making the codeword estimates and corresponding angular metric update in a recursive manner. The final results are picked with the largest noncoherent likelihood.

***Step 3: Final beamforming vector generation.*** After *Step 2*, $\mathbf{w}_H^{opt}$ and $\mathbf{w}_V^{opt}$ are obtained. We can then construct the final beamforming vector

$$
\mathbf{w}^{opt} = vec(\mathbf{w}_H^{opt}(\mathbf{w}_V^{opt})^T) . \tag{14}
$$

$\mathbf{w}^{opt}$ belongs to the KPC $W_K$.

Figure 3 presents the procedure of the KPC CSI quantization.

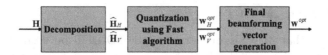

**Fig. 3.** CSI quantization of the KPC CSI.

## 4.3  Complexity

In the quantization procedure, *Step 1* and *Step 3* have complexity $O(M_t)$. The complexity of *Step 2* is mainly due to the noncoherent PSK sequence detection. The complexity of the algorithm is dominated by the sorting operation of cross over angels. The number of cross over angels equals to the length of the vector waiting to be detected. In our case, we use the noncoherent PSK sequence detection in parallel to quantify $\mathbf{w}_H^{opt}$ and $\mathbf{w}_H^{opt}$. Their length are $M_{tH}$ and $M_{tV}$. According to [8], for $\mathbf{w}_H^{opt}$ the complexity is $O(M_{tH} \log M_{tH})$ and for $\mathbf{w}_V^{opt}$ the complexity is $O(M_{tV} \log M_{tV})$. Therefore, the complexity of *Step 2* is $O(M_{tH} \log M_{tH}) + O(M_{tV} \log M_{tV})$. If $M_{tH} > \log M_{tV}$ and $M_{tV} > \log M_{tH}$, the overall complexity of channel quantization is $O(M_t)$.

Compared with traditional exponentially search complexity, our quantization complexity is linear to the number of antennas. However, it is worth noting that we obtain reduced complexity by decomposing the channel vector. This will certainly bring the performance loss. We will evaluate the performance loss in the Sect. 7.

## 5  Simulation Results and Discussions

### 5.1  Simulation Setup

Quadrature phase shift keying (QPSK) modulation is adopted in simulations. The BER is estimated using at least 10000 iterations per SNR point, where $2^{14}$ QPSK symbols are used for each iteration. Channels are generated according to (2). The antenna spacing is usually set to be $0.5\lambda$, where $\lambda$ is the wavelength of carriers. The spatial correlation $\rho$ is calculated according to [7], which is 0.66. $\rho$ is mainly related with the antenna spacing, the azimuth angle spread (AS) and elevation angle spread (ES). In common case, $\rho$ increases as the antenna spacing, the AS and the ES decrease.It is worth noting that since the BSs in FD-MIMO systems deploys a large scale antenna array within a limited space, the distance between antennas may be smaller than $0.5\lambda$, and the AS and the ES will also accordingly decrease [7]. Therefore, $\rho$ will likely be higher than 0.66 in future FD-MIMO systems.

We first compare the bit error rate (BER) performance of our proposed limited feedback scheme (3D-PSK) with traditional DFT codebooks based limited feedback scheme (2D-DFT) in two antenna configuration to show the efficiency of our scheme in the vertical freedom utilization. Then, we compare our 3D-PSK scheme with the 3D limited feedback scheme in [4] under four spatial correlation to show our 3D-PSK strike the balance between performance and complexity.

## 5.2    3D-PSK vs. 2D-DFT

Figure 4 shows that 3D-PSK outperforms the 2D-DFT by 0.8 dB and 1.2 dB coding gain respectively under both the two transmission configuration. This result shows that 3D-PSK makes full use of the vertical freedom of 3D channels, which will improve the system capacity. It can also be seen that as the number of antennas increases, the coding gain gets larger, which proves the superiority of 3D-PSK scheme in large scale FD-MIMO systems.

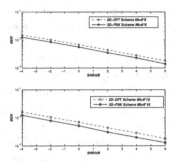

**Fig. 4.** BER versus SNR comparison with 2D-DFT when $\rho = 0.66$.

## 5.3    3D-PSK vs. 3D-DFT

Figure 5 compares 3D-PSK with 3D-DFT under four spatial correlation: $\rho = 0.91$, $\rho = 0.73$, $\rho = 0.69$ and $\rho = 0.61$. When $\rho = 0.91$, 3D-PSK earns about 1 dB coding gain compared with the 3D-DFT. As the correlation decreases to $\rho = 0.73$, the coding gain is down to about 0.4 dB. When $\rho = 0.66$, the two schemes perform nearly the same. When $\rho$ is down to 0.61 3D-DFT outperforms 3D-PSK. This validates our inference in Sect. 4 that our 3D-PSK is more appropriate for highly correlated systems, especially when $\rho$ is above 0.66. SInce $\rho$ will likely be higher than 0.66 in future FD-MIMO systems, 3D-PSK will have a very promising future.

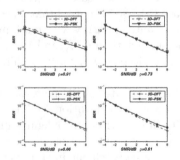

**Fig. 5.** BER versus SNR comparison between 3D-PSK and 3D-DFT when transmit antennas $M_t = 8 * 8$.

## 6   Conclusion

In this paper, an effective limited feedback scheme for FD-MIMO has been proposed to explore the vertical freedom of 3D channels with moderate CSI quantiaztion complexity. We first employ KPC to extend the limited feedback from 2D to 3D. Then, we use NCSD to quantify the CSI which includes both the vertical and horizontal channel information and reduce the complexity from exponential to linear with the number of antennas. Simulation results validate the efficiency of our quantization scheme and demonstrate the better performance of our scheme in high correlated environments, making it more promising for FD-MIMO systems.

## References

1. Younsun, K., Hyoungju, J., Juho, L., Young-Han, N.: Full dimension MIMO (FD-MIMO): the next evolution of MIMO in LTE systems. IEEE Wirel. Commun. $21(2)$, 26–33 (2014)
2. Xie, Y., Jin, S., Wang, J., Zhu, Y., Gao, X., Huang, Y.: A limited feedback scheme for 3D multiuser MIMO based on kronecker product codebook. In: IEEE International Symposium on Personal Indoor and Mobile Radio Communications (PIMRC), pp. 1130–1135. IEEE (2013)
3. Ying, D., Vook, F.W., Thomas, T.A., Love, D.J., Ghosh, A.: Kronecker product correlation model and limited feedback codebook design in a 3D channel model. In: IEEE International Conference on Communications (ICC), pp. 5865–5870. IEEE (2014)
4. Wang, Y., Jiang, L., Chen, Y.: Kronecker product-based codebook design and optimisation for correlated 3D channels. Trans. Emerg. Telecommun. Technol (2014). doi:10.1002/ett.2914
5. Ryan, D.J., Clarkson, I.V.L., Collings, I.B., Guo, D., Honig, M.L.: QAM and PSK codebooks for limited feedback MIMO beamforming. IEEE Trans. Commun. $57(4)$, 1184–1196 (2009)
6. Choi, J., Chance, Z., Love, D.J., Madhow, U.: Noncoherent trellis coded quantization: a practical limited feedback technique for massive MIMO systems. IEEE Trans. Commun. $61(12)$, 5016–5029 (2013)
7. Yong, S.K., Thompson, J.S.: Three-dimensional spatial fading correlation models for compact MIMO receivers. IEEE Trans. Wirel. Commun. $4(6)$, 2856–2869 (2005)
8. Sweldens, W.: Fast block noncoherent decoding. IEEE Commun. Lett. $5(4)$, 132–134 (2001)

# Two-Stage Precoding Based Interference Alignment for Multi-cell Massive MIMO Communication

Jianpeng Ma, Shun Zhang, Hongyan Li[(⊠)], and Weidong Shao

State Key Laboratory of Integrated Services Networks,
Xidian University, Xi'an 710071, People's Republic of China
jpmaxdu@gmail.com, zhangshunsdu@gmail.com, hyli@mail.xidian.edu.cn

**Abstract.** The two-stage precoding scheme was proposed to reduce the high overhead of channel estimation and channel state information (CSI) feedback for frequency division duplexing (FDD) massive MIMO systems. However, most of recent works focus only on single cell scenery. In this paper, we examine two-stage precoding for multi-cell FDD massive MIMO system. To manage the inter-cell interference and improve the data rate for cell-edge users, we propose a two-stage precoding based Interference alignment (IA) scheme for multi-cell massive MIMO system. Both theoretical analysis and numerical results show that proposed two-stage precoding based IA scheme can sufficiently improve the data rate for cell-edge users.

**Keywords:** Interference alignment · Two-stage precoding · Massive MIMO · Channel covariance matrix

## 1 Introduction

Massive multiple-input multiple-output (MIMO) technology has been widely considered as a promising technology to achieve the capacity requirement in 5G system [1–4]. The main idea of massive MIMO is that the base station (BS) employs a large number of antennas, which make the independently distributed channel vectors for different users become pairwise orthogonal. In this case, simple linear precodings, such as the matched-filtering (MF) and zero-forcing (ZF), become nearly optimal [5].

Channel state information (CSI) at BS side plays a principal role for downlink precoding and uplink detection in MIMO system. In time-division duplex (TDD) systems, the CSI at BS side can be obtained through uplink training

This work is supported by the National Science Foundation (91338115, 61231008), National S&T Major Project (2015ZX03002006), the Fundamental Research Funds for the Central Universities (WRYB142208, JB140117), Program for Changjiang Scholars and Innovative Research Team in University (IRT0852), the 111 Project (B08038), SAST (201454).

ⓒ ICST Institute for Computer Sciences, Social Informatics and Telecommunications Engineering 2018
Q. Chen et al. (Eds.): ChinaCom 2016, Part I, LNICST 209, pp. 34–43, 2018.
DOI: 10.1007/978-3-319-66625-9_4

by uplink-downlink reciprocity. Under this situation, the overhead of training is proportional to the total number of user antennas. However, in FDD system where uplink-downlink reciprocity does not exist, the CSI at BS side should be acquired by downlink training, channel estimation at user side, and CSI feedback. In this case, both the number of orthogonal training symbols and the amount of CSI feedback are in scale with the number of BS antennas. Therefore, the large amount of BS antennas in FDD massive MIMO system will lead to unacceptable overhead.

However, FDD dominant current wireless cellular system. To overcome this difficulty and make massive MIMO practical in FDD system, a two-stage precoding scheme called "Joint Spatial Division and Multiplexing (JSDM)" was first proposed in [6]. The concept behind two-stage precoding is: (i) users are grouped into different clusters, and the users in the same cluster have almost similar covariance matrices; the covariance matrices of different cluster are independent and occupy different subspaces; (ii) the downlink precoding is divided into two stages: a prebeamforming stage and an inner precoding stage. The prebeamforming, which only depends on channel covariance matrices, is used to eliminate inter-cluster interference. After the prebeamforming stage, the high dimensional massive MIMO channel links for different clusters are partitioned into several independently equivalent channels of reduced dimensions. Then each cluster separately performs the inner precoding to eliminate the intra cluster interferences.

Many researchers followed the two-stage precoding for FDD massive MIMO. In [7], The authors developed a low complexity online iterative algorithm to track the prebeamforming matrix. The iterative algorithm minimizes the total interference power minus weighted total desired power step by step, and converge to global optimal solution under static channels. In [8], the signal-to-leakage-plus-noise ratio (SLNR) is considered to design prebeamforming matrix, an iterative algorithm was proposed to design prebeamforming matrix by maximizing the SLNR. In [9], the JSDM algorithm was adopted in mm-Wave communication.

Almost all above mentioned works [6–9] only considered single cell scenario. To the best of our knowledge, the two-stage precoding in multi-cell scenario is only considered in [7]. In this paper, we examine the two-stage precoding for multi-cell systems. We focus on inter-cell interference management and improving data rate for cell-edge users. Interference alignment (IA) is a promising interference management scheme for multi-cell cellular system [10]. However, BS need to know global CSI to preform IA, which lead to unaffordable signaling overhead in massive MIMO system. Fortunately, two-stage precoding can efficiently reduce the channel dimension, which makes it possible to perform IA in massive MIMO system. Therefore, IA can eliminates interference and improve data rate for users under two-stage precoding, and two-stage precoding can in turn reduces signaling overhead for IA. In this paper we combine the two technologies together and propose a two-stage precoding based IA scheme for multi-cell massive MIMO system. Both theoretical analysis and numerical results show that proposed scheme can sufficiently improve the data rate for cell-edge users.

The rest of this paper is organized as follows. The system model is described in Sect. 2. Section 3 illustrates proposed scheme and analyzes its performance. Numerical results and conclusion are given in Sects. 4 and 5 separately.

**Notations:** We use lowercase (uppercase) boldface to donates column vector (matrix). $(\cdot)^H$ denotes the complex conjugate transpose operation, and $(\cdot)^T$ denotes the transpose operation. $\mathbf{I}_N$ donates a $N \times N$ identity matrix. $\mathbb{C}^{N \times M}$ is the $N \times M$ complex number space. $\mathbb{E}\{\cdot\}$ means expectation operator. We use $\det\{\cdot\}$ and $rank\{\cdot\}$ to donate determinant and rank of a matrix. $\mathbf{n} \sim \mathcal{CN}(0, \mathbf{I}_N)$ means $\mathbf{n}$ is complex circularly-symmetric Gaussian distributed with zero mean and covariance $\mathbf{I}_N$.

## 2    System Model

We consider the typical three-cell FDD system to implement full spectrum reuse, where each cell consists of one BS at the geometric center position. Each BS is equipped with $N_t \gg 1$ antennas in the form of uniform linear array (ULA). The corresponding BSs are separately donated as $BS_1$, $BS_2$, $BS_3$. Thus, as illustrated in Fig. 1, only the three adjacent sectors with mutual interference are analyzed for simplicity. Users, each with $N_r$-antennas, are randomly distributed. According to geographic information, we can partition the users into $G$ groups, and the users in one specific cluster are almost co-located. The $k$-th user in group $j$ can be donated as $(g, k)$, $k = 1, 2, \ldots, K_j$, and $j = 1, 2, \ldots, G$, where $K_j$ is the number of users in group $j$.

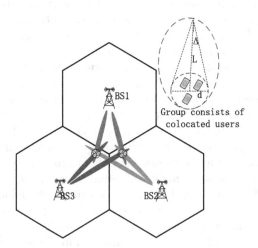

**Fig. 1.** A three cell massive MIMO cellular system. Users are partitioned into groups and three BSs jointly transmit data for each group.

We suppose that BSs antennas are elevated at a very high amplitude, such that there is not enough local scattering around the BS antennas. In this case, antenna correlation at BS side should be considered. Since users in same group are almost co-located, such that it is reasonable to assume that user in group $g$ have the same channel covariance matrix $\mathbf{R}_g$. Then, the channel between BS $i$ and user $k$ in group $g$ is given by

$$\mathbf{H}_{g,k} = \mathbf{W}^i_{g,k} \{\mathbf{R}^i_g\}^{\frac{1}{2}} = \mathbf{W}^i_{g,k} \{\mathbf{\Lambda}^i_g\}^{\frac{1}{2}} \{\mathbf{E}^i_g\}^H \tag{1}$$

where $\mathbf{W}^i_{g,k} \in \mathbb{C}^{N_r \times r^i_g} \sim \mathcal{CN}(0, \mathbf{I})$, $\mathbf{\Lambda}^i_g$ is an diagonal matrix whose elements are nonzero eigenvalues of $\mathbf{R}^i_g$, $\mathbf{E}^i_g \in \mathbb{C}^{N_t \times r^i_g}$ is the tall unitary matrix of the eigenvectors of $\mathbf{R}^i_g$ corresponding to the nonzero eigenvalues, and $r^i_g$ is rank of $\mathbf{R}^i_g$. We adopt one ring channel model where users group is surrounded by a ring of scatters with radius $d$ [11]. Under this model, the $(m, n)$th entry of $\mathbf{R}^i_g$ is given by

$$[\mathbf{R}^i_g]_{m,n} = \frac{1}{2\Delta^i_g} \int_{\theta^i_g - \Delta^i_g}^{\theta^i_g + \Delta^i_g} \exp\left[\frac{-2i\pi(p-q)\sin(\alpha)\tau}{\lambda}\right] d\alpha \tag{2}$$

where $\alpha$ is the angle of departure (AoD) of one path from BS to scattering ring with interval $[\theta^i_g - \Delta^i_g, \theta^i_g + \Delta^i_g]$, $\theta^i_g$ is the azimuth angle of central point of scattering ring, $\tau$ is the antenna element spacing, and $\lambda$ is the carrier wavelength. $\Delta^i_g \approx \arctan(d/L^i_g)$ is the angular spread (AS) and $L^i_g$ is the distance between BS $i$ and group $g$.

Interestingly, in the massive MIMO system, the toeplitz matrix $\mathbf{R}^i_j$ asymptotically approaches to a circulant matrix, and $\mathbf{E}^i_j$ can be constructed by $r^i_j$ columns of the $N_t \times N_t$ unitary discrete Fourier transform (DFT) matrix $\mathbf{F}_{N_t}$ as [6]

$$\mathbf{E}^i_g = [\mathbf{f}_n : n \in \mathcal{I}^i_g] \tag{3}$$

where $\mathbf{f}_n$ represents $n$-th column of $\mathbf{F}_{N_t}$, and the index set $\mathcal{I}^i_g$ is defined as

$$\mathcal{I}^i_j = \left\{ n : 2n/N_t - 1 \in [\frac{\tau}{\lambda}\sin(\theta^i_g + \Delta^i_g). \right.$$
$$\left. \frac{\tau}{\lambda}\sin(\theta^i_g - \Delta^i_g)], n = 0, 1, \cdots, N_t - 1 \right\}. \tag{4}$$

Moreover, we have $r^i_g = \lfloor N_t \min\{1, \rho^i_g\} \rfloor$, where

$$\rho^i_g = \left| \frac{\tau}{\lambda}\sin(\theta^i_g + \Delta^i_g) - \frac{\tau}{\lambda}\sin(\theta^i_g - \Delta^i_g) \right|$$
$$= 2\frac{\tau}{\lambda} \left| \cos(\theta^i_g) \right| \sin(\Delta^i_g). \tag{5}$$

Since the AS $\Delta^i_g$ is relatively small, $\mathbf{R}^i_g$ possesses low rank property, i.e., $r^i_g \ll N_t$.

# 3   Two-Stage Precoding Based IA Scheme

## 3.1   Proposed Transmission Scheme

To improve the data rate for cell-edge users, we let three BSs to jointly transmit data for each users group. Then the received signal at group $g$ is given by,

$$\mathbf{y}_g = \sum_{i=1}^{3} \mathbf{H}_g^i \mathbf{P}_g^i \mathbf{x}_g^i + \sum_{i=1}^{3} \sum_{g'=1,g'\neq g}^{G} \mathbf{H}_{g'}^i \mathbf{P}_{g'}^i \mathbf{x}_{g'}^i + \mathbf{n}_g \tag{6}$$

where $\mathbf{H}_g^i = \left[ \{\mathbf{H}_{g,1}^i\}^T \{\mathbf{H}_{g,1}^i\}^T \cdots \{\mathbf{H}_{g,K_g}^i\}^T \right]^T \in \mathbb{C}^{K_g N_t \times N_r}$ is the channel matrix associates with the BS $i$ and group $g$, $\mathbf{P}_g^i \in \mathbb{C}^{N_r \times S_g^i}$ is the precoding matrix, $\mathbf{x}_g^i \in \mathbb{C}^{S_g^i \times 1}$ is the data vector transmitted by BS $i$ to group $g$, and $\mathbf{n}_g \sim \mathcal{CN}(0, \mathbf{I}_{N_t})$ is the additive complex Gaussian noise. In this paper, we adopt the two-stage precoding framework, where the precoding process can be divided into two stages as

$$\mathbf{P}_g^i = \mathbf{B}_g^i \mathbf{V}_g^i, \tag{7}$$

where the prebeamforming matrix $\mathbf{B}_g^i$, related to spatial correlation matrices, is utilized to eliminate the inter-cluster interferences; the $M_g^i \times S_g^i$ matrix $\mathbf{V}_g^i$ denotes the inner precoder dealing with the intra-cluster interferences, which depends on $K_g N_r \times M_g^i$ effective equivalent channel matrix $\overline{\mathbf{H}}_g^i = \mathbf{H}_g^i \mathbf{B}_g^i$; $M_g^i$ is the rank of $\overline{\mathbf{H}}_g^i$ seen by the inner precoder, which satisfies $S_g^i \leq M_g^i \leq r_g^i$. It can be found that $\overline{\mathbf{H}}_g^i$ possesses a much smaller number of unknown parameters than the original channel matrix $\mathbf{H}_g^i$.

The designing of the prebeamforming matrix $\mathbf{B}_g^i$ is the key task of two-stage precoding and has been examined in [6,8] for single-cell system.

Clearly, treating all groups in the whole system as one big group, we can directly calculate the $\mathbf{B}_g^i$ with the methods for the single-cell system. Without loss of generality, we adopt the DFT based prebeamforming, and achieve the prebemforming matrices through concentrating the subspace span$\{\mathbf{B}_g^i\}$ into the null-space of span$\{\boldsymbol{\Xi}_g^i\}$, where $\boldsymbol{\Xi}_g^i$ is constructed by $\mathbf{E}_{g'}^i$ of all but the group $g$ in the system as

$$\boldsymbol{\Xi}_g^i = \left[ \mathbf{f}_n : n \in \bigcup_{g'=1,g'\neq g}^{G} \mathcal{I}_{g'}^i \right]. \tag{8}$$

Utilizing the orthogonality of columns of DFT matrix, $\mathbf{B}_g^i$ for group $g$ is given by

$$\mathbf{B}_g^i = \left[ \mathbf{f}_n : n \in \left( \mathcal{I}_g^i - \bigcup_{g'=1,g'\neq g}^{G} \mathcal{I}_{g'}^i \right) \right]. \tag{9}$$

where the set $\mathcal{A} - \mathcal{B}$ contains all the elements that are in set $\mathcal{A}$ but not in set $\mathcal{B}$, i.e., $\mathcal{A} - \mathcal{B} = \{x : x \in \mathcal{A} \text{ and } x \notin \mathcal{B}\}$. It can be learned from the computation of

$\mathbf{B}_g^i$ that $M_g^i$ equals the number of columns of $\mathbf{E}_g^i$ that linearly independent with columns of $\Xi_g^i$, namely,

$$M_g^i = \text{rank}\{\mathbf{B}_g^i\} = \left| \mathcal{I}_g^i - \bigcup_{g'=1,g'\neq g}^{J} \mathcal{I}_{g'}^i \right|, \tag{10}$$

where $|\mathcal{A}|$ donates the number of elements in set $\mathcal{A}$. The resultant prebeamforming matrices $\mathbf{B}_g^i$ satisfies the following constraint:

$$\{\mathbf{E}_{g'}^i\}^T \mathbf{B}_g^i = 0, \forall g' \neq g, \tag{11}$$

which means that the transmitted signal to group $g$ will not cause interference to other groups. Then the inter-group interference terms in (6) are eliminated, and the received signals can be simplified as

$$\mathbf{y}_g = \sum_{i=1}^{3} \overline{\mathbf{H}}_g^i \mathbf{V}_g^i \mathbf{x}_g^i + \mathbf{n}_g \tag{12}$$

where $\overline{\mathbf{H}}_g = \mathbf{H}_g \mathbf{B}_g$, of dimension $K_g N \times D_g^i$, is the reduced dimensional effective channel between BS $i$ and group $g$. As 3 BSs jointly server one group, the received signal is superposition of signal transmitted by 3 BSs. For simplicity of expression, we assume that the number of user in each group is same as number of BSs. But the scheme can be easily extended to the general case. In this case, each BS serves one specific user in each group. Thus we can rewrite the received signal in (12) separately for each user.

$$\mathbf{y}_{g,1} = \overline{\mathbf{H}}_{g,1}^1 \mathbf{V}_g^1 \mathbf{x}_g^1 + \sum_{i=2,3} \overline{\mathbf{H}}_{g,1}^i \mathbf{V}_g^i \mathbf{x}_g^i + \mathbf{n}_{g,1} \tag{13}$$

$$\mathbf{y}_{g,2} = \overline{\mathbf{H}}_{g,2}^2 \mathbf{V}_g^2 \mathbf{x}_g^2 + \sum_{i=1,3} \overline{\mathbf{H}}_{g,2}^i \mathbf{V}_g^i \mathbf{x}_g^i + \mathbf{n}_{g,2} \tag{14}$$

$$\mathbf{y}_{g,3} = \overline{\mathbf{H}}_{g,3}^3 \mathbf{V}_g^3 \mathbf{x}_g^3 + \sum_{i=1,2} \overline{\mathbf{H}}_{g,3}^i \mathbf{V}_g^i \mathbf{x}_g^i + \mathbf{n}_{g,3} \tag{15}$$

Obviously, with prebeamforming and joint transmission, the effective channel of each group becomes a 3 BS and 3 users MIMO X channel [10]. A promising interference management scheme named interference alignment (IA) has been proposed to efficiently achieve multiple signaling dimensions under MIMO X channel [10]. The inner precoder $\mathbf{V}_g^1$, $\mathbf{V}_g^2$ and $\mathbf{V}_g^3$ are carefully chosen to consolidate the interference at each receiver into a reduced-dimensional subspace space, while keep the desired signals separable from interference. An $N \times S_g^k$ suppression matrix $\mathbf{U}_{g,k}$ whose columns are orthonormal to the interference subspace is used at each user to eliminate interference. When IA is feasible [10], the following conditions are met

$$rank\{\mathbf{U}_{g,k}^H \overline{\mathbf{H}}_{g,k}^k \mathbf{V}_g^k\} = S_g^k, \tag{16}$$

$$\mathbf{U}_{g,k}^H \overline{\mathbf{H}}_{g,k}^i \mathbf{V}_g^i = \mathbf{0}, \forall k \neq i. \tag{17}$$

Thus, the intra-group interference is completely eliminated and the desired signal of user $k$ in group $g$ can be rewrote as

$$\underline{\mathbf{y}}_{g,k} = \underline{\mathbf{H}}_{g,k}^k \mathbf{x}_g^k + \underline{\mathbf{n}}_{g,k} \tag{18}$$

where $\underline{\mathbf{y}}_{g,k} = \mathbf{U}_{g,k}^H \mathbf{y}_{g,k}$, $\underline{\mathbf{H}}_{g,k}^k = \mathbf{U}_{g,k}^H \overline{\mathbf{H}}_{g,k}^k \mathbf{V}_g^k$ is the $S_g^k \times S_g^k$ full rank effective channel between $k$th BS and user $k$ in group $g$, $\underline{\mathbf{n}}_{g,k} = \mathbf{U}_{g,k}^H \mathbf{n}_{g,k}$ is the effective Gaussian noise with distribution $\mathcal{CN}(0, \mathbf{I}_{S_g^k})$.

## 3.2   Performance Analysis

In this subsection, we provide performance analysis of proposed transmission scheme in term of number of data streams, achievable rate and signaling overhead. For simplicity of expression, we consider a symmetric scenario with same rank $r_g^i = r$ of the channel covariance matrix, same dimension $M_g^i = M$ of the prebeamforming matrix, and same number $S_g^i = S$ of data streams per group. However, the analysis can be easily extended to the general case.

To meet the IA feasible condition (16) and (17), the number of data streams should satisfy the follow constrain,

$$S \leq \frac{M + N}{K_g + 1}. \tag{19}$$

As 3 BSs transmit data for one user group simultaneously, the total number of data streams for each group is $3S$.

We assume that the intra-group interference is exactly eliminated by IA. By carefully considering the leaked inter-group interference, the achievable rate of group $g$ is given by

$$R_g = \sum_{k=1}^{3} \log \det \left\{ \mathbf{I}_S + \mathbf{K}_{g,k}^{-1} \underline{\mathbf{H}}_{g,k}^k \mathbf{Q}_g^k \left( \underline{\mathbf{H}}_{g,k}^k \right)^H \right\}. \tag{20}$$

where

$$\mathbf{K}_{g,k} = \mathbf{I}_S + \sum_{i=1}^{3} \sum_{g'=1, g' \neq g}^{G} \mathbf{H}_{g,k}^i \mathbf{P}_{g'}^i \mathbf{Q}_{g'}^i \left( \mathbf{H}_{g,k}^i \mathbf{P}_{g'}^i \right)^H \tag{21}$$

is the covariance matrix of inter-group interference pluse noise, and $\mathbf{Q}_g^k = \mathbb{E}\{\mathbf{x}_g^i [\mathbf{x}_g^i]^H\}$ is the covariance matrix of data vector.

In the prebeamforming stage, the dominant eigenmodes $\{\mathbf{E}_g^i\}$ is necessary. It is fact the channel statistical informations remain unchanged within a long time, such that the acquisition of $\{\mathbf{E}_g^i\}$ has low overhead. We focus on the analysis for acquisition of the effective channel $\{\overline{\mathbf{H}}_g^i\}$, which are essential to the design of inner precoding. Thanks to the prebeamforming, the effective channel of different groups are independent. Training symbols can be reuse between groups. But it should be note that 3 BSs transmit data to each group simultaneously. Therefore, the training symbols of different BSs for a specific group should be orthogonal. In this case, we need $3M$ orthogonal dimensions to train the effective channels. To perform IA, the BSs need to know not only the intended channels but also the interference channels. Therefore, each group need to feedback $9 \times M \times N$ complex channel coefficients, which is 3 times of that without IA. We assume that each complex channel coefficient is quantized into $Q$ bits, the channel coherent block length is $T$, and the rate of the feedback channel is $F$ bits per symbol. Taking into consideration of overhead of training and feedback, the effective achievable rate of group $g$ is given by

$$R_{g,ohd} = \max \left\{ 1 - \frac{3M}{T} - \frac{9MNQ}{FT}, 0 \right\} R_g. \qquad (22)$$

## 4   Numerical Result

In this section, we evaluate the proposed two-stage precoding based IA scheme for multi-cell massive MIMO communication through numerical simulation. We consider a three cell cellular system with 3 groups in cell-edge. The number of users in each group is 3. The radius of the cell is 1 km. The distance between user groups and BS is 800 m. Each BS is equipped with a ULA with $M = 128$ antennas, and each user is equipped with $N = 2$ antennas. The BS antenna elements spacing equal to half wavelength. The carrier frequency is 2 GHz. We generate massive MIMO channel according to (1) and (2). The variance of the noise is 1. A total number of $10^4$ Monte Carlo runs are used to numerically average the achievable rate.

Firstly, we compare the performance of two-stage precoding without IA (each user group is served by only on BS) and the proposed two-stage precoding based IA transmission scheme. In this example, the rank $D$ of effective channel is 2, such that if IA is not applied, each group can only receive 2 data streams, which is less than the number of users in group. Whereas, the total number of streams for each group with IA is 3. In this case, the proposed scheme achieves an improvement factor of 3/2 in number of data streams. Figure 2 compares the sum rate per group of the two-stage precoding transmission with IA against the two-stage precoding transmission without IA. The simulation results show that the sum rate is obviously improved by IA.

To uncover the impact of training and CSI feedback overhead on the performance, we consider a numerical example of effective sum rate in (22), where SNR = 30 dB, $F = 4$ and $Q = 16$. Figure 3 shows the effective sum rate per group versus channel coherent block length $T$. From Fig. 3 we can observe that the proposed two-stage precoding with IA is still efficient when overhead is considered. But the gaps between transmission with IA and that without IA become smaller when $T$ decreases. The efficient sum rate of transmission with IA become lower than that without IA when $T$ is extremely small. The reasons behind this is that BS need to know more CSI to perform interference alignment, which increases the overhead of channel estimation and feedback.

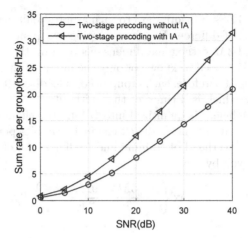

**Fig. 2.** Sum rate per group over two-stage precoding transmission with IA and that without IA versus SNR.

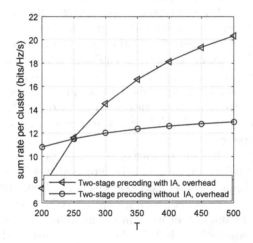

**Fig. 3.** Effective sum rate per group versus channel coherent block length T (SNR = 30 dB, $F = 4, Q = 16$).

## 5    Conclusion

In this paper, we investigated two-stage precoding for multi-cell FDD massive MIMO systems, where multiple antennas at user side is considered. We proposed a two-stage precoding based interference alignment scheme. The performance of proposed transmission scheme was evaluated by theoretical analysis. Numerical simulation showed that the proposed scheme can efficiently improve the data rate of cell-edge users with affordable overhead.

# References

1. Jungnickel, V., Manolakis, K., Zirwas, W., Panzner, B., Braun, V., Lossow, M., Sternad, M., Apelfrojd, R., Svensson, T.: The role of small cells, coordinated multipoint, and massive MIMO in 5G. IEEE Commun. Mag. **52**, 44–51 (2014)
2. Boccardi, F., Heath, R.W., Lozano, A., Marzetta, T.L., Popovski, P.: Five disruptive technology directions for 5G. IEEE Commun. Mag. **52**, 74–80 (2014)
3. Larsson, E.G., Edfors, O., Tufvesson, F., Marzetta, T.L.: Massive MIMO for next generation wireless systems. IEEE Commun. Mag. **52**, 186–195 (2014)
4. Andrews, J.G., Buzzi, S., Choi, W., Hanly, S.V., Lozano, A., Soong, A.C.K., Zhang, J.C.: What will 5G be? IEEE J. Sel. Areas Commun. **32**, 1065–1082 (2014)
5. Gao, X., Edfors, O., Rusek, F., Tufvesson, F.: Linear pre-coding performance in measured very-large MIMO channels. In: IEEE VTC-Fall, pp. 1–5 (2011)
6. Adhikary, A., Nam, J., Ahn, J.-Y., Caire, G.: Joint spatial division and multiplexing the large-scale array regime. IEEE Trans. Inf. **59**, 6441–6463 (2013)
7. Chen, J., Lau, V.K.N.: Two-tier precoding for FDD multi-cell massive MIMO time-varying interference networks. IEEE J. Sel. Areas Commun. **32**, 1230–1238 (2014)
8. Kim, D., Lee, G., Sung, Y.: Two-stage beamformer design for massive MIMO downlink by trace quotient formulation. IEEE Trans. Commun. **63**, 2200–2211 (2015)
9. Adhikary, A., Safadi, E.A., Samimi, M.K., Wang, R., Caire, G., Rappaport, T.S., Molisch, A.F.: Joint spatial division and multiplexing for mm-Wave channels. IEEE J. Sel. Areas Commun. **32**, 1239–1255 (2014)
10. Cadambe, V.R., Jafar, S.A.: Interference alignment and degrees of freedom of the-user interference channel. IEEE Trans. Inf. Theory **54**, 3425–3441 (2008)
11. Zhang, M., Smith, P., Shafi, M.: An extended one-ring MIMO channel model. IEEE Trans. Wirel. Commun. **6**, 2759–2764 (2007)

# MAC Schemes

# Adaptive Energy-Saving Mechanism for SMAC Protocol in Wireless Sensor Network

Zhou Jieying[✉], Peng Shi, Liu Yinglin, and Huang Shaopeng

School of Data and Computer Science, Sun Yat-sen University,
Guangzhou 510006, Guangdong, China
isszjy@mail.sysu.edu.cn

**Abstract.** This paper proposes an Adaptive Energy-Saving mechanism to improve the performance of SMAC protocol (AES-SMAC). AES-SMAC is composed of two mechanisms, adaptive synchronous period (ASP) and dual element adaptive contention window (DEACW). In ASP, the cache queue of SMAC is simplified into a limited capacity of M/M/1 queuing model to calculate the node's service efficiency. ASP also introduced a parameter called sleep conflict rate to evaluate the performance of node synchronization. Then ASP adjusts the length of synchronous period reasonably to achieve better performance. AES-SMAC protocol was compared with SMAC, ASP and DEACW via the simulation software NS2 in a scenario of Multi-hop topology. Simulation results show that AES-SMAC achieved better performance with higher throughput, lower average delay and higher energy utilization efficiency.

**Keywords:** Wireless sensor network · SMAC protocol · Queuing theory · Synchronous period · Contention window

## 1 Introduction

In the development of wireless sensor network (WSN), MAC (Media Access Control) which provides reliable communication links has been a hot research topic. There are many MAC protocols that have been developed, such as the time division multiple access (TDMA), code division multiple access (CDMA), and contention-based protocols like IEEE 802.11 [1]. Because of the special environment of WSN application, traditional MAC protocol which is based on minimum delay and maximum throughput is not applicable for WSN [2, 3]. WSN focuses on reducing energy consumption while a certain throughput is guaranteed. Based on the characteristic that WSN has limited energy and unique channel access technology, SMAC (sensor-MAC) with dormancy mechanism and based on IEEE802.11 is proposed [4–6]. It aims to reduce energy consumption, enhance scalability of the network and adapt to the dynamic topology changes that it would be suitable for wireless sensor networks. The disadvantages of SMAC are that the throughput, delay and fairness are not considered in this mechanism and fixed synchronous period and contention window cannot adapt to the dynamic changes of the network environment [7, 8]. Therefore an improved protocol–AES-SMAC is introduced

© ICST Institute for Computer Sciences, Social Informatics and Telecommunications Engineering 2018
Q. Chen et al. (Eds.): ChinaCom 2016, Part I, LNICST 209, pp. 47–57, 2018.
DOI: 10.1007/978-3-319-66625-9_5

in this paper to solve the above problems. The rest of this paper is organized as follows: the improved SMAC protocol with adaptive energy saving mechanism (AES-SMAC) is proposed in Sect. 2. Section 3 introduces the simulation of AES-SMAC, DEACW, ASP and SMAC via the software NS2 in a scenario of Multi-hop topology, the simulation results of the four mechanisms are compared and analyzed in this section. Sect. 4 draws a conclusion of this paper.

## 2   Adaptive Energy-Saving Mechanism for SMAC

To overcome the shortcomings of SMAC, this paper proposes an adaptive energy saving mechanism–AES-SMAC to improve the performance of the WSN network which adjusts the synchronous period and the contention window adaptively. AES-SMAC is composed of adaptive synchronous period (ASP) and dual element adaptive contention window (DEACW). In ASP mechanism, to reduce the extra energy consumption resulting from packet re-transmission for packet loss during nodes sleep period, the current network state and synchronization state between nodes are measured based on queuing theory [9] and sleep conflict rate which are used to adjust synchronous period reasonably. While DEACW measures the network channel occupancy and fairness with conflict free ratio and node channel occupancy which are used to adjust contention window adaptively. AES-SMAC improves overall performance of WSN network and reduces energy consumption by combining the advantages of ASP and DEACW mechanisms.

### 2.1   Introduction of ASP

To overcome the deficiency in the synchronization mechanism of SMAC protocol, this paper proposes the ASP mechanism which measures the network and node synchronization state and adjusts the synchronous period adaptively.

In order to measure the state of the network and adjust the synchronous period adaptively, data packet service rate is used in this paper to measure the traffic flow of the network after a node performs synchronization. It is based on queuing theory and reflects the congestion of the network. In order to reflect the synchronization state between nodes, this paper introduces a parameter col_s to represent the conflict ratio of data packets caused by sleeping nodes. At the same time, a new symbol is added in the control packet to monitor the synchronous time among nodes in the switching process of controlling packet. Once time difference is found to be too large, it immediately performs synchronization at the next sleep/listen cycle. The improved mechanism will calculate the average $\mu$ and col_s at the end of a synchronous period. Two values are used to analyze the network congestion and synchronization state, so as to adjust the synchronous period reasonably. ASP mechanism increases the network throughput, reduces the average end-to-end delay and also reduces energy consumption [10], therefore the performance of the network is improved.

(1)   **Calculation of $\mu$ and col_s**

First, the service rate $\mu$ is defined as

$$\mu = \lambda \left( \sqrt{ \left( \frac{1}{4} + \frac{1}{L_q} \right) } + \frac{1}{2} \right) \tag{1}$$

where $\lambda$ refers to the arrival rate of data packets, $L_q$ refers to number of packets in buffer. It can be seen from formula (1) that the value of $\mu$ is proportional to the value of the input rate $\lambda$, is inversely proportional to the length of the packet in the queue. In SMAC protocol, if the current network is congested and the clock difference with the next hop is large, the current node can not send out packet. It has to wait for a long time for synchronization, which leads to the increasing of data packets waiting in the buffer queue. Even if the clock drift is small, it still can not complete data transmission when network congestion occur. The value of $\mu$ will decrease which reflects that current network load is heavy. When the network load is relatively light, if the input rate of the data packet is great, there may be two kinds of situation occur. In the first situation, synchronization between nodes is very good, data packet in the queue is almost zero, therefore, the value $\mu$ will be very large, reflecting that processing speed of the node is fast. In the second situation, the node synchronization is relatively bad, the data packets are stuck in conflict, the the value of $\mu$ will decrease, reflecting that processing speed of the node is slow.

Sleep conflict ratio is defined as the ratio of the sleeping conflict to the total conflict in the synchronous period, i.e.

$$col\_s = \frac{col_{sleep}}{\left( col_{sleep} + col_{other} \right)} \tag{2}$$

where $col_{sleep}$ is the length of conflict caused by sleep, $col_{other}$ is the length of conflict caused by other reasons.

From the definition of col_s we know that, when col_s is large, the value of $col_{sleep}$ is too large in comparison with the $col_{other}$. This situation occurs because the clock difference of the nodes in the network increases along with time passes by. And the long synchronous period is unable to prevent the occurrence of this situation, resulting in the packet loss caused by node sleep, at this time it is necessary to reduce the synchronous period. And when col_s is small, there are two situations, one is the value of $col_{other}$ is too large in comparison with $col_{sleep}$, which means that great conflicts are caused by the network congestion although the node synchronous state is good. At this time it is necessary to increase the synchronous period. The other situation is that the network load is very light, the probability of $col_{sleep}$ and $col_{other}$ is relatively small.

In order to measure the current state of the network reasonably, we should take two parameters into consideration when deciding how to adjust the synchronous period. Because col_s is based on the average value of a synchronous cycle, while the value of $\mu$ depends on the average number of packets in the buffer queue and the average rate of entry. Therefore it is necessary to record the two values in each sleep /listen cycle. The calculation is as follows: Calculation of service rate $\mu$:

$$E(L_q) = \frac{\left(L_q^{(1)} + L_q^{(2)} + \cdots L_q^{(syncperiod)}\right)}{syncperiod} \tag{3}$$

$$\lambda = \frac{\left(p^{(1)} + p^{(2)} + \cdots p^{(syncperiod)}\right)}{(syncperiod \times cycletime)} \tag{4}$$

$$\mu = \lambda\left(\sqrt{\left(\frac{1}{4} + \frac{1}{E(q)}\right)} + \frac{1}{2}\right) \tag{5}$$

Calculation of sleep conflict rate col_s:

$$col\_s = \left(\frac{\left(col_{sleep}^{(1)} + col_{sleep}^{(2)} + \ldots + col_{sleep}^{syncperiod}\right)}{\left(col_{all}^{(1)} + col_{all}^{(2)} + \ldots + col_{all}^{syncperiod}\right)}\right) \tag{6}$$

where

$$col\_all^{(n)} = col\_sleep^{(n)} + col\_other^{(n)} \tag{7}$$

where synchronous period is the number of listening cycle in a synchronous period, cycletime is a monitoring cycle, p is the number of received packages in a listening period.

## (2) Adjustment of synchronous period

When a synchronous cycle is over, the node will calculate the average service rate and the average sleep conflict ratio in a cycle, and then adaptively adjusts the synchronous period according to the following mechanism, as shown in Algorithm 1:

The parameters of $\theta$, $\omega$, $\beta$, $\alpha$, $\gamma$ and $\delta$ are used to balance the jitters of the col_s and $\mu$ where SYNC_MIN and SYNC_MAX are the maximum and minimum values of a synchronous cycle.

In Algorithm 1, the code calculates the value of col_s at first. There are two situations, if col_sleep and col_other are not zero at the same time, then it will calculate the value of col_s. When two value are zero, there is no data exchange in the network or the load of network is light, then col_s is $-1$. The algorithm adjusts the synchronous period reasonably by analyzing the current network state and node synchronization. So as to achieve the goal of increasing the throughput, reducing delay and improving energy efficiency.

After calculating the value of col_s, if the average number of packets in the buffer area is more than 45 (the queue length of simulation setting is 50), the network is considered to be extremely congested regardless of the value of $\mu$. Considering the relationship among the synchronous period, time delay and the throughput, at this time, it is necessary to reduce the probability of the occurrence of the clock difference.

Therefore, the synchronous period should be appropriately reduced. When average number of data packets waiting in the buffer area is in the range of 10 to 45, the network is considered to be in good state. If $\mu \geq \beta + \omega$, it means that the network state is very good. If col_s < δ + θ at the same time, the probability of the increasing clock difference is small. So we can appropriately increase the synchronous period and reduce the energy caused by sending SYNC packets. When col_s > γ + θ, we should reduce the synchronous period and keep synchronization between nodes. When α ≤ μ < β, network load and synchronization are both in balanced state, therefore overall performance of the network will be better without changing synchronous cycle. When μ < α, the network load is heavy. If col_s < δ + θ at the same time, then synchronization between nodes is very good. So we can increase the synchronous period appropriately to reduce the occurrence of more conflicts caused by sending SYNC packets. At last, when the average number of packets in the buffer area is less than 10, the load of the network is light. When col_s > γ + θ, in order to reduce the packet loss caused by sleep, we should reduce the synchronous period to improve the throughput. If col_s = −1 at the same time, then the network load is considered to be extremely light. In order to reduce the energy consumption of nodes, we should increase the period of the synchronization.

```
Algorithm 1 ASP
01: if (col_other !=0) then
02:    col_s=col_sleep / (col_sleep + col_other);
03: else
04:    if (col_sleep==0) col_s=-1;
05:    else col_s=col_sleep / (col_sleep + col_other);
06: end if
07: if (L_q ≥ 45) then
08:    if(col_s≥γ+θ)
09:    syncperiod=max(syncperiod-2,SYNC_MIN);
10: else if ( L_q< 45&& L_q ≥ 10 ) then
11:    μ=(sqrt(1/L_q+ 0.25)+0.5)*suc/cycleTime_/count;
12:    if (μ ≥ β+ ω) then
13:        if(col_s<δ+θ)
14:        syncperiod=min((syncperiod+1),SYNC_MAX);
15:        if(col_s>γ+θ)
16:        syncperiod=max((syncperiod-1),SYNC_MIN);
17:    else if ( col_s < δ+θ && μ < α+ω) then
18:        syncperiod=min((syncperiod+1), SYNC_MAX);
19:    end if
20: else
21:    if ( col_s > γ+θ )
22:    syncperiod=max((syncperiod-2),SYNC_MIN);
23:    else if(col_s=-1)
24:    syncperiod=min((syncperiod+2),SYNC_MAX);
25: end if
```

The basic algorithm is described above. From the analysis, it can be seen that, in order to calculate the sleep conflict ratio and service rate at the end of the period, the node must record the length of a cycle and the number of packets in the buffer area. And then, we can adjust the length of the synchronous cycle and improve the performance of overall network.

### (3) Synchronous monitoring of the node

For the above algorithm, there are some situations that are not considered. If the synchronous period fluctuates frequently and dramatically, the performance of the whole network becomes worse. So the synchronous monitoring mechanism is proposed in RTS/CTS exchange to monitor clock drift between nodes. If the clock drift exceeds a threshold value, it directly sends SYNC packages in the next waking-up without waiting for the end of the cycle. Specific ideas are as follows (Fig. 1):

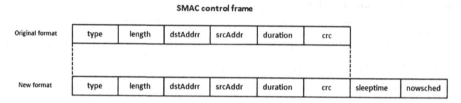

**Fig. 1.** SMAC control frame modification

First, two values are inserted in the RTS control frame. The monitoring mechanism needs to add two values in the control frame. Sleeptime is used to record the time left for the node to sleep, nowsched records the current scheduling table of this node. After the node receives RTS control frame, according to the two values, it can be judged whether two nodes are in the same scheduling table and clock difference can be calculated. If it is larger than the threshold value, then the node sends a synchronizing packet at the next waking-up.

Therefore nodes may encounter the following situations, as shown in Fig. 2. The receiving node sends the SYNC packet to achieve synchronization in the next waking up. We don't use the source node to send SYNC packet because the transmission may be start when the receiving node still sleeps. The synchronization is very good without the need to send SYNC packet. The threshold value will be set larger than before the sudden SYNC broadcast may affect data transmission of other nodes.

## 3    Simulation Results and Performance Analysis

In this section, AES-SMAC protocol is compared with three other schemes: SMAC, ASP and DEACW. Multi-hop topology is used to simulate the four schemes in this paper. CBR model is used to generate the data stream in the network. Sending interval is used to simulate the load of the network. The smaller the interval is, the more data is transmitted in unit time, then load of the network is more heavier. For each of these

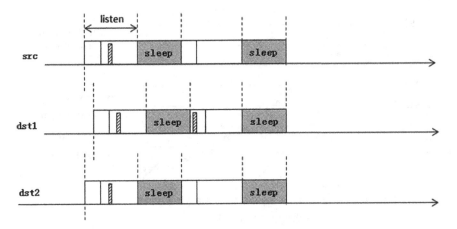

**Fig. 2.** Node synchronization

schemes, the simulation is carried out separately in each scenario. Results of these protocols are analyzed and compared after the simulation. In WSN, data usually needs to be transmitted to the sink node through multi-hop. In this paper, this situation is simulated by the topology of multi hop in Fig. 3. The topology is composed of 10 nodes. The distance between two nodes is 200 m. The simulation time is 1000 s. The CBR data stream starts at 50 s and ends at 800 s.

**Fig. 3.** Multi-hop transmission topology

In this simulation, the transmission range of each node is 250 m. The distance between nodes is determined according to the setting of the scene. And CBR (Constant Bit Rate) is used as the generator of the data stream in this simulation. Packet size of the data stream is 256 bytes. UDP protocol is used as transport layer protocol.

Figure 4 shows that in the multi-hop topology, the through put of SMAC, DEACW, ASP, and AES-SMAC changes with the increase of sending interval. For AES-SMAC, in heavy load area, the node adjusts the contention window adaptively and reduces the probability that multiple nodes simultaneously compete the channel. At the same time, AES-SMAC monitors network traffic situation through ASP mechanism, increases synchronous period and reduces the transmission of controlling packet. So the throughput of AES-SMAC is better than ASP and DEACW in heavy load area.

Figure 5 shows that in the multi-hop topology, the delay of four mechanisms changes with the increase of sending interval. In the heavy load area, the network delay

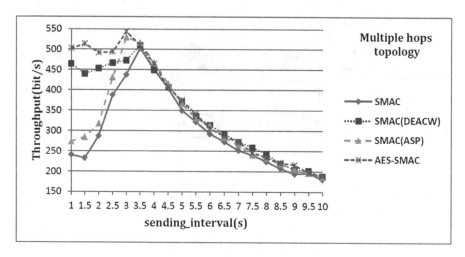

**Fig. 4.** Throughput variation under different sending interval

is mainly caused by conflicts, exposed and hidden terminal problems. In ASP, conflicts increase easily when the exposed and hidden terminal problems occur, because it adopts the mechanism of fixed contention window, so the improvement is not great. In light load area, ASP which focuses on synchronization has smaller delay. In the heavy

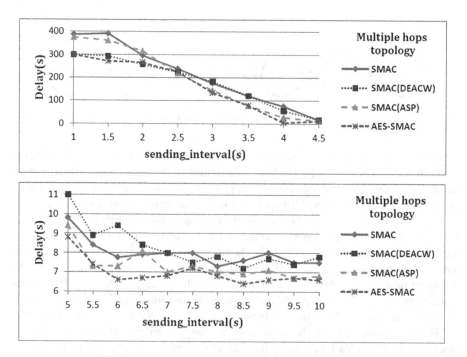

**Fig. 5.** Delay variation under different sending interval

load area, because a large amount of conflicts and SYNC packet transmission are reduced, the delay of AES-SMAC is significantly better than SMAC and ASP. While in light load area, because the ASP mechanism reduces the impact of sleeping delay, the delay of AES-SMAC is better than the other 3 mechanisms.

Figure 6 shows that in the multi-hop topology, the energy consumption of the four mechanisms changes when sending interval increases. Since throughput and SYNC packet transmission are increased in the adjusting process, the overall energy consumption of ASP is larger than DEACW. In the heavy load area, because the increase of throughput is great, the energy consumption of DEACW is larger than ASP.

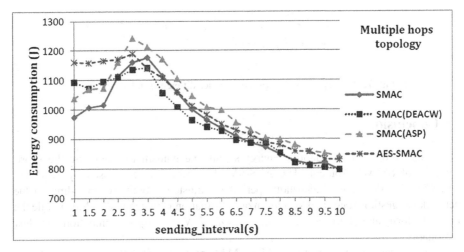

**Fig. 6.** Energy consumption variation under different sending interval

In light load area, energy consumption of AES-SMAC is between DEACW and ASP. Because DEACW reduces energy consumption caused by the idle listening time, while the ASP increases the energy consumption because of sending control frame. The energy required for transmission is much more than idle listening, so the energy consumption of AES-SMAC is slightly more than that of SMAC in light load area.

Figure 7 shows that in the multi-hop topology, the energy efficiency of the four mechanisms changes when sending interval increases. In heavy load area, AES-SMAC reduces conflicts of data packets by adjusting the contention window according to the network state, meanwhile it reduces the transmission of SYNC packets by slightly increasing the synchronous period according to the network load, therefore AES-SMAC reduces the energy consumption from two aspects so energy efficiency is very good. In light load area, idle listening is the main reason of energy consumption. Therefore, AES-SMAC needs to consider the energy consumption caused by idle listening. But because ASP mechanism increases the synchronous period in light load area, the energy efficiency of AES-SMAC is better than DEACW in light load area.

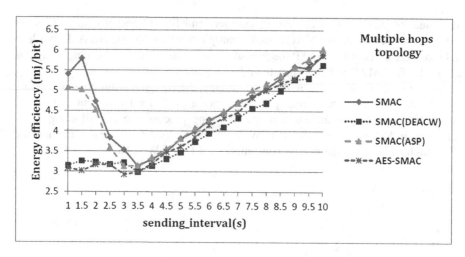

**Fig. 7.** Energy efficiency variation under different sending interval

# 4  Conclusion

This paper proposed an adaptive energy-saving mechanism to overcome the short-comings of SMAC protocol. The AES-SMAC protocol is composed by ASP and DEACW. In ASP, the synchronous period is adjusted adaptively according to the network congestion states and synchronization situation between nodes. Meanwhile the network load and fairness are used in DEACW to adjust contention window reasonably.

The comparison experiments of AES-SMAC protocol with other relative protocols are carried out via simulation software NS2. Different network topologies are used in the experiment. Simulation results show that AES-SMAC protocol achieves higher throughput, lower average delay and higher energy utilization efficiency than SMAC and other relative protocols, therefore the performance of the network is improved efficiently.

**Acknowledgement.** This paper is financially supported by the program of Guangdong Science and Technology (Grant No. 2015A010103007) and the program of Guangzhou Science and Technology (Grant No. 2015A010103007).

# References

1. LAN MAN Standards Committee of the IEEE Computer Society: Wireless LAN medium access control (MAC) and physical layer (PHY) specification, IEEE Std 802.11-1997 edition. IEEE, New York (1997)
2. Yang, O., Heinzelman, W.B.: Modeling and performance analysis for duty-cycled MAC protocols with applications to S-MAC and X-MAC. IEEE Trans. Mob. Comput. **11**(6), 905–921 (2012)

3. Feng, H., Ma, L., Leng, S.: A low overhead wireless sensor networks MAC protocol. In: 2010 2nd International Conference on Computer Engineering and Technology (ICCET) (2010)
4. Estrin, D., Ye, W., Heidemann, J.: An energy-efficient mac protocol for wireless sensor networks. In: Proceedings of Twenty-First Annual Joint Conference of the IEEE Computer and Communications Societies, pp. 1567–1576. IEEE (2002)
5. Heidemann, J., Ye, W.: Medium access control in wireless sensor networks. In: Raghavendra, C.S., Sivalingam, K.M., Znati, T. (eds.) Wireless Sensor Networks, pp. 73–91. Springer, Boston (2004). doi:10.1007/978-1-4020-7884-2_4
6. Estrin, D., Ye, W., Heidemann, J.: Medium access control with coordinated adaptive sleeping for wireless sensor networks. IEEE ACM Trans. Netw. 12(3), 493–506 (2004)
7. Yang, O., Heinzelman, W.: Modeling and throughput analysis for SMAC with a finite queue capacity. In: 2009 5th International Conference on Intelligent Sensors, Sensor Networks and Information Processing (ISSNIP) (2009)
8. Heinzelman, W., Ray, S., Demirkol, I.: ADV-MAC: advertisement-based MAC protocol for wireless sensor networks. In: 5th International Conference on Mobile Ad-hoc and Sensor Networks, MSN 2009 (2009)
9. Chouhan, L., Trivedi, A.: Priority based MAC scheme for cognitive radio network: a queuing theory modelling. In: 2012 Ninth International Conference on Wireless and Optical Communications Networks (WOCN) (2012)
10. Pottie, G.J., Kaiser, W.J.: Embedding the internet: wireless integrated network sensors. Commun. ACM. 43(5), 51–58 (2000)

# A Transmission Rate Optimized Cooperative MAC Protocol for Wireless Sensor Networks

Pengfei Zhao[1,2,3(✉)], Kai Liu[1,2,3], Feng Liu[1,2,3], and Ruochen Fang[4]

[1] School of Electronics and Information Engineering,
Beihang University, Beijing, China
{pf_zhao,liuk,liuf}@buaa.edu.cn
[2] Beijing Key Lab for Network-Based Cooperative Air Traffic Management,
Beijing, China
[3] Collaborative Innovation Center of Geospatial Technology, Wuhan, China
[4] School of Software, Beihang University, Beijing, China
82343445@qq.com

**Abstract.** In order to enhance throughput in wireless sensor networks (WSNs), we propose a transmission rate optimized cooperative MAC (TRO-CMAC) protocol. The protocol always adopts the cooperative transmission with high transmission rates to replace the direct transmission with low transmission rate. A sender preselects two best candidate relays from its relay information table according to recent equivalent transmission rate and channel condition for use in cooperative transmission. These two relays contend to become the final best relay with instantaneous cooperative transmission rate and channel condition. Simulation results show that TRO-CMAC protocol can obtain higher throughput than those of the RCF-CMAC and 2rcMAC protocols.

**Keywords:** Cooperative communication · Cooperative MAC protocol · Relay selection · Network lifetime · Wireless sensor networks

## 1 Introduction

With the rapidly increasing data from more and more sensor nodes in wireless sensor networks (WSNs), there is a rising demand for a higher transmission rate over the whole wireless network [1]. This situation can be solved by introducing the cooperative communication technique to WSNs. The cooperative communication can improve throughput and decrease the transmission time by acquiring the space diversity gain. The 2rc-MAC protocol [2] makes use of two cooperative relays to achieve better throughput and delay performance. This improves throughput while guaranteeing transmission reliability. In RCF-CMAC Protocol [3], source node preselects two optimal candidate relays through its local relay information table, and sets different priorities to them in cooperative request-to-send (C-RTS) packet according to relay efficiency which reflects the level of its saved time, but it does not consider the channel condition and transmission power. ORS-MAC protocol [4] takes MAC overhead caused by retransmission into consideration. CoopMAC [5] similarly attempt to

Q. Chen et al. (Eds.): ChinaCom 2016, Part I, LNICST 209, pp. 58–66, 2018.
DOI: 10.1007/978-3-319-66625-9_6

increase transmission rates by a high-date-rate relay. That is to say, a high-data-rate node is employed to help a low-data-rate node to transmit data packet. The design of high transmission rate medium access control (MAC) protocols and the issue of multiple rates has become a research hotspot, and more and more researches pay attention to these aspects.

Giving preference to those nodes with optimal channel quality under the condition of high transmission rate in a multiple-rate situation is our motivation to design the TRO-CMAC protocol. The protocol uses two-hop links with a high transmission rate to replace one low-rate hop to enhance the network throughput. Taking channel condition and novel access methods into consideration effectively reduce the interference and avoid the collision.

The rest of the article is organized as follows. In Sect. 2, we introduce the network model. TRO-CMAC protocol with relay selection algorithm is shown in Sect. 3. The simulation results is presented in Sect. 4, and the conclusion is given in Sect. 5.

## 2 Network Model

This article investigates a typical WSNs, and nodes placed randomly in a circle with a radius of 100 m, which is the communication range. Each node is a half-duplex transceiver. As shown in Fig. 1, it's assumed that the transmission rates are 1, 2, 5.5 or 11 Mbps respectively, which corresponds the range of $r_1$, $r_2$, $r_{5.5}$ or $r_{11}$ under the condition that Bit Error Rate (BER) is not less than $10^{-5}$. The relation between the data rates and the ranges is listed in Table 1 [5]. The nodes in regions 1 and 2 can transmit at high rates (e.g., nodes A and B (11, 5.5 Mbps)), while those in regions 3 and 4 are low rate nodes (e.g., nodes C and D (2, 1 Mbps)). In this paper, we use S, R and D represent sender, relay and recipient, while $R_{sr}$, $R_{rd}$, $R_{sd}$ and $G_{sr}$, $G_{rd}$, $G_{sd}$ denote as the data transmission rate and channel-gain between the S and R, R and D, S and D, respectively [3].

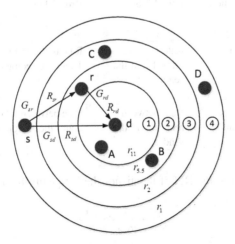

**Fig. 1.** Network model

**Table 1.** Physical model table (path loss exponent = 3).

| Data rate | 11 Mbps | 5.5 Mbps | 2 Mbps | 1 Mbps |
|---|---|---|---|---|
| Range ($BER \geq 10^{-5}$) | 48.2 m | 67.1 m | 74.7 m | 100 m |

# 3  TRO-CMAC Protocol

## 3.1  Relay Information Table (RIT)

Each node should have a relay information table (RIT) that maintain the information about potential relays. It can be used to select a better relay for a transmission process. Due to the broadcasting specialty of wireless communication, RIT can be created and updated by overhearing all ongoing transmission of neighbor nodes. For example, S always passively listen both control frame and data frame of R and D, of which locate in the communication region, while R is corresponding with D.

The information contained in the RIT is described in Table 2. The first column is the ID field, which stores the MAC address of the potential relay. The next column is the Time field storing the time of the last frame transmission. As it is shown below, $R_{sr}$ and $R_{rd}$ store the data rate from R to D, and from S to R, respectively. Both of them can be estimated by signal noise ratio (SNR) of cooperative request-to-send (C-RTS) frame and cooperative clear-to-send (C-CTS) frame. The last column in Fig. 2 is Num of Failures field, counts the number of transmission failures. When the counter expires, which is defined to 3 in our protocol, the related information of this relay will be removed from the RIT. The value of Num of Failures is incremented after every failed transmission process in cooperative mode, and this value will be reset to zero after a successful transmission. Each of these relays is updated timely to reflect the current channel status.

**Table 2.** Relay information table.

| MAC address (48 bits) | Update time (8 bits) | Rsr (2 bits) | Rrd (2 bits) | Num of failures (3 bits) |
|---|---|---|---|---|
| Relay 1 | Time of the last update process | Rate between relay 1 and the sender | Rate between relay 1 and the recipient | Counts of transmission failures |
| ... | ... | ... | ... | ... |
| Relay n | Time of the last update process | Rate between relay n and the sender | Rate between relay n and the recipient | Counts of transmission failures |

A relay will be stored in the RIT if it satisfies the inequality below:

$$\frac{1}{R_{sr}} + \frac{1}{R_{rd}} > \frac{1}{R_{sd}} \tag{1}$$

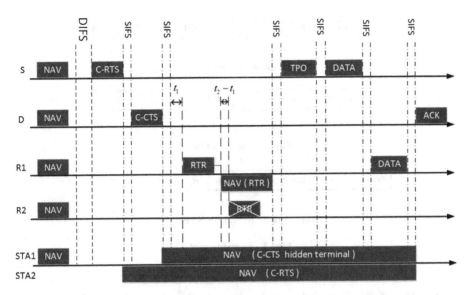

C-RTS : cooperative – request-to-send     C-CTS : cooperative – clear-to-send
TPO : transmission power optimization     RTR : ready-to-relay

**Fig. 2.** NAV settings in TRO-CMAC

where $R_{sd}$, which can be extracted from corresponding field of C-CTS frame, is the rate for direction mode between S and D. If these three parameters $R_{sr}$, $R_{rd}$ and $R_{sd}$ satisfy the inequality, it means that the cooperative transmission with high transmission rates can replace the direct transmission with low transmission rate, moreover, these nodes which meet the inequality may bring some performance enhancement.

### 3.2 TRO-CMAC Protocol and Relay Selection Algorithm

The sender S detects channels' status when S has data to transmit. It should have been waiting until the channel is idle or available. Our proposed TRO-CMAC seeks two best relays as preselected relay from RIT.

Obviously, the bigger rate is, the better relay selects. When many relays have the same value of rate, the one with better channel condition will be selected as the cooperative relay. If only one relay exists in the RIT, thus, it is necessary for the cooperation. Otherwise, the direct transmission mode will be chosen.

The exchange of control message in TRO-CMAC and the opposite NAV settings are depicted in Fig. 2. The corresponding frame format shows in Fig. 3.

**Operation in the Sender S**

- If there is more than one data frame in the buffer queue, S will attempt to transmit. After ending its back-off time, S inserts the ID information of the preselected relays (at least one relay) into the C-RTS frame (shown in Fig. 3) and sends it to D.

| Frame Control | Duration | DA | SA | Relay ID1 | Relay ID2 | FCS |

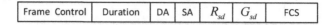

(a)    Frame format for C-RTS

| Frame Control | Duration | DA | SA | $R_{sd}$ | $G_{sd}$ | FCS |

(b)    Frame format for C-CTS

| Frame Control | Duration | DA | SA | $R_{sr}$ | $R_{rd}$ | FCS |

(c)    Frame format for RTR

**Fig. 3.** Frame format

Otherwise, if no suitable relay can be chosen as the relay node, S will adopt direct transmission mode. Similar to that in IEEE 802.11. S sends C-RTS and sets Network Allocation Vectors (NAVs) in the duration field of C-RTS frame as follows:

$$NAV = 6SIFS + T_{C-CTS} + 2T_{RTR} + t_2 + T_{TPO} + \frac{L_{data}}{R_{sr}} + \frac{L_{data}}{R_{rd}} + T_{ACK} \qquad (2)$$

where SIFS is Short Inter-frame Space, $T_{C\text{-}CTS}$, $T_{RTR}$, $T_{TPO}$ and $T_{ACK}$ are the overhead of sending C-CTS frame, RTR frame, TPO frame and ACK frame, respectively. $t_i$ is the delay time of sending $i$th RTR frame, and relevant detail is in Sect. 3.3.

- Due to a collision, if either a C-CTS frame (shown in Fig. 3) or a RTR frame (shown in Fig. 3) is not received after a desired time, S will go into a regular back-off for a retransmission.
- If C-CTS and RTR frames are successfully received, the sender transmits data to the relay R at the rate of $R_{sr}$.
- If an ACK is received from D, this transmission is successful. Then it continues transmitting residual data in the buffer queue. Otherwise, this transmission fails and the sender should perform back-off.

**Operation in the Relay R**

- If both a C-RTS frame and a C-CTS frame are received, all neighbor nodes interpret them by overhearing. And then the two preselected relays contend to relay by their priority and channel condition. In addition, $G_{sr}$ and $G_{rd}$ should also be calculated by SNR in this process, indicating the timely obtained channel state information (CSI) between S and R, and between R and D, respectively. The winning relay sends RTR frame, while other nodes set NAV according to NAV (RTR), it defines below:

$$NAV = t_2 - t_1 + T_{RTR} + SIFS \tag{3}$$

- As soon as the winning relay receives the data from S, it forwards the data to D at the rate of $R_{rd}$ specified in RTR frame.
- The transmission is successful if ACK is received. Otherwise the relay tries to retransmit the data after a random back-off.

**Operation in the Recipient D**

- If a C-RTS frame is received, the recipient D replies a C-CTS frame at the rate of $R_{sd}$. What's more, $G_{sd}$ should also be calculated by SNR in this process, indicating the timely obtained channel state information (CSI) between S and R. It sets NAV in the duration field of C-CTS frame as follows:

$$NAV = 5SIFS + 2T_{RTR} + t_2 + T_{TPO} + \frac{L_{data}}{R_{sr}} + \frac{L_{data}}{R_{rd}} + T_{ACK} \tag{4}$$

- After receiving a RTR frame from winning relay, and the winning relay R, then D wait for the data from R. Otherwise, it choose the direct transmission mode.
- When the data is successfully received, D replies an ACK frame to S.

### 3.3 Access Method of Cooperative Node

For decreasing the interference and the collision probability, the node with high-quality channel should have priority to access. The energy of once data transmission $E_{PKTi}$ shows below:

$$E_{PKTi} = (P_s + P_r) \times L/(2RB) \tag{5}$$

where $L$ is data packet length, $B$ is bandwidth, and $R$ is the bandwidth utilization. The sender transmits the data packets using the optimized transmission power $P_s$ and cooperative relay R forwards the data packets using the optimized transmission power $P_r$. According to Shannon's theorem, the specific formulas are as follows.

$$P_s = \frac{(2^{2R} - 1)N_0}{\|G_{sr}\|^2} \tag{6}$$

$$P_r = (2^{2R} - 1)N_0 \frac{\|G_{sr}\|^2 - \|G_{sd}\|^2}{\|G_{rd}\|^2 \|G_{sr}\|^2} \tag{7}$$

where $N_0$ is the Gaussian white noise power.

Formulas (6) and (7) make $E_{PKTi}$ obtain the minimum value. The better quality of channels, the smaller value of $E_{PKTi}$. Each node ordered by the time of sending RTR that should be consistent with the sequence of $E_{PKTi}$, the access delay $t_{ri}$ for $i$th relay shows below:

$$t_i = \frac{E_{PKTi}}{2P_{\max}\frac{L}{2RB}}T_W \tag{8}$$

where $T_W$ is the longest time that waiting for nodes to access.

Each node calculates the access delay $t_i$ and starts to wait, respectively. Meanwhile, nodes overhear the state of channel, the node decreases the time counter when it hears that channel is idle, and it sends the RTR frame to recipient D when the time counter decreases to zero.

# 4 Performance Evaluation

## 4.1 Simulation Environment

Assuming that all nodes in the network are randomly distributed in a circle with a radius of 100 m. Each node generates data packets with a fixed length according to a Poisson distribution with the arrival rate. The wireless channel is a common Rayleigh fading channel and the path loss exponent is 3. In order to guarantee that the transmission rates from the sender to its recipient are the same in different protocols, if the direct transmission is used, the bandwidth utilization is R, and if the cooperative transmission is used, the bandwidth utilization is 2R. The default value of R is 2 bit/s/Hz. Table 3 gives the default parameter settings used in the simulation.

**Table 3.** Parameter settings.

| Parameter | Value | Parameter | Value |
|---|---|---|---|
| $B$ | 10 kHz | $P_{\max}$ | 50 mW |
| $N_0$ | −80 dbm | $L_{MAC}$ | 272 bits |
| $L_{PHY}$ | 192 bits | $L_{C\text{-}CTS}$ | 304 bits |
| $L_{DATA}$ | 9120 bits | $L_{C\text{-}RTS}$ | 448 bits |
| $L_{ACK}$ | 304 bits | SIFS | 10 μs |
| Slot time | 20 μs | DIFS | 50 μs |

## 4.2 Performance Metrics

We propose three performance metrics to evaluate the TRO-CMAC protocol, including saturation throughput ($S_c$), average packet delay ($D_c$) and packet dropping ratio ($p_d$). $S_c$ is defined as the average data transmission rate. $D_c$ is defined as the average duration of a packet from generation to getting sent. $p_d$ is the ratio of discarded packets to total existing packets. The relevant formulas are as follows.

$$S_c = \frac{L_{PKT} \times N_{success}}{t_{sim}},$$

$$D_c = \frac{\sum_{i=1}^{N_{success}} D_i}{N_{success}},$$

$$p_d = \frac{N_{failure}}{N_{failure} + N_{success}}. \tag{9}$$

where $L_{PKT}$ is the length of a data packet, $N_{success}$ is the number of packets that are sent successfully, $N_{failure}$ is the number of dropped packets owing to collisions, $t_{sim}$ is the simulation duration, and $D_i$ is the delay of the $i$th packet.

### 4.3 Simulation Results

We compare our proposed TRO-CMAC protocol with RCF-CMAC and 2rcMAC in a one-hop situation that only consists of three terminals (sender, relay and recipient).

Figure 4 shows the throughput comparison of TRO-CMAC, RCF-CMAC and 2rcMAC protocols when varying the number of nodes N in the network and packet arrival rate. The data packet length $L_{PKT}$ is set to 1024 bytes. It is obvious that the throughput of our proposed TRO-CMAC is always much higher than RCF-CMAC and 2rcMAC protocols. This is because we take channel gain and collision avoidance into consideration, TRO-CMAC selects the best relay to participate in the transmission, enhancing the throughput markedly. The throughputs of all protocols increase with the increase of packet arrival rate, and the throughput reaches a peak when the network is almost saturated. In addition, the throughput of 100 nodes reaches the peak earlier than 50 nodes. This is because more data packets can be transmitted in a fixed time when N increases, meaning that a larger number of nodes N accounts for a higher throughput when the network is unsaturated.

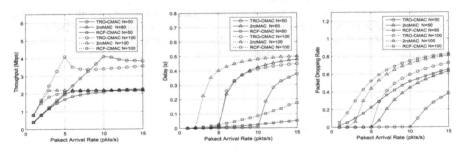

**Fig. 4.** Throughput　　　　　**Fig. 5.** Delay　　　　　**Fig. 6.** Packet dropping rate

Figure 5 shows the delay of all protocols under a serious of different packet arrival rates. When the packet arrival rates is small, the delay of TRO-CMAC is nearly zero. A sharp rise generates when the traffic load is more than 500, the reason to this case is that the throughput is saturated. When the network is saturated, packet dropping ratio is increased sharply. Figure 6 shows the packet dropping rate of all protocols under a serious of different packet arrival rates. The dropping rate of our proposed TRO-CMAC is lower than RCF-CMAC and 2rcMAC protocols with the consideration of channel quality and collision avoidance.

## 5   Conclusion

In this paper, we have proposed a transmission rate optimized cooperative MAC protocol for WSNs. The performance is enhanced significantly by introducing TRO-CMAC mechanism, relay selection algorithm and the novel access method into this protocol. We preselect two candidate relays for a cooperative transmission from the RIT, then choose the best relay for the three terminals (sender, relay and recipient) by the relay selection algorithm. Our simulation results have demonstrated that TRO-CMAC can obviously improve the performances comparing with RCF-CMAC and 2rcMAC protocol.

**Acknowledgements.** This work is supported by the National Natural Science Foundation of China under Grant Nos. 61231013, 61271195 and 61301083, the National Science Foundation for Innovative Research Groups of China under Grant No. 61521091, and the State Scholarship Fund of CSC under Grant No. 201406025008.

## References

1. Demirkol, I., Ersoy, C., Alagoz, F.: MAC protocols for wireless sensor networks: a survey. IEEE Commun. **44**, 115–121 (2006)
2. Khalid, M., Wang, Y., Ra, I., Sankar, R.: Two-relay-based cooperative MAC protocol for wireless ad hoc networks. IEEE Trans. Veh. Technol. **60**, 3361–3373 (2011)
3. Liu, Y., Liu, K., Zeng, F.: A relay-contention-free cooperative MAC protocol for wireless networks. In: 2011 IEEE CCNC, pp. 388–392 (2010)
4. Cao, B., Feng, G., Li, Y., Wang, C.G.: Cooperative media access control with optimal relay selection in error-prone wireless network. IEEE Trans. Veh. Technol. **63**, 252–265 (2014)
5. Liu, P., Tao, Z.F., Narayanan, S., Korakis, T., Panwar, S.S.: CoopMAC: a cooperative MAC for wireless LANs. IEEE JSAC **25**, 340–354 (2007)

# Heterogeneous Control and Data Split Network for Precision Formation Flying of Distributed Spacecraft

Haiyan Jiao[✉], Liqiang Zhao, and Xiaoxiao Zhang

State Key Laboratory of ISN, Xidian University, Xi'an 710071, Shaanxi, China
18700409921@163.com, lqzhao@mail.xidian.edu.cn,
anypoint2009@163.com

**Abstract.** In order to support Precision Formation Flying (PFF) mission, distributed spacecraft requires inter-satellites communication links with reliable and efficient performance. An optimized Mobile Ad hoc Network (MANET) is used to provide high-quality broadband service with high reliability and system capacity. It separates the whole network into two sub-networks, including a control sub-network in mesh architecture for time-critical control messages, and a data sub-network in Point-to-Multipoint (PMP) architecture for high speed data messages. In this paper, an event-driven Medium Access Control (E-MAC) protocol for control sub-network to deal with PFF high priority messages is proposed. E-MAC protocol is based on the event-driven mechanism: spacecraft adjust the contention parameters to the arrival of primary events and secondary events. Analysis and simulation results indicate that the proposed E-MAC protocol can achieve real-time ability as well as spectrum and energy efficiency.

**Keywords:** Formation flying · Distributed spacecraft communications · Event-driven · Heterogeneous

## 1 Introduction

The concept of Distributed Satellites System (DSS) has been intensively researched in recent years, promising revolutionary advancement by enabling the collective use of multiple small mini- or micro-satellites to create a single, large, virtual space borne instrument [1, 2].

Distributed Spacecraft Communications (DSC) system can adopt several technical architectures, such as data link system and MANET [3]. The capacity of the current data link system is limited, and cannot implement high-speed transmission. MANET communication protocols are presented as possible candidates for the future DSC systems [4]. However, it cannot support high-speed real-time data transmissions in DSC system [5].

Generally, there are two kinds of messages in PFF: real-time control messages and massive data messages. Due to the highly dynamic property of PFF network topology, the transmission of control messages should meet low delay, high reliability and omnidirectional coverage. However, data messages have lower latency and should be

© ICST Institute for Computer Sciences, Social Informatics and Telecommunications Engineering 2018
Q. Chen et al. (Eds.): ChinaCom 2016, Part I, LNICST 209, pp. 67–76, 2018.
DOI: 10.1007/978-3-319-66625-9_7

transmitted directionally. In the existing techniques, the mentioned two kinds of messages are coupled in the same channel to transmit, which is of conflict with the requirements above. Besides, in traditional PFF systems, spacecraft may loss contact with the control center due to the constraints of communication conditions or unexpected failure. Therefore, efficient control and data split mechanism (to guarantee the QoS of control messages and high-speed transmission of data messages simultaneously) is needed [6]. In this paper, we present a heterogeneous control and data split network that supports both the instantaneity of control messages and the high-speed transmission of data messages simultaneously at separate channels.

Moreover, when satellites use loose formations flying, DSC requires low QoS of control messages. However, when spacecraft fly in a circular formation, PFF can be easily influenced by environmental factors, which may cause spacecraft in danger [7]. Hence, a proactive scheme is needed for the DSC to deliver such critical messages instantly to the whole DSS. Here, the emergent spacecraft named primary spacecraft which faces the danger of ruin, should have higher priority to access to the network than the other spacecraft named secondary spacecraft. In order to provide different levels of spacecraft with different QoS guarantee, an event-driven MAC protocol named E-MAC is proposed in this paper. Different from IEEE 802.11e which differentiates packets according packet types or protocol classes, E-MAC promotes the priorities just according to whether a triggering event is coming no matter what the packet type is.

The paper is organized as follows. In Sect. 1, the architecture of heterogeneous control and data split network for PFF-based distributed spacecraft is presented. In Sect. 2, event-driven MAC protocol for control sub-network is discussed. In Sect. 3, simulations are carried out to evaluate the performance of the proposed network architecture and event-driven MAC protocol. Finally, conclusions are drawn in Sect. 4 based on the analysis and simulation results.

## 1.1    Architecture of Heterogeneous Control and Data Split Network for Distributed Spacecraft

As shown in Fig. 1, the architecture of DSC system is a combination of two logical sub-networks: control sub-network for transmitting satellite operational messages as well as signaling messages, and data sub-network for high speed data transmission. Control sub-network is the basis of DSC system, which transmits control data for the whole network to operate. Control messages feature small amount, periodical, omnidirectional transmission as well as highly real-time. Data sub-network deals with payload data, which are of great quantity, and should be transmitted directionally.

## 1.2    Optimize the MANET Protocol Stack

In IEEE 802.11x, there are two access modes, one is the fundamental contention-based Distributed Coordination Function (DCF), and the other is the optional polling-based Point Coordination Function (PCF).

Since in DCF mode, wireless users have to contend to access the wireless medium, each user has fair opportunity to transmit messages and is strongly adaptable to the

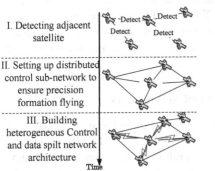

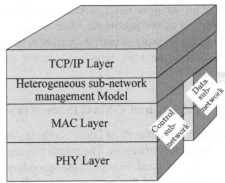

**Fig. 1.** Network structure of the DSC system.

**Fig. 2.** Optimized MANET protocol stack.

highly dynamic DSC network topology. Control sub-network adopts the decentralized mesh architecture and works in DCF without central coordination node. This structure provides multiple end-to-end transmission paths, and the redundancy of the paths can assure that operational control packets can reach the destination spacecraft by single-hop or multi-hops. In addition, if one spacecraft fails, it will not affect the operation of the whole network, which means the survivability of the network arises.

PCF is based on a centralized polling protocol where a point coordinator controls the access to the radio resource. Data sub-network adopts Point to Multi-Point (PMP) structure and works in PCF mode. Each spacecraft can upload payload data to the central module via allocated transmission channel. Specifically, the load spacecraft are responsible for collecting observing data, and the central spacecraft is in charge of processing data from other spacecraft and communicating with the control center.

In order to build flexible DSC network and to avoid complex systems or heavy equipment, we need to optimize MANET protocol stack, as shown in Fig. 2. Control sub-network adopts DCF mode, and data sub-network adopts PCF mode. The function of the heterogeneous sub-network management model is to maintain users' information obtained through control sub-network, including position, velocity and so on. Then by analyzing the topological location information storied in the heterogeneous sub-network management model, data sub-network could realize high-speed data transmission by digital beamforming.

## 2   Event-Driven MAC Protocol for Control Sub-network

DCF is the fundamental MAC mechanism of IEEE 802.11x. Besides, DCF uses a basic acknowledgment mechanism for verifying successful transmissions as well as an optional RTS/CTS handshaking mechanism for decreasing overhead from collisions. In both cases a binary exponential back-off mechanism is used. Where the back-off time is slotted and the number of back-off slots is randomly chosen in the range [0, CW]. At the first transmission attempt, the contention window CW is set to the minimum contention window $CW_{min}$. After several unsuccessful transmissions, $CW$ is finally doubled up to the maximum value $CW_{max} = 2^m CW_{min}$. Once $CW$ reaches $CW_{max}$, it will remain unchanged until the packet is transmitted successfully or the retransmission time reaches the retry limit r. Once the retry limit is reached, the packet will be discarded.

## 2.1 Description of E-MAC Protocol in Control Sub-network

In control sub-network of DSC, two kinds of spacecraft need to transmit packets with different access strategies. The primary spacecraft follow IEEE 802.11× to contend for the channel as usual. However, the secondary spacecraft make their contention window larger than that of the primary spacecraft in order to defer its transmission after the emergency ones.

Let i represent the types of spacecraft, and i = 1 for primary spacecraft, i = 2 for the secondary spacecraft. According to IEEE 802.11x, the contention window is defined as:

$$W_{i,j} = \begin{cases} CW_{i,min} & j = 0 \\ 2CW_{i,j-1} & 0 < j < m. \\ CW_{i,m} & m \le j < r \end{cases} \qquad (1)$$

where j denotes back-off stage, m denotes the maximum back-off stage. The current value of the back-off slot can be obtained as:

$$Backoff_{i,j} = rand(0, W_{i,j}) + x. \qquad (2)$$

where x means an additional variable to distinguish different priorities. For the primary events, x equals zero, otherwise probabilities should be optimized to improve the spectrum and energy efficiency.

## 2.2 Analytical Model of E-MAC Protocol

Let's consider the contention procedure of a given event of the i-th priority. The tri-dimensional Markov chain in [4, 5] of the back-off process can be represented by (i, s(t), b(t)), where i represents the priority, s(t) stands for the back-off stage and b(t) denotes the back-off count value. In this Markov chain, two special states are added: one is the idle state, which means the MAC queue is empty, and the other is D state, which means the medium is sensed to be idle for a time interval greater than DIFS. A spacecraft can send a packet only at state $(i, j, 0)$ or D state.

Let $d_{i,0}$ be the probability that the MAC queue is empty, let $P_{i,b}$ be the probability that the given slot is busy, and let $P_{i,c}$ be the collision probability when the given slot is busy. Define $W_{i,0} = W_{i,min}$ for convenience and adopt $W_{i,j} = 2^j W_{i,0}$.

The transition probabilities from the idle state to idle, D and $(i, 0, k)$ state are shown respectively as the following:

$$P(idle|idle) = d_{i,0}. \tag{3}$$

$$P(D|idle) = (1 - d_{i,0})(1 - p_{i,b}). \tag{4}$$

$$P((i,0,k)|idle) = (1 - d_{i,0})p_{i,b}/W_{i,0}, \ x \leq k \leq W_{i,0} + x - 1. \tag{5}$$

The transition probabilities from the D state to idle and $(i, 0, k)$ states are respectively:

$$P(idle|idle) = d_{i,0}(1 - p_{i,c}). \tag{6}$$

$$P((i,0,k)|D) = \left[ p_{i,c} + (1 - p_{i,c})(1 - d_{i,0}) \right]/W_{i,0}, \ x \leq k \leq W_{i,0} + x - 1. \tag{7}$$

Based on the fact that the sum of the steady-state probabilities of all states must be equal to 1, we can get

$$1 = b_{i,0} + b_{i,D} + \sum_{j=0}^{r} \left( \sum_{k=0}^{W_{i,j}+x-1} b_{i,j,k} \right). \tag{8}$$

By obtaining $b_{i,0,0}$, we can express the probability $\tau$ that a satellite transmits in a randomly chosen slot time. As a satellite can send a packet only at $(i, j, 0)$ or D state, then

$$\tau_i = b_{i,D} + \sum_{j=0}^{r} b_{i,j,0}. \tag{9}$$

Consider a fixed number n of contending spacecraft, therefore $n = n_1 + n_2$. The probability that at least one i-th urgency event is transmitted in a given time slot can be derived as follows

$$P_{tr,i} = 1 - (1 - \tau_i)^{n_i}. \tag{10}$$

The probability that exactly one i-th urgency spacegraft generates packets on the channel (assuming that at least one i-th urgency event will happen), can be expressed as

$$P_{s,i} = \frac{n_i \tau_i (1 - \tau_i)^{n_i - 1} \prod_{h=1, h \neq i}^{2} (1 - \tau_h)^{n_h}}{P_{tr,i}}. \tag{11}$$

As regards to the status of packet transmission in a given time slot, there are three possibilities. Firstly, there may be no transmission with the probability of $P_{idle} = (1 - \tau_1)^{n_1}(1 - \tau_2)^{n_2}$, whose average time is $\sigma = aSlotTime$. Hence the average consumed energy is $E_i = nW_{Rx}\sigma$. Secondly, it contains a successful transmission. The probability that an i-th urgency spacecraft transmits successfully is $P_{tr,i}P_{s,i}$, whose average time is $T_s$. In the basic acknowledgement mechanism, $T_s = F_i + SIFS + 2\sigma + ACK + DIFS$, where $F_i$ is the average time length of the i-th priority data frame. And then the average consumed energy is $E_s = (W_{Tx} + W_{Rx} + (n-2)W_{Lx})T_s$. Finally, there may be collision with the probability of $P_c = 1 - P_{idle} - P_{tr,1}P_{s,1} - P_{tr,2}P_{s,2}$, whose average time is $T_c = F^* + DIFS + \sigma$, where $F^*$, the average length of the longest frame involved in the collision, was discussed in detail in [4]. The average consumed energy is

$$E_c = \sum_n C_n^c \tau_i^c (1 - \tau_i)^{n-n_c} (n_c W_{Tx} + (n - n_c) W_{Rx}) T_c. \tag{12}$$

Let the average bit size of payloads in the i-th urgency be $B_i$. Thus, the system spectrum efficiency $\eta_{spectrum}$ and energy efficiency $\eta_{energy}$ can be expressed respectively as

$$\eta_{spectrum} = \frac{\sum_{i=1}^{2} P_{tr,i} P_{s,i} B_i}{\left(P_e \sigma + \sum_{i=1}^{2} P_{tr,i} P_{s,i} T_s + P_c T_c\right)}. \tag{13}$$

$$\eta_{energy} = \frac{\sum_{i=1}^{2} P_{tr,i} P_{s,i} B_i}{\left(P_e E_i + \sum_{i=1}^{2} P_{tr,i} P_{s,i} E_s + P_c E_c\right)}. \tag{14}$$

### 2.3   Spectrum and Energy Efficiency of E-MAC Protocol

From the analysis in the previous subsections, we present the event-driven MAC protocol, E-MAC, to improve the viability of DSC by adjusting the contention parameters according to the number of spacecraft in emergent circumstances and normal flights respectively. From equations above, we can explicitly compute the optimal values of x to guarantee the QoS of emergent spacecraft which has higher priority. The relationship between x and energy efficiency as well as the relationship between x and spectrum efficiency is shown in Fig. 3. As we can see, along with the increasing of x, the peak of the energy efficiency and that of the spectrum efficiency are not at the same x, but we can find a relatively optimum x, at which the energy efficiency and spectrum efficiency can be both at a relatively high level.

We can get a range of x, between which the spectrum efficiency is not smaller than Q time of the maximum of the spectrum efficiency and the energy efficiency is not smaller than Q time of the maximum energy efficiency. Here we choose Q as 99.8%. For instance, $[x_{1,min}, x_{1,max}]$ satisfies the required spectrum efficiency, and $[x_{2,min}, x_{2,max}]$ satisfies the required energy efficiency. Then choose a value in the intersection of $[x_{1,min}, x_{1,max}]$ and $[x_{2,min}, x_{2,max}]$, i.e. satisfying the below formulation:

$$x \in [x_{1,min}, x_{1,max}] \cap [x_{2,min}, x_{2,max}]. \tag{15}$$

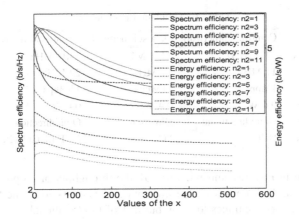

**Fig. 3.** Energy and spectrum efficiency versus x.

## 3 Performance Evaluation

In order to evaluate the proposed E-MAC protocol, the following simulations are made in OPNET. In the simulations, we consider two different scenarios.

### 3.1 Scenario I

Consider a rectangular area of 30 km × 30 km × 30 km with 20 spacecraft shown in Fig. 4 (left). For comparison, we consider two network architectures, one is the proposed heterogeneous control and data split network, and the other is the traditional network, where both control and data packets are tightly coupled to transmit over the IEEE 802.11x-based system [3]. The main parameters of the simulation are shown in Table 1.

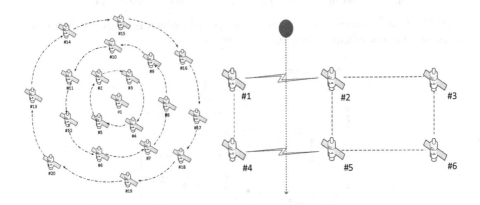

**Fig. 4.** Network topology for scenario I (left) and scenario II (right).

**Table 1.** Simulation parameters.

| Parameters | Control sub-network | Data sub-network | Traditional network |
|---|---|---|---|
| Carrier frequency | 2431 MHz | 2401 MHz | 2401 MHz |
| bandwidth | 11 MHz | 11 MHz | 22 MHz |
| Data rate | 1Mbps | 11Mbps | 11Mbps |
| Transmit power | 0.4 W | 0.4 W | 0.4 W |
| Antenna mode | Omnidirectional | Directional | Omnidirectional |
| Access method | DCF | PCF | DCF (default)/PCF (optional) |

As is shown in Fig. 5, compared with [3], the throughput of proposed network is slightly improved. And along with the improving of network load, the throughput of the proposed network continues to grow but that of the traditional slightly decreases. As to delay, the proposed network structure has a better delay property, and with the network load increasing, the performance of the proposed network has more advantage than that of the traditional network.

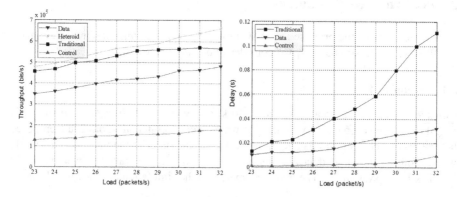

**Fig. 5.** Throughput (left) and delay (right) properties in diverse loads.

In Fig. 6, it is obvious that the proposed network, which is an overall index, has larger transmission efficiency than general network.

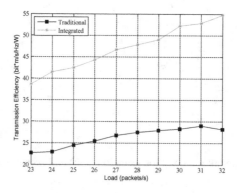

**Fig. 6.** Transmission efficiency property in diverse loads.

## 3.2   Scenario II

For simplicity, we consider a PFF with 6 spacecraft, of which the relative speed is 30 km/h, and an obstacle, which could be a space junk or a small meteorite, flies through the formation, just as shown in Fig. 4 (right). The orbits of the micro-satellite #1, #2, #4, #5 are influenced by the obstacle, so they would become the primary spacecraft according to the proposed E-MAC protocol.

As shown in Fig. 7, the average delay of primary spacecraft is about 8 ms, a bit lower than that of the secondary spacecraft (around 1.35 ms on average). As the primary spacecraft have a shorter back-off time, and the collision probability can be significantly reduced, so the emergency messages can be transmitted timely.

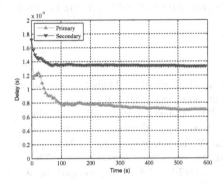

**Fig. 7.** Average delay of the primary and secondary spacecraft in control sub-network.

Figure 8 compares the energy and spectrum efficiency between CSMA/CA and the proposed E-MAC protocol. Obviously, spectrum efficiency in the proposed protocol is almost equal to CSMA/CA, at around 0.0117 bit/s/Hz. Besides, the energy efficiency of the proposed protocol is also close to that of CSMA/CA, fluctuating between 0.028 and 0.031 bit/s/Hz/W. Both indicate that the proposed protocol can reduce the collision of the DSC system effectively without obvious deterioration of energy consumption.

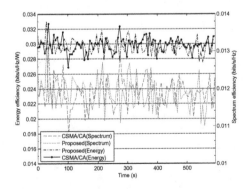

**Fig. 8.** Energy and spectrum efficiency of control sub-network.

## 4 Conclusion

In this paper, a heterogeneous network architecture using E-MAC protocol is proposed for PFF-based DSS. Two sub-networks can transmit control messages and data messages in DCF and PCF mode respectively. Then, we propose event-driven MAC protocol for control sub-network, which enables the DSC to response to the triggering events and guarantee the QoS of the control sub-network. Simulation results demonstrate that the proposed network structure can achieve better overall performance.

**Acknowledgements.** This work was supported in part by National Natural Science Foundation of China (61372070), Natural Science Basic Research Plan in Shaanxi Province of China (2015JM6324), Ningbo Natural Science Foundation (2015A610117), National High-tech R&D Program of China (863 Program-2015AA015701), and the 111 Project (B08038).

## References

1. Scharf, D.P., Keim, J.A., Hadaegh, F.Y.: Flight-like ground demonstrations of precision maneuvers for spacecraft formations—Part I. IEEE Syst. J. **4**(1), 84–95 (2010)
2. Sanjeeviraja, T., Dash, P.K.: Estimation of precision formation flying using position of the spacecraft. In: 2012 IEEE Aerospace Conference, pp. 157–160 (2012)
3. Liang, K., Zhao, L., Liu, Y.: Enhanced IEEE 802.11 MAC protocol for precision formation flying-based distributed spacecraft. Wirel. Pers. Commun. **79**(1), 375–388 (2014)
4. Yang, X.: Enhanced DCF of IEEE 802.11e to support QoS. In: Wireless Communications and Networking, vol. 2, pp. 1291–1296 (2003)
5. Du, H.Q., Yixi, L., Chang, G., et al.: An improved analytical model for WLANs under unsaturated traffic conditions. In: Global Mobile Congress, pp. 1–4. IEEE (2009)
6. Hofestadt, H.: GSM-R: global system for mobile radio communications for railways. In: International Conference on Electric Railways in a United Europe, pp. 111–115. IET (1995)
7. Mirrezaei, S.M., Faez, K., Ghasemi, A.: Performance analysis of network coding based two-way relay wireless networks deploying IEEE 802.11. Wirel. Pers. Commun. **76**(1), 41–76 (2013)
8. Yuan, Z., Muntean, G.M.: A prioritized adaptive scheme for multimedia services over IEEE 802.11 WLANs. IEEE Trans. Netw. Serv. Manag. **10**(4), 340–355 (2013)

# A Novel Feedback Method to Enhance the Graphical Slotted ALOHA in M2M Communications

Yu Hanxiao, Jia Dai, Zhang Zhongwei, Sun Ce,
Huang Jingxuan, and Fei Zesong$^{(\boxtimes)}$

Beijing Institute of Technology, Beijing 100081, China
superkk@bit.edu.cn

**Abstract.** The multiple access issue caused by the massive connections of devices is the key design aspect in the machine-to-machine communication system. As an uncoordinated access scheme, coded slotted ALOHA (CSA) is proposed and well studied to enable random access and high throughput simultaneously with no grant process. It shows efficient performance when the payloads are small. However, the CSA does suffer from the stopping set problem: the Successive Interference Cancellation (SIC) decoding process of CSA would come to a jam when normalized offered traffic is large. We propose an enhanced scheme based on CSA, that is, adding a novel physical layer feedback scheme on CSA to initiate the SIC decoding when there is no degree-1 slot. Considering the overhead of the feedback, simulations show that the proposed scheme can increase the number of successfully accessed devices in one frame.

**Keywords:** M2M · Coded slotted ALOHA · Feedback · Random access

## 1 Introduction

Machine-to-Machine(M2M) communications enable the trillions of devices communicate with each other with a mechanical automation. Many scenarios like intelligent transportation and home automation require the communications between the applications such as sensors, actuators, smartphones and so on. The number of M2M devices supported by the cellular networks in the future will be ten times more than now, it is the essential requirement in M2M communication. Many of devices have no/low mobility in M2M communications, what's more, the traffic involves a large number of short-lived sessions containing only few hundred bits, which is distinct from the human-to-human communications [1–3].

Solving severe congestions is the most critical challenge of M2M communications, so seeking a random access (RA) approach which can avoid the transmission collisions and reduce the access delay is the research priority. Several schemes are proposed to support M2M communications considering the signaling overhead and practical deployment [4,5]. Generally, two kinds of system-level

© ICST Institute for Computer Sciences, Social Informatics and Telecommunications Engineering 2018
Q. Chen et al. (Eds.): ChinaCom 2016, Part I, LNICST 209, pp. 77–86, 2018.
DOI: 10.1007/978-3-319-66625-9_8

designs can be adopted in M2M communication: (i) a one-stage design, where the data payload is communicated over a random access channel, and (ii) a conventional two-stage design, where the identity of devices is established over a random access channel and the payload is communicated during a scheduled stage [6].

In M2M communication, with smaller data packet, the ratio of signaling becomes larger. Theoretical research has proved that the one stage methods can achieve larger throughput. It's easy to understand this result since the signaling overhead is kind of fixed in each transmission. Thus as a result, the aforementioned one-stage technologies are varying promising in future M2M communication scenario.

As a typical one stage access technology, slotted ALOHA (SA) is a traditional random access scheme as an uncoordinated multiple access technique. In [7], a improvement of ALOHA is proposed, named contention resolution diversity slotted ALOHA (CRDSA), where users transmit their packets within two different slots randomly, and successive interference cancellation (SIC) is applied to reuse the collision slots. A more effective scheme irregular repetition slotted ALOHA (IRSA) is provided in [8,9], where each user sends multiple replicas instead of two within different slots randomly according to a predefined probability distribution function. [10] provides a further generalization, named coded slotted ALOHA(CSA). It encodes the packets via linear block code instead of the replicas, and combines the iterative SIC with decoding algorithm of linear block code to recover the packets. [11] provides a CSA scheme using rateless codes. It should be noted that, IRSA is a special case of CSA which uses repetition codes and has low complexity decoding algorithm and is easy to achieve without significant degradation of performance.

CSA draws interest for that it can provide high throughput. It has become one of the alternative offers for the RA in M2M. The common shortage of these methods is that the SIC only starts at the packet which does not have collision, resulting in low throughput under high traffic load when the collision problem is serious. In this paper, we proposed an enhanced scheme of CSA based on feedback design to overcome the problem.

The reminder of this paper is organized as follows. The description of the system model is given in Sect. 2. Section 3 provides the details of the proposed scheme and formulates the overhead. Then, numerical and simulation results are given in Sect. 4. Finally, Sect. 5 concludes the paper.

## 2    System Model

Consider a typical M2M communication system, where cell radius is $r_0$ and the base station is in the origin, while there are $D$ devices distributed in the cell evenly. Devices connect with the base station (BS) by contention, and send the packet with a random access pattern without the assigned resource by the BS.

Frame structure is used in this system, and the duration of each frame is $T_F$. Each frame is divided into $N_{SA}$ slots, resulting that the length of the slot can be presented as $T_{SA} = \frac{T_F}{N_{SA}}$. We assume only $M$ devices represented by $\{u_1, u_2, \cdots, u_M\}$ are active in one frame, and each transmits one information package to the base station during the duration of one frame. Further define the normalized offered traffic as $G = M/N_{SA}$ representing the average number of packets loaded per slot and the normalized throughput as $T$ representing the average number of packets can be accepted successfully per slot. Device $u_i$ chooses the value of replicas $r_i$ of its packet, which is named after degree of device, according to a predefined degree distribution, then selects $r_i$ slots randomly to transmit its packet repeatedly. We can define $\Lambda_r$ as the probability of the device transmitting the packet for $r$ times. Then the degree distribution can be expressed by

$$\Lambda(x) = \Lambda_1 x + \Lambda_2 x^2 + \cdots + \Lambda_{N_{SA}} x_{SA}^N \tag{1}$$

we have $\sum_r \Lambda_r = 1$. And the average degree of devices is given by

$$\bar{r} = \Lambda^{'}(1) = \sum_r \Lambda_r r. \tag{2}$$

The received signal in slot $s_i$ is given by

$$Y_i = \sum_{i=1}^{M} a_{i,j} X_i + N_j, 1 \leq j \leq M \tag{3}$$

where $N_j$ is the additive gaussian white noise and $a_{i,j}$ represents the corresponding coefficient between the i-th device and the j-th slot, $a_{i,j} = 1$ means the i-th device transmits its packet in the j-th slot, otherwise it's 0. The process of the access can be represented by a bipartite graph $\mathcal{G} = (\mathcal{B}, \mathcal{S}, \mathcal{E})$ like Fig. 1. $\mathcal{B}$ represents the set of devices $U = \{u_1, u_2, \cdots, u_M\}$, $\mathcal{S}$ represents the set of slots in one frame, and $\mathcal{E}$ is the set of edges in which the edge connecting a device node and a slot node indicates that the device transmits its packet in corresponding slot. The number of the edge connected to one slot is defined as the degree of the slot. This results in a collision when more than one devices connect to the same slot, in traditional ALOHA protocol the collision packets will be abandoned, but in [9] the collision packets may be decoded with inter-slot SIC.

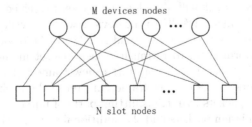

**Fig. 1.** System model of CSA

Firstly, the packets transmitted in degree-one slots can be recovered immediately, and edges connecting to the corresponding devices can be removed at the same time, since their carrying packets are decoded now. The degrees of the slots are updating as the process of the decoding. Repeat the above steps until that there is no evidence of the slot with degree one or all the packets are recovered.

Figure 2 shows an example about the process of SIC, where the frame consists of 4 slots and 3 devices, represented by circles and squares separately. The solid circles mean that the packets of these devices have been or can be already recovered in this step, and the hollow circles mean the packets still remain unrecovered.

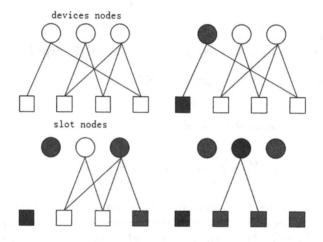

**Fig. 2.** Graph representation of the SIC procedure

## 3    Feedback Enhanced Design

In traditional CSA, high SNR is assumed, so we don't consider the effect of noise. BS will send ACK to the whole devices after SIC decoding when all the packets in this frame are recovered and then each device transmits a new packet in following frame. Otherwise, when the BS fails to recover some the packets in the decoding process, it will abandon the packets received now and start a new frame. The BS will send ACK to the devices whose packet is resolved to let them transmit their next packets and send NACK to the devices whose packet is unresolved to inform them to retransmit their packet in the next frame. In the feedback based model, it will not start a new frame but continue and add some additional slots to the current frame, and reuse the packets received and try to recover more packets by retransmitting parts of unrecovered packets. The number of retransmission packets and the additional slots are the same, and it is named retransmission number which is represented by $N_{RE}$. The retransmission procedure is detailed below.

When SIC procedure terminates with no evidence of degree-one slot, the BS sorts the devices with the updated degree in descending order, and informs the first $N_{RE}$ devices to retransmit their packets sequentially. The number $N_{RE}$ can be optimized by the simulation in Sect. 4. The packets of the devices with higher degree contain more information, and can be more useful in the SIC decoding algorithm comparing to these of the devices with lower degree. So, the BS chooses the more useful packets as the feedback information to recover the packets stored in the buffer.

As an example in Fig. 3. The SIC algorithm stops, remaining some packets unrecovered whose corresponding device nodes are represented by hollow circles in the final step. The BS finds $N_{RE}$ devices with largest degree, informs them to retransmit their packets by sequence in the following $N_{RE}$ slots and assigns specific slots for the retransmission packets individually. As an example, the set of devices $u_{i_1}, u_{i_2}, \cdots, u_{i_{N_{RE}}}$ are called to retransmit their packets, then $u_{i_1}$ transmits its packet in the first additional slot, $u_{i_2}$ transmits its packet in the next additional slot, and so on. The not involved devices wait for the next frame and don't transmit packets in the additional slots. The additional slots should be taken into account when calculating the normalized offered traffic, is given by $G = M/N$, where $N = N_{SA} + N_{RE}$, so as the normalized throughput. The BS continues the SIC algorithm after receiving the retransmitting packets, labels the packets recovered and removes the edges connecting to the corresponding devices. With the retransmitted packets, the performance of the system can be promoted and number of access devices can be increased to satisfy the system requirements.

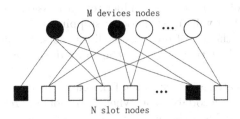

**Fig. 3.** Example of interrupting of SIC

## 3.1  Motivation of Feedback on CSA

Here we state the motivation of adding feedback in CSA transmission. When offered traffic load becomes close to 1, e.g. $G = 0.85 \sim 0.9 * N$, the collisions are significant. In this situation, applying SIC between slots will meet the stopping set problem [12], a term used in fountain coding, where no degree-one slot can be decoded due to circles between device nodes and slot nodes. If we just abandon the received slots, the system throughput would drop dramatically. To fully use the received signals, retransmissions of some transmitted packets with large degree will help to initiate the SIC decoding, and thus able the rebuilding of the previous received data packets. The retransmission order is announced by the receiver in dedicated feedback physical channel.

## 3.2   Overhead Analysis

When the SIC stops without recovering all the packets, the BS should send messages to all the devices to coordinate the transmission condition in the next $N_{RE}$ slots. The chosen devices are required to retransmit their packets sequentially by the order received from the BS. There should be $\lfloor log(M) \rfloor * N_{RE}$ bits used for the instructions, where $\lfloor . \rfloor$ represents selecting the minimum integer larger than the value inside. Compared to the packets transmitted by the devices, the waste of the instructions is negligible, and the instructions can be transmitted in the traditional feedback channel.

The proposed scheme always wastes some slots to retransmit the unrecovered packets. However, the waste of slots for retransmitting is considered in the calculation of the normalized offered traffic and the normalized throughput.

## 3.3   Analysis on the Optimal $N_{RE}$ value

In the papers about ALOHA random access, the highest achievable throughput is always regarded as one important metric to show the advancement of one access method. So in this section, we make some qualitative analysis in the optimal $N_{RE}$ value to achieve highest throughput.

As aforementioned, when the decoder meets problem resulting from the stopping set, a number of $N_{RE}$ devices conduct retransmission sequentially. For one specific feedback slot, it will either unlock a stopping set, or happen to be a slot decoded by BS with the aid of previous feedback slots, except for the very first feedback slot. Thus the latter a slot is retransmitted, the more possible this slot is a waste of resource.

When $N_{RE}$ slots are feed back to the BS, define function $f(\Lambda, N, G, N_{RE})$ as the average number of decodable slots when $N_{RE}$ slots are retransmitted, which is affected by $\Lambda, N, G$. Then the optimization problem can be shown by:

$$\max_{N_{RE}} \frac{N * T(G) + f(\Lambda, N, G, N_{RE})}{N + N_{RE}} \tag{4}$$

where $T(G)$ is the normalized throughput achieved by SIC decoder. The main challenge remains in the calculation of function $f(\Lambda, N, G, N_{RE})$, which is highly correlated to the stopping set distribution. Paper [7] studies the stopping set with low $G$, however, when $G$ grows, the situation is pretty complex and become hard to derivate the analytic expression. In the following part of the paper, Montel-Carlo simulation is made to analysis the suboptimal value of $N_{RE}$, while fixings $\Lambda$ with a classical formulation.

## 4     Numerical Results

We perform the simulation to verify the performance of our scheme, the simulation results are shown in the following. We adopted the degree distribution function $\Lambda(x) = 0.5x^2 + 0.28x^3 + 0.22x^8$, and set the maximum iteration as 100 and the frame size as $N_{SA} = 200$ slots. Select the retransmission number as $N_{RE} = 1, 5, 10, 15, 20$, plot the throughput vs. traffic load curves, and compare the performance with traditional CSA. The curves are presented in Fig. 4. It can be seen that when the retransmission number is 5 or 10, the performance outperforms others. The proposed scheme has performance gains compared to CSA for that the largest peak throughput reaches $T \approx 0.83$, while the CSA is $T \approx 0.77$. The $N_{RE}$ must be chosen suitably, in avoiding the case where although the retransmission packets promote the SIC decoding procedure, the peak throughput point still decreases since the retransmission cost too much resources. On the other hand, when the $N_{RE}$ value is too small, performance gains will be inapparent. Choosing the optimal $N_{RE}$ by theoretical calculations is quite hard, we changed the $N_{SA}$, and found the functional relation between the suboptimal $N_{RE}$ and $N_{SA}$ by simulation.

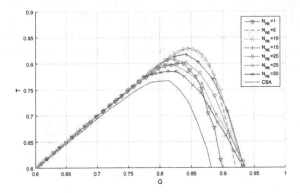

**Fig. 4.** Simulated throughput for $\Lambda(x) = 0.5x + 0.28x^2 + 0.22x^3$, $N_{SA} = 200$

As mentioned in Sect. 3, the higher-degree packets can be better able to promote the gain of throughput. As a comparison, we compare the situation where retransmitting the higher-degree packets to that randomly selecting the retransmitting packets, and prove that the scheme proposed in this paper is better than selecting the packets purposelessly. Comparison is shown in Fig. 6.

We simulated the following four scenarios where $N_{SA} = 200, 500, 1000, 2000$ respectively, and the degree distribution function remained unchanged as before. The simulation results of $N_{SA} = 200, 500$ are shown in Figs. 4 and 5. When $N_{SA} = 200$, the performance gain is obvious for about 10%. There is also a performance gain for more than 5% in the scenario where $N_{SA} = 2000$. As a summary, plot the variation of the peak throughput with different values of

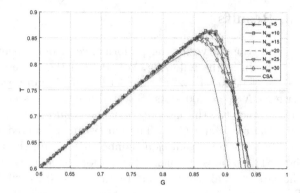

**Fig. 5.** Simulated throughput for $\Lambda(x) = 0.5x + 0.28x^2 + 0.22x^3$, $N_{SA} = 1000$

retransmission number $N_{RE}$ in the four scenarios in Fig. 7. The peak throughput is increasing quickly when $N_{RE}$ is quite small and the growth rate becomes slow as the increase of $N_{RE}$. There is an suboptimal value of $N_{RE}$ promoting the throughput reaching the largest peak that when the $N_{RE}$ is higher than it, the peak throughput will descend. Find the suboptimal values of $N_{RE}$ in different scenarios. It's clear that the relation of suboptimal $N_{RE}$ and $N_{SA}$ is not linear. When the $N_{SA}$ is really high, the suboptimal $N_{RE}$ nearly remains unchanged. The performance is really similar when the $N_{RE}$ ranging around 10, so we can choose the suboptimal $N_{RE}$ as 10.

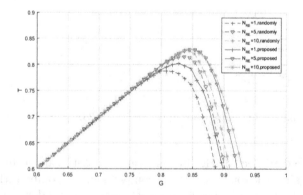

**Fig. 6.** Comparison of retransmitting the higher-degree packets to randomly selecting the retransmitting packets

Intuitively thinking, when a degree-8 user's packet is retransmitted, more packets is expected to be decoded, since this user may form a number of different stopping sets far more than 2 or 3. Once the degree-8 users are all retransmitted, with the growing of $N_{RE}$, the normalized throughput is expected to experience a

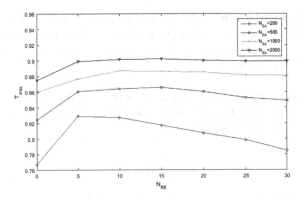

**Fig. 7.** Peak throughput as a function of $N_{RE}$ in four scenarios

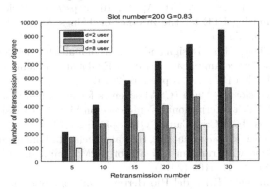

**Fig. 8.** Comparison of retransmitting the higher-degree packets to randomly selecting the retransmitting packets

dramatic decline. To this end, simulation is made considering number of different degree users out of retransmission users, as shown in Fig. 8. In the simulation result shown above, we observe that

1. When $N_{RE}$ becomes larger, more degree-8 user is retransmitted, the system performance tends to grow. However, when $N_{RE}$ is pretty large (i.e. larger than 15), more degree-2 or 3 users are retransmitted, meanwhile, the normalized throughput decreases.

2. Compare the situation $N_{RE} = 10$ with $N_{RE} = 15$, although the latter situation retransmitted more degree-8 users, which leads to decoding of more packets, it does cost more resources (almost 2%). Thus the best $N_{RE}$ is chosen to be the tradeoff between the retransmission resource and decoded packets by retransmission, which happen to be 10 in the proposed scenario.

## 5    Conclusion

In this paper, we proposed an enhancement of the CSA to improve the throughput of the system meeting the demand of M2M communications. This is achieved by feedback scheme which make use of the abandoned packets of the traditional CSA. We calculated the overhead of the feedback and optimized the retransmission scheme. The simulations show the performance improvement of the proposed scheme compared to CSA.

**Acknowledgments.** This work is supported by the 863 project No. 2015AA01A706, 111 Project of China under Grant B14010, and National Natural Science Foundation of China under Grant No. 61421001.

# References

1. M2M Whie Paper: The Interoperability Enabler for the Entire M2M and IoT Ecosystem, April 2016. http://www.onem2m.org
2. Cellular Networks for Massive IoT, April 2016. https://www.ericsson.com
3. LTE-M - Optimizing LTE for the Internet of Things: White Paper, April 2016. https://networks.nokia.com
4. Chang, C.H., Chang, R.Y.: Design and analysis of multichannel slotted ALOHA for machine-to-machine communication. In: IEEE Global Communications Conference (GLOBECOM), San Diego, CA, pp. 1–6 (2015)
5. Yuan, J.: Coded slotted Aloha (CSA) schemes for machine-to-machine communications. In: 2015 9th International Conference on Signal Processing and Communication Systems (ICSPCS), Cairns, QLD, pp. 1–2 (2015)
6. Dhillon, H., Huang, H., Viswanathan, H., Valenzuela, R.: Fundamentals of throughput maximization with random arrivals for M2M communications. IEEE Trans. Commun. **62**(11), 4094–4109 (2014)
7. Cassini, E., Gaudenzi, R.D., del Rio Herrero, O.: Contention resolution diversity slotted ALOHA (CRDSA): an enhanced random access scheme for satellite access packet networks. IEEE Trans. Wirel. Commun. **6**(4), 1408–1419 (2007)
8. Liva, G.: Graph-based analysis and optimization of contention resolution diversity slotted ALOHA. IEEE Trans. Commun. **59**(2), 477–487 (2011)
9. Ghanbarinejad, M., Schlegel, C.: Irregular repetition slotted ALOHA with multiuser detection. In: 2013 10th Annual Conference on Wireless On-demand Network Systems and Services (WONS), 18–20 March 2013, pp. 201–205 (2013)
10. Paolini, E., Liva, G., Chiani, M.: High throughput random access via codes on graphs: coded slotted ALOHA. In: Proceedings of IEEE International Conference on Communications, Kyoto, Japan, pp. 1–6, January 2011
11. Stefanovic, C., Popovski, P.: ALOHA random access that operates as a rateless code. IEEE Trans. Commun. **61**(11), 4653–4662 (2013)
12. Ivanov, M., Brannstrom, F., Amat, A.G., Popvski, P.: Error floor analysis of coded slotted ALOHA over packet erasure channels. IEEE Commun. Lett. **19**(3), 419–422 (2015)

# A Hybrid Automatic Repeat reQuest Scheme Based on Maximum Distance Separable Codes

Shangguan Chenglin, Jia Dai, Yang Yanbao,
Yu Hanxiao, Sun Ce, and Fei Zesong[(✉)]

Beijing Institute of Technology, Beijing 100081, China
feizesong@bit.edu.cn

**Abstract.** For communication systems, a good error control technology is expected to get higher data transmission rate without reducing the quality of service. This paper presents a Hybrid Automatic Repeat reQuest (HARQ) scheme based on Maximum Distance Separable (MDS) codes to improve the ability of error correction. We divide the file into several segments, i.e., information packets and get a check packet using a kind of MDS codes before we transmit the file. Then we try our best to recover the file with the help of the check packet and information packets at the receiver. It is shown that our proposed HARQ scheme has better Block Error Rate (BLER) performance when compared to the traditional HARQ scheme, but the average slots cost per file does not increase significantly.

**Keywords:** Error control · HARQ · MDS

## 1 Introduction

In communication systems, higher data transmission rate and higher quality of service are the two important aspects of both research and application. Error control technologies are developed to get higher data transmission rate, without reducing the quality of service. Forward Error Correction (FEC) and Automatic Repeat reQuest (ARQ) are two of the most important error control technologies [1].

But in wireless communication systems, the channel condition is complicated and unpredictable, while the interference and the distortion is serious. These factors reduce the quality of communication systems significantly, making simple FEC and ARQ useless.

As the combination of FEC and ARQ, Hybrid Automatic Repeat reQuest (HARQ) is one of the important link adaptive technology which could improve the efficiency of data transmission. Nowadays, there are three kinds of HARQ technologies used in error control retransmission mechanism, namely Type-I HARQ, Type-II HARQ and Type-III HARQ [2–4].

Lots of people have done the research about HARQ and some achievements have been made. In [4], the authors obtained the close-form solutions of Type-I HARQ and Type-II HARQ, and the integral solution of Type-III HARQ

© ICST Institute for Computer Sciences, Social Informatics and Telecommunications Engineering 2018
Q. Chen et al. (Eds.): ChinaCom 2016, Part I, LNICST 209, pp. 87–96, 2018.
DOI: 10.1007/978-3-319-66625-9_9

by applying the latest theory and channel coding theorem. Furthermore, they proved that the performance of Type-III HARQ scheme is always better than that of Type-II HARQ scheme, and the performance of Type-II HARQ scheme is always better than that of Type-I HARQ scheme.

In another paper [5], someone confirmed that a variable-rate HARQ-IR scheme would provide gains when compared to a fix-rate transmission in terms of increased throughput and decreased average number of transmissions.

In [6], the paper investigates the throughput performance of HARQ systems under finite block length constraint and presents a framework to compute the maximum achievable rate with HARQ over the Rayleigh fading channel for a given probability of error.

Paper [7] studied the throughput of a power-limited communication system using incremental redundancy HARQ. The results show that, for a large range of HARQ feedback delays, the throughput is increased by finite-length coding incremental redundancy HARQ, if the sub-codeword lengths are properly designed.

This paper is organized as follows. Section 2 puts forward the system model of our work and the encoding process of the proposed scheme is also given in this part. Section 3 introduces the decoding process of the proposed scheme in detail and some analysis is done. Simulations are presented in Sect. 4. And Sect. 5 concludes the paper.

## 2    System Model and Encoding

As stated earlier in this paper, Hybrid Automatic Repeat reQuest (HARQ) is an important technology which can reduce the block error rate effectively and improve the system throughput performance as well. The system block diagram of HARQ is shown in Fig. 1.

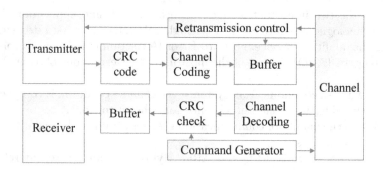

**Fig. 1.** System block diagram of HARQ

There are three kinds of HARQ. In the Type-I HARQ scheme, those packets which fail to match the Cyclic Redundancy Check (CRC) are discarded directly and the retransmission packets are exactly the same as the packet which is transmitted at the first time. So the Type-I HARQ scheme can't adapt to the channel condition well. In order to overcome the disadvantages of the Type-I HARQ scheme, the Type-II HARQ scheme changes the code rate adaptively according to the current channel condition. Specially, in the Type-II HARQ scheme, the packets which fail to match the CRC are deposited into the buffer at the receiver, rather than discarded directly. If the packet does not match the CRC, the receiver would try to complete the decoding process after receiving a retransmission packet, using the retransmission packet as well as the information stored in the buffer. This is the so-called soft-combined. But the Type-II HARQ scheme still has shortcomings that the retransmission packet can't be decoded alone. Then the Type-III HARQ scheme is proposed to solve the problem. The main advantage of the Type-III HARQ scheme is that any retransmission packets can be self-decoding.

In this paper we mainly consider Type-II HARQ using incremental redundancy combining. That is to say, each retransmission packet contains the same information bits and different parity bits. Actually we use rate matching to obtain different redundant version which satisfies the retransmission request.

Although retransmission could reduce the block error rate effectively, it doesn't solve everything. A packet may be incorrect in a very poor channel condition, even if the retransmission number reaches the maximum retransmission number. On the other hand, a file is usually divided into several packets and the file is invalid as long as any of the packets is incorrect.

In order to further improve the performance of HARQ, we develop a HARQ scheme based on maximum distance separable (MDS) codes [8–10].

In the situation that the code length $n$ and the code dimension $k$ is fixed, MDS codes have the best error correction ability among all $(n,k)$ codes. The minimum distance $d$ of MDS codes is the code length $n$ minus the code dimension $k$ plus 1, i.e., MDS codes meet the Singleton-type bound. An $(n,k)$ MDS code has an important property: if a file is divided into $k$ segments and then coded into $n$ segments using an $(n,k)$ MDS code, any $k$ out of $n$ segments could recover the whole file.

Single Parity Check (SPC) code [11,12] is a class of MDS codes. In this case, the number of information bits is $k$, and the check bit is the exclusive-or of all the information bits.

In traditional HARQ scheme, a file is divided into several information packets. Similarly to SPC code, we can get the exclusive-or of all the information packets and the exclusive-or result is the so-called check packet. If the file is still unrecovered after the maximum retransmission number of all the information packets is reached, the check packet is transmitted to the receiver. According to the property of SPC code, receiver could try to recover the entire file using the information packets and the check packet as well.

An example is given to show how to calculate the check packet. Assuming that a file is divided into 5 information packets, and then the 6th packet, i.e. check packet is obtained. The 5 information packets are marked as $I_1$, $I_2$, $I_3$, $I_4$ and $I_5$, respectively, while the check packet is marked as $C$. The relationship between the information packets and the check packet can be represented as follows.

$$C = I_1 + I_2 + I_3 + I_4 + I_5 \tag{1}$$

## 3   Decoding Process

The flow diagram of our proposed HARQ scheme is shown in Fig. 2. In our proposed scheme, the transmitter sends the information packets to the receiver at first. If an information packet doesn't match the CRC, this information packet is retransmitted until the maximum retransmission number is reached. The file is recovered successfully if all the information packets match the CRC. In this case, the check packet is not necessary for the file recovery and there is no need to send it. In fact, the transmitter sends the information packets of the next file to the receiver immediately.

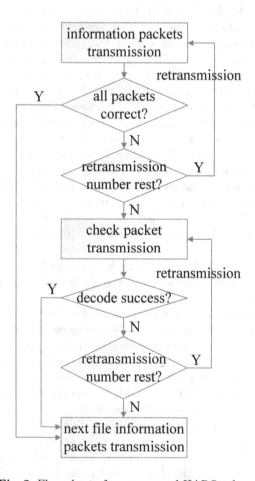

**Fig. 2.** Flow chart of our proposed HARQ scheme

Sometimes, some of the information packets couldn't match the CRC even if the retransmission number is used up, due to the poor channel condition. Compared with retransmitting the whole file, transmitting one more packet (check packet) would be quickly and effectively and the relationship between the information packets and the check packet can be used to recover the file.

The check packet can also be retransmitted. The retransmission check packet is soft-combined with the former ones and then the combined result is used to calculate the revised sequence. Here the method is described in detail.

Assuming that the information packets $I_1$, $I_2$, $I_3$ and $I_4$ is correctly received, as well as the check packet $C$. That is to say, the information packet $I_5$ is the only one which could not match the CRC after all the retransmission times is used. According to Eq. (1), we can see that

$$I_5 = I_1 + I_2 + I_3 + I_4 + C \tag{2}$$

Then we obtain the information packet $I_5$ by simple exclusive-or operation and we recover the whole file.

The poorer the channel condition is, the more information packets are likely to be incorrect. If two information packets is incorrect, the check packet is still be sent to the receiver.

As is known to all, in the decoding part, soft information or the so-called Logarithmic Likelihood Ratio (LLR) is widely used. So the receiver could choose the packet which is more likely to be correct from the two incorrect packets and update its LLRs.

To find the packet which is more likely to be correct, we calculate the sum of squares of all the LLRs in each incorrect packet. Assuming that two information packets $I_1$ and $I_4$ are incorrect, and we calculate the sum of squares of all the LLRs in packet $I_1$ and $I_4$. The length of each LLR sequence is represented as $L$.

$$LLR_{sum}(I_j) = \sum_{k=1}^{L} LLR(k)^2, j = 1, 4 \tag{3}$$

The packet whose result of the summation is larger is the one we want to find. If packet $I_1$ is more likely to be correct, we then calculate a revised sequence of the LLRs of information packet $I_1$ and update it. Finally, the information packet $I_1$ can be decoded again with the help of other information packets and check packet.

$$LLR(I_1)_{revised} = 2 * arctanh \left\{ tanh \left[ \frac{LLR(C)}{2} \right] \right.$$

$$\left. * \prod_{j=2}^{5} tanh \left[ \frac{LLR(I_j)}{2} \right] \right\} \tag{4}$$

$$LLR(I_1)_{new} = LLR(I_1)_{old} + LLR(I_1)_{revised} \tag{5}$$

If packet $I_4$ is more likely to be correct, we do the similar operations to packet $I_4$. In a situation that the packet we choose from the two incorrect packets is decoded successfully, we could recover the whole file using Eq. (2).

If the number of incorrect packets is three or more, we would find the packet which is most likely to be correct using Eq. (3). Then we try to decode the packet we choose using Eqs. (4) and (5). If the packet we choose is decoded successfully, we would try to find the next packet among all the remaining incorrect packets in the same way. The file is recovered as soon as the receiver recovers $k$ packets with the help of the check packet. The maximum retransmission number of the check packet is set to be the same as the information packets.

According to Eq. (5), $LLR(I_1)_{old}$ and $LLR(I_1)_{revised}$ can be seen as two different transmission results of the same packet $I_1$ in different channel conditions. Although the results of $LLR(I_1)_{old}$ or $LLR(I_1)_{revised}$ can't be decoded correctly, their soft-combined result may be decoded successfully. Now we explain the reason why the updated LLRs may be decoded successfully.

According to the definition of the LLR, we can know that

$$LLR = \frac{2y}{\sigma^2} = \frac{2(x + \sigma N)}{\sigma^2} \tag{6}$$

where $\sigma^2$ is the channel noise power and $N$ represents a Gaussian variable whose mean value is zero and variance is 1. The value of $x$ is $-1$ or 1 and $y$ is the received result at the receiving end. It is easy to prove that LLR is also a Gaussian variable. The mean value and variance of LLR can be calculated.

$$\mu_{LLR} = \frac{2x}{\sigma^2} \qquad \sigma_{LLR}^2 = \frac{4}{\sigma^2} \tag{7}$$

where $\sigma^2$ is the channel noise power and the value of $x$ is $-1$ or 1.

As mentioned earlier, $LLR_{old}$ and $LLR_{revised}$ can be seen as two different transmission results of the same packet in different channel conditions. Obviously, the channel noise power $\sigma^2$ is different in different channel conditions. Then we can get the relationship between the variance of channel noise and the variance of LLRs.

$$\sigma_{LLR_{old}}^2 = \frac{4}{\sigma_{old}^2} \qquad \sigma_{LLR_{revised}}^2 = \frac{4}{\sigma_{revised}^2} \tag{8}$$

When we update the LLRs using Eq. (5), we add the variance of $LLR_{revised}$ to the variance of $LLR_{old}$ and get the variance of $LLR_{new}$.

$$\sigma_{LLR_{new}}^2 = \sigma_{LLR_{old}}^2 + \sigma_{LLR_{revised}}^2 \tag{9}$$

Then we can calculate the equivalent channel noise power after soft-combining.

$$\sigma_{new}^2 = \frac{\sigma_{old}^2 \sigma_{revised}^2}{\sigma_{old}^2 + \sigma_{revised}^2} \tag{10}$$

We can easily prove that the variance after soft-combining is smaller than any of the variance before soft-combining.

$$\sigma^2_{new} < \sigma^2_{old} \qquad \sigma^2_{new} < \sigma^2_{revised} \tag{11}$$

As is shown in Fig. 3, the smaller the channel noise power is, the better the channel condition is. That is to say, soft-combining makes us complete the decoding process under a better channel condition. That is the reason why our proposed scheme has better block error rate performance than traditional HARQ scheme.

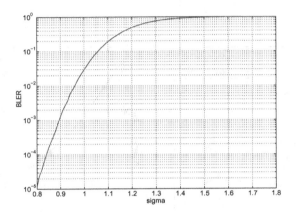

**Fig. 3.** Sigma vs. BLER in AWGN channel

# 4 Simulations

In this section, the advantages of our proposed Hybrid Automatic Repeat reQuest (HARQ) scheme based on maximum distance separable (MDS) codes is verified by simulating a simple communication system. A simplest MDS code, i.e., Single Parity Check (SPC) code is employed for simplicity.

The file is divided into 5 segments and each segment is seen as an information packet. In traditional HARQ scheme, we just transmit the information packets. But in our HARQ scheme, we transmit the information packets as well as the check packet. The maximum retransmission number of both the information packets and the check packet is 4. The channel used in the communication system is assumed to be Additive White Gaussian Noise (AWGN) channel and the channel coding method we choose is Turbo code.

The simulation is completed in two situations and the code rate of Turbo code is 1/3 and 1/2, respectively. The performances we focus on are block error rate which indicates the probability of a correct file transmission and the average slots cost per file in a file transmission.

### 4.1 Case 1

In this case, the code rate of Turbo code is 1/3. The block error rate (BLER) and average slots vs. the signal to noise ratio (SNR) are shown in Figs. 4 and 5, respectively. According to the results in Fig. 5, it can be seen that the poorer the channel condition is, the more average slots is cost to transmit a file in both traditional HARQ scheme and proposed HARQ scheme. For example, when SNR is −8 dB, the average slots cost per file in traditional HARQ scheme is 24.5010, while the average slots cost per file in proposed HARQ scheme is 28.5710. That is to say, almost every packet in both schemes has been retransmitted 4 times. As the channel condition gets better, the average slots cost per file of both schemes decrease.

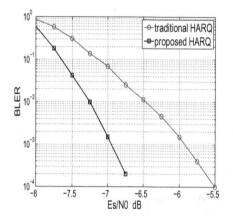

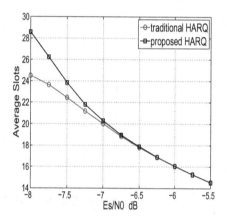

**Fig. 4.** BLER vs. SNR for 1/3 code rate Turbo code

**Fig. 5.** Average Slots vs. SNR for 1/3 code rate Turbo code

In the region where SNR is greater than −7 dB, the gap of the average slots cost per file between traditional HARQ scheme and proposed HARQ scheme is very small, but the BLER performance in proposed HARQ scheme is much better than that in traditional HARQ scheme. We take the situation when SNR equals −7 dB as an example. The average slots cost per file in traditional HARQ scheme is 20.0220, while the average slots cost per file in proposed HARQ scheme is 20.2995. The BLER of the proposed HARQ scheme is 0.0015, and the BLER of the traditional HARQ scheme is 0.069. When BLER is $10^{-3}$, our proposed HARQ scheme has about 1 dB gain compared to traditional HARQ scheme.

### 4.2 Case 2

In this case, the code rate of Turbo code is 1/2. The block error rate (BLER) and average slots vs. the signal to noise ratio (SNR) are shown in Figs. 6 and 7, respectively. As the same as case 1, almost every packet in both schemes has been retransmitted 4 times when the channel condition is poor and the average slots cost per file of both schemes decrease when the channel condition gets better.

In the region where SNR is greater than −4.5 dB, the gap of the average slots cost per file between traditional HARQ scheme and proposed HARQ scheme is negligible, but the BLER performance in proposed HARQ scheme is much better than that in traditional HARQ scheme. We take the situation when SNR equals −4.5 dB as an example. The average slots cost per file in traditional HARQ scheme is 18.6930, while the average slots cost per file in proposed HARQ scheme is 18.8777. The BLER of the proposed HARQ scheme is 0.0018, and the BLER of the traditional HARQ scheme is 0.067. When BLER is $10^{-3}$, our proposed HARQ scheme has about 1.1 dB gain compared to traditional HARQ scheme.

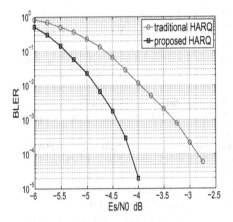 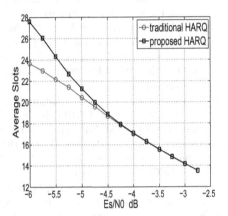

**Fig. 6.** BLER vs. SNR for 1/2 code rate Turbo code

**Fig. 7.** Average slots vs. SNR for 1/2 code rate Turbo code

The results show that our proposed HARQ scheme has much better BLER performance than traditional HARQ scheme, and the average slots cost per file in proposed HARQ scheme does not increase.

## 5  Conclusion

In this paper, we have proposed a Hybrid Automatic Repeat reQuest (HARQ) scheme based on Maximum Distance Separable (MDS) codes to improve the ability of error correction. The system model and the detailed simulation results have been presented to verify the advantages of our proposed HARQ scheme. Compared to traditional HARQ scheme, our proposed HARQ scheme has better BLER performance, but the average slots cost per file does not increase significantly.

**Acknowledgments.** This work is supported by the 863 project No. 2015AA01A706, 111 Project of China under Grant B14010, and National Natural Science Foundation of China under Grant No. 61421001.

# References

1. Tian, Z., Yuan, D., Liang, Q.: Energy efficiency analysis of error control schemes in wireless sensor networks. In: International Wireless Communications and Mobile Computing Conference, IWCMC 2008, pp. 401–405. IEEE (2008)
2. de Oliveira Brante, G.G., Uchoa, A.G.D., Souza, R.D.: Cooperative coded partial retransmission scheme using type-I HARQ and LDPC codes. In: IEEE 21st International Symposium on Personal Indoor and Mobile Radio Communications (PIMRC), pp. 123–128. IEEE (2010)
3. Uzawa, F., Koyama, T., Mitsuyama, K., et al.: PCI reduction method suitable for type-II HARQ with SR-ARQ. In: 2015 IEEE International Workshop Technical Committee on Communications Quality and Reliability (CQR). IEEE (2015)
4. Yafeng, W., Lei, Z., Dacheng, Y.: Performance analysis of type III HARQ with Turbo codes. In: IEEE 38th Vehicular Technology Conference, vol. 4, pp. 2740–2744 (2003)
5. Szczecinski, L., Correa, C., Ahumada, L.: Variable-rate transmission for incremental redundancy hybrid ARQ. In: 2010 IEEE Global Telecommunications Conference, GLOBECOM 2010, pp. 1–5. IEEE (2010)
6. Sahin, C., Liu, L., Perrins, E.: On the finite blocklength performance of HARQ in modern wireless systems. In: 2014 IEEE Global Communications Conference (GLOBECOM), pp. 3513–3519. IEEE (2014)
7. Makki, B., Svensson, T., Zorzi, M.: Finite block-length analysis of the incremental redundancy HARQ. IEEE Wirel. Commun. Lett. **3**(5), 529–532 (2014)
8. Krishna, A., Sarwate, D.V.: Pseudocyclic maximum-distance-separable codes. IEEE Trans. Inf. Theory **36**(4), 880–884 (1990)
9. Solomon, G.: Generation of maximum distance separable codes. In: Proceedings of 1991 IEEE International Symposium on Information Theory (papers in summary form only received) (Cat. No. 91CH3003-1), p. 8. IEEE (1991)
10. Tolhuizen, L.M.G.M.: On maximum distance separable codes over alphabets of arbitrary size. In: Proceedings of 1994 IEEE International Symposium on Information Theory (1994)
11. Xu, H., Takawira, F.: A new structure of single parity check product codes. In: 7th AFRICON Conference in Africa, AFRICON, vol. 1, pp. 67–70. IEEE (2004)
12. Kurkoski, B.M., Yamaguchi, K., Kobayashi, K.: Turbo equalization with single-parity check codes and unequal error protection codes. IEEE Trans. Magn. **42**(10), 2579–2581 (2006)
13. Shen, C., Liu, T., Fitz, M.P.: On the average rate performance of hybrid-ARQ in quasi-static fading channels. IEEE Trans. Commun. **57**(11), 3339–3352 (2009)
14. Chelli, A., Alouini, M.S.: Performance of hybrid-ARQ with incremental redundancy over relay channels. In: 2012 IEEE Globecom Workshops (GC Wkshps), pp. 116–121. IEEE (2012)
15. Kasami, T., Lin, S.: On the probability of undetected error for the maximum distance separable codes. IEEE Trans. Commun. **32**(9), 998–1006 (1984)
16. Chee, Y.M., Ji, L., Han, M.K., et al.: Maximum distance separable codes for symbol-pair read channels. IEEE Trans. Inf. Theory **59**(11), 7259–7267 (2012)

# Energy-Efficient Resource Allocation in Distributed Antenna Systems

Xiaoge Huang, Weipeng Dai, Zhifang Zhang,
Qiong Huang, and Qianbin Chen[(✉)]

School of Communication and Information Engineering,
Chongqing University of Posts and Telecommunications, Chongqing, China
{Huangxg,Huangqiong,Chenqb}@cqupt.edu.cn, daiweipeng@hotmail.com

**Abstract.** In this paper, we introduce an energy-efficient resource allocation scheme in distributed antenna systems (DASs). Throughout the paper, the resource allocation includes distributed antenna units (DAU) selection, subcarriers assignment and power allocation. Our aim is to optimize energy efficiency (EE) of the whole system, which is defined as the ratio of total data rate to total consumed power, under the constraints of the overall transmit power of each DAU and minimum required data rate of each user. Due to the mixed combinatorial features of the formulation, we focus on low-complexity suboptimal algorithm design. Firstly, a joint DAU selection and subcarriers assignment algorithm is developed with equal power allocation. Secondly, EE maximization problem is a non-convex fractional programming problem, we transform the problem into a subtractive form, then solve it by using the Lagrangian dual decomposition. The simulation results show the convergence performance, and demonstrate the advantage of the proposed resource allocation scheme compared with the random resource allocation scheme.

**Keywords:** Distributed antenna systems · Energy efficiency · Resource allocation

## 1 Introduction

With the rapid development of economy and society, the proliferation of mobile devices and diverse mobile applications demand high data rate and ubiquitous access. To meet such mobile data challenges, DAS has been considered as a promising candidate for future wireless communication networks. Due to its advantages of reducing access distance, transmit power, and co-channel interference, DAS can increase the network capacity and expand coverage, thus it is considered as a key technology for next generation communications in the future

This work is supported by the National Natural Science Foundation of China (NSFC) (61401053, 61201205), the 863 project No. 2014AA01A701, and Changjiang Scholars and Innovative Research Team in University (IRT1299), Special Fund of Chongqing Key Laboratory (CSTC).

© ICST Institute for Computer Sciences, Social Informatics and Telecommunications Engineering 2018
Q. Chen et al. (Eds.): ChinaCom 2016, Part I, LNICST 209, pp. 97–106, 2018.
DOI: 10.1007/978-3-319-66625-9_10

[1,2]. In DAS, a certain number of distributed antenna units (DAU) are located in different positions in cell and connected to a central processing unit via optical fibers or high speed cable. The central processing unit is used to process information and resource allocation.

Recently, due to the rapid growth of global energy consumption and the environmental problems, EE has attracted more attention in both academia and industry [3,4]. EE is proposed as a metric which is defined as the sum-rate divided by the total power consumption measured in bits/Hz/Joule. In [5], a scheme of maximizing EE is proposed, the authors demonstrate that there is a tradeoff between EE and spectrum efficient transmission. [6,7] study EE maximization in DAS through optimal power allocation. In [6] the authors consider multi-cell DAS and use successive Taylor expansion to formulate subproblems which are solved by iterative power allocation algorithm; [7] studys a practical case where the channel state information (CSI) is slowly-varying, the authors propose an iterative algorithm to achieve the global optimal solution. On the other hand, orthogonal frequency division multiplexing (OFDM) is regarded as a potential transmission technology for the future wireless network due to its flexibility in resource allocation and effectiveness in anti-multipath fading. There are many relevant research works on EE optimization and resource allocation. In [8], the authors develop an energy-efficient resource allocation scheme including subcarriers allocation and power allocation under different constraints with fixed DAU assignment. [9] investigates EE optimization problem and the authors consider power consumption of the transmitter and receiver to capture the impact of subcarriers and users on EE, and propose a joint optimization method for optimal solution.

Different from existing works, in this paper, we study the energy-efficient resource allocation optimization, joint antenna units selection, subcarriers assignment and power allocation for a downlink multiuser OFDM DAS. The optimization objective is to maximize EE under the constraints of total transmit power of each BS and minimum rate requirement of each user. Nevertheless, due to the non-convex nature of the problem, it is especially challenging to manage DAUs and subcarriers assignment, thus the optimal solution is extremely computationally complicated. Therefore, we divide the optimization problem into two suboptimal problems. Namely, DAU-subcarrier assignment optimization and power allocation optimization. In the DAU-subcarrier optimization process, we ensure that each user can be served by at least one DAU, and optimize the DAU-subcarrier assignment with equal allocation power to maximize EE of network. In the power allocation optimization process, we transform the fractional programming problem into an equivalent optimization problem in subtractive form, which can easily be solved by using the Lagrangian dual decomposition.

The rest of the paper is organized as follows. We describe the system model and formulate the problem of EE optimization in Sect. 2. Section 3 gives the EE resource allocation algorithm consisting of two sub-optimization algorithms that are DAU-subcarrier assignment and power allocation optimization. Simulation results and performance evaluation are given in Sect. 4. Followed by the conclusion drawn in Sect. 5.

## 2    System Model and Problem Formulation

A. System Model Description

We consider a downlink single-cell OFDM DAS, where both $M$ DAUs and $K$ users ($M \geq K$) with single antenna are uniform randomly distributed in the cell area. $N$ orthogonal subcarriers are used for serving users simultaneously. The bandwidth of each subcarrier is $B = \frac{W}{N}$, $W$ is the total bandwidth. All DAUs are physically connected with a central processing unit via optical fibers. The received signal for the user $k$ on the $n$th subcarrier from the $m$th DAU is written as

$$y_{k,n,m} = \sqrt{p_{k,n,m}}h_{k,n,m}x_{k,n,m} + z_{k,n,m} \tag{1}$$

where $p_{k,n,m}$ is the transmit power allocated to the $m$th DAU on the $n$th subcarrier. $h_{k,n,m}$ denotes composite flat-fading channel impulse response between the $m$th DAU on $n$th subcarrier and user $k$. It consists of small-scale and large-scale fading, which is modeled as $h_{k,n,m} = g_{k,m} \cdot l_{k,n,m}$, $g_{k,m} = \sqrt{s_{k,m} \cdot d_{k,m}^{-\alpha}}$ represents the large-scale fading, $s_{k,m}$ is a lognormal shadow fading variable, $10\log_{10} s_{k,m}$ is a zero-mean gaussian random variable with standard deviation $\sigma_{sh}$, $d_{k,m}$ is the distance between DAU $m$ and user $k$, $\alpha$ is the path-loss exponent. $l_{k,n,m}$ denotes the small-scale fading of channel which is an independent and identically distributed complex gaussian random variable with zero mean and unit variance. $z_{k,n,m}$ is additive white gaussian noise with zero mean and variance equal to 1.

B. EE Optimization Problem Formulation

According to Shannon's Theorem, the overall data rate of user $k$ can be expressed as

$$r_k = B \sum_{m=1}^{M} \sum_{n=1}^{N} a_{k,m}b_{n,m} \log_2(1 + \frac{p_{k,n,m}|h_{k,n,m}|^2}{\Gamma\sigma_z^2}) \tag{2}$$

where $a_{k,m}$ and $b_{n,m}$ are binary variables. $a_{k,m} = 1$ indicates that DAU $m$ is assigned to user $k$, otherwise, $a_{k,m} = 0$. $b_{n,m} = 1$ denotes that subcarrier $n$ is assigned to DAU $m$, otherwise, $b_{n,m} = 0$. $\Gamma = -\frac{1.5}{\ln(5P_{BER})}$ is a constant for a specific probability of a BER ($P_{BER}$) requirement. The overall data rate of the system is

$$R_{tot} = \sum_{k=1}^{K} r_k \tag{3}$$

Furthermore, the total power consumption of the system is modeled as

$$P_{tot} = \tau p_t + Mp_c + p_o \tag{4}$$

where $p_t = \sum_{k=1}^{K} \sum_{m=1}^{M} \sum_{n=1}^{N} a_{k,m}b_{n,m}p_{k,n,m}$, $\tau$ is the drain efficiency of the radio-frequency power amplifier. $p_c$ is the circuit power consumption. $p_o$ is the dissipated power by the fiber-optic transmission. We define EE of an OFDM DAS as the ratio of the total data rate $R_{tot}$ to the total power consumption $P_{tot}$, i.e.

$$EE = R_{tot}/P_{tot} \tag{5}$$

Our goal is to maximize EE while meet the minimum rate requirement of each user, as well as the total transmit power constraint of each DAU. The EE optimization problem for a downlink multiuser OFDM DAS is given as

$$\textbf{P1:} \max_{\mathbf{a,b,P}} \quad EE = \frac{R_{tot}(\mathbf{a,b,P})}{P_{tot}(\mathbf{a,b,P})} \tag{6}$$

$$\text{s.t.} \quad C1 : r_k \geq R_k^{req}, \forall k$$

$$C2 : \sum_{n=1}^{N} a_{k,m} b_{n,m} p_{k,n,m} \leq p_m^{max}, \forall k, m$$

$$C3 : 1 \leq \sum_{m=1}^{M} a_{k,m} \leq M - K + 1, \forall k$$

$$C4 : \sum_{k=1}^{K} a_{k,m} \leq 1, \forall m; \sum_{m=1}^{M} b_{n,m} \leq 1, \forall n$$

$$C5 : \sum_{n=1}^{N} b_{n,m} \leq N_m, \forall m$$

$$C6 : a_{k,m} \in \{0,1\}, b_{n,m} \in \{0,1\}, \forall k, n, m$$

$$C7 : p_{k,n,m} \geq 0, \forall k, n, m$$

The constraints $C1$ and $C2$ ensure that each user's data rate requirement and each DAU's maximum transmit power budget are satisfied. The constraint $C3$ guarantees that each user can be served by at least one DAU. The constraints $C4$ and $C6$ indicate that each DAU and each subcarrier can only be allocated to one user and one DAU respectively. $C5$ denotes the number of subcarriers assigned to each DAU is $N_m$. Notice that if the parameter setting on $R_k^{req}$ and $p_m^{max}$ is not appropriate, the optimization problem **P1** is infeasible, here we assume that the optimization problem **P1** is always feasible.

## 3 Energy Efficient Resource Allocation with Distributed Antennas

Notice that problem **P1** with nonlinear constraints is a mixed integer nonlinear programming problem, due to problem's high computation complexity, we focus on low-complexity algorithm. Therefore, we divide the optimization problem into two sub-optimization problems, which are joint DAU-subcarrier assignment and power allocation optimization.

## 3.1   Joint DAU and Subcarrier Assignment

A. Number of subcarriers per DAU

In general, the closer the distance between user and DAU is, the better the channel condition is. The contribution to throughput is greater and the probability of serving this user is also larger [10]. For unity transmit power, $SNR$ of user $k$ from DAU $m$ on subcarrier $n$ is given by $snr_{k,n,m} = |h_{k,n,m}|^2/\sigma_z^2$. Similarly, we can get $M \times K \times N$ $SNRs$ of the whole network, then construct a $M \times K \times N$ three dimensional matrix denoted by $SNR_{k,n,m}(K, N, M)$, for a specific subcarrier $n$, the matrix can be expressed as

$$SNR_{k,m}(n) = \begin{bmatrix} snr_{1,n,1} & snr_{2,n,1} & \cdots & snr_{K,n,1} \\ snr_{1,n,2} & snr_{2,n,2} & \cdots & snr_{K,n,2} \\ \vdots & \vdots & \ddots & \vdots \\ snr_{1,n,M} & snr_{2,n,M} & \cdots & snr_{K,n,M} \end{bmatrix} \tag{7}$$

Summing up all elements by row of matrix $SNR_{k,m}(n)$, we can get a new matrix

$$SNR_m(n) = \left[ \sum_{k=1}^{K} snr_{k,n,1}, \sum_{k=1}^{K} snr_{k,n,2}, \cdots, \sum_{k=1}^{K} snr_{k,n,M} \right]^T \tag{8}$$

Let $p_m^n$ denotes the accessing probability of DAU $m$ on subcarrier $n$, given by

$$p_m^n = \sum_{k=1}^{K} snr_{k,n,m} / \sum_{m=1}^{M} \sum_{k=1}^{K} snr_{k,n,m} \tag{9}$$

The accessing probability of each DAU on subcarrier $n$ is a vector, i.e. $\mathbf{p}^n = [p_1^n, p_2^n, \cdots, p_M^n]^T$. For $N$ subcarriers, the total accessing probability of DAU $m$ is $\mathbf{P}_m = \sum_{n=1}^{N} p_m^n = p_m^1 + p_m^2 + \cdots + p_m^N$, thus we can get $\varnothing_m = \frac{\sum_{n=1}^{N} p_m^n}{\sum_{m=1}^{M} \sum_{n=1}^{N} p_m^n}$, where $\varnothing_m$ denotes the ratio of the total accessing probability of DAU $m$ to the total accessing probability of all the DAUs. Hence, the number of subcarriers of assigning to DAU $m$ is expressed as $N_m = \lfloor \varnothing_m \cdot N \rfloor$.

B. Optimal DAU selection and subcarriers allocation

We assign DAUs to users based on the CSI. Assignment procedure is consisted of following steps:

- Step 1: Sorting DAUs based on the CSI and assign the best DAU with the best subcarrier to the corresponding user, then the pairs of DAU-subcarrier will be erased from the selection list. Repeating until all the users are served by one DAU.
- Step 2: Assigning the rest of DAUs in the selection list based on the CSI until all remaining DAUs are assigned to users.
- Step 3: Assigning the rest of subcarriers to DAUs until the number of subcarriers of DAU is $N_m$.

The proposed optimal algorithm is summarized in Algorithm 1.

---

**Algorithm 1.** Joint DAU selection and Subcarriers Assignment Algorithm

1: **Initialization** : $S_k = \emptyset$, $\Omega_m = \emptyset$, let $\overline{M} = \{1, \cdots, M\}$, $\overline{K} = \{1, \cdots, K\}$,
　　$\overline{N} = \{1, \cdots, N\}$;
2: Step 1: Construct a three-dimensional matrix H(K, N, M).
　2.1 Find maximum $h_{k^*,n^*,m^*} \in H$; let $m^* \in S_{k^*}$, $n^* \in \Omega_{m^*}$; $\Omega_{m^*} = \Omega_{m^*}+1$,
　　　$S_{k^*}=S_{k^*}+1$; $i=k$, then $\overline{M}= \overline{M} - m^*$, $\overline{K} = \overline{K} - k^*$, $\overline{N} = \overline{N} - n^*$;
　2.2 Remove H(:, :, m$^*$), H(k$^*$, :, :) and H(:, n$^*$, :). Set $i=i-1$, Repeat 2.1.
　2.3 Until $|\overline{M}|_r=M - K$, $|\overline{N}|_r=N - K$, $i=0$.
3: Step 2: Based on step 1, construct matrix H$'$(K, N − K, M − K).
　3.1 Find maximum $h_{k^*,n^*,m^*} \in$ H$'$(K, N − K, M − K); let $m^* \in S_{k^*}$, $n^* \in \Omega_{m^*}$;
　　　$\Omega_{m^*} = \Omega_{m^*}+1$; $\overline{M} = M - K - m^*$, $\overline{N} = N - K - n^*$;
　3.2 Remove H$'$(:, :, m$^*$) and H$'$(:, n$^*$, :). Set $M=M - K - 1$, Repeat 3.1.
　3.3 Until $|\overline{M}|_r=0$; $|\overline{N}|_r=N - M$; $\Omega_m = 1, \forall m$.
4: Step 3: Get $S_k \neq \emptyset$, and $\sum_{k=1}^{K} |S_k| = M$, $\sum_{m=1}^{M} \Omega_m = M$;
　4.1 Construct matrix H$_k$(k, N − M, |S$_k$|);
　4.2 Traverse $H_k$, find maximum channel gain $h_{k^*,n^*,m^*}$,$m^* \in S_{m^*}$; Let
　　　$n^* \in \Omega_{m^*}$, remove H$_k$(k, n$^*$, :). $\overline{N}=\overline{N} - M - n^*$, when $|\Omega_m|=N_m$, stop.

---

### 3.2 Power Allocation Optimization

Based on the optimal DAU selection and subcarriers allocation algorithm, we determine the set of DAU $S_k$ to serve user $k$ and the set of subcarriers to DAU $m$ is denoted as $\Omega_m$. Therefore, the Eqs. (2) and (4) can be changed into (10) and (11), respectively.

$$r_k = B \sum_{m \in S_k} \sum_{n \in \Omega_m} \log_2(1 + \frac{p_{k,n,m}|h_{k,n,m}|^2}{\Gamma \sigma_z^2}) \tag{10}$$

$$P_{tot} = \sum_{k=1}^{K} \sum_{m \in S_k} \sum_{n \in \Omega_m} \tau p_{k,n,m} + Mp_c + p_o \tag{11}$$

Thus, the optimization problem **P1** is converted to optimization problem **P2**

$$\max_{\boldsymbol{P}} \quad EE = R_{tot}(\boldsymbol{P})/P_{tot}(\boldsymbol{P}) \tag{12}$$

$$\text{s.t.} \quad C1 : r_k \geq R_k^{req}, \forall k$$

$$C2 : \sum_{n \in \Omega_m} p_{k,n,m} \leq p_m^{max}, \forall k, m$$

$$C7 : p_{k,n,m} \geq 0, \forall k, n, m$$

Due to the non-convexity of problem **P2**, it is difficult to solve. However, the numerator and denominator of Eq. (12) are differentiable concave and affine functions with respect to $\boldsymbol{P}$ respectively. So problem **P2** can be transformed into a equivalent subtractive form, and solved by using Lagrangian dual decomposition method [11]. The subtractive form problem **P3** is given as

$$\max_{\boldsymbol{P}} \quad U(q) = R_{tot}(\boldsymbol{P}) - q \cdot P_{tot}(\boldsymbol{P}) \tag{13}$$

$$\text{s.t.} \quad C1, C2, C7.$$

**Theorem 1.** There is $q^* = \max \frac{R_{tot}(\boldsymbol{P}^*)}{P_{tot}(\boldsymbol{P}^*)}$, if and only if, $U(q^*) = R_{tot}(\boldsymbol{P}^*) - q^* \cdot P_{tot}(\boldsymbol{P}^*) = 0$.

In Theorem 1, $q^*$ is the optimal EE to be determined, $\boldsymbol{P}^*$ is the optimal power to be allocated. The Lagrangian function of optimization problem (13) can be expressed as

$$L(\boldsymbol{P}, \boldsymbol{\alpha}, \boldsymbol{\beta}) = B \sum_{k=1}^{K} \sum_{m \in S_k} \sum_{n \in \Omega_m} \log_2(1 + \frac{p_{k,n,m}|h_{k,n,m}|^2}{\Gamma \sigma_z^2}) - \sum_{k=1}^{K} \alpha_k (R_k^{req} - r_k)$$

$$-q(\sum_{k=1}^{K} \sum_{m \in S_k} \sum_{n \in \Omega_m} \tau p_{k,n,m} + M p_c + p_o) - \sum_{m=1}^{M} \beta_m (\sum_{n \in \Omega_m} p_{k,n,m} - p_m^{max}); \tag{14}$$

where $\boldsymbol{\alpha} = [\alpha_1, \alpha_2, \cdots, \alpha_K]^T$ and $\boldsymbol{\beta} = [\beta_1, \beta_2, \cdots, \beta_M]^T$ are non-negative Lagrange multipliers. The optimal power $p_{k,n,m}^*$ can be obtained through differentiating with respect to $p_{k,n,m}$, which is given as

$$p_{k,n,m}^* = \left[ \frac{(1+\alpha_k)B}{(q\tau + \beta_m)\ln 2} - \frac{\Gamma \sigma_z^2}{|h_{k,n,m}|^2} \right]^+. \tag{15}$$

where $[x]^+ = \max(0, x)$, the power allocation scheme can be regarded as the classical water-filling policy. Notably that there is a zero duality gap between the primal problem and its dual problem, if the problem is convex. For the optimization problem **P3**, the Lagrange dual function is derived by

$$g(\boldsymbol{\alpha}, \boldsymbol{\beta}) = max \ L(\boldsymbol{P}, \boldsymbol{\alpha}, \boldsymbol{\beta}) \tag{16}$$

$$s.t. \ C1, C2, C7.$$

and we have the dual problem which is

$$\min_{\boldsymbol{\alpha}, \boldsymbol{\beta}} g(\boldsymbol{\alpha}, \boldsymbol{\beta}) \quad s.t. \boldsymbol{\alpha} \geq 0, \boldsymbol{\beta} \geq 0 \tag{17}$$

The sub-gradient method could be employed to solve the problem, The sub-gradient of dual function can be expressed as

$$\Delta \alpha_k^{(i)} = B \sum_{m \in S_k} \sum_{n \in \Omega_m} \log_2(1 + \frac{p_{k,n,m}^{*(i)}|h_{k,n,m}|^2}{\Gamma \sigma_z^2}) - R_k^{req}, \tag{18}$$

$$\Delta \beta_m^{(i)} = p_m^{max} - \sum_{n \in \Omega_m} p_{k,n,m}^{*(i)}. \tag{19}$$

where $p_{k,n,m}^{*(i)}$ is optimal allocation power in the $i$ iteration. The multipliers $\alpha_k$ and $\beta_m$ can be updated through following formulas

$$\alpha_k^{(i+1)} = \left[ \alpha_k^{(i)} - \delta^{(i)} \Delta \alpha_k^{(i)} \right]^+, \ \beta_m^{(i+1)} = \left[ \beta_m^{(i)} - \xi^{(i)} \Delta \beta_m^{(i)} \right]^+. \tag{20}$$

where $i$ is iteration index, $\delta^{(i)}$ and $\xi^{(i)}$ are sufficiently small positive step size. In the paper, we assume $\delta^{(i)} = \xi^{(i)} = \frac{0.1}{i}$, According to all the above analysis and procedure, the process of optimal power allocation algorithm is outlined in Algorithm 2.

---

**Algorithm 2.** Energy Efficient Power Allocation Optimization Algorithm

---

1: **Initialization** : $\alpha, \beta$, the maximal iterations $I_{max}, T_{max}$, error tolerance threshold $\epsilon, \kappa$, set $t = 0$, $q^{(0)} = 0$, $i = 0$.

2: **repeat**

3:    Given $q^{(0)}$, Solve (15) to obtain $p^*_{k,n,m}$

4: **repeat**

5:    Update $\alpha, \beta$ from (20), respectively.

6:    $i = i + 1$;

7: **If** $|\alpha_k^{(i+1)} - \alpha_k^{(i)}| \leq \kappa$, $|\beta_m^{(i+1)} - \beta_m^{(i)}| \leq \kappa$ **then**

8:       **break.**

9: **end if**

10: **until** $i \geq I_{max}$

11: **If** $|R_{tot}(\boldsymbol{P}^*) - q^{(t)} P_{tot}(\boldsymbol{P}^*)| \leq \epsilon$ or $t \geq T_{max}$ **then**

12:    $\boldsymbol{P}^{opt} = \boldsymbol{P}^*$. $EE^{opt} = q^{(t)} = \frac{R_{tot}(\boldsymbol{P}^*)}{P_{tot}(\boldsymbol{P}^*)}$.

13: **break.**

14:    **else**

15:    Set $q^{(t+1)} = \frac{R_{tot}(\boldsymbol{P}^*)}{P_{tot}(\boldsymbol{P}^*)}$, $t = t + 1$.

16: **end if.**

17: **until** $t \geq T_{max}$

---

## 4    Simulation Results

In this section, we evaluate the performance of the proposed energy-efficient resource allocation scheme through Monte Carlo simulations. We consider a circular coverage area with radius equals to $\sqrt{112/3}$ km, in which DAUs and users are random uniformly distributed. We set DAU $P_m^{max} = 30$ dBm, noise power $\sigma_z^2 = -50$ dBm, $p_c = 0.03$ w, $p_o = 0.01$ w. Shadow fading $\sigma_{sh} = 8$ dB, path loss exponent $\alpha = 3.7$, user data rate $R^{req} = 20$ kbps, subcarrier bandwidth $B = 15$ kHz.

Figures 1 and 2 depict the EE versus the number of iterations in proposed scheme. It can be seen that the EE converge to the maximum value around seven iterations. In Fig. 1, we compare EE for different number of users and DAUs with $N = 8$. From the results, the EE with $M = 4$, $K = 3$ is higher compared with other conditions. Comparing with the case $M = 5$, $K = 3$, the fewer number of DAUs the less system power consumption which leads higher EE of the system. Similarly, with increasing number of users, the proposed scheme is able to achieve higher EE by the larger user diversity gain. Specifically, power consumption of DAUs have larger effect on EE of the system than diversity gain of users. In

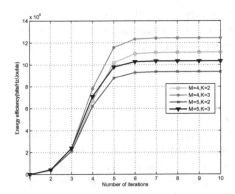
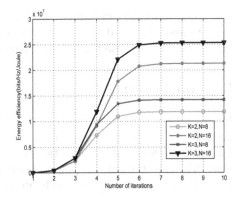

**Fig. 1.** EE versus number of iterations     **Fig. 2.** EE versus number of iterations

Fig. 2, we obtain EE for different users and subcarriers with given DAU number. From the Fig, we can see that increase of the number of subcarriers can improve EE greatly, e.g., with fixed number of users. when subcarrier increases from 8 to 16, the performance of the system improved around 50%.

Figure 3 compares the EE of two algorithms which are the proposed algorithm and random selection algorithm, namely randomly allocating DAUs with subcarriers and users. EE of two algorithms increases with increasing number of subcarriers. Notably, the more number of subcarriers rises, the larger gap of EE between two algorithms. Therefore, Fig. 3 demonstrates the effectiveness of the proposed algorithm.

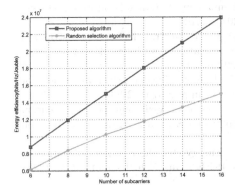
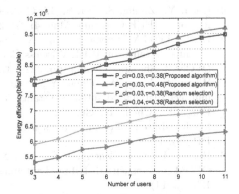

**Fig. 3.** EE versus number of sucarriers     **Fig. 4.** EE versus number of users

Figure 4 shows the EE versus the number of users of two algorithms. We can see that the EE increases with the number of users with different parameters, the proposed algorithm can always achieve higher performance than random selection algorithm. Meanwhile, we evaluate the EE at different circuit power $p_c$

and power amplifier efficiency $\tau$. It is seen that larger circuit power consumption leads to lower EE, and larger power amplifier efficiency can improve EE. This is because the larger power amplifier efficiency can increase data rate of the system.

## 5    Conclusion

In this paper, we formulated and studied a mixed combinatorial programming problem for EE optimization in a downlink multiuser OFDM DAS. We divided the optimization problem into two subproblems, which are DAU selection, and subcarriers assignment and power allocation optimization. Firstly, an energy efficient resource allocation scheme is presented. Then, we transform the optimization problem into a subtractive form, and solve it by Lagrangian dual decomposition. From simulation results, we can see that the proposed algorithm has better performance. In the future, the inter-cell interference and cell-edge users' performance will be taken into consideration to how to design EE optimization scheme.

## References

1. Feng, W., Li, Y., Gan, J., Zhou, S., Wang, J., Xia, M.: On the deployment of antenna elements in generalized multi-user distributed antenna systems. ACM Mob. Netw. Appl. **16**(1), 35–45 (2011)
2. Zhu, H.: Performance comparison between distributed antenna and microcellular systems. IEEE J. Sel. Areas Commun. **29**(6), 1151–1163 (2011)
3. Correia, L.M., et al.: Challenges and enabling technologies for energy aware mobile radio networks. IEEE Commun. Mag. **48**(11), 66–72 (2010)
4. Chen, Y., Zhang, S., Xu, S., Li, G.Y.: Fundamental trade-offs on green wireless networks. IEEE Commun. Mag. **49**(6), 30–37 (2011)
5. He, C., Li, G.Y., Sheng, B., You, X.: Energy and spectral efficiency of distributed antenna systems. In: IEEE Wireless Communications and Networking Conference (WCNC), Shanghai, China, pp. 3225–3229 (2013)
6. Wang, J., Feng, W., Chen, Y., Zhou, S.: Energy efficient power allocation for multicell distributed antenna systems. IEEE Commun. Lett. **20**(1), 177–180 (2016)
7. Feng, W., Chen, Y., Ge, N., Lu, J.: Optimal energy-efficient power allocation for distributed antenna systems with imperfect CSI. IEEE Trans. Veh. Technol. **PP**(99), 1
8. He, C., Li, G.Y., Zheng, F.C., You, X.: Energy-efficient resource allocation in OFDM systems with distributed antennas. IEEE Trans. Veh. Technol. **63**(3), 1223–1231 (2014)
9. Wu, Q., Chen, W., Tao, M., Li, J., Tang, H., Wu, J.: Resource allocation for joint transmitter and receiver energy efficiency maximization in downlink OFDMA systems. IEEE Trans. Commun. **63**(2), 416–430 (2015)
10. Ge, X., Jin, H., Leung, V.C.M.: Opportunistic downlink scheduling with fair resource sharing for distributed antenna systems. In: 2014 IEEE International Conference on Communications (ICC), Sydney, NSW, pp. 5000–5005 (2014)
11. Dinkelbach, W.: On nonlinear fractional programming. Manag. Sci. **13**(7), 492–498 (1967)

# Traffic Engineering and Routing Algorithms

# Applications of Genetic Algorithms in BGP-Based Interdomain Traffic Engineering

Jiyun Yan[1(✉)], Zhenqiang Li[2], and Xiaohong Huang[1]

[1] Beijing University of Posts and Telecommunications,
No. 10, Xitucheng Road, Haidian District, Beijing, China
yanjybupt@163.com, huangxh@bupt.edu.cn
[2] China Mobile Research Institute,
No. 32, West Street, Xuanwumen, Xicheng District, Beijing, China
lizhenqiang@chinamobile.com

**Abstract.** With the rapid development of the Internet, widely deployed new services such as high definition videos and voice over IP (VoIP) require higher performance guarantees. Traffic engineering can improve end to end service quality, help large autonomous systems (AS) operators improve network resource utilization and meet the challenge. At the interdomain level, traffic engineering is more challenging. Most network operators still rely on changing routing policies and BGP attributes manually. In this paper, we discuss the existing systematic techniques in BGP-based interdomain traffic engineering and propose an improved algorithm based on a multi-objective genetic algorithm. Our algorithm is scalable and efficient. We apply our solution to a provincial network of China Mobile and discuss the influence of different parameters on the performance and validity of the algorithm.

**Keywords:** Genetic algorithms · Interdomain traffic engineering · BGP

## 1 Introduction

Today, the Internet has been developing rapidly. The traffic of the Internet is growing at a high speed while widely deployed new services such as high definition videos and voice over IP (VoIP) require higher performance guarantees. With the rapid growth of traffic and the emergence of various kinds of new services, the network operation is facing a big challenge. Nowadays more and more Internet Service Providers (ISP) rely on traffic engineering to control the flow of traffic into, out of, and across their networks. The main objective of traffic engineering is to optimize the performance of the network. Intradomain traffic engineering is mature and several techniques exist such as MPLS based traffic engineering and OSPF based traffic engineering [1]. Due to the incomplete information of the network topology and state and the complex interactions between the BGP decision process and IGP routing, the current state-of-the-art in interdomain traffic engineering is primitive. An efficient multi-objective evolutionary algorithm to evenly distribute the interdomain traffic has been proposed in [3–5]. As described in [5], the algorithm has one manifest drawback. If multiple eBGP peers in a

Q. Chen et al. (Eds.): ChinaCom 2016, Part I, LNICST 209, pp. 109–118, 2018.
DOI: 10.1007/978-3-319-66625-9_11

same AS are attached to one egress router, it cannot guarantee a good balance among those peers. We design an improved genetic algorithm based on the multi-objective evolutionary heuristic. We solved this problem and reduced the running time of the algorithm by adding filtering mechanism for the selection of exit routers. Another key contribution in our paper is that we apply our method to a provincial network of China Mobile. We also discuss the influence of different parameters on the performance and validity of the algorithm which has great practical significance to network operators.

The remainder of this paper is organized as follows. Section 2 introduces the interdomain traffic engineering. Section 3 presents the related work in BGP-based interdomain traffic engineering. Section 4 introduces the improved multi-objective genetic algorithm. Section 5 presents the application of our solution to a provincial network of China Mobile. The last section summarizes the content of this paper.

## 2 Interdomain Traffic Engineering

The Internet is composed of Autonomous Systems (AS). A transit AS is mainly to transit packets from a neighbor domain to another. A stub AS does not provide transit service and only sends or receives packets produced by or destined to their hosts. Stub ASes represent the majority of the Internet and they have two types: single-homed ones and multi-homed ones. Today, Border Gateway Protocol (BGP) is the de facto standard interdomain routing protocol used in the Internet. BGP is a path vector protocol that works by sending routing advertisements. There are two variants of BGP. The external BGP (eBGP) variant is used to announce the reachable prefixes on a link between routers that are part of distinct ASes. The internal BGP (iBGP) variant is used to distribute the best routes learned from neighboring ASes inside an AS. A key feature of BGP is that it allows each network operator to define its routing policies implemented by configuring the BGP attributes. BGP routing attributes include Next-hop, AS-Path, Local-Preference, MED (Multi-Exit Discriminator), Origin, etc.

Before designing traffic engineering techniques, we must study the stability of interdomain routing and the characteristics of interdomain traffic. As explained in [2], most of the network prefixes do not change for several days or even a few weeks and the routes modified by the interdomain traffic engineering are guaranteed to remain constant over a long period of time. Many studies show that most of the traffic is concentrated in a small part of the prefixes [2]. Only by selecting popular prefixes reasonably, interdomain traffic engineering can redistribute a large amount of traffic. Popular prefixes with large volume traffic, the relative stability of traffic and interdomain routing are the preconditions of interdomain traffic engineering.

There are two main solutions in interdomain traffic engineering, MPLS (Multi-Protocol Label Switching) based solution and BGP based solution [1]. The MPLS based solution is generally an extension of intradomain traffic engineering based on MPLS and follows its framework. The deployment of the solution needs all the ASes within the traffic engineering, which is very difficult. There are still some unsolved problems in this kind of solution. The BGP based solution is divided into incoming traffic engineering and outgoing traffic engineering. Modifying the flow of the inbound traffic with BGP requires changing how remote ASes choose their best

BGP routes to reach the local AS. Since it is relatively difficult to influence the route policy in remote ASes, more of the current effort has been spent on outbound aspects. The outbound traffic engineering is generally implemented by influencing the decision process of BGP. In this paper, we focus on BGP-based outbound interdomain traffic engineering.

## 3 Related Work

The traffic engineering objectives that an AS may want to optimize will depend on its size, the type of business it focuses on and the relationships with other ASes. Stub ASes care more about aspects related to the distribution of the traffic over egress points than end-to-end properties. They also want to maintain the lowest communication cost at the same time. The stub ASes whose main business is to provide access to contents may prefer to optimize the outgoing traffic while the stub ASes whose main business is to provide dial-up, broadband access services may want to optimize how the traffic enter their network. For transit ASes, they care about both the distribution of traffic inside their ASes and among their interdomain links. We should build different models for stub ASes and transit ASes.

BGP-based outbound traffic engineering is essentially a problem of egress router selection and a NP problem. So we need heuristic algorithms to solve this problem. A systematic BGP-based traffic engineering for the outbound traffic of stub ASes at a very limited cost in terms of iBGP messages are presented in [3]. They use an efficient multi-objective evolutionary algorithm to evenly distribute the total traffic over the available providers and minimize the cost of the traffic. The cost of the traffic models the volume-based billing performed by transit ISPs. The multi-objective evolutionary heuristic is described in detail in [4]. The objectives considered in [4] are the following: minimizing the burden on BGP and optimizing one or several objectives defined on the traffic exchanged with other ASes or on the distribution of the traffic inside the AS. They implement a NSGA-II like algorithm. To avoid making the search space grow very large by sampling the whole search space, their heuristic iterate over the BGP routing changes by trying to add one BGP routing changes at each generation. The evolutionary heuristic is also used in [5]. The problem tackled in [5] consists in balancing the outbound traffic of a transit AS over its Internet connections while minimizing the cost of the traffic to cross its internal topology. They propose Tweak-it, a tool that based on the steady-state view of BGP routing inside the AS and the traffic demands of the AS, computes the BGP updates to be sent to the ingress routers of a transit AS to engineer its interdomain traffic over time. Tweak-it is based on two components: a scalable BGP simulator (C-BGP) [6] that reproduces the steady-state behavior of BGP routing and the multi-objective evolutionary heuristic. The work of this paper is based on this tool.

Taking into account the stability of BGP routing and the difficulty of real-time collection of traffic and routing updates, it is more practical to provide an offline tool for large ASes. The tool provided by this paper is offline.

## 4   A Multi-objective Genetic Algorithm

We design our method based on the Tweak-it tool proposed in [5]. Tweak-it is composed of two parts: C-BGP and the multi-objective evolutionary heuristic algorithm. Our contributions in this paper are the optimization and improvements of the algorithm and the re-development of C-BGP to apply a systematic BGP-based interdomain traffic engineering to a real network.

C-BGP is an efficient open-source BGP simulator written in C programming language which can model networks as large as the Internet. The network is represented as a graph where nodes are routers, and edges are links between routers. Each edge is weighted by the IGP metric of the corresponding link. C-BGP uses Dijkstra's Shortest Path First (SPF) to model IGP routing instead of modeling the specific implementation details in IGP. C-BGP is aimed at computing the outcome of the BGP decision process and it computes for each router the routes selected toward all the interdomain prefixes. This output can then be used to replay how the traffic was routed by the routers of the AS. To model BGP, the nodes which are considered as BGP routers are fitted out with additional data structures: a local RIB (Loc-RIB) and adjacent RIBs (Adj-RIBs). The Loc-RIB is used to store the best BGP routes while the Adj-RIBs contain alternative routes. These data structures form the basis of the algorithm. C-BGP is easily configurable through a CISCO-like command-line interface. To verify the simulation results, we add a command to C-BGP which will be explained in Sect. 5.

The second part of the tool is the multi-objective genetic algorithm. As practical traffic engineering objectives can be conflicting, the interdomain traffic engineering problem is intrinsically a multi-objective optimization problem. The algorithm we use as a basis can deal with one or several objectives definede tffic ehanged wher ASes or on the distribution of the traffic inside the AS. We define the imbalance ratio to measure the balance of interdomain traffic, specified as

$$(\max(tr_i) - \min(tr_i)) / \sum_{i=1}^{n} tr_i i = 1, \ldots, n \tag{1}$$

where n denotes the number of eBGP peers and $tr_i$ denotes the amount of traffic sent to the peer i. In this paper, for the provincial network of China Mobile, our first traffic objective is to reduce the imbalance ratio as much as possible to evenly distribute the interdomain traffic. The second objective is minimizing the IGP cost of the traffic inside the transit AS, specified as

$$\sum_{\forall(i,p)}^{n} \text{traffic}(i, p) * IGP\_cost(i, p, e) \tag{2}$$

where $\text{traffic}(i, p)$ denotes the amount of traffic received by ingress router i having as destination external prefix p and $IGP\_cost(i, p, e)$ represents the IGP cost for ingress i to reach egress router e.

Unlike the general genetic algorithms, this algorithm doesn't encode the possible solutions and has no crossover and mutation. Instead, the steady-state policy routing made by BGP constitutes the search space of the multi-objective genetic algorithm. We do not describe this algorithm in detail but refer to [5] for the original idea and to [3, 4] for a thorough explanation. The core points of the algorithm are briefly mentioned here. This algorithm is implemented as a Perl script. The first phase of the script is the initialization interacting with C-BGP. It takes the internal topology, IGP weights, and BGP routing policies of each BGP router. Then the Perl script can build the C-BGP configuration file which will be injected into C-BGP. And after we inject RIBs of the border routers, C-BGP will populate the BGP routing tables and reproduce the steady-state policy routing made by BGP which constitutes the search space of the genetic algorithm. Then the multi-objective genetic algorithm will compute the tweakings to be performed to engineer the interdomain traffic. A tweaking is a <ingress, prefix, exit> tuple. The genetic algorithm relies on a population of individuals. Each individual is a potential solution, i.e. a set of tweakings to be applied. At the first generation, we start with a population of individuals initialized at the default solution found by BGP routing containing no BGP routing changes. At each generation, we parse the whole population and for each individual we choose an additional randomly <ingress, prefix> pair. Then, we try to apply the tweaking by computing the new values of the traffic objectives for every reachable exit peer. If the objectives have been optimized, we accept the tweaking. The number of generations is upper bounded by MAXGEN, the maximum number of tweakings allowed. Finally, after MAXGEN generations, we can select the best solution according to our optimization objectives.

Here we focus on our improvements of the algorithm. The paper improves the algorithm on two aspects: adding filtering mechanism and expanding the scope of application of the algorithm by solving the defects of the original algorithm.

## 4.1 Adding Filtering Mechanism

At each generation, the original algorithm tries to add one tweaking. It randomly chooses a <ingress, prefix> and tries every reachable exit peer to test whether the traffic objectives are optimized. Taking into account the fact that we usually tweak the traffic to the exit routers whose traffic on its interdomain link is smaller than average, we can add filtering mechanism for the selection of exit routers. In our algorithm, we only try the reachable exit peers whose traffic is below average. This will narrow the search space largely and shorten the running time of the algorithm.

## 4.2 Expanding the Scope of Application of the Algorithm

The original algorithm cannot efficiently deal with the following kind of scenario. Multiple eBGP peers belonging to a same AS are attached to one egress router, as shown in Fig. 1. The router R1 and R2 are egress routers. The router R3 and R4 are ingress routers. The best BGP routes chosen by each ingress router in the transit AS to reach prefix p are also shown in Fig. 1. As we can see in Fig. 1, the router R2 has two eBGP peers R6 and R7 in AS A.

To tackle the problem exists in the original algorithm, we must also record the corresponding eBGP peers when recording the best and alternative routes the ingress routers use to reach the prefixes. For instance, both R2 and R3 use R6 as the exit peer. Since C-BGP only stores the Next-hop and AS-Path attributes for the BGP routes, we need to do additional work in the algorithm. For routers like R2 whose Next-hop is just

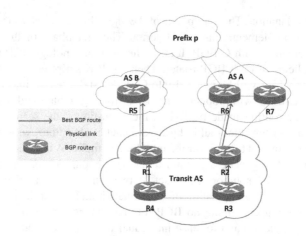

**Fig. 1.** The scenario that the original algorithm cannot deal with

the eBGP peer, we can simply record the Next-hop as the exit peer. But for routers like R3 whose Next-hop is a router inside the AS, we should find the exact exit peer. Taking into account the propagation of BGP and the interactions between IGP and BGP, we find the fact that if the BGP Next-hop is a router inside the AS, the exit peer the Next-hop router use to reach the prefix is actually the exit peer we are looking for. This is a key point here. For instance, we can find the exit peer R6 for R3 through R2. In the original algorithm, an egress router has only one eBGP peer in a neighboring AS by default and tweakings are defined in terms of egress routers. In our algorithm, through the additional information of exit peers, we can define tweakings in terms of exit peers, tweak the traffic more accurately and expand the scope of application of the algorithm.

## 5   Applications of the Genetic Algorithm

After we solve the problem exists in the original algorithm, we can apply our method to a provincial network of China Mobile. AS shown in Fig. 2, the simplified architecture is an abstraction of one provincial network of China Mobile. All the routers in the provincial network are both ingress routers and egress routers at the same time. The traffic objectives we consider here are evenly distributing the traffic over the interdomain links and minimizing the IGP cost of the traffic inside the provincial network as described in Sect. 4.

The first thing we should do is gathering the information of the network to inject into C-BGP which will build the search space of the genetic algorithm. It is necessary to collect the information such as: internal topology (including nodes, links and link weights), BGP routing policies and the RIBs of the border routers to be injected into C-BGP.

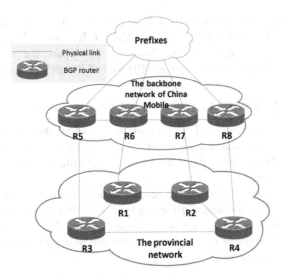

**Fig. 2.** The provincial network

## 5.1 Gathering the Information of Topology and IGP Weights

Large scale ISPs usually use IS-IS as the intradomain routing protocol and the provincial network of China mobile is no exception. We can extract information of all the nodes and links inside this network and the corresponding IGP weights from the IS-IS link-state database. We can get the database from any of the routers inside the AS. For reasons of confidentiality, the IP addresses, node names and link weights are changed.

We design a Python script to parse the file and output a C-BGP configuration file as shown in Fig. 3 by which C-BGP will compute the shortest paths from one router to another. In order to save space, we will not introduce the parsing process in detail.

```
1  IS-IS level 1 link-state database:
2  IS-IS level 2 link-state database:
3
4 ⊟RT01-M320-RE0.00-00 Sequence: 0x16949, Checksum: 0xb93b, Lifetime: 27438 secs
5    IPV4 Unicast IS neighbor:RT02-M320-RE0.00 Metric:    305
6    IPV4 Unicast IS neighbor:RT03-M320-RE0.00 Metric:    5180
7    IPV6 Unicast IS neighbor: RT02-M320-RE0.00 Metric:   20000
8    IP IPV4 Unicast prefix: 1.0.0.1/32   Metric:       0 Internal Up
9    V6 IPV6 Unicast prefix: 2409:8080::1b3/128 Metric:    0 Internal Up
```

```
1  net add domain 1 igp
2  net add node 1.0.0.1
3  net node 1.0.0.1 domain 1
4  net add node 1.0.0.2
5  net node 1.0.0.2 domain 1
6  net add node 1.0.0.3
7  net node 1.0.0.3 domain 1
8  net add node 1.0.0.4
9  net node 1.0.0.4 domain 1
10 net add link 1.0.0.1 1.0.0.2
11 net link 1.0.0.1 1.0.0.2 igp-weight --bidir 305
12 net add link 1.0.0.1 1.0.0.3
13 net link 1.0.0.1 1.0.0.3 igp-weight --bidir 5180
```

**Fig. 3.** The IS-IS database and the C-BGP configuration file

## 5.2 Gathering the Information of BGP Routing

To model the routing of BGP, we must get the information of all the BGP sessions established by the routers first. In our example, the iBGP sessions are full mesh and each BGP router has an eBGP peer belong to the backbone network of China Mobile as we can see in Fig. 2. C-BGP can load into one BGP router a dump of RIB captured on a real router and the RIB dump must be provided in ASCII MRT format. In the same way, we get the RIBs of the real routers and write Python scripts to parse the files. To ensure the correctness of BGP routing, we should get RIBs of all the BGP routers inside the AS.

### 5.3    Collecting Traffic and the Validation of the Algorithm

After gathering the information of the network, we also need the information of traffic. We collected a day of the traffic of the province and we can see that a limited fraction of the prefixes carry the vast majority of the interdomain traffic and these popular prefixes have stable BGP routes.

Then we can use the multi-objective genetic algorithm to compute the BGP updates to optimize the traffic objectives. C-BGP can load traffic but cannot analyze the traffic. To verify the simulation results, we add a command to C-BGP as shown in Fig. 4. With the comparison of imbalance ratio before and after the BGP updates, we can verify the effectiveness of the algorithm.

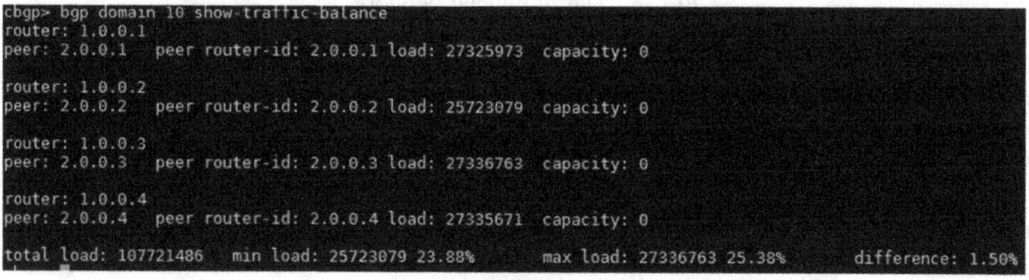

```
cbgp> bgp domain 10 show-traffic-balance
router: 1.0.0.1
peer: 2.0.0.1   peer router-id: 2.0.0.1 load: 27325973  capacity: 0

router: 1.0.0.2
peer: 2.0.0.2   peer router-id: 2.0.0.2 load: 25723079  capacity: 0

router: 1.0.0.3
peer: 2.0.0.3   peer router-id: 2.0.0.3 load: 27336763  capacity: 0

router: 1.0.0.4
peer: 2.0.0.4   peer router-id: 2.0.0.4 load: 27335671  capacity: 0

total load: 107721486   min load: 25723079 23.88%        max load: 27336763 25.38%        difference: 1.50%
```

Fig. 4.  The command added to C-BGP

### 5.4    Comparison with the Original Algorithm

Under the same parameter condition, we run the original algorithm and our algorithm separately. In Table 1, we show the results of the two algorithms where we optimized the balance of the outgoing traffic of the provincial network while minimizing the cost of the traffic to cross its network (IGP cost metric), by relying on as few BGP routing changes as possible.

Table 1.  Results of two algorithms.

| Results | Original algorithm | Improved algorithm |
| --- | --- | --- |
| Imbalance ratio | 2.49% | 1.18% |
| Running time | 19.89 s | 16.24 s |

The imbalance ratio is 43.17% by default in our provincial network. We will say the interdomain traffic is well balanced when the ratio is under 10%. As we can see, the traffic can both be well balanced by the two algorithms but the running time of our algorithm is decreased because of the reduced search space of the algorithm.

## 5.5    Discussion on Different Parameters

As most of the traffic is concentrated in a small part of the prefixes, we just need to tweak some popular prefixes carrying the vast majority of the traffic. The algorithm takes as a parameter a percentage of the total traffic. This will greatly reduce the search space. But percentage is not as small as possible to ensure adequate search space and good optimization results. In this section, we focus on discussing the influence of different percentages on the performance and validity of the algorithm.

First, we talk about the relationship between the percentage parameter and the number of prefixes needed to tweak. As presented in Fig. 5 we can see a sharp decrease in the numbers of early period and a good percentage will greatly reduce the search space of the algorithm. When the percentage of the total traffic is decreased from 100 to 95, the number of prefixes is almost down to 1/5. When the percentage is below 70%, there are not enough prefixes.

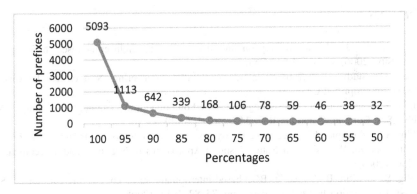

**Fig. 5.** Relationships between the percentage parameter and the number of prefixes

In Fig. 6, we can see the relationships among the percentage parameter, the imbalance ratio and the running time. All the different parameters can get a good balance of the interdomain traffic and the results are all acceptable. In our example,

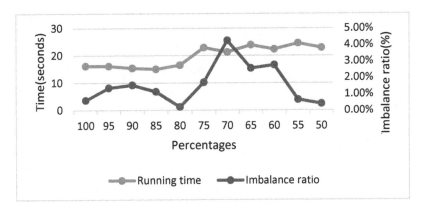

**Fig. 6.** Relationships among the percentage parameter, the imbalance ratio and the running time

85% to 95% of total traffic to be considered have relatively less running time. In a word, 85% to 95% can get relatively good optimization results and less time used for our example network. The percentage parameter should not be too big nor too small. Network operators can adjust the parameter according to their actual demands.

## 6  Conclusions

In this paper, we introduce the genetic algorithms in BGP-based interdomain traffic engineering. Then we propose an improved genetic algorithm and apply it to a provincial network of China Mobile. At last, we discuss the influence of different parameters in practical application. This systematic method in BGP-based interdomain traffic engineering has great practical significance for the network operators.

## References

1. Luo, W., Wu, J., Xu, K.: Survey on inter-domain traffic engineering research. Tsinghua University (2006). (in simplified Chinese)
2. Wang, D.: Study on BGP-based interdomain traffic engineering. Northeastern University (2006). (in simplified Chinese)
3. Uhlig, S., Bonaventure, O.: Designing BGP-based outbound traffic engineering techniques for stub ASes. Comput. Commun. Rev. 34(5), 89–106 (2004)
4. Uhlig, S.: A multiple-objectives evolutionary perspective to interdomain traffic engineering in the internet. In: Workshop on Nature Inspired Approaches to Networks and Telecommunications (2004)
5. Uhlig, S., Quoitin, B.: Tweak-it: BGP-based interdomain traffic engineering for transit ASs. In: Next Generation Internet Networks, pp. 75–82. IEEE (2005)
6. Quoitin, B., Uhlig, S.: Modeling the routing of an autonomous system with C-BGP. IEEE Netw. 19(6), 12–19 (2005)

# MP-SDWN: A Novel Multipath-Supported Software Defined Wireless Network Architecture

Chuan Xu[1(✉)], Wenqiang Jin[1], Yuanbing Han[1], Guofeng Zhao[1],
and Huaglory Tianfield[2]

[1] School of Communication and Information Engineering,
Chongqing University of Posts and Telecommunications, Chongqing, China
{xuchuan,jinwq,hanyb,zhaogf}@cqupt.edu.cn
[2] School of Engineering and Built Environment,
Glasgow Caledonian University, Glasgow, UK
h.tianfield@gcu.ac.uk

**Abstract.** The wireless access networks have witnessed an explosive growth in home and enterprise applications. However, to meet the tough performance requirements, such as seamless handover, higher throughput, and agile programing, there still exists many challenges in WiFi networks. In this paper, we propose a novel MP-SDWN (multipath-supported Software Defined Wireless Network), to provide mobility handover, throughput enhancement, and flow-level transmission control as well as programmable system control interfaces. Furthermore, the effectiveness and efficiency of MP-SDWN is evaluated on an experimental prototype.

**Keywords:** SDN · NFV · MP-SDWN · Multipath · Handover · Flow control

## 1 Introduction

In support of mobility and cloud services provisioning wireless LAN is growing rapidly in quantity as well as its high throughput. The increasing WLAN users bring new requirements, e.g., burst user access, seamless handover, quality of service, high throughput and security. However, most of existing WLAN networks are often deployed in an unplanned and uncoordinated way, and different ISPs often adopt their private protocol and architecture to operate their WLAN systems. As a result, the management and operation of today's WLAN is very inflexible, and with limited support to mobility and specific need of new applications. Meanwhile, WLAN has still suffered from the traditional wireless problems such as radio frequency interference, Ping-Pong effect and energy saving, which are not well solved either.

Software-defined network (SDN) [4–6], an innovative paradigm for programmable network, advocates decoupling the control plane and data plane of networks, which dramatically simplifies network control and enables innovation and evolution by abstracting the control functions of the network into a logically centralized control plane. Moreover, the concept of network function virtualization (NFV) [7–9]

© ICST Institute for Computer Sciences, Social Informatics and Telecommunications Engineering 2018
Q. Chen et al. (Eds.): ChinaCom 2016, Part I, LNICST 209, pp. 119–128, 2018.
DOI: 10.1007/978-3-319-66625-9_12

effectively separates the abstraction of functionalities from the network hardware and substrate. SDN and NFV technologies provide wireless networks with the needed flexibility to evolve according to the ever-changing application contexts. By extending SDN to mobile and wireless networks, it leads to a new trend, i.e. software-defined wireless network (SDWN). SDWN is very promising to address challenges in mobile wireless network, such as wireless resource optimization, convergence of heterogeneous networks, fine-grained controllability, and efficient programmability for network innovation and smooth evolution [10].

Recently, SDWN has been studied in wireless access networks and cellular networks with different emphasizes [11–18]. To separate the network service from the underlying physical infrastructure and allow rapid innovation of WLAN services, a number of SDWN architectures are proposed. OpenRoads [11, 12] uses OpenFlow to separate control from the data path through an open API, and FlowVisor to create network slices. OpenRadio [13] proposes a programmable wireless data plane to provide modular programming capability for the entire wireless stack, and utilizes multi-core DSP architecture to achieve NFV functionalities. OpenRF [14] proposes a software defined cross-layer architecture for managing MIMO signal processing with commodity Wi-Fi cards. OpenRF adopts the SDN idea and enables access points to control MIMO signal processing at physical layer. CloudMAC [15] is a distributed architecture, which consists of virtual APs, wireless termination points and an Open-Flow switch. Furthermore, the 802.11 WLAN MAC processing in which is partially performed in data centers on virtual machines connected by an OpenFlow controlled network. Odin [16, 17] is an SDN framework that proposes to simplify the implementation of high-level enterprise WLAN services, by introducing light virtual access point (LVAP), which is similar to the virtual access points used in CloudMAC. In [18], the LVAP is extended to a set of programming abstractions to model the fundamental aspects of a wireless network, including state management, resource provisioning, network monitoring, and network reconfiguration. In summary, SDWN architectures mainly focus on abstracting the details of the underlying wireless physical technologies and moving as much as intelligence to the center of the network. However, the additional processing functions required of the less-capable AP devices and centralized controller architecture of SDN might slow down the response to PHY or MAC layer incidents and reduce the WLAN system throughput significantly.

In this paper, to improve the system performance, we propose a novel WLAN system, namely, MP-SDWN, and present the design, implementation, and evaluation. MP-SDWN could provide seamless mobility handover, flow-level QoS control and high throughput for clients as well as programmable interface to meet the needs from enterprise applications and ISP deployments.

The rest of the paper is organized as follows. Section 2 presents the system architecture, and describes typical use cases of MP-SDWN. In Sect. 3, we evaluate its performance on an experimental prototype. We conclude our work in Sect. 4.

# 2  MP-SDWN Architecture

## 2.1  Architecture of MP-SDWN

MP-SDWN is constructed based on SDN and NFV using open-source wireless network devices.

As shown in Fig. 1, MP-SDWN comprises a logically centralized Controller entity and distributed AP Daemons residing on physical AP devices for virtualizing and programming the wireless components, and the Controller and AP Daemons are connected through OpenFlow switch. The entities are described as follows.

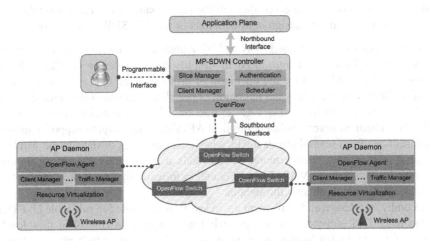

Fig. 1.  The architecture of MP-SDWN.

*Controller.* As an SDN controller, the Controller enables applications to orchestrate the underlying physical wireless network entities, which provides a set of interfaces (the northbound interface) to the applications and translates their requests into a set of commands (the southbound interface) to the network devices. It maintains a view of the network components including clients, APs, applications and OpenFlow switches, and provides a set of centralized functions including user authentication; creating, migrating and releasing of MVAP (*multi-connection virtual access point, which forms the same virtual AP over different physical APs*) for per-client; client and network-slice management; network performance monitoring and resources scheduling; etc.

*AP Daemon.* AP Daemon runs on the physical APs, executes the command from the Controller to orchestrate the wireless network, measures and reports the MVAP performance of Clients on APs. Firstly, it takes over the WiFi devices and virtualizes high-level wireless functions of 802.11 MAC protocol for different network slices; secondly, it maintains MVAP and WFTR for each client, dispatching and forwarding his/her traffic flow according to flow-tables in MVAP, and differentiating flow priorities among diverse applications according to the rules in WFTR; thirdly, as the status of client changes frequently, it sniffers the wireless frames in real time for monitoring the performance of MVAPs, to support a publish-subscribe information system when a certain frame event triggered.

*Programmable Interface.* We provide a set of open programmable interfaces for systems administrator, they can create multiple independent network slices, and inject their own routing or scheduling algorithms into network slices. Moreover, applications can access the statistics at different granularity including frame, flow, MVAP, client, OpenFlow and network slice. The programmable interface allows administrator to share the network control, e.g., load balancing, troubleshooting, and supports researchers to inject customized routing, flow assignment or migration algorithm into MP-SDWN core module to testify their idea. In addition, the performance of customized algorithm can be observed through the performance monitoring module.

In summary, the major design considerations of the MP-SDWN are as follows.

- Firstly, a unified and extended SDN and NFV abstraction, multi-connection virtual access point (MVAP) is introduced to simplify the complexity of IEEE 802.11 protocol stack and to move the operation of protocol stack into application layer, and facilitate easy handling and migration of per-client state cross different physical APs. Different from the single VAP abstraction, MVAP maintains the same VAP for each client on several adjacent physical APs simultaneously, to support multiple connections from several physical APs when client migrates or stays in the wireless signal overlap area. Furthermore, MVAP adds a collaborative hierarchical flow table distributed on all VAPs for each client, to forward all flows from the client in parallel to improve client's throughput.
- Secondly, we design and implement a wireless flow transmission rule table (WFTR) into mac80211 subsystem to achieve wireless transmission control in flow-level, similar to the packet forwarding control on wired network, which allows administrators to differentiate flow priorities of diverse applications from the same user. Adding control parameters including transmission power, transmission rate and priorities into WFTR, MP-SDWN can provide flow-level QoS control to satisfy the needs from various applications.
- Thirdly, MP-SDWN introduces a programmable interface which allows ISPs to share the network control, e.g., load balancing, QoS policy, troubleshooting. Moreover, the interface supports researcher to inject customized routing or scheduling algorithm into MP-SDWN core module to simulate their idea. We implement MP-SDWN, and evaluate the feasibility and efficiency of our framework by conducting several typical WiFi application experiments using the prototype deployed at our university.

## 2.2   Use Cases

MP-SDWN is designed to provide seamless access in the dense deployment scenarios, and there typical use cases are shown in Fig. 2.

*Mobility and Migration.* Based on the virtualization of 802.11 MAC protocol, MP-SDWN supports seamless user mobility and dynamic resource management for each client. During the handover, the changes in wireless signal strength are captured

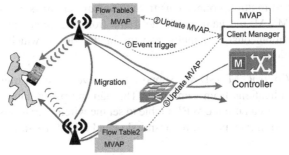

(a) Mobility and migration, the state and MVAP of client can be migrated seamlessly or work on the two APs simultaneously during the handover.

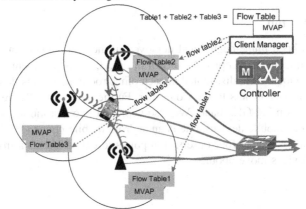

(b) Multipath transmission, for each client, multiple connections and transmission paths are provided when it stays in the wireless signal overlap area of several APs.

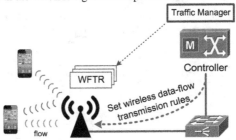

(c) Transmission control, *administrator* can set specific wireless transmission rules for per-flow to each client through the controller.

**Fig. 2.** The typical use cases based on MP-SDWN.

on nearby APs, then the migration event will be triggered and send to Controller by APs, and at last, the Controller will dispatch the resources according to the status of mobility and performance demand from the client.

*Multipath Transmission.* When the client roams around the wireless signal overlap area from several adjacent physical APs, MP-SDWN provides a unified abstraction –

MVAP to support multiple connections from these adjacent physical APs for the client. Based on the MVAP mechanism, all the traffic from the client can be assigned and transmitted simultaneously on multiple paths in flow-level, which can improve the throughput obviously.

*Transmission Control.* MP-SDWN supports flow-level wireless transmission control for different applications from same user. Through the programmable interface, network administrator can use the WFTR table to set the wireless transmission parameters, such as transmission rate, power, retransmission and RTC/CTS strategy, to per-packet.

# 3 Performance Evaluation

## 3.1 Test-Bed Setup

MP-SDWN has been implemented and deployed in the real network at third floor of YiFu building in CQUPT campus. As shown in Fig. 3, the deployment consists of 20 IEEE 802.11n enabled APs, distributed in each office room across this floor, connected with the OpenFlow switchers to the Controller. Furthermore, all APs are restricted to the same channel on 2.4 GHz band. We also deployed two test mobile devices and a number of random mobile devices, one is an android mobile phone (M2), and another is a notebook (M1). We set four observation points to collect the data from controller when the test devices move about.

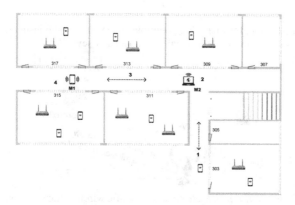

**Fig. 3.** The deployment of MP-SDWN system in YiFu building.

Deployed on Netgear WNDR3800 device, APs run OpenWRT release 14.07 with the ath9k Linux driver, the embeded linux version is 3.10.49, user-level click modular router 2.0.1 [19], and OpenvSwitch (OvS) version 2.3.90 supporting OpenFlow (OF) version 1.3. MP-SDWN controller runs on Ubuntukylin-14.04 with floodlight version 1.2 with dual 4-cores CPU and 16G RAM Dell Server supported.

## 3.2   Benchmark Performance of MVAP

As a key technology to provide mobility and performance for users in MP-SDWN, we perform experiments to measure the effectiveness of MVAP. The goal is to understand the benchmark performance for mobile user, including user association and performance improvement.

### *Delay of Association*

For each client, association is the first step to connect to the WLAN network. Different to traditional WLAN, MP-SDWN needs to create new MVAP identification and choose APs to serve for the client, and the performance of association will affect the user experience directly. Regarding, we compare the latency to standard WiFi system without authentication.

In MP-SDWN system, we provide several APs' connection to the client according to the position where the client stays. To the client, the association can be established when the first connection finishes, and the client only perceives one connection although other connections running in the background. Figure 4 shows the time by which the association is established successfully to the client with different number of connections to APs. For regular WiFi, the association time is around 100 ms. In our system, for one AP, most of the association time is slightly larger than 100 ms, the median value is 125 ms; for two APs, the association time is smaller than the value with one AP, and the median value is 118 ms, and the second AP establishes the connection which is 20 ms after the first one; but for four APs, to our surprise, the association time is very stable and close to the regular WiFi, the median value is 102 ms, and the second, third and fourth APs are connected to the client within 10 ms. Evidently, MVAP sets up more connections serving the client, and the total association time is almost the same as the regular WiFi.

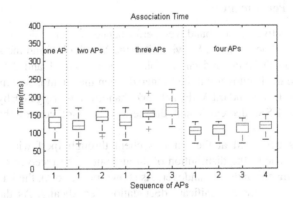

**Fig. 4.** The Delay of association.

### *Performance Improvement with MVAP*

Since the MVAP provides multiple paths to transmit the traffic from the client, it will improve the performance significantly especially when the bandwidth from a single AP cannot satisfy the throughput requirement of client. To verify the performance improvement, we restrict the bandwidth of each AP to 5 Mbps, and use Iperf on the client to generate several different UDP and TCP flows. When slowly moving the client from observation point 1 to 4, we obtain the throughput changes from Iperf.

The UDP throughput is shown in Fig. 5(a), when only one AP serving the client, due to the bandwidth constraint, the throughput varies around 5 Mbps. Afterwards, when more APs serving the client, the throughput increases to 10 Mbps with two APs and nearly 15 Mbps with three APs. As shown in Fig. 5(b), similar to UDP throughput, the TCP throughput increases with more APs serving the client, 10 Mbps with two APs and nearly 15 Mbps with three APs. Since the wireless environment is unstable when the client moves about, the throughput increases with fluctuations, nevertheless, the TCP throughput is more stable than the UDP throughput.

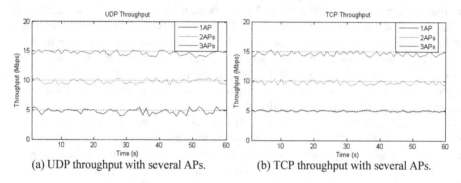

(a) UDP throughput with several APs.          (b) TCP throughput with several APs.

**Fig. 5.** Performance improvement with MVAP.

### 3.3  Handover Performance

To assess the effectiveness of handover performance, we consider a standard WiFi network as the baseline scenario. So we switch the MP-SDWN and the standard WiFi system running on the APs, and choose observation points 1 and 2 to perform the evaluation, where the handover will be triggered when the client is moving a round trip between the two. In a standard WiFi network, handover is triggered by the wireless clients when the RSSI decreases and the network cannot control the mobility of wireless clients.

The traffic is generated at the wireless client through Iperf with a fixed speed 5 Mbps. Figure 6 shows the distribution of throughput at the receiver's side when the client is performing a round trip handover. As shown in Fig. 6(a), the UDP throughput of standard wifi performs a significant degradation periodically. As the handover is triggered, the client would take 1–2 s to re-establish the association with the new AP, which can effectively lead to the throughput degradation. We also tested the handover performance with TCP traffic, the same results are observed in Fig. 6(b). On the other hand, with completely seamless handovers supported by the MP-SDWN system, the UDP and TCP throughputs remain stable on 5 Mbps.

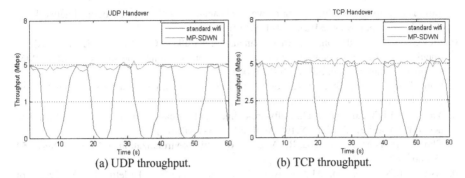

(a) UDP throughput.                    (b) TCP throughput.

**Fig. 6.** Throughput at the receiver side when the client is performing a round trip handover.

# 4   Conclusion

To improve the performance of WLAN networks, we have proposed a novel WLAN system based on SDN and NFV, called Multipath-Supported Software Defined Wireless Network (MP-SDWN) to meet the needs from different applications. First, the MVAP simplifies the complexity of IEEE 802.11 stack and handle per-client state cross different physical APs. Take the advantage of the multiple connections on several adjacent APs simultaneously, client can obtain high throughput whether it migrates or stays in the wireless signal overlap area. Then, the WFTR running in mac80211 subsystem provides wireless transmission control in flow-level to meet the QoS requirements from different applications on the same client. Lastly, the programmable interface is presented for network administrator to exert the network control, e.g., load balancing, QoS policy, troubleshooting. We have deployed the system in an experimental network to evaluate the performance improvement and stability of MP-SDWN, and believed that the home and enterprise networks can benefit from the capabilities as demonstrated in this research.

**Acknowledgments.** This work is supported by the National Science Foundation of China (NSFC) under grant 61402065, Chongqing Key Science and Technology Program (No. cstc2014jcsf70001), the China Scholarship Council and Young Backbone Academics Funding Program of Chongqing Municipal Education Commission.

# References

1. Cisco. Cisco service provider Wi-Fi.: a platform for business innovation and revenue generation. J. Cisco (2015)
2. Valerio, P.: Using carrier Wifi to offload IoT networks. J. Inf. Week: Netw. Comput. (2014)
3. CNNIC.: 37th Development Statistics Report of Internet Network in China (2016). https://www.cnnic.net.cn
4. Yu, M., Rexford, J., Freedman, M.J., Wang, J.: Scalable flow- based networking with difane. J. SIGCOMM Comput. Commun. Rev. **41**(4), 351–362 (2015)

5. Kim, H., Feamster, N.: Improving network management with software defined networking. J. IEEE Commun. Mag. **51**(2), 114–119 (2013)
6. McKeown, N., Anderson, T., Balakrishnan, H., Parulkar, G., Peterson, L., Rexford, J., Shenker, S.: Turner.: openflow: enabling innovation in campus networks. J. SIGCOMM Comput. Commun. Rev. **38**(2), 69–74 (2008)
7. Chowdhury, N., Boutaba, R.: Network virtualization: state of the art and research challenges. J. IEEE Commun. Mag. **47**(7), 20–26 (2009)
8. Yang, M., Li, Y., Jin, D., et al.: Software-defined and virtualized future mobile and wireless networks: a survey. J. Mob. Netw. Appl. **20**(1), 4–18 (2014)
9. Chowdhury, N.M.K., Boutaba, R.: A survey of network virtualization. J. Comput. Netw. **54** (5), 862–876 (2012)
10. Astuto, B.N., Mendon, M., Nguyen, X.N., Obraczka, K., Turletti, T.: A survey of software-defined networking: past, present, and future of programmable networks. J. IEEE Commun. Surv. Tutor. **16**(3), 1617–1634 (2014)
11. Yap, K.K., Kobayashi, M., Sherwood, R., Huang, T.Y., Chan, M., Handigol, N., McKeown, N.: Openroads: empowering research in mobile networks. J. SIGCOMM Comput. Commun. Rev. **40**(1), 125–126 (2010)
12. Yap, K.K., Sherwood, R., Kobayashi, M., Huang, T.Y., Chan, M., Hand-igol, N., McKeown, N., Parulkar, G.: Blueprint for introducing innovation into wireless mobile networks. In: Proceedings of the 2nd ACM SIGCOMM Workshop on Virtualized Infrastructure Systems and Architectures, Series VISA 2010, New York, USA, pp. 25–32 (2010)
13. Bansal, M., Mehlman, J., Katti, S., Levis, P.: Openradio: a programmable wireless dataplane. In: Proceedings of the 1st Work-Shop on Hot Topics in Software Defined Networks, Series HotSDN 2012, New York, pp. 109–114 (2012)
14. Kumar, S., Cifuentes, D., Gollakota, S., Katabi, D.: Bringing cross-layer mimo to today's wireless lans. J. SIGCOMM Comput. Commun. Rev. **43**(4), 387–398 (2013)
15. Dely, P., Vestin, J., Kassler, A., et al.: Cloudmac—an openflow based architecture for 802.11 MAC layer processing in the cloud. In: 2012 IEEE GlobeCom Workshops, pp. 186–191. IEEE (2012)
16. Suresh, L., Schulz-Zander, J., Merz, R., Feldmann, A., Vazao, T.: Towards programmable enterprise WLANS with odin. In: Proceedings of the 1st Workshop on Hot Topics in Software Defined Networks, Series HotSDN 2012, New York, pp. 115–120 (2012)
17. Schulz-Zander, J., et al.: OpenSDWN: programmatic control over home and enterprise WiFi. In: Proceedings of the 1st ACM SIGCOMM Symposium on Software Defined Networking Research, pp. 1–12. ACM (2015)
18. Riggio, R., Marina, M.K., Schulz-Zander, J., et al.: Programming abstractions for software-defined wireless networks. IEEE Trans. J. Netw. Serv. Manag. **12**(2), 146–162 (2015)
19. Click modular router project. http://read.cs.ucla.edu/click

# Performance Analysis of Routing Algorithms Based on Intelligent Optimization Algorithms in Cluster Ad Hoc Network

Chenguang He[1,2], Tingting Liang[1(✉)], Shouming Wei[1,2],
and Weixiao Meng[1,2]

[1] Communication Research Center, Harbin Institute of Technology,
Harbin, China
{hechenguang, weishouming, wxmeng}@hit.edu.cn,
wslttl992@sina.com
[2] Key Laboratory of Police Wireless Digital Communication,
Ministry of Public Security, People's Republic of China, Harbin, China

**Abstract.** In this paper, a mobile cluster Ad Hoc network model is presented for scenarios with large nodes number and high mobility. Intelligent optimization algorithms perform better than traditional routing algorithms in such scenarios but papers about performance comparison of these algorithms are rare. So we pick the most widely used intelligent optimization algorithms ACO, PSO and GA and describe the routing search process of these three algorithms in detail. Then we analyze performance of them together with AODV for comparison. Simulation results show that ACO, PSO and GA algorithms perform better than AODV in average throughput, packet loss rate, success link rate and average link hop.

**Keywords:** Ad Hoc network · Intelligent optimization · Cluster · Performance analysis

## 1 Introduction

Mobile Ad Hoc networks, where users can communicate with each other directly when infrastructures are unavailable, were proposed for military purpose in 1970s and 1980s. Since 1990s Ad Hoc networks were adopted widely in emergency communications, commercial and civil communications [1, 2]. Ad Hoc networks have some significant characteristics [2]: Ad Hoc networks have dynamic topology; nodes in the network are self-organized and can have various functions; communication links between nodes are multi-hop, etc.

The topology of Ad Hoc network is dynamic and generally can be divided into two types: flat and hierarchical structure [3], according to whether there is logic hierarchical relationship among nodes. All the nodes in the flat structure have equal status, and every node needs to know the information of all the other nodes in the network. For small and medium-sized network, it's easy to manage and maintain network in the flat structure. However, when there is a large amount of nodes, especially when nodes have

© ICST Institute for Computer Sciences, Social Informatics and Telecommunications Engineering 2018
Q. Chen et al. (Eds.): ChinaCom 2016, Part I, LNICST 209, pp. 129–137, 2018.
DOI: 10.1007/978-3-319-66625-9_13

high mobility, the control overhead becomes severe and routing interrupts frequently; management and control of the network become difficult, too. So for scenarios of large node number and high node mobility, the hierarchical structure is usually adopted. In the hierarchical structure nodes will be divided into several clusters [4] and each cluster has one cluster head responsible for relaying business between member nodes and the control node. Other member nodes don't need to maintain complex routing information, which greatly reduces the number of routing control information, therefore the network has good scalability.

Traditional Ad Hoc network routing algorithms are mostly based on distance vector or link-state and can be divided into table driven and on-demand routing protocols. In table driven routing protocols, each node periodically broadcasts its information and updates the local routing table continuously to ensure that the information in the routing table are the newest in order to directly search path when the routing request message is launched. The most representative protocols of table driven routing protocols include DSDV [5], OLSR [6]. In on-demand routing protocols, nodes don't need to maintain routing information periodically, only when the source node has data to send the routing search mechanism starts. These protocols reduce the excessive consumption of network bandwidth and energy compared to table driven routing protocols. The best known on-demand routing protocols are DSR [7], and AODV [8]. When the network topology changes frequently, table driven routing protocols have more control information leading to system performance degradation. Therefore, for Ad Hoc networks, although having a certain delay, on-demand routing protocols are more practical.

With nodes' high mobility in Ad Hoc network, the traditional wireless Ad Hoc network routing protocols cannot adapt to the changeable topology and the performance of protocols also becomes poor. Artificial intelligence algorithms and swarm intelligence algorithms with the characteristics of distributed, self-organized and intelligent are increasingly applied in Ad Hoc network routing search. The most prominent intelligent algorithms are Genetic Algorithm (GA), Ant Colony Optimization (ACO), Particle Swarm Optimization (PSO), etc.

GA algorithm, proposed by Michigan University professor Holland and his students in 1975, is a kind of random search algorithm based on biological natural selection and genetic mechanism. Reference [9] is a survey on application of GA for QoS routing in Ad Hoc networks and gives a comparison between GA-based routing algorithms GAMAN and GLBR. ACO algorithms proposed by Italian scholar Dorigo. M in 1996. The algorithm simulates the foraging behavior of ant colony in the nature. A routing discovering algorithm RACO is proposed in [10] to solve the limitation of ACO by using the characteristics of the network and the concept related-node. Simulation shows RACO can reduce the convergence time and iteration of algorithm. PSO algorithm is a kind of evolutionary computation technology, proposed by Kennedy in 1995, imitating social behavior of animals or insects, such as birds, fish, etc. A novel approach based on PSO for solving the minimum energy broadcast problem in Ad Hoc networks was proposed in Ref. [11] and the simulation results show that it can compete and outperform state-of-the-art works.

The majority of researches above can play an important guide role for routing algorithms based on intelligent optimization algorithms in cluster Ad Hoc network. It should be noted, however, that there have been few attempts to compare network performance results with different intelligent optimization algorithms. In this paper, we introduce several intelligent optimization algorithms and compare performance of routing protocols based on these intelligent optimization algorithms in Ad Hoc networks. After performance analysis we get accurate network performance results, which provide theoretical basis for the practical application of cluster Ad Hoc networks in the future.

This paper has three purposes: (a) to establish a cluster system model; (b) to give an introduction of the routing process based on the most representative intelligent optimization algorithms in Ad Hoc networks; (c) to analyze and compare the performance of these routing algorithms. The remainder of the paper is organized as follows. In Sect. 2, we establish a cluster system model. Then in Sect. 3, we introduce how the routing algorithms work in Ad Hoc networks. And in Sect. 4, we simulate the performance of these routing algorithms on average throughput, packet loss rate, success link rate and average link hop. Finally we draw a conclusion in Sect. 5.

## 2 Cluster Ad Hoc Network Model

In cluster-structure Ad Hoc network, three kinds of nodes are used including control node, relay node and user node. Control node is in charge of controlling and managing relay nodes and user nodes, so in our mobile model control node is limited to move in the area near network center in order to better manage network nodes in different positions. Relay node is responsible for relaying business between user nodes and the control node, so we make all the relay nodes uniformly distribute in the network to ensure that all user nodes can transmit data to the control node with the aid of relay nodes, and avoid the case that some relay nodes' burden overweight, and some are out of use. Movement of user nodes has high randomness and independence, so the moving range is the entire network.

Three kinds of nodes have different move range according to their function, but on the whole each node moves using random waypoint mobile model (RWP). RWP model works as follows:

Node moves in a limited area, usually a rectangular or circular area. Node in the network first randomly selects an initial position, known as the "waypoint", and pauses in the current position for a random time, and then selects a random location in the network as target location, and moves to the target location with a random velocity. After arriving at the target location it stays for a randomly period of time, and then repeats the process. The waypoint in every section of the movement is chosen randomly, and has nothing to do with the history and the current waypoint location, and this is also fit for the velocity. Figure 1 shows the model of cluster Ad Hoc network.

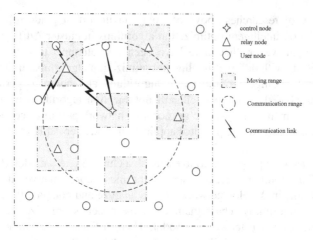

control node
relay node
User node

Moving range

Communication range

Communication link

**Fig. 1.** Cluster Ad Hoc network model

# 3 Principle of Intelligence Algorithms

There are many intelligent optimization algorithms that are adopted in Ad hoc network routing protocols and the most prominent of them are Genetic Algorithm (GA), Ant Colony Optimization (ACO), Particle Swarm Optimization (PSO). So next we will describe the working process of these three algorithms in routing search problem.

## 3.1 Genetic Algorithm

In genetic algorithm search starts from a set of randomly generated initial "chromosome" (called population), then the population is put in the environment of the question, and a "chromosome" is chosen to replicate according to the principle of survival of the fittest, next through the crossover and mutation process produce a new generation of "chromosome" group that adapt to the environment much better. The performance of "chromosome" is measured by fitness, according to the value of fitness a certain number of individuals are chosen from the previous generation and future generation as the next generation of population, and then continue to evolve. After several generations, the algorithm converges to the most adaptable "chromosome" and it is the optimal solution of the problem.

Its basic steps for routing search are shown as follow:

(i) Initialize population size, crossover probability, mutation probability and iteration number.
(ii) Randomly generate initial population; Calculating the fitness of initial population.
(iii) Choose the parent body 1 and the parent body 2 according to a certain selection strategy.

(iv)   Produce a random number in [0,1]. If it is greater than the crossover probability, the parent body 1 and the parent body 2 execute crossover to generate son 1 and 2; Otherwise the parent body 1 and the parent body 2 are replicated as child 1 and 2 directly.
(v)   Produce a random number in [0,1]. If it is greater than the mutation probability, child 1 and 2 execute mutation.
(vi)   Judge whether the number of children is equal to the population size, if so turn to step vii; else to step iii.
vii)   Evaluation the fitness of new population; Children become parents.
(viii)   Judge whether it meets termination conditions, if so stop the process; else turn to step iii.

Genetic algorithm has the advantages of simple and easy to implement and it can achieve parallel processing and has the ability to global search. So it is suitable for solving complex and nonlinear problems that are difficult for traditional search. Deficiencies are shown as precocious phenomenon and poor local optimization ability.

### 3.2   Ant Colony Optimization

During foraging ants leave pheromones on the path they walk and they tend to move in the direction of high pheromones, which volatilize as time goes. The more ants walk on a path, the more pheromones left on this path and in return will attract more ants walk through this path. Take advantage of this positive feedback, ants will eventually find an optimal path.

The working process of ACO is roughly listed as follows:

(i)   Initialize pheromones concentration on each path;
(ii)   Place several ants on the source node. Each ant first judges whether destination node is the neighbor node of the current node, if so then directly builds routing from source node to destination node, otherwise chooses the next node in the neighbor nodes collection according to a certain probability and records it in the routing table, meanwhile clears the chosen node in the neighbor node table in case of visiting repeatedly;
(iii)   When ants reach the next node, repeat step ii, until all the ants arrive at the destination node or reach the end conditions, then stop this iteration. Then, compute length of all the available paths and select the optimal path in this iteration;
(iv)   After one iteration update pheromones on each path based on the ant's visit (including volatilization);
(v)   Then begin the next iteration, repeat step ii–iv, until reach the iteration number. Select the shortest path in optimal paths of all iterations.

ACO has significant advantages in converging speed and stability of the optimal solution, but the performance of ACO is determined by the pheromones. Shortage of the initial pheromone makes it easy to cause converging speed slower. Inappropriate pheromones setting can also cause slow convergence or converging to a local optimal solution.

### 3.3   Particle Swarm Optimization

PSO is a kind of optimization tool based on iteration. System is initialized to a group of random solutions and searches for the optimal solution through iteration. Instead of crossover and mutation in genetic algorithm, in PSO the particles in the solution space follow the optimal particle to search. Compared with genetic algorithm, the advantage of PSO is simple and easy to implement, and it doesn't have many parameters to adjust. PSO has been widely used in function optimization.

A group is composed of $m$ particles fly at a certain speed in $d$ dimension search space. During search time, each particle considers both its own best point and the best point of the entire group in search history to update location and speed. The location of particle $i$ is $x_i = (x_{i1}, x_{i2}, \ldots, x_{id})$, its speed is $v_i = (v_{i1}, v_{i2}, \ldots, v_{id})$, the best point in its search history is $p_i = (p_{i1}, p_{i2}, \ldots, p_{id})$, $1 \leq i \leq m$, the best point of all the particles in their search history is $p_g = (p_{g1}, p_{g2}, \ldots, p_{gd})$. Generally speaking, the particle's position and speed belong to continuous real number, each particle's position and speed update according to the formulas (1) and (2).

$$v_{id} = w \times v_{id} + c_1 \times rand() \times (p_{id} - x_{id}) + c_2 \times rand() \times (p_{gd} - x_{gd}) \qquad (1)$$

$$x_{id} = x_{id} + v_{id} \qquad (2)$$

In (1) $w$ is called inertia weight, the value of $w$ indicates how much the inheritance of the current speed, so appropriate value can make particles have a balanced exploration and search ability. $c_1$ and $c_2$ are called learning factors, generally $c_1 = c_2 = 2$. Learning factors make particles have self-summary and the ability to learn from excellent individuals in groups, so that the particles move towards best point of their own and the entire group in search history. Rand() is pseudo-random number uniformly distributed in [0, 1], that is $rand() \in U[0, 1]$.

The main steps of PSO are given as follows:

  (i)   Initialize particles size and iteration number; randomly generate initial particles.
 (ii)   Calculate the fitness of initial particles. Choose the individual best point and the global best point according to the particles fitness.
(iii)   Update position and velocity of each particle according to the individual best point and the global best point.
 (iv)   During each iteration, repeat step ii, iii, until reach the limitation of iterations. The final global best point is the best routing from source node to destination node.

In these three routing algorithms, GA and PSO use fitness and ACO use pheromones to choose best solution. Fitness and pheromones are calculated with "distance" between two adjacent nodes. In our model "distance" is calculated with signal to interference plus noise ratio (SINR) between two adjacent nodes, as formula (3) shows. $Q$ is a constant, whose value shows the influence of "distance" while calculating probability and in our model it is set to 1, $A_j$ is the adjacent nodes collection of node $j$. Formula (3) demonstrates "distance" between node $i$ and $j$ in conditions whether node $i$ belongs to $A_j$. The better channel condition is, the bigger SINR is between two nodes and therefore the shorter "distance" is.

$$d_{ij} = \begin{cases} \dfrac{Q}{SINR_{ij}}(i \in A_j) \\ \infty(i \notin A_j) \end{cases} \tag{3}$$

## 4 Network Performance Analysis

In our simulation the network coverage area is 1000 km * 1000 km, node speed is 200–300 m/s and routing updates per second. There are one control node, 10 relay nodes and 150 user nodes in the network. Using AODV routing protocol for comparison, we simulate ACO, PSO, GA and AODV routing protocols in MATLAB to analyze the average throughput of three kinds of nodes, packet loss rate, successful routing rate and the average link hop performance.

As shown in Figs. 2, 3, 4, using ACO, PSO and GA algorithm, the average throughput of three kinds of nodes is higher than that of AODV respectively. In addition, ACO and PSO are better than GA for average throughput of relay nodes.

Figure 5 shows average system packet loss rate for different routing algorithms. As seen, with GA, ACO and PSO the system packet loss rates are close and a little bit bigger than that of AODV, but using these four routing algorithms the system packet loss rates are all within 1%.

Figures 6 and 7 respectively show under different number of nodes, the rate that four algorithms successfully find routing and the average link hop of four algorithms. Apparently, the successful rates for four algorithms under different number of nodes are all very high, but GA algorithm performs poorer than the other three algorithms. As for average link hop, ACO and PSO perform exceed than GA, and AODV has the worst performance.

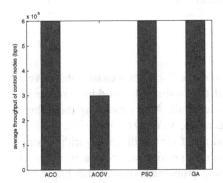

**Fig. 2.** Average throughput of control nodes for different routing algorithm

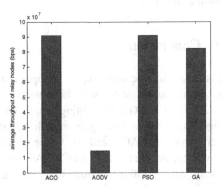

**Fig. 3.** Average throughput of relay nodes for different routing algorithm

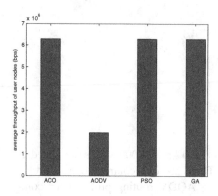

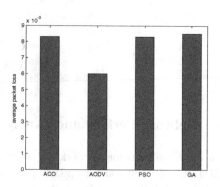

**Fig. 4.** Average throughput of user nodes for different routing algorithm

**Fig. 5.** Average system packet loss for different routing algorithm

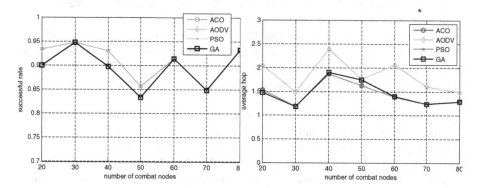

**Fig. 6.** Successful routing rate of different routing algorithm

**Fig. 7.** Average link hop of different routing algorithm

## 5  Conclusion

In cluster Ad Hoc network, we set up a mobile model suitable for scenarios that have a large amount of nodes with high mobility, and demonstrate the working process of ACO, PSO and GA for routing search problem in detail. After simulating these three algorithms and comparing them with AODV algorithm, we draw a conclusion. Overall, performance of ACO and PSO exceeds GA and all of the intelligent algorithms simulated perform better than AODV. As few papers give performance comparison among intelligent algorithms in Ad Hoc network routing problems, work of this paper can provide theoretical basis for the practical application of cluster Ad Hoc networks in the future.

**Acknowledgment.** This work was supported by the National Science and Technology Major Specific Projects of China (Grant No. 2015ZX03004002-004) and the Fundamental Research Funds for the Central Universities (Grant No. HIT. NSRIF. 201616).

# References

1. Xu, B., Hischke, S., Walke, B.: The role of Ad hoc networking in future wireless communications. In: Proceedings ICCT2003, pp. 1353–1358 (2003)
2. Sterbenz, J.P., Krishnan, R., Hain, R.R., et al.: Survivable mobile wireless networks: issues, challenges, and research directions. In: ACM International Conference on Proceedings of the 1st ACM Workshop on Wireless Security, pp. 31–40 (2002)
3. Baker, D., Ephremides, A.: The architectural organization of a mobile radio network via a distributed algorithm. Commun. IEEE Trans. **29**(11), 1694–1701 (1981)
4. Yu, J., Chong, R.: A survey of clustering schemes for mobile ad hoc networks. IEEE Commun. Surv. Tutor. **7**(1), 32–48 (2005)
5. Perkins, C., Bhagwat, P.: Highly dynamic destination-sequenced distance-vector routing (DSDV) for mobile computers. In: ACM SIGCOMM
6. RFC 3626. Optimized Link State Routing Protocol (OLSR). http://www.ietf.org/rfc/rfc3626.txt (2003)
7. Johnson, D., Maltz, D., Hu, Y.-C.: The dynamic source routing protocol for mobile Ad hoc networks (DSR). IETF Internet Draft, draft-ietf-manet-dsr-09.txt
8. Perkins, C., Belding-Royer, E., Das, S.: Ad hoc on-demand distance vector (AODV) Routing. IETF RFC 3561, July 2003
9. Barolli, A., Takizawa, M., Xhafa, F., et al.: Application of genetic algorithms for QoS routing in mobile Ad Hoc networks: a survey. In: 2010 International Conference on Broadband, Wireless Computing, Communication and Applications (2010)
10. Ping, Y., Ziyan, M., Minglai, Y.: Routing discovering based on ant colony algorithm in Ad Hoc networks. In: 2012 International Conference on Computer Science and Electronics Engineering (2012)
11. Hsiao, P.-C., Chiang, T.-C., Fu, L.-C.: Particle swarm optimization for the minimum energy broadcast problem in wireless Ad-Hoc networks. In: 2012 IEEE World Congress on Computational Intelligence (2012)

# Incentive Mechanism for Crowdsensing Platforms Based on Multi-leader Stackelberg Game

Xin Dong, Xing Zhang[✉], Zhenglei Yi, and Yiran Peng

Wireless Signal Processing and Network Laboratory, Key Lab of Universal Wireless Communications, Ministry of Education, Beijing University of Posts and Telecommunications, Beijing, China
hszhang@bupt.edu.cn

**Abstract.** Nowadays, the exponential growth of smartphones creates a potential paradigm of mobile crowdsensing. A sensing task originator accomplishes its sensing data collection work by publishing them on crowdsensing platforms. All the platforms want to attract the task originator to use their services in order to make higher profit. Thus, the issue of competition arises. In this paper, we study the incentive mechanism based on pricing strategy for crowdsensing platforms. We formulate the competition among platforms as a dynamic non-cooperative game and use a multi-leader Stackelberg game model, where platforms are leaders and the task originator is the follower. In the real world, it is difficult for a platform to know the strategies of others. So we propose an iterative learning algorithm to compute its Nash equilibrium. The iterative learning algorithm is that each platform learns from its historic strategy and the originator's response. Through extensive simulations, we evaluate the performance of our incentive mechanism.

**Keywords:** Incentive mechanism · Crowdsensing · Pricing strategy · Stackelberg game · Nash equilibrium

## 1 Introduction

Nowadays smartphones are highly ubiquitous. There were over 6.8 billion mobile phones in use all over the world in 2013 [1]. Meanwhile, with the technological advances, smartphones are programmable and equipped with a set of useful embedded sensors, such as GPS, accelerometer, microphone, camera and so on. These sensors can record a variety of sensing data. Therefore, the proliferation of smartphones provides facilities for applying their sensing data in a wide variety of domains, such as transportation, medical research and social networks, which emerges a new frontier called mobile crowdsensing.

As a special form of crowdsourcing [2], mobile crowdsensing aims to provide a mechanism to involve participants from the general public to effectively contribute and utilize sensing data from their mobile devices in solving specific

© ICST Institute for Computer Sciences, Social Informatics and Telecommunications Engineering 2018
Q. Chen et al. (Eds.): ChinaCom 2016, Part I, LNICST 209, pp. 138–147, 2018.
DOI: 10.1007/978-3-319-66625-9_14

problems in collaborations [3]. Crowdsensing leverages human intelligence to collect sensing data by employing mobile devices. It is obvious that crowdsensing has much significant benefit, such as overcoming the limits of space-time, low cost and so on.

In the real world, a mobile crowdsensing system generally consists of three parts. The first part is sensing task originator who initiates many mobile crowdsensing tasks. The second part is crowdsensing platform which is an intermediary between smartphone users and the sensing task originator. Meanwhile, the platforms provide some related services, such as pushing crowdsensing tasks to smartphone users. The last part is the set of smartphone users who provide sensing data according to crowdsensing task requirements published on platforms.

A key factor for the success of crowdsening lies in the users' participation in data sensing activities. A number of works have studied the incentive mechanisms to motivate users to participate in crowdsensing. In [4], Reddy et al. investigated how different payment schemes affect user participation. In [5], Danezis et al. developed a seal-bid second-price auction to motivate user participation. In [6], Yang et al. studied two types of incentive mechanisms for a crowdsensing system: crowdsourcer-centric incentive mechanisms and user-centric incentive mechanisms. They considered that crowdsourcer resided in the cloud and consisted of multiple sensing servers. In [7], Peng et al. studied the price competition of multiple crowdsourcers. Multiple crowdsourcers competed with each other to purchase crowdsourcing service from smartphone users. Koutsopoulos [8] developed a random incentive mechanism to minimize the total payment to the participating users while guaranteeing certain quality of service level. Although the above papers have studied different incentive goals or considered different objectives, they all just studied the relationship between crowdsourcers and smartphone users.

In this paper, we focus on the relationship between crowdsensing platforms and the sensing task originator who demands on sensing data. The above papers considered that crowdsensing platforms and sensing task originators as a whole named crowdsourcer. We consider an actual scenario where multiple crowdsensing platforms compete for a sensing task originator by pricing strategy. An incentive mechanism is designed for crowdsensing platforms which have absolute control over the service pricing strategy. We formulate the price competition among platforms as a dynamic non-cooperative game, where each platform independently decides its own price aiming at highest profit. Therefore we model the incentive mechanism as a multi-leader single-follower Stackelberg game and propose an iterative learning algorithm to achieve the Nash equilibrium among platforms as their optimal pricing strategy profile.

The rest of this paper is organized as follows. Section 2 presents the system model and utility functions of platforms and task originator. In Sect. 3, we model system as a Stackelberg game and proposed an algorithm to calculate Nash equilibrium. Simulation results are presented and analyzed in Sect. 4. Finally, Sect. 5 concludes the paper.

## 2  System Model

The system consists of many crowdsensing platforms which provide sensing data collection services, and a sensing task originator with many crowdsensing tasks. Using services of platforms incurs costs, such as reward for smartphone users, platform maintenance costs and so on. Hence platforms look forward to getting some return for their services. Meanwhile, the sensing task originator makes its crowdsensing tasks assignment strategy considering payment and return aiming at maximizing its utility. We assume that platforms belong to different companies, so they are selfish and rational that just want to maximize their own utility.

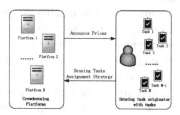

**Fig. 1.** System model

In our model, there is just one sensing task originator with $M$ crowdsensing tasks and $N$ crowdsensing platforms as shown in Fig. 1. The crowdsensing platforms first announce their own prices of data collection respectively to attract the sensing task originator to use their services. According to the prices that platforms announced, sensing task originator maximize utility by making its sensing tasks assignment strategy.

Let the price strategy profile of crowdsensing platforms be $P = (p_1, p_2, \cdots, p_j, \cdots p_N)$. The variable $p_j$ represents the unit price of data on platform $j$. The sensing task originator's sensing tasks assignment strategy profile is $X = (x_1, x_2, \cdots, x_i, \cdots x_M)$, where $x_i = (x_{i1}, x_{i2}, \cdots, x_{ij}, \cdots x_{iN})$. $x_i$ is total amount of data in task $i$ and $x_{ij}$ means amount of data of task $i$ collected in platform $j$.

According to our model and decision variables, we define the following utility functions:

1. The total utility of the sensing task originator is

$$F(P, X) = \sum_{i=1}^{M} f_i(P, x_i),\qquad(1)$$

$f_i(P, x_i)$ is utility of crowdsensing task $i$ as

$$f_i(P, x_i) = \alpha_i \log(1 + \sum_{j=1}^{N} \beta_j x_{ij}) - \sum_{j=1}^{N} p_j x_{ij},\qquad(2)$$

Where $\alpha_i$ is utility parameter of task $i$ and $\beta_j$ is data quality parameter of platforms $j$.

The utility function of sensing task $i$ is comprised of two parts. The first part is the tasks' diminishing return on the data collected from platforms. The second part is total payment for platforms.

2. The utility of crowdsensing platform $j$ is

$$g_j(p_j, X) = p_j \sum_{i=1}^{M} x_{ij}, \tag{3}$$

which is total return getting from each crowdsensing task and parameter $C_j$ means the resources quantity of platform $j$, requiring $\sum_{i=1}^{M} x_{ij} \leq C_j$.

## 3 Optimal Pricing Strategy Dealing with a Non-cooperative Game

Our incentive mechanism for crowdsensing platforms is based on optimizing their pricing strategies. We model our crowdsensing platforms-task originator incentive mechanism as a multi-leader single-follower Stackelberg game [9] and Nash Equilibrium is the solution of the game. There are two stages in this mechanism: in the first stage, crowdsensing platforms announce their own unit prices; in the second stage, the sensing task originator makes crowdsensing tasks assignment strategy to maximize its own utility. Therefore the crowdsensing platforms are leaders and the sensing task originator is the follower in this Stackelberg game. Both platforms and sensing task originator are players.

Then we define the equilibrium concepts.

*Definition 1 (Nash equilibrium):* A set of strategies profile $(p_1^*, p_2^*, \cdots, p_N^*)$ is the Nash equilibrium of the non-cooperative game among platforms if for any platform $j$,

$$g_j(p_j^*, p_{-j}^*) \geq g_j(p_j, p_{-j}^*)$$

In our model, there exists a non-cooperative game among platforms. In the crowdsensing platform level, Nash equilibrium is that any platform can not improve its own utility unilaterally, if the other platforms' strategy profiles are fixed.

In order to make the optimal pricing strategy at Nash equilibrium of crowdsensing platforms, the platform needs to know other platforms' utility functions and the sensing task originator's responding strategy. But these information may not be obtained in real world. So each platform can just adjust its own strategy by observing the reaction of other platforms and the sensing task originator, eventually reach a steady state.

Based on the above reasons, an iterative learning algorithm is proposed to achieve the Nash equilibrium. Assuming that pricing strategy profile of crowdsensing platforms at $t$ moment is $P(t)$. Then the sensing task originator needs to adjust its sensing tasks assignment strategy $X(t)$ to maximize its utility. After sensing task originator utility reaches maximum, crowdsensing platforms adjust their price strategy $P(t+1)$ at $t+1$ moment by learning from its historic strategy $P(t)$ and sensing task originator's strategy $X(t)$. The price iterative equation for platform $j$ is

$$p_j(t+1) = p_j(t) + v_j(\frac{\partial g_j(p_j(t), X(t))}{\partial p_j(t)}), \tag{4}$$

where, $v_j > 0$ is platform pricing strategy adjustment step length, and

$$\frac{\partial g_j(P(t),X(t))}{\partial p_j(t)} \approx \frac{g_j([\cdots,p_j(t)+\varepsilon,\cdots],X(t)) - g_j([\cdots,p_j(t)-\varepsilon,\cdots],X(t))}{2\varepsilon}, \tag{5}$$

Thus the whole iteration process loop illustrated as follow:

---

**Algorithm 1.** Iterative Learning Algorithm

---

    Initialize the $v_j, \forall j = 1, 2, \cdots, N$.
2: **for** crowdsensing platforms **do**
    Initialize platform prices $P = (p_1, p_2, \cdots, p_N)$;
4: **end for**
    **while** maximum iterations **do**
6:    **for** each crowdsensing platform $j$ **do**
        Update $p_j$ by equation (4) and (5)
8:    **end for**
        Update sensing task assignment strategy $X^*$
10:    Calculate the utility of each crowdsensing platform
    **end while**
12: **for** each crowdsensing platform $j$ **do**
    Calculate its best responding pricing strategy curve
14: **end for**
    Calculate intersection of best responding pricing strategies among platforms as optimal pricing strategy
**Ensure:** optimal pricing strategy $p^*$ for platforms

---

In the iterative learning algorithm, task originator makes its optimal strategy $X^*$ to obtain the maximum utility given platforms pricing strategies in Algorithm 1 row 9. The optimization problem can be written as follow:

$$\max_X F(X, P)$$
$$s.t. \begin{cases} X \geq 0 \\ \sum_{i=1}^{M} x_{ij} \leq C_j \end{cases} \tag{6}$$

To solve this optimization problem, Genetic Algorithm (GA) and Newton method is applied. Genetic Algorithm [10] is a powerful stochastic algorithm based on the principles of nature selection and natural genetics. Genetic Algorithm maintains a population of individuals which also called strings representing candidate solutions to the optimization problems, and probabilistically modifies the population by some genetic operators, for example, selection, crossover, mutation, with the intent of finding a near-optimal solution to the problem.

But in some cases, its convergence rate is slow. This is mainly because of the parameter selection in Genetic Algorithm. For instance, if initial population size of individuals is too large, the algorithm takes up a lot of system resources leading to low convergence rate. When it is too small, optimal process terminates in sub-optimal solution. There is still no effective method for selecting these parameters.

To improve the calculation accuracy and convergence rate of optimization process, we adopt a typical method that using Genetic Algorithm to obtain a rough solution first, and then using Newton method to calculate precisely based on the rough solution. This process is relatively stable. It effectively avoids the convergence in the local optimal solution, and ensures enough precision.

## 4   Simulations and Discussions

In this section, we present simulations with Matlab to evaluate the performance of the incentive mechanism. Our performance metrics includes (a) optimal pricing strategies of crowdsensing platforms; (b) utility of platforms; and (c) utility of sensing task originator. In order to facilitate simulation, there are just two crowdsensing platforms called platform 1 and platform 2 in our simulation. But these results can be easily extended to the model having multiple platforms.

### 4.1   Nash Equilibrium Between Crowdsensing Platforms

Set data quality parameter $\beta_1 = 0.6$, $\beta_2 = 0.7$, quantity of resource for platforms $C_1 = C_2 = 50$, number of crowdsensing tasks $M = 5$ and utility parameter $\alpha$ of sensing task originator is uniformly distributed over $[1, 10]$.

Figure 2 shows the utility of platforms as a function of their own price respectively. We observe that utility curves of both crowdsensing platform 1 and platform 2 first increase and then decrease as their own price becomes higher. When price of the crowdsensing platform is too high, sensing task originator is willing to complete their crowdsensing tasks on the other platform leading to little utility. While the price of crowdsensing platform is too low, even if the number of tasks platform completed is saturated, its utility is still low. The best response is the price which results in the highest utility when the other is fixed.

Figure 3 shows the Nash equilibrium between platform 1 and platform 2. These two curves mean the best responding pricing strategy of the two platforms respectively. Thus the intersection of two curves is Nash equilibrium, as well as the optimal pricing strategy, because in this intersection both platforms achieve their optimal utility and no one can improve its own utility unilaterally.

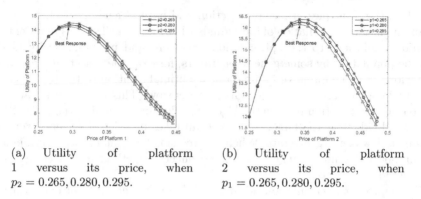

(a) Utility of platform 1 versus its price, when $p_2 = 0.265, 0.280, 0.295$.

(b) Utility of platform 2 versus its price, when $p_1 = 0.265, 0.280, 0.295$.

**Fig. 2.** The relationship between price and utility in platforms.

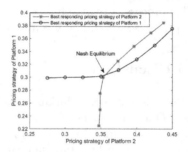

**Fig. 3.** Nash equilibrium between platform 1 and platform 2, when $\beta_1 = 0.6$, $\beta_2 = 0.7$

### 4.2 Optimal Pricing Strategy of Crowdsensing Platforms

We show the impact of data quality parameter $\beta$, number of crowdsensing tasks $M$ and range of utility parameter $\alpha$ on the optimal prices of crowdsensing platforms respectively in Figs. 4 and 5.

In Fig. 4, We observe that the optimal price of platform 1 decreases and platform 2 increases as the data quality of platform 2 improves. Both trends gradually become steady. This is because when the quality of data improves, sensing task originator's demand of data will decrease. It weakens influence of quality data on platforms' optimal price. Then we compare the changes in optimal price between different quantities of platform resources. We assume these two platforms having the same quantity of resources. It is obvious that the fewer quantity of platform resources is the more considerably the prices vary. This can be explained by the reason that when the quantity of platform resources is few, it is a seller's market. Thus platforms have initiative and their quality of data is influential.

In Fig. 5(a), it can be observed that both optimal prices of platforms increase with sensing task originator's number of tasks $M$ and gradually becomes steady as $M$ becomes larger.

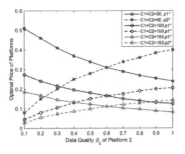

**Fig. 4.** Optimal prices of platforms versus $\beta_2$ for different quantities of platform resources, $\beta_1 = 0.6$, $M = 5$

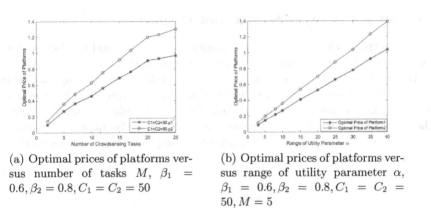

(a) Optimal prices of platforms versus number of tasks $M$, $\beta_1 = 0.6, \beta_2 = 0.8, C_1 = C_2 = 50$

(b) Optimal prices of platforms versus range of utility parameter $\alpha$, $\beta_1 = 0.6, \beta_2 = 0.8, C_1 = C_2 = 50, M = 5$

**Fig. 5.** $M$ and $\alpha$ impact on optimal prices of platforms.

In Fig. 5(b), we observe that when the range of tasks' utility parameter $\alpha$ increases, the optimal prices for both platforms increase almost linearly. The reason is that increment range of utility parameter means the sensing task originator can get more return from the data collected by platforms, thus the price it can afford is higher.

### 4.3  Optimal Utility of Crowdsensing Platforms

We study the effect of data quality parameter $\beta$ on the crowdsensing platform utility in diverse quantities of platform resources situation in Fig. 6. We assume that there are same quantities of resources between platform 1 and platform 2. The results show that the optimal utility of b platforms varies little in different quantities of resources, as data quality of platform 2 increases. And the increment of resource quantities just makes a slightly improvement of the platforms' utility. The reason is that both quantities of resources for platforms increase, leading to reduction of their optimal prices.

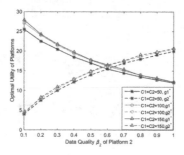

**Fig. 6.** Optimal utility of platforms versus $\beta_2$ for different $C$ , $\beta_1 = 0.6$

### 4.4   Optimal Utility of Sensing Task Originator

Then we explore the impact of data quality parameter $\beta$ and number of crowd-sensing tasks $M$ on optimal utility of sensing task originator.

In Fig. 7(a), it is obvious that the sensing task originator's optimal utility increases almost linearly as data quality of platform 2 improves. The growth rate of sensing task originator utility is basically same in different source situation. The reason for diminishing increment is that when the quantity of resource grows to a certain degree, data demand of sensing task originator approaches to saturation.

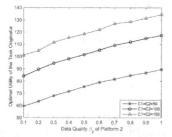
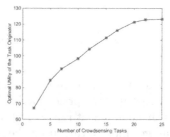

(a) Optimal utility of Sensing task originator versus $\beta_2$ for different quantities of platform resources, $\beta_1 = 0.6$

(b) Optimal utility of sensing task originator versus number of crowdsensing tasks $M$, $\beta_1 = 0.6, \beta_2 = 0.8, C_1 = C_2 = 50$

**Fig. 7.** Impact of data quality parameter $\beta$ and number of crowdsensing tasks $M$ on optimal utility of sensing task originator

In Fig. 7(b) sensing task originator optimal utility raises diminishingly as the number of crowdsensing tasks $M$ increase. It can be explained that although number of tasks increases, the quantity of resources is fixed. Therefore sensing task originator utility raises to a certain degree and becomes steady.

# 5 Conclusion

In this paper, we study the incentive mechanism for crowdsensing platforms that maximizes their utility through pricing strategy. The situation that multiple crowdsensing platforms compete for providing data collection service for the sensing task originator is considered. A dynamic non-cooperative game, specifically a Stackelberg game is used to model this situation. For the reason that a crowdsensing platform may not know the strategies of others which are unrevealed information, we propose an iterative learning algorithm to find the optimal pricing strategy profile for platforms at Nash equilibrium. We also evaluate the performance and analyze influence factors of pricing strategy of crowdsensing platforms.

**Acknowledgments.** This work is supported by the National Science Foundation of China (NSFC) under grant 61372114, 61571054, the New Star in Science and Technology of Beijing Municipal Science and Technology Commission (Beijing Nova Program: Z151100000315077).

# References

1. List of countries by number of mobile phones in use. http://en.wikipedia.org/wiki/
2. Howe, J.: The rise of crowdsourcing. Wired Mag. **14**(6), 1–4 (2006)
3. Ganti, R.K., Ye, F., Lei, H.: Mobile crowdsensing: current state and future challenges. IEEE Commun. Mag. **49**(11), 32–39 (2011)
4. Reddy, S., Estrin, D., Hansen, M., Srivastava, M.: Examining micropayments for participatory sensing data collections. In: Proceedings of ACM Ubiquitous Computing, pp. 33–36 (2010)
5. Danezis, G., Lewis, S., Anderson, R.: How much is location privacy worth? In: Proceedings of the Workshop on the Economics of Information Security Series (WEIS) (2005)
6. Yang, D., Xue, G., Fang, X., Tang, J.: Incentive mechanisms for crowdsensing: crowdsourcing with smartphones. IEEE/ACM Trans. Netw. **PP**(99), 1–13 (2015)
7. Peng, J., Zhu, Y., Shu, W., Wu, M.Y.: How multiple crowdsourcers compete for smartphone contributions? In: 2015 Computer Communications Workshops (INFOCOM WKSHPS), Hong Kong, pp. 516–521 (2015)
8. Koutsopoulos, I.: Optimal incentive-driven design of participatory sensing systems. In: Proceedings of IEEE INFOCOM, pp. 1402–1410 (2013)
9. Fudenberg, D., Tirole, J.: Game Theory. MIT Press, Cambridge (1991)
10. Holland, J.H.: Genetic algorithms and the optimal allocations of trials. SIAM J. Comput. **2**(2), 88–105 (1973)

# Master Controller Election Mechanism Based on Controller Cluster in Software Defined Optical Networks

Jie Mi[1(✉)], Xiaosong Yu[1], Yajie Li[1], Yongli Zhao[1], Jie Zhang[1], Chuan Liu[2], and Gang Zhang[2]

[1] State Key Laboratory of Information Photonics and Optical Communications, Beijing University of Posts and Telecommunications, Beijing, China
{mijie,xiaosongyu,yajieli,yonglizhao,
lgr24}@bupt.edu.cn
[2] Global Energy Interconnection Research Institute, Beijing, China

**Abstract.** In large-scale software defined optical networks (SDON) with tens of thousands of network elements, multiple controllers have to be deployed simultaneously, because single controller cannot bear too many service requests. Then, survivability of controller becomes an important issue for SDON. Controller cluster deployed with master and slave controllers is considered as an effective solution for this issue. A SDON controller cluster architecture is given in the paper, based on which a master controller election mechanism (MCEM) is proposed. Simulation results show that MCEM can get better performance in terms of operation time, traffic loads and fault tolerance compared with Paxos algorithm.

**Keywords:** SDON · Survivability · Controller election · Master/slaves mode

## 1 Introduction

With the growth of cloud computing, mobile Internet, Internet of things, as well as the sharp increase of the network traffic, network complexity and the continuous emergence of new business, the broadband business represented by video and massive data aggregation model represented by large data centers all drive the development of communication network. However, legacy optical network with poor flexibility and intelligence in network operation which can not adapt to the present network environment and needs revolution [1]. In traditional networking, the routing control and packets forwarding services are on the same hardware, this unified network structure makes communication mechanism becomes sophisticated. In order to change the embarrassment of such relatively closed and cumbersome network architecture, the concept of intelligent and open software defined network (SDN) is quickly introduced. In software defied networking, the most significant improvement is that the control function is separated from the hardware, it allows control plane to perform more flexible control function over the whole software defined network, and the data plane is merely forwarding packets conducted by control plane. Since legacy optical network

© ICST Institute for Computer Sciences, Social Informatics and Telecommunications Engineering 2018
Q. Chen et al. (Eds.): ChinaCom 2016, Part I, LNICST 209, pp. 148–155, 2018.
DOI: 10.1007/978-3-319-66625-9_15

with rigid, non-programming transport capacity blocks the service innovation, vendors and service providers combines SDN with latest optical transport technologies to provide more responsive and flexible optical networks which produces software defined optical networks (SDON). In SDON, it allows network operators to program the optical layer to a set of shared, common resources, that can be used on demand.

In SDON, especially the large-scale SDON architecture, the control layer is the kernel part of the whole system, which is very important for achieving a reliable network. However, a single-controller SDON system has a limited processing capacity to forward routing decisions for each new flow in the data path, therefore, a single-controller structure would easily become a bottleneck for network extending. Some researchers consider that a controller is unable to handle plenty of new flows with OpenFlow protocol in 10 Gbps speed networks is a big problem [2]. At present, the speed of most optical transport networks reaches over 100 Gbps, so introduction of multiple controllers to form a controller cluster is a reasonable method to solve this problem for SDON. HyperFlow is a first logically centralized but physically distributed control plane for OpenFlow, it is based on Nox and implements event-based services [3]. FlowVisor is another similar control plane comprises multiple controllers which slices network resources and delegates the control of each slice to a single controller [4]. Kandoo is a hierarchy-based control plane contains two types of controllers: root controller and local controllers. Root controller is responsible for non-local services and global network management such as harmonize local distributed information, and local controllers make routing decision for their own network devices [5]. Master and slave controllers is a distributed control system with high reliability, scalability and good performance.

In this paper, we study on the master controller survivability issue in master and slave controllers. As a distributed multiple-controllers structure, the master controller election is a complex issue and requires corresponding distributed consensus algorithm to complete the election procedure. It is proposed a master controller election algorithm named Master Election and a customized Master Controller Election Mechanism (MCEM). The preparation work before starting an algorithm is detailed introduced, then we describe the inputs, main body of the algorithm and final outputs. In the end, we conduct a stand-alone simulation, in which compares Paxos algorithm with proposed Master Election algorithm in terms of operation time, traffic loads and fault tolerance to verify that Master Election algorithm can solve the problem of master controller election in SDON Master/Slaves system, meanwhile, guarantees high efficiency, reliability and fault tolerance for election mechanism.

## 2 Master/Slaves Mode and Controller Election

In Master and slaves structure, shown as below in Fig. 1, JGroups is applied for communications between the controllers, the node management and data cache in cluster are achieved by IGMP and Hazelcast technologies respectively. The master controller in cluster is responsible for maintenance and update controller-switch device mapping function in the global network scope. [6] In the operation process of master and slaves system, there are three abnormal scenarios: the system initialization, the slave controller failure and the master controller failure. To solve these problems, we propose corresponding solutions. When a slave controller is invalid, the failed node should be removed, then the master node distributes the traffic load to the rest slaves to balance network load. When the system initiates or the master node is disabled, it should start a master controller election mechanism in the system to find a new master controller to guarantee the system works properly, in addition, the entire failover process is transparent to all switches in the bottom data layer.

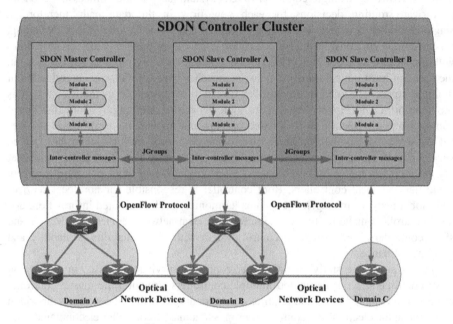

**Fig. 1.** A master/slaves structure.

Controller election is a complex issue in Master and slaves structure because it is a distributed structure which need introduce a message consistent distributed algorithm into the issue. One of the most classical consistent distributed algorithms is Paxos algorithm, which is the foundation of other distributed algorithms [7]. However, Paxos has three weaknesses for the master controller election. First, livelock problem means there are multiple Proposers initiate proposals to the same Acceptor would result in vicious circle of system resource occupation [8]. Second, each controller in Paxos (a Proposer) recommends itself to acceptors without reviewed, which contributes to heavy traffic loads. Last, Learners must learn the value of the determined proposal in the end, therefore, it would cause large bandwidth resources wasting [9]. We propose a master controller election algorithm named Master Election to solve the controller election issue in master/slaves mode of SDON.

## 3 Design and Implementation of MCEM

MCEM is a distributed master controller election mechanism which chooses a master controller from qualified slave controllers. Master Election algorithm is the core technology in this mechanism, it contains two main procedures and two roles for each of controller. Before implementing Master Election algorithm, it should carry some judgment procedures for preparation works. The whole process of MCEM is shown in Fig. 2 below.

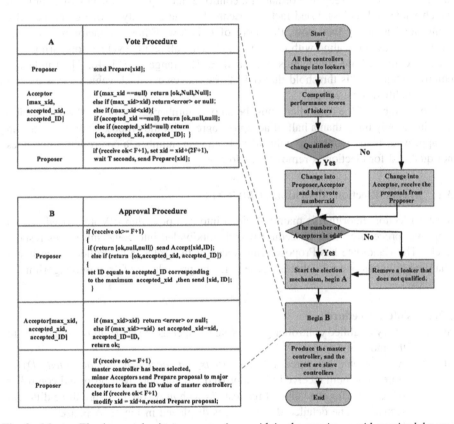

**Fig. 2.** Master Election mechanism process. (*max_xid is the maximum xid received by an Accetor, accepted_xid is the approved xid, accepted_ID is the approved controller ID*)

### 3.1 Election Qualifications for MCEM

In this algorithm, there are three types of roles of controllers: Master, Slave and Candidate. When the master and slaves system initiates, all the controllers change into Candidates. When the master controller fails, the rest are Slaves. Before start election, all the Slaves should be reviewed whether they meet the MCEM standard or not. The controller which qualifies for standard becomes a Candidate, otherwise, a Slave.

MCEM sets the standard for Candidates: the performance scores of qualified controllers must be in [x, 1) (x is the threshold of the score). In this paper, we propose a performance calculating formula shown as follows.

$$P = S + \alpha D + \beta E \tag{1}$$

According to this formula, $P$ represents the performance score of a controller. $S$, $D$, $E$ represent stability factor, load factor and the efficiency factor respectively. $S$ is the rate that a controller keeping normal, if a controller has higher frequency of disable, of which value of $E$ is less. Load factor presents the load capacity of one controller, if a controller has heavy load now, the score of $D$ is low. Efficiency factor presents the speed of controller dealing with requests. $S$, $D$, $E$ are all relative values comparing with a base score. $\alpha, \beta$ are coefficients of D and E. The range of $P$ is [0, 1], 0 indicates controller failure. $x$ is threshold that only those Slaves of which value of $P$ is greater than $x$ qualified for election.

The number of the controllers must be an odd number (2F + 1). In Master Election algorithm, only more than a half of acceptors agree with the proposal, the proposal can be approved. If the number of controllers is an even number, a controller which does not qualified for election is removed randomly.

## 3.2    Master Election Algorithm of MCEM

Master Election algorithm is mainly divided into two procedures: Vote procedure and Approval procedure. Each procedure is then subdivided into some sub stages respectively. The Candidate has Proposer and Acceptor two roles, a controller which is not qualified only has one role, that is, Acceptor. The procedures of proposed algorithm is as follows.

### 3.2.1    Vote Procedure

Step1:    Every qualified controller gets a vote number as *xid*. A *Proposer* sends *xid* to the most of *Acceptors*

Step2:    An *Acceptor* has three variables (*max_xid, accepted_xid, accepted_ID*) to store maximum received xid, approved xid and approved proposed controller ID. Comparing the value of request *xid* with *max_xid*, there are three different scenarios. The detailed description is displayed in Fig. 2, A phase.

Step3:    If *Proposer* does not receive ok messages from most of the *Acceptors*, *xid* adds *(2F + 1)* ((2F + 1) is the number of controllers), then waits *T* (random waiting time) milliseconds, repeat Step 1.

### 3.2.2    Approval Procedure

Step4:    If *Proposer* receives *ok* messages from the most of *Acceptors*, then sends messages to all Acceptors that reply to its vote requests. Message contents are vary according to the received *ok* messages in step 2. The detailed description is shown in Fig. 2, B phase.

Step5:    *Acceptors* reply messages to the *Proposer*, the process is described in Fig. 2, B phrase.

Step6:   If a *Proposer* receives *ok* messages over *a half of* Accepters' number, the proposal raised by this Proposer is approved, a master controller has been elected. Otherwise, repeat Step 3.

# 4   Simulation Results

We use Core2 Duo CPU PC, 2.93 GHz, 4 GB memory of PC and Linux Ubuntu14 operating system in this experimental environment. This simulation experiment chooses C language as the main programming language to achieve the classic Paxos algorithm and Master Election algorithm, and uses multiple terminal windows to simulate the role of multiple controllers. There are some Proposers and 5 Acceptors. These following technical appraisals are usually chosen for performance evaluation in distributed consensus algorithms.

## 4.1   The Evaluation Indicators in Experiment

Running time reflects speed of consistency algorithm to achieve the agreement. In this experiment, we set $\alpha = 0.6$, $\beta = 0.5$, $x = 0.6$, that is, only those controllers of which $P$ is in $[0.6, 1)$ qualified for election. After Calculating, there are 2 qualified out of 3 controllers group, and 3 qualified out of 5 controllers group.

Traffic load reflects the internal system communication load, the more number of messages, the heavier communication load, and the lower work efficiency it has. We take communication message number as indicator of traffic load.

Fault tolerance means whether a controller failure or abnormal data transmission condition would cause drastic effect on the system. In this experiment, we use 3 and 5 terminals to carry out simulation experiments for 10 times. In 3 terminals system, we suspend a terminal after the $5^{th}$ time experiment. In 5 terminals system, we choose a machine incapable after the $3^{rd}$ time and the $7^{th}$ time operation respectively.

## 4.2   The Analysis of Numerical Results

Figure 3 illustrates the value of running time of 3 terminals operating Paxos and Master Election algorithm. The value of running time decreases after $5^{th}$ experiment, for one terminal is closed. Figure 4 illustrates the value of running time of 5 terminals. After $3^{rd}$ and $7^{th}$ experiments, the value of time decreases progressively. Comparing Figs. 3 and 4, it is concluded that Election Master algorithm works more efficient than the Paxos algorithm.

Figure 5 illustrates the number of messages communicate between 3 controllers, the number of messages reduces after $5^{th}$ experiment. Figure 6 illustrates the number of messages communicate between 5 controllers, we also notice that there are twice abatement messages number after $3^{rd}$ and $7^{th}$ experiments. Comparing Figs. 5 and 6, it is obvious that the Master Election algorithm operates lower traffic load than Paxos algorithm, because its number of communication messages between each controller is less than the Paxos thus results in higher system efficiency.

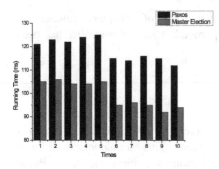

**Fig. 3.** Running time of 3 terminals

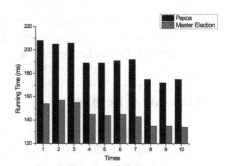

**Fig. 4.** Running time of 5 terminal

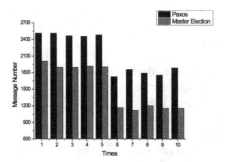

**Fig. 5.** Message number of 3 terminals

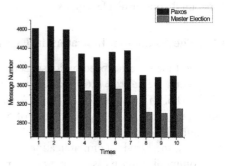

**Fig. 6.** Message number of 5 terminals

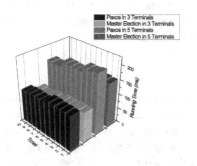

**Fig. 7.** Running time of 3 and 5 terminals

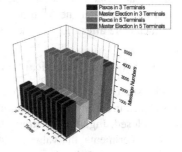

**Fig. 8.** Message number of 3 and 5 terminals

According to the simulation results, we conclude that Master Election mechanism meets fault tolerance requirement. In master and slave controllers system, when the number of failed controller reaches a half of sum, both Paxos algorithm and Election Master algorithm still work normally and guarantee the system stability and robustness. In 3 terminal windows simulation experiments, when 1 controller becomes disabled and reaches the a half of total number. As the simulations results show, this system also keeps stable and implements master controller election internally. In 5 terminal windows experiments, there are two terminals closed and the system also works properly, which proves that both Master Election and Paxos algorithm implement good performance in fault tolerance. Figures 7, 8 are the two-dimensional figure of the running time, messages number of 3, 5 terminals in Paxos and Master Election algorithm.

## 5 Conclusion

In this experiment, we compare Master Election algorithm with Paxos and get conclusion that Master Election algorithm can solve the master controller election problem. According to the three performance indicators of distributed algorithm, we find Master Election algorithm meets fault tolerance requirement. For in a master and slave controllers system, when the number of failed controllers reaches the half of the total controllers, both Paxos algorithm and Election Master algorithm can ensure system normal operation. In addition, Master Election has shorter running time, lower traffic load than Paxos which proves that we proposed algorithm has superiority in master controller election for SDON system.

**Acknowledgements.** This work is supported by NSFC project (61271189, 61571058), Open Fund of State Key Laboratory of Information Photonics and Optical Communications, BUPT (IPOC2014ZZ03), and supported by Key Technology Research of Software Defined Optical Network Oriented to Multi-domain Interaction of Power Communication Project.

## References

1. Mingming, C., Guochu, S., Yihong, H., Zhigang, G.: Enabling software-defined optical networks based on openflow extension. In: Opto-Electronics and Communications Conference, pp. 1–3. IEEE Press, Shangha (2015)
2. Michael, J., Simon, O., Daniel, S., Rastin, P.: Modeling and performance evaluation of an OpenFlow architecture. In: 2011 23rd International Teletraffic Congress, pp. 1–7. IEEE Press, San Francisco (2011)
3. Amin T., Yashar G.: HyperFlow: a distributed control plane for OpenFlow. In: Proceedings Internet Networking Management Conference Resolution Enterprise Network, p. 3. USENIX Assoc., CA, USA (2010)
4. Rob, S., Glen, G., Kok-Kiong, Y.: FlowVisor: a network virtualization layer. In: OpenFlow Switch Consortium, Stanford, CA, USA (2009)
5. Soheil Hassas, Y., Yashar G.: Kandoo: a framework for efficient and scalable offloading of control applications. In: Proceedings of the First Workshop on Hot Topics in Software Defined Networks, New York, pp. 19–24 (2012)
6. Yazici, V., Sunay, M.O., Ercan, A.O.: Controlling a software-defined network via distributed controllers. In: Proceedings of the 2012 NEM Summit, Turkey, pp. 16–20 (2012)
7. Leslie, L.: Paxos Made Simple (2001)
8. WenCheng, S., JianPing, L.: Research on consistency of distributed system based on Paxos algorithm. In: 2012 International Conference on Wavelet Active Media Technology and Information Processing, pp. 257–259. IEEE Press, Chengdu (2012)
9. Barbieri, R.R., Vieira, G.M.: Hardened Paxos through consistency validation. In: 2015 Brazilian Symposium on Computing Systems Engineering, pp. 13–18. IEEE Press, Foz do Iguacu (2015)

# Security

# Performance Evaluation of Black Hole Attack Under AODV in Smart Metering Network

Yanxiao Zhao$^{(\boxtimes)}$, Suraj Singh, Guodong Wang$^{(\boxtimes)}$, and Yu Luo

Department of Electrical and Computer Engineering, South Dakota School of Mines
and Technology, Rapid City 57701, USA
{yanxiao.zhao,guodong.wang}@sdsmt.edu

**Abstract.** In this paper, we thoroughly investigate the impact of black
hole attacks under Ad hoc On-Demand Distance Vector (AODV) routing
in smart metering network. Specifically, the impact of black hole attack
is fully examined by adjusting AODV parameters such as Hello message
interval, route lifetime and positions of malicious meters, which have been
under explored so far. Two critical performance metrics including packet
delivery ratio and end-to-end delay are used to measure the impact.
Extensive simulations are conducted in a topology based on an actual
suburban neighborhood. Simulation results demonstrate that by carefully adjusting AODV parameters, it increases resistance against black
hole attack. The position of malicious meters also plays a critical role to
prevent black hole attack and is studied as well.

**Keywords:** Smart metering network · Black hole attack · AODV ·
Throughput · End-to-end delay

## 1 Introduction

Smart grid is generally referred to the next-generation power system that fully
integrates high-speed and two-way communications. To evolve from a legacy
power system to smart grid successfully, smart meters play a critical role because
they are capable of recording consumption of electricity, gas and water for monitoring and billing. It is reported that nearly 50 million networked smart meters,
about 43% of the county, have been installed and are running across USA as of
July 2014 [1]. This number is expected to continually rise in the near future.

The security issue of smart grid heavily impacts its performance and has
drawn considerable attention from academia, industry and government. Specifically, a variety of security attacks including denial of service, spoofing, and
eavesdrop deserve an in-depth investigation in the context of smart grids. In this
paper, we focus on black hole attack, which is one kind of denial of service and
severely impairs the performance of a smart metering network.

A smart metering network is typically a wireless mesh network that consists
of a data aggregation point (DAP) and a large number of smart meters [2–4].
The DAP is responsible for collecting information from smart meters. Some

© ICST Institute for Computer Sciences, Social Informatics and Telecommunications Engineering 2018
Q. Chen et al. (Eds.): ChinaCom 2016, Part I, LNICST 209, pp. 159–168, 2018.
DOI: 10.1007/978-3-319-66625-9_16

smart meters have to serve as relay nodes to help deliver information to the DAP through multiple hops. During a black hole attack, a malicious meter discards packets from other meters instead of relaying packets as expected. This could occur due to a compromised meter from various causes.

Since a smart metering network is essentially a multi-hop network, a routing protocol is required to find the best route to the DAP for each smart meter. Ad hoc On-Demand Distance Vector (AODV) Routing is a widely-used protocol for mobile and wireless ad hoc networks, which is also recommended in the smart metering network [5]. Therefore, we adopt AODV as the routing protocol and evaluate black hole attacks under AODV in smart metering network.

In the literature, the impact of malicious meters has been studied for black hole attack under AODV including the impact of the number of malicious meters [6,9]. Distinct from the existing work, our paper aims at carrying out a comprehensive investigation for the effect of malicious meters on network performance including Hello packet interval, route lifetime and positions of malicious meters, which have received limited attention. The performance metrics including packet delivery radio (PDR) and end-to-end delay will be calculated to measure the impact on system performance.

In brief, the main contributions of this paper are summarized as below.

- Black hole attacks are simulated by modifying AODV functions to generate a fake route reply with a high sequence number and a low hop count. Data packets sent by source meters will be simply discarded by the malicious meters.
- The performance under black hole attacks is thoroughly evaluated by adjusting several factors. Specifically, the impact of AODV parameters including Hello message interval and route lifetime as well as positions of malicious meters are fully examined. To the best of our knowledge, it is the first time to conduct such a comprehensive investigation of black hole attacks under AODV in the context of smart metering network.
- Extensive simulations are conducted in a topology based on an actual suburban neighborhood in Rapid City, SD, USA. Simulation results show that performance varies when changing AODV parameters. By carefully adjusting AODV parameters, it increases resistance against black hole attack. In addition, the position of malicious meters affects networking performance and is examined as well. Findings from simulation will shed light on improving security in smart metering networks including malicious meters detection and robust routing protocol design.

The rest of the paper is organized as follows. Section 2 presents how to simulate the black hole attacks under AODV. The simulation setup and results are presented in Sects. 3 and 4, respectively. Concluding remarks are made in Sect. 5.

## 2    Black Hole Attack in Smart Metering Network

In this section, we will present how to trigger the black hole attacks under AODV in smart metering network. The AODV routing protocol will be briefly introduced followed by how to simulate black hole attacks under AODV.

### 2.1    AODV Routing Protocol

AODV is a reactive routing protocol designed to find a route between a source and a destination. In AODV, multiple types of messages are used, e.g., Route Request (RREQ), Route Reply (RREP), Route Error (RERR) and Hello message [7]. The source node initiates a route request RREQ and intermediate nodes are responsible for forwarding the RREQ message until the message is delivered to the destination node or an intermediate node that has a fresh route to the destination. In the latter case, the intermediate node sends a reply, i.e., RREP message back to the source node. After a route is established, the source and destination establish a communication and start transmitting data packets. When a link is broken, RERR message is sent to all nodes to notify a lost of link. Hello messages are used by nodes to monitor and detect links to neighbors. Once a node fails to receive Hello messages from its neighbor, a down link is detected.

### 2.2    Black Hole Attack Under AODV

Black hole attack falls into the category of Denial of Service (DoS) in which a malicious node exploits the route discovery process of AODV and advertises itself the shortest path to the destination. Malicious nodes on receiving route request initiated by a source node, replies with a fake RREP. The source node then forwards data packets to the malicious node which drops all the packets instead of forwarding. In our paper, malicious meters will send a tampered RREP that has 1 as the value of hop count and an extremely high value of destination sequence

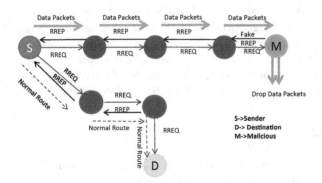

**Fig. 1.** Black hole attack under AODV: the malicious meter tricks the sender to send data packet towards itself and then drop the packets

number because a RREP message with a higher destination sequence number is always considered as a fresh route. Figure 1 illustrates the effect of black hole attack under AODV. It can be seen that with a malicious meter, the normal route is not adopted. Instead, the malicious meter misleads the source/sender to send data towards itself by relying with a higher destination sequence number and then drops the sender's packets. As a result, the performance of sender's PDR is severely degraded.

## 3   Simulation Setup and Performance Metrics

In this section, a simulation platform is set up using a popular Network Simulator 3 (NS3). To imitate a real smart metering network, a suburban neighborhood with 100 houses is selected from Rapid City, South Dakota, USA, as shown in Fig. 2.

**Fig. 2.** An actual suburban neighborhood selected from Rapid City, SD (color figure online)

It is assumed that each house installs a smart meter and a DAP is placed at the center of this neighborhood, which is marked as a green dot. In our simulations, the geographical information of this real neighborhood is imported to NS3 and the resulting smart metering network is created accordingly. The longitudes and latitudes of houses are obtained from Google map and the distance between any two smart meters is calculated by Haversine formula [8], presented by Eq. (1).

$$
\begin{aligned}
\Delta lat &= |lat2 - lat1| \\
\Delta lon &= |lon2 - lon1| \\
a &= (sin(\tfrac{\Delta lat}{2}))^2 + cos(lat1) \times cos(lat2) \times (sin(\tfrac{\Delta lon}{2}))^2 \\
c &= 2 * \arctan 2(\sqrt{(a)}, \sqrt{(1-a)}) \\
d &= R \times c
\end{aligned}
\tag{1}
$$

where $R$ is 6373 km, the radius of the earth.

IEEE 802.11 is recommended as a promising option for smart metering neighborhood network and we adopt IEEE 802.11 for smart meters as well [3]. The transmission range of the smart meters is set to 50 m. To achieve the coverage distance of 50 m for each station, Eq. (2) is utilized [12] as follows.

$$P = \left(\frac{4\pi D}{0.12476}\right)^2 X 10^{-12.5}, \tag{2}$$

where $P$ is the transmission power and $D$ is the coverage distance, which is 50 m in our paper.

The transmission pattern is carefully scheduled so that every smart meter periodically sends data to the DAP with 10 s interval between consecutive smart meters. AODV is chosen as the routing protocol for this scenario. The major parameters for the simulation setup are listed in Table 1.

**Table 1.** Specific parameters for simulations

| Parameter | Attributes |
|---|---|
| Number of DAP | 1 |
| Number of smart meters | 100 |
| Packet size | 1024 |
| Transmission range | 50 m |
| Routing protocol | AODV |
| Mobility model | Static |
| Traffic | Constant bit rate |
| MAC/PHY | IEEE 802.11b |

To evaluate the black hole attacks under AODV, two widely used performance metrics [10,11] will be examined and they are presented in the following.

- Packet Delivery Ratio (PDR): the ratio of the successfully delivered packets compared with the total packets that have been sent. It is formulated as:

$$PDR = \frac{\sum number\ of\ packet\ received}{\sum number\ of\ packet\ sent}$$

- End-to-end Delay: the average time taken by a data packet transmitted from a source to the destination. It is comprised of the delay caused by route discovery process and the queue in data packet transmission.

$$Delay = \frac{\sum (arrival\ time\ -\ sent\ time)}{\sum number\ of\ successful\ transmission}$$

Note that the end-to-end delay is counted only for the successfully delivered data packets.

## 4    Simulation Results

In this section, extensive simulations are carried out to evaluate the impact of black hole attack under AODV protocol based on the topology shown in Fig. 2. The objective of the simulation is to evaluate how different parameters, such as Hello packet interval and Active Route Timeout (ART), affect the PDR and end-to-end delay of smart metering network in presence and absence of a black hole attack. In AODV, ART refers to as the rout state hold time, which means after such a time period nodes will remove the route states [12]. From simulation results, we attempt to draw general conclusions and provide insights how to choose an appropriate parameter to achieve a desirable performance.

In the simulation, we set three different values for ART, which are 3 s (i.e., the default value in AODV), 300 s and 3000 s. Note that when ART = 3000 s, all of the smart meters will not change route states for the entire simulation duration.

### 4.1    Effect of Variation of ART and Hello Packet Interval on PDR

First, the impact of ART and Hello packet interval on PDR is evaluated with and without malicious meters. Without malicious behaviors, all meters behave normally and send data successively to the DAP. Figure 3 demonstrates the average PDR of all senders with varied ART and Hello packet interval without malicious meters. It can be observed that the PDR is about 100% for all settings and no significant difference is observed when ART and Hello packet interval are changed. This result is expected since the meters are stationary and changing ART value and Hello interval will not significantly affect the PDR.

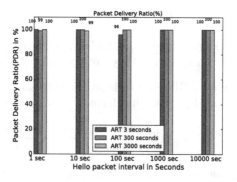

**Fig. 3.** Average packet delivery ratio without malicious activities

Figure 4 shows the PDR of the same topology under a single malicious meter, whose position is marked in Fig. 2. The PDR falls down to 57% for the default AODV setting (i.e., Hello packet interval = 1s and ART = 3 s). For ART = 300 s and ART = 3000 s, the results show some resistance to black hole attacks. It can

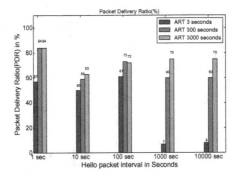

**Fig. 4.** Average packet delivery ratio with malicious activities

be seen that PDR is generally improved with the increase of ART in presence of malicious meters. This is because increasing the route lifetime can counter-measure a black hole attack. More specifically, the route discovery process is minimum when the ART value is larger and hence it shows resistance to black hole attacks to some degree. In addition, PDR changes with variation of Hello packet interval but this depends on a specific topology and meter polling frequency. In our case, PDR is maximized when $ART = 3000\,s$ and Hello packet interval $= 1\,s$. In general, this simulation result suggests that higher PDR values could be achieved with a higher ART under a black hole attack.

### 4.2 Effect of Variation of ART and Hello Packet Frequency on Average End-to-End Delay

In this subsection, we evaluate the impact of black hole attacks on end-to-end delay of the network. The average end-to-end delay is calculated from all normal senders with or without the malicious meter, based on the topology illustrated in Fig. 2. The results are plotted in Figs. 5 and 6 while changing the ART and Hello packet interval.

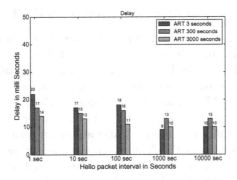

**Fig. 5.** Average delay without malicious activities

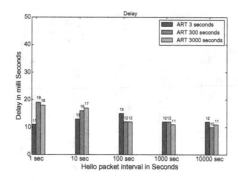

**Fig. 6.** Average delay with malicious activities

Without malicious meters, Fig. 5 demonstrates that a smaller ART usually results in a larger delay. It can be found that the average end-to-end delay decreases at a higher value of ART and Hello interval. For the default AODV setting (i.e., Hello packet interval $= 1$ s and ART $= 3$ s), the delay reaches 22 ms and is the largest one for all settings. This is because the meters frequently update the route state and the short Hello interval (i.e., 1 s) causes flooding the network every second, which ultimately results in the increase of delay. In general, this simulation result discovers that minimum delay can be achieved by increasing ART value since with a large ART, the meters will keep route states for a long time. In addition, the Hello packet interval can be tuned according to a specific topology to achieve a minimum delay. The appropriate Hello packet interval is 1000 s in our topology.

Figure 6 illustrates the average end-to-end delay with the malicious meter, whose position is marked in Fig. 2. The average delay in Fig. 6 is smaller than that observed in Fig. 5 due to that most of packets are dropped by the malicious meter and they fail to be transmitted to DAP. It is also shown that the average end-end delay decreases when Hello packet interval and ART are increased, which is similar to the trend in Fig. 5.

### 4.3   Effect of Position of Malicious Meters on PDR

In this subsection, we evaluate the PDR while changing the position of malicious meters in Fig. 2. Two different scenarios are considered: (1) only one specific source meter sends data to the DAP and (2) all meters take turn to send data to the DAP. In the first scenario, one specific sender is the attacking target, which is marked as "*" and DAP is marked as "red dot" as shown in Fig. 7. Each time, assume there is only one malicious meter, and the sender's PDRs are recorded by making all other smart meters as a malicious one in turn. The 3-D result for the first scenario is shown in Fig. 7, in which the z-axis represents the sender's PDR when the meter at the position (x, y) is compromised. It is clearly seen that the PDR varies when attacker changes its location. By intuition, we expect a reduction of PDR when the malicious meters are physically close to the sender

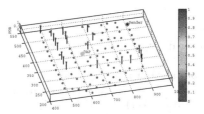

**Fig. 7.** Effect of position of malicious meters on PDR for a specific sender (Color figure online)

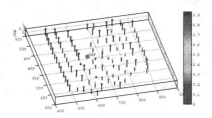

**Fig. 8.** Effect of position of malicious nodes on PDR for overall senders

or the destination. Unfortunately, from this figure, there is no obvious trend to support that intuition. The PDR can still reach 0 even when the malicious meter is far away to both sender and DAP.

In the second scenario, one malicious meter is assumed and all other meters successively send data to the DAP. The average PDR is recorded for all regular meters when the malicious meter changes the position. The 3-D result for this scenario is shown in Fig. 8, in which the z-axis represents the average PDR when the meter at the position (x, y) is compromised while all other meters are good meters. It is observed that the average PDR also changes if malicious meter is placed at different locations, but no general trend is concluded.

## 5   Conclusions

In this paper, we have evaluated the black hole attack from new perspectives, by changing the AODV routing parameters including Hello message interval and rout lifetime as well as positions of malicious meters. Simulation results demonstrate that different AODV parameters will result in different performance. Hence parameter of AODV can be tuned according to a specific topology to achieve better performance. We have also studied the impact of the position of malicious meters on black hole attack. These findings will provide insights into security improvement in smart metering networks, e.g., malicious meters detection and robust routing protocol design.

# References

1. Utility-scale smart meter deployments: building block of the evolving power grid. IEI report (2014)
2. Erol-Kantarci, M., Mouftah, H.T.: Energy-efficient information and communication infrastructures in the smart grid: a survey on interactions and open issues. IEEE Commun. Surv. Tutor. **17**(1), 179–197 (2015)
3. Ho, Q.-D., Gao, Y., Le-Ngoc, T.: Challenges and research opportunities in wireless communication networks for smart grid. IEEE Wirel. Commun. **20**(3), 89–95 (2013)
4. Xu, J., Zhang, R.: CoMP meets smart grid: a new communication and energy cooperation paradigm. IEEE Trans. Veh. Technol. **64**(6), 2476–2488 (2015)
5. Bennett, C., Wicker, S.B.: Decreased time delay and security enhancement recommendations for AMI smart meter networks. In: IEEE Innovative Smart Grid Technologies (ISGT), pp. 1–6 (2010)
6. Esmaili, H., Shoja, M., et al.: Performance analysis of AODV under black hole attack through use of OPNET simulator. World Comput. Sci. Inf. Technol. J. (WCSIT) **1**, 49–52 (2011)
7. Klein-Berndt, L.: A quick guide to AODV routing. In: NIST, Wireless Communications Technologies Group (2011). http://w3.antd.nist.gov/wctg/aodv_kernel/
8. Gellert, W.: The VNR Concise Encyclopedia of Mathematics. Springer Science and Business Media, Heidelberg (2012)
9. Yi, P., Zhu, T., Zhang, Q., Wu, Y., Li, J.: A denial of service attack in advanced metering infrastructure network. In: IEEE International Conference on Communications (ICC), pp. 1029–1034 (2014)
10. Wang, G., Ren, Y., Dou, K., Li, J.: IDTCP: an effective approach to mitigating the TCP incast problem in data center networks. Inf. Syst. Front. **16**, 35–44 (2014)
11. Wang, G., Ren, Y., Li, J.: An effective approach to alleviating the challenges of transmission control protocol. IET Commun. **8**(6), 860–869 (2014)
12. Al-Mandhari, W., Gyoda, K., Nakajima, N.: Performance evaluation of active route time-out parameter in ad-hoc on demand distance vector (AODV). In: The 6th WSEAS International Conference on Applied Electromagnetic, Wireless and Optical Communications, pp. 2–4 (2008)

# An Entropy-Based DDoS Defense Mechanism in Software Defined Networks

Yajie Jiang[1(✉)], Xiaoning Zhang[1], Quan Zhou[1], and Zijing Cheng[2]

[1] Qingshuihe Campus of UESTC, No. 2006, Xiyuan Ave, West Hi-Tech Zone,
Chengdu 611731, Sichuan, People's Republic of China
jiangyj319@163.com, xnzhang@uestc.edu.cn,
634466414@qq.com
[2] Beijing Institute of Information Engineering,
Beijing, People's Republic of China
linuxdemo@126.com

**Abstract.** The issue on defensing against Distributed Denial of Service (DDoS) attacks in Software Defined Networks (SDN) has been highly concerned by academe and industry. The existing studies cannot eliminate the false positives by using the simple classification algorithms. In this paper, we analyze the essential difference between DDoS attacks and flash crowds which causes some similar consequences to DDoS. Accordingly we design a novel effective Entropy-based DDoS Defense Mechanism (EDDM) running on the SDN controller, which including a two-stage DDoS detection method. Compared with the existing works, the EDDM avoids the dropping of legitimate packets and minimizes the losses of legitimate users. Simulations demonstrate that the EDDM can distinguish the DDoS attacks from flash crowds, find the locations of bots, and block attack packets at source effectively.

**Keywords:** DDoS defense · Flash crowd · SDN · Entropy

## 1 Introduction

In the Distributed Denial of Service (DDoS) [1] flooding attacks, the attacker takes control of some hosts distributed in the network which are called zombie hosts or bots, then instructs them to send huge attack packets with legitimate looking. The target will be busy processing the attack traffic, cannot deal with the legitimate packets, meanwhile, network bandwidth is occupied by the attack traffic. From the users' perspectives, the target is unable to provide service as usual. In addition, it is difficult to trace to the zombie hosts, as the attack packets are filled with forged source IP addresses to conceal zombies' locations. With the development of network technology, the cost of DDoS attacks is getting lower and lower, while the attacker hides more easily. Enterprises and Operators have always been focusing on the topic *How to effectively defend against DDoS attacks*, due to the significant losses caused by DDoS attacks.

In traditional networks, the security strategies are complex, not easy to manage, and the upgrading is time-consuming, which needs the participation of vendors. The

© ICST Institute for Computer Sciences, Social Informatics and Telecommunications Engineering 2018
Q. Chen et al. (Eds.): ChinaCom 2016, Part I, LNICST 209, pp. 169–178, 2018.
DOI: 10.1007/978-3-319-66625-9_17

emerging network architecture, Software Defined Network (SDN), has the characteristics of centralized control and programmable logic, which makes the upgrading quite easy.

There are emerging studies on DDoS attacks defense methods for SDN [1–10]. However, these studies didn't give a simple, complete and feasible defense mechanism against DDoS attacks. Most of them are unable to distinguish the DDoS attacks traffic from the flash crowd traffic.

Our contributions can be summarized as follows: (1) we examine the essential difference between DDoS attacks and flash crowds. (2) We propose a two-stage detection method based on the entropy of the destination and the essential difference mentioned above, which can detect DDoS accurately. (3) We present a novel DDoS defense mechanism (EDDM) deployed in the SDN controller, thus can trace to the bots, block attack traffic at source, and prevent the network from being overwhelmed by the attack traffic.

The rest of the paper is organized as follows. Section 2 summarizes some related studies. Section 3 describes the principles of entropy-based DDoS detection methods, analyzes the essential difference between DDoS and flash crowds. Sections 4, 5 present the proposed mechanism and simulation results, respectively. Finally, Sect. 6 summarizes our conclusions.

## 2    Related Work

To minimize the impacts on the SDN controller and the network bandwidth from attack traffic, the attack packets should be blocked at source after a rapid detection of DDoS. Therefore, the key of mitigating DDoS attack is how to distinguish attack packets from legitimate packets.

The existing DDoS detection schemes in SDN can be divided into two categories: pattern matching and anomaly-based detection.

Pattern matching methods extract the features of input flows, and match with the attack features library. Once a match is found, the flow must belong to DDoS attack traffic. Pattern matching methods [2, 3] will never lead to false positives, but they are invalid against the variants beyond the library.

Anomaly-based DDoS detection methods [4–10] can distinguish abnormal network traffic, but they may cause false positives. For example, flash crowds caused by the network hot events may be misjudged as DDoS attacks. Among anomaly-based detection methods, the flow-based attack detection [4–6] mechanisms deployed in the controller without proper aggregation of network traffic could overload the communication among control and data plane [8]. The existing entropy-based detection methods [7–10] take the entropy values as the sole indicator, which can also cause false positives. So we propose the EDDM to eliminate false positives.

## 3    Principle of Entropy-Based DDoS Detection in SDN

Compared with traditional networks, SDN has the characteristics of centralized control and programmable logic, which makes the upgrading and maintaining of the network strategies easy.

### 3.1   SDN Profile

In SDN networks, switches only need to forward data flows quickly following the flow table entries which are issued by controller through secure channel [11].

When a packet enters into OpenFlow switch, it is matched with the flow table entries and follows the entry with the highest priority. Otherwise, when the packet doesn't match any existing entries in OpenFlow switch, the switch will send a Packet-in to controller. Then controller determines forwarding strategy according to network state, and sends Packet-out to instruct relevant OpenFlow switches to establish corresponding flow table entries.

So, when controller receives a Packet-in, that means a newly launched flow wants to enter into the network. If there is DDoS attack in SDN network, the controller will be busy dealing with the attack flows, the secure channel will be occupied by Packet-ins of attack flows, and the legitimate flows will be delayed or dropped.

### 3.2   Principle of Entropy-Based DDoS Detection

In information theory, the entropy is a measure of the uncertainty associated with a random variable [12]. Suppose $X$ represents a random event, it has some possible results $\{x_1, x_2, \ldots, x_n\}, x_i$ has a probability $p(x_i)$ to occur, then the entropy value of $X$ is given by the formula:

$$H(X) = E[I(x_i)] = E[\log_2^{p(x_i)}] = -\sum_{i=1}^{n} p(x_i) \log_2^{p(x_i)}. \tag{1}$$

Formula (1) validates that the bigger of the event's uncertainty, the higher of its entropy value.

In normal network communications, a host may connect to any other host distributed in the whole network. Each IP has the same probability to appear in the destination IP field of packet-in. But if the network is under a DDoS attack, the SDN controller can receive a large number of *Packet-ins*, the target host's IP will appear in destination IP field with a high frequency.

Thus, if we calculate the entropy of destination IP address, with a specific window size, it will be found that the entropy value descends visibly under a DDoS attack [7].

### 3.3   The Essential Difference Between DDoS Attacks and Flash Crowds

However, some network hot events may cause many hosts communicating with the server, which is called flash crowd [13], has the similar characteristics of the soaring network traffic, with the declining entropy value of the destination IP addresses. Hence, using entropy variation of the destination IP addresses as sole indicator in DDoS attacks detection may lead to false positives.

Accordingly, we investigate the essential difference between DDoS attack packets and flash crowd packets. We found that the flash crowd packets, with real source IP, are from legitimate hosts distributed in the whole network, but the DDoS packets, usually with huge forged source IP, are from specific zombies. Therefore, the mapping relationships from the source MAC to the source IP, flash crowd packets use the actual source IP with the actual MAC, while DDoS packets use many spoofed source IPs with the actual MAC.

# 4   Proposed Mechanism: EDDM

The EDDM is deployed in the SDN controller. There are three phases in EDDM, *Window Construction Phase, DDoS Detection Phase* and *DDoS Mitigation Phase*. The flow chart is shown in Fig. 1.

## 4.1   Initialization and Window Construction Phase

*Initialization and Window Construction Phase* collects and extracts some relevant arguments from *Packet-ins*. It is shown as Initialization and Step 1 in Fig. 1.

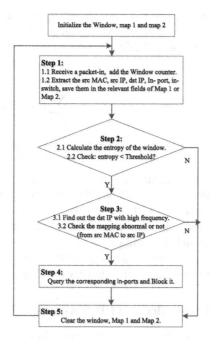

**Fig. 1.**  The main flow chart of EDDM

The principles of entropy-based DDoS attacks detection, the essential difference between DDoS attacks and flash crowds, are introduced in the previous section. For the purpose of detecting DDoS attacks accurately, we propose a new two-stage detection method in the DDoS attack detection phase (see the next subsection), which need to collect and save the relevant arguments in Map with the customized value field (as shown in Fig. 2).

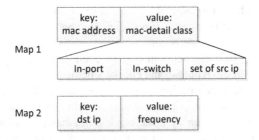

**Fig. 2.** Data structures of Map 1 and Map 2

The EDDM detects DDoS attacks by analyzing header information (such as the source IP, the destination IP and the source MAC) of *Packet-ins*. As proved in [9], we calculate the entropy of the destination IP address with a specific **Window** size 50. As shown in Fig. 2, we use two kinds of Map to store different arguments for different purposes in the SDN controller. Each pair in *Map 1* is used to store arguments of the packet(s) with the same source MAC address. The *key* field is filled with the source MAC address, and the *value* field is customized with the *mac-detail class* which is defined with three instance variables, *In-switch, In-port,* and *set of src ip. In-switch* represents the number of the OF switch where the *Packet-in* sent from. *In-port* represents the ingress port of the flow on the *In-switch*. The *set of src ip* stores the source IP address(es) with the same source MAC address, which is the critical indicator in the second stage of the detection phase (the Step 3 in Fig. 1) because the attack packets from a zombie host always have various source IP addresses. Each pair in the *Map 2* is used to store the destination IP addresses and their frequencies in the *Window*. The *Map 2* is used to calculate the entropy value of the *Window* in the first stage of *Detection Phase* (the Step 2 in Fig. 1).

When controller receives a *Packet-in*, it will check whether the *Window* is full or not. If the *Window* is not full, controller will extract relevant header information and store them in the relevant fields in *Map 1* or *Map 2*. When the *Window* is full of 50 *Packet-ins*, controller will go to the *Attack Detection Phase*.

### 4.2  DDoS Attack Detection Phase

*DDoS Detection Phase* detects the DDoS attack accurately by the two-stage detection method. Step 2 and Step 3 in Fig. 1 are included in this phase.

The SDN controller can receive many *Packet-ins* with the same destination IP when DDoS attack is in progress. But the flash crowd can also cause similar consequence. It's inaccurate to take the entropy of destination IP as the sole indicator in DDoS detection. After found the essential difference between DDoS attack packets and flash crowd packets, we propose a two-stage detection method as the second phase of EDDM.

In the first stage (see the Step 2 in Fig. 1), controller calculates the *entropy* of the destination IP using the arguments in *Map 2* (according to the mathematical *formula* (1)). If the entropy is higher than the preset **Threshold** (we chose 1.31 as proved in [9]), the flows which are represented by the *Packet-ins* in the *Window* are legitimate, and controller will execute the Step 5. If not, they are abnormal flows which need to go to the second stage for further detection.

In the second stage (see the Step 3 in Fig. 1), controller finds out the destination IP with a high frequency in the *Window*, and checks whether the corresponding *Packet-ins* have informal mapping relationships (from the source MAC to the source IP) by checking the *size* of *set of src ip* (the instance variable of the *mac-detail* class customized in the *value* field of *Map 1*). If the *size* is more than two (which means the host sends packets with more than two source IPs), controller can determine that the corresponding *In-port* of the *In-switch* (both in the *value* field of *Map 1*) is connected to a zombie host. Otherwise, that means there is a flash crowd caused by some hot events in network.

If there is no zombie host found in the *Window*, controller will clear the *Window*, *Map 1* and *Map 2* to prepare to build the next *Window*. Or else it goes to the *Attack Mitigation Phase*.

### 4.3   DDoS Attack Mitigation Phase

*DDoS Mitigation Phase* blocks the attack flows. It is shown as the Step 4 in Fig. 1.

In theory, the best way to mitigate DDoS attacks is blocking the attack packets at source, which minimizes impacts on the network bandwidth and the SDN controller. The existing studies have not considered tracing to the attack sources effectively, in this way dropping packets is a general method to mitigate DDoS attacks, but they may drop some legitimate flows that cause QoS and SLA degraded. Besides, the zombie hosts send legitimate looking packets with forged source IP addresses to conceal their locations, so tracing to the bots and blocking attack packets at source is difficult to achieve. The inevitable result is massive packets with forged source IP entering into the OpenFlow switches. As a result, the SDN controller is busy in processing attack flows, cannot deal with legitimate flows normally.

However, the EDDM can find out the bots and query corresponding *In-port* of the *In-switch* (stored in the *value* field of the *Map 1*). Then, the SDN controller can issue *Packet-outs* to relevant switches to establish corresponding flow table entries, and the ingress ports connected to those bots will be blocked, the attack packets cannot enter into the network to affect the SDN controller and the target host.

## 5   Simulation Results

This study presents EDDM developed with the Floodlight [14], a Java-based SDN controller, which is one of the mainstream SDN controllers at present. In order to evaluate the proposed novel EDDM, a virtual scenario is simulated. Mininet [15] is a great way to develop, share, and experiment with OpenFlow and SDN systems. It can create a realistic virtual network, running real kernel, switch and application code, on a single machine (VM, cloud or native), in seconds, with a single command. Besides, sFlow [16] can display and monitor the traffic on the network, which is used in virtual networks but also in real ones.

The simulations use a custom Mininet script for the network topology. The test topology configuration is shown in Fig. 3. We test the effectiveness of EDDM which is running over the Floodlight controller in a small SDN network, which contains a Floodlight controller, 3 OpenFlow switches and 12 hosts. The bots (signed with "B") are generating huge traffic with forged source IP addresses towards the target nodes (signed with "T"). sFlow is used to display the real-time traffic at some specific ports to illustrate the traffic state in the network.

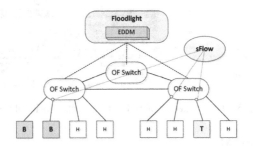

**Fig. 3.** The test network topology

In order to verify the impacts of the EDDM on DDoS defense, we simulate the following three scenarios: *DDoS without any defense mechanisms, DDoS with EDDM, the flash crowd and DDoS with EDDM*. We use sFlow to display the packets rate of specific ports connected to the attack zombie host, the legitimate host and the target host (see Fig. 3), and the situation of each scene can be compared visually.

### 5.1 DDoS Without Any Defense Mechanisms

For a better comparison, we set a reference basis. So we first simulate that the DDoS attacker attacks the SDN network without any defense mechanisms in Floodlight.

The attack packets are sent from specified bots at a high transmission rate with forged source IP addresses. The transmission rate remains high for a long while, as shown in Fig. 4, because there is no defense mechanism in the SDN network.

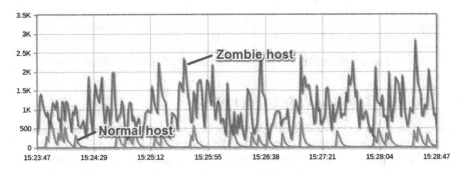

**Fig. 4.** The packet rate of the zombie host and the normal host without EDDM

We use the Wireshark [17], which is a free and open source packet analyzer, to capture the attack packets at the ingress port connected to a zombie host. As shown in Fig. 5, the destination IPs in the fourth column are all the same, but the source IPs (shown in the third column) are various fake IP addresses.

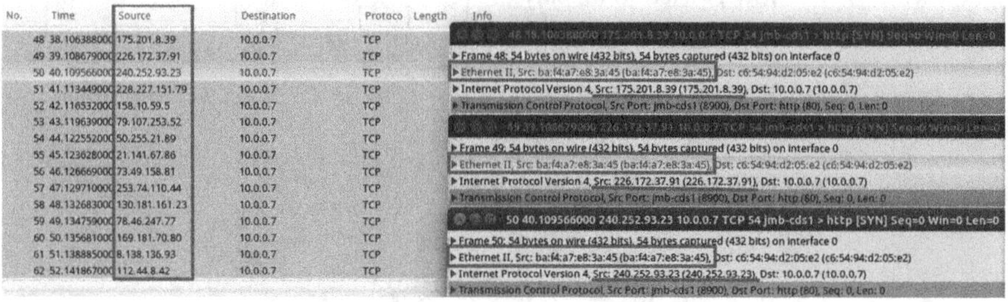

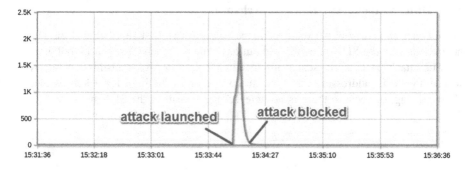

**Fig. 5.** The packets captured at the attack port in DDoS

## 5.2    DDoS with EDDM

When we run the EDDM in Floodlight, the defense mechanism can detect DDoS attacks accurately, trace to the bots and block the attack traffic at source.

Compared with the scene without any DDoS defense mechanisms, the attack packets are blocked at the ingress port of access OpenFlow switch almost immediately, as shown in Fig. 6. As a result, the attack packets cannot be delivered the *Packet-ins* to burden the controller through the secure channel between controller and switches, and cannot occupy the network bandwidth too.

**Fig. 6.** The packet rate of a zombie host in DDoS with EDDM

## 5.3    The Flash Crowd and DDoS with EDDM

Moreover, in order to prove that EDDM is able to distinguish DDoS traffic from flash crowd flows, we simulate the flash crowd and DDoS with the EDDM. Every host in the network sends packets to the server with a high transmission rate, 3 hosts of them as the bots sending spoofed packets, while the remaining 8 hosts send legitimate packets.

As shown in Fig. 7, with the EDDM running on Floodlight, the attack flows are all blocked in the access switch, while the legitimate flows belonged to flash crowd are forwarded normally, and the packets rate of the legitimate host is unaffected. It demonstrates that the proposed EDDM can protect flash crowd flows from being misjudged as the DDoS attacks, and avoid the dropping of flash crowd packets.

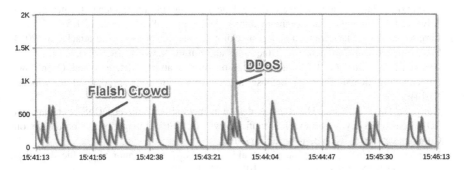

**Fig. 7.** The packet rate of a zombie host and a normal host with EDDM

### 5.4 Discussions

In [7], they confirm the DDoS attacks after the abnormal entropy in five consecutive windows, but we can detect the abnormal flows according to the entropy of one window, our decision process is quite short. In [9], they try to use the conditional entropy as a sole measure to distinguish DDoS attack from flash crowd. But they misunderstand the essential difference. The false alarm rate was up to 8.4% in the simulation. The EDDM can defense DDoS attacks with forged source IPs, distinguish DDoS attacks from flash crowd, and block attack packets at source. Thus it is able to protect the bandwidth of the secure channel, and the processing capacity of controller. Therefore, it can minimize the losses of legitimate users in the SDN networks.

## 6   Conclusion

In this paper, we analyze the essential difference between DDoS packets and flash crowd packets, design a two-stage DDoS detection method included in EDDM. The simulation results demonstrate that the EDDM can distinguish the DDoS from flash crowd, find out the locations of bots, and block the attack packets at source effectively. The only flaw is the processing delay is undesirable.

In the future, we will focus on the optimization of processing delay, investigate on the influences of the EDDM using different topologies with larger scale, and test it on a real physical network.

# References

1. Vizváry, M.: Mitigation of DDoS attacks in software defined networks
2. Braga, R., Mota, E., Passito, A.: Lightweight DDoS flooding attack detection using NOX/OpenFlow. In: 2010 IEEE 35th Conference on. IEEE Local Computer Networks (LCN) (2010)
3. Van Trung, P., Huong, T.T, Van Tuyen, D., et al.: A multi-criteria-based DDoS-attack prevention solution using software defined networking. In: International Conference on Advanced Technologies for Communications (ATC), pp. 308–313. IEEE (2015)
4. Lim, S., et al.: A SDN-oriented DDoS blocking scheme for botnet-based attacks. In: 2014 Sixth International Conference on Ubiquitous and Future Networks (ICUFN). IEEE (2014)
5. García de la Villa, A.: Distributed denial of service attacks defenses and OpenFlow: implementing denial-of-service defense mechanisms with software defined networking (2014)
6. Dong, P., Du, X., Zhang, H., et al.: A detection method for a novel DDoS attack against SDN controllers by vast new low-traffic flows. In: IEEE International Conference on Communications (ICC), pp. 1–6. IEEE (2016)
7. Mingxin, W., Huachun, Z., Jia, C., et al.: An entropy based anomaly traffic detection approach in SDN. Telecommun. Sci. 31(9), 2015217 (2015)
8. Mousavi, S.M., St-Hilaire, M.: Early detection of DDoS attacks against SDN controllers. In: 2015 International Conference on Computing, Networking and Communications (ICNC). IEEE (2015)
9. Shu, Y., Mei, M., Huang, H.: Research on DDoS attack detection based on conditional entropy in SDN environment. Wirel. Internet Technol. 5, 75–76 (2016)
10. Jantila, S., Chaipah, K.: A security analysis of a hybrid mechanism to defend DDoS attacks in SDN. Proc. Comput. Sci. 86, 437–440 (2016)
11. Hwang, T., Liu, J., Wei, L.: SDN Core Principles and Application Practice, 36–37. Post & Telecom Press, Beijing (2014)
12. Information Entropy. https://en.wikipedia.org/wiki/Entropy_(information_theory)
13. Luo, K., Luo, J., Yi, M.: Survey on distinction between flash crowd and DDoS attacks. Comput. Sci. 11A, 313–316 (2015)
14. Floodlight. http://www.projectfloodlight.org/floodlight/
15. Mininet Study Guide. http://www.sdnlab.com/11495.html
16. sFlow Overview Documents. http://www.sflow.org/about/index.php
17. About Wireshark. https://www.wireshark.org/#learnWS

# Protecting Location Privacy Through Crowd Collaboration

Zhonghui Wang, Guangwei Bai$^{(\boxtimes)}$, and Hang Shen

College of Computer Science and Technology,
Nanjing Tech University, Nanjing 211816, China
bai@njtech.edu.cn

**Abstract.** Location-based services (LBSs) enable users to sense their surroundings at the risk of exposing coordinates to attackers. Worse yet, a strong adversary with arbitrary knowledges probably derive more privacy especially in continuous query scenarios. To address the problems, a multi-player privacy game mechanism is proposed to satisfy users' location privacy against adaptive attacks while maximizing utility, building upon which a heuristic algorithm is applied to iteratively converge to the optimal equilibrium point. The gain stems from the collaboration of mobile devices: users share information and forward queries for each other. We evaluate our mechanism against the Bayesian localization attack and maximum possible moving speed attack. The simulations with real map data and mobility traces indicate that our mechanism is effective to preserve privacy at an acceptable price of utility and time complexity.

**Keywords:** Location-based service · Multi-player privacy game · Joint differential-distortion privacy · Inference privacy · Adaptive attack

## 1    Introduction

Users are enabled to query the LBS servers for the purpose of searching points of interest (POIs, like restaurants, stores, etc.), real-time traffic information or navigation related to the current position, which is observable to attackers [1,2]. Sensitive coordinates may be exposed during the queries. Even worse, the strong adversary [3,4] with arbitrary knowledges probably traces and models the queries to predict users' following behaviors and derive more privacy.

Data confusion is an excellent mechanism for hiding sensitive data by misleading, extra or ambiguous information, resulting in extra extracting overhead. A number of obfuscation mechanisms have been proposed [5,6]. One of the most important is Stackelberg Game proposed in [7], where the focus is on two rivals solved by linear programming. Another important contribution is joint differential-distortion privacy metric. The privacy achieved through joint metric against optimal attacks is the maximum privacy that can be achieved by either of these metrics separately. The utility cost is also not larger than what

© ICST Institute for Computer Sciences, Social Informatics and Telecommunications Engineering 2018
Q. Chen et al. (Eds.): ChinaCom 2016, Part I, LNICST 209, pp. 179–188, 2018.
DOI: 10.1007/978-3-319-66625-9_18

either of them imposes. However, it fails to preserve privacy in continuous query scenarios. When observing queries continuously issued, the adversary may run overlapping rectangle attack [9], continuous query attack [10] or maximum possible moving speed attack [11] by linking historical cloaking regions with users' mobility patterns to infer more privacy than obtained from an isolated query.

Even worse, cooperations between the adversary and LBS providers greatly weaken users' privacy. Fortunately, with the rapid advance in mobile devices and their embedded sensors, users in local area can help each other to enhance privacy protection without a trusted central server [8]. We enable users to randomly select neighbors for forwarding queries through a transition probability matrix $P$. Thus users are supposed to negotiate with each other over $P$ so that more privacy can be preserved.

To address the above concerns, we propose a multi-palyer game mechanism to minimizing users' utility loss with respect to privacy measured by both inference and joint differential-distortion privacy metrics, where the adversary runs adaptive attacks to minimize users' privacy by inverting users' strategies. On the basis, a heuristic algorithm is proposed to iteratively converge to the optimal equilibrium point on $P$. The simulations with real map data and mobility traces indicate that our mechanism is effective to preserve privacy at an acceptable price of utility and time complexity. Additionally, compared with the existing joint differential-distortion privacy metric, employing both inference and joint privacy metrics significantly improves the privacy level.

The remainder of this paper is organized as follows. Section 2 defines some important concepts and states problems. In Sect. 3, an optimal obfuscation mechanism is designed for multi-palyer game scenarios, followed by thorough analysis and evaluation in Sect. 4. Finally, Sect. 5 concludes the paper.

## 2    Problem Statement

We assume a user wants to protect sensitive information when communicating with untrusted LBS providers, and refer to his sensitive information as *secret*, which can be protected by collaboration. More specifically, the user may asks others (assuming there's no spiteful users) to issue LBS queries for him according to $P$. Figure 1 illustrates the information flow. The joint probability distribution

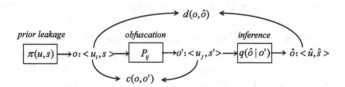

**Fig. 1.** The information sharing framework. A user-secret pair $<u, s>$ denoted by $o$ is obfuscated into observable $o'$ by the mechanism according to $P$. The adaptive adversary runs inference attack $q$ on $o'$ and draws a probability distribution over estimates $\hat{o}$. Distance function $d$ stands for privacy level, and $c$ denotes the utility cost.

$\pi$ is estimated by observing the users' exposed information in the past. Thus we need to update $\pi$ whenever any user shares his information. In the following sections, we define several important concepts and state the problems based on the information sharing framework.

### 2.1   Weighed Distance

In fact, a user could bear much smaller distance error if he is at a bus stop or other POIs with less sensitivity. In order to reduce unnecessary computational cost, we provide adjustable protection level.

Thus the notion of weighed distance is introduced to provide flexibility. POIs are classified into several levels from extremely sensitive to not sensitive. The coefficient of $i$th level is $w_i$, which is defined by users before entering in or modified during the game. The weighed distance is calculated as

$$d^{w_i} = w_i \cdot d, w_i \in [0, 1] \tag{1}$$

The smaller $w_i$ is, the more sensitive related POIs are.

### 2.2   Joint Differential-Distortion Privacy Metric

After an observable $o'$ was released, the adversary will speculate about the original content of the query and get an estimate $\hat{o}$. Therefore we use the distance between $o$ and $\hat{o}$ to define distortion privacy. A user would be less worried about revealing $o \sim p\,(o'|o)$, if the portrait of his secret $o$ in the eyes of the adversary is an estimate $\hat{o}$ with a large distance $d^w(o, \hat{o})$.

Given inference algorithm $q$ and specific secret $o$, the user's privacy obtained through a protection mechanism $p$ is computed by

$$\sum_{o'} p(o'|o) \sum_{\hat{o}} q(\hat{o}|o')d^w(o, \hat{o}). \tag{2}$$

The expected distortion privacy of the users is

$$\sum_{o} \pi(o) \sum_{o'} p(o'|o) \sum_{\hat{o}} q(\hat{o}|o')d^w(o, \hat{o}). \tag{3}$$

A generic definition of differential privacy is adopted in this paper, assuming arbitrary distance function $d^\epsilon$ on the users. A protection mechanism is differentially private if for all users $u, u' \in U$ with distinguishability $d^\epsilon(u, u')$, and for all observables $o' \in O$, we have

$$p\,(o'|\,\langle u, s\rangle) \leqslant \epsilon d^\epsilon\,(u, u') \cdot p\,(o'|\,\langle u', s'\rangle). \tag{4}$$

In fact, the differential privacy metric guarantees that, given the observation, there is not enough convincing evidence to prefer to one user than others.

## 2.3   Inference Privacy Metric

Users usually continuously issue queries. The adversary with background knowledges can infer more information aftering comparing adjacent queries. Given that the protection mechanism $p$ releases $o'_t$ at time $t$ and last output is $o'_{t-1}$, $\varepsilon$-privacy can be saved if the following inequality holds.

$$q\left(\hat{o}_t | o'_t, o'_{t-1}\right) \leqslant e^\varepsilon q\left(\hat{o}_t | o'_t\right), \tag{5}$$

where more privacy is preserved when $\varepsilon$ getting smaller.

## 2.4   Utility Cost

Through obfuscation mechanism, users may gain more privacy while incurring more utility loss. On one hand, it leads to additional communication cost denoted by $c_d$ when user $i$ asks $j$ to forward the query instead of issuing it personally. On the other hand, we explain the heterogeneity between two secrects by an r-range query (considering users will most likely issue r-range queries or kNN queries and both of them are related to circle regions). Figure 2 describes how $j$ handles the query from $i$. The mechanism increases the cost of data transmission and the workload of the result refinement process. All these expenditure are proportional to the size of superset, depending on the quantity of POIs within this range. Because there is locally even distribution in POIs, we calculate the extra refinement cost $c_r$ with density and area instead of the quantity of POIs.

$$c_r = \frac{\rho \cdot \pi \cdot r'^2}{\rho \cdot \pi \cdot r^2} \geqslant \frac{(r + d_{ij})^2}{r^2}, \tag{6}$$

where $\rho$ is density of POIs and $d_{ij}$ is the linear distance between $u_i$ and $u_j$.

To simplify the problem, we employee function $c$ to denote the overall utility cost calculated by $c_d$ and $c_r$.

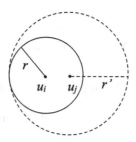

**Fig. 2.** Processing procedure of a range query. Firstly, $u_i$ issues a range query with radius $r$ and selects $u_j$ to forward the query. Aftering receiving the original request $o$, $u_j$ computes a new radius $r'$ and repacks it into $o'$. Then LBS providers will return a result superset after processing $o'$. Finally, $u_j$ needs to extract the exact results what $u_i$ requests and send it back to finish the entire procedure.

## 2.5   Objective

The objective is to find the optimal balance between privacy and utility, and to construct the protecting mechanism that achieves such an equilibrium point. In other words, it is to find a vector of probability distribution function $p^*$ to minimize the overall utility cost, on average,

$$p^* = \min \sum_i \pi(u_i) \sum_{j,s} \pi(u_i, s) P_{ij} c_{ij} \tag{7}$$

under users' privacy constraints.

Let $d_m$ be the minimum desired distortion privacy level and $\epsilon_m$ be the differential privacy budget associated with the minimum desired privacy of the users. The users' joint privacy is guaranteed if $p$ satisfies

$$\sum_{o'} p(o'|o) \sum_{\hat{o}} q^*(\hat{o}|o') d^w(o, \hat{o}) \geqslant d_m, \forall o \in O, \tag{8}$$

$$p(o'|\langle u, s \rangle) \leqslant \epsilon_m d^\epsilon(u, u') p(o'|\langle u', s' \rangle), \forall u, u', o'. \tag{9}$$

Let $\varepsilon_m$ be the desired inference privacy of the users. The users' inference privacy is guaranteed if

$$q^*(\hat{o}_t|o'_t, o'_{t-1}) \leqslant e^{\varepsilon_m} q^*(\hat{o}_t|o'_t), \forall t. \tag{10}$$

With the objective, the following multi-player game minimizes the overall cost when satisfying the above constraints.

## 3   Privacy Game

**Definition 1** *(Privacy Game). A strategic game consists of*

1. *A finite set $M$: the set of players,*
2. *For each player $i \in M$, a nonempty set $A_i$: the set of actions available to player $i$,*
3. *For each player $i \in M$, a preference relation $\succeq_i$ on $A$.*

$\succeq_i$ *is defined by a utility cost function $c_i$. For any $a \in M, b \in M$, $c_i(a) \leqslant c_i(b)$ if $a \succeq_i b$.*

Each player wants to maximize the objective according to his preference relation. A user's action space is all users he can request for forwarding queries. The adversary's action space is all possible requesters when observing outcomes of obfuscation mechanism. Assuming that the obfuscation mechanism is not oblivious and is available to all players, the adversary takes the upper hand in the conflict for making decisions after users. Therefore, an obfuscation mechanism against a fixed attack is always suboptimal. The best obfuscation mechanism should be designed against any adaptive attack which is tailored to each specific obfuscation mechanism. After the adversary designs the best inference attack, users' goal is the obfuscation against the adversary. Accordingly, we do not model any particular adversary but the one who minimizes users' privacy according to observation.

Given secret $o$, we denote a mixed strategy for user $u_i$ by

$$p_i = p\left(\cdot|o\right) = \left\{p\left(o_1'|o\right), p\left(o_2'|o\right), ..., p\left(o_j'|o\right), ...\right\},$$
$$\forall o_j' \in O, p\left(o_j'|o\right) \geqslant 0, \text{and} \sum_j p\left(o_j'|o\right) = 1. \tag{11}$$

Similarly, let $q$ be the set of the adversary's mixed strategy of finding out the original requester when observing $o'$,

$$q = q\left(\cdot|o'\right) = \left\{q\left(\hat{o}_1|o'\right), q\left(\hat{o}_2|o'\right), ..., q\left(\hat{o}_j|o'\right), ...\right\},$$
$$\forall \hat{o}_j \in O, q\left(\hat{o}_j|o'\right) \geqslant 0, \text{and} \sum_j q\left(\hat{o}_j|o'\right) = 1. \tag{12}$$

$p, q$ and $\pi$ are available to all players. With these information, users want to figure out the mutually optimal $\langle p^*, q^* \rangle$, which is the solution of the game. In the following sections, we design the optimal attack $q^*$ and the best obfuscation mechanism $p_i^*$ for each user $u_i$ against $q^*$ under his privacy constraints.

### 3.1  Optimal Strategies

The adversary's objective is to minimize the users' privacy, i.e., to minimize error between the estimation $\hat{o}$ and original secret $o$. The optimal attack is

$$q^* = \min_q \sum_{\hat{o}} p^*\left(o'|o\right) q\left(\hat{o}|o'\right) d\left(o, \hat{o}\right), \tag{13}$$

where $q$ is not only a Bayesian probability inverse, but also considering mobile pattern attack(MPA) like maximum possible moving speed attack to infer more privacy in continuous query scenarios.

Against the adversary, users cooperate with each other to minimize overall cost under the premise of satisfying every user's privacy. Thus we can formulate the protection as

$$p^* = \min_p \sum_{o,o'} p\left(o'|o\right) q^*\left(\hat{o}|o'\right) c\left(o, \hat{o}\right) \tag{14a}$$

$$\text{s.t.} \sum_{o'} p(o'|o) \sum_{\hat{o}} q^*(\hat{o}|o') d^w(o, \hat{o}) \geqslant d_m, \forall o \in O, \tag{14b}$$

$$p\left(o'|o_i\right) \leqslant \epsilon_m d^\epsilon\left(o_i, o_j\right) \cdot p\left(o'|o_j\right), \forall i, j, o', \tag{14c}$$

$$q^*\left(\hat{o}_t|o_t', o_{t-1}'\right) \leqslant e^{\varepsilon_m} q^*\left(\hat{o}_t|o_t'\right), \forall t. \tag{14d}$$

Equation (14a) is to minimize overall cost of all queries; constraints (14b), (14c) and (14d) represent the desired distortion, differential and inference privacy level of all users.

## 3.2   Optimal Equilibrium Point

The solution is to find the mutually optimal $\langle p^*, q^* \rangle$ among all pairs. Assuming that there are $n$ users involved in this game, the time complexity of enumerating all $\langle p, q \rangle$ is $O(n^3)$, which is infeasible when $n$ is large enough.

To reduce the complexity, a heuristic algorithm is proposed to iteratively converge to the optimal equilibrium point. Considering hiring a remote user for forwarding queries will take much higher utility cost, users prefer to give closer neighbors a higher forwarding probability. Thus an appropriate initial probability density function is

$$f(x,y) = \frac{1}{\sqrt{2\pi\sigma^2}\sqrt{1-\varrho^2}} e^{-\frac{1}{2\sigma^2(1-\varrho^2)}\left[(x-y)^2+(1-2\varrho)(x-a)(y-b)\right]}, \qquad (15)$$

where $a, b$ is the coordinate (usually marked with latitude and longitude in maps) of requester $u(a,b)$, $\sigma$ and $\varrho$ are parameters for adjusting probability distribution. The neighbors of $u(a,b)$ are ordered by distance as a sequence: $u(x_0, y_0), u(x_1, y_1), ...u(x_i, y_i), u(x_{i+1}, y_{i+1})...$ (where $u(x_0, y_0)$ is $u(a,b)$). The probability of chosing $u_i$, i.e., $u(x_i, y_i)$, is calculated as

$$\iint_D f(x,y)\,dxdy,$$
$$D : (x_i - a)^2 + (y_i - b)^2 \leqslant (x-a)^2 + (y-b)^2 < (x_{i+1} - a)^2 + (y_{i+1} - b)^2. \qquad (16)$$

After $n$ users get their own probability transition matrix, the multi-player game has taken the first step to get the initial $P$ before releasing queries like $p(u_j|u_i)$. The adversary runs $q(\hat{u}_i|u_j)$ to find out the original requesters. Afterwards, obfuscation mechanism will modify $P$ by

$$P'(u_j|\hat{u}_i) = \left(1 - \frac{1}{n}\right) q(\hat{u}_i|u_j) P(u_j|\hat{u}_i), \qquad (17)$$

if $u_j$' secret is exposed to the adversary. Players repeat the above steps to converge to the equilibrium point, with convergence rate determined by $n$ and $q$.

## 4   Performance Evaluation

In this section, the effectiveness of our proposed mechanism are experimentally evaluated under several system settings, with data of Beijing that contains various categories of POIs [12]. To the best of our knowledge, due to privacy and commercial interest reasons, no real suitable data sets have been publicly released. Therefore, in most of our experiments, we randomly generate a group of users as players. In addition, we adapt the real devices data to validate the mechanism. There is no inference attack being specified, but the maximum possible moving speed attack is employed in the experiments to illustrate the crucial problems. The evaluation metrics include privacy level, utility cost and time cost. All algorithms are implemented with Matlab and run on a desktop PC with Intel Core i3 2.53 GHz processor and 8 GB memory.

## 4.1   Case 1: Impacts of POI Density

This section examines the impacts of POI density, while the other parameters keeping constant. Let a group of users experience LBSs in three different districts, where Haidian is downtown with the highest POIs density, and Yanqing is suburban with the lowest density. We compare the utility cost and privacy of users located in the three districts. In Fig. 3, it is interesting to observe that users can achieve more privacy at lower utility cost when being in Haidian. However, staying in Yanqing probably results in much more expensive cost when satisfying the same privacy level, which means users in districts with higher POIs density can preserve much more privacy with the same cost limitation. That is to say, our proposed mechanism performs better in districts with higher POIs density, though it protects at least 79% privacy in the suburbs.

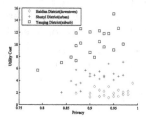

**Fig. 3.** Impacts of POI density.

## 4.2   Case 2: Impacts of Privacy Level

In this section, we investigate the impacts of privacy level from two aspects: increasing the average minimum desired distortion privacy level $d_m$ and inference privacy budget $\varepsilon_m$. The differential privacy metric $\epsilon_m$ is set as 0.05 for being a static metric with little impacts on indicators. In addition, we analyse the impacts of the group size on indicators, including privacy, utility cost and time cost. Figure 4 depicts impacts of different privacy level restrained by $d_m, \epsilon_m$ and $\varepsilon_m$, with POIs data of Shunyi district. Increasing $d_m$ by 0.4 km has much deeper influence than decreasing $\varepsilon_m$ by 0.3. We are glad to see the average privacy of 50 users reaches up to 96% when $d_m = 0.5$ km, $\epsilon_m = 0.05$ and $\varepsilon_m = 0.1$. With group size growing from 5 to 50, the average privacy increases by 30%, while utility cost increases at a low speed. Nevertheless, the exponential growth in initialization time raises concerns about choice on group size, though 18 ms might seem to be acceptable. From the analysis, we realize that gathering 20 devices into a group will incur relatively low utility cost and initialization time consuming under privacy constraints.

## 4.3   Case 3: Tracing Real Devices

As mentioned earlier, no real suitable data sets are publicly available. Thus we develop a software tool to collect trajectory data from 50 real mobile devices and

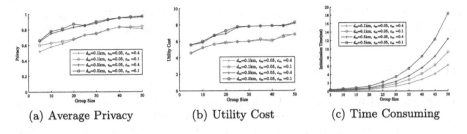

| (a) Average Privacy | (b) Utility Cost | (c) Time Consuming |

**Fig. 4.** Impacts of privacy level.

take the data as input to evaluate our mechanism. Figure 5 indicates that our obfuscation mechanism can provide a better protection when employing both inference and joint privacy metrics by increasing about 10% privacy. We believe that such a mechanism would be acceptable in terms of privacy level of mobile users.

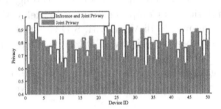

**Fig. 5.** Tracing data of 50 real devices.

## 5    Conclusions

This paper contributes to the extensive field of research that concerns obfuscation mechanisms, e.g., in the context of privacy metric, attack algorithm and anonymity in distributed mobile systems without a trusted central server. The proposed obfuscation mechanism is able to preserving users' location privacy against adaptive attacks when maximizing utility. Another important contributions is the optimization with respect to both joint differential-distortion and inference privacy metrics, as well as weighed distance. The simulations with real map and mobility traces corroborate that it is effective to preserve privacy at an acceptable price of utility and time cost. Additionally, it proves that users in districts with higher POIs density can preserve much more privacy with the same cost limitation.

**Acknowledgements.** The authors gratefully acknowledge the support and financial assistance provided by the National Natural Science Foundation of China under Grant Nos. 61502230 and 61073197, the Natural Science Foundation of Jiangsu Province under Grant No. BK20150960, the Innovation Project for Postgraduates of Jiangsu

Province under Grant No. KYLX16_0600, the Natural Science Foundation of the Jiangsu Higher Education Institutions of China under Grant No. 15KJB520015.

# References

1. Hashem, T., Kulik, L., Zhang, R.: Countering overlapping rectangle privacy attack for moving kNN queries. Inf. Syst. **38**(3), 430–453 (2013)
2. Rathi, N., Ghosh, S., Iyengar, A., et al.: Data privacy in non-volatile cache: Challenges, attack models and solutions. In: 2016 Proceedings of 21st IEEE Asia and South Pacific Design Automation Conference, Macao, pp. 348–353 (2016)
3. Wen, F., Li, X.: An improved dynamic ID-based remote user authentication with key agreement scheme. Comput. Electr. Eng. **38**(2), 381–387 (2012)
4. Guo, M., Pissinou, N., Iyengar, S.S.: Pseudonym-based anonymity zone generation for mobile service with strong adversary model. In: 2015 Proceedings of 12th IEEE Annual Consumer Communications and Networking Conference (CCNC), Las Vegas, USA, pp. 335–340 (2015)
5. Garg, S., Gentry, C., Halevi, S., et al.: Candidate indistinguishability obfuscation and functional encryption for all circuits. In: Proceedings of 54th IEEE Annual Symposium on Foundations of Computer Science, Berkeley, USA, pp. 40–49 (2013)
6. Ardagna, C.A., Cremonini, M., di Vimercati, S.D.C., et al.: An obfuscation-based approach for protecting location privacy. IEEE Trans. Dependable Secure Comput. **8**(1), 13–27 (2011)
7. Shokri, R.: Privacy games: optimal user-centric data obfuscation. In: Proceedings of Privacy Enhancing Technologies, Philadelphia, USA, vol. 2015, no. 2, pp. 299–315 (2015)
8. Ghinita, G., Kalnis, P., Skiadopoulos, S.: PRIVE: anonymous location-based queries in distributed mobile systems. In: Proceedings of 16th ACM International Conference on World Wide Web, Banff, Canada, pp. 371–380 (2007)
9. Ma, C., Zhou, C., Yang, S.: A voronoi-based location privacy-preserving method for continuous query in LBS. Int. J. Distrib. Sensor Net. **2015**, 1 (2015)
10. Gustav, Y.H., Wu, X., Ren, Y., Wang, Y., Zhang, F.: Achieving absolute privacy preservation in continuous query road network services. In: Luo, X., Yu, J.X., Li, Z. (eds.) ADMA 2014. LNCS, vol. 8933, pp. 279–292. Springer, Cham (2014). doi:10.1007/978-3-319-14717-8_22
11. Xu, J., Tang, X., Hu, H., Du, J.: Privacy-conscious locationbased queries in mobile environments. IEEE Trans. Parallel Distrib. Syst. **21**(3), 313–326 (2010)
12. POIs Data of Beijing (2016). http://www.datatang.com/data/44484

# A Measurement and Security Analysis of SSL/TLS Deployment in Mobile Applications

Yu Guo[1], Zigang Cao[1(✉)], Weiyong Yang[2], and Gang Xiong[1]

[1] Institute of Information Engineering, Chinese Academy of Sciences,
Beijing, China
caozigang@iie.ac.cn
[2] NARI Group Corporation, Nanjing, China

**Abstract.** Secure Socket Layer (SSL) and Transport Layer Security (TLS) have been widely used to provide security in communications. With the rapid development of mobile Internet, they are progressively applied in mobile applications. It is interesting to study the security of their usage. However, most of existed researches on SSL/TLS focus on the whole ecosystem, while few of them have in-depth study on the status quo of mobile security about SSL/TLS. In this paper, we measure the network behaviors of top 50 popular applications on Android and iOS platforms to reveal the security problems of SSL/TLS deployment in mobile Internet. A system is implemented which can extract the handshake parameters and inspect SSL deployment status. We also demonstrate some typical severe problems by performing man-in-the-middle (MITM) attacks against six applications. We believe our study is very consequential for SSL deployment on mobile platforms and the design of secure applications in the future.

**Keywords:** SSL · TLS · Mobile application security · Measurement · Android · iOS

## 1 Introduction

According to the report [1] published by China Internet Network Information Center (CNNIC) in December 2015, the amount of Chinese Internet users has reached 688 million and mobile Internet users account for 90.1% of it, which leads to a ubiquitous usage of mobile applications in people's daily life. However, almost every application has access to users' private information, and the problems raised by applications leaking users' sensitive data occur frequently. Therefore, it is legitimate to assess the security of mobile applications and improve it.

Secure Sockets Layer (SSL) and its successor Transport Layer Security (TLS) are widely used to provide end-to-end communication security for mobile applications. Although SSL/TLS protocols can be effectively against many types of network attacks, there are still various security problems due to unrated deployment of SSL/TLS in applications. As were shown in previous works [2], some mobile applications leak users' personally identification information (PII), while some applications suffer from the risk of being attacked by MITM [3].

© ICST Institute for Computer Sciences, Social Informatics and Telecommunications Engineering 2018
Q. Chen et al. (Eds.): ChinaCom 2016, Part I, LNICST 209, pp. 189–199, 2018.
DOI: 10.1007/978-3-319-66625-9_19

According to the previous works [2–4] on the usage of SSL/TLS protocols, we summarize three main factors that can jeopardize applications into insecure situations:

(1) Improper SSL/TLS deployment on an application.
(2) The usage of low-security parameters in SSL handshake, such as protocol version, cipher suites and so on. Early SSL/TLS versions have protocol flaws, and some of the algorithms used by SSL/TLS are weak, like DES or MD5 algorithms. In addition, the use of self-signed certificates results in risks.
(3) Incomplete certificate validation.

Considering that Android and iOS now account for the major share of the global mobile operating system market, we perform our measurement on Android and iOS mobile platforms. We choose the popular top 50 applications on each platform. We get the dataset via combining manual and automated methods, capturing each application's packets while it is used. Then we design and implement a system that can analyze these packets, detecting whether an application deploys SSL/TLS protocols, and extracting its SSL handshake parameters as well as certificate chains. Apart from the statistics and analysis, we also perform MITM experiments against applications using self-signed certificates and several representative applications.

In summary, this paper makes the following contributions:

- We demonstrate that sensitive data can be accessed easily in some applications, emphasizing the great significance of deploying SSL/TLS properly in mobile applications. We find that there are even a few applications leaking passwords over plain text.
- We design and implement a system for detecting the status of SSL deployment in applications and its security.
- We make statistics on the selection of SSL handshake parameters. We find that 14% of Android apps and 24% of iOS apps use a set of low-security parameters, which is vulnerable when facing attacks.
- We discover some certificate validation problems in several applications. Applications with self-signed certificates fail to resistant MITM attacks.
- Based on our results, we propose concrete recommendations on SSL deployment for application designers to provide more secure applications.

The remainder of this paper is structured as follows: in Sect. 2, we discuss related work. Section 3 explains the origin of our dataset and the methodology of our measurement. Our system is presented in this section as well. In Sect. 4, we illustrate our measurement results, propose concrete recommendations for SSL deployment and describe our future work. Finally, we conclude our study in Sect. 5.

## 2   Related Work

There have been a few previous works studying the ecosystem of SSL/TLS protocols and analyzing the improper usage of SSL/TLS. He et al. [4] designed a system for vetting the improper SSL usage which may cause vulnerabilities. Their system detects the source code to find design flaws of applications. Sounthiraraj et al. [5] also found

SSL validation vulnerabilities in the source code from Android applications. Thus, the major difference between their work and ours is that we focus on the network traffic generated by applications instead of the source code.

As for the disclosure of sensitive information, recent studies [2, 6] show that when using applications, the user is tracked by third parties. At the same time, the applications being used is leaking users' personally identifiable information without the users' knowledge. Balebako et al. [6] performed a study to reveal and control privacy leaks in mobile network traffic. Roesner et al. [7] presented a method to detect and resistant privacy leaks by the third party trackers. Egele et al. [8] detected privacy leaks in iOS applications. We also have concerns about privacy leaks from mobile applications. However, in this paper, we only discuss the privacy leaks resulted from improper SSL deployment.

Many works in the past have studied the correlation between the SSL handshake parameters and the SSL/TLS server's security. Levillain et al. [9] assessed the quality of https server by analyzing parameters included in the server's response after sending a stimuli to the server. He proposed criteria for assessing TLS quality, which consist of the protocol version, cipher suite, TLS extension, quality of certificate chain and so on. Pukkawanna et al. [10] conducted a research to classify the SSL servers into different security levels using SSL handshake parameters. We reference their understanding of SSL handshake parameters.

Pukkawanna et al. also proposed certificate CA to be an important measure to assess the security of SSL/TLS servers [10]. A certificate issued by a CA offering low-price or free certificates is likely to be a risky certificate. Besides, Georgiew et al. [11] tried MITM attacks against several applications and found over twenty certificate and hostname verification vulnerabilities. Trummer and Dalvi [3] used BurpSuite to detect applications' certificate validation. They found that 43 applications failed to validate trust chain and 59 applications failed to validate hostname matched. We also attempted MITM attack against applications using self-signed certificates, to reveal the security problems existing in mobile applications.

## 3  Measurement Method

In this paper, we focus on the mobile application security in terms of SSL/TLS protocols. This section describes the data sources and how we performed our measurement in detail.

### 3.1  Data Collection

Considering the better representation of all applications, we choose the top 50 applications on two major operating systems, iOS and Android. We use a spider to obtain the popular top applications list in the apple app store on Nov 12, 2015. The list contains applications' name, ranking, version, etc. We try to obtain the Android top popular application list at the same time. Because Google has no cooperation with the Chinese mainland, application rankings in Google play cannot represent the use of applications in China. So we select three main application markets in China, namely

360 mobile assistant, Tencent yingyongbao and Baidu mobile assistant. Then we combine the application rankings of these three markets and choose the top 50 popular applications on Android platform.

The basic method of obtaining the dataset is to capture packets when an application is used. First, we set up a wireless environment with 360 portable Wi-Fi. Then when the experimental device connects to the wireless, we capture the traffic flowing through the virtual wireless network card, which is generated by the device.

It should be noted that we not only capture the entire traffic of applications, but also keep the specific traffic of "critical behaviors" for further analysis. We define critical behaviors as operations involving or probably involving users' sensitive information when using applications. We list all critical behaviors used in our measurement in Table 1.

**Table 1.** List of critical behaviors.

| Critical behavior | Sensitive information it may involve |
|---|---|
| Register | User account, password, phone number, email address, user's personal information |
| Login | User account, password, phone number, email address |
| Modify password | Old password, new password, phone number, email address |
| Pay | User account, payment password |
| Upload/Download file | Document content |
| Chat on line | Conversation content |
| Send/Receive emails | Senders and recipients' email address, content of emails |

For applications on iOS platform, we capture packets of each application manually. The experiment device is an apple iPad air1 and its system is iOS 9.1. We try almost all functions of an application and capture packets with Wireshark and Commview.

For applications on Android device, we achieve a semi-automatic capture. We develop an application named Simulator. It consists of a client on the computer and a server on an Android device. We root a Nexus 5 with Android 5.0 system and install Simulator's server on it. Simulator can help us capture traffic generated by the device and send packets to the computer to save automatically. The only thing we have to do manually is to click the figures corresponding to the functions of each application.

### 3.2    Measurement System

After the data collection process, we get 1000 ".pcap" files (2000000 packets). According to the factors we proposed in Sect. 1, we wish to know how an application deploys SSL/TLS and what parameters its server selects during the SSL handshake. To address this problem, we design and implement a system.

Figure 1 presents the architecture of the system. In the pcap platform we put packets which were saved as ".pcap" format into it. These packets will be replayed and directed to a network card. Then the traffic flows into the TCP parser module. TCP parser module reassembles the TCP segments and restores the message. When the complete message is sent to the next module, the SSL parser module will recognize SSL traffic and discard non-SSL traffic. After that, SSL traffic is further parsed. It will extract parameters of three phases, Client Hello, Server Hello and Certificate. Parameters in Client Hello include client protocol version, host, cipher suites, compression methods, extensions and so on. So does this in server hello. In certificate phase, the module extracts the length of certificates, algorithm, issuer, subject and the validity. All these parameters are saved in "JSON" format and uniquely identified by the four-tuple (source IP address, destination IP address, source port and destination port). Moreover, the module extracts the corresponding certificate chain. The JSON files will be further processed and put into MongoDB database automatically. Finally, the analysis module does statistics and gives a preliminary statistical result.

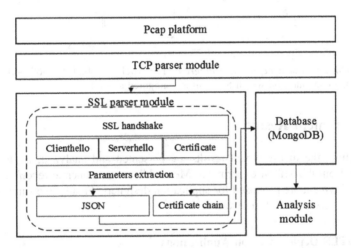

**Fig. 1.** System *Architecture*. Put the dataset into Pcap platform, then the data is parsed by TCP parser module and SSL parser module sequentially, generating JSON format files. These files are imported into the Database and analyzed by the Analysis module in the end.

### 3.3   MITM Experiment

As mentioned in Sect. 3.2, besides the parameters of Client Hello and Server Hello, we also extract certificate details and certificate chains. Generally, if an application uses a validated certificate issued by a well-known certificate authority (CA) for the server side, and the client side performs a correct certificate validation, it can protect users from man-in-the-middle (MITM) attack. Otherwise, it provides opportunities to MITM attacks. We perform MITM attack experiments to applications whose certificates are self-signed since they are probably vulnerable to MITM attacks.

We exploit SSLsplit [12], an open-source tool for MITM attacks against SSL/TLS encrypted network connections, to do the experiment. We use 360 portable Wi-Fi to build a wireless network and configure SSLsplit on Ubuntu. As described in Fig. 2, when the mobile device connects to the wireless, the traffic is intercepted by SSsplit. We keep the logs of that using a python script. If there is a non-empty log about 443 TCP ports and the applications on the device can be used normally, that means SSL traffic is decrypted and the communication has been compromised. In contrast, if there is no log about 443 TCP port or the size of 443 port log is zero, the application can resistant MITM attacks.

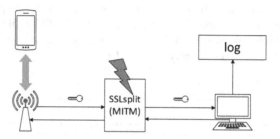

**Fig. 2.** MITM experiment *deployment diagram*. The wireless is built by 360 portable Wi-Fi plugged on the computer, on which SSLsplit is configured as well.

## 4    Measurement Results

In this section, the measurement results are presented and analyzed, as well as the discoveries from the MITM experiment. Meanwhile, some concrete recommendations on SSL deployment are proposed for application designers. Finally, we summarize our research and describe the future work.

### 4.1    SSL/TLS Deployment on Applications

Through the measurement, we discover that the SSL deployment status on applications can be classified into three types:

a. Deploy SSL/TLS protocols on all critical behaviors. *We name this type "all"*.
b. Only deploy SSL/TLS protocols on some of the critical behaviors. *We name this type "part"*.
c. Not deploy SSL/TLS protocols on any critical behaviors. This type includes two different cases. If an application uses proprietary protocols to encrypt communications, it is relatively secure although it does not deploy SSL/TLS protocols. However, applications using http or other protocols on all critical behaviors may have serious security problems. *We name these two cases "none-security" and "none-insecurity" separately*.

Among top 50 applications on iOS platform, 28 applications deploy SSL/TLS protocols on all critical behaviors. Three applications only deploy SSL/TLS on part of critical behaviors, still exposing sensitive data on non-SSL/TLS deployment critical behaviors. Finally, 19 applications do not deploy SSL/TLS protocols on any critical behaviors. Nine of them use proprietary protocols, Wechat, QQ, QQ music and other applications published by Tencent cooperation included. The rest of ten applications use http protocol on critical behaviors, causing lots of security problems. For example, MengDian, an e-commerce application, exposes users' payment password by plaintext. Table 2 lists applications on iOS platform which leak users' sensitive data.

**Table 2.** List of applications leaking users' sensitive data on iOS platform.

| Application | SSL deployment | Sensitive data exposed | Form (in http packets) |
|---|---|---|---|
| Baiduyun | None-insecurity | File uploaded and downloaded | Ciphertext |
| Mengdian | None-insecurity | Payment password | Plaintext |
| Dazhongdianping | None-insecurity | User name, login password | Ciphertext |
| Kuwo music | None-insecurity | User name, login password | Ciphertext |
| Kuaishou | None-insecurity | User name, login password | Ciphertext |
| XimalayaFM | None-insecurity | Phone number; login password | Plaintext; Ciphertext |
| Kugou music | None-insecurity | Phone number; login password | Plaintext; Ciphertext |
| Mojitianqi | None-insecurity | Phone number | Plaintext |
| Souhu vedio | None-insecurity | Login password | Plaintext |
| QQ mail | None-insecurity | Some details of email | Ciphertext |
| Qunaer travle | Part | Login password | Plaintext |
| Fanli | Part | Login password | Plaintext |
| Mogujie | Part | Login password | Ciphertext |

SSL deployment on Android platform has similar status with that on iOS. As shown in Fig. 3, 32 applications deploy SSL/TLS protocols on all critical behaviors. Six applications only deploy SSL/TLS on part of critical behaviors and 12 applications do not deploy SSL/TLS on any critical behavior, of which nine use proprietary protocols and three use http protocol. Table 3 lists applications leaking users' sensitive data on Android platform in detail.

In addition, applications with navigation functions such as Baidu map leak users' accurate location by plaintext in http packets. However, considering the large cost of deploying SSL/TLS on navigation, we do not define navigation as critical behavior. But these applications still need to make improvements on protecting users' location privacy.

From the results, we can see that there are a large number of applications that expose users' sensitive data. Specially, entertainment applications account for a substantial amount. E-commerce and tool applications with security issues also account for

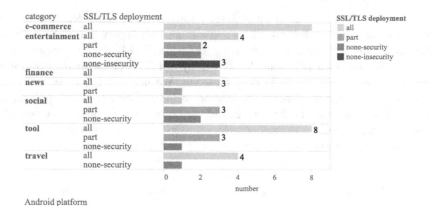

Android platform

**Fig. 3.** SSL deployment of different categories on Android platform

**Table 3.** List of applications leaking users' sensitive data on Android platform.

| Application | SSL deployment | Sensitive data exposed | Form (in http packets) |
|---|---|---|---|
| Kuwo music | None-insecurity | User account; login password | Plaintext |
| Souhu video | None-insecurity | Login password | Plaintext |
| Letv video | None-insecurity | User account, login password | Plaintext |
| XimalayaFM | Part | Phone number; login password | Plaintext; ciphertext |
| Baofeng video | Part | Phone number; login password | Plaintext; ciphertext |
| Baidu map | Part | User name; login password | Plaintext; ciphertext |
| Baidutieba | Part | User name; login password | Plaintext; ciphertext |
| Baiduyun | Part | User name; login password | Plaintext; ciphertext |
| Sina weibo | Part | Some detail of chat content | Plaintext; |

a large number. Application designers should be aware of the significance of deploying SSL/TLS protocols on critical behaviors and pay particular attention to those categories with serious security problems.

## 4.2 SSL Handshake Parameters

On iOS platform, 37.84% applications use TLS 1.0 version. Sina weibo and Qunaer travel completely use TLS 1.0 version and the others use a mix of TLS 1.0, 1.1 and 1.2 version. 5.4% applications use version 1.1 and 56.76% use version 1.2. There are 12 applications using RC4 encryption algorithm, which is weak and should not be used anymore [13]. Among them, Sina weibo and ICBC mobile bank use TLS 1.0 version as well as RC4 algorithm. This combination of parameters has great risks of being compromised. It is especially dangerous for ICBC mobile bank as a finance application. Besides, one application, 12306 railway, uses self-signed certificates.

On Android platform, 18.75% applications use TLS 1.0 version and the rest use TLS 1.2 version. There are seven applications using RC4 algorithm and two applications using self-signed certificates, which are 12306 railway and Iqiyi.

Table 4 shows the selection of SSL handshake parameters on iOS and Android. Due to many applications use not only one type of encryption algorithm, the sum of three algorithms in Table 4 is more than 100%.

**Table 4.** Selection of SSL handshake parameters on iOS and Android.

| Platform | TLS1.0 | TLS1.1 | TLS1.2 | AES_GCM | AES_CBC | RC4 |
|----------|--------|--------|--------|---------|---------|-----|
| iOS      | 37.84% | 5.4%   | 56.76% | 75.68%  | 27.03%  | 32.43% |
| Android  | 18.75% | \      | 81.25% | 71.05%  | 34.21%  | 18.42% |

The result shows that most applications prefer to use TLS 1.2 version and AES_GCM algorithm, which is a good phenomenon for application security. Thankfully, there is no application using SSL 2.0 or 3.0 version on neither of platforms. However, there are still many applications using the insecure algorithm, RC4. A combination of low TLS version and insecure algorithm can greatly reduce application security. The designers should attach importance to this.

### 4.3 MITM Experiment Results

In Sect. 4.2 we find that two applications use self-signed certificates, 12306 railway and Iqiyi. We perform MITM experiments on them, as well as four widely used applications from e-commerce and finance categories.

First, 12306 railway and Iqiyi can be compromised. When MITM attack is performed, there is no warning of abnormality and we can use the applications as usual. SSLsplit intercepts their SSL traffic and decrypts it. We can see sensitive data by ciphertext in decrypted packets.

Secondly, two e-commerce applications, Taobao and Jingdong cannot be compromised. SSLsplit hasn't intercepted their SSL traffic and they can work normally. We owe it to their use of proprietary protocols. However, there are still serious problems in Taobao. We can login a user's Taobao account using cookies in http packets instead of the user's account and password.

Finally, the finance application, Jingdong finance, can be compromised as well. But another finance application, Zhifubao, can resist MITM attack successfully. It warns the user with a certificate problem notification and prevents users to use it unless there is no MITM attack any more.

Therefore, the use of self-signed certificates is very dangerous and may be easily compromised by MITM attacks. Of course a successful resistance to MITM attack cannot guarantee communication security completely. However, the designers should avoid using self-signed certificates in applications.

## 4.4   Discussion

With the measurement results in Sect. 4.1, we try to compare the differences of application security between iOS and Android. However, we find that such a comparison is irrelevant. The first reason is that the popular top 50 applications are different on two platforms. The second reason is that we cannot guarantee an application has the same version on two top application lists. Without variable controlled, the comparison is meaningless.

Moreover, the measurement results in Sect. 4.2 are not complete. There are other correlations between SSL handshake parameters and communication security that we haven't taken into account.

Therefore, in the future, we plan to perform a variable controlled experiment to explore the differences of mobile security in terms of SSL/TLS among different platforms. Besides, we will improve our measurement on SSL handshake parameters and certificate validation of mobile applications.

## 5   Conclusion

In this paper, we measure the SSL/TLS deployment of the popular top 50 applications on iOS and Android platform. A system is designed and implemented to detect whether an application deploys SSL/TLS protocol and extract the SSL handshake parameters. The results show that 28% of the applications on iOS platform and 20% on Android platform have problems in deploying SSL/TLS protocols on critical behaviors, which can cause severe sensitive data exposure. By analyzing the SSL handshake parameters, we find that most applications use a high TLS version, but some still use weak algorithms and insecure certificates. Then, we perform MITM experiments against applications deploying insecure certificates and several representative applications. The results prove our guess that the former can be easily compromised by MITM attack. We propose concrete recommendations to designers based on our measurement results. Finally, we summarize the shortcomings of our measurement and describe the future work.

**Acknowledgments.** This work is supported by the Strategic Priority Research Program of the Chinese Academy of Sciences (No. XDA06030200), Xinjiang Uygur Autonomous Region Science and Technology Project (No. 201230123), and Beijing Natural Science Foundation (4164089).

## References

1. CNNIC 37th Statistical Report on Chinese Internet. http://tech.sina.com.cn/z/CNNIC37/
2. Ren, J., Rao, A., Lindorfer, M., et al.: Recon: revealing and controlling privacy leaks in mobile network traffic. arXiv preprint arXiv:1507.00255 (2015)
3. Trummer, T., Dalvi, T.: Mobile SSL failures (2015)
4. He, B., Rastogi, V., Cao, Y., et al.: Vetting SSL usage in applications with SSLINT. In: 2015 IEEE Symposium on Security and Privacy (SP), pp. 519–534. IEEE (2015)

5. Sounthiraraj, D., Sahs, J., Greenwood, G., et al.: SMV-hunter: large scale, automated detection of SSL/TLS man-in-the-middle vulnerabilities in android apps. In: Proceedings of the 21st Annual Network and Distributed System Security Symposium, NDSS 2014 (2014)
6. Balebako, R., Jung, J., Lu, W., et al.: Little brothers watching you: raising awareness of data leaks on smartphones. In: Proceedings of the Ninth Symposium on Usable Privacy and Security, p. 12. ACM (2013)
7. Roesner, F., Kohno, T., Wetherall, D.: Detecting and defending against third-party tracking on the web. In: Proceedings of the 9th USENIX Conference on Networked Systems Design and Implementation, p. 12. USENIX Association (2012)
8. Egele, M., Kruegel, C., Kirda, E., et al.: PiOS: detecting privacy leaks in iOS applications. In: NDSS Network and Distributed System Security Symposium (2011)
9. Levillain, O., Ébalard, A., Morin, B., et al.: One year of SSL internet measurement. In: Proceedings of the 28th Annual Computer Security Applications Conference, pp. 11–20. ACM (2012)
10. Pukkawanna, S., Kadobayashi, Y., Blanc, G., et al.: Classification of SSL servers based on their SSL handshake for automated security assessment (2014)
11. Georgiev, M., Iyengar, S., Jana, S. et al.: The most dangerous code in the world: validating SSL certificates in non-browser software. In: Proceedings of the 2012 ACM Conference on Computer and Communications Security, pp. 38–49. ACM (2012)
12. Transparent SSL/TLS interception. http://www.roe.ch/SSLsplit
13. Sheffer, Y., Holz, R., Saint-Andre, P.: Summarizing known attacks on transport layer security (TLS) and datagram TLS (DTLS) (2015)

# A Method for Countering Snooping-Based Side Channel Attacks in Smart Home Applications

Jingsha He, Qi Xiao[✉], and Muhammad Salman Pathan

School of Software Engineering, Beijing Engineering Research Center for IoT
Software and Systems, Beijing University of Technology, Beijing 100124, China
jhe@bjut.edu.cn, xqnssa@emails.bjut.edu.cn,
muhammad.salman@nu.edu.pk

**Abstract.** In recent years, with the rapid development of the Internet of Things (IoT), the information technology has been widely used in smart home applications. On the other hand, smart home technology closely related to people's privacy, which is not much considered by smart home vendors, making the privacy protection of smart home a hot research topic. Traditional encryption methods can ensure the security of the transmission process, but it can hardly resist the side channel attacks. Adversaries can analyze the radio frequency signals of wireless sensors and timestamp series to acquire the Activity of Daily Living (ADL). The most simple and efficient way to counter side channel attacks is to add noise into the transmitted data sequence. In this paper, we propose an improved method based on Logistic Regression (LR), which can be adapted to network status to protect the privacy of residents in smart home environments. Compared with other similar approaches, our method has the advantage of low energy consumption, low latency, strong adaptability and good effect of privacy protection.

**Keywords:** Smart home · Side channel attack · Privacy · Logistic Regression

## 1 Introduction

Smart home is one of the important branches of the Internet of Things (IoT) which relies on wireless sensors to sense and collect activity and status information. These sensors can sense particular phenomena, convert the sensed information into data, process the data and then transmit the data onto a sink node for further analysis [1]. For example, the measurement of temperature, humidity, luminosity, noise levels, presence, etc., can provide useful data to interpret a physical activity in space and time in order to determine the activity of a person and thus can contribute in detecting unusual situations and emergency cases [2]. The sensed data contains much private information of the resident, however, while the societal concerns of smart home technology evolution in relation to the privacy and security of the citizen appear to be still at an embryonic stage [3]. The acquired ADLs can help to improve the quality of life, but it can also be exposed to the attacker, therefore, the issue of privacy protection in smart home environments has become one of the most challenging issues.

© ICST Institute for Computer Sciences, Social Informatics and Telecommunications Engineering 2018
Q. Chen et al. (Eds.): ChinaCom 2016, Part I, LNICST 209, pp. 200–207, 2018.
DOI: 10.1007/978-3-319-66625-9_20

Compared to other wireless sensor networks, the type and number of sensors in the smart home are similar to general homes. And most sensors are operated in the event-triggered mode, where sensor data is transmitted only when a relevant event is detected. We can image that when an event occurs, the transmission will be triggered immediately. While data encryption algorithms can only ensure the security of the sensor data during the transmission, however the radio frequency of the transmission can be revealed to the adversary who has the ability to listen to the global transmission state. The adversary can use a side channel attack method to analyze the transmission sequence and can acquire the ADLs of the resident. For example, Fingerprint And Timing-based Snooping (FATS) attacks only need the timestamp and the fingerprint of each radio message, where a fingerprint is a set of features of an RF waveform that are unique to a particular transmitter [4]. The most simple and effective method to resist side channel attacks is to add fake message onto the transmission sequence to make the adversary unable to distinguish between fake and real messages. However, due to the limitations of the communication bandwidth, battery energy and computing power of wireless sensor nodes, the amount of fake data should be added as low as possible.

There has been an extensive study of the approaches to protect the privacy of residents in a smart home environment. These solutions are mainly based on a fixed frequency or probability models, thus having the major drawbacks like delaying in reporting the real events until the next scheduled transmission. For smart home scenarios, such delay of reporting real sensed data can cause the degradation of the quality of service (QoS) in many applications [5]. Some of the applications like intelligent sensing, the delay can generally not be tolerated, where the states of the sensors must be received in a real timely fashion for making the corresponding responses. As the delay problem is concerned, Park et al. proposed an improved method based on behavioral semantics. But the method heavily depends on the accuracy of prediction, if the prediction of the next activity provides an inaccurate answer, the added fake messages will not be enough to affect the statistical analysis. In this paper, we propose an improved method to resist the side channel attacks based on logistic regression that can be adapted to the network state. That is, when the traffic is heavy and no ADL happens, the frequency of adding fake data should be automatically reduced. When the real event occurs, right time will be chosen to add noise to protect the real events.

The rest of this paper is organized as follows. In Sect. 2, we review some existing solutions. In Sect. 3, we describe our method in detail. In Sect. 4, we will compare our method to some other solutions. In Sect. 5, we have given the conclusion of this approach.

## 2 Related Work

The ConstRate (Sending packets at a fixed frequency) model, all the sensor nodes send the packets according to the same transmission intervals. Thus, the real events must send the packets until the next transmission. So the method can achieve the remarkable work to resist the static analysis attack. Obviously, the ConstRate model has a congenital deficiency: the delay depends on the transmission interval which is half of the interval. Also it is difficult to determine an appropriate transmission interval in the

ConstRate Model. The delay will vary with the time interval. When the time interval increases, the delay time will also increase. And the amount of fake messages and additional energy consumption will be increased significantly.

Shao et al. proposed the FitProbRate model that aims to improve the deficiencies of ConstRate model. The core idea is to make the intervals follow the specific probability distribution. When a real event occurred, the algorithm will start looking for a minimum interval which obey the distribution of index distribution to send. When the real event is sparse, the FitProbRate model will get a good performance, and compared with the ConstRate model the delay will be reduced. On the contrary, the real event triggered frequently, the delay will bigger than other models.

Park et al. proposed a model which based on adding several fake packets to the transmission sequence [6]. The model adds fake packets lie on the events that will happen in the future. The first step is to forecast the activity through the status of the sensor nodes and then the fake messages will be generated according to the prediction. Even an attacker has the ability to listen to the transmission of all the sensors, it could only predict the wrong ADLs. However, the shortcoming of the model is that the effect depends on the answer of the prediction. If the prediction model gives a wrong forecast, the fake packets will pall on the protection of the ADLs. Obviously, the stability of the model is lower than these two models mentioned above.

The purpose of adding fake packets to the transmission sequence is to make the attacker can't pick out the fake packets from all the RF radios. For the top two models above, the interval of all the packets is obey to the same distribution. It is assumed that the attacker have the ability to listen to the RF radio of the whole wireless sensor network. And make the model effectively, the transmission sequence must have the significant confidence to make sure that the adversary couldn't determine the real radio is contained in which intervals [7]. That is, if the transmission sequence which contains the fake packets in sending real messages has the sufficient randomness, the adversary cannot recognize the fake data from the real messages, and the ADLs of the residents will be protected. In our method, we have made enough randomness between fake and real data to ensure the attacker couldn't recognize the fake messages. As for the load of traffic is concerned, the more closer to the sink node, the larger data is needed to forward. If all the sensors send the packets follow the same distribution, the sensor node near the sink node will be too heavy to forward packets. Therefore, it is necessary to make the sensor node sends fake data packets adaptively according to the network status.

Considering the particularity of the wireless sensor network and the sensitivity of the smart home, it is important to think over the privacy, energy consumption and latency of the WSN while designing the noisy based privacy protection models. For the effect of privacy protection, the noise data should not be recognized, but also makes the correct recognition rate of the behavior low enough. In other words, either the identification of the behavior should be wrong, or can't recognize the true behavior. As for energy consumption, it cannot be a good privacy protection model, if the implementation of the model greatly reduces the lifetime of the WSN. We should consider the average of traffic load to prolong the lifetime of the sensor network. Latency is the main indicator of the QoS. If the latency is too long, it can lose the meaning of intelligence. As for the delay, a good model should make the delay as small as possible. Especially in the automatic adjudication environment, the sink node use the long delayed messages is meaningless.

## 3  Proposed Method

In this section, we have introduced our method. The logistic regression will be used to judge whether the fake messages should be sent or not, and named as hypothesis function. At first, the sensor node will acquire the current state, and normalize the data by a simple process. Then, input the processed data to the hypothesis function to decide whether to send the fake message. For each sensor node, the parameters of the hypothesis function will be different. And the different parameter will be trained by the sink node through supervised learning.

At the very beginning of our method. All of the sensor nodes in the sensor network will send fake messages with a fixed time-window. The detailed procedure is described in Fig. 1. The sensor node needs three variables to plug into the hypothesis function, to determine whether the fake data should be sent or not. These three variables are traffic state, time and send density, represented by $x_1$, $x_2$, $x_3$. We collected the traffic state and send density in the period of the block time. We present the real-time transmission times as TT, which consists of the send times of themselves and the forwarding times from other sensor nodes. And we use TT to divide by TrMax to represent the current traffic situation, where the TrMax is the max transmission times of all the sensor nodes in the block time. In order to unify the time, we map the current timestamp to the region of [0, 24], and presents as $x_2$. As for the send density, we use the Send Times (ST) to be divided by BlockMax to represent the send density, where the BlockMax is the block interval divided by time-window. When these three parameters are collected, the ANS could be calculated by the hypothesis function. If the ANS is greater than 0.5, fake

---

**Algorithm 1:** Sensor node checks for sending fake messages
**Repeat**
$x_1 = TT/TrMax$ ;
$x_2 = (nowtime - date(now))/3600$;
$x_3 = ST/BlockMax$;
$ANS = 1/(1 + exp(-\theta^T x))$
**if** $ANS \geq 0.5$ **then**
    wait (rand (0, window));
    send ({sensor_id : sensor_id, traffic_load: $x_1$,time: $x_2$,is_fake:1});
    fail_fake = 0;
    window = initial window;
  **else**
    fail_fake = fail_fake+1; //record does not send fake data times
    **if** $fail\_fake \geq max\_times$ **then** window =2*window;
    //the time window becomes double
**end if**
**until** next window

---

**Fig. 1.** Sensor node checks for sending fake messages

massage should be sent after a random time interval. Otherwise the algorithm will judge whether to send the messages at long intervals, if so, the time-window would be increased. Once the real data is sent, the time-window will be recovered again.

Figure 2 Shows the detail of the learning algorithm. Each sensor node has its own different parameters, the learning algorithm will deal with all the data and calculates θ for each sensor node respectively. As for each dataset from different sensor nodes are concerned. Before the learning algorithm, the received data should be labeled. The main purpose of labels is to mark the fake data, labeled with 1 indicates that fake data should be sent, labeled with 0 indicates that the fake data should not be sent. As for the learning algorithm, Firstly, we calculate the cost by using the square difference method, just as the J(θ) in the Algorithm 2, the m in J(θ) is the number of training samples. And then the gradient descent algorithm is used to find the θ that makes the J(θ) obtain the global minimum [9]. When the learning algorithm is completed, the θ should be handed out to the sensor node and should be plugged into the hypothesis function.

---

**Algorithm 2: Sink node training the sensor data**
**Input: the set of all sensor data X**
**Output: $\theta$**
**Foreach X as $X_i$**
Label the $x_i$ *by* traffic status
**End Foreach**
**Foreach X as $X_i$**

$$J(\theta) = \frac{1}{2m} \sum_{i=1}^{m} \left( h_\theta \left( X^{(i)} \right) - y^i \right)^2$$

Repeat

$$\theta_j^{(i)} := \theta_j^{(i)} - \alpha \frac{\partial}{\partial \theta_j} J(\theta)$$

Until Convergent
**End Foreach**
Hand out all parameters

---

**Fig. 2.** Sink node training sensor data

## 4    Evaluation

In this section, we will first introduce the method and settings of the experiment. And then will do the experiment to compare the effect of privacy protection and delay with the ConstRate Model and FitProbRate Model. We have used the public dataset related to accurate activity recognition in a Home Setting [8] for our experiment.

In order to evaluate the effects of the privacy, we studied the side channel attack method in a smart home. The common step of the side channel attack is to cluster the sensor data to the reasoning for the number of rooms in the home. The purpose of the FitProbRate model and ConstRate model are to disturb the attacker to cluster the sensor to a wrong classification. In our experiment we use the cluster accuracy to evaluate the protection model [5]. If the clustering accuracy is approximate to 1, the clustering results will equal to the number of rooms and the sensor distribution is the same as the clustering results. In contrast, if the clustering results are completely inconsistent with the actual room distribution, the ADL will be perfectly protected. Consequently, the lower the cluster accuracy will be, the better effect of privacy protection will be achieved. In addition, the Ratio is calculated by the number of fake messages divided by the number of real messages.

As shown in Fig. 3, with the incensement of the Ratio, the clustering accuracy of these three model decreased gradually. The clustering accuracy of the ConstRate model maintained at a low level. Our method and the FitProbRate model are affected by the Ratio, because when the Ratio is increased, the clustering accuracy is declined, And when the ratio is in the range of (5, 15), the clustering accuracy between our method and FitProbRate model has a wide margin, and the FitProbRate model has a good performance than our method. When the amount of fake messages is low, the Fit-ProbRate model has been well-distributed than our method. So our method is lower in accuracy than the FitProbRate model in terms of clustering accuracy in the range of (5, 15). When the Ratio is greater than 15, the gap between our method and FitPro-bRate model is very small. Also, we have ensured that when the clustering accuracy is lower than 0.4, the side channel attack will be hard to analyze the ADL.

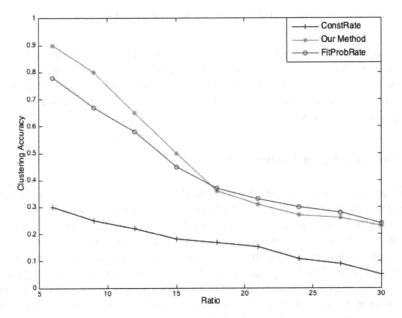

**Fig. 3.** The relation between ratio and clustering accuracy

As shown in Fig. 4 with the incensement of the Ratio, the latency of ConstRate model and FitProbRate model decreased gradually, and the latency of the ConstRate model is the longest of the three models or method, which is the half of the trans-mission interval. Compared with the ConstRate model, the FitProbRate model has significantly declined the latency. Figure 4 displays the average of the latency of these

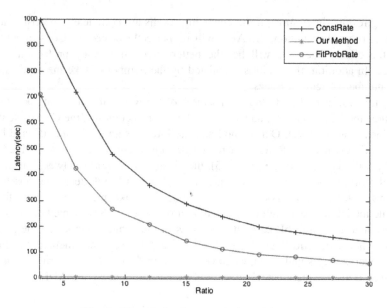

**Fig. 4.** The relation between ratio and latency

three model, the latency of the FitProbRate model related to the density of the transmission, when the transmission frequency of the real event is raised up, the latency will be increased. On the contrary, when the transmission is sparse, the latency time will be declined. Consequently, the latency of the FitProbRate model is affected by the frequency of the real events.

## 5   Conclusion and Future Work

In this paper, we have proposed a new method to resist the side channel attack. Compared with other models, our method has the advantage of adaptive network status, low latency and low power consumption. In the context of the smart home environment, when the user goes to work and when comes back to home from work or when go to sleep etc., these are likely to be the scope of privacy protection. The attacker can infer these living habits through analyzing the density of the transmission sequence. In the future, we plan to make our method fit the daily routines to the popular routine of almost people. Even if the attacker gains the daily routines, also cannot distinguish the routines of the particular prey. In a word, the privacy plays an essential role in the smart home, we should pay more attention to the privacy protection in smart home.

**Acknowledgement.** The work in this paper has been supported by Beijing Natural Science Foundation (4142008), National Nature Science Foundation of China (61272500) and National High-tech R&D Program (863 Program) (2015AA017204).

# References

1. Theoharidou, M., Tsalis, N., Gritzalis, D.: Smart Home Solutions: Privacy Issues. Handbook of Smart Homes, Health Care and Well-Being, pp. 1–14. Springer, Cham (2014)
2. Alami, A., Benhlima, L., Bah, S.: An overview of privacy preserving techniques in smart home wireless sensor networks. In: 10th International Conference on Intelligent Systems: Theories and Applications, pp. 1–4. IEEE Press, Rabat (2015)
3. Sanchez, I., Satta, R., Fovino, I.N., Baldini, G.: Privacy leakages in smart home wireless technologies. In: International Carnahan Conference on Security Technology, pp. 1–6. IEEE Press, Rome (2014)
4. Srinivasan, V., Stankovic, J., Whitehouse, K.: Protecting your daily in-home activity information from a wireless snooping attack. In: International Conference on Ubiquitous Computing, pp. 202–211. ACM Press, Seoul (2008)
5. Park, H., Park, T., Sang, H.S.: A comparative study of privacy protection methods for smart home environments. Int. J. Smart Home 7, 1–12 (2013)
6. Park, H., Basaran, C., Park, T., Son, S.H.: Energy-efficient privacy protection for smart home environments using behavioral semantics. J. Sens. 14, 16235–16257 (2014)
7. Yang, Y., Shao, M., Zhu, S., Cao, G.: Towards statistically strong source anonymity for sensor networks. In: 27th Conference on Computer Communications. pp. 51–55. IEEE INFOCOM, Phoenix (2008)
8. Van Kasteren, T., Noulas, A., Englebienne, G.: Accurate activity recognition in a home setting. In: International Conference on Ubiquitous Computing, pp. 1–9. ACM Press, Seoul (2008)
9. Song, Y., Cai, Q., Nie, F., Zhang, C.: Semi-supervised additive logistic regression: a gradient descent solution. J. Tsinghua Sci. Technol. 12, 638–646 (2007)

# Coding Schemes

# FPGA-Based Turbo Decoder Hardware Accelerator in Cloud Radio Access Network (C-RAN)

Shaoxian Tang[✉], Zhifeng Zhang, Jun Wu[✉], and Hui Zhu

College of Electronics and Information Engineering,
Tongji University, Shanghai 201804, People's Republic of China
{1433273,zhangzf,wujun,1433250}@tongji.edu.cn

**Abstract.** In the Cloud Radio Access Network (C-RAN), the Software Defined Radio (SDR) is combined with multi-mode base stations (BSs) together. A lot of BSs are centralized in a Cloud center, the centralized BSs need high bandwidth and cost-effective resource allocation. Since BSs may also run on the virtualized machines, the hardware accelerator can provide faster signal processing speed. This paper uses the Xen virtualization to set up a C-RAN platform, where the SDR and the FPGA hardware connected with PCIe interface to server as the signal processing hardware accelerator. Experimental results demonstrate the turbo decoder accelerator based on the FPGA and Xen platform has good performance to support the SDR signal processing with high bandwidth. The turbo decoder hardware accelerator solved the timing constraints in C-RAN.

**Keywords:** C-RAN · SDR · Xen · FPGA · Hardware accelerator · Turbo decoder

## 1 Introduction

Radio Access Network (RAN) is wireless communication infrastructure. However, with the costs of distributed base stations deployment increasing, the mobile operators have to develop a new evolved network architecture. Centralized base station pool with the cloud computing-based architecture supports 2G, 3G, 4G and future wireless communication standards. C-RAN is an eco-friendly and energy efficient infrastructure. The base stations can be reduced with centralized processing of this architecture [5]. The C-RAN emerged to offer a low cost, high reliability, low latency and high bandwidth green network architecture [8].

In order to support multi-network, the operators usually should establish multi-mode base stations (such as GSM, UMTS and LTE), which increase costs. The SDR meets the multi-standards for low cost operation by software reconfiguration. The SDR platform can be implemented when the large scale Baseband Unit (BBU) pool has high-speed and low-latency interconnection. The BBU

© ICST Institute for Computer Sciences, Social Informatics and Telecommunications Engineering 2018
Q. Chen et al. (Eds.): ChinaCom 2016, Part I, LNICST 209, pp. 211–220, 2018.
DOI: 10.1007/978-3-319-66625-9_21

with virtual BS pool is shown in Fig. 1. Therefore, the SDR with open platform will become one of the mainstream products.

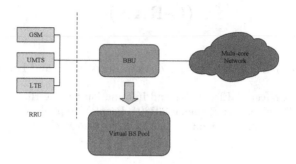

**Fig. 1.** Virtual base station pool

In the SDR base stations, the baseband process includes some computation intensive tasks. Therefore, using the hardware accelerator instead of software can reduce the processing time of these tasks such as turbo decoder, MIMO decoder and FFT etc. Since the speed of the hardware operation has greatly improved, taking advantage of hardware resources is a good option. Virtualization is the technology to create a virtual version of something, such as computer hardware platforms, operating system, storage devices and network resources. Through the virtualization, we can replace many small physical servers by several larger physical servers to increase the utilization of hardware resources such as CPU and FPGA. Therefore, using the virtual base stations can reduce the cost and fully utilize the hardware resources. Xen is a hypervisor that allows multiple computer operating systems to execute on the same computer hardware concurrently. Xen has para-virtualization, which uses special API instead of simulate hardware to modify the guest OS [1]. So we can use the guest OS to access hardware through the hypervisor with the special API. Using the para-virtualization can minimize the performance loss.

The BS based on the SDR platform has more choices to implement the signal processing, not only uses CPU in the server. The multi-core GPP-SDR platform was proposed in Sora, a programmable software radio platform on PC architectures [6]. However, it only has single terminal to use the platform. Digital Signal Processor (DSP) have high capabilities of floating point, which combined with the GPP has improved the BBU processing density and reduced the power consumption effectively. There are some SDR platforms based on FPGA [4] and DSP [3].

FPGA virtualization, such as [2] brings FPGA as a shareable resources in the cloud, which demonstrate that FPGA can be used in the C-RAN for the signal processing with good performance. pvFPGA [7] also runs in the Xen virtualized environment and uses FPGA to accelerate the process. It uses the accelerator to compute FFT with Xilinx IP core. So using the accelerator for decoding in the SDR base stations can reduce the overall time effectively.

In this paper, we design a turbo decoder hardware accelerator in the SDR base stations based on FPGA and Xen virtualization. The rest of paper is organized as follows. Section 2 is the system design. Section 3 is the detailed design of the turbo decoder in FPGA. Section 4 gives simulation and evaluation of the turbo decoder hardware accelerator. Finally, Sect. 5 concludes the paper.

## 2 System Design

The system has the structure shown in Fig. 2, which includes the SDR platform based on general purpose computer server, and the custom designed hardware accelerators. Virtualization is utilized to support multiple BSs on one physical server. Figure 2 is a simplified SDR platform with only one single virtual machine. The Guest OS is based on Xen virtualization. Although only one guest OS is showed, the platform supports multiple guest OS running on the host OS, each corresponds to one virtualized BS. The system has hardware accelerators to meet the requirement of high bandwidth baseband signal processing. The accelerator is implemented with FPGA, using Verilog HDL and IP cores provided by Xilinx. PCIe interface is used to support data exchanges between the hardware accelerator and the host OS. The Xen VMM and the PCIe backend driver is located in the host OS, and the front-end driver is in the Guest OS, which is used for transfer the data between the SDR platform and backend driver.

### 2.1 Virtualized SDR Platform

The general server system runs Xen hypervisor, also called Virtual Machine Monitor (VMM), to build the virtualized SDR platform. The architecture of Xen is shown in Fig. 3. The SDR platform is located in the Guest OS (VM), uses the front-end driver to communicate with Dom0 (a privileged virtual domain). The

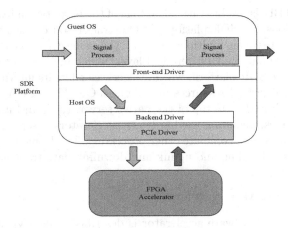

**Fig. 2.** System design

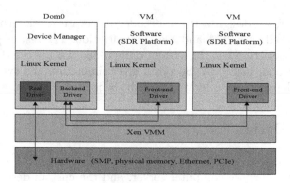

**Fig. 3.** Xen architecture

data transfer in Xen VMM is made up of three different paths, namely the shared memory, the event channel and grant table. Large data is exchanged through shared memory to achieve high throughput without memory copy, and the message use event channel and grant table to transfer requests and small amount of information between Dom0 and other VMs. Supporting virtually centralized BS, or in other words, supporting multiple BS in one physical server requires a significant higher throughput of encoded and decoded data in compares with the traditional distributed BS structure. To meet such a requirement, PCIe is used as data transfer interface between server and the FPGA-based hardware accelerator. For the virtual platform, we implement the PCIe backend driver in Dom0 and front-end driver in VMs. The SDR platform can use the front-end driver as the real PCIe driver to write encoded data and read decoded data after computing process.

## 2.2 Cloud Base Stations

The centralized BBUs need to take advantage of the base station resources. In the cloud base stations, the SDR platform can abstract resources as a open interface and share them between multiple users at the same time. In the cloud base station, we care about the LTE physical layer, which includes signal processing. In our system, the SDR platform within the server offers its interface to users to take advantage of virtual resources in the guest OS. The FPGA are connected to the server with PCIe. On top of the native server, the VMM manages all the hardware resources, including the hardware accelerators. Users in the VMs use the accelerator and then complete other processing. The Dom0 is responsible for the accelerators scheduling and uplink and downlink data transmission control.

## 2.3 FPGA Hardware Accelerator

In this section, the hardware accelerator is described. Xilinx virtex-6 FPGA is used as the hardware resources to implement the turbo decoder and the PCIe interface. The design of hardware accelerator include two sub-modules: PCIe interface and turbo decoder logic.

**PCIe Interface.** For supporting high channel bandwidth, the LTE needs to finish decoding process as fast as possible. The requirement is to finish it in 1 ms for a sub-frame. We use Xilinx PCIe IPcore v1.7 for the PCIe and DMA design. The PCIe interface has a transfer speed of 400 MB/s. Based on the calculation, a data transfer interface based on PCIe can meet the bandwidth requirement of our experimental system, supporting read and write operation at the same time. The actual data driver transfer data with FPGA module via the PCIe data acquisition card. The PCIe interface use DMA to control the encoded data transform the server data pool to the FIFO in FPGA decoder layer. The block size in data pool is from 4 KB to 1 MB, we can reconfigure it when the driver is loaded.

**Turbo Decoder Logic.** The detailed design of turbo decoder is shown in next section.

## 3 Turbo Decoder Design

The decoder is used with a compared encoder to provide an extremely effective way of transmitting data reliably over noisy data channels. The turbo decoder operates very well under low signal-to-noise conditions and provides a performance close to the theoretical optimal performance. The turbo code has good error correction performance, it has been widely used in wireless communication.

Turbo decoder has long interleaving length and need iterate many times, so it has large delay to get the decoding results. For the CPU, it takes very long time to process the decoding operation. We use FPGA instead of CPU for turbo decoding. The FPGA has high clock frequency and parallel processing, all of which can speed up the decoding operation.

### 3.1 Interface Design

The data needs to use the soft decision input and output, the data received from the SDR platform is 16 bits. Through the quantization, 8 bits (include 5 integer bits and 3 fractional bits) data is input to the decoder accelerator. The PCIe interface has 64 bits width and it can transfer 64 bits data in one clock cycle. So we can use it transfer two groups data at the same clock cycle. The algorithm is known as the Max-scale algorithm, which is a simplified algorithm based on the Log-Map algorithm.

### 3.2 Design of Turbo Decoder

Figure 4 shows the architecture of turbo decoder. It has three layers.

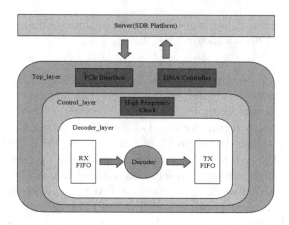

**Fig. 4.** Turbo decoder design

**Top Layer.** PCIe hardware interface and the DMA controller is in the top layer. The PCIe driver in the FPGA coordinates with the driver in server to transfer data and control signal.

**Control Layer.** FPGA reset the decoder core upon the power is on, and it is always waiting for the encoded data and signals input. When the data and parameters are delivered into the FPGA through PCIe, the control layer sends the parameters to the decoder layer first, such as the data block size, reset signal and data count information. Then the encoded data is sent to decoder layer for decoding. This layer also catch the decoded data from decoder layer and send it to the PCIe driver in server with the DMA controller.

**Decoder Layer.** The decoder layer includes the turbo decoder intellectual property core (IP core) which is the Xilinx IP core for the 3GPP LTE turbo decoder. The main interfaces of the IP core are data input, data output and control signals. We use FIFO to cache data and isolate asynchronous clock between DMA and decoder. The decoder core use 250 MHz clock frequency to achieve higher data throughput while the data transfer clock frequency is 62.5 MHz. When the control layer receives control signal and the encoded data, the information is written into the corresponding RX FIFO in the decoder layer. If the decoder core is free and the data is in the RX FIFO, the data would be transferred into the core.

The decoder layer masks the invalid data into the RX FIFO, which comes from the entire block data transfer through the DMA. After the decoding operation, the decoded data is put into the TX FIFO. At the same time, control layer detect the TX FIFO status and the valid data is read. When the SDR platform receives the decoded data from the PCIe driver, the whole operation is completed.

### 3.3    Pipeline Process

We write and read data simultaneously with the full-duplex mode by PCIe interface. For the encoded data, the data length ranges from to 24 KB for all 188 different code length in the range of 40 to 6144 bits. The average time for writing data into decoder is about 24 μs and for the reading data from decoder is 10 μs. Taking the decoding stage into consideration, we can make the overall process pipelined. Figure 5 shows the pipelined process for the data write, decoding computation and data read. For the pipelined process, each data block decoding time can be the maximum of reading data, decoding and writing data. In order to use the pipeline operation and adapt to single user, the decoder will compute every data block independently.

**Fig. 5.** Pipeline process

### 3.4    Implementation of Turbo Decoder

The proposed layers of the hardware accelerator is implemented by Verilog HDL at a structural level and then synthesized with Xilinx Synthesis Technology (XST). Then it was placed and routed using ISE Implement Design. After that, the programming file is generated for the FPGA to process the turbo decoder. The implementation results can be illustrated by the Table 1. It shows the utilization of the FPGA resources.

**Table 1.** Resource utilization

| Resource | Used | Available | Utilization |
|----------|------|-----------|-------------|
| Slice register | 45208 | 301440 | 14% |
| Slice LUT | 28955 | 150720 | 19% |
| 36 Kb block RAM | 98 | 416 | 23% |
| 18 Kb block RAM | 56 | 832 | 6% |

There are a number of factors which influence the throughput of the FPGA accelerator, such as the processing clock frequency, iterations and algorithm type. Table 2 shows the factors we set to increase the decoder throughput. Within the decoder layer, we use higher clock frequency to decode than the data transfer. The accelerator has the same number of iterations and algorithm type with software implementation, which can compare the performance fairly. We use the

**Table 2.** Throughput factors

| Factors | Settings |
|---|---|
| Data transfer clock frequency | 62.5 MHz |
| Processing clock frequency | 250 MHz |
| Iterations | 6 |
| Algorithm type | Max-scale |
| Processing units | 8 |
| Parallel data input/output width | 2 words (64 bits) |

maximum processing units and the parallel data input/output width in the IP core to achieve higher throughput. The number of processing units is six, and the parallel data input/output width is 64 bits which matches PCIe interface width.

# 4    Simulation and Evaluation

In order to minimize the overhead and reduce the time consumption, we can simulate the turbo decoder to evaluate the costs. Xilinx ISE and Modelsim are used to design and simulate the turbo decoder.

Table 3 shows the simulation decoding time for the code length from 40 bits to 6144 bits, including write data time, decoding time and read data time. Because the turbo code rate is 1/3, so the encoded data length is 3 times longer than the decoded data. The input data can be calculated immediately while all the valid data input into the RX FIFO, and the invalid data can be masked by the decoder layer. However, because of the characteristic of the DMA, all the block data should be send to the data pool, and then the driver can read the decoded data from this block. So the read data time is 10 μs for every single code length. In order to reduce this time consumption, we choose the minimize block size: 4 KB for the DMA data transmission.

**Table 3.** Simulation decoding time

| Code length | Data input | Decoding | Data output |
|---|---|---|---|
| 40 bits | 0.5 μs | 25.1 μs | 10 μs |
| 512 bits | 4.2 μs | 30.1 μs | 10 μs |
| 1024 bits | 8.3 μs | 31.8 μs | 10 μs |
| 2048 bits | 16.5 μs | 32.5 μs | 10 μs |
| 3008 bits | 24.2 μs | 38.4 μs | 10 μs |
| 4032 bits | 32.4 μs | 45.2 μs | 10 μs |
| 5184 bits | 41.6 μs | 52.1 μs | 10 μs |
| 6016 bits | 48.3 μs | 59.5 μs | 10 μs |

Figure 6 shows the experimental results of decoding time for the code length from 40 bits to 6016 bits. The hardware accelerator decoding time for the max code length is almost one tenth of the software decoding. And the average decoding time is one eighth of the software decoding. So we can use the hardware accelerator to support at least 5 M bandwidth of LTE platform. While the software decoding of LTE platform cannot support even the 2.5 M bandwidth because the total time exceeds 2 ms.

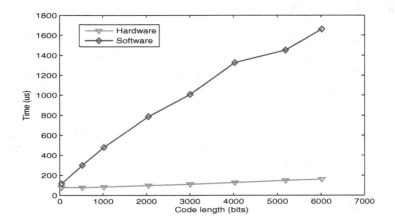

**Fig. 6.** Decoding time

We run the LTE physical layer in VM and native server respectively to evaluate the overhead of virtualization. Table 4 shows the overhead of Xen virtualization. For the long code length, the overhead can be relatively small (about 10 µs), which can be accepted. For the short length, we can change the algorithm to combine multiple data blocks together to improve the performance.

**Table 4.** Xen virtualization overhead

| Code length | Native | VM | Xen VM overhead |
|---|---|---|---|
| 40 bits | 68.3 µs | 77.6 µs | 13.6% |
| 512 bits | 69.2 µs | 77.2 µs | 11.6% |
| 1024 bits | 78.9 µs | 83.9 µs | 6.3% |
| 2048 bits | 87.1 µs | 95.5 µs | 9.6% |
| 3008 bits | 103.1 µs | 110.1 µs | 6.8% |
| 4032 bits | 117.4 µs | 127.1 µs | 8.3% |
| 5184 bits | 135 µs | 148.2 µs | 9.8% |
| 6016 bits | 150.8 µs | 160.4 µs | 6.4% |

## 5    Conclusions and Future Work

This paper designs and implements a FPGA-based turbo decoder hardware accelerator for C-RAN. Xen virtualization is used to support multiple virtual BSs on the C-RAN platform, and the FPGA hardware connected with PCIe interface to server as hardware accelerator. Experimental results demonstrate the turbo decoder accelerator based on the FPGA and Xen platform has much better performance to support the real time signal process with high bandwidth. The turbo decoder hardware accelerator can solve the timing constraints well in the C-RAN.

We believe the accelerators can be used for all VMs in C-RAN. So we will design the scheduling algorithm and make the accelerators support parallel processing of multitasking. And we will also design more accelerators for the C-RAN such as FFT and MIMO decoder to further reduce overall processing latency of C-RAN.

**Acknowledgments.** This work was supported in part by National Science and Technology Major Project of China under Grant 2014ZX03003003, in part by the National Natural Science Foundation of China under Grant 61390513.

## References

1. Barham, P., Dragovic, B., Fraser, K., Hand, S., Harris, T., Ho, A., Neugebauer, R., Pratt, I., Warfield, A.: Xen and the art of virtualization. ACM SIGOPS Oper. Syst. Rev. **37**(5), 164–177 (2003)
2. Chen, F., Shan, Y., Zhang, Y., Wang, Y., Franke, H., Chang, X., Wang, K.: Enabling FPGAs in the cloud. In: Proceedings of the 11th ACM Conference on Computing Frontiers, p. 3. ACM (2014)
3. Glossner, J., Hokenek, E., Moudgill, M.: The sandbridge sandblaster communications processor. In: Tuttlebee, W.H.W. (ed.) Software Defined Radio, pp. 129–159. Wiley (2004)
4. Haruyama, S.: FPGA in the software radio. IEEE commun. Mag. **37**, 109 (1999)
5. China Mobile. C-RAN: the road towards green RAN, version 2 . White Paper (2011)
6. Tan, K., Liu, H., Zhang, J., Zhang, Y., Fang, J., Voelker, G.M.: Sora: high-performance software radio using general-purpose multi-core processors. Commun. ACM **54**(1), 99–107 (2011)
7. Wang, W.: Accessing an FPGA-based hardware accelerator in a paravirtualized environment. Ph.D. thesis, Université d'Ottawa/University of Ottawa (2013)
8. Wu, J., Zhang, Z., Hong, Y., Wen, Y.: Cloud radio access network (C-RAN): a primer. IEEE Netw. **29**(1), 35–41 (2015)

# Iterative Detection and Decoding for Spatially Coupled Multiuser Data Transmission

Xiaodan Wang[✉], Sijie Wang, Zhongwei Si,
Zhiqiang He, Kai Niu, and Chao Dong

Key Laboratory of Universal Wireless Communications, Ministry of Education,
Beijing University of Posts and Telecommunications, Beijing 100876, China
xiaodanwang@bupt.edu.cn

**Abstract.** Non-orthogonal multiple access (NOMA) is a candidate multiple access scheme for 5G wireless communication. In this paper we consider applying the principle of spatially coupling in a NOMA system, where coupled data streams from different users transmit via the additive white Gaussian noise (AWGN) multiple access channel. A data stream is constructed by replicating each encoded bit for several times and then permuting the replicated bits. We propose an message-passing algorithm (MPA) based iterative multiuser detection combining with channel decoding, which is illustrated and analysed by the factor graph representation and the extrinsic information transfer (EXIT) chart, respectively. Numerical results show that lower node degree of the spatially coupled structure, higher number of iterations of the detector, and an appropriate encoding/decoding scheme jointly contribute to a better performance of the multiuser transmission system.

**Keywords:** NOMA · Spatially coupling · Message-passing · Iterative · Detection and decoding

## 1 Introduction

Different orthogonal multiple access (OMA) schemes have been applied in current wireless communication networks. However, due to the increasing demand of mobile Internet, the 5th generation (5G) wireless communication is required to support massive connectivity of users and/or devices. In a non-orthogonal multiple access (NOMA) system, signals from different users are allowed to be superimposed in the time/frequency resource [1,2]. Therefore, NOMA has gained much attention as a key technique for 5G due to its higher spectral efficiency comparing to OMA.

The technique of spatial graph coupling was first discovered for convolutional low-density parity-check (LDPC) codes [3] and proved to achieve the same limits as the optimum maximum likelihood (ML) decoding [4]. The concept has attracted considerable interests from the area of iterative processing and found applications in many areas of communication including compressive sensing [5], quantum coding [6] and multiuser data transmission [7].

© ICST Institute for Computer Sciences, Social Informatics and Telecommunications Engineering 2018
Q. Chen et al. (Eds.): ChinaCom 2016, Part I, LNICST 209, pp. 221–231, 2018.
DOI: 10.1007/978-3-319-66625-9_22

Applying spatial graph coupling to multiple access communication, a sequence of coupled symbols at the transmitter is formed as the sum of equal-power data streams from different users. A data stream is constructed by replicating each encoded bit for several times and then permuting the replicated bits. The data coupling is accomplished by a linear superposition of data streams (in the real or complex domain) from different users transmitted with time offsets. The interconnection of the coupled symbols and the data bits can be described by means of a factor graph [9]. It has been demonstrated in [8] that the system with spatial coupling can achieve the capacity of AWGN multiple access channel even for the case that all the users transmit with equal power and equal rate.

The receiver discussed in [8], which combines minimal-mean squared error (MMSE) with successive interference cancellation (SIC), is capacity-approaching in theory. However, the same performance cannot be achieved in practice since Gaussian assumptions are not appropriate when the number of users is small, and error propagation is inevitable in the SIC. Thus the iterative receiver based on belief propagation (BP) [7,10,11], which is also known as message-passing algorithm (MPA), turns out to be a candidate receiver applied for the multiuser detection in this paper.

Joint multiuser detection and decoding (JMUDD) proposed in [12] is an MPA based receiver. However, the optimization of its joint sparse graph needs complex calculation; otherwise the performance of the receiver may not be satisfying, for example, when using regular LDPC code. In this paper, we focus on the iterative detection and decoding for spatially coupled multiuser data transmission instead of JMUDD. With the help of EXIT chart [13], we investigate the spatially coupling structure and analyse the system performance by varying the number of inner iterations of the detector (and the LDPC decoder) and the outer iterations between the detector and the decoder, as well as the encoding schemes.

The rest of the paper is organized as follows. The system model of the spatially coupled structure is described in Sect. 2. Section 3 introduces the factor graph representation to illustrate corresponding structure and the EXIT chart to analyse the iterative process between the detector and decoders. EXIT chart analysis and numerical results are given in Sect. 4. Section 5 concludes the paper.

## 2    System Model

We consider a spatially coupling system based on the model of the generalized modulation [14], in which the signal transmitted over the channel is formed by a superposition of different data streams, and each stream contains several data packets.

The data coupling of $L$ users is shown as in Fig. 1. Take the $l$th user as the example, where $l \in \{1, 2, \ldots, L\}$. First the $P$ packets of the binary information sequence $\mathbf{x}_l = \left[\mathbf{x}_{l,0}^T, \mathbf{x}_{l,1}^T, \ldots, \mathbf{x}_{l,P-1}^T\right]^T$ are fed into a binary channel encoder of code rate $R = K/N$, respectively, where $\mathbf{x}_{l,p} = [x_{l,p,0}, x_{l,p,1}, \ldots, x_{l,p,K-1}]^T$, and $p \in \{0, 1, \ldots, P-1\}$. Without loss of generality, BPSK will be used as

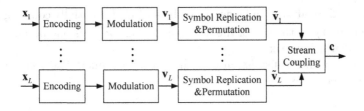

**Fig. 1.** Block diagram of the coupled signal generation for $L$ users.

the modulation scheme in this paper. Then each packets of the modulated sequence $\mathbf{v}_l = \left[\mathbf{v}_{l,0}^T, \mathbf{v}_{l,1}^T, \ldots, \mathbf{v}_{l,P-1}^T\right]^T$, where $\mathbf{v}_{l,p} = [v_{l,p,0}, v_{l,p,1}, \ldots, v_{l,p,N-1}]^T$, is replicated $M$ times and the symbols in different packets are permuted by different interleavers, producing the transmitting packets of the $l$th user $\left\{\tilde{\mathbf{v}}_{l,0}^{(0)}, \tilde{\mathbf{v}}_{l,0}^{(1)}, \ldots, \tilde{\mathbf{v}}_{l,0}^{(M-1)}, \ldots, \tilde{\mathbf{v}}_{l,P-1}^{(0)}, \ldots, \tilde{\mathbf{v}}_{l,P-1}^{(M-1)}\right\}$. Finally the coupled signal to be transmitted $\mathbf{c}$ is the superposition of the data packets of different users.

Without loss of generality, we assume that each user utilizes two streams to transmit his data packets in this paper. The process of stream coupling is realized as follows. At time $t = 0$, the first user starts to transmit his first 2 packets, then after a delay of $\tau$ symbol intervals the second user joins the transmission. At time $t = 2\tau$, the third user joins and so on. Thus there will be $J = 2L$ modulated data streams overlapping with time offsets. This process is illustrated in Fig. 2 for the case $M = 3$ and $J = 6$ where each row stands for one data stream, and $\tilde{\mathbf{v}}_{l,p}^{(m)}$ denotes the $m$th replica of $\mathbf{v}_{l,p}$ permuted by the interleaver $\boldsymbol{\pi}_{l,p}^{(m)}$, namely, $\tilde{\mathbf{v}}_{l,p}^{(m)} = \boldsymbol{\pi}_{l,p}^{(m)} \mathbf{v}_{l,p}$ where $m \in \{0, 1, \ldots M-1\}$. In each data stream a transmitted packet is immediately followed by the next packet. The total transmit data rate equals $RJ/M = \alpha R$ information bits per channel use, where $\alpha = J/M$ is called the modulation load.

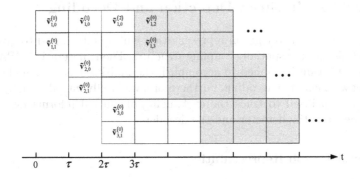

**Fig. 2.** Coupling process of data streams for different users in the channel. In this case each packet is replicated $M = 3$ times and there are $L = 3$ users with $J = 6$ data streams in total.

The procedure above can be described by an $(M, J)$-spatially coupling matrix $\mathbf{H}$ as given in (1) on the top of the next page, where $\boldsymbol{\pi}_{l,p}^{(m)}$ is one permutation of the $\tau \times \tau$ identity matrix.

We consider the transmission over an AWGN channel. The received signal can be represented as (2).

$$
\mathbf{H} = \begin{bmatrix}
\boldsymbol{\pi}_{1,0}^{(0)} & \cdots & \boldsymbol{\pi}_{1,0}^{(M-1)} & \cdots\cdots & \boldsymbol{\pi}_{1,P-2}^{(0)} & \cdots & \boldsymbol{\pi}_{1,P-2}^{(M-1)} \\
\boldsymbol{\pi}_{1,1}^{(0)} & \cdots & \boldsymbol{\pi}_{1,1}^{(M-1)} & \cdots\cdots & \boldsymbol{\pi}_{1,P-1}^{(0)} & \cdots & \boldsymbol{\pi}_{1,P-1}^{(M-1)} \\
& \boldsymbol{\pi}_{2,0}^{(0)} & \cdots & & & \cdots & \boldsymbol{\pi}_{2,P-2}^{(M-1)} \\
& \boldsymbol{\pi}_{2,1}^{(0)} & \cdots & & & \cdots & \boldsymbol{\pi}_{2,P-1}^{(M-1)} \\
& & \ddots & & \ddots & & \ddots \\
& & \boldsymbol{\pi}_{L,0}^{(0)} & \cdots & \cdots\cdots & \cdots & \boldsymbol{\pi}_{L,P-1}^{(M-1)} \\
& & \boldsymbol{\pi}_{L,1}^{(0)} & \cdots & \cdots\cdots & \cdots & \boldsymbol{\pi}_{L,P-1}^{(M-1)}
\end{bmatrix} \tag{1}
$$

$$
\mathbf{y} = \sqrt{\frac{Q}{J}}\mathbf{c} + \mathbf{n}, \tag{2}
$$

where $\mathbf{c} = \mathbf{H}^T\mathbf{v}$ is the coupled signal with

$$
\begin{aligned}
\mathbf{v} = \big[\mathbf{v}_{1,0}^T, \mathbf{v}_{1,1}^T, \ldots, \mathbf{v}_{L,0}^T, \mathbf{v}_{L,1}^T, \ldots, \\
\mathbf{v}_{1,P-2}^T, \mathbf{v}_{1,P-1}^T, \ldots, \mathbf{v}_{L,P-2}^T, \mathbf{v}_{L,P-1}^T\big]^T,
\end{aligned} \tag{3}
$$

and $\mathbf{n}$ is the additive white Gaussian noise with variance $\sigma^2$.

Note that the coupled signal $\mathbf{c}$ is multiplied by the power normalizing amplitude $\sqrt{Q/J}$, where $Q = 1$ is the constraint power.

## 3    Iterative Multiuser Detection and Decoding

In this section, the factor graph representation will be introduced to give more insight details into the spatially coupling structure. Then an iterative MPA-based detection algorithm is applied to accomplish the multiuser detection effectively combining with channel decoding. Furthermore, we briefly introduce EXIT chart which can be utilized to track the exchanging of mutual information at each iteration between the detector and the decoders.

### 3.1    Factor Graph Representation

The coupling process in the previous section can be illustrated by a factor graph. As shown in Fig. 3, each encoded bit $v_{l,n}$ where $l \in \{1, 2, \ldots, L\}$, $n \in \{0, 1, \ldots, PN - 1\}$, corresponds to a variable node represented by a circle, whereas each coupled symbol $c_t$, $t \in \{0, 1, 2, \ldots\}$ is denoted by a square called channel node. To be specific, in Fig. 3 there are $L = 2$ users with data bits encoded independently.

An edge connects a variable node to a channel node in the factor graph if that encoded bit is added to the coupled symbol correspondingly. Thus there is a one-to-one correspondence between a factor graph and a spatially coupling matrix. In other words, the number of edges connecting the channel nodes and the variable nodes is equal to the number of 1s in the spatially coupling matrix.

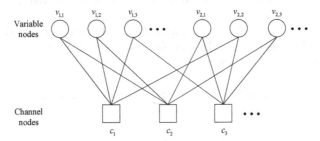

**Fig. 3.** Factor graph representation for a spatially coupled multiple access system of $L = 2$ users, where channel node degree is 4 and variable node degree is 2.

Define the degree of a node as the number of edges the node connected to other kinds of nodes, thus for the $(M, J)$-spatially coupled structure, the degrees of the variable nodes and the channel nodes are $M$ and $J$, respectively.

## 3.2   Iterative Detection and Decoding Based on MPA

In this subsection, the process of iterative detection and decoding based on MPA is introduced, where the detector exchanges the extrinsic message with the decoders of different users. First, the variable nodes exchange the extrinsic information with the channel nodes inside the detector using *a priori* information which has been received from the corresponding decoders. Then based on the received *a priori* information from the detector, the decoders update the extrinsic information which will be passed to the detector for the next iteration. Define the inner iteration as the message passing process inside the detector or the decoder, while the outer iteration as the message passing process between them. The log-likelihood ratios (LLRs) of the inner iteration and the outer iteration can be calculated as follows.

**Inner Iterations of the Detector.** During each iteration inside the detector, the extrinsic messages is exchanged between the channel nodes and the variable nodes. Note that the information received from one edge cannot be used to update the information to be transmitted onto that edge. Let the subset $\partial(l, n) \setminus t$ denote the indices of the channel nodes connected directly to the variable node $v_{l,n}$, called its neighborhood, excluding $c_t$, while the subset of index pairs $\partial t \setminus (l, n)$ stands for the neighborhood of the channel node $c_t$, excluding $v_{l,n}$.

At the channel node $c_t$, the conditional probability density function of the received symbol $y_t$ is given by [15]

$$p\left(y_t|\mathbf{v}^{[t]}\right) = \frac{1}{\sqrt{2\pi}\sigma} \exp\left(-\frac{1}{2\sigma^2}\left\|y_t - \mathbf{h}^{[t]T}\mathbf{v}^{[t]}\right\|^2\right), \tag{4}$$

where $\mathbf{v}^{[t]}$ and $\mathbf{h}^{[t]}$ denote the vector containing the symbols overlapped on the $t$th coupled symbol and their corresponding fraction of effective received signature values, respectively.

Let $LLR_{c_t \to v_{l,n}}$ and $LLR_{v_{l,n} \to c_t}$ be the LLR delivered from the channel node $c_t$ to the variable node $v_{l,n}$ and the LLR from the variable node $v_{l,n}$ to the channel node $c_t$, respectively. Then we have

$$LLR_{v_{l,n} \to c_t} = \sum_{t' \in \partial(l,n) \backslash t} LLR_{c_{t'} \to v_{l,n}}. \tag{5}$$

where

$$LLR_{c_t \to v_{l,n}} = \log \frac{p_t\left(v_{l,n} = +1|y_t, \mathbf{v}^{[t]}\backslash v_{l,n}\right)}{p_t\left(v_{l,n} = -1|y_t, \mathbf{v}^{[t]}\backslash v_{l,n}\right)} \tag{6}$$

$$= \log \frac{p\left(y_t|\mathbf{v}^{[t]}, v_{l,n} = +1\right) p_t\left(\mathbf{v}^{[t]}|v_{l,n} = +1\right)}{p\left(y_t|\mathbf{v}^{[t]}, v_{l,n} = -1\right) p_t\left(\mathbf{v}^{[t]}|v_{l,n} = -1\right)}, \tag{7}$$

Note that (7) is derived from (6) by using Bayes' rule written as

$$p\left(\mathbf{x}|\mathbf{y}\right) = \frac{p\left(\mathbf{y}|\mathbf{x}\right) p\left(\mathbf{x}\right)}{p\left(\mathbf{y}\right)} \propto p\left(\mathbf{y}|\mathbf{x}\right) p\left(\mathbf{x}\right), \tag{8}$$

where the symbol $\propto$ denotes "is proportional to" and the conditional probability density function (pdf) is calculated as

$$p_t\left(\mathbf{v}^{[t]}|v_{l,n}\right) = \prod_{(l',n') \in \partial t \backslash (l,n)} p_t\left(v_{l',n'}\right), \tag{9}$$

with a priori probability given by

$$p_t\left(v_{l',n'}\right) = \exp\left(\frac{v_{l',n'}}{2} LLR_{v_{l',n'} \to c_t}\right). \tag{10}$$

Combining (7), (9) and (10), the information of the channel node $c_t$ sent to the variable node $v_{l,n}$ can be written as (12) on the top of the next page, where $\max^*$ operation, is a numerically stable operation suggested in [16].

**Outer Iterations Between the Detector and the Decoder.** The iterative process between the detector and the decoder is shown as Fig. 4.

In Fig. 4, $LLR_{ext}^{DET[i]}$ and $LLR_{ext}^{DEC_l[i]}$, $l \in \{1, 2, \dots, L\}$ are the output of the detector and $L$ decoders at the $i$th iteration, respectively, $i = \{1, 2, \dots, I_{max}\}$

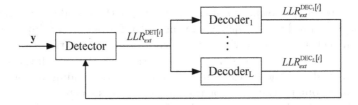

**Fig. 4.** Block diagram of the iteration between the detector and $L$ decoders.

with $I_{\max}$ defined as the max number of the outer iteration. The subscript "ext" denotes that only the extrinsic information is exchanged during each iteration.

Since we use different encoding scheme in this paper, thus we only focus on the input and output of the decoder in this section, both of which are given as

$$LLR_{ext,v_{l,n}}^{\mathrm{DEC}[i]} = LLR_{v_{l,n}}^{I_{\mathrm{DEC}}} - LLR_{ext,v_{l,n}}^{\mathrm{DET}[i]}, \tag{11}$$

where the left hand side of the equation denotes the output extrinsic information of the decoder at the $i$th outer iteration. In the right hand side of the equation,

$$LLR_{c_t \rightarrow v_{l,n}} = \max_{\substack{\mathbf{v}^{[t]} \\ v_{l,n}=+1}}^{*} \left( \sum_{(l',n') \in \partial t \backslash (l,n)} \frac{v_{l',n'}}{2} LLR_{v_{l',n'} \rightarrow c_t} - \frac{1}{2\sigma^2} \left\| c_t - \mathbf{h}^{[t]T} \mathbf{v}^{[t]} \right\|^2 \right)$$

$$- \max_{\substack{\mathbf{v}^{[t]} \\ v_{l,n}=-1}}^{*} \left( \sum_{(l',n') \in \partial t \backslash (l,n)} \frac{v_{l',n'}}{2} LLR_{v_{l',n'} \rightarrow c_t} - \frac{1}{2\sigma^2} \left\| c_t - \mathbf{h}^{[t]T} \mathbf{v}^{[t]} \right\|^2 \right) \tag{12}$$

the minuend is the LLR of the variable node $v_{l,n}$ after $I_{\mathrm{DEC}}$ inner iterations of the decoder, which can be used for bit decision. Note that $I_{\mathrm{DEC}} = 1$ for the decoder of convolutional code. The subtrahend denotes *a priori* input information derived from the detector written as

$$LLR_{ext,v_{l,n}}^{\mathrm{DET}[i]} = \sum_{t \in \partial(l,n)} LLR_{c_t \rightarrow v_{l,n}}^{I_{\mathrm{DET}}} - LLR_{ext,v_{l,n}}^{\mathrm{DEC}[i-1]}, \tag{13}$$

where $LLR_{c_t \rightarrow v_{l,n}}^{I_{\mathrm{DET}}}$ is the soft information sent to the variable node $v_{l,n}$ from its neighborhood channel node $c_t$ after $I_{\mathrm{DET}}$ inner iterations of the detector. Note that at the first outer iteration, *a priori* input information received by the detector from the decoders $LLR_{ext,v_{l,n}}^{\mathrm{DEC}[0]}$ is set to be 0 initially.

## 3.3  EXIT Chart

EXIT chart is a valuable tool to track the mutual information at each iteration between the soft-input soft-output (SISO) constituents, and it gives an excellent visual representation of the process of belief propagation.

To measure the performance of the detector (or the decoder) and determine whether it does produce an increase in mutual information, an input extrinsic information vector is created with the known mutual information $I_A$ and passed into the detector (or the decoder). The detection (or the decoding) algorithm is then employed and the mutual information $I_E$ corresponding to the extrinsic information output by the detector (or the decoder) is calculated. This process is repeated for several different extrinsic information input vectors with different mutual information content, producing corresponding curve in the EXIT chart.

## 4    EXIT Chart Analysis and Numerical Results

In this paper, we focus on different setup of degree distributions, inner iterations and outer iterations. The system performance can be analysed with the help of EXIT chart.

Generally speaking, with a fixed load, the variable node degree and the channel node degree affect the performance of multiuser detection simultaneously. On the one hand, a higher variable node degree means that each information bit is transmitted in more channel uses, which corresponds to a higher diversity. On the other hand, a higher channel node degree means that there are more transmission bits imposed in one channel use, resulting in a higher interference.

Figure 5 illustrates the EXIT chart over AWGN channel at $E_b/N_0 = 8\,\mathrm{dB}$. For a fair comparison, we keep the modulation load $\alpha = 2$ and the same number of inner iteration $T_{\mathrm{DET}} = 2$ of the detector but varying the degree distribution. It can be seen that as the degrees of variable node and channel node increase, the average mutual information between the transmitted bits and the output

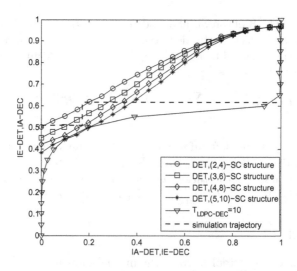

**Fig. 5.** EXIT chart analysis for detectors with 2 inner iterations for different spatially coupled (SC) structure and the LDPC decoder over AWGN Channel at $E_b/N_0 = 8\,\mathrm{dB}$.

of the detector is reduced, which demonstrates that the interference, instead of diversity, is the dominating factor affecting the performance of the detector. For a fixed load, lower degrees lead to a better performance. The iteration between the detector of a $(2,4)$-spatially coupled structure and the LDPC decoder is traced in Fig. 5, which is marked by the dashed line.

In the following we study the behavior of the inner iteration within the detector and the decoder respectively. The EXIT curves of the detector for a $(2,4)$-spatially coupled structure with different number of inner iterations at 6 dB are drawn in Fig. 6. The mutual information between the output of the detector and the transmitted bits increases when allowing more inner iterations of the detector. Moreover, two encoding schemes are considered in the simulation, i.e. convolutional code and LDPC code both with length $N = 1800$ bits and rate $R = 1/2$. Similar to the observation of the detector, the LDPC decoder performs better when there are more inner iterations. The convolutional decoder achieves a better performance than the LDPC decoder with 2 inner iterations, $T_{\text{LDPC-DEC}} = 2$, while it is not as good as the LDPC decoder with $T_{\text{LDPC-DEC}} = 10$ since its output mutual information is smaller than that of the latter when $I_{A-\text{DEC}} > 0.6$. Accordingly, we expect the best BER performance of receivers with the three decoders by using the LDPC decoder with 10 inner iterations.

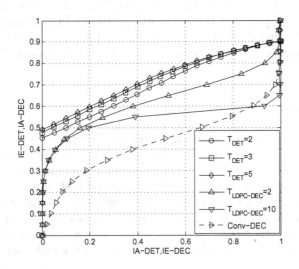

**Fig. 6.** EXIT chart of detectors with different inner iterations for $(2,4)$-spatially coupling structure and different decoders over AWGN Channel at $E_b/N_0 = 6$ dB.

The average bit error rates (BER) of all the users' data coupled with $(2,4)$-matrix is illustrated in Fig. 7. The max number of outer iteration between the detector and the decoder $T_{\max}$ is set to be 20 during the simulation to ensure sufficient iterations at low SNRs. It can be observed that with a fixed decoder, the system achieves better performance as the number of iteration within the

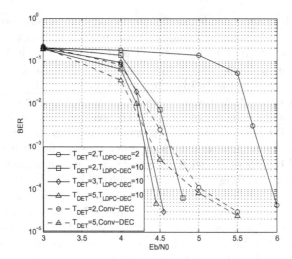

**Fig. 7.** Average BER performance over AWGN Channel for multiuser data coupled by $(2, 4)$-spatially coupling matrix.

detector $T_{DET}$ increases. Meanwhile, with fixed $T_{DET}$, the system using the convolutional decoder performs better than using the LDPC decoder with 2 inner iterations, and using the LDPC decoder with 10 inner iterations achieves the best BER performance, which is consistent with the analysis of EXIT chart in Fig. 6.

## 5    Conclusion

In this paper we consider a signaling format for NOMA system where information is coupled via the superposition of data streams for different users. Each stream is formed by replication and permutation of the encoded bits. An MPA-based iterative detection combining with channel decoding is applied to multiuser detection. The EXIT charts and BER simulation results show that lower node degree of the spatially coupled structure, higher number of iterations of the detector (and the LDPC decoder), and an appropriate encoding/decoding scheme jointly contribute to a better performance of the multiuser transmission system.

## References

1. Dai, L., Wang, B., Yuan, Y., Han, S., Chih-Lin, I., Wang, Z.: Non-orthogonal multiple access for 5G: solutions, challenges, opportunities, and future research trends. IEEE Commun. Mag. **53**(9), 74–81 (2015)
2. Chen, S., Peng, K., Jin, H.: A suboptimal scheme for uplink NOMA in 5G systems. In: Wireless Communications and Mobile Computing Conference (IWCMC), Dubrovnik, Croatia (2015)

3. Truhachev, D., Lentmaier, M., Zigangirov, K.S.: Mathematical analysis of iterative decoding of LDPC convolutional codes. In: Proccedings of 2001 IEEE International Symposium on Information Theory, Washington, USA, June 2001

4. Kudekar, S., Richardson, T., Urbanke, R.: Threshold saturation via spatial coupling: why convolutional LDPC ensembles perform so well over the BEC. In: Proceedings of IEEE International Symposium on Information Theory (2010)

5. Kudekar, S., Pfister, H.D.: The effect of spatial coupling on compressive sensing. In: Proceedings of Allerton Conference on Communications, Control, and Computing, Monticello, IL, September 2010

6. Hagiwara, M., Kasai, K., Imai, H., Sakaniwa, K.: Spatially coupled quasi-cyclic quantum LDPC codes. In: Proceedings of IEEE International Symposium on Information Theory, St. Petersburg, Russia (2011)

7. Takeuchi, K., Tanaka, T., Kawabata, T.: Improvement of BP-based CDMA multiuser detection by spatial coupling. In: Proceedings of IEEE Interantional Symposikum on Informationa Theory, St. Petersburg, Russia (2011)

8. Truhachev, D.: Achieving Gaussian multiple access channel capacity with spatially coupled sparse graph multi-user modulation. In: Proceedings of Information Theory and Applications Workshop (ITA), pp. 331–337 (2012)

9. Kschischang, F.R., Frey, B.J., Loeliger, H.-A.: Factor graphs and the sum-product algorithm. IEEE Trans. Inf. Theory **47**(2), 498–519 (2001)

10. Guo, D., Wang, C.-C.: Multiuser detection of sparsely spread CDMA. IEEE J. Sel. Areas Commun. **26**(3), 421–431 (2008)

11. Takeuchi, K., Tanaka, T., Kawabata, T.: Performance improvement of iterative multiuser detection for large sparsely spread CDMA systems by spatial coupling. IEEE Trans. Inf. Theory **61**(4), 1768–1794 (2015)

12. Wen, L., Razavi, R., Imran, M.A., Xiao, P.: Design of joint sparse graph for OFDM system. IEEE Trans. Wirel. Commun. **14**(4), 1823–1836 (2015)

13. Johnson, S.J.: Iterative Error Correction: Turbo, Low-Density Parity-Check and Repeat-Accumulate Codes. Cambridge University Press, New York (2010)

14. Schlegel, C., Burnashev, M., Truhachev, D.: Generalized superposition modulation and iterative demodulation: a capacity investigation. Hindawi J. Electr. Comput. Eng. **2010**, 1 (2010)

15. Hoshyar, R., Wathan, F., Tafazolli, R.: Novel low-density signature for synchronous CDMA systems over AWGN channel. IEEE Trans. Sig. Process. **56**(4), 1616–1626 (2008)

16. Hochwald, B., Brink, S.: Achieving near-capacity on multiple-antenna channel. IEEE Trans. Commun. **51**(3), 389–399 (2003)

# Two Degree Forest Based LT Codes with Feedback

Liang Liu[1,2,3,4(✉)] and Feng Liu[1,2,3,4]

[1] School of Electronic and Engineering, Beihang University, Beijing, China
{Liuliang1945,liuf}@buaa.edu.cn
[2] The Collaborative Innovation Center of Geospatial Technology, Wuhan, China
[3] Beijing Key Laboratory for Network-Based Cooperative Air Traffic
Management (No. BZ0272), Beijing, China
[4] Beijing Laboratory for General Aviation Technology,
Beijing, People's Republic of China

**Abstract.** The performance of belief propagation (BP) decoding algorithm for LT codes is significantly deteriorated, as the data-block length decreases, since the randomly encoding of LT codes causes lots of wasted output symbols, which is helpless for decoding. To solve this problem, this paper provides two degree forest based LT codes in order to help the sender to send badly needed symbols to accelerate decoding throughout entire receiving process. Through gathering two degree output symbols into separable trees, the decoder can easily get and feedback the indexes of the badly needed input symbols. Simulation results show that, in the short data-block length case, two degree forest based LT codes achieve much lower coding overhead, consume much smaller storage resources, and need less feedback opportunities compared with current LT codes algorithms.

**Keywords:** LT codes · Two degree forest · Feedback channel · Robust soliton distribution

## 1 Introduction

LT codes are the simplest kind of fountain codes [1] with capacity achieving performance on erasure channels [1–3]. The biggest advantage of LT codes is that it is simultaneously near optimal for different erasure channels with time varying or unknown erasure rate [1]. Moreover, due to the character of sparsity for encoding [1], the decoder can achieve linear decoding complex, according to a belief propagation (BP) decoding algorithm. In addition, only one single bit feedback is needed from the decoder to the sender during entire transmission process. Due to above advantages, LT codes are widely used in different scenarios of communications.

However, it should not be ignored that the performance of LT codes is compromised considerably when the data block length is relatively small [1, 4, 5]. Such situation happens frequently. For one thing, in some applications, it is not needed to transmit large amount of data bits. For another, in some energy limited equips, such as

© ICST Institute for Computer Sciences, Social Informatics and Telecommunications Engineering 2018
Q. Chen et al. (Eds.): ChinaCom 2016, Part I, LNICST 209, pp. 232–241, 2018.
DOI: 10.1007/978-3-319-66625-9_23

small wireless sensors [9] and satellites in low earth orbits [10], there are not sufficient storage resource to buffer large amount of data bits. Hence, it is needed to enhance the performance of LT code when data block length is relatively small.

To enhance the performance of LT code with relatively small data block length, former researchers have proposed some improvements based on limited feedback. In the work by [6], the decoder transmits feedback message about the number of original symbols that are already recovered, so that the sender can shift the degree distribution of LT code to accelerate data recovery, such method is called shifted LT code or SLT code for short. However, the performance of SLT code is limited due to following two aspects. For one thing, although average degree increases when some original symbols are recovered at decoder, it still has large probability that newly generated output symbols are useless for decoder. For another, as average degree increases, the probability of degree one decreases, which is negative for traditional BP decoding algorithm.

To better accelerate the decoding process, LT codes with alternating feedbacks (LT-AF codes) is proposed [7, 8]. In this algorithm, not only the currently decoded number of original symbols, but also the needed input symbol index is feedback from the decoder, to further enhance decoding process. The second kind of feedback is useful, if some input symbol is badly needed for the decoder. To better figure out the suitable input symbol index, three different principles are proposed is [8]. However, in [7, 8], the feedback message about index of input symbol is only used when the number of output symbols received by decoder is larger than the number of original symbols, which is negative for decoding process. Since traditional decoding algorithm can only recover a small fraction of input symbols, when number of received output symbols is less than the number of input symbols [1], then it is inevitable that the storage costs for decoder is huge. Moreover, it is reasonable for the decoder to obtain the badly needed input symbols in the whole receiving and decoding process.

This paper proposes the two degree forest based LT codes (TBLT codes) with feedback to enhance the performance of LT codes with relatively small data block length. TBLE codes work as follows. First, in order to provide appropriate feedback for indexes of input symbols, the two degree forest (TDF), which consists of output symbols with two adjacent input symbols, is formulated and maintained throughout entire decoding process. The feedback message about the badly needed index of input symbol is sent to the sender, as long as the size of some two degree tree (TDT) is larger than certain threshold. If the badly needed input symbol arrives at destination, all input symbols, which is included in that TDT, can be recovered, and the iterative decoding algorithm can be accelerated to recovery more input symbols. Notice that, although the idea of two degree chains is mentioned in [8] as one kind of principle to get the indexes of needed input symbols, which is similar to the two degree trees in our methods, the function of two degree forest is not fully explored and analyzed in [8].

Simulation results show that TBLT codes have following advantages. First, the average coding overhead, which is defined as proportion of additional data bits needed for transmission, can be reduced by about 40%, compared with traditional LT codes and SLT codes [6]. Second, the peak value of restore cost during entire decoding process can be reduced by about 35%. Finally, compared with SLT codes, TBLT codes require much less feedback times.

The paper is organized as follows. Section 2 presents basic knowledge about LT codes. Section 3 presents the design of two degree forest based LT codes. The simulation results with comparison are given in Sect. 4. Section 5 concludes the paper.

## 2  Preliminary

First, for simplicity without losing generalization, assume that all input and output symbols are binary symbols, which may include thousands of bits. The encoding and decoding procedures of LT codes are as follows.

**LT Encoding:** Let $k$ be the number of input symbols for encoding. Let $U = \{u_1, \ldots, u_k\}$ be the set of input symbols. First, an output symbol degree $d$ is chosen from the Robust-Soliton distribution [1], $M = \{\mu_1, \mu_2, \ldots, \mu_k\}$, where $\mu_i$ is the probability that $d = i$, such that $\sum_{i=1}^{k} \mu_i = 1$. Next, uniformly and randomly chose $d$ input symbols. Then the output symbol $v$ is generated through XORing those $d$ input symbols. Those $d$ input symbols refer to the neighbors of $v$. The encoding procedure repeats until the single-bit feedback comes. The RS distribution is obtained by combining ideal-soliton (IS) distribution $\rho_i$ and distribution $\tau$ given by

$$\rho_i = \begin{cases} 1/k & i = 1 \\ 1/i(i-1) & i = 2, \ldots, k \end{cases} \tag{1}$$

and

$$\tau_i = \begin{cases} R/ik & i = 1, \ldots, k/R - 1 \\ R/k \ln(R/\delta) & i = k/R \\ 0 & i = k/R + 1, \ldots, k \end{cases}$$

respectively, where $R = c \ln(k/\delta)\sqrt{k}$, $\delta$ and $c$ are two tunable parameters. Then, RS distribution is obtained through

$$\mu_i = \frac{\rho_i + \tau_i}{\beta}, i = 1, \ldots, k, \tag{2}$$

where, $\beta = \sum_{i=1}^{k} \rho_i + \tau_i$.

**LT Decoding:** Currently, the basic decoding algorithm for LT codes is the belief propagation, which works iteratively as follows. When decoder finds an output symbol, such that the value of all but one of its neighboring input is known, the unknown input symbol can be obtained by bitwise XOR operations and removes all edges incident to that output symbol. This process is repeated until no such output symbols exist. Notice that the set of output symbols that are reduced to degree one is called ripple, which is critical for LT decoding. If the ripple is empty, the decoding stops and waits for new output symbols of degree one to proceed the decoding. If all $k$ input symbols are recovered, the decoder sends a single-bit feedback message to the sender to inform the success of decoding.

Let $\gamma$ be the number of output symbols during transmission. Let $\gamma_S$ be the average number of output symbols when successful recovery of $k$ input symbols can be obtained. As shown in [1], $\gamma_S \geq k$ holds. Let $\eta$ and $\varepsilon$ be the redundancy and overhead for LT codes, such that $\eta = \gamma_S/k$, and $\varepsilon = \eta - 1$. It is obvious that $\eta \geq 1$ and $\varepsilon \geq 0$.

Although LT codes with RS distribution can asymptotically achieve, i.e. $\eta \to 1$, as $k \to \infty$, $\eta$ is significantly larger than 1 when $k$ is finite [4, 5]. Hence, it is needed to improve the performance when $k$ is finite.

# 3   Design of Two Degree Forest Based LT Codes

In this section, the two degree forest based LT (TBLT) codes are proposed. The encoding process is the same as the LT codes, while the decoding process is changed. First, the structure of two degree forest for decoder is introduced. Then, the updating procedure for two degree forest is proposed. Finally, based on the feedback rule, the decoding algorithm for TBLT is proposed.

## 3.1   Two Degree Forest

As mentioned before, the decode process can be promoted considerably if appropriate input symbol can be sent to destination. However, which input symbol is most important for decoder is unclear. To solve this problem, the two degree forest of output symbols is formulated at decoder as follows.

**Definition 1.** *Two degree tree (TDT)*: a TDT, $\Gamma$, is a tree, which has following properties: First, the nodes of the tree are output symbols, which have exact two neighbors as input symbols. Second, let $v_1$ and $v_2$ be two nodes in $\Gamma$, then one link exists between $v_1$ and $v_2$, if and only if $v_1$ and $v_2$ have exactly one same neighbor. Third, as a tree, $\Gamma$ has no loop path.

Moreover, let $V_\Gamma$ and $U_\Gamma$ be the set of output symbols in $\Gamma$ and set of neighbor input symbols in $\Gamma$, respectively. Let $|V_\Gamma|$ and $|U_\Gamma|$ be the number of elements in $V_\Gamma$ and $U_\Gamma$ respectively, then it is obviously that $|U_\Gamma| = |V_\Gamma| + 1$.

**Definition 2.** *Two degree forest (TDF)*: a TDF, $\Omega$, is a graph consists of two degree trees, such that $\Omega = \{\Gamma_1, \ldots \Gamma_{N_\Omega}\}$, which has following property. Let $\Gamma^{(1)}$ and $\Gamma^{(2)}$ be any two TDTs in $\Omega$. Let $v^{(1)} \in V^{(1)}$ and $v^{(2)} \in V^{(2)}$ be any two output variables, which lie in $\Gamma^{(1)}$ and $\Gamma^{(2)}$ respectively. Then, $v^{(1)}$ and $v^{(2)}$ have no same neighbor input symbol.

For example as shown in Fig. 1, a TDF with two TDTs is formulated at decoder.

The most important feature for TDF is that, for each TDT, $\Gamma \in \Omega$, the input symbols in $U_\Gamma$ can be recovered with breadth first search, if any input symbol in $U_\Gamma$ is obtained. For example as shown in Fig. 2, if the input symbol, $u_2$ is obtained, then $u_4$ can be recovered, since $u_2$ and $u_4$ are neighbor input symbols of the output symbol indexed by 2,4 in Fig. 2. Next, $u_{14}$, $u_8$ and $u_{12}$ can be recovered, since output symbols indexed by 2,14, 2,8, and 4,12 are adjacent to the output symbol indexed by 2,4. Finally, $u_{18}$ and $u_{16}$ can be recovered, since output symbols indexed by 8,18 is adjacent to output symbols indexed by 2,8, and output symbols indexed by 4,16 is adjacent to output symbols indexed by 4,12.

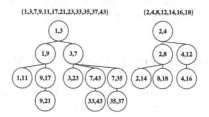

**Fig. 1.** Simple example of two degree forest.

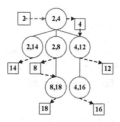

**Fig. 2.** Recovery of input symbols within one two degree tree

## 3.2  Updating Two Degree Forest

In the receiving and decoding process, the two degree forest is updated according to following operations.

(1) Tree adding: Let $\Gamma^{(1)} \in \Omega$. Let $\tilde{v}$ be the new output symbol that reaches destination, such that $\tilde{v}$ has two neighbor input symbols, $\tilde{u}_1$ and $\tilde{u}_2$. If $\tilde{u}_1 \in U_{\Gamma^{(1)}}$, and $\tilde{u}_2 \notin U_{\Gamma^{(1)}}$, then $\Gamma^{(1)}$ can be added with a new output symbol such that $V_{\Gamma^{(1)}} = V_{\Gamma^{(1)}} \cup \{\tilde{v}\}$ and $U_{\Gamma^{(2)}} = U_{\Gamma^{(2)}} \cup \{\tilde{u}_2\}$.

(2) Tree combining: Let $\Gamma^{(1)}, \Gamma^{(2)} \in \Omega$. Let $\tilde{v}$ be the new output symbol that reaches destination, such that $\tilde{v}$ has two neighbor input symbols, $\tilde{u}_1$ and $\tilde{u}_2$. If $\tilde{u}_1 \in U_{\Gamma^{(1)}}$ and $\tilde{u}_2 \in U_{\Gamma^{(2)}}$, then $\Gamma^{(1)}$ and $\Gamma^{(2)}$ can be combined to formulate a new tree $\tilde{\Gamma}$, such that $V_{\tilde{\Gamma}} = V_{\Gamma^{(1)}} \cup V_{\Gamma^{(2)}} \cup \{\tilde{v}\}$, and $U_{\tilde{\Gamma}} = U_{\Gamma^{(1)}} \cup U_{\Gamma^{(2)}}$.

(3) Tree removing: Let $\Gamma^{(1)} \in \Omega$ be one TDT, such that all input symbols in $U_{\Gamma^{(1)}}$ are recovered by decoder, then $\Gamma^{(1)}$ is removed from TDF, namely, $\Omega = \Omega/\Gamma^{(1)}$.

Entire updating procedure for two degree forest is as follows.

| **Algorithm 1**: TDF Updating Procedure |
|---|
| Input: Current TDF $\Omega = \{\Gamma_1,...,\Gamma_N\}$, one output symbol $\tilde{v}$ with two neighbor input symbols, $\tilde{u}_1$ and $\tilde{u}_2$. |
| If two TDT $\Gamma^{(1)}, \Gamma^{(2)} \in \Omega$, such that $\tilde{u}_1 \in U_{\Gamma^{(1)}}$, and $\tilde{u}_2 \notin U_{\Gamma^{(1)}}$: <br><br> Then, get one combined tree, $\tilde{\Gamma}$, according to tree combining operation. Let $\Omega^* = \Omega \cup \tilde{\Gamma}$, and let $\tilde{\Omega} = \Omega^* / \Gamma^{(1)} \cup \Gamma^{(2)}$. <br> Else if one $\Gamma^{(1)} \in \Omega$ exists, such that $\tilde{u}_1, \tilde{u}_2 \in U_{\Gamma^{(1)}}$: <br><br> Then, discard $\tilde{v}$, and let $\tilde{\Omega} = \Omega$. <br> Else if only one $\Gamma^{(1)} \in \Omega$ exists, such that $\tilde{u}_1 \in U_{\Gamma^{(1)}}$, and $\tilde{u}_2 \notin U_{\Gamma^{(1)}}$: <br><br> Then, add $\Gamma^{(1)}$ with $\tilde{v}$, according to tree adding operation. <br> Else if no $\Gamma^{(1)} \in \Omega$ exists, such that $\tilde{u}_1 \in U_{\Gamma^{(1)}}$, or $\tilde{u}_2 \in U_{\Gamma^{(1)}}$: <br><br> Then, formulate one new TDT, $\Gamma^*$, such that $V_{\Gamma^*} = \{\tilde{v}\}$ and $U_{\Gamma^*} = \{\tilde{u}_1, \tilde{u}_2\}$. |
| Output: $\tilde{\Omega}$ |

### 3.3 Feedback Rule and Decode Process

As mentioned before, for any $\Gamma^{(1)} \in \Omega$, all the input symbols within $U_{\Gamma^{(1)}}$ can be recovered with a breadth first search, if one of them is obtained. Furthermore, more input symbols can be recovered iteratively with those input symbols within $U_{\Gamma^{(1)}}$, according to the belief propagation decoding algorithm. Hence, it is reasonable for the decoder to inform the sender to send one symbol $\tilde{u} \in U_{\Gamma^{(1)}}$, when $|U_{\Gamma^{(1)}}|$ is large enough. The feedback rule is as follows.

Let $\beta > 0$ be one integer. Then, if one $\Gamma^{(1)} \in \Omega$ exists, such that $|U_{\Gamma^{(1)}}| \geq \beta$, the decoder send a feedback message to the sender, that the sender should send one original input symbol $\tilde{u}$, such that $\tilde{u} \in U_{\Gamma^{(1)}}$. Such feedback rule is called $F_\beta(\tilde{u})$, where $\beta$ is called the feedback threshold.

Based on the two degree forest and feedback rule, the decoding algorithm is proposed as follows.

---

**Algorithm 2**: TDF Based Decoding Algorithm for TBLT Codes

---

Input: Current TDF $\Omega = \{\Gamma_1, ..., \Gamma_N\}$, current set of output symbols, $V$, and

current set of recovered symbols $\widetilde{U} \subset U$, newly arrived output symbol

$\widetilde{v}$, with the set of index of neighbor input symbols $\Lambda_{\widetilde{v}}$, and $\beta$.

---

If $|\Lambda_{\widetilde{v}}| \geq 3$:  let $V = V \cup \{\widetilde{v}\}$.

Else if $|\Lambda_{\widetilde{v}}| = 2$:

   Then update $\Omega$ according to algorithm1.

   If one $\Gamma^{(1)} \in \Omega$ exists, such that $|U_{\Gamma^{(1)}}| \geq \beta$: send $F_{\beta}(\widetilde{u})$ to sender.

Else if $|\Lambda_{\widetilde{v}}| = 1$:

   Take BP decoding algorithm to obtain new $\widetilde{U}$ and $V$.

   If $\widetilde{U} = U$:

      Then, inform the sender that decoding succeeds.

   Else if $|\widetilde{U}| < |U|$:

      Then, for any $\Gamma \in \Omega$, if $U_{\Gamma^{(1)}} \subset \widetilde{U}$, let $\Omega = \Omega / \{\Gamma\}$.

---

Compared with the traditional BP decoding algorithm, additional cost for TDF based decoding algorithm is small. For one thing, the two degree forest doesn't need much storage resource, since, the decoder only needs to restore the index information of input symbols and output symbols to maintain the structure for TDF. For another, since each output symbol in TDF has exactly two adjacent input symbols, it doesn't need much calculation cost to put each output symbols into suitable TDT.

## 4  Simulation Results and Analysis

As mentioned before, the basic aim for the proposed algorithm in this paper is to reduce the redundancy of LT codes, when $k$ is relatively small, hence, let $k = 500, 1000$, in simulation. Next, the classical robust soliton distribution is used through simulation, where it is set that $\delta = 0.1$, and $c = 0, 0.1, 0.2$ for comparison. Moreover, in our algorithm, the feedback threshold, $\beta$, is set to be 10, 20, 30, 40, 50 for comparison.

Following two algorithms are used for comparison:

(1) The classical BP decoding algorithm for LT codes [1].
(2) The SLT codes [6], which is based on the idea that relative larger degree should be generated, if the sender is informed of the number of input symbols that have already recovered.

The simulation results are obtained through getting average values of 10000 tests, for each simulation condition.

Comparison of simulation results for overhead is proposed in Fig. 3. TBLT codes achieve lower overhead than traditional LT codes and SLT codes, no matter what feedback threshold value is. When $k = 500$, compared with the best case of SLT codes that the overhead is about 0.25, the best case of TBLT codes is about 0.15, which is about 40% lower. Moreover, it should be noticed that TBLT codes get the smallest overhead, when $c = 0$, while LT codes and SLT codes get the smallest overhead when $c = 0.1$. Such results can be explained as follows. The two degree output symbols are of great importance for the decode process in TBLT codes. However, according to the definition of robust soliton distribution [1], the probability of degree two decreases as $c$ increases, which is negative for the efficiency of two degree forest.

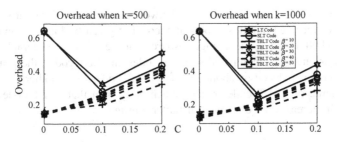

**Fig. 3.** Comparison of simulation results of overhead when packet error rate is zero of degree

Comparison of simulation results of overhead when packet error rate is larger than 0 is shown in Fig. 4. It is naturally that, the larger packet error rate is, the larger the overhead is. The overhead of TBLT codes are still lower than that of the traditional LT codes and SLT codes under different $c$ values, no matter what the packet error rate is.

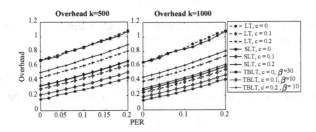

**Fig. 4.** Comparison of simulation results of overhead when packet error rate is larger than 0.

The simulation results for decode process is expressed through the relationship between average decoded number of input symbols and the number of output symbols received at decoder, as shown in Fig. 5. For simplicity, the best case, $c = 0.1$, is used for LT codes and SLT codes. While, when $c = 0$, TBLT codes achieve smallest overhead. Compared with LT codes and SLT codes, TBLT codes can accelerate the decoding process. When number of received output symbols at decoder equals $k$, LT and SLT can only recover a small fraction of input symbols, while, TBLT can recover majority of input symbols.

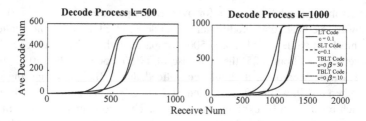

**Fig. 5.** Comparison of simulation results for the relationship between average decoded number of input symbols and the receive number of output symbols.

Simulation results for the relationship between average stored output symbols and the number of received output symbols at decoder is given by Fig. 6. Compared with LT codes and SLT codes, the storage resource can be saved considerably by TBLT algorithm. For one thing, compared with LT codes and SLT codes, the peak value of storage resource is reduced by about 35% for TBLT codes. For another, the amount of storage resource of TBLT codes reduce much early than that of LT codes and SLT codes, which increases the efficiency of buffer's usage.

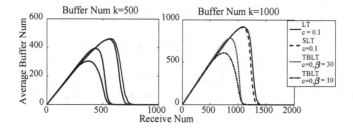

**Fig. 6.** Comparison of simulation results for the relationship between average stored output symbols and the number of received output symbols at decoder.

Simulation results for the relationship between average feedback times and the number of received output symbols at decoder is given by Fig. 7. Compared with SLT

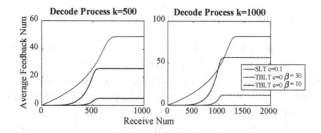

**Fig. 7.** Comparison of simulation results for the relationship between average feedback times and the number of received output symbols at decoder.

codes, TBLT codes require much less feedback times. Especially, when $\beta = 30$, the average feedback times can be reduced by about 80%, compared with SLT codes.

## 5 Conclusion

This paper proposes two degree forest based LT codes to enhance the performance of LT codes in the relatively small data-block length case. To help the sender to send the appropriate output symbols to accelerate decoding, the two degree output symbols are gathered into separable trees, so that decoder can get the indexes of badly needed input symbols if the size of some tree is larger than certain threshold value.

Simulation results show that TBLT codes can reduce coding overhead by about 40%, compared with traditional LT codes and SLT codes. Moreover, the storage cost during entire decoding process can be reduced considerably. Finally, compared with SLT codes, TBLT codes require much less feedback opportunities.

**Acknowledgments.** This work is supported in part by National Natural Science Foundation of China (Grant Nos. 61231013, 91438206, 91538202 and 61521091) and Fundamental Research Funds for the Central Universities (Grant No. YMF-14-DZXY-027).

## References

1. Luby, M.: LT codes. In: The 43rd Annual IEEE Symposium on Foundations of Computer Science, pp. 271–280 (2002)
2. Shokrollahi, A.: Raptor codes. IEEE Trans. Inf. Theory **52**, 2551–2567 (2006)
3. Maymounkov, P.: Online codes, NYU Technical report TR2003-883 (2002)
4. Bodine, E., Cheng, M.: Characterization of Luby transform codes with small message size for low-latency decoding. In: IEEE International Conference on Communications, ICC, pp. 1195–1199 (2008)
5. Hyytia, E., Tirronen, T., Virtamo, J.: Optimal degree distribution for LT codes with small message length. In: 26th IEEE International Conference on Computer Communications, pp. 2576–2580 (2007)
6. Hagedorn, A., Agarwal, S., Starobinski, D., Trachtenberg, A.: Rateless coding with feedback. In: INFOCOM, pp. 1791–1799 (2009)
7. Talari, A., Rahnavard, N.: LT-AF codes: LT codes with alternating feedback. In: IEEE International Symposium on Information Theory Proceedings, pp. 2646–2650 (2013)
8. Talari, A., Rahnavard, N.: Robust LT codes with alternating feedback. Comput. Commun. **49**(1), 60–68 (2014)
9. Younis, O., Fahmy, S.: HEED: a hybrid, energy-efficient, distributed clustering approach for ad hoc sensor networks. IEEE Trans. Mob. Comput. **3**(4), 366–379 (2004)
10. Hu, Y.F., Berioli, M., Pillai, P., Cruickshank, H., Giambene, G., Kotsopoulos, K., Guo, W., Chan, P.M.L.: Broadband satellite multimedia. IET Commun. **4**(13), 1519–1531 (2010)

# Joint Spatial Diversity and Network Coding in Satellite Communications

Cui-Qin Dai[1,2(✉)], Qingyang Song[1], Lei Guo[1], and Nan-Nan Huang[2]

[1] School of Computer Science and Engineering Northeastern,
University Shenyang, Shenyang, China
daicq@cqupt.edu.cn,
{songqingyang,guolei}@mail.neu.edu.cn
[2] Chongqing University of Posts and Telecommunications, Chongqing, China
1471904661@qq.com

**Abstract.** In this paper, we focus on the transmission reliability in satellite communications. In current algorithms, traditional Spatial Diversity (SD) was investigated to resist wireless channel fading. However, intermittent connections between satellites lead to the higher system outage probability. To solve this problem, we propose a novel joint SD and Systematic Random Linear Network Coding (SRLNC) transmission scheme, namely SD-SRLNC. For time-varying satellite channels, we assume that all the source-satellite links are ON/OFF channels, and then model the satellite transmission between ON and OFF states by using the two-state Markov chain. Following this, we discuss the procedure of SD-SRLNC, and provide a theoretical analysis on its effectiveness of resisting the fading in satellite channel. Furthermore, the expressions of outage probability and Bit Error Rate (BER) for the proposed scheme are derived respectively. Simulation results show that the proposed SD-SRLNC can improve the BER performance and reduce the outage probability compared with other existing transmission schemes.

**Keywords:** Satellite communication · Spatial diversity · Network coding · BER · Outage probability

## 1 Introduction

The presence of wireless channel fading raises more and more practical difficulties on transmission reliability in satellite communications [1–3]. As well known, Spatial Diversity (SD) has been proved as an effective way to combat the transmission failures in wireless fading channels [4–6]. Additionally, Network Coding (NC) has attracted much attention to mitigate the effect of wireless fading channel caused by its advantage in improving the network reliability and its application in the cooperative diversity communication. The author in [7] employed the XOR network coding in two-way relay satellite communication for the asymmetric data transmission. In [8], the authors applied Random Linear Network Coding (RLNC) to the multi-beam satellite communication scenario to provide enhanced and robust load-balancing to unequal load demands between beams. Therefore, the existing NC schemes proposed in the satellite communication mostly considered the XOR network coding and RLNC.

© ICST Institute for Computer Sciences, Social Informatics and Telecommunications Engineering 2018
Q. Chen et al. (Eds.): ChinaCom 2016, Part I, LNICST 209, pp. 242–253, 2018.
DOI: 10.1007/978-3-319-66625-9_24

Recently, a novel network coding named Systematic Network Coding (SNC) using XORs was introduced in [9] to provide the closer performance of completion time and the added advantage of requiring fewer and simpler operations during the decoding process compared with the RLNC scheme. But, when using XORs, a direct link between the source and the destination must be existed. The author in [10] proposed a SNC using RLNC scheme, namely Systematic Random Line Network Coding (SRLNC), where the source could transmit data just via relay, and denoted the proposed approach reduced the packet loss compared with the traditional RLNC scheme. With SNC using RLNC, the author demonstrated the less computation time in encoding & decoding in [11] and showed higher decoding probability than traditional RLNC in [12]. Distinguished from [10–12], SNC using RLNC was applied to satellite communication scenarios to jointly optimize throughput and packet drop rate in [13].

In order to make further improvement of system performance, several works have focused on studying how to introduce NC along with SD into the wireless communication to reduce the effect of fading and increase the transmission reliability [14–16]. In [14], the XOR network coding was applied to the distributed wireless network and better diversity performance was obtained. In [15], a protocol named network coding cooperative MAC was introduced to obtain the better network throughput and delay by employing RLNC in the distributed cooperative network. The author in [16] presented several important contributions to the improvement of overall performance of combining analog network coding with SD in wireless relay networks. As a result, the combinational scheme of SD and NC has been applied widely for wireless channel transmission to improve system performance effectively. Therefore, as above mentioned, the existing joint schemes mainly considered the combination of SD and XORs, SD and RLNC, even SD and analog network coding, few have introduced SRLNC into the SD up till the present. And also, most of them mainly focused on the terrestrial communications, few papers on the satellite communications [13], where the wireless link is intermittent, the error probability is higher, and the transmission outage is more possible compared with terrestrial communications.

In light of above problems, we propose a novel joint SD and SRLNC (SD-SRLNC) scheme based on the ON/OFF satellite channels by taking comprehensively into account the advantages of SD and SRLNC. In the following, we assume that the destination can receive data from two sources simultaneously. All links between sources and satellite are modeled as ON/OFF channels, the link between satellite and ground terminal is assumed reliable. Based on the proposed satellite communication model, we discuss the procedure of data transmission for SD-SRLNC, and provide a theoretical analysis on its effectiveness of resisting the fading in satellite channel. Also, the expressions of outage probability and BER are derived. Simulation results show that SD-SRLNC has much better outage probability performance than the traditional SD scheme and the SD-RLNC scheme, but does not outperform SD-RLNC with respect to BER. Through the paper, we can help the readers decide which type of NC should be employed to be jointed with SD according to the performance they need optimize.

The rest of the paper is organized as follows. Section 2 introduces the system model and the transmission procedure of the SD-SRLNC scheme. In Sect. 3, the system outage probability and BER of the proposed scheme are derived by analyzing the model feature. The simulation results are given in Sect. 4.

## 2  System Model

In this section, we describe the system model and state the primary procedure of the SD-SRLNC scheme in the satellite communication.

As shown in Fig. 1, we consider a cooperative satellite model consisting of four parts: two source areas A and B, a satellite relay R and a destination D. In this model, sources only can transmit their information to D via R. We let the set $\{S_1, S_2, \ldots S_{|s|}\}$ and $\{S_{-1}, S_{-2}, \ldots S_{-|s|}\}$ respectively denote the sources included in A and B areas. The data that is going to be transmitted are composed by $N$ packets, expressed by the set $P_1, P_2, \ldots P_N$. Each source and relay use 4-QAM modulation. Also, we assume that the two areas have the same transmission process.

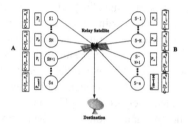

**Fig. 1.**  The model of SD-SRLNC

In addition, the links between sources and satellite are assumed to suffer from shadowed-Rician fading, and modeled as ON/OFF channels, meanwhile the link between satellite and ground terminal is reliable. During the ON states, the relay satellite receives packets from the sources correctly and during the OFF states, packets are lost. Let $E_G$ and $E_B$ be the expected durations in seconds of the good and bad states respectively. For a mean transmission rate of $R$ packets per second, the mean durations in packets of the good $D_G$ and bad $D_B$ states are derived and given by $D_G = R \cdot E_G, D_B = R \cdot E_B$ respectively [17]. The probabilities are expressed as $P_G = D_G/(D_G + D_B) \ P_B = D_B/(D_G + D_B)$. In this paper we assume uncorrelated channels but with identical channel statistics.

Following above assumptions and known conditions, we take just the transmission in one area as an example to state the primary procedure of the SD-SRLNC scheme. The transmission can be divided into two substeps: (1) each source from $S_1$ to $S_N$ sends R a different uncoded packet $P_1$ to $P_N$, then sources $S_{N+1}, S_{N+2}, \ldots S_{|s|}$ correspondingly send $P_1, P_2, \ldots P_{|s| \bmod N}$; (2) the sources send coded packets to R that are generated from $N$ native packets using RLNC. The R handles these packets and transmits them to D.

As for the traditional SD, each source sends an uncoded packet to R. The SD-RLNC scheme employs RLNC to generate a single coded packet from $N$ native packets, and uses SD to send the coded packets to R.

## 3 Performance Analysis of SD-SRLNC

In this section, we analyze and derive the system outage probability and BER of the SD-SRLNC scheme, and also compare the performance of the proposed scheme with the existing schemes including the traditional SD and SD-RLNC.

### 3.1 The Outage Probability

**The Outage Probability of SD-SRLNC.** Firstly, we derive the expression of outage probability in the A area through analyzing the transmission process of SD-SRLNC, and then according to the feature of the communication model, we obtain the system outage probability. We focus on the transmission of $N$ different packets. Let the set of packets to be transmitted be $P = \{P_1, P_2, \ldots P_N\}$. Let $n_{Pj}$ denote the number of sources sending the packet $P_j$ with $1 \leq j \leq N$.

As the description in Sect. 2, the SD-SRLNC scheme transmission is divided into two stages. If both of the two stages occur outage, the whole transmission will be fail. So the outage probability of this scheme at the area A is expressed as,

$$P_{out1}^{SNC} = P_{out1}^{SD} \cdot P_{out1}^{NC} \tag{1}$$

The system outage probability is given by,

$$P_{out}^{SNC} = 1 - \left( \left(1 - P_{out1}^{SNC}\right) \cdot \left(1 - P_{out1}^{SNC}\right) \right) \tag{2}$$

where $P_{out1}^{SD}$ detonates the outage probability when the sources send uncoded packets at the first stage, and $P_{out1}^{NC}$ is the outage probability when sending coded packets at the second stage.

In the following, we introduce the expressions of $P_{out1}^{SD}$ and $P_{out1}^{NC}$. At the first stage, sources employ SD scheme to send their uncoded packets to R, and a system outage occurs when any of the $N$ packets is not received. The outage probability of SD in area A is given by,

$$P_{out1}^{SD}(N, |S|) = 1 - \sum_{i=N}^{|S|} P_G^i P_B^{|S|-i} T_{i,N} \tag{3}$$

where $i$ denotes the number of links between sources and satellite in good sate and $T_{i,N}$ computes the number of ways of getting $N$ different packets taking into account the cases where repeated versions of the same packet would be received. To compute $T_{i,N}$, we should first get the integer solutions of the following expression,

$$x_{P1} + \ldots + x_{PN} = i, 1 \leq x_{Pj} \leq n_{Pj}, j = 1, \ldots N \tag{4}$$

The equation can be solved through standard algorithms [16]. Let $x_{l,Pj}^*, \ldots, x_{l,PN}^*$ be one of the $N_s$ solutions of (5), then we can obtain $T_{i,N}$ given by,

$$T_{i,N} = \sum_{l=1}^{N_s} \left( \prod_{j=1}^{N} \binom{n_{Pj}}{x_{l,Pj}^*} \right) \tag{5}$$

Plugging (5) into (3), we obtain the expression for $P_{out1}^{SD}$.

At the second stage, the sources transmit coded packets which are generated from the $N$ native packets to R. We use $L$ to denote the length in bits of a native packet, and the payload of each packet is split into blocks of $m'$ bits. The $k - th$ coded block of a coded packet is given by,

$$C_K = \sum_{j=1}^{N} c_j b_{jk}, \forall k = \left\{ 1, \ldots, L/m' \right\} \tag{6}$$

where $b_{jk}$ denotes the $k - th$ block of $j - th$ packet, with $1 \leq k \leq L/m'$, and $c_j$ denotes encoding coefficients chosen from $F_q$, with $q = 2^m$. The encoding coefficients $c_1, \ldots, c_N$ are added in the header of the packet. At the relay, at least $N$ coded packets must be received to retrieve the original packets. The parameter $m$ is the size of the finite field and should be big enough to ensure that the probability of generating two linearly dependent (l.d.) coded packets is negligible. The outage occurs when less than $N$ coded packets are received at the relay in the A area,

$$P_{out1}^{NC}(N, |s|) = 1 - \sum_{i=N}^{|s|} P_G^i P_B^{|s|-i} \binom{|s|}{i} \tag{7}$$

For a given $i \geq N$, the term $P_G^i P_B^{|s|-i}$ denotes the probability of having $i$ links between sources and satellite in good state and $\binom{|s|}{i}$ computes the number of distinct $i$ link subsets from the $|s|$ links between sources and satellite.

Plugging (3), (7) into (1) and combining (2), we can obtain the system outage probability for the SD-SRLNC scheme.

**The Outage Probability of Traditional SD.** From the analysis in part above, we know the outage probability for area A by using traditional SD. Now that the two areas have the same transmission, the system outage probability with traditional scheme is shown as,

$$P_{out}^{SD} = 1 - \left( \left( 1 - P_{out1}^{SD} \right) \cdot \left( 1 - P_{out1}^{SD} \right) \right) \tag{8}$$

Plugging (3) into (8), we have,

$$P_{out}^{SD} = 1 - \sum_{i=N}^{|s|} P_G^i P_B^{|s|-i} T_{i,N} \cdot \sum_{i=N}^{|s|} P_G^i P_B^{|s|-i} T_{i,N} \tag{9}$$

**The Outage Probability of SD-RLNC.** The main idea of SD-RLNC is that each source sends a single coded packet. We have known the outage probability for area A from above, so the system outage probability by using SD and RLNC is computed as,

$$P_{out}^{NC} = 1 - \left( \left( 1 - P_{out1}^{NC} \right) \cdot \left( 1 - P_{out1}^{NC} \right) \right) \tag{10}$$

Plugging (7) into (10), we have,

$$P_{out}^{NC} = 1 - \sum_{i=N}^{|s|} P_G^i P_B^{|s|-i} \binom{|s|}{i} \cdot \sum_{i=N}^{|s|} P_G^i P_B^{|s|-i} \binom{|s|}{i} \tag{11}$$

### 3.2   The BER Performance

**The BER Performance of SD-SRLNC.** A coded packet is composed of $l_0 = h + L_n + Ng$, where $h$ represents the number of bits allocates for the packet's header, $L_n$ denotes the number of bits for the linear combination of all $N$ data packets, and $g = \log_2 q$ is the number of bits used to represent the randomly chosen coding coefficients for each data packet. In the SD-SRLNC scheme, according to the definition of BER we provide the computational formula of the system using SRLNC in area A,

$$P_{AR}^{SNC} = \frac{P_{AR}^{SD} \times L_n + P_{AR}^{NC} \times |s| \times (h + L_n + \log_2 q)}{L_n + |s| \times (h + L_n + \log_2 q)} \tag{12}$$

$$P_{BR}^{SNC} = \frac{P_{BR}^{SD} \times L_n + P_{BR}^{NC} \times |s| \times (h + L_n + \log_2 q)}{L_n + |s| \times (h + L_n + \log_2 q)} \tag{13}$$

The system BER for SD-SRLNC scheme is expressed as,

$$\begin{aligned} P_e^{SNC} = {} & (1 - P_{RD}^{SNC})(P_{AR}^{SNC}(1 - P_{BR}^{SNC} + (1 - P_{AR}^{SNC})P_{BR}^{SNC} + P_{BR}^{SNC} P_{AR}^{SNC}) + \\ & P_{RD}^{SNC}(1 - (P_{AR}^{SNC}(1 - P_{BR}^{SNC}) + (1 - P_{AR}^{SNC})P_{BR}^{SNC} + P_{BR}^{SNC} P_{AR}^{SNC})) \end{aligned} \tag{14}$$

where $P_{RD}^{SNC} = P_{RD}^{NC} = P_{RD}$ denotes the BER of link $R \to D$ with SD-SRLNC, $P_{AR}^{SD}, P_{BR}^{SD}$ respectively denotes the BER using traditional SD scheme in area A and B, $P_{AR}^{NC}$ and $P_{BR}^{NC}$ respectively denote the BER from A and B areas to the relay in the case of SD-RLNC.

In the following, we introduce the expression of $P_{AR}^{SD}, P_{BR}^{SD}$ and $P_{AR}^{NC}, P_{BR}^{NC}$. Throughout the paper, the links between satellite and ground are assumed to suffer from shadowed-Rican fading. Adopting the shadowed Rican model, Nakagami-$m_0$

random variables with average power $\Omega$, where $m_0$ describes the severity of shadowing varying over the range $m_0 \geq 0$. Let $h_{xy}$ denote the coefficient of channel fading, and $r_{xy}$ denotes the average SNR from node x to node y. The Probability Density Function (PDF) of is shown as (8), where $x \in \{A, B, R\}$, $y \in \{R, D\}$,

$$f_{r_{xy}}(r_{xy}) = \alpha \sum_{l=0}^{c} \binom{c}{l} \beta^{c-1} \left( F\left(r_{xy}, l, d, \bar{r}_{xy}\right) + \varepsilon \delta F\left(r_{xy}, l, d+1, \bar{r}_{xy}\right) \right) \tag{15}$$

where

$$F(r_{xy}, l, d, \bar{r}_{xy}) = \frac{(\beta - \delta)^{\frac{l-d}{2}}}{\bar{r}_{xy}^{\frac{d-l}{2}} \Gamma(d-l)} r_{xy}^{\frac{l-d}{2}-1} e^{\frac{\beta-\delta}{2\bar{r}_{xy}} r_{xy}} \\ \times M_{\frac{d+l}{2}, \frac{d-l-1}{2}} \left( \frac{\beta-\delta}{\bar{r}_{xy}} r_{xy} \right) \tag{16}$$

$$\bar{r}_{xy} = \frac{E_b}{N_0} E\left[ |h_{xy}|^2 \right] \tag{17}$$

$$\begin{cases} \beta = (0.5/b) \\ c = (d - N_0^+) \\ \varepsilon = m_0 - d \\ \delta = 0.5\Omega/(2b^2 + b\Omega) \\ \alpha = 0.5(2bm_0/(2bm_0 + \Omega))m_0/b \end{cases} \tag{18}$$

where $N_0$ denotes the antenna numbers equipped at the relay and destination, $d = \max\{1, \lfloor m_0 \rfloor\}$, $\lfloor m_0 \rfloor$ denotes the largest integer not greater than $m_0$; $(d - N_0^+)$ indicates that if $(d - N_0) \leq 0$, then use $d - N_0 = 0$; $\max\{1, \lfloor m_0 \rfloor\}$ chooses the greatest of the two positive integers; $\Gamma(\cdot)$ denotes the Gamma function [17], and $M_{u,v}(\cdot)$ represents the Whittaker function [17].

We assume that at the two areas each link between source and satellite has the same BER $P_{A1R}$, $P_{B1R}$ expressed by (15) during the good state, and during the bad state, the BER is equal to 1.

According to [1],

$$P_{A1R} = P_{B1R} = \alpha \sum_{l=0}^{c} \binom{c}{l} \beta^{c-1} \times \\ [T(1, l, d, \bar{r}_{A1R}) + \varepsilon \delta T(1, l, d+1, \bar{r}_{A1R})] \tag{19}$$

$$P_{RD} = \alpha \sum_{l=0}^{c} \binom{c}{l} \beta^{c-1} \times [T(1, l, d, \bar{r}_{RD}) + \varepsilon \delta T(1, l, d+1, \bar{r}_{RD})] \tag{20}$$

where

$$T(1,l,d,\bar{r}_{xy}) = \frac{\Gamma(d-l+1/2)}{2\sqrt{\pi} \times (1/2)^{d-l} \times \bar{r}_{xy} \times \Gamma(d-l+1)} \times$$
$$_3F_2\left(d, d-l, d-l+\frac{1}{2}; d-l+1, d-l; -\frac{(\beta-\delta)}{1/2\bar{r}_{xy}}\right)$$

(21)

where $_3F_2(\cdot,\cdot,\cdot;\cdot,\cdot;\cdot)$ represents the generalized Hypergeometric function. The expression of BER from A to R is the following,

$$P_{AR}^{SD} = P_L \times \frac{L \times P_{A1R} + (N-L)}{N}$$

(22)

$$P_L = \sum_{i=L}^{|s|} P_G^L P_B^{|s|-L} T_{i,L}, 0 \leq i \leq L, 0 \leq L \leq N$$

(23)

The first term in (22) represents the number of methods to send $L$ packets to relay successfully, the second term denotes the BER of sending $L$ packets one time.

Similarly to A, the BER of B is calculated as

$$P_{BR}^{SD} = P_L \times \frac{L \times P_{B1R} + (N-L)}{N}$$

(24)

The $P_{AR}^{NC}$, $P_{BR}^{NC}$ respectively denote the BER from A or B area to the relay in the case of SD-RLNC, and are expressed as,

$$P_{AR}^{NC} = \sum_{i=0}^{|s|} C_{|s|}^i P_G^i P_B^{|s|-i} P_{A1R}$$

(25)

$$P_{BR}^{NC} = \sum_{i=0}^{|s|} C_{|s|}^i P_G^i P_B^{|s|-i} P_{B1R}$$

(26)

**The BER Performance of Traditional SD.** With the traditional SD, at the relay, the satellite obtains the data from A and B, then recodes and sends them to D using RLNC. The error occurs at the destination when either of the two data is transmitted incorrectly or the relay sends incorrect data, so the system BER is expressed as,

$$P_e^{SD} = (1 - P_{RD}^{SD})(P_{AR}^{SD}(1 - P_{BR}^{SD}) + (1 - P_{AR}^{SD})P_{BR}^{SD} + P_{AR}^{SD}P_{BR}^{SD}) +$$
$$P_{RD}^{SD}(1 - (P_{AR}^{SD}(1 - P_{BR}^{SD}) + (1 - P_{AR}^{SD})P_{BR}^{SD} + P_{AR}^{SD}P_{BR}^{SD}))$$

(27)

where $P_{RD}^{SD} = P_{RD}$ that computed by (20) denotes the BER of transmitting data from relay to destination, and $P_{AR}^{SD}, P_{BR}^{SD}$ that expressed in (22) and (24) respectively means the BER from A or B to the relay.

Plugging (20), (22) and (24) into (27), we can obtain the system BER of SD.

**The BER Performance of SD-RLNC** The SD-RLNC scheme employs RLNC to deal with the signal at each source and the encoded packets will be sent to the relay. Under the condition that each area at less $N$ packets are received at the relay, then the relay decodes the packets using RLNC, finally sends packets to the destination. The expression of BER of SD-RLNC is given by,

$$P_e^{NC} = \left(1 - P_{RD}^{NC}\right)\left(P_{AR}^{NC}\left(1 - P_{BR}^{NC}\right) + \left(1 - P_{AR}^{NC}\right)P_{BR}^{NC} + P_{BR}^{NC}P_{AR}^{NC}\right) + \\ P_{RD}^{NC}\left(1 - \left(P_{AR}^{NC}\left(1 - P_{BR}^{NC}\right) + \left(1 - P_{AR}^{NC}\right)P_{BR}^{NC} + P_{BR}^{NC}P_{AR}^{NC}\right)\right) \tag{28}$$

where $P_{RD}^{NC} = P_{RD} P_{AR}^{NC}$ and $P_{BR}^{NC}$ shown in (25) and (26) respectively denote the BER from A or B area to the relay in the case of SD-RLNC. Plugging (20), (25) and (26) into (28), we can obtain the BER of SD-RLNC system.

## 4   Simulation Results

In this section, we verify the performance of our proposed scheme and compare it with that of the traditional SD, the SD-RLNC. Throughout the simulation, the number of antenna equipped at the relay and destination is $N_0 = 1$; the number of transmitted packets $N = 2$; the number of data bits in a packet $L = 1600$; the number of header bits $h = 80$ and the number of sources in one area is from 2 to 10. Moreover, the field size is set $q = 2^8$, $E_G = 1200, E_B = 600$ and the transmission rate R = 10 kbps, transmission rate is very low since the uplink for this scenario is typically used for sending command message. The channel is assumed to suffer from the average shadowing (AS) Rican fading unless mentioned otherwise.

In Fig. 2, we compare the system outage probability of three schemes. We can observe clearly under the condition of $|s| = 2$, the outage probability is almost identical of the three schemes. As the increase of the number of sources, the outage probability decreases for all of these schemes. In addition, it is obviously indicated that the performance of SD-SRLNC is much better than that of another two schemes as sources increase. The SD-RLNC outperforms than SD, from which we conclude combining SD and NC should be employed widely in satellite communication to reduce outage probability and improve the satellite communication reliability.

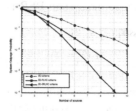

**Fig. 2.** The outage probability of SD, SD-SRLNC and SD-RLNC

The BER performance of these three schemes are simulated and compared in Fig. 3. It can be obtained that our proposed scheme behaves much better than that of SD, but does not outperform than SD-RLNC. The reason for the better performance of SD-RLNC scheme is that RLNC avoids duplicated versions of the same packets are received, and RLNC provides fair protection of the packets. Each coded packet stores information from $N$ original packets, then if one source-satellite link is in bad state, it equally affects to all the $N$ packets and not to a single packet. The SD-SRLNC and SD may provide duplicated versions. The Fig. 2 indicates that our proposed SD-SRLNC reduces the outage probability by sacrificing the BER performance. We can determine which combination scheme should be employed in satellite communication depending on the different optimized goal.

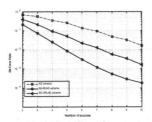

**Fig. 3.** The BER of SD, SD-SRLNC and SD-RLNC

In Fig. 4, we compare the BER performance for three schemes in the case of frequent heavy shadowing (FHS), average shadowing (AS) and infrequent light shadowing (ILS). The simulated paratemers under these shadowing enviroments are shown in Table 1. From Fig. 4, we can observe that the BER performance in AS and ILS environments is much better than that in the FHS environment. Also, the BER performance of SD-RLNC in the AS environment approximates to that in the ILS when the number of sources is 2 to 5. As the increasing of number of sources, the distinction is obvious. When using SRLNC, the BER performance of AS and ILS is always closer.

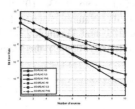

**Fig. 4.** The BER for SD-SRLNC in different shadowing environment

**Table 1.** Different shadowing environment parameter

| Shadowing | $b$ | $m_0$ | $\Omega$ |
|---|---|---|---|
| Frequent heavy shadowing (FHS) | 0.063 | 0.739 | $8.97 \times 10^{-4}$ |
| Average shadowing (AS) | 0.126 | 10.1 | 0.835 |
| Infrequent light shadowing (ILS) | 0.158 | 19.4 | 1.29 |

The $E_G$ and $E_B$ is the expected durations in seconds of the good and bad states respectively. In Fig. 5, we investigate the effect of the variation on the performance in terms of the outage probability for the aforementioned schemes. We can obtain the better system performance with the variation of $E_G$ from 600 to 1200. Additionally, the figure indicates that lower outage probability is obtained when $E_G > E_B$ than that of $E_G = E_B$.

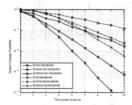

**Fig. 5.** The outage probability with different $E_G$ and $E_B$

## 5   Conclusion

In this paper, considering the issue on transmission failures due to the deep fading produced by the randomness of the surrounding environment, we have analyzed the existed traditional schemes and proposed the SD-SRLNC scheme in the scene of multiple sources-single relay-single destination. In addition, we derive the outage probability and BER expressions of these schemes. Simulation results show that the proposed scheme outperforms SD-RLNC scheme and traditional SD in terms of outage probability, and the performance will be promoted as the increase of the numbers of sources. However, the SD-RLNC scheme provides the best BER performance. The simulation results will be helpful to make the decision for choosing the appropriate scheme according to different requirements in satellite communications.

**Acknowledgment.** This work was jointly supported by the National Natural Science Foundation of Major Research Project in China (No. 91438110), the National Natural Science Foundation in China (No. 61601075), the Natural Science Foundation Project of CQ CSTC (No. cstc2016jcyjA0174), the Scientific and Technological Research Program of Chongqing Municipal Education Commission (No. KJ1500440), the Natural Science Foundation Project of CQUPT (No. A2014-111).

## References

1. Bhatnagar, M.R., Arti, M.K.: On the closed-form performance analysis of maximal ratio combining in shadowed-rician fading LMS channels. IEEE Commun. Lett. **18**, 54–57 (2014)
2. Bhatnagar, M.R., Arti, M.K.: Performance analysis of AF based hybrid satellite-terrestrial cooperative network over generalized fading channels. IEEE Commun. Lett. **17**, 1912–1915 (2013)

3. Seyedi, Y., Shirazi, M., Moharrer, A., et al.: Use of shadowing moments to statistically model mobile satellite channels in urban environments. IEEE Trans. Wirel. Commun. **12**, 3760–3769 (2013)

4. Brante, G., Souza, R.D., Garcia-Frias, J.: Spatial diversity using analog joint source channel coding in wireless channels. IEEE Trans. Commun. **61**, 301–311 (2013)

5. Chau, Y.A., Huang, K.Y.: Spatial diversity with a new sequential maximal ratio combining over wireless fading channels. In: 12th IEEE International Workshop on Signal Processing Advances in Wireless Communication, pp. 241–245. IEEE Press, San Francisco (2011)

6. Vien, N.H., Nguyen, H.H., Le-Ngoc, T.: Diversity analysis of smart relaying over Nakagami and Hoyt generalized fading channels. In: IEEE 69th Vehicular Technology Conference. pp. 1–5. IEEE Press, Barcelona (2009)

7. Zhang, X., Ghrayeb, A., Hasna, M.: On hierarchical network coding versus opportunistic user selection for two-way relay channels with asymmetric data rates. IEEE Trans. Commun. **61**, 2900–2910 (2013)

8. Vieira, F., Lucani, D.E., Alagha, N.: Codes and balances: multibeam satellite load balancing with coded packets. In: IEEE International Conference on Communications. pp. 3316–3321. IEEE Press, Ottawa (2012)

9. Lucani, D.E., Medard, M., Stojanovic, M.: Systematic network coding for time-division duplexing. In: IEEE International Symposium on Information Theory Proceedings, pp. 2403–2407. IEEE Press, Texas (2010)

10. Prior, R., Rodrigues, A.: Systematic network coding for packet loss concealment in broadcast distribution. In: International Conference on Information Networking, pp. 245–250. IEEE Press, kuala lumpur (2011)

11. Li, Y., Chan, W.Y., Blostein, S.D.: Systematic network coding for transmission over two-hop lossy links. In: 27th Biennial Symposium on Communications, pp. 213–217. IEEE Press, kingston (2014)

12. Khan, A.S., Chatzigeorgiou, I.: Performance analysis of random linear network coding in two-source single-relay networks. In: International Conference on Communication Workshop, pp. 991–996. IEEE Press (2015)

13. Esmaeilzadeh, M., Aboutorab, N., Sadeghi, P.: Joint optimization of throughput and packet drop rate for delay sensitive applications in TDD satellite network coded systems. IEEE Trans. Commun. **62**, 676–690 (2013)

14. Chen, Y., Kishore, S., Li, J.T.: Wireless diversity through network coding. In: IEEE Wireless Communications and Networking Conference, pp. 1681–1686. IEEE Press, Las Vegas (2006)

15. Qin, H., Zhang, R., Li, B., et al.: Distributed cooperative MAC for wireless networks based on network coding. In: IEEE Wireless Communications and Networking Conference, pp. 2050–2055. IEEE Press, New Orleans (2015)

16. Upadhyay, P.K.: Spatial Diversity for Analog Network Coding: Outage Characterization over Wireless Channels. LAP LAMBERT Academic Publishing, Saarbrücken (2012)

17. Lutz, E.: A Markov Model for Correlated Land Mobile Satellite Channels. Int. J. Sat. Commun. **14**, 333–339 (1996)

# Interference Alignment in Cognitive Relay Networks Under CSI Mismatch

Weiwei Yang[✉], Tao Zhang, Yueming Cai, and Dan Wu

College of Communications Engineering, PLA University of Science and Technology,
Nanjing 210007, China
wwyang1981@163.com, ztcool@126.com, caiym@vip.sina.com

**Abstract.** Interference alignment (IA) is an effective method that can eliminate interferences in wireless networks, and has been applied to spectrum sharing in cognitive radio (CR) networks recently. However, the availability of perfect network channel state information (CSI) is necessary for most existing IA schemes, which is not practical in general due to the realistic communication scenarios and deployment challenges. In this paper, we apply IA to cognitive relay networks under CSI mismatch where the variance of the CSI measurement error depends on signal-to-noise ratio (SNR). An adaptive Max-SINR IA algorithm has been introduced to improve the performance of the secondary network by using the knowledge of CSI error variance. Finally, we analyze the performance of the secondary network in terms of the end-to-end equivalent transmission rate and outage probability. Simulation results indicate that our proposed adaptive Max-SINR IA scheme can greatly improve the performance of the secondary network.

**Keywords:** Cognitive relay networks · Interference alignment · CSI mismatch · Outage probability

## 1 Introduction

Recently, due to the ability of alleviating the spectrum shortage problem of wireless communications, spectrum sharing techniques have received substantial interests [1,2]. In spectrum sharing networks, the secondary users (SUs) are allowed to access the licensed spectrum as long as the interference power generated by the secondary communications does not exceed the predefined threshold at the primary user (PU). In parallel, cooperative relay has been demonstrated as an effective way to combat channel fading and improve systems transmission performance. In [3,4], the performance of an underly cognitive relay networks has been studied. Using $N$-th best relay selection, the outage probability was

This work is supported by the National Natural Science Foundation of China (Nos. 61371122, 61471393, and 61501512), Jiangsu Provincial National Science Foundation (BK20150718) and China Postdoctoral Science Foundation under a Special Financial Grant (No. 2013T60912).

© ICST Institute for Computer Sciences, Social Informatics and Telecommunications Engineering 2018
Q. Chen et al. (Eds.): ChinaCom 2016, Part I, LNICST 209, pp. 254–263, 2018.
DOI: 10.1007/978-3-319-66625-9_25

further analyzed for spectrum-sharing relaying networks in [5]. However, to the best of the authors' knowledge, the SU receivers have ignored the interference that caused by primary transmission in above works. In most of practical scenario, both the interference between PU receivers and SU transmitters and the interference between SU receivers and PU transmitters should be considered simultaneously.

Recently, interference alignment (IA) has been proposed as an effective method not only to eliminate the interference to PU receivers but also the interference to SU receivers [6]. However, the application of IA should satisfy some conditions. First of all, the application of IA needs global channel state information (CSI) and it is difficult to maintain. To deal with this issue, the authors in [7] proposed the distributed iterative algorithm to achieve IA, in which the proposed algorithm only need the local CSI and can simplify the implementation of IA. Unfortunately, it will affect the achievable throughput and the total full degrees of freedom (DoF) of the network that only can obtain partial CSI due to the realistic communication scenarios. Thus, IA under CSI mismatch has received great interests. However, due to the complex nature of the issue, different works deal with various CSI uncertainty aspects, such as correlated channels [8], analog channel state feedback [9], and constant variance of the CSI error [10]. The authors of [11] investigate the performance of IA techniques in multiple-input multiple-output (MIMO) interference channels in the presence of CSI mismatch, in which the CSI mismatch model is versatile and treats the channel error variance either as a function of SNR or as independent of it. Moreover, to the best of authors' knowledge, no existing literatures have considered the application of IA in cognitive relay networks under CSI mismatch.

Motivated by these observation, we apply IA to spectrum sharing relay network under the similar CSI mismatch model in [11]. The adaptive Max-SINR algorithm has been introduced to improve the performance of the secondary network by using the knowledge of CSI error variance. Finally, we investigate the performance of the secondary network in terms of the end-to-end equivalent transmission rate and outage probability and derive that IA can increase the sum rate and decrease the outage probability of the secondary network. Simulation results are provided to demonstrate the validity of our analysis and indicate that our proposed adaptive Max-SINR IA scheme can greatly improve the performance of the secondary network.

*Notation:* $\mathbf{A}^H$ represents the conjugate transpose of matrix $\mathbf{A}$. $rank(\mathbf{A})$ is the rank of matrix $\mathbf{A}$. $\mathbf{I}_n$ denotes the $n \times n$ identity matrix.

## 2   System Model

### 2.1   Network Description

We consider a spectrum sharing relay network, where the PU network containing a PU source that equipped with $M_p$ antennas and a PU destination that equipped with $N_p$ antennas. Secondary network including three nodes coexists with the PU network. Moreover, the SU network contains a secondary source (SS), a secondary relay (SR) and a secondary destination (SD) that equipped with $M_s$, $M_r$ and $M_d$ antennas, respectively. Specifically, the PU source transmit information to PU destination directly while the SS transmit information to SD with the help of SR using decode-and-forward (DF) protocol. In the first phase, the received signals at the PU receiver, the SR and the SD are respectively given by

$$\mathbf{y}_{p,1} = \mathbf{H}_{pp}\mathbf{V}_{p,1}\mathbf{x}_p + \mathbf{H}_{ps}\mathbf{V}_{s,1}\mathbf{x}_s + \mathbf{n}_{p,1} \tag{1}$$

$$\mathbf{y}_{r,1} = \mathbf{H}_{rs}\mathbf{V}_{s,1}\mathbf{x}_s + \mathbf{H}_{rp}\mathbf{V}_{p,1}\mathbf{x}_p + \mathbf{n}_{r,1} \tag{2}$$

$$\mathbf{y}_{d,1} = \mathbf{H}_{ds}\mathbf{V}_{s,1}\mathbf{x}_s + \mathbf{H}_{dp}\mathbf{V}_{p,1}\mathbf{x}_s + \mathbf{n}_{d,1} \tag{3}$$

In the second phase, if the SR can decode the message from the SS successfully, the SR will forward the signal to the SD. The received signals of PU destination and SD are respectively expressed as

$$\mathbf{y}_{p,2} = \mathbf{H}_{pp}\mathbf{V}_{p,2}\mathbf{x}_p + \mathbf{H}_{pr}\mathbf{V}_{r,2}\mathbf{x}_r + \mathbf{n}_{p,2} \tag{4}$$

$$\mathbf{y}_{d,2} = \mathbf{H}_{dr}\mathbf{V}_{r,2}\mathbf{x}_r + \mathbf{H}_{dp}\mathbf{V}_{p,2}\mathbf{x}_r + \mathbf{n}_{d,2} \tag{5}$$

In the formulas above, $\mathbf{H}_{ab} \in C^{N_a \times M_b}$ denotes the channel fading matrix from node $b$ to node $a$, $\mathbf{x}_b \in C^{d_b \times 1}$ and $\mathbf{V}_{b,t} \in C^{M_b \times d_b}$ are the transmitting data and the precoding matrix at node $a$ in the $t$th phase, and $\mathbf{n}_{a,t} \sim N_C\left(\mathbf{0}, \sigma^2\mathbf{I}_{N_a}\right)$ is the noise vector at node $a$ in the $t$th phase, where $b \in \{p, s, r\}$, $a \in \{p, r, d\}$ and $t \in \{1, 2\}$.

Using the interference suppression matrix to null the interference at receiver, the recovered signal vector can be expressed as

$$\mathbf{r}_{d,t} = \mathbf{U}_{d,t}^H \mathbf{y}_{d,t} \tag{6}$$

where $\mathbf{U}_{d,t} \in C^{N_d \times d_d}$ is the truncated unitary interference suppression matric. And the SD will use maximum ratio combination (MRC) protocol to combine the recovered signals of the two phases to recover the message.

For notational convenience, we assume that the transmit power of all nodes is $P$, and $\rho = P/\sigma^2$ is the nominal transmitting SNR.

## 2.2   CSI Mismatch Model

According to the assumption in [11], we assume that all precoding matrixs are defined with the knowledge of unified CSI mismatch. And the CSI mismatch model can be expressed as

$$\hat{\mathbf{H}}_{ab} = \mathbf{H}_{ab} + \mathbf{E}_{ab} \tag{7}$$

where the channel measurement error $\mathbf{E}_{ab}$ is thought to be independent of actual channel matrix $\mathbf{H}_{ab}$. We consider $\mathbf{E}_{ab}$ as a Gaussian matrix, which consists of i.i.d. elements with mean zero and variance $\tau$, i.e.,

$$
\begin{aligned}
vec\left(\mathbf{E}_{ab}\right) &\sim \mathrm{N}_C\left(\mathbf{0}, \tau \mathbf{I}\right) \\
with\, \tau &\overset{\Delta}{=} \beta \rho^{-\alpha}, \beta > 0, \alpha \geq 0
\end{aligned}
\tag{8}
$$

where $\alpha \neq 0$ denotes the error variance depends on SNR and $\alpha = 0$ denotes the error variance is independent of SNR.

## 3   Iterative Algorithm for Interference Alignment in Cognitive Relay Networks

In this section, we give the iterative IA algorithm in cognitive relay networks under CSI mismatch model.

For the CSI mismatch case, we assume that all precoding matrices are derived based on imperfect CSI $\hat{\mathbf{H}}_{ab}$. According to the perfect CSI case that in [7], in the first phase, the precoding matrices should satisfy

$$\hat{\mathbf{U}}_{p,1}^{H}\hat{\mathbf{H}}_{ps}\hat{\mathbf{V}}_{s,1} = 0, \quad rank\left(\hat{\mathbf{U}}_{p,1}^{H}\hat{\mathbf{H}}_{pp}\hat{\mathbf{V}}_{p,1}\right) = d_p \tag{9}$$

$$\hat{\mathbf{U}}_{r,1}^{H}\hat{\mathbf{H}}_{rp}\hat{\mathbf{V}}_{p,1} = 0, \quad rank\left(\hat{\mathbf{U}}_{r,1}^{H}\hat{\mathbf{H}}_{rs}\hat{\mathbf{V}}_{s,1}\right) = d_s \tag{10}$$

$$\hat{\mathbf{U}}_{d,1}^{H}\hat{\mathbf{H}}_{dp}\hat{\mathbf{V}}_{p,1} = 0, \quad rank\left(\hat{\mathbf{U}}_{d,1}^{H}\hat{\mathbf{H}}_{ds}\hat{\mathbf{V}}_{s,1}\right) = d_s \tag{11}$$

Similarly, in the second phase, the precoding matrices should satisfy

$$\hat{\mathbf{U}}_{p,2}^{H}\hat{\mathbf{H}}_{pr}\hat{\mathbf{V}}_{r,2} = 0, \quad rank\left(\hat{\mathbf{U}}_{p,2}^{H}\hat{\mathbf{H}}_{pp}\hat{\mathbf{V}}_{p,2}\right) = d_p \tag{12}$$

$$\hat{\mathbf{U}}_{d,2}^{H}\hat{\mathbf{H}}_{dp}\hat{\mathbf{V}}_{p,2} = 0, \quad rank\left(\hat{\mathbf{U}}_{d,2}^{H}\hat{\mathbf{H}}_{dr}\hat{\mathbf{V}}_{r,2}\right) = d_r \tag{13}$$

To derive the precoding matrices, we firstly derive the normalized interference plus noise covariance matrix the following Lemma.

**Lemma 1.** The normalized interference plus noise covariance matrix associated with the $l$th stream of node $k$ is derived as

$$
\begin{aligned}
\hat{\mathbf{Q}}_k^l = &\sum_{d=1}^{d_j} \hat{\mathbf{H}}_{kj}\hat{\mathbf{V}}_j^{[*d]}\hat{\mathbf{V}}_j^{[*d]H}\hat{\mathbf{H}}_{kj}^{H} + \sum_{d=1,d\neq l}^{d_k} \hat{\mathbf{H}}_{kk}\hat{\mathbf{V}}_k^{[*d]}\hat{\mathbf{V}}_k^{[*d]H}\hat{\mathbf{H}}_{kk}^{H} \\
&+ \underbrace{\left(\left(d_s + d_p - 1\right)\tau\left(1+\tau\right) + \rho^{-1}\left(1+\tau\right)^2\right)}_{\mu_1}\mathbf{I}_{N_k},
\end{aligned}
\tag{14}
$$

*Proof.* The interference plus noise covariance matrix associated with the $l$th stream of user $k$ can be shown as that in (15).

$$
\begin{aligned}
\mathbf{Q}_k^l =& \sum_{d=1}^{d_j} P\mathbf{H}_{kj}\hat{\mathbf{V}}_j^{[*d]}\hat{\mathbf{V}}_j^{[*d]H}\mathbf{H}_{kj}^H + \sum_{d=1,d\neq l}^{d_k} P\mathbf{H}_{kk}\hat{\mathbf{V}}_k^{[*d]}\hat{\mathbf{V}}_k^{[*d]H}\mathbf{H}_{kk}^H + \sigma^2\mathbf{I}_{N_k} \\
=& \sum_{d=1}^{d_j} P\left(\tfrac{1}{1+\tau}\hat{\mathbf{H}}_{kj} + \breve{\mathbf{H}}_{kj}\right)\hat{\mathbf{V}}_j^{[*d]}\hat{\mathbf{V}}_j^{[*d]H}\left(\tfrac{1}{1+\tau}\hat{\mathbf{H}}_{kj} + \breve{\mathbf{H}}_{kj}\right)^H \\
&+ \sum_{d=1,d\neq l}^{d_k} P\left(\tfrac{1}{1+\tau}\hat{\mathbf{H}}_{kk} + \breve{\mathbf{H}}_{kk}\right)\hat{\mathbf{V}}_k^{[*d]}\hat{\mathbf{V}}_k^{[*d]H}\left(\tfrac{1}{1+\tau}\hat{\mathbf{H}}_{kk} + \breve{\mathbf{H}}_{kk}\right)^H + \sigma^2\mathbf{I}_{N_k} \\
=& \sum_{d=1}^{d_j} \tfrac{P}{(1+\tau)^2}\hat{\mathbf{H}}_{kj}\hat{\mathbf{V}}_j^{[*d]}\hat{\mathbf{V}}_j^{[*d]H}\hat{\mathbf{H}}_{kj}^H + \sum_{d=1,d\neq l}^{d_k} \tfrac{P}{(1+\tau)^2}\hat{\mathbf{H}}_{kk}\hat{\mathbf{V}}_k^{[*d]}\hat{\mathbf{V}}_k^{[*d]H}\hat{\mathbf{H}}_{kk}^H \\
&+ \underbrace{\sum_{d=1}^{d_j} \tfrac{P}{1+\tau}\left(\hat{\mathbf{H}}_{kj}\hat{\mathbf{V}}_j^{[*d]}\hat{\mathbf{V}}_j^{[*d]H}\breve{\mathbf{H}}_{kj}^H + \breve{\mathbf{H}}_{kj}\hat{\mathbf{V}}_j^{[*d]}\hat{\mathbf{V}}_j^{[*d]H}\hat{\mathbf{H}}_{kj}^H\right)}_{J_1} \\
&+ \underbrace{\sum_{d=1,d\neq l}^{d_k} \tfrac{P}{1+\tau}\left(\hat{\mathbf{H}}_{kk}\hat{\mathbf{V}}_k^{[*d]}\hat{\mathbf{V}}_k^{[*d]H}\breve{\mathbf{H}}_{kk}^H + \breve{\mathbf{H}}_{kk}\hat{\mathbf{V}}_k^{[*d]}\hat{\mathbf{V}}_k^{[*d]H}\hat{\mathbf{H}}_{kk}^H\right)}_{J_2} \\
&+ \underbrace{\sum_{d=1}^{d_j} P\breve{\mathbf{H}}_{kj}\hat{\mathbf{V}}_j^{[*d]}\hat{\mathbf{V}}_j^{[*d]H}\breve{\mathbf{H}}_{kj}^H + \sum_{d=1,d\neq l}^{d_k} P\breve{\mathbf{H}}_{kk}\hat{\mathbf{V}}_k^{[*d]}\hat{\mathbf{V}}_k^{[*d]H}\breve{\mathbf{H}}_{kk}^H + \sigma^2\mathbf{I}_{N_k}}_{J_3}
\end{aligned} \tag{15}
$$

All precoders and combiners are constructed upon channel $\hat{\mathbf{H}}_{kj}$ and are independent of $\breve{\mathbf{H}}_{kj}$, therefore $E_{\hat{\mathbf{H}}_{kj},\breve{\mathbf{H}}_{kj}} J_1 = 0$, $E_{\hat{\mathbf{H}}_{kj},\breve{\mathbf{H}}_{kj}} J_2 = 0$, $E_{\hat{\mathbf{H}}_{kj},\breve{\mathbf{H}}_{kj}} J_3 = P(d_j + d_k - 1)\frac{\tau}{1+\tau}\mathbf{I}$ based on that in [7]. This way, we can normalized $\mathbf{Q}_k^l$ by divided $\frac{P}{(1+\tau)^2}$ in (14) and approximate it with a simpler from, i.e., $\hat{\mathbf{Q}}_k^l$, as follows that in (14).

Given randomly initialized precoders and with respect to the fact that only imperfect channel estimates are available, in the cognitive relay network considered in this paper in the first phase, the normalized interference plus noise covariance matrices for stream $l$ at the PU receiver, the SR and SD can be evaluated as

$$
\begin{aligned}
\hat{\mathbf{Q}}_{p,1}^l =& \sum_{d=1}^{d_s} \hat{\mathbf{H}}_{ps}\hat{\mathbf{V}}_{s,1}^{[*d]}\hat{\mathbf{V}}_{s,1}^{[*d]H}\hat{\mathbf{H}}_{ps}^H + \sum_{d=1,d\neq l}^{d_p} \hat{\mathbf{H}}_{pp}\hat{\mathbf{V}}_{p,1}^{[*d]}\hat{\mathbf{V}}_{p,1}^{[*d]H}\hat{\mathbf{H}}_{pp}^H \\
&+ \underbrace{\left((d_s + d_p - 1)\tau(1+\tau) + \rho^{-1}(1+\tau)^2\right)}_{\mu_1}\mathbf{I}_{N_p},
\end{aligned} \tag{16}
$$

$$\hat{\mathbf{Q}}_{r,1}^l = \sum_{d=1}^{d_p} \hat{\mathbf{H}}_{rp} \hat{\mathbf{V}}_{p,1}^{[*d]} \hat{\mathbf{V}}_{p,1}^{[*d]H} \hat{\mathbf{H}}_{rp}^H + \sum_{d=1,d\neq l}^{d_s} \hat{\mathbf{H}}_{rs} \hat{\mathbf{V}}_{s,1}^{[*d]} \hat{\mathbf{V}}_{s,1}^{[*d]H} \hat{\mathbf{H}}_{rs}^H$$
$$+ \underbrace{\left( (d_s + d_p - 1) \tau (1+\tau) + \rho^{-1}(1+\tau)^2 \right) \mathbf{I}_{N_r}}_{\mu_1} \tag{17}$$

$$\hat{\mathbf{Q}}_{d,1}^l = \sum_{d=1}^{d_p} \hat{\mathbf{H}}_{dp} \hat{\mathbf{V}}_{p,1}^{[*d]} \hat{\mathbf{V}}_{p,1}^{[*d]H} \hat{\mathbf{H}}_{dp}^H + \sum_{d=1,d\neq l}^{d_s} \hat{\mathbf{H}}_{ds} \hat{\mathbf{V}}_{s,1}^{[*d]} \hat{\mathbf{V}}_{s,1}^{[*d]H} \hat{\mathbf{H}}_{ds}^H$$
$$+ \underbrace{\left( (d_s + d_p - 1) \tau (1+\tau) + \rho^{-1}(1+\tau)^2 \right) \mathbf{I}_{N_d}}_{\mu_1}, \tag{18}$$

respectively. In the reciprocal network, the normalized interference plus noise covariance matrices for stream $l$ for the second phase at the PU transmitter and the SS are given by

$$\tilde{\mathbf{Q}}_{p,1}^l = \sum_{d=1}^{d_s} \tilde{\mathbf{H}}_{pr} \tilde{\mathbf{V}}_{r,1}^{[*d]} \tilde{\mathbf{V}}_{r,1}^{[*d]H} \tilde{\mathbf{H}}_{pr}^H + \sum_{d=1}^{d_d} \tilde{\mathbf{H}}_{pd} \tilde{\mathbf{V}}_{d,1}^{[*d]} \tilde{\mathbf{V}}_{d,1}^{[*d]H} \tilde{\mathbf{H}}_{pd}^H$$
$$+ \sum_{d=1,d\neq l}^{d_p} \tilde{\mathbf{H}}_{pp}^H \tilde{\mathbf{V}}_{p,1}^{[*d]} \tilde{\mathbf{V}}_{p,1}^{[*d]H} \tilde{\mathbf{H}}_{pp} + \underbrace{\left( (d_s + d_d + d_p - 1) \tau (1+\tau) + \rho^{-1}(1+\tau)^2 \right) \mathbf{I}_{N_p}}_{\tilde{\mu}_1} \tag{19}$$

$$\tilde{\mathbf{Q}}_{s,1}^l = \sum_{d=1}^{d_p} \tilde{\mathbf{H}}_{sp} \tilde{\mathbf{V}}_{p,1}^{[*d]} \tilde{\mathbf{V}}_{p,1}^{[*d]H} \tilde{\mathbf{H}}_{sp}^H + \sum_{d=1,d\neq l}^{d_r} \tilde{\mathbf{H}}_{sr} \tilde{\mathbf{V}}_{r,1}^{[*d]} \tilde{\mathbf{V}}_{r,1}^{[*d]H} \tilde{\mathbf{H}}_{sr}^H$$
$$+ \sum_{d=1,d\neq l}^{d_d} \tilde{\mathbf{H}}_{sd} \hat{\mathbf{V}}_{d,1}^{[*d]} \tilde{\mathbf{V}}_{d,1}^{[*d]H} \tilde{\mathbf{H}}_{sd}^H + \underbrace{\left( (d_s + d_d + d_p - 1) \tau (1+\tau) + \rho^{-1}(1+\tau)^2 \right) \mathbf{I}_{N_s}}_{\tilde{\mu}_1} \tag{20}$$

As mentioned earlier, due to the coupled nature of the problem, finding precoders and combiners requests an iterative algorithm in general. With respect to the fact that only imperfect channel estimates are available, and with knowledge of error variance $\tau$ in advance, the proposed adaptive Max-SINR algorithm in the first phase can be concisely presented as follows:

---

## Adaptive Max-SINR in the first phase

---

1. Set the adaptive factors $\mu_1 = (d_s + d_p - 1) \tau (1+\tau) + \rho^{-1}(1+\tau)^2$, $\tilde{\mu}_1 = (d_s + d_d + d_p - 1) \tau (1+\tau) + \rho^{-1}(1+\tau)^2$.
2. The PU source and SS respectively set arbitrary precoding matrices $\hat{\mathbf{V}}_{p,1}$ and $\hat{\mathbf{V}}_{s,1}$ under CSI mismatch, which satisfies $\hat{\mathbf{V}}_{p,1}^H \hat{\mathbf{V}}_{p,1} = \mathbf{I}_{d_p}$, $\hat{\mathbf{V}}_{s,1}^H \hat{\mathbf{V}}_{s,1} = \mathbf{I}_{d_s}$.
3. According to (16)–(18), the PU destination, the SR and the SD compute their interference plus noise covariance matrices $\hat{\mathbf{Q}}_{p,1}$, $\hat{\mathbf{Q}}_{r,1}$ and $\hat{\mathbf{Q}}_{d,1}$, respectively.

4. The PU destination, the SR and the SD calculate their interference suppression vectors $\hat{\mathbf{U}}_{p,1}^{[*d]}$, $\hat{\mathbf{U}}_{r,1}^{[*d]}$ and $\hat{\mathbf{U}}_{d,1}^{[*d]}$ under CSI mismatch by

$$\hat{\mathbf{U}}_{i,1}^{[*d]} = \frac{\left(\hat{\mathbf{Q}}_{i,1}^{l}\right)^{-1} \hat{\mathbf{H}}_{i,j} \hat{\mathbf{V}}_{i,1}^{[*d]}}{\left\| \left(\hat{\mathbf{Q}}_{i,1}^{l}\right)^{-1} \hat{\mathbf{H}}_{i,j} \hat{\mathbf{V}}_{i,1}^{[*d]} \right\|} \tag{21}$$

where $i \in \{p, r, d\}$ and $j \in \{p, s\}$.

5. Setting $\tilde{\mathbf{V}}_{i,1} = \hat{\mathbf{U}}_{i,1}$ ($i \in \{p, r, d\}$). Then, according to (19) and (20), we compute the interference plus noise covariance matrices at the PU source and SS, i.e. $\tilde{\mathbf{Q}}_{p,1}$, $\tilde{\mathbf{Q}}_{s,1}$, respectively.

6. The PU source and SS compute their interference suppression matrices $\tilde{\hat{\mathbf{U}}}_{p,1}^{[*d]}$, $\tilde{\hat{\mathbf{U}}}_{s,1}^{[*d]}$ under CSI mismatch, respectively, satisfying

$$\tilde{\hat{\mathbf{U}}}_{a,1}^{[*d]} = \frac{\left(\tilde{\hat{\mathbf{Q}}}_{a,1}^{l}\right)^{-1} \tilde{\hat{\mathbf{H}}}_{a,b} \tilde{\hat{\mathbf{V}}}_{a,1}^{[*d]}}{\left\| \left(\tilde{\hat{\mathbf{Q}}}_{a,1}^{l}\right)^{-1} \tilde{\hat{\mathbf{H}}}_{a,b} \tilde{\hat{\mathbf{V}}}_{a,1}^{[*d]} \right\|} \tag{22}$$

where $a \in \{p, s\}$ and $b \in \{p, r, d\}$.

7. Reverse the communication direction again and set $\hat{\mathbf{V}}_{a,1} = \tilde{\hat{\mathbf{U}}}_{a,1}$ ($a \in \{p, s\}$).
8. Repeat the procedure from 2 to 7 till convergence.

In the second phase, the adaptive Max-SINR algorithm can be proposed as that in the first phase. And the detailed analysis is omitted due to space constraints.

## 4   Performance Analysis

According to [12], we evaluate the achievable rate for each user in this section. Specifically, the achievable rates for the transmission from SS to SR and SS to SD in the first phase can be derived as

$$\begin{aligned} R_{rs} &= \tfrac{1}{2}\log_2 \det \left( \mathbf{I}_{d_r} + \left( \mathbf{I}_{d_r} + \hat{\boldsymbol{\Phi}}_{r,1} \right)^{-1} \hat{\boldsymbol{\Psi}}_{r,1} \right) \\ &= \tfrac{1}{2}\log_2 \det \left( \mathbf{I}_{d_r} + \hat{\boldsymbol{\Theta}}_{r,1} \right) \end{aligned} \tag{23}$$

where $\boldsymbol{\Phi}_{r,1} = P\hat{\mathbf{U}}_{r,1}^{H}\mathbf{H}_{rp}\hat{\mathbf{V}}_{p,1}\hat{\mathbf{V}}_{p,1}^{H}\mathbf{H}_{rp}^{H}\hat{\mathbf{U}}_{r,1}$, $\boldsymbol{\Psi}_{r,1} = P\hat{\mathbf{U}}_{r,1}^{H}\mathbf{H}_{rs}\hat{\mathbf{V}}_{s,1}\hat{\mathbf{V}}_{s,1}^{H}\mathbf{H}_{rs}^{H}\hat{\mathbf{U}}_{r,1}$.

$$\begin{aligned} R_{ds} &= \tfrac{1}{2}\log_2 \det \left( \mathbf{I}_{d_d} + \left( \mathbf{I}_{d_d} + \hat{\boldsymbol{\Phi}}_{d,1} \right)^{-1} \hat{\boldsymbol{\Psi}}_{d,1} \right) \\ &= \tfrac{1}{2}\log_2 \det \left( \mathbf{I}_{d_d} + \hat{\boldsymbol{\Theta}}_{d,1} \right) \end{aligned} \tag{24}$$

where $\Phi_{d,1} = P\hat{\mathbf{U}}_{d,1}^H \mathbf{H}_{dp} \hat{\mathbf{V}}_{p,1} \hat{\mathbf{V}}_{p,1}^H \mathbf{H}_{dp}^H \hat{\mathbf{U}}_{d,1}$, $\Psi_{d,1} = P\hat{\mathbf{U}}_{d,1}^H \mathbf{H}_{ds} \hat{\mathbf{V}}_{s,1} \hat{\mathbf{V}}_{s,1}^H \mathbf{H}_{ds}^H \hat{\mathbf{U}}_{r,1}$.

In the second phase, the achievable rate for the transmission from SR to SD can be written as

$$R_{dr} = \frac{1}{2}\log_2 \det\left(\mathbf{I}_{d_d} + \left(\mathbf{I}_{d_d} + \hat{\Phi}_{d,2}\right)^{-1} \hat{\Psi}_{d,2}\right)$$
$$= \frac{1}{2}\log_2 \det\left(\mathbf{I}_{d_d} + \hat{\Theta}_{d,2}\right) \tag{25}$$

where $\Phi_{d,2} = P\hat{\mathbf{U}}_{d,2}^H \mathbf{H}_{dp} \hat{\mathbf{V}}_{p,2} \hat{\mathbf{V}}_{p,2}^H \mathbf{H}_{dp}^H \hat{\mathbf{U}}_{d,2}$, $\Psi_{d,2} = P\hat{\mathbf{U}}_{d,2}^H \mathbf{H}_{dr} \hat{\mathbf{V}}_{r,2} \hat{\mathbf{V}}_{r,2}^H \mathbf{H}_{dr}^H \hat{\mathbf{U}}_{d,2}$.

Hence, the transmission rate and the outage probability of the spectrum sharing relay network are derived as

$$R = \min\left\{\frac{1}{2}\log_2 \det\left(\mathbf{I}_{d_r} + \hat{\Theta}_{r,1}\right), \frac{1}{2}\log_2 \det\left(\mathbf{I}_{d_d} + \hat{\Theta}_{d,1} + \hat{\Theta}_{d,2}\right)\right\} \tag{26}$$

and

$$P_{out} = \Pr\{R < R_{th}\} \tag{27}$$

respectively, where $R_{th}$ represents the target transmission rate of the spectrum sharing relay network.

## 5 Numerical Results

In this section, Monte Carlo simulation results are performed to evaluate the performance of the proposed IA algorithm in the spectrum sharing relay network. For notational convenience, we assume that each user has equal power. We focus on two representative cases: $\alpha = 0$ (the error variance is independent of SNR), and $\alpha = 0.5$ (the error variance is depend on SNR).

Figure 1 shows the transmission rate of the spectrum sharing relay network when adopting different algorithms. In this figure, we observe that the transmission rate of the adaptive Max-SINR algorithm is better than that of the original Max-SINR algorithm described in [7]. We also analyze the transmission rate of Alt-Min algorithm given in [7] and observe that Max-SINR algorithm outperforms Alt-Min algorithm when the CSI is perfect. However, due to CSI mismatch, the adaptive Max-SINR achieves notably better performance than both Max-SINR and Alt-Min algorithms. And it demonstrates the validity of our proposed adaptive Max-SINR scheme in the cognitive relay system with CSI mismatch.

Figure 2 shows the outage probability of the spectrum sharing relay network when $R_{th} = 1bit/s/Hz$. As observed, the Max-SINR algorithm achieves better outage performance than the Alt-Min algorithm when the CSI is perfect. Moreover, when the CSI is imperfect, the achieved outage performance improvement of Max-SINR algorithm can be negligible compared to Alt-Min algorithm especially at high SNRs, while the adaptive Max-SINR algorithm achieves greatly better outage performance. Therefore, similar to that in Fig. 1, the adaptive Max-SINR algorithm is high necessary when the CSI is imperfect.

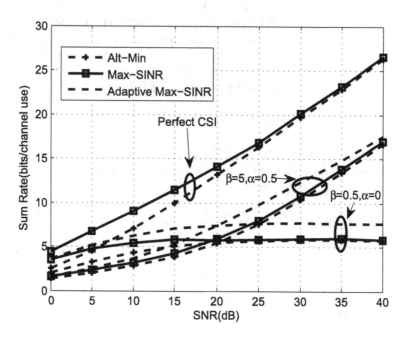

**Fig. 1.** Average sum rate for $d = 2$, $M = 4$ and for the cases $\beta = 0.5, \alpha = 0$ and $\beta = 5, \alpha = 0.5$.

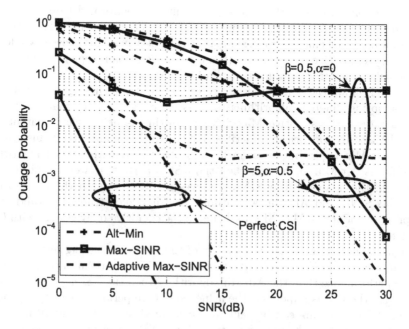

**Fig. 2.** Outage probability for $d = 2$, $M = 4$ and for the cases $\beta = 0.5, \alpha = 0$ and $\beta = 5, \alpha = 0.5$.

# 6    Conclusions

In this paper, we apply IA to relay network to improve the performance of the secondary system. The results show that interference between the PU network and the SU network can be nulled using the iterative IA algorithm. We further quantify the performance of IA under CSI mismatch where the variance of the CSI measurement error depends on the SNR. Then, we propose an adaptive Max-SINR to improve the performance of the spectrum sharing relay network under CSI mismatch. Finally, we investigate the performance of the spectrum sharing relay network and conclude that IA can improve the sum rate and outage performance of the considered network, which demonstrates that IA is a promising solution to interference avoidance in the spectrum sharing relay network.

# References

1. Mitola, J.: Cognitive radio: an integrated agent architecture for software defined radio. Ph.D. dissertation, Royal Institute of Technology (KTH), Stockholm, Sweden (2000)
2. Akyildiz, I.F., Lee, W.-Y., Vuran, M.C., Mohanty, S.: Next generation dynamic spectrum access cognitive radio wireless networks: a survey. Comput. Netw. **50**(13), 2127–2159 (2006)
3. Lee, K., Yener, A.: Outage performance of cognitive wireless relay networks. In: Proceedings of IEEE GLOBECOM, pp. 1–5 (2006)
4. Yan, Z., Wang, W., Zhang, X.: Exact outage performance of cognitive relay networks with maximum transmit power limits. IEEE Commun. Lett. **15**(12), 1317–1319 (2011)
5. Zhang, X., Xing, J., Yan, Z., Gao, Y., Wang, W.: Outage performance study of cognitive relay networks with imperfect channel knowledge. IEEE Commun. Lett. **17**(1), 27–30 (2013)
6. Jafar, S.A.: Interference alignment: a new look at signal dimensions in a communication network. Found. Trends Commun. Inf. Theory **7**(1), 1–136 (2011)
7. Gomadam, K., Cadambe, V.R., Jafar, S.A.: A distributed numerical approach to interference alignment and applications to wireless interference networks. IEEE Trans. Inf. Theory **57**(6), 3309–3322 (2011)
8. Makouei, B.N., Andrews, J.G., Heath, R.W.: MIMO interference alignment over correlated channels with imperfect CSI. IEEE Trans. Sig. Process. **59**(6), 2783–2794 (2011)
9. Ayach, O.E., Heath, R.W.: Interference alignment with analog channel state feedback. IEEE Trans. Wirel. Commun. **11**(2), 626–636 (2012)
10. Tresch, R., Guillaud, M.: Cellular interference alignment with imperfect channel knowledge. In: Proceedings of IEEE International Conference on Communications, pp. 1–5 (2009)
11. Razavi, S.M., Ratnarajah, T.: Performance analysis of interference alignment under CSI mismatch. IEEE Trans. Veh. Technol. **63**(9), 4740–4748 (2014)
12. Blum, R.S.: MIMO capacity with interference. IEEE J. Sel. Areas Commun. **21**(5), 793–801 (2003)

# Joint User Grouping and Antenna Selection Based Massive MIMO Zero-Forcing Beamforming

Wang Qian[✉], Hua Quan, Zhou Yingchao, and Shen Bin

Chongqing Key Lab of Mobile Communications,
Chongqing University of Postsand Telecommunications,
Chongqing 400065, People's Republic of China
qian2010140@163.com

**Abstract.** In massive MIMO systems where the number of antennas at base station (BS) is larger than that of users, the existing beamforming schemes generally choose all users as receivers. Howerver, due to the fact that the various channels may be significantly different, the existing schemes are not appropriate for the condition where the number of users becomes large, the system throughput is not optimal at that condition with transtional scheme. In addition, if a large number of antennas equipped at BS are selected to transmit data streams, the requirement of the hardware complexity will become higher, which results in the waste of RF links and transmit power. In this paper, a new zero-forcing beamforming algorithm is proposed based on joint user grouping and antenna selection for massive MIMO systems. When the number of antennas at BS and that of the users in the cell are large, we will deal with the anntenas and the users. The simulation results show that the proposed algorithm provides a better trade-off between rate performance and hardware compexity in massive MIMO systems.

**Keywords:** Massive MIMO · User grouping · Antenna selection · Zero-forcing beamforming · Hardware complexity

## 1 Introduction

The basic characteristic of massive MIMO is that a base station (BS) equipped with multiple antennas serves a number of users. Compared with the number of antennas in 4G, which is utmost four for LTE and up to eight for LTE-A, the number of antennas of massive MIMO systems increases by one or two orders of magnitude [1,2]. The users located in the coverage of BS use the degrees of freedom provided by large scale antennas to simultaneously communicate with BS in the same time-frequency resource, which not only significantly increases the throughput [3,4], and improves the spectrum efficiency by orders of magnitude [5–7] to solve the problem of limited spectrum resources, but also reduces the interference and enhances the robustness of the system [8,9]. Meanwhile,

© ICST Institute for Computer Sciences, Social Informatics and Telecommunications Engineering 2018
Q. Chen et al. (Eds.): ChinaCom 2016, Part I, LNICST 209, pp. 264–273, 2018.
DOI: 10.1007/978-3-319-66625-9_26

diversity gain and array gain it provides enable us to reduce the transmitted power and improve power efficiency significantly [10,11].

The BS is equipped with orders of magnitude more antennas, e.g., one hundred or more. On one hand, in order to support transmission through a large-scale antenna array, the massive MIMO system requires high hardware complexity in digital and RF/analog domains [12]. Thus, it consumes more energy than conventional small-scale MIMO technologies. So it is particularly necessary to look for an antenna selection technology with low-cost and low-complexity. In the system, some channels contribute little for throughput because of the difference of channel state information, that inevitably results in the waste of RF chains and transmit power without selecting effective channels for transmission. On the other hand, when the number of users is large, selecting all users as receivers may be unable to achieve the highest system throughput, due to the fact that the various channels may be significantly different. That means some processing schemes are necessary for the users, such as user grouping. By the reason of some users' channel conditions being superior to others, only sending the signal to the user group with better channel conditions at any moment can improve the efficiency of resource allocation and the system capacity or rate performance.

In this paper we propose a new zero-forcing beamforming algorithm based on joint user grouping and antenna selection for massive MIMO system. On one hand in the cell, we divided all users into two groups: one group contains the target users to receive signal, and the other for users is in idle mode, not to receive signal. With an aim to achieve a higher sum rate by selecting the users with a better channel condition. On the other hand at the BS, we process the transmit antennas by selecting an optimal antenna combination for each transmit data stream, in order that we can obtain the lower complexity of hardware with a little loss of performance, further lower RF circuit cost and save power consumption in massive MIMO systems.

**Notations:** Boldface lower and upper case symbols represent vectors and matrices, respectively. The transpose and Hermitian transpose operators are denoted by $(\cdot)^T$ and $(\cdot)^H$, respectively. The Moore-Penrose pseudoinverse operator is denoted by $(\cdot)^{-1}$. The 0-norm and 2-norm of a vector is denoted by $\| \cdot \|_0$ and $\| \cdot \|_2$ or $\| \cdot \|$, respectively. The size of a set is denoted by $| \cdot |$.

## 2    System Model

Consider a single cell quasi-static flat-fading MIMO downlink channel with $N$ transmit antennas at BS serving $M$ single antenna users $(N \geq M)$. Let $\mathbf{H} = [\mathbf{h}_1^H, \mathbf{h}_2^H, \ldots, \mathbf{h}_N^H]^H \in \mathbb{C}^{M \times N}$ be the channel matrix of all users, where $\mathbf{h}_k = [h_{k1}, h_{k1}, \ldots, h_{kN}] \in \mathbb{C}^{1 \times N}$ is the channel vector of user $k$. Generally, the system operates in TDD mode to obtain the perfect downlink channel state information (CSI) form the uplink CSI, relying on reciprocity between the uplink and downlink channels.

Assume $\mathbb{U}_{all} = \{1, 2, \cdots, M\}$ is the set of indexes of all users in the cell, and $\mathbb{S} = \{\pi(1), \pi(2), \cdots, \pi(|\mathbb{S}|)\}$ is the set of indexes of the optimal users selected to receive signals, for any $\mathbb{S} \subset \mathbb{U}_{all}$, where $\pi(i)$ is the $i$-th element of the optimal user index set $\mathbb{S}$, and the $\pi(i)$-th element of $\mathbb{U}_{all}$, corresponding to the $\pi(i)$-th user in the cell. Denote $|\mathbb{S}|$ as the size of set $\mathbb{S}$, that is the number of optimal users. The transmit signal vector $\mathbf{x}$ is a linear combination of all selected users date streams $\mathbf{s}$ with the zero-forcing beamforming (ZFBF) matrix $\mathbf{W}_{\mathbb{S}}$, constructed as

$$\mathbf{x} = \mathbf{W}_{\mathbb{S}} \mathbf{P}_{\mathbb{S}}^{\frac{1}{2}} \mathbf{s} = \sum_{i=1}^{|\mathbb{S}|} \mathbf{w}_{\pi(i)} \sqrt{p_i} s_i, \tag{1}$$

where $\mathbf{W}_{\mathbb{S}} = [\mathbf{w}_{\pi(1)}, \mathbf{w}_{\pi(2)}, \ldots, \mathbf{w}_{\pi(|\mathbb{S}|)}] \in \mathbb{C}^{N \times |\mathbb{S}|}$ is the ZFBF weight matrix for the optimal users, with $\mathbf{w}_{\pi(i)} = [w_{\pi(i)1}, w_{\pi(i)2}, \ldots, w_{\pi(i)N}]^T \in \mathbb{C}^{N \times 1}$. $p_i$ is the transmit power scaling factor for $\mathbf{P} = diag(p_1, p_2, \cdots, p_{|\mathbb{S}|})$ and $\mathbf{s}$ is the symbol vector at the transmitter. So the received vector for the optimal user set is

$$\mathbf{y} = \mathbf{H}_{\mathbb{S}} \mathbf{x} + \mathbf{n} = \mathbf{H}_{\mathbb{S}} \mathbf{W}_{\mathbb{S}} \mathbf{P}_{\mathbb{S}}^{\frac{1}{2}} \mathbf{s} + \mathbf{n}, \tag{2}$$

where $\mathbf{H}_{\mathbb{S}} = [\mathbf{h}_{\pi(1)}^H, \mathbf{h}_{\pi(2)}^H, \cdots, \mathbf{h}_{\pi(|\mathbb{S}|)}^H]^H \in \mathbb{C}^{|\mathbb{S}| \times N}$ is the channel matrix of the optimal users, and $\mathbf{h}_{\pi(i)} = [h_{\pi(i)1}, h_{\pi(i)2}, \cdots, h_{\pi(i)N}] \in \mathbb{C}^{1 \times N}$. $\mathbf{n} = [n_1, n_2, \cdots, n_{|\mathbb{S}|}]^H \in \mathbb{C}^{|\mathbb{S}| \times 1}$ is white Gaussian noise with zero mean and unit variance, that is $\mathbf{n} \sim CN(0, 1)$. Specifically, the received signal at user $i$ is given by

$$y_i = \mathbf{h}_{\pi(i)} \mathbf{w}_{\pi(i)} \sqrt{p_i} s_i + \sum_{l=1, l \neq i}^{|\mathbb{S}|} \mathbf{h}_{\pi(i)} \mathbf{w}_{\pi(l)} \sqrt{p_l} s_l + n_i. \tag{3}$$

The ZF beamforming matrix is

$$\mathbf{W}_{\mathbb{U}} = [\mathbf{w}_{\pi(1)}, \mathbf{w}_{\pi(2)}, \cdots, \mathbf{w}_{\pi(\mathbb{U})}] = \mathbf{H}_{\mathbb{U}}^H (\mathbf{H}_{\mathbb{U}} \mathbf{H}_{\mathbb{U}}^H)^{-1}, \tag{4}$$

where $\mathbb{U} = [\pi(1), \pi(2), \ldots, \pi(|\mathbb{U}|)]$ is the index set of users to be selected, with $\mathbb{U} \subset \mathbb{U}_{all}$. And the initial $\mathbb{U}$ represents all users, that means $\mathbb{U} = \mathbb{U}_{all}$. Similarly, the channel matrix and beamforming matrix for $\mathbb{U}$ are $\mathbf{H}_{\mathbb{U}} = [\mathbf{h}_{\pi(1)}^H, \mathbf{h}_{\pi(2)}^H, \cdots, \mathbf{h}_{\pi(|\mathbb{U}|)}^H]^H \in \mathbb{C}^{|\mathbb{U}| \times N}$ and $\mathbf{W}_{\mathbb{S}} = [\mathbf{w}_{\pi(1)}, \mathbf{w}_{\pi(2)}, \ldots, \mathbf{w}_{\pi(|\mathbb{U}|)}] \in \mathbb{C}^{N \times |\mathbb{U}|}$. Assuming that $\mathbb{U} \backslash \{n\}$ denotes the new set that deletes the element $n$ from the set $\mathbb{U}$, $\mathbf{H}_{\mathbb{U} \backslash \{n\}}$ is the row-reduced channel matrix of all the selected users except user $n$ and $\mathbf{W}_{\mathbb{U} \backslash \{n\}}$ is the column-reduced beamforming matrix. The sum rate of the user set $\mathbb{U}$ is:

$$R(\mathbb{U}) = log_2[\det(\mathbf{I}_{\mathbb{U}} + \mathbf{H}_{\mathbb{U}} \mathbf{W}_{\mathbb{U}} \mathbf{P}_{\mathbb{U}} \mathbf{W}_{\mathbb{U}}^H \mathbf{H}_{\mathbb{U}}^H)]$$

$$= \sum_{\substack{\pi(i) \in \mathbb{U}, \\ p_i : \sum_{\pi(i) \in \mathbb{U}} \lambda_i^{-1} p_i \leq P}} log_2(1 + p_i), \tag{5}$$

where

$$\lambda_i = \frac{1}{\|\mathbf{w}_i\|^2}, \tag{6}$$

is the effective channel gain of user $\pi(i)$ [14], and $\lambda_i^{-1}p_i$ is the transmit power allocated to user $\pi(i)$, the optimal power scaling factor $p_i$ can be found by waterfilling and $P$ represents the total transmit power. $\mathbf{I}_U$ is the $|\mathbb{U}| \times |\mathbb{U}|$ identity matrix.

## 3   Joint Beamforming Algorithm

Joint user grouping and antenna selection beamforming algorithm is proposed in this paper for massive MIMO transmission systems, as shown in Fig. 1. In this scheme, we consider combining schemes of user grouping within a cell and antenna selection at BS, which means that at the side of the cell all users are divided into two groups: one group is selected to receive signal, namely the target user set $\mathbb{S}$, and the other group is not, as $\mathbb{S}_0$; at the same time selecting antennas at BS for transmission significantly reduces the hardware complexity with a little loss of system performance.

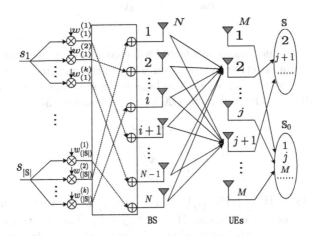

**Fig. 1.** Illustration of joint user grouping and antenna selection ZF beamforming algorithm

The design problem is formulated as follows.

$$maximize \quad R(\mathbb{U}) \tag{7}$$

$$subject \; to \quad \mathbb{U} \subset \mathbb{U}_{all} \tag{8}$$

$$\|\mathbf{w}_{\pi(i)}\|_0 = k, \qquad\qquad i = 1, 2, \cdots, |\mathbb{S}| \tag{9}$$

$$\sum_{i=1}^{|\mathbb{S}|} \|\mathbf{w}_{\pi(i)}\|_2^2 p_i \leq P, \qquad i = 1, 2, \cdots, |\mathbb{S}| \tag{10}$$

where (8) is the constraint of user grouping, and (9) and (10) are respectively the constraints of antenna selection. The 0-norm in (9) represents that in the set each column of the beamforming matrix has $k$ nonzero elements and all the rest elements are zero, that means the number of transmit antennas selected at BS. Equation (10) stands for the power constraints.

## 3.1 User Grouping at the Receiver Side

The proposed scheme at the receiver side uses a decremental user grouping scheme, which means deleting the user with the minimum effective channel gain of the beamforming matrix per iteration. The algorithm works as follows: it starts by selecting all users as the target users to receive signal, then deletes the user with the minimum effective channel gain $\lambda_n$ per iteration until the sum rate increment $\triangle R = R(\mathbb{U}\backslash\{n\}) - R(\mathbb{U}) < 0$, and subsequently calculates the set $\mathbb{S}$ of indexes of optimal users and the ZF beamforming matrix $\mathbf{W}_\mathbb{S}$. The power allocation matrix $\mathbf{P}_\mathbb{S}$ is given by waterfilling in previous section.

Without the constraints (9) and (10) in user grouping, we only need consider:

$$maximize \quad R(\mathbb{U})$$
$$subject \quad to \quad \mathbb{U} \subset \mathbb{U}_{\text{all}}$$

The set of users indexes to be selected will change because of deleting the user with the minimum effective channel gain. Denote the updated set of indexes of the users $\mathbb{U}$ as $\tilde{\mathbb{U}}$, and $\tilde{\mathbb{U}} = \mathbb{U} \backslash \{n\}$. The beamforming vector $\mathbf{w}_i$ can be obtained through the effective channel vector(ECV) $\mathbf{v}_i$ defined by [13]

$$\mathbf{v}_i = \mathbf{h}_i \mathbf{P}_i^\perp, \tag{11}$$

$$\mathbf{w}_i = \frac{\mathbf{v}_i^H}{\|\mathbf{v}_i\|^2}, \tag{12}$$

where $\mathbf{P}_i^\perp = \mathbf{I}_N - \mathbf{H}_{\mathbb{U}\backslash\{i\}}^H (\mathbf{H}_{\mathbb{U}\backslash\{i\}}\mathbf{H}_{\mathbb{U}\backslash\{i\}}^H)^{-1}\mathbf{H}_{\mathbb{U}\backslash\{i\}}$ is the orthogonal projector matrix on the subspace $\mathbf{V}_n = span\{\mathbf{h}_j | j \in \mathbb{U}, j \neq n\}$. The effective channel gain of user $i$ is $\lambda_i = \|\mathbf{v}_i\|^2$. The updated effective channel vector is given by

$$\begin{aligned}
\tilde{\mathbf{v}}_i &= \mathbf{h}_i(\mathbf{I}_N - \mathbf{H}_{\mathbb{U}\backslash\{i\}}^H(\mathbf{H}_{\mathbb{U}\backslash\{i\}}\mathbf{H}_{\mathbb{U}\backslash\{i\}}^H)^{-1}\mathbf{H}_{\mathbb{U}\backslash\{i\}}) \\
&= \mathbf{h}_i \begin{bmatrix} \mathbf{v}_i^H & \mathbf{v}_n^H \end{bmatrix} \begin{bmatrix} \mathbf{v}_i\mathbf{v}_i^H & \mathbf{v}_i\mathbf{v}_n^H \\ \mathbf{v}_n\mathbf{v}_i^H & \mathbf{v}_n\mathbf{v}_n^H \end{bmatrix}^{-1} \begin{bmatrix} \mathbf{v}_i \\ \mathbf{v}_n \end{bmatrix} \\
&= \begin{bmatrix} \mathbf{h}_i\mathbf{v}_i^H & 0 \end{bmatrix} \frac{1}{\|\mathbf{v}_i\|^2\|\mathbf{v}_n\|^2 - \|\mathbf{v}_i\mathbf{v}_n^H\|^2} \\
&\quad \cdot \begin{bmatrix} \mathbf{v}_n\mathbf{v}_n^H & -\mathbf{v}_i\mathbf{v}_n^H \\ -\mathbf{v}_n\mathbf{v}_i^H & \mathbf{v}_i\mathbf{v}_i^H \end{bmatrix} \begin{bmatrix} \mathbf{v}_i \\ \mathbf{v}_n \end{bmatrix} \\
&= \frac{\|\mathbf{v}_i\|^2\|\mathbf{v}_n\|^2}{\|\mathbf{v}_i\|^2\|\mathbf{v}_n\|^2 - \|\mathbf{v}_i\mathbf{v}_n^H\|^2}(\mathbf{v}_i - \frac{\mathbf{v}_i\mathbf{v}_n^H}{\|\mathbf{v}_n\|^2}\mathbf{v}_n),
\end{aligned} \tag{13}$$

So the updated effective channel gain and effective channel vector are respectively:

$$\tilde{\lambda}_i = \|\tilde{\mathbf{v}}_i\|^2 = \lambda_i \frac{\|\mathbf{v}_i\|^2 \|\mathbf{v}_n\|^2}{\|\mathbf{v}_i\|^2 \|\mathbf{v}_n\|^2 - \|\mathbf{v}_i \mathbf{v}_n^H\|^2},$$
$$= \frac{\lambda_i^2 \lambda_n}{\lambda_i \lambda_n - \|\mathbf{v}_i \mathbf{v}_n^H\|^2} \tag{14}$$

$$\tilde{\mathbf{v}}_i = \frac{\lambda_i \lambda_n}{\lambda_i \lambda_n - \|\mathbf{v}_i \mathbf{v}_n^H\|^2} \left( \mathbf{v}_i - \frac{\mathbf{v}_i \mathbf{v}_n^H}{\lambda_n} \mathbf{v}_n \right). \tag{15}$$

By plugging $\mathbf{w}_i = \frac{\mathbf{v}_i^H}{\|\mathbf{v}_i\|^2}$ and $\lambda_i = \|\mathbf{v}_i\|^2$ into (14) and (15), we can get the updated $\tilde{\lambda}_i$ based on the beamforming vector $\mathbf{w}_i$ as

$$\tilde{\lambda}_i = \frac{\lambda_i}{1 - \lambda_n \lambda_i |\mathbf{w}_n^H \mathbf{w}_i|^2}, \tag{16}$$

$$\tilde{\mathbf{w}}_i = \mathbf{w}_i - \lambda_n \mathbf{w}_n^H \mathbf{w}_i \mathbf{w}_n. \tag{17}$$

## 3.2   Antenna Selection at BS

Based on the proposed user grouping algorithm, the strategy of antenna selection is considered in this subsection for designing the joint scheme. A major critical factor in increasing the number of antennas in massive MIMO system is the cost of the RF chain consisting of low noise amplifiers, mixers and analog to digital converters (ADCs) and the hardware complexity we want to reduce mainly lies in the number of ADCs in this paper. In the proposed beamforming scheme, each of the data streams for MIMO transmission is multiplied by $k$ complex gains and assigned to $k$ out of the available transmit $N$ antennas, and signals assigned to the same transmit antenna are added and transmitted through the assigned antenna as shown in Fig. 2. That means each of the channel beamforming column vectors has $k$ nonzero elements and all the rest elements are zero. The main difficulty in this beamformer design lies in finding $k$ best antennas for each data stream.

The best way of finding $k$ would be the exhaustive search method, i.e., selecting a best one from all the possible antenna combinations to maximize the throughput. However, because the complexity order of this optimal method is $O((C_N^k)^M)$, which requires $C_N^k$ operations per section, the larger the number of antennas, the higher the complexity, which results in that the actual system cannot realize the data real-time processing. In this paper the algorithm we proposed uses the maximum correlation method (MCM) based on vector modulus. Compared with the exhaustive search method, the algorithm reduces the computational complexity with the feasible realization of antenna selection.

The sum rate with antenna selection is:

$$R(\mathbb{S}) = \log_2[\det(\mathbf{I}_{|\mathbb{S}|} + \mathbf{H}_{\mathbb{S}} \mathbf{W}_{\mathbb{S}} \mathbf{P}_{\mathbb{S}} \mathbf{W}_{\mathbb{S}}^H \mathbf{H}_{\mathbb{S}}^H)], \tag{18}$$

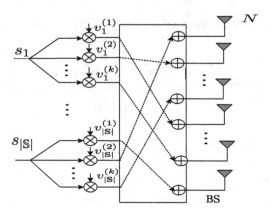

**Fig. 2.** The antenna selection architecture at BS for massive MIMO

where, $\mathbf{H}_{\mathbb{S}}$ is the channel matrix, $\mathbf{W}_{\mathbb{S}}$ is the beamforming matrix for the set of the optimal users, and $\mathbf{P}_{\mathbb{S}}$ is the transmit power scaling matrix for the optimal users.

The maximum correlation method is formulated as follows:

$$maximize \quad |\langle \boldsymbol{\psi}_i, \mathbf{w}_{\pi(i)}\rangle| \tag{19}$$

$$subject \quad to \quad \|\mathbf{w}_{\pi(i)}\|_0 = k, i = 1, 2, \cdots, |\mathbb{S}|, \tag{20}$$

$$\sum_{i=1}^{|\mathbb{S}|} \|\mathbf{w}_{\pi(i)}\|_2^2 p_i \leq P, i = 1, 2, \cdots, |\mathbb{S}|, \tag{21}$$

where $|\langle \cdot, \cdot \rangle|$ denotes the inner product operation and $\boldsymbol{\psi}_i = [\psi_{i1}, \psi_{i2}, \cdots, \psi_{iN}]^H$ is the first $k$ beamforming vector.

The solution to the MCM problem is to select the first $k$ largest absolute values of elements of the beamforming vectors:

$$\psi_{ij} = \begin{cases} \mathbf{w}_{\pi(i)j}, & i \in 1, 2, \cdots, |\mathbb{S}|, \quad j \in \mathcal{K} \\ 0, & otherwise \end{cases}, \tag{22}$$

where $\mathcal{K}$ is the set of indices of the elements of $\mathbf{w}_{\pi(i)}$ with the first $k$ largest absolute values.

### 3.3    Complexity Analysis

The complexity of joint user grouping and antenna selection beamforming algorithm lies mainly in the initialization step of the Moore-Penrose pseudo-inverse of $\mathbf{W}$, which involves a complexity of $O(NM^2)$. The corresponding $\lambda_i$ initialization in Step (1) involves $M$ 2-norms of $1 \times N$ vectors, which include complex multiplications. The updating of $\mathbf{w}_i$ and $\lambda_i$ in Step (2) involves $|\mathbb{S}| - 1$ vector-vector multiplications and $|\mathbb{S}| - 1$ 2-norms, which include $2N(|\mathbb{S}| - 1)$ complex

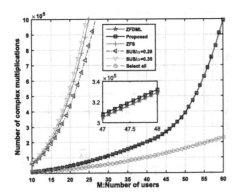

**Fig. 3.** The computational complexity about number of complex multiplications.

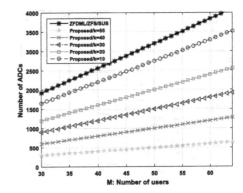

**Fig. 4.** The hardware complexity about ADCs of RF chains.

multiplications. While the computational complexity of antenna selection lies in the finding of the first $k$ nonzero elements with largest absolute values, it involves a complexity of $O(N|\mathbb{S}|)$. The total complexity of the proposed scheme is (Fig. 3)

$$O\left(NM^2 + MN + \sum_{n=|\mathbb{S}|}^{K} 2N(n-1) + N|\mathbb{S}|\right).$$

We have shown that the complexity of Select All is $O(NM^2)$, due to the Moore-Penrose pseudo-inverse of $\mathbf{H}_{U_{all}}$, which is lower with poor performance. From Fig. 5, we can see the computational complexity of proposed scheme is basically the same as Select All. This is a significant improvement over previous user selection algorithms, such as ZFS and SUS, which all have the complexity of $O(NM^3)$.

## 4    Simulation Results

In this section, we compare the performance of DML, ZFS, SUS (with $\alpha = 0.28$ and $\alpha = 0.35$), 'Select All', and the proposed scheme (with $k = 55$ and $k = 40$) with ZFBF serving a fixed number of users. The BS is equipped with $N = 64$ antennas. The transmit SNR is 20 dB, and the number of users $M$ ranges from 30 to 64. All curves are obtained by averaging over $10^3$ independent channel matrices with each entry being a zero-mean unit-variance circular symmetric complex Gaussian random variable.

From Fig. 6, we can see that when the number of users in the cell is small, that is $M < 45$, the user grouping phenomenon of other schemes are not obvious, except SUS related with the threshold $\alpha$. We also can see that the proposed algorithm have a certain extent in antenna selection with almost the same performance in this range. However, according to Fig. 4, when $k = 55$, selecting 55

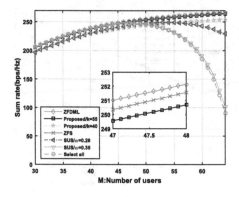 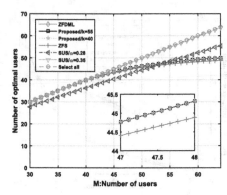

**Fig. 5.** Sum rate performance comparison serving a fixed number of users.

**Fig. 6.** The comparison of the number of optimal user grouping serving a fixed number of users.

antennas from the massive antennas at BS for each transmit date stream, the proposed scheme greatly reduces the hardware complexity. When the number of users is larger, the schemes with superior performance are DML, ZF, and the proposed scheme with $k = 55$ and $k = 40$, which have almost the same rate and computational complexity. The proposed algorithm provides a better trade-off between rate performance and hardware complexity in massive MIMO systems with the same set of users and rate performance as shown in Figs. 5 and 6. The simulation results also show that when $k = 55$ and $k = 40$, the utilization of degrees of freedom are respectively 85.9% and 62.5%. As expected, for the antenna selection, still a large portion of antennas are not connected to signals for reasonably small $k$ values. This aspect of the proposed scheme can be exploited to reduce the hardware complexity in addition to the reduction in the number of required multiplications or multipliers.

## 5   Conclusion

In this paper, we have considered a joint user grouping and antenna selection zero-forcing beamforming algorithm and analyzed it from throughput, computational complexity and hardware complexity. In this algorithm, we lower the hardware complexity with the number of ADCs by selecting a optimal antenna subset for each transmit data stream, subject to maximize system throughput with low computational complexity by user grouping when the number of users in the cell is large for massive MIMO system. The proposed scheme provides a better trade-off between rate performance and hardware complexity with a small $k$.

**Acknowledgments.** This work was supported by the National Science and Technology Major Project of the Ministry of Science and Technology of China (Grant No. 2015ZX03001033-002).

# References

1. Yang, L.X., He, S.W., Wang, Y.: Summary of key technologies for 5G wireless communication system. J. Data Acquis. Process. **30**(3), 469–485 (2015)
2. You, L., Gao, X.Q.: The key technologies of massive MIMO wireless communication. ZTE Technol. J. **20**(2), 26–28 (2014)
3. Guthy, C., Utschick, W., Honig, M.L.: Large system analysis of sum capacity in the gaussian MIMO broadcast channel. IEEE J. Sel. Areas Commun. **31**(31), 149–159 (2013)
4. Ngo, H.Q., Larsson, E.G., Marzetta, T.L.: Energy and spectral efficiency of very large multiuser MIMO systems. IEEE Trans. Commun. **61**(4), 1436–1449 (2011)
5. Rusek, F., Persson, D., Lau, B.K.: Scaling up MIMO: opportunities and challenges with very large arrays. IEEE Sig. Process. Mag. **30**(1), 40–60 (2012)
6. Huh, H., Caire, G., Papadopoulos, H.C.: Achieving "massive MIMO" spectral efficiency with a not-so-large number of antennas. IEEE Trans. Wirel. Commun. **11**(9), 3226–3239 (2011)
7. Lu, L., Li, G.Y., Swindlehurst, A.L.: An overview of massive MIMO: benefits and challenges. IEEE J. Sel. Top. Sig. Process. **8**(5), 742–758 (2014)
8. Marzetta, T.L.: Massive MIMO: an introduction. Bell Labs Tech. J. **20**, 11–22 (2015)
9. Larsson, E.G., Tufvesson, F., Edfors, O., Marzetta, T.L.: Massive MIMO for next generation wireless systems. IEEE Commun. Mag. **52**(2), 186–195 (2014)
10. Bjornson, E., Kountouris, M., Debbah, M.: Massive MIMO and small cells: improving energy efficiency by optimal soft-cell coordination. In: Proceedings of 20th ICT, pp. 1–5 (2013)
11. Qian, M., Wang, Y., Zhou, Y.: A super BS based centralized network architecture for 5G mobile communication systems. DCAN **1**(2), 152–159 (2015)
12. Lee, G., Park, J., Sung, Y., Seo, J.: A new approach to beamformer design for massive MIMO systems based on k-regularity. In: IEEE Globecom Workshops, pp. 686–690 (2012)
13. Huang, S., Yin, H., Wu, J., Leung, V.C.M.: User selection for multi-user MIMO downlink with zero-forcing beamforming. IEEE Trans. Veh. Technol. **62**, 3084–3097 (2013)
14. Yoo, T., Goldsmith, A.: On the optimality of multi-antenna broadcast scheduling using zero-forcing beamforming. IEEE J. Sel. Areas Commun. **24**, 528–542 (2006)
15. Wang, J.Q., Love, D.J., Zoltowski, M.D.: User selection with zeroforcing beamforming achieves the asymptotically optimal sum rate. IEEE Trans. Sig. Process. **56**, 3713–3726 (2008)

# Relay Systems

# Utility-Based Resource Allocation in OFDMA Relay Systems with Half-Duplex Transmission

Huanglong Teng[1], Binjie Hu[2], Hongming Yu[1], Miao Cui[1,3(✉)], and Guangchi Zhang[3]

[1] China Electronics Technology Group Corporation No. 7 Research Institute, Guangzhou 510310, China
single450@163.com
[2] School of Electronic and Information Engineering, South China University of Technology, Guangzhou 510641, China
[3] School of Information Engineering, Guangdong University of Technology, Guangzhou 510006, China

**Abstract.** This paper considers resource allocation in an Orthogonal Frequency Division Multiple Access (OFDMA) relay system, which uses either direct transmission or nonregenerative relay transmission strategies in each subchannel. An optimization problem is developed to handle joint dynamic subchannel assignment (DSA), adaptive power allocation (APA), transmission strategy selection and relay selection in the downlink of OFDMA relay system exploiting half-duplex transmission. We aim to obtain the fair usage of the relays with the assumption that one relay's maximum subchannels and the relay power in each subchannel are fixed. A suboptimal greedy algorithm is proposed to optimize all users' overall sum utility, where resources are allocated to the user with the greatest utility increment potential one at a time. Simulation results illustrate that the proposed algorithm significantly outperforms the fixed resource allocation schemes.

**Keywords:** Resource allocation · Relay transmission · OFDMA · Utility function · Half-duplex

## 1 Introduction

Wireless relay attracts great interest in wireless communication research [1]. The two main types of relay transmission strategies are the regenerative and the nonregenerative [2]. Orthogonal Frequency Division Multiplexing (OFDM) is robust against frequency selective fading and Orthogonal Frequency Division Multiple Access (OFDMA) is one of the promising multiple-access schemes for future broadband wireless networks, e.g., IEEE 802.16.

The OFDMA systems that employ relays have attracted notable attention [3, 4]. The systems investigated in this paper are used in cellular networks, and are called OFDMA relay systems. Efficient resource allocation schemes can greatly improve system performance, and it is natural to ask the questions: which user transmits at which subchannel, which relay forwards information at which subchannel, how much

© ICST Institute for Computer Sciences, Social Informatics and Telecommunications Engineering 2018
Q. Chen et al. (Eds.): ChinaCom 2016, Part I, LNICST 209, pp. 277–284, 2018.
DOI: 10.1007/978-3-319-66625-9_27

power is allocated to each subchannel etc. By means of optimizing the utility function, the balance between efficient and fair resource allocation can be achieved [4, 5].

Using nonregenerative relay transmission, Han et al. [6] proposed an algorithm to handle dynamic subchannel assignment (DSA), adaptive power allocation (APA) and relay selection in an OFDM Time-Division Multiple Access relay system to reduce transmission power. In [3], Li and Liu investigated joint DSA and relay selection with fixed power allocation and transmission strategy in the uplink of an OFDMA relay system. Ng and Yu [4] considered joint DSA, APA, transmission strategy selection and relay selection in an OFDMA relay system with full-duplex transmission. Although the digital full-duplex operation is implemented in wireline systems [7], it cannot be used in wireless systems because the transmitted signal drowns out the received signal [1].

This paper investigates joint DSA, APA, transmission strategy selection and relay selection in the downlink of an OFDMA nonregenerative relay system with half-duplex transmission. A greedy algorithm is proposed to maximize the overall sum utility on the condition that the maximum number of subchannels one relay can assist and the relay power in each subchannel are fixed. These conditions are necessary for ensuring fair usage of the relays. Note that our proposed algorithm is different from the dual decomposition method in [4].

## 2   System Model and Problem Formulation

### 2.1   System Model

The downlink of the broadband OFDMA relay system consists of one base station and $K$ half-duplex users. Denote the user set as $\mathcal{K} = \{1, 2, \ldots, K\}$. In addition to receiving information of their own, the users in a subset of $\mathcal{K}$ serve as relays. Denote $\mathcal{V}$ as the relay set with $\mathcal{V} \subset \mathcal{K}$, $|\mathcal{V}| = L$ ($1 \leq L \leq K/2$), and $\bar{\mathcal{V}} = \mathcal{K} - \mathcal{V}$ as the non-relay user set[1]. The slow fading wireless channel is divided into $N$ subchannels, and denote $\mathcal{N} = \{1, 2, \ldots, N\}$ as the set of all subchannels. The OFDM frames are synchronized [3, 4, 6]. The base station allocates resources according to full channel state information.

The downlink transmission slot includes two subslots of equal length. In the first subslot, the base station transmits in all subchannels, and all relay users listen; in the second subslot, the relay users forward the amplified signals in relay transmission subchannels, the non-relay users listen. For simplicity, assume that a relay user transmits the information at the same subchannel where it receives information. It is assumed that one relay user assists one subchannel at most [3, 4].

For $i \in \mathcal{K}$, denote $\mathcal{A}_i$ as the subchannel set where user $i$ selects direct transmission, and $\mathcal{B}_{ii}$ as the subchannel set where user $i$ selects relay transmission and $\mathcal{S}_i = \mathcal{A}_i \cup \mathcal{B}_i$ as subchannel set of user $i$. $\mathcal{A}_i \cap \mathcal{B}_i = \emptyset$. As the relay users transmit in the second subslot, they cannot receive at the same time due to the half-duplex constraint. Therefore they only select direct transmission in their subchannels, e.g., $\mathcal{B}_j = \emptyset$ for $j \in \mathcal{V}$, while non-relay users may select both direct transmission and relay transmission in their different subchannels.

---

[1] The procedure of determining $\mathcal{V}$ is out of the scope of this paper.

With direct transmission, user $i$ receives from the base station in the first subslot in the subchannels of $\mathcal{A}_i$. The direct transmission rate in subchannel $n$ is given by

$$R_{i,n}^{direct} = \frac{W}{2} \log_2 \left( 1 + \frac{p_{0,n}|H_{0i,n}|^2}{N_0 W} \right), \quad n \in \mathcal{A}_i, \tag{1}$$

where $W$ is the subchannel bandwidth, $p_{i,n}$ is the power that user $i$ allocates to subchannel $n$, $H_{ji,n}$ is the channel gain of subchannel $n$ from user $j$ to user $i$, and $N_0$ is the power spectral density of the additive white Gaussian noise. User 0 denotes the base station.

With relay transmission, user $i$ receives the amplified signal from its relays in the second subslot in the subchannels of $\mathcal{B}_i$. The relay transmission rate in subchannel $n$ is given by [2]

$$R_{i,n}^{relay} = \frac{W}{2} \log_2 \left( 1 + \frac{p_{0,n}p_{j,n}|H_{0j,n}|^2|H_{ji,n}|^2}{N_0 W (p_{0,n}|H_{0j,n}|^2 + p_{j,n}|H_{ji,n}|^2 + N_0 W)} \right), \quad n \in \mathcal{B}_i, \tag{2}$$

where user $j$ is the relay in the subchannel. The total rate of user $i$ is given by

$$R_i = \sum_{n \in A_i} R_{i,n}^{direct} + \sum_{n \in B_i} R_{i,n}^{relay}. \tag{3}$$

## 2.2  Problem Formulation

To optimize all users' sum utility, the resource allocation scheme determines the subchannel set of each user, e.g., $\mathcal{S}_i$ for $i \in \mathcal{K}$, the subchannel set that each relay assists, denoted as $\mathcal{Q}_i$ for $i \in \mathcal{V}$, and power allocated at each subchannel. Note that $\mathcal{B}_i = \mathcal{S}_i \cap \left( \bigcup_{j \in V} \mathcal{Q}_j \right)$. The problem is formulated as

$$\max_{p_{j,n},S_i,Q_i} \sum_{i=1}^{K} U_i(R_i) \tag{4}$$

$$\text{subject to} \quad \sum_{n=1}^{N} p_{j,n} \leq P_j^{tot}, \; \forall j \in \{0\} \cup \mathcal{V} \tag{5}$$

$$p_{j,n} \geq 0, \; \forall j \in \{0\} \cup \mathcal{V}, \; \forall n \in \mathcal{N} \tag{6}$$

$$\bigcup_{i \in \mathcal{K}} \mathcal{S}_i \subseteq \mathcal{N} \tag{7}$$

$$\bigcup_{j \in V} \mathcal{Q}_j \subseteq \mathcal{N} - \bigcup_{i' \in V} \mathcal{S}_{i'} \tag{8}$$

$$S_i \cap S_{i'} = \varnothing, \forall i, i' \in \mathcal{K} \tag{9}$$

$$Q_j \cap Q_{j'}\varnothing = \forall j, j' \in \mathcal{V} \tag{10}$$

In Eq. (4), $y = U_i(R_i)$ is the utility function of user $i$, which is concave increasing in this paper [4, 5]. In Eq. (5), $P_j^{tot}$ is the total transmission power. Equation (8) guarantees that the relay users cannot select relay transmission; Eqs. (9) and (10) guarantee that each subchannel is assigned to one user and assisted by at most one relay [3, 4].

## 3   Greedy Algorithm for Resource Allocation

The above problem is combinatorial, and the optimal solution is hard to find. To prevent that some relays are used in excess [3], our algorithm guarantees that each relay assists at most $\Omega$ subchannels, and that the relay power at each relay transmission subchannel is $p_{j,n} = p_r, j \in \mathcal{V}$, so the maximum transmission power of each relay user is $P_j^{tot} = \Omega p_r, j \in \mathcal{V}$.

The greedy algorithm allocates resources to the user with the greatest utility increment potential under the available resources one at a time. Similar to [8], the user rate is updated with water-filling power allocation given in the Appendix. The algorithm continues until all the resources have been allocated. The proposed algorithm is given below, where $P_i$ is the total power allocated to user $i$ from the base station, e.g., $P_i = \sum_{n \in S_i} p_{0,n}$, $[R_i, \{p_{0,n}\}_i] = \mathrm{WF}(P_i, \mathcal{A}_i, \mathcal{B}_i)$ denotes water-filling power allocation for user $i$ based on subchannels and transmission strategy of it, and $\{p_{0,n}\}_i$ denotes the allocated power by the base station to the subchannels of user $i$.

Greedy algorithm for resource allocation:

1. Initialization. $C = \mathcal{N}$, $S_i = \varnothing$, $Q_i = \varnothing$, $\mathcal{A}_i = \varnothing$, $\mathcal{B}_i = \varnothing$, $P_i = 0$ for $i \in \mathcal{K}$.
2. Calculate the maximum possible rate $R_i^{pos}$ for each user.
   (a) Find subchannel $n$ with the greatest channel gain, $n \in C$;

$$[R_{i,1}^{pos}, \{p_{0,n}\}_i] = \mathrm{WF}(P_i + P_0^{tot}/N, \mathcal{A}_i \cup \{n\}, \mathcal{B}_i).$$

   (b) If $i \in \mathcal{V}$, $R_i^{pos} = R_{i,1}^{pos}$. Else, find $(n, j)$ where the maximum rate is achieved with relay $j$ at subchannel $n$, $n \in C$ and $j \in \{k|k \in \mathcal{V}, |Q_k| < \Omega\}$;

$$[R_{i,2}^{pos}, \{p_{0,n}\}_i] = \mathrm{WF}(P_i + P_0^{tot}/N, \mathcal{A}_i, \mathcal{B}_i \cup \{n\}); \ R_i^{pos} = \max(R_{i,1}^{pos}, R_{i,2}^{pos}).$$

3. Resource allocation on the user with maximum utility increment potential.
   (a) Find $i^*$ that $U_{i^*}(R_{i^*}^{pos}) - U_{i^*}(R_{i^*}) \geq U_k(R_k^{pos}) - U_k(R_k), \forall i^*, k \in \mathcal{K}$;

$$P_{i^*} = P_{i^*} + P_0^{tot}/N; \ R_{i^*} = R_{i^*}^{pos}.$$

   (b) Subchannel $n^*$ is the best, $S_{i^*} = S_{i^*} \cup \{n^*\}$, $C = C - \{n^*\}$. If $i^* \notin \mathcal{V}$, $R_{i^*,1}^{pos} < R_{i^*,2}^{pos}$ and the user $j^*$ is the best relay, $Q_{j^*} = Q_{j^*} \cup \{n^*\}$,

$$\mathcal{B}_{i^*} = \mathcal{B}_{i^*} \cup \{n^*\}; \quad \text{Else } \mathcal{A}_{i^*} = \mathcal{A}_{i^*} \cup \{n^*\}.$$

If $\mathcal{C}$ is not empty, go to step 2; else water-filling power allocation for each user and stop.

## 4 Simulation Results

We have conducted a simulation to evaluate the proposed algorithm. In the simulation, our algorithm was compared with two other resource allocation schemes: the fixed resource allocation (FRA) scheme and the fixed subchannel assignment with adaptive power allocation (FSA-APA) scheme. In the FRA scheme, all resource allocations are fixed. The FSA-APA scheme is the same with the FRA except adaptive water-filling power allocation.

The OFDM relay system has $N = 128$ subchannels with 5 MHz bandwidth. Each channel has a six-tap multipath, where each tap component is simulated by Clarke's model [9]. The path loss exponent is 3, and the energy of the $t$th tap is

$$E[|h_t|^2] = \left(\frac{d_0}{d}\right)^3 e^{-(t-1)}, \ t = 1, 2, \ldots, 6, \tag{11}$$

where $d$ is the distance with $d_0 = 10$ m as the reference. The utility function of each user is $U_i(R_i) = \ln R_i$, so the resource allocations are proportionally fair [10]. $P_0^{tot} = 1$ W, $P_j^{tot} = 0.25$ W, $\Omega = 32$, $p_{j,n} = p_r = 7.8125$ mW ($j \in \mathcal{V}$) and $N_0 = -80$ dBW/Hz.

In the two-user case, all users locate in the same line. User 1, the relay, locates between the base station and user 2. The distance from base station to the user 1 is fixed at $D_{01} = 100$ m. Figure 1 shows the average rate of each user versus the distance from base station to user 2 $D_{02}$. The rates of both users with our algorithm are much higher than the other two schemes. Figure 2 shows that our algorithm achieves greater sum utility.

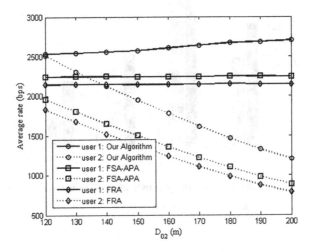

**Fig. 1.** Average rate of each user in the two-user case.

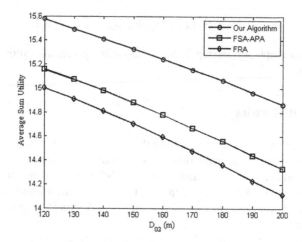

**Fig. 2.** Average sum utility in the two-user case.

In the four-user case, users 0 to 4 are located at (0, 0), (60, 80), (48, 36), (102, 136) and (160, 120), and the unit of measurement is meter. User 1 and 2 are relays. Figure 3 shows that with our algorithm, although user 2 suffers a slight rate loss, the other three users have significant rate gain. The average sum utility of our algorithm is 28.521, greater than the ones of the FSA-APA and FRA which are 26.857 and 26.698 respectively.

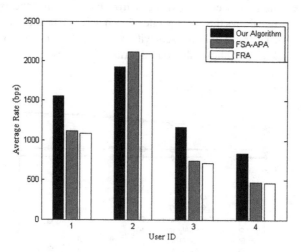

**Fig. 3.** Average rate of each user in the four-user case.

## 5  Conclusions

In this paper, by fixing the maximum number of subchannels that a relay assists and relay power at each subchannel, a utility-based resource allocation algorithm is proposed for joint DSA, APA, transmission strategy selection and relay selection in an OFDMA relay system. Simulation results show that the greedy and suboptimal algorithm significantly outperforms the fixed resource allocation schemes.

**Acknowledgments.** This work was supported by the National Natural Science Foundation of China under Grand 61571138, the Natural Science Foundation of Guangdong Province under Grand 2015A030313481, the Science and Technology Plan Project of Guangdong Province under Grands 2016A050503044, 2016KZ010101, 2016KZ010107, 2016KZ010101 and 2016B 090904001, Science and Technology Plan Project of Guangzhou City under Grand 201604020 127, and the Scientific Talent Development Project of Guangdong University of Technology under Grand 220411321.

## Appendix

The water-filling power allocation problem for user $i$ is given by

$$\begin{aligned} \max_{p_{0,n}} \quad & R_i \\ \text{s. t.} \quad & \sum_{n \in S_i} p_{0,n} = P_i, p_{0,n} \geq 0. \end{aligned} \tag{A.1}$$

Using the Karush–Kuhn–Tucker (KKT) conditions [11], after some algebraic manipulations, we get

$$p_{0,n} = \left( \lambda - \frac{N_0 W}{|H_{0i,n}|^2} \right)^+, \quad n \in A_i, \tag{A.2}$$

$$p_{0,n} = \frac{N_0 W}{|H_{0r,n}|^2} \left[ \frac{p_{r,n}|H_{ri,0}|^2}{2N_0 W} \left( \sqrt{1 + \frac{4|H_{0r,n}|^2}{\lambda p_{r,n}|H_{ri,n}|^2}} - 1 \right) - 1 \right]^+, \quad n \in B_i, \tag{A.3}$$

where $r$ denotes the relay in each subchannel, and constant $\lambda$ is chosen to satisfy $\sum_{n \in S_i} p_{0,n} = P_i$.

## References

1. Laneman, J.N., Tse, D.N.C., Wornell, G.W.: Cooperative diversity in wireless networks: efficient protocols and outage behavior. IEEE Trans. Inf. Theory **50**, 3062–3080 (2004)

2. Hammerstrom, I., Wittneben, A.: On the optimal power allocation for nonregenerative OFDM relay links. In: IEEE International Conference on Communications 2006 (ICC 2006), pp. 4463–4468 (2006)
3. Li, G., Liu, H.: Resource allocation for OFDMA relay networks with fairness constraints. IEEE J. Sel. Areas Commun. 24, 2061–2069 (2006)
4. Ng, T.C.-Y., Wei, Y.: Joint optimization of relay strategies and resource allocations in cooperative cellular networks. IEEE J. Sel. Areas Commun. 25, 328–339 (2007)
5. Song, G., Li, Y.: Cross-layer optimization for OFDM wireless networks-Part I: theoretical framework. IEEE Trans. Wireless Commun. 4, 614–624 (2005)
6. Han, Z., Thanongsak, H., Siriwongpairat, W.P., et al.: Energy-efficient cooperative transmission over multiuser OFDM Networks: who helps whom and how to cooperate. In: 2005 IEEE Wireless Communications and Networking Conference, pp. 1030–1035 (2005)
7. Sjoberg, F., Isaksson, M., Nilsson, R., et al.: Zipper: a duplex method for VDSL based on DMT. IEEE Trans. Commun. 47, 1245–1252 (1999)
8. Mohanram, C., Bhashyam, S.: A sub-optimal joint subcarrier and power allocation algorithm for multiuser OFDM. IEEE Commun. Lett. 9, 685–687 (2005)
9. Rappaport, T.S.: Wireless Communications: Principles and Practice, 2nd edn. Prentice Hall PTR, Upper Saddle River (2002)
10. Han, Z., Ji, Z., Liu, K.J.R.: Fair multiuser channel allocation for OFDMA networks using nash bargaining solutions and coalitions. IEEE Trans. Commun. 53, 1366–1376 (2005)
11. Nocedal, J., Wright, S.: Numerical Optimization. Springer, Boston (2000)

# Joint Time Switching and Power Allocation for Secure Multicarrier Decode-and-Forward Relay Systems with Wireless Information and Power Transfer

Xiancai Chen[1]([✉]), Gaofei Huang[2], Yuan Lin[3], Zijun Liang[1], and Jianli Huang[4]

[1] School of Electronics and Information Technology, Sun Yat-sen University,
Guangzhou 510006, Guangdong, China
chenxc6@mail2.sysu.edu.cn
[2] School of Mechanical and Electrical Engineering, Guangzhou University,
Guangzhou 510006, Guangdong, China
huanggaofei@gzhu.edu.cn
[3] Information System Development, E Fund Management Co., Ltd.,
Guangzhou 510620, Guangdong, China
linyuan@efunds.com.cn
[4] Electric Power Research Institute, CSG, Guangzhou 510080, Guangdong, China
huangjl2@csg.cn

**Abstract.** Secure communication is critical in wireless networks due to the openness of the wireless transmission medium. In this paper, we study the secure communication in a multicarrier orthogonal frequency division multiplexing (OFDM) decode-and-forward (DF) relay network with an energy-constrained relay node which operates with a time-switching (TS) protocol. By jointly designing TS ratios of energy harvesting (EH) and information-decoding (ID) at the relay, TS ratio of signal forwarding from relay to destination and power allocation (PA) over all subcarriers at source and relay, we aim at maximizing the achievable secrecy rate of the DF relay network subject to a maximum transmit power constraint at source and an EH constraint at relay. The formulated optimization problem is a non-convex problem. We decouple it into a convex problem and a non-convex problem, where the non-convex problem can be solved by a constrained concave convex procedure (CCCP) based iterative algorithm to achieve a local optimum. Simulation results verify that our proposed joint TS and PA scheme achieves nearly global optimal resource allocation and outperforms the existing resource allocation scheme.

**Keywords:** Time switching (TS) · Power allocation (PA) · Energy harvesting (EH) · Relay networks · Secure communication

## 1 Introduction

Allowing battery operated wireless communication systems to harvest energy from radio signals, wireless information and energy transfer (WIET) is a

© ICST Institute for Computer Sciences, Social Informatics and Telecommunications Engineering 2018
Q. Chen et al. (Eds.): ChinaCom 2016, Part I, LNICST 209, pp. 285–294, 2018.
DOI: 10.1007/978-3-319-66625-9_28

promising energy harvesting (EH) technique to solve the energy scarcity problem in energy-constrained wireless networks [1–5]. In [2], a multiple-input-multiple-output (MIMO) system with WIET was studied and a power-splitting (PS) or time-switching (TS) EH scheme was proposed. By employing PS-based EH receiver at the relay, a decode-and-forward (DF) relay system with multiple source-destination pairs was studied in [3]. In [4], the authors aim for maximizing achievable rate of DF relay networks with WIET. It was shown that the proposed scheme is superior to the scheme with fixed time-switching ratios from the simulations. An EH relay network was investigated in [5]. With the aid of relay node, communication between sources and destinations can perform efficiently.

Secure communications had been investigated in [6,7]. The secure resource allocation in a multicarrier half-duplex relay system was studied in [6]. In [7], a full-duplex DF relay network was studied, whose objective is to maximize the achievable secrecy rate of the system. Unfortunately, there is still short of study on the secure communication in wireless relay systems with WIET.

In this paper, we investigate secure multicarrier communication in OFDM DF relay systems with WIET. As in [4], we assume that the EH relay will reallocate the energy amongst all the sub-channels. By jointly optimizing TS factors and power allocations on sub-channels, where the TS factors are consisted of energy harvesting, information-decoding at the relay node and signals transmitted to destination node, we aim to maximize the achievable secrecy rate subject to maximum transmit power constraint at source node and energy harvesting constraint at relay node. The formulated optimization problem is non-convex because both the objective function and the energy harvesting constraint at relay node are non-convex. By transforming the non-convex original problem into a solvable convex problem and a non-convex problem, the non-convex problem can be solved by a constrained concave convex procedure (CCCP) based iterative algorithm to achieve a local optimum. Simulation results show that our proposed joint TS ratios and PA allocation scheme can achieve nearly global optimal resource allocation and has a superior performance over the existing resource allocation scheme.

## 2   System Model and Problem Formulation

In Fig. 1, we consider a multicarrier DF relay system which contains a source node, a relay node, a legitimate destination node and a eavesdropper node. The relay node harvests energy from the source node [4,11]. The direct links between the source node and the two receivers are unavailable [11]. The reliable communication from source to destination is established by EH relay. At the eavesdropper node, it attempts to eavesdrop the signals which are transmitted from the EH relay to the destination [11].

In the network, we assume that the relay operates in time-division half-duplex mode. There is no inner energy supply at the relay node. So it will gather energy from the source node. In this paper, we adopt the time-switching protocol for

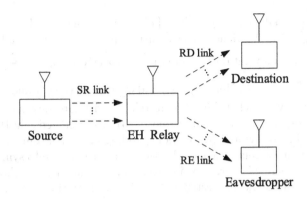

**Fig. 1.** The system model of multicarrier secure communications in the DF relay.

WIET. Each transmission block of time $T$ is split into three parts with TS ratios. We denote them as $\alpha_1$, $\alpha_2$, and $\alpha_3$, where $\alpha_1 + \alpha_2 + \alpha_3 = 1$. To be specific, $\alpha_1 T$, $\alpha_2 T$ and $\alpha_3 T$ are the continuance of the 1st phase, 2nd phase and the 3rd phase, respectively.

In this paper, the entire bandwidth is equally split into $N$ orthogonal sub-channels. On the $n$th ($n \in \mathcal{N} = \{1, 2, \cdots, N\}$) sub-channel, we denote $h_n^{SR}$, $h_n^{RD}$ and $h_n^{RE}$ as the responses between SR link, RD link and the RE link, respectively. We assume that both the source node and the relay node can obtain the instantaneous channel state information of the entire system [11].

In the 1st phase, the relay harvests energy from the source node. It can be written as [4]

$$E = \alpha_1 T \tau \sum_{n=1}^{N} p_n^{S,1} \left| h_n^{SR} \right|^2 \tag{1}$$

where $p_n^{S,1}$ and $\tau$ denote the power transmitted from the source node on $n$th sub-channel for wireless energy transfer and energy conversion efficiency factor ($0 < \tau < 1$), respectively. For maximizing harvested energy at the EH relay node, transmitting power of the source node will be allocated to the sub-channel with the best channel gain [11]. Hence, (1) can be rewritten as $E = \alpha_1 T G$, where

$$G = \tau P_{stot} \left| h_k^{SR} \right|^2, \tag{2}$$

$P_{stot}$ meams the maximum transmission power at the source node for WIET, and $h_k^{SR}$ means $k$th sub-channel has best channel gain. In the 2nd phase, the source node transfers message to the relay node on all sub-channels. As in [4], at the relay node, it will decode the signals transmitted from the source node. Then, it will forward the decoded signals to the destination after reallocating them on sub-channels. Accordingly, the achievable secrecy rate is given by

$$R = \{\min[\sum_{n=1}^{N} \alpha_2 \log_2 \left(1 + p_n^{S,2} \gamma_n^{SR}\right), \sum_{n=1}^{N} \alpha_3 \log_2 \left(1 + p_n^{R} \gamma_n^{RD}\right)] - R'\}^+ \tag{3}$$

where $R' = \sum_{n=1}^{N} \alpha_3 \log_2\left(1 + p_n^R \gamma_n^{RE}\right)$, $\{x\}^+$ denotes $\max\{x, 0\}$ for a real scaler $x$ and $p_n^{S,2}$, $p_n^R$, $n \in \mathcal{N}$, denote the transmit power of source and relay over $n$th subcarrier for information transmission, respectively, $\gamma_n^{SR} = \frac{|h_n^{SR}|^2}{\sigma_R^2}$, $\gamma_n^{RD} = \frac{|h_n^{RD}|^2}{\sigma_D^2}$, and $\gamma_n^{RE} = \frac{|h_n^{RE}|^2}{\sigma_E^2}$. Here, $\sigma_R^2$, $\sigma_D^2$ and $\sigma_E^2$ denote the variances of additive Gaussian noises over each subcarrier at relay, legitimate destination and the eavesdropper, respectively. It is noted that in (3), it is assumed that the DF relay is only responsible for symbol-by-symbol decoding and forwarding as in [6]. The source rather than the relay encodes the secret information into symbols. In the 3rd phase, the consumed energy for information transmission at relay should be less than or equal to the harvested energy in the first time slot, so it should satisfy,

$$\alpha_3 T \sum_{n=1}^{N} p_n^R \leq E. \tag{4}$$

In this paper, our objective is to maximize the achievable secrecy rate of the DF relay network subject to the power constraint at source and the EH constraint at relay. The optimization problem is formulated as

$$\max_{\{\alpha_1, \alpha_2, \alpha_3, p_n^{S,2} \geq 0, p_n^R \geq 0, n \in \mathcal{N}\}} R \tag{5a}$$

$$\text{s.t. } \sum_{n=1}^{N} p_n^{S,2} \leq P_{stot}, \ \alpha_3 T \sum_{n=1}^{N} p_n^R \leq \alpha_1 T G, \tag{5b}$$

$$0 \leq \alpha_i \leq 1, i \in \{1, 2, 3\}, \ \alpha_1 + \alpha_2 + \alpha_3 = 1. \tag{5c}$$

## 3    The Proposed Jiont TS and PA Scheme

The problem (5) is non-convex because the objective function and EH constraint at relay are both non-convex. In the following, we will make it tractable by decoupling the non-convex optimization problem into two subproblems.

It is noted that if $\gamma_n^{RD} \leq \gamma_n^{RE}$, we have $\min\{p_n^{S,2}\gamma_n^{SR}, p_n^R\gamma_n^{RD}\} \leq p_n^R\gamma_n^{RE}$. In this case, in order to achieve more achievable secrecy rate, we should not allocate any transmit power over the $n$th subcarrier. Let $\Omega$ be

$$\Omega = \{n | \gamma_n^{RD} > \gamma_n^{RE}, n \in \mathcal{N}\}. \tag{6}$$

The problem is recasted as follows

$$\max_{\{\alpha_1, \alpha_2, \alpha_3, p_n^{S,2} \geq 0, p_n^R \geq 0, n \in \Omega\}} \hat{R} \tag{7a}$$

$$\text{s.t. } \sum_{n \in \Omega} p_n^{S,2} \leq P_{stot}, \ \alpha_3 T \sum_{n \in \Omega} p_n^R \leq \alpha_1 T G, \tag{7b}$$

$$0 \leq \alpha_i \leq 1, i \in \{1, 2, 3\}, \ \alpha_1 + \alpha_2 + \alpha_3 = 1 \tag{7c}$$

where

$$\hat{R} = \left\{ \min \left[ \sum_{n\in\Omega} \alpha_2 \log_2 \left(1 + p_n^{S,2} \gamma_n^{SR}\right), \sum_{n\in\Omega} \alpha_3 \log_2 \left(1 + p_n^R \gamma_n^{RD}\right) \right] \right.$$
$$\left. - \sum_{n\in\Omega} \alpha_3 \log_2 \left(1 + p_n^R \gamma_n^{RE}\right) \right\}^+. \qquad (8)$$

**Proposition 1.** *The optimal solution* $\left(\alpha_1, \alpha_2, \alpha_3, p_n^{S,2}, p_n^R\right)$, $n \in \Omega$, *to problem* (7) *should satisfy*

$$\sum_{n\in\Omega} \alpha_2 \log_2 \left(1 + p_n^{S,2} \gamma_n^{SR}\right) = \sum_{n\in\Omega} \alpha_3 \log_2 \left(1 + p_n^R \gamma_n^{RD}\right). \qquad (9)$$

*Proof.* By using reduction to absurdity, we will demonstrate Proposition 1. Let the optimum solutions $\left(\alpha_1, \alpha_2, \alpha_3, p_n^{S,2}, p_n^R\right)$ meet $\sum_{n\in\Omega} \alpha_2 \log_2 \left(1 + p_n^{S,2} \gamma_n^{SR}\right) \geq \sum_{n\in\Omega} \alpha_3 \log_2 \left(1 + p_n^R \gamma_n^{RD}\right)$. Thus, the achievable secrecy rate of DF relay networks is

$$\hat{R} = \sum_{n\in\Omega} \alpha_3 \log_2 \left(\frac{1 + p_n^R \gamma_n^{RD}}{1 + p_n^R \gamma_n^{RE}}\right). \qquad (10)$$

By decreasing $\alpha_2$ and increasing $\alpha_1$, $\alpha_3$, which satisfies $\alpha_3 T \sum_{n\in\Omega} p_n^R \leq \alpha_1 TG$, the achievable secrecy rate of the networks $\hat{R}$ in (10) will increase. Consequently, it will contradict the previous setting that $\left(\alpha_1, \alpha_2, \alpha_3, p_n^{S,2}, p_n^R\right)$ are the optimum solutions.

For another, let the optimum solutions $\left(\alpha_1, \alpha_2, \alpha_3, p_n^{S,2}, p_n^R\right)$ meet inequality $\sum_{n\in\Omega} \alpha_2 \log_2 \left(1 + p_n^{S,2} \gamma_n^{SR}\right) \leq \sum_{n\in\Omega} \alpha_3 \log_2 \left(1 + p_n^R \gamma_n^{RD}\right)$. Thus, the achievable secrecy rate of DF relay networks is

$$\hat{R} = \sum_{n\in\Omega} \alpha_2 \log_2 \left(1 + p_n^{S,2} \gamma_n^{SR}\right) - \sum_{n\in\Omega} \alpha_3 \log_2 \left(1 + p_n^R \gamma_n^{RE}\right). \qquad (11)$$

Based on inequality $\alpha_3 T \sum_{n\in\Omega} p_n^R \leq \alpha_1 TG$, by decreasing $p_n^R$, and holding $\alpha_3$ constant, $\alpha_1$ will decrease, too. With $\alpha_1 + \alpha_2 + \alpha_3 = 1$, $\alpha_2$ will increase. So, the achievable secrecy rate of the networks $\hat{R}$ in (11) will increase, too. Consequently, it will contradict the previous setting that $\left(\alpha_1, \alpha_2, \alpha_3, p_n^{S,2}, p_n^R\right)$ are the optimum solutions. $\qquad \square$

From Proposition 1, the optimal $\alpha_2$ and $\alpha_3$ satisfy $\alpha_2 = \lambda \alpha_3$, where

$$\lambda = \frac{\sum_{n\in\Omega} \log_2 \left(1 + p_n^R \gamma_n^{RD}\right)}{\sum_{n\in\Omega} \log_2 \left(1 + p_n^{S,2} \gamma_n^{SR}\right)}. \qquad (12)$$

Furthermore, according to the EH constraint at relay $\alpha_3 T \sum_{n\in\Omega} p_n^R \leq \alpha_1 TG$ and $\alpha_1 + \alpha_2 + \alpha_3 = 1$, we obtain

$$\alpha_3 \leq \frac{G}{(1+\lambda)G + \sum_{n\in\Omega} p_n^R}. \qquad (13)$$

According to Proposition 1, we equivalently transform the problem (7) into

$$\max_{\{\alpha_3, p_n^{S,2} \geq 0, p_n^R \geq 0, n \in \Omega\}} \hat{R} = \sum_{n \in \Omega} \alpha_3 \log_2 \left( \frac{1 + p_n^R \gamma_n^{RD}}{1 + p_n^R \gamma_n^{RE}} \right) \tag{14a}$$

$$\text{s.t.} \quad \sum_{n \in \Omega} p_n^{S,2} \leq P_{stot}, (13), 0 \leq \alpha_3 \leq 1. \tag{14b}$$

From (14a), we can observe that achievable secrecy rate $\hat{R}$ increases with the increase of $\alpha_3$. So, for the sake of getting the maximum, $\alpha_3$ is

$$\alpha_3 = \frac{G}{(1 + \lambda) G + \sum_{n \in \Omega} p_n^R}. \tag{15}$$

Substituting (12) and (15) into the objective function (14a), the optimization problem becomes

$$\max_{\{p_n^{S,2} \geq 0, p_n^R \geq 0, n \in \Omega\}} \frac{G \sum_{n \in \Omega} \log_2 \left( \frac{1 + p_n^R \gamma_n^{RD}}{1 + p_n^R \gamma_n^{RE}} \right)}{\left[ 1 + \frac{\sum_{n \in \Omega} \log_2 (1 + p_n^R \gamma_n^{RD})}{\sum_{n \in \Omega} \log_2 (1 + p_n^{S,2} \gamma_n^{SR})} \right] G + \sum_{n \in \Omega} p_n^R} \quad \text{s.t.} \quad \sum_{n \in \Omega} p_n^{S,2} \leq P_{stot}. \tag{16}$$

In order to solve the problem (16), we decompose this non-convex problem into two problems, i.e.,

$$\max_{\{p_n^{S,2} \geq 0, n \in \Omega\}} \sum_{n \in \Omega} \log_2 \left( 1 + p_n^{S,2} \gamma_n^{SR} \right) \quad \text{s.t.} \quad \sum_{n \in \Omega} p_n^{S,2} \leq P_{stot} \tag{17}$$

and

$$\max_{\{p_n^R, n \in \Omega\}} \frac{G \sum_{n \in \Omega} \log_2 \left( \frac{1 + p_n^R \gamma_n^{RD}}{1 + p_n^R \gamma_n^{RE}} \right)}{\left[ 1 + \frac{\sum_{n \in \Omega} \log_2 (1 + p_n^R \gamma_n^{RD})}{t^o} \right] G + \sum_{n \in \Omega} p_n^R} \quad \text{s.t.} \quad p_n^R \geq 0, n \in \Omega \tag{18}$$

where $t^o$ denotes the optimal objective value of problem (17). For optimization problem (17), we can know that it is convex from [4,12]. And we express its closed-form solution as

$$p_n^{S,2} = \left( 1/\nu - 1/\gamma_n^{SR} \right)^+, n \in \Omega \tag{19}$$

where $\nu$ is the lagrange multiplier introduced by $\sum_{n \in \Omega} p_n^{S,2} \leq P_{stot}$.

It is noted that the numerator of objective function (18) is concave respect to $p_n^R$ and the denominator is neither convex nor concave respect to $p_n^R$. To our best of knowledge, the problem (18) has no globally optimal solution currently. Therefore, we develop a constrained concave convex procedure (CCCP) [9] based iterative algorithm to achieve the local optimum of the problem (18). Let

$$f \left( \mathbf{p^R} \right) = \sum_{n \in \Omega} \log_2 \left( 1 + p_n^R \gamma_n^{RD} \right) \tag{20}$$

where $\mathbf{p^R} = \left(p_1^R, p_2^R \ldots, p_n^R\right), n \in \Omega$. The first-order Taylor expansion of (20) around $\tilde{\mathbf{p}}^{\mathbf{R}}$ is computed as [8]

$$\hat{f}\left(\mathbf{p^R}, \tilde{\mathbf{p}}^{\mathbf{R}}\right) = f\left(\tilde{\mathbf{p}}^{\mathbf{R}}\right) + \nabla f\left(\tilde{\mathbf{p}}^{\mathbf{R}}\right)\left(\mathbf{p^R} - \tilde{\mathbf{p}}^{\mathbf{R}}\right) \tag{21}$$

where $\tilde{\mathbf{p}}^{\mathbf{R}} = \left(\tilde{p}_1^R, \tilde{p}_2^R \ldots, \tilde{p}_n^R\right), n \in \Omega$, and

$$\nabla f\left(\tilde{\mathbf{p}}^{\mathbf{R}}\right) = \left(\frac{1}{\ln 2}\frac{\gamma_1^{RD}}{1+\tilde{p}_1^R\gamma_1^{RD}}, \frac{1}{\ln 2}\frac{\gamma_2^{RD}}{1+\tilde{p}_2^R\gamma_2^{RD}}, \cdots, \frac{1}{\ln 2}\frac{\gamma_n^{RD}}{1+\tilde{p}_n^R\gamma_n^{RD}}\right), n \in \Omega. \tag{22}$$

In the $(i+1)$th iteration of the proposed CCCP based iterative algorithm [10], we solve the following quasi-convex optimization problem

$$\max_{\{p_n^R, n\in\Omega\}} \frac{G\sum_{n\in\Omega}\log_2\left(\frac{1+p_n^R\gamma_n^{RD}}{1+p_n^R\gamma_n^{RE}}\right)}{G + \frac{G}{t^o}\hat{f}\left(\mathbf{p^R}, \tilde{\mathbf{p}}^{\mathbf{R}^{(i)}}\right) + \sum_{n\in\Omega}p_n^R} \quad \text{s.t.} \quad p_n^R \geq 0, n \in \Omega \tag{23}$$

where $\tilde{\mathbf{p}}^{\mathbf{R}^{(i)}}$ denotes the solution to the problem (23) at the $i$th iteration. Inversing the objective function of problem (23) and introducing a slack variable $\mu$, the problem (23) is equivalently rewritten as

$$\min_{\{\mu\geq 0, p_n^R\geq 0, n\in\Omega\}} \mu \tag{24a}$$

$$\text{s.t.} \quad G + \frac{G}{t^o}\hat{f}\left(\mathbf{p^R}, \tilde{\mathbf{p}}^{\mathbf{R}^{(i)}}\right) + \sum_{n\in\Omega}p_n^R - \mu\left[G\sum_{n\in\Omega}\log_2\left(\frac{1+p_n^R\gamma_n^{RD}}{1+p_n^R\gamma_n^{RE}}\right)\right] \leq 0 \tag{24b}$$

then solve it by following Algorithm 1.

---

**Algorithm 1** The Proposed CCCP Based Iterative Algorithm Using Bisection Search to Solve Problem (18)

---

1: **Initialization:** $\mu_L = 0$, $\mu_U = u$, where u is large enough to problem (24), tolerance $\epsilon > 0$, $k = 0$;
2: **Repeat:** $\mu^{(k)} = \frac{1}{2}(\mu_L + \mu_U)$, and substitute $\mu^{(k)}$ into the subproblem (25);
3: **Initialization:** $i = 0$, $\tilde{\mathbf{p}}^{\mathbf{R}^{(0)}}$;
4: **Repeat:** Solve subproblem (25):

$$\min_{\{p_n^R, n\in\Omega\}} G + \frac{G}{t^o}\hat{f}\left(\mathbf{p^R}, \tilde{\mathbf{p}}^{\mathbf{R}^{(i)}}\right) + \sum_{n\in\Omega}p_n^R - \mu^{(k)}\left[G\sum_{n\in\Omega}\log_2\left(\frac{1+p_n^R\gamma_n^{RD}}{1+p_n^R\gamma_n^{RE}}\right)\right] \tag{25a}$$

$$\text{s.t.} \quad p_n^R \geq 0, n \in \Omega; \tag{25b}$$

5: $i = i+1$, and update $\tilde{\mathbf{p}}^{\mathbf{R}^{(i)}} = \mathbf{p^{R*}}$, where $\mathbf{p^{R*}}$ is the optimal solution of (25);
6: **Until:** Convergence;
7: **If** $U^* < 0$, where $U^*$ is the optimal value of (25)
8: $\mu_U = \mu^{(k)}$;
9: **Else**
10: $\mu_L = \mu^{(k)}$;
11: **End**
12: $k = k+1$;
13: **Until:** $\mu_U - \mu_L < \epsilon$.

---

## 4   Simulation Results

In this paper, we assume that the entire bandwidth is equally split into $N = 16$ sub-channels. On the $n$th ($n \in \mathcal{N} = \{1, 2, \cdots, N\}$) sub-channel, all the channel responses $h_n^{SR}$, $h_n^{RD}$ and $h_n^{RE}$ are independent and identically distributed (i.i.d.) complex Gaussian random variables with zero mean [4,11]. Their variances are $d_{SR}^{-2}$, $d_{RD}^{-2}$ and $d_{RE}^{-2}$, respectively, through the use of a path loss model. $d_{SR}$ means the distance between the source node and the relay node. $d_{RD}$ means the distance between the relay node and the legitimate destination node and its value is 20 m. $d_{RE}$ means the distance between the relay node and the eavesdropper node and its value is also 20m. To be specific, we make the following settings, $d_{SR} = \eta d_{RD}$ ($\eta = d_{SR}/d_{RD}$), $\sigma_R^2 = \sigma_D^2 = \sigma_E^2 = \sigma^2/N = 0.001 \, \text{mW}$, and $\tau = 0.9$.

In Fig. 2, we show the achievable secrecy rate comparison of our proposed joint time switching and power allocation scheme (denoted as "Proposed Joint TS and PA" in the legend), the scheme with two-dimensional search (denoted as "Two-Dimensional Search"), which can get the optimal solution of the original optimization problem with very high complexity, and the scheme with $\alpha_1 = \alpha_2 = \alpha_3 = 1/3$ and equal power allocation (denoted as "Equal TS and PA") versus $\eta$ ($\eta = 10^{-1}$ to $\eta = 10^1$) with $P_{stot} = 100 \, \text{mW}$. From the result of Fig. 2, we can see that the scheme proposed in this paper has a superior performance over the scheme with equal time switching factors and power allocation. We can also find that our proposed scheme is very close to the scheme with two-dimensional

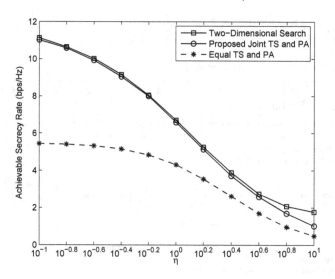

**Fig. 2.** Achievable secrecy rate versus $\eta$; performance comparison of our proposed joint time switching and power allocation scheme, the scheme with two-dimensional search and the scheme with equal time switching factors and power allocation for DF relay network where $P_{stot} = 100 \, \text{mW}$ and $\sigma^2 = 0.001 \, \text{mW}$.

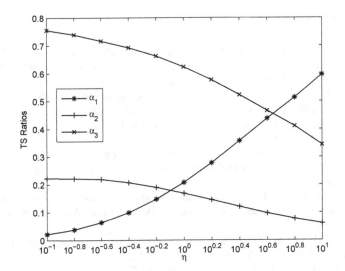

**Fig. 3.** Time switching factors versus $\eta$; obtained by our proposed joint time switching and power allocation scheme for the DF relay network where $P_{stot}$ =100 mW and $\sigma^2$ =0.001 mW.

search when the distance between the SR and RD links is not large ($\eta < 10^{0.4}$). However, with the larger $\eta$, the our proposed scheme performs worse.

In Fig. 3, we show the time switching factors, i.e., $\alpha_1$, $\alpha_2$ and $\alpha_3$ versus $\eta$ ($\eta = 10^{-1}$ to $\eta = 10^1$). And they can be found by using the scheme proposed in this paper. From Fig. 3, it is found that both $\alpha_2$ and $\alpha_3$ decrease as $\eta$ increases. On the contrary, $\alpha_1$ increases with $\eta$. This is because in order to achieve more achievable secrecy rate, $\alpha_1$ should be larger as $\eta$ increases. Besides, the sum of $\alpha_1$, $\alpha_2$ and $\alpha_3$ is 1.

## 5    Conclusions

In this paper, considering the DF scheme, we study the joint TS and PA for multicarrier secure communication with an energy harvesting relay. Simulation results have shown that our proposed joint TS and PA scheme achieves nearly global optimal resource allocation and has a superior performance over the existing resource allocation scheme.

**Acknowledgments.** The research work was supported by the Guangdong science and technology project (No. 2016A010101032), Guangzhou science and technology project (No. 2014J4100142) and Guangzhou college and university science and technology project (No. 1201421329).

# References

1. Zhang, R., Ho, C.K.: MIMO broadcasting for simultaneous wireless information and power transfer. IEEE Trans. Wireless Commun. **12**(5), 1989–2001 (2013)
2. Zhou, X., Zhang, R., Ho, C.: Wireless information and power transfer: architecture design and rate-energy tradeoff. IEEE Trans. Commun. **61**(11), 4754–4767 (2013)
3. Ding, Z., Krikidis, I., Sharif, B., Poor, H.V.: Wireless information and power transfer in cooperative networks with spatially random relays. IEEE Trans. Wirel. Commun. **13**(8), 4440–4453 (2014)
4. Huang, G., Zhang, Q., Qin, J.: Joint time switching and power allocation for multicarrier decode-and-forward relay networks with SWIPT. IEEE Sig. Process. Lett. **22**(12), 2284–2288 (2015)
5. Ding, Z., Perlaza, S., Esnaola, I., Poor, H.: Power allocation strategies in energy harvesting wireless cooperative networks. IEEE Trans. Wirel. Commun. **13**(2), 846–860 (2014)
6. Jeong, C., Kim, I.-M.: Optimal power allocation for secure multicarrier relay systems. IEEE Trans. Sig. Process **59**(11), 5428–5442 (2011)
7. Huang, X., He, J., Li, Q., Zhang, Q., Qin, J.: Optimal power allocation for multicarrier secure communications in full-duplex decode-and-forward relay networks. IEEE Commun. Lett. **18**(12), 2169–2172 (2014)
8. Magnus, J.R., Neudecker, H.: Matrix Differential Calculus with Applications in Statistics and Econometrics. Wiley, New York (1988)
9. Smola, A.J., Vishwanathan, S.V.N., Hofmann, T.: Kernel methods for missing variables. In: Proceedings of 10th International Workshop on Artificial Intelligence and Statistics, pp. 325–332 (2005)
10. Li, Q., Zhang, Q., Qin, J.: Secure relay beamforming for simultaneous wireless information and power transfer in non-regenerative relay networks. IEEE Trans. Veh. Technol. **63**(5), 2462–2467 (2014)
11. Lin, Y., Huang, J., Chen, H., Chen, L., Zhang, F., Jiang, Y., Xu, A., Guo, X., Chen, B.: Resource allocation for multicarrier secure communications in energy harvesting decode-and-forward relay network. In: IEEE Conference on Industrial Electronics and Applications, pp. 848–851 (2016)
12. Boyd, S., Vandenberghe, L.: Convex Optimization. Cambridge University Press, Cambridge (2004)
13. Goldsmith, A.: Wireless Communications. Cambridge University Press, Cambridge (2005)

# Joint Relay Processing and Power Control for Two-Way Relay Networks Under Individual SINR Constraints

Dongmei Jiang[1(✉)], Balasubramaniam Natarajan[2], and Haisheng Yu[1]

[1] Department of Communication Engineering, Qingdao University, Qingdao, China
jiangdm@sdu.edu.cn, yu.hs@163.com
[2] Department of Electrical and Computer Engineering, Kansas State University,
Manhattan, KS, USA
bala@ksu.edu

**Abstract.** This paper proposes an iterative algorithm, with which the relay processing matrix and power control can be realized jointly in two-way relay networks consisting of multiple pairs of single-antenna users and one multi-antenna relay station (RS). The users pairs in these networks exchange their information through the half-duplex RS. The joint processing scheme is formulated by including the design of the processing scheme at the RS and the transmit power of each node. Take the consideration of fairness among users, the scheme is written as an optimization problem which is formulated to minimize the total transmit power of all nodes subject to the individual signal to interference plus noise ratio (SINR) of each user. An iterative algorithm is proposed to solve the formulated non-convex joint optimization problem. The relay processing matrix is designed to maximize the SINR of each transmission link by using the uplink-downlink duality theory. In addition, theoretical analysis and simulation results demonstrate that with the given processing matrix at the RS, the total transmit power is a convex function with respect to the amplifying factor at the RS. The proposed algorithm is proved to converge efficiently.

**Keywords:** Two-way · Relay processing · Power control · Signal to interference plus noise ratio

## 1 Introduction

Two-way relay networks [1,2] have attracted much attention for its double spectrum efficiency comparing with conventional one-way relaying. In a two-way relaying, a bidirectional communication is established between two users, which takes two time slots. In the first time slot, users transmit signals to the relay station (RS) simultaneously. And in the second time slot, the RS processes the

H. Yu—This work was supported by Postdoctoral Application and Research Foundation of Qingdao.

© ICST Institute for Computer Sciences, Social Informatics and Telecommunications Engineering 2018
Q. Chen et al. (Eds.): ChinaCom 2016, Part I, LNICST 209, pp. 295–304, 2018.
DOI: 10.1007/978-3-319-66625-9_29

received signals and broadcast to all of the users. In [3], the capacity region of two-way relay networks with one pair of users and single RS is obtained. [4] extended the capacity region analysis to the case with multiple pairs of users. Resource allocation in two-way relaying systems has also been studied widely to improve the system performance. In [5], the optimal relay power allocation problem is investigated to maximize an arbitrary weighted sum rate of all users for a multiuser two-way relaying system with decode-and-forward (DF), amplify-and-forward (AF) and compress-and-forward (CF) protocols. The optimal resource allocation to maximize the sum rate for a two-way relay orthogonal frequency-division multiple access (OFDMA) system is studied in [6].

Multiple-input multiple-output (MIMO) can improve the system capacity or reliability of data transmission without additional power or bandwidth expenditure [7]. It has been widely studied in two-way relaying. For the network with one pair of users and multiple single-antenna RS, two optimal distributed beamforming methods at the RS are studied in [8]. One is to minimize the total transmit power whereas the other is to maximize the minimum of the two transceiver signal to noise ratios (SNRs) with the total power constraint. And the problem of maximizing the minimum of the two SNRs is also discussed with per-node power constraints by joint power control and distributed beamforming in [9]. In addition, the achievable rate region of such kind of networks via designing joint power allocation and collaborative beamforming scheme is studied in [10]. [11] considers a two-way relay network consisting of multiple pairs of users and multiple single-antenna relays and get two closed-form expressions for zero-forcing beamforming weights. One scheme is to null out every inter-pair interference and the other one is to cancel the total inter-pair interference. In [12], a low-complexity joint beamforming and power management scheme is proposed for a two-way relay network with one pair of multiantenna users and one multi-antenna RS to maximize the sum-rate and minimize the total transmission power. With the same network structure, [13] proposes a beamforming scheme with limited feedback. For the network with multiple pairs of users and one multi-antenna RS, relay processing based on zero forcing (ZF) and minimum mean square error (MMSE) criteria is studied in [14], and two power control strategies are proposed for ZF system to achieve fairness among all users and the maximum system SNR. In [15], a joint power allocation and beamforming is proposed to minimize the MSE by a iterative algorithm. In [16], a iterative algorithm is proposed to minimize the total transmit power of users with employing MMSE relay processing scheme. [17] proposed the signal to interference plus noise ratio (SINR) balancing and interference minimization relay beamforming schemes with imperfect channel state information for an cognitive relay network consisting of a secondary network with multiple cognitive relay nodes and a primary network.

In this paper, we focus on a multiuser two-way relay system with a multi-antenna RS. Considering the fairness among all users and energy efficiency, we try to minimize the total transmit power of all nodes in the same time satisfying the SINR requirements of each user. The problem is formulated as joint optimizing the relay processing matrix and the power control policy. As the joint optimization problem is non-convex, an iterative algorithm is proposed to solve the problem. The relay processing matrix is obtained to maximize the SINR of each user by using the uplink-downlink duality theory, and with this given processing matrix, the total transmit power is a convex function with respect to the amplifying factor at the RS. Simulations show that the algorithm converge efficiently and can minimize the total transmit power under the target SINRs for users.

In the text followed, matrices and vectors are denoted by bold upper- and lower-case letters. $tr(\cdot)$, $(\cdot)^{\mathrm{T}}$ and $(\cdot)^{\mathrm{H}}$ denote trace of a matrix, transpose and complex conjugate transpose of a matrix, respectively. $|\cdot|$ and $\|\cdot\|_2$ denote the absolute value and Euclidian norm, respectively.

## 2   System Model

Consider a two-way relay network which consists of $K$ pairs of users and a RS, as shown in Fig. 1. The RS is equipped with $N_r > 1$ antennas while each user has a single antenna. Each pair of users exchange their information via the RS. Without loss of generality, we assume $user_{2i}$ and $user_{2i-1}, i \in \{1, 2, \cdots, K\}$ are two users exchanging their information via the RS. Denote $\boldsymbol{h}_k \in \mathbb{C}^N, k \in \{1, 2, \cdots, 2K\}$ as the channel vector from $user_k$ to the RS.

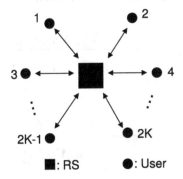

**Fig. 1.** A two-way relay network with K pairs of users

In the first phase, users transmit signals to the relay station simultaneously. The received signal at the relay station can be written as

$$\boldsymbol{r} = \boldsymbol{H}\sqrt{\boldsymbol{P}}\boldsymbol{s} + \boldsymbol{n}_r \in \mathbb{C}^N, \tag{1}$$

where $\boldsymbol{s} = [s_1, \ldots, s_{2K}]$ is the transmitted signals with unit power from all users. $\boldsymbol{P} = diag\{P_1, \cdots, P_{2K}\}$ accounts for power loading. $\boldsymbol{H} = [\boldsymbol{h}_1, \cdots, \boldsymbol{h}_{2K}] \in \mathbb{C}^{N_r \times 2K}$ is the channel matrix obtained by stacking all channel vectors seen from users to the RS. Besides, $\boldsymbol{n}_r \in \mathbb{C}^{N_r}$ is the additive white Gaussian noise with zero mean and variance $E[\boldsymbol{n}_r \boldsymbol{n}_r^{\mathrm{H}}] = \boldsymbol{I}\sigma^2$.

In the second phase, the signals are first processed at the RS, which can be modelled as

$$x = \beta V r, \tag{2}$$

where $\beta$ and $V \in \mathbb{C}^{N_r \times N_r}$ are the amplifying factor and the processing matrix at the RS, respectively. The relay processing matrix is designed to perform data exchanging between a user pair and to suppress inter- and intra-pair interference. Then, the transmit power at the RS can be written as

$$P_r = \beta^2 tr(V\Phi V^H), \tag{3}$$

where $P_r$ is the transmit power at the RS, $\Phi = HPH^H + \sigma^2 I$.

After processing, the RS broadcasts the processed signals to users. Due to the reciprocity of the channel between the uplink and downlink, the received signals at the users in this phase can be written as

$$y = H^T x + n, \tag{4}$$

where $n = [n_1, \cdots, n_{2K}]^T \in \mathbb{C}^{2K \times 1}$ with $n_k, \forall k$ is Gaussian distributed with zero mean and variance $\sigma^2$. Then, the received noise power at user $k$ is presented as

$$\sigma_k^2 = (\beta^2 \|h_k^T V\|_2^2 + 1)\sigma^2. \tag{5}$$

Till now, we can write the expressions of SINR at $User_{2i-1}$ and $User_{2i}, \forall i$, which are given by

$$SINR_{2i-1} = \frac{\beta^2 |h_{2i-1}^T V h_{2i}|^2 P_{2i}}{\sum\limits_{j=1, j \neq 2i}^{2K} \beta^2 |h_{2i-1}^T V h_j|^2 P_j + \sigma_{2i-1}^2}, \tag{6}$$

and

$$SINR_{2i} = \frac{\beta^2 |h_{2i}^T V h_{2i-1}|^2 P_{2i-1}}{\sum\limits_{j=1, j \neq 2i-1}^{2K} \beta^2 |h_{2i}^T V h_j|^2 P_j + \sigma_{2i}^2}, \tag{7}$$

respectively.

## 3    Joint Power Control and Relay Processing Scheme

Considering the fairness among all users and the energy efficiency, the optimization problem is designed to minimize the total transmit power of users and the RS while satisfying SINR constraints at each user. Let $P_{total} = \sum\limits_{k=1}^{2K} P_k + P_r$, the optimization problem is written as

$$\{V, p, \beta\} = \arg \min_{V, p, \beta} P_{total}$$
$$s.\,t. \qquad SINR_k \geq \gamma_k, \tag{8}$$

where $p = diag\{P\}$ and $\gamma_k$ is the target SINR of user $k$. From the above expressions, we can get that when the processing matrix is given, the minimum total transmit power can only be obtained with equality in their constraints, which is written in matrix form as follows

$$\beta^2 (W - D\Psi) p = D \left( \beta^2 \sigma_1 + \sigma_2 \right), \tag{9}$$

where $W$, $D$, $\Psi$ and $\sigma$ are defined as follows

$$W = blockdiag \left( \begin{bmatrix} 0 & 1 \\ 1 & 0 \end{bmatrix}, \cdots, \begin{bmatrix} 0 & 1 \\ 1 & 0 \end{bmatrix} \right) \in \mathbb{C}^{2K \times 2K}, \tag{10}$$

$$[D]_{k,j} = \begin{cases} \frac{\gamma_k}{|h_k^T V h_{k+1}|^2}, & k = 2i - 1, j = k \\ \frac{\gamma_k}{|h_k^T V h_{k-1}|^2}, & k = 2i, j = k \\ 0, & otherwise. \end{cases} \tag{11}$$

$$[\Psi]_{k,j} = \begin{cases} |h_k^T V h_j|^2, & k = 2i - 1, j \neq k + 1 \\ |h_k^T V h_j|^2, & k = 2i, j \neq k - 1 \\ 0, & k = 2i - 1, j = k + 1 \\ 0, & k = 2i, j = k - 1. \end{cases} \tag{12}$$

$$\sigma_1^2 = \left[ \|h_1^T V\|_2^2 \sigma^2, \cdots, \|h_{2K}^T V\|_2^2 \sigma^2 \right]^T. \tag{13}$$

$$\sigma_2^2 = \left[ \sigma^2, \cdots, \sigma^2 \right]^T \tag{14}$$

Denote $\lambda_{max}(\cdot)$ as the maximum eigenvalue of a matrix. If $\lambda_{max}(D\Phi) < 1/\gamma$, Eq. (9) has feasible solution. It means that with this condition, there exist a positive power vector $p$ and a positive value of $\beta$ satisfying the SINR constraints. Given the processing matrix $V$, it is easy to get the solution to this problem being

$$p = \Omega \left( \sigma_1 + \beta^{-2} \sigma_2 \right). \tag{15}$$

where $\Omega = (W - D\Psi)^{-1} D$. From the above equation, we get the solution is a function of $\beta$. To determine the value of $p$ is to determine $\beta$. Substitute (15) into the objective function in (8), the optimization problem is then reduced to

$$\beta = \arg\min_{\beta} \ \beta^2 tr \left( V \Phi V^H \right) + i\Omega \left( \sigma_1 + \beta^{-2} \sigma_2 \right).$$

$$s. t. \quad \beta > 0, \tag{16}$$

where $i = [1, \cdots, 1]^T$. We can prove easily that the objective function in the above optimization problem is convex with respect to $\beta$. Then, its optimal solution is

$$\beta = \sqrt[4]{i\Omega \sigma_2^2 / tr \left( V \Phi V^H \right)} \tag{17}$$

Substituting (17) into (15) and (3), we can get the transmit power at users and at the RS, respectively.

Given the obtained transmit power, the processing scheme at the RS can then be established. Firstly, we get the receive filter $\boldsymbol{V}_{rx}$ at RS, which is designed to maximize the individual SINRs of users in the first transmission phase. Define $\boldsymbol{R}_k = \boldsymbol{h}_k \boldsymbol{h}_k^{\mathrm{H}} / \sigma^2$, $\boldsymbol{Q} = \sum_{i=1, i \neq k}^{K} \boldsymbol{R}_i P_i + \boldsymbol{I}$. The optimization problem is formulated as follows

$$\boldsymbol{V}_{rx,k} = \arg \max_{\boldsymbol{V}_{rx,k}} \frac{\boldsymbol{V}_{rx,k}^{\mathrm{H}} \boldsymbol{R}_k \boldsymbol{V}_{rx,k}}{\boldsymbol{V}_{rx,k}^{\mathrm{H}} \boldsymbol{Q}_k \boldsymbol{V}_{rx,k}} \tag{18}$$

It is solved by the dominant generalized eigenvectors of the matrix pairs $(\boldsymbol{R}_k, \boldsymbol{Q}_k)$. Denote $\boldsymbol{V}_{tx}$ as the downlink transmit processing matrix at the RS. According to the uplink-downlink duality theory, it is easy to get $\boldsymbol{V}_{tx} = \boldsymbol{V}_{rx}^{\mathrm{T}}$. Then, the processing matrix at the RS can be written as

$$\boldsymbol{V} = \boldsymbol{V}_{tx} \boldsymbol{W} \boldsymbol{V}_{rx}. \tag{19}$$

After this two processes, the global optimal relay processing matrix and the power control strategy can be finally obtained via an iterative algorithm, which is summarized in Table 1.

**Table 1.** Iterative algorithm for the solution to the problem in (8)

---
1: Initialize: $t = 0, P_k(0) \neq 0, \forall k$

2: Obtain the processing scheme $\boldsymbol{V}(0)$ based on (19).

**3: Repeat**

3: $t \leftarrow t + 1$

4: Construct $\boldsymbol{\Psi}(t)$, $\boldsymbol{D}(t)$, $\boldsymbol{\Phi}(t)$ and $\boldsymbol{\sigma_1}(t)$ based on $\boldsymbol{V}(t-1)$.

5:    if $\lambda_{max}(\boldsymbol{D}(t)\boldsymbol{\Psi}(t)) \geq 1$

6:       Set $\gamma \leftarrow \gamma'$ such that $\lambda_{max}(\boldsymbol{D}(t)\boldsymbol{\Psi}(t)) < 1$.

8:       Update $\boldsymbol{D}(t)$.

9:    **end if**

10: Obtain $\boldsymbol{p}(t), \beta(t)$ and the total transmit power $P_{total}(t)$.

11: **Until** $\frac{P_{total}(t) - P_{total}(t-1)}{P_{total}(t)} < \epsilon$

---

## 4    Computer Simulations

In this section, the performance of the proposed algorithm is investigated by computer simulations. To set up the system, we assume that there are 4 single antenna users and a 4 antennas RS. We also assume that the channel state information (CSI) between the RS and users are known perfectly at the RS. The elements of $\boldsymbol{h}_k$ is modelled as Rayleigh distributed variables with zero mean and unit variance. In all simulations, the noise variance $\sigma^2 = 10^{-3}$ and the stopping criterion $\epsilon$ is set to be $10^{-3}$. The initial transmit power of users is 0.1 W. All results are obtained by taking the average of 1000 simulation runs.

We firstly investigate the convergence property of the proposed algorithm. The target SINRs are set to be the same, i.e. $\gamma_1 = \gamma_2 = \gamma_3 = \gamma_4 = 10$ dB. From Fig. 2, we can see that the transmit power of all nodes as well as the total transmit power converge to constants as the number of iterations increases. We have observed that the typical number of iterations is between 5 to 10, which is a fast convergence. The power assignments of users are the same as shown in Fig. 2 is due to the same assumptions on distances between users and the RS and the target SINRs. Different results will be achieved if those values are set to be different. In addition, the converged values of power is dependent on the initial transmit power.

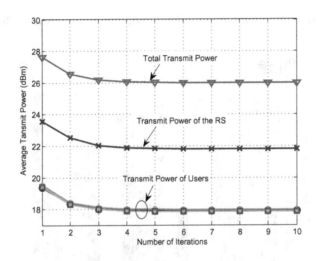

**Fig. 2.** Convergence of the average transmit power.

We then investigate how the amplifying factor $\beta$ affect the total transmit power $P_{total}$. Results are shown in Fig. 3 showing that the value of $\beta$ has a great impact on the total transmit power and telling that the total power can be minimized by carefully choosing the value of $\beta$. The results also tell that as $\beta$ increases, the total transmit power first decreases, and then increases, showing that there must be a point the total power is minimum.

Figure 4 presents the converged total transmit power $P_{total}$ and the user transmit power $P_k, \forall k$ as functions of the target SINRs $\{\gamma_1, \gamma_2, \gamma_3, \gamma_4\}$. It can be observed that when the target SINRs increases, the corresponding transmit power increases as expected. From the first and the third group data, we can see that when the target SINRs are the same, the transmit power assigned to users is also the same. Comparing the first group with the second group, we

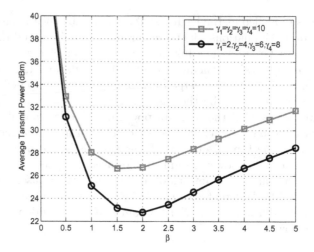

**Fig. 3.** Total transmit power versus relay amplifying factor $\beta$ with different target SINRs $\{\gamma_1, \gamma_2, \gamma_3, \gamma_4\}$ (dB).

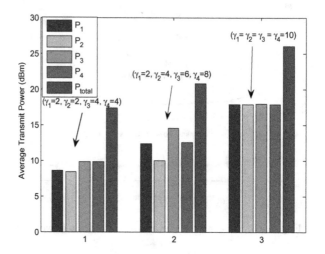

**Fig. 4.** Transmit power versus target SINRs $\{\gamma_1, \gamma_2, \gamma_3, \gamma_4\}$ (dB).

know that with the same target SINR of $user_1$ the transmit power of $user_2$ increases when the target SINRs of the others increase. The reason is that when the target SINRs of the rest users increase, the corresponding transmit power of their partners increases, then the interference power between users increases. $User_2$ has to raise its transmit power to guarantee the received SINR by $user_1$. In the first and the third group data, the values of total transmit power are about 20.78 dBm and 26.01 dBm, smaller than the minimum values given in Fig. 3, which are about 22.77 dBm and 26.70 dBm respectively.

# 5  Conclusions

In this paper, we have proposed an iterative algorithm to jointly optimize the processing matrix and power control policy in a two-way relay networks. Take the fairness among all users into account, the optimization problem is formulated to minimize the total transmit power of users and the RS while satisfying the SINR constraints of users. We get the processing matrix and the power control policy separately at first and then get the global optimal solution iteratively. The algorithm can converge quickly and the minimum total transmit power can be found efficiently with the proposed scheme.

# References

1. Rankov, B., Wittneben, A.: Spectral efficient protocol for half-duplex fading relay channels. IEEE J. Sel. Areas Commun. **25**(2), 379–389 (2007)
2. Chen, M., Yener, A.: Multiuser two-way relaying: detection and interference management strategies. IEEE Trans. Wireless Commun. **8**(8), 4296–4303 (2009)
3. Zhang, R., Chai, C., Liang, Y., Cui, S.: On capacity region of two-way multi-antenna relay channel with analogue network coding. In: Proceedings of IEEE ICC, pp. 1–5 (2009)
4. Kim, S.J., Smida, B., Devroye, N.: Capacity bounds on multi-pair two-way communication with a base-station aided by a relay. In: Proceedings of IEEE ISIT, pp. 425–529 (2010)
5. Chen, M., Yener, A.: Power allocation for F/TDMA multiuser two-way relay networks. IEEE Trans. Wireless Commun. **9**(2), 546–551 (2010)
6. Jitvanichphaibool, K., Zhang, R., Liang, Y.: Optimal resource allocation for two-way relay-assisted OFDMA. IEEE Trans. Veh. Technol. **58**(7), 3311–3321 (2009)
7. Vishwanath, S., Jindal, N., Goldsmith, A.: Duality, achievable rates, and sum-rate capacity of Gaussian MIMO broadcast channels. IEEE Trans. Inf. Theory **49**(10), 2658–2668 (2003)
8. Havary-Nassab, V., Shahbazpanahi, S., Grami, A.: Optimal distributed beamforming for two-way relay networks. IEEE Trans. Signal Process. **58**(3), 1238–1250 (2010)
9. Jing, Y., ShahbazPanahi, S.: Max-min optimal joint power control and distributed beamforming for two-way relay networks under per-node power constraints. IEEE Trans. Sig. Process. **60**(12), 6576–6589 (2012)
10. Zeng, M., Zhang, R., Cui, S.: On design of collaborative beamforming for two-way relay networks. IEEE Trans. Sig. Process. **59**(5), 2284–2295 (2011)
11. Wang, C., Chen, H., Yin, Q.: Multi-user two-way relay networks with distributed beamforming. IEEE Trans. Wireless Commun. **10**(10), 3460–3471 (2011)
12. Leow, C.Y., Ding, Z., Leung, K.K.: Joint beamforming and power management for nonregenerative MIMO two-way relaying channels. IEEE Trans. Veh. Technol. **60**(9), 4374–4383 (2011)
13. Chun, K., Love, D.J.: Optimization and tradeoff analysis of two-way limited feedback beamforming systems. IEEE Trans. Wireless Commun. **8**(5), 2570–2579 (2009)
14. Joung, J., Sayed, A.H.: Multiuser two-way amplify-and-forward relay processing and power control methods for beamforming systems. IEEE Trans. Signal Process. **58**(3), 1833–1846 (2010)

15. Khafagy, M., El-Keyi, A., ElBatt, T., Nafie, M.: Joint power allocation and beam-forming for multiuser MIMO two-way relay networks. In: Proceedings of IEEE PIMRC, pp. 1692–1697 (2011)
16. Jiang, D., Zhang, H., Yuan, D.: Joint relay processing and power control in two-way relay networks. In: Proceedings of IEEE ICCT, pp. 66–69 (2011)
17. Safavi, S.H., Ardebilipour, M., Salari, S.: Relay beamforming in cognitive two-way networks with imperfect channel state information. IEEE Wireless Commun. Lett. **1**(4), 344–347 (2012)

# Capacity Region of the Dirty Two-Way Relay Channel to Within Constant Bits

Zhixiang Deng[(✉)], Yuan Gao, Wei Li, and Changchun Cai

College of Internet of Things Engineering, Hohai University, Changzhou, China
dengzhixiang@gmail.com

**Abstract.** In this paper, we consider a dirty Gaussian two-way relay channel, where the two user nodes exchange messages with the help of a relay node. The three nodes experience two independent additive interferences which are assumed to be known at some nodes. We consider two cases: (1) the two user nodes know each of the two interferences respectively; (2) the relay node knows both the interferences. With nested lattice coding and compute-and-forward relaying, we derive achievable rate regions for the above two cases. The achievable rate regions are shown to be within constant bits from the cut-set outer bound for all channel parameters regardless of the interferences. Comparing the two achievable rate regions of the above two cases, it is shown that more information about the interferences the relay node knows more interferences will be canceled, larger achievable rate region can be achieved.

**Keywords:** Two-way relay channel · Dirty paper channel · Nested lattice coding · Compute-and-forward

## 1 Introduction

The channel with channel state information causally known at the source node was first considered by Shannon [1]. For the channel with state information non-causally known at the encoder, Gel'fand and Pinsker [2] derived the capacity for general discrete memoryless channels and Costa [3] derived the capacity of the Gaussian dirty channel with dirty-paper coding.

The two-way relay channel in which two users wish to exchange messages with the help of a third relay node is a practical channel model for wireless communication systems. A number of coding schemes and relaying strategies have been proposed for the two-way relay channels. Lattice coding which has been shown to be good for almost everything [4] was applied to two-way relay channels during recent years and was demonstrated to be capacity-approaching [5–9]. Nam *et al.* [6] proposed a scheme based on nested lattice codes formed from a lattice chain. They exploited the structural gain of computation coding and derived the capacity region for the two-way relay channel to with 1/2 bit. In [7], a lattice-based achievability strategy was proposed to derive a symmetric rate which is within $\frac{1}{2}\log(3)$ bits of the capacity for the two-way two-relay channel.

© ICST Institute for Computer Sciences, Social Informatics and Telecommunications Engineering 2018
Q. Chen et al. (Eds.): ChinaCom 2016, Part I, LNICST 209, pp. 305–315, 2018.
DOI: 10.1007/978-3-319-66625-9_30

For some certain classes of channels with side information, Zamir *et al.* [9] used lattice codes to derive the capacity of these channels. The nested approach of [9] for the dirty-paper channels is extended to multi-user dirty-paper channels, e.g. the authors in [10] showed that lattice-based binning seemed to be necessary to achieve capacity of the dirty multiple access channel (MAC). In [11], Song *et al.* studied the two-hop Gaussian relay channel with a source, a relay and a destination. The destination experienced an additive interference which is known to the source non-causally. They proposed a new achievable scheme based on nested lattice code and decode-and-forward (DF) relaying. This strategy used the structure provided by nested lattice codes to cancel part of the interference at the source and achieved a rate to within 1/2 bit of the clean channel.

In this paper, we consider a Gaussian two-way relay channel with channel state information. The two user nodes (node 1 and node 2) exchange messages with the help of a relay node (node 3). The three nodes experience two independent additive Gaussian interferences $S_1$ and $S_2$ which can be viewed as the signals transmitted from the primary users in cognitive radio systems. We assume that only part of the nodes in the two-way relay channel are capable of acquiring some knowledge about the interferences $S_1$ and $S_2$. Thus, the state-dependent two-way relay channel studied in this paper can be viewed as a secondary relay communication with some cognitive nodes. The nodes knowing the interference $S_1$ or $S_2$ may adapt their coding schemes to mitigate the interferences caused by the primary communication. We consider the following two cases: (1) user node 1 and user node 2 know the interferences $S_1$ and $S_2$ respectively; (2) the relay node knows both interferences $S_1$ and $S_2$. We generalize the lattice coding schemes used in [6,11], and derive corresponding inner bounds for the capacity regions of the above two cases based on compute-and-forward relaying at the relay node and nested lattice coding with interferences pre-cancellation at the nodes which know the interference. With these achievable schemes, the achievable rate regions derived for the above two cases are within constant bits from the cut-set outer bounds for all channel parameters regardless of the interferences.

## 2 Channel Model and Lattice Coding Preliminaries

### 2.1 Channel Model

As shown in Fig. 1, we consider a two-way relay channel with interferences. We assume that there is no direct path between the two user nodes. The channel is corrupted by two independent additive Gaussian interferences $S_1$ and $S_2$ known non-causally at some of the nodes. The message $w_i \in \{1, 2, ..., 2^{nR_i}\}$ is uniformly distributed over the message set $\mathcal{W}_i = \{1, 2, ..., 2^{nR_i}\}$, where $i \in \{1, 2\}$, $n$ is the number of channel uses, and $R_i$ denotes the rate of message $w_i$. The messages $w_1$ and $w_2$ are independent of each other. We let $\mathbf{X}_i^n = (X_i(1), X_i(2), ..., X_i(n))$ where $X_i(k)$ denotes the input from node $i$ at channel use $k$ (and similarly for the channel outputs $\mathbf{Y}_i^n$ of node $i$) where $i \in \{1, 2, 3\}$. Node $i$ transmits $X_i(k)$ at time $k$ to the relay through the channel specified by

$$Y_3(k) = X_1(k) + X_2(k) + S_1(k) + S_2(k) + Z_3(k) \tag{1}$$

where $Z_3(k)$ is an independent identically distributed (i.i.d.) Gaussian random variable with zero mean and variance 1, $S_1$ and $S_2$ are the two additive i.i.d. Gaussian interferences with zero mean and variance $Q_1$ and $Q_2$ respectively.

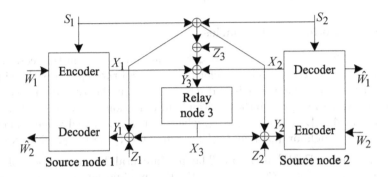

**Fig. 1.** Dirty two-way relay channel

The relay node 3 transmits $X_i(k)$ to user node 1 and user node 2 through the channel specified by

$$Y_i(k) = X_3(k) + S_1(k) + S_2(k) + Z_i(k) \qquad (2)$$

where $Z_i(k)$ is an additive white Gaussian noise with zero mean and variance 1.

For the first case when user node 1 and user node 2 know the channel state information non-causally, a $(2^{nR_1}, 2^{nR_2}, n)$-code consists of message $w_i$ uniformly distributed over the message set $\mathcal{W}_i = \{1, 2, ..., 2^{nR_i}\}$; two encoding functions at node 1 and node 2

$$f_i^n : \{1, 2, ..., 2^{nR_i}\} \times \mathcal{S}_i^n \to \mathbb{R}^n \qquad (3)$$

such that $\frac{1}{n} \sum_{k=1}^n E(x_{i,k}^2) \leq P_i$, where $i = 1, 2$; a series of encoding functions $\{f_3^{(k)}\}_{k=1}^n$ at the relay node 3 such that $X_3(k) = f_3^{(k)}(\mathbf{Y}_3^{k-1})$ and $\frac{1}{n} \sum_{k=1}^n (X_3(k))^2 \leq P_3$; decoding functions at node 1 and node 2

$$g_i^n : \mathcal{Y}_i^n \times \mathcal{S}_i^n \times \mathcal{W}_i \to \{1, 2, ..., 2^{nR_{\bar{i}}}\} \qquad (4)$$

where, $i, \bar{i} \in \{1, 2\}, i \neq \bar{i}$.

The definition of $(2^{nR_1}, 2^{nR_2}, n)$-code for the second case when the relay node knows both $S_1$ and $S_2$ is similar to that for the first case, except that the encoding functions and decoding functions at node 1 and node 2 should be replaced by $f_i^n : \{1, 2, ..., 2^{nR_i}\} \to \mathbb{R}^n$ and $g_i^n : \mathcal{Y}_i^n \times \mathcal{W}_i \to \{1, 2, ..., 2^{nR_{\bar{i}}}\}$, $i, \bar{i} \in \{1, 2\}, i \neq \bar{i}$, respectively, and encoding functions at the relay node should be replaced by $X_3(k) = f_3^{(k)}(\mathbf{Y}_3^{k-1}, \mathbf{S}_1^n, \mathbf{S}_2^n)$.

The decoding error probability is defined as

$$P_{n,e} = \frac{1}{2^{n(R_1+R_2)}} \sum_{w_1 \in \mathcal{W}_1, w_2 \in \mathcal{W}_2} \Pr\left((w_1, w_2) \neq (\hat{w}_1, \hat{w}_2) \,|\, (w_1, w_2) \text{ was sent}\right)$$

For any $\varepsilon > 0$ and sufficiently large $n$, if there exists $(2^{nR_1}, 2^{nR_2}, n)$-code such that $P_{n,e} < \varepsilon$, the rate pair $(R_1, R_2)$ is said to be achievable. The capacity region for the dirty two-way relay channel is defined as the supremum of the set of all achievable rate pairs.

## 2.2  Lattice Coding Preliminaries

We briefly outline the notations and definitions for nested lattice codes. For details of the lattice coding, please refer to [4,12] and the references therein.

An $n$-dimensional lattice $\Lambda$ is a discrete group in the Euclidian space $\mathbb{R}^n$ which is closed with respect to the addition and reflection operations. The lattice is specified by $\Lambda = \{\lambda = G \cdot \mathbf{i} : \mathbf{i} \in \mathbb{Z}^n\}$, where $G$ is a $n \times n$ real valued matrix.

The nearest neighbor quantizer $Q_\Lambda(\cdot)$ is defined by $Q_\Lambda(\mathbf{x}) = \arg\min_{\lambda \in \Lambda} \|\mathbf{x} - \lambda\|$, where $\|\cdot\|$ denotes Euclidian norm. The fundamental Voronoi region of $\Lambda$ is defined as $\mathcal{V}(\Lambda) = \{\mathbf{x} \in \mathbb{R}^n : Q_\Lambda(\mathbf{x}) = 0\}$. The modulo lattice operation with respect to $\Lambda$ is defined as $\mathbf{x} \bmod \Lambda = \mathbf{x} - Q_\Lambda(\mathbf{x})$. The second moment of a lattice $\Lambda$ is given by $\sigma^2(\Lambda) = \frac{1}{V} \cdot \frac{1}{n} \int_{\mathcal{V}} \|\mathbf{x}\|^2 d\mathbf{x}$, and the normalized second moment of lattice $\Lambda$ is given by $G(\Lambda) = \frac{\sigma^2(\Lambda)}{V^{\frac{2}{n}}}$, where $V$ is the volume of the Voronoi region.

A lattice $\Lambda$ is said to be Rogers-good if $\lim_{n \to \infty} G(\Lambda) = \frac{1}{2\pi e}$ and Poltyrev-good if $\Pr\{Z \notin \mathcal{V}\} \leqslant e^{-nE_p(\mu)}$ for any $Z \in \mathcal{N}(0, \sigma^2 \mathbf{I})$, where $\mu = \frac{(\text{Vol}(\mathcal{V}))^{2/n}}{2\pi e \sigma^2}$ is the volume-noise ratio.

A nested lattice code is defined in terms of two $n$-dimensional lattices $\Lambda$ and $\Lambda_c$ such that $\Lambda \subseteq \Lambda_c$ with fundamental regions $\mathcal{V}$, $\mathcal{V}_c$ of volumes $V := \text{Vol}(\mathcal{V})$, $V_c := \text{Vol}(\mathcal{V}_c)$ respectively. Lattice $\Lambda$ is called the coarse lattice which is a sub-lattice of the fine lattice $\Lambda_c$. The set $\mathcal{C}_{\Lambda_c, \Lambda} = \{\Lambda_c \cap \mathcal{V}\}$ can be employed as the codebook using $\Lambda_c$ as codewords and the Voronoi region $\mathcal{V}$ of $\Lambda$ as a shaping region. The coding rate $R$ is defined as $R = \frac{1}{n} \log |\mathcal{C}_{\Lambda_c, \Lambda}| = \frac{1}{n} \log \frac{V}{V_c}$.

# 3  Main Results

## 3.1  Achievable Rate Region When the Two User Nodes Know $S_1$ and $S_2$ Respectively

Since the two user nodes 1 and 2 know only part of the interferences, each user node pre-cancels part of the interferences according to their own knowledge about the interferences using the nested lattice codes. The relay node decodes and forwards the function of the codewords transmitted from the two user nodes exploiting the structure property of the nested lattice codes. The two user nodes decode the message from the other node using their own messages as side information. Combining the structured interference pre-cancelation technique in [11] and the compute-and-forward relaying used to derive the achievable rate region for the two-way relay channel by Nam in [6], an achievable rate region is derived for the dirty two-way relay channel studied in this paper as shown in the following theorem.

**Theorem 1.** *For the dirty Gaussian two-way relay channel with partial channel state information known at the user nodes as shown in Fig. 1, the rate region which is the closure of the set of all points $(R_1, R_2)$ satisfying*

$$R_1 < \min \left\{ \left[ \frac{1}{2} \log \left( \frac{P_1}{\frac{P_1 + P_2}{P_1 + P_2 + 1} + \frac{P_2}{P_2 + 1}} \right) \right]^+, \left[ \frac{1}{2} \log \left( \frac{P_3}{\frac{2P_3}{2P_3 + 1} + \frac{P_3}{P_3 + 1}} \right) \right]^+ \right\}$$
$$R_2 < \min \left\{ \left[ \frac{1}{2} \log \left( \frac{P_2}{\frac{P_1 + P_2}{P_1 + P_2 + 1} + \frac{P_2}{P_2 + 1}} \right) \right]^+, \left[ \frac{1}{2} \log \left( \frac{P_3}{\frac{2P_3}{2P_3 + 1} + \frac{P_3}{P_3 + 1}} \right) \right]^+ \right\} \tag{5}$$

*is achievable and is within 1 bit from the cut-set outer bound, where $[x]^+ \triangleq \max \{x, 0\}$.*

*Remark 1.* Compared with the achievable rate region of the two-way relay channel with no interference considered in [6] which is shown to be within 1/2 bit from the outer bound, the achievable rate region of the two-way relay channel with two additional interferences derived in this paper is within 1 bit from the outer bound. This 1/2 bit larger gap is due to the fact that the two user nodes know only part of the interference.

*Proof.* Without loss of generality, we assume $P_1 \geq P_2$. We will prove the theorem in two cases: (1) $P_3 \geq P_2$; (2) $P_2 \geq P_3$.

(1) the first case: $P_3 \geq P_2$
For the first case, let us consider a good nested lattice chain $\Lambda_1 \subset \Lambda_2 \subset \Lambda_c \subset \Lambda_q$ as in Sect. 2.2, where the second moment of each lattice is constrained to be $\sigma^2(\Lambda_1) = \min(P_1, P_3)$, $\sigma^2(\Lambda_2) = P_2$, $\sigma^2(\Lambda_c) = \sigma_c^2$ and $\sigma^2(\Lambda_q) = \sigma_q^2$. The lattices $\Lambda_1$, $\Lambda_2$ and $\Lambda_q$ are both Rogers good and Poltyrev good, while $\Lambda_c$ is Poltyrev good. The proof in [13] ensures the existence of such lattice chain. The Voronoi regions of the lattices $\Lambda_1$, $\Lambda_2$, $\Lambda_c$, $\Lambda_q$ are denoted by $\mathcal{V}_1$, $\mathcal{V}_2$, $\mathcal{V}_c$, $\mathcal{V}_q$ of volumes $V_1$, $V_2$, $V_c$, $V_q$ respectively.

**Encoding at the User Nodes.** We use $\mathcal{C}_1 = \{\Lambda_c \cap \mathcal{V}_1\}$ for node 1, $\mathcal{C}_2 = \{\Lambda_c \cap \mathcal{V}_2\}$ for node 2. For node $i$, each message $w_i \in \{1, 2, ..., 2^{nR_i}\}$ is one-to-one mapped to the lattice point $\mathbf{t}_i \in \mathcal{C}_i$, where $R_i = \frac{1}{n} \log(\frac{V_i}{V_c})$. We also define two sets $\mathcal{C}_{q,1} = \{\Lambda_q \cap \mathcal{V}_1\}$ and $\mathcal{C}_{q,2} = \{\Lambda_q \cap \mathcal{V}_2\}$ for quantizing the interferences at node 1 and node 2 with quantization rates $R_{q,1} = \frac{1}{n} \log(\frac{V_1}{V_q})$ and $R_{q,2} = \frac{1}{n} \log(\frac{V_2}{V_q})$ respectively. To transmit a message $w_i$, node $i$ chooses $\mathbf{t}_i$ associated with the message and sends

$$\mathbf{X}_i = (\mathbf{T}_i - \alpha \mathbf{S}_i + \mathbf{U}_i) \mod \Lambda_i$$

where $\mathbf{T}_i = (\mathbf{t}_i - Q_{\Lambda_q}(\alpha_i \mathbf{S}_i + \mathbf{U}_{q_i})) \mod \Lambda_i \in \mathcal{C}_{q,i}$, $\mathbf{U}_i$ is the channel coding dither uniformly distributed over $\mathcal{V}_i$ and is known to the relay node, $\mathbf{U}_{q_i}$ is the quantization dither uniformly distributed over $\mathcal{V}_q$. From the dithered quantization property, $\mathbf{X}_i$ is uniformly distributed over $\mathcal{V}_i$ and is independent of $\mathbf{T}_i$.

**Encoding at the Relay Nodes.** The relay receives $\mathbf{Y}_3 = \mathbf{X}_1 + \mathbf{X}_2 + \mathbf{S}_1 + \mathbf{S}_2 + \mathbf{Z}_3$ and computes

$$
\begin{aligned}
\tilde{\mathbf{Y}}_3 &= (\alpha \mathbf{Y}_3 - \mathbf{U}_1 - \mathbf{U}_2) \bmod \Lambda_1 \\
&= [\mathbf{T}_1 + \mathbf{T}_2 - Q_{\Lambda_2}(\mathbf{T}_2 - \alpha \mathbf{S}_2 + \mathbf{U}_2) - (1 - \alpha)(\mathbf{X}_1 + \mathbf{X}_2) + \alpha \mathbf{Z}_3] \bmod \Lambda_1 \\
&= [\mathbf{T}_3 - (1 - \alpha)(\mathbf{X}_1 + \mathbf{X}_2) + \alpha \mathbf{Z}_3] \bmod \Lambda_1
\end{aligned}
$$

where $\mathbf{T}_3 = (\mathbf{T}_1 + \mathbf{T}_2 - Q_{\Lambda_2}(\mathbf{T}_2 - \alpha \mathbf{S}_2 + \mathbf{U}_2)) \bmod \Lambda_1$. Since $\Lambda_1 \subset \Lambda_2 \subset \Lambda_c \subset \Lambda_q$, it follows that $\mathbf{T}_3 \in \mathcal{C}_{q1}$. Using the crypto-lemma, $\mathbf{T}_3$ is uniformly distributed over $\mathcal{C}_{q1}$ and independent of $-(1 - \alpha)(\mathbf{X}_1 + \mathbf{X}_2)$ and $\alpha \mathbf{Z}_3$ which can be seen as two independent noise terms. According to Theorem 3 in [6], choosing $\alpha = \frac{\min(P_1, P_3) + P_2}{\min(P_1, P_3) + P_2 + 1}$, the relay can decode $\hat{\mathbf{T}}_3$ successfully with the error probability $\Pr\{\hat{\mathbf{T}}_3 \neq \mathbf{T}_3\}$ vanishes as $n \to \infty$ if

$$
\begin{aligned}
R_{q1} &< \left[ \tfrac{1}{2} \log \left( \min(P_1, P_3) / (\min(P_1, P_3) + P_2) + \min(P_1, P_3) \right) \right]^+ \\
R_{q2} &< \left[ \tfrac{1}{2} \log \left( P_2 / (\min(P_1, P_3) + P_2) + P_2 \right) \right]^+
\end{aligned}
\tag{6}
$$

Following that $R_{qi} = \frac{\sigma^2(\Lambda_i)}{\sigma^2(\Lambda_q)}$, the following inequality must be satisfied.

$$
\sigma_q^2 = \sigma^2(\Lambda_q) > \min(P_1, P_3) + P_2 / (\min(P_1, P_3) + P_2 + 1)
\tag{7}
$$

The relay transmits $\mathbf{X}_3 = (\hat{\mathbf{T}}_3 + \mathbf{U}_3) \bmod \Lambda_1$ where $\mathbf{U}_3$ is the channel coding dither known at the user nodes 1 and 2. Again, according to the crypto-lemma, $\mathbf{X}_3$ is uniformly distributed over $\mathcal{V}_1$ and independent of $\hat{\mathbf{T}}_3$.

**Decoding at the User Node 1.** The user node 1 estimates the message $\hat{w}_2$ by its received vector $\mathbf{Y}_1 = \mathbf{X}_3 + \mathbf{S}_1 + \mathbf{S}_2 + \mathbf{Z}_1$.

Since the user node 1 has known the interference $\mathbf{S}_1$ in advance, it subtracts it from $\mathbf{Y}_1$ to derive $\mathbf{Y}'_1 = \mathbf{X}_3 + \mathbf{S}_2 + \mathbf{Z}_1$. It then computes

$$
\begin{aligned}
\tilde{\mathbf{Y}}_1 &= (\alpha_2 \mathbf{Y}'_1 + \mathbf{U}_{q2} - \mathbf{U}_3 - \mathbf{T}_1) \bmod \Lambda_2 \\
&= [(\mathbf{T}_3 + \mathbf{U}_3) \bmod \Lambda_1 - (1 - \alpha_2) \mathbf{X}_3 \\
&\quad + \alpha_2(\mathbf{S}_2 + \mathbf{Z}_1) + \mathbf{U}_{q2} - \mathbf{U}_3 - \mathbf{T}_1] \bmod \Lambda_2 \\
&\overset{(a)}{=} [\mathbf{T}_2 - (1 - \alpha_2) \mathbf{X}_3 + \alpha_2 \mathbf{S}_2 + \alpha_2 \mathbf{Z}_1 + \mathbf{U}_{q2}] \bmod \Lambda_2 \\
&= \mathbf{t}_2 + (\alpha_2 \mathbf{S}_2 + \mathbf{U}_{q2}) \bmod \Lambda_q - (1 - \alpha_2) \mathbf{X}_3 + \alpha_2 \mathbf{Z}_1 \bmod \Lambda_2
\end{aligned}
\tag{8}
$$

where (a) follows from the facts that $\mathbf{T}_3 = (\mathbf{T}_1 + \mathbf{T}_2 - Q_{\Lambda_2}(\mathbf{T}_2 - \alpha \mathbf{S}_2 + \mathbf{U}_2)) \bmod \Lambda_1$ and the mod-lattice operation $(\mathbf{x} \bmod \Lambda_1) \bmod \Lambda_2 = \mathbf{x} \bmod \Lambda_2$ resulting from the fact $\Lambda_1 \subset \Lambda_2$.

From (8), it is easy to find that $(\alpha_2 \mathbf{S}_2 + \mathbf{U}_{q2}) \bmod \Lambda_q$ is a random variable uniformly distributed over $\mathcal{V}_q$ and independent of all the others. Thus, $(\alpha_2 \mathbf{S}_2 + \mathbf{U}_{q2}) \bmod \Lambda_q$, $-(1 - \alpha_2) \mathbf{X}_3$ and $\alpha_2 \mathbf{Z}_1$ can be seen as three independent noise terms with variance $\sigma_q^2$, $(1 - \alpha)^2 \min(P_1, P_3)$ and $\alpha_2^2$ respectively. Choosing $\alpha_2 = \frac{\min(P_1, P_3)}{\min(P_1, P_3) + 1}$, node 1 decodes $\mathbf{t}_2$ by lattice decoding $\hat{\mathbf{t}}_2 = Q_{\Lambda_c}(\tilde{\mathbf{Y}}_1)$ where

$Q_{\Lambda_c}(\cdot)$ denotes the nearest neighbor lattice quantizer associated with $\Lambda_c$. The error probability $\Pr\{\hat{\mathbf{t}}_2 \neq \mathbf{t}_2\}$ vanishes as $n \to \infty$, if

$$R_2 < \frac{1}{2}\log\left(P_2/\left(\sigma_q^2 + \frac{\min(P_1, P_3)}{\min(P_1, P_3) + 1}\right)\right) \tag{9}$$

Considering the inequality (7), we have

$$R_2 < \frac{1}{2}\log\left(P_2/\left(\frac{\min(P_1, P_3) + P_2}{\min(P_1, P_3) + P_2 + 1} + \frac{\min(P_1, P_3)}{\min(P_1, P_3) + 1}\right)\right) \tag{10}$$

**Decoding at the User Node 2.** The user node 2 estimates the message $\hat{w}_1$ by its received vector $\mathbf{Y}_2$. Taking similar steps as decoding at the user node 1, we can derive the following achievable rate of the message $w_1$

$$R_1 < \frac{1}{2}\log\left(\min(P_1, P_3)/\left(\frac{\min(P_1, P_3) + P_2}{\min(P_1, P_3) + P_2 + 1} + \frac{\min(P_1, P_3)}{\min(P_1, P_3) + 1}\right)\right) \tag{11}$$

(2) the second case $P_2 \geq P_3$,
For the case $P_2 \geq P_3$, we let $\Lambda_1 = \Lambda_2$ of the nested lattice chain $\Lambda_1 \subset \Lambda_2 \subset \Lambda_c \subset \Lambda_q$ used in the first case. The second moments of both the two lattices $\Lambda_1$ and $\Lambda_2$ are restricted to be $P_3$. In this case, all the three nodes will transmit with the same average power $P_3$. Taking the same encoding and decoding steps as in the first case, we can derive the following achievable rate pair $(R_1, R_2)$.

$$R_1 = R_2 < \frac{1}{2}\log\left(P_3/\left(\frac{2P_3}{2P_3 + 1} + \frac{P_3}{P_3 + 1}\right)\right) \tag{12}$$

Therefore, according to Eqs. (10)–(12), we conclude that the following rate pair $(R_1, R_2)$ is achievable

$$
\begin{aligned}
R_1 &< \min\left\{\left[\frac{1}{2}\log\left(\frac{P_1}{\frac{P_1+P_2}{P_1+P_2+1} + \frac{P_2}{P_2+1}}\right)\right]^+, \left[\frac{1}{2}\log\left(\frac{P_3}{\frac{2P_3}{2P_3+1} + \frac{P_3}{P_3+1}}\right)\right]^+\right\} \\
R_2 &< \min\left\{\left[\frac{1}{2}\log\left(\frac{P_2}{\frac{P_1+P_2}{P_1+P_2+1} + \frac{P_1}{P_1+1}}\right)\right]^+, \left[\frac{1}{2}\log\left(\frac{P_3}{\frac{2P_3}{2P_3+1} + \frac{P_3}{P_3+1}}\right)\right]^+\right\}
\end{aligned}
\tag{13}
$$

Next, we will show that the above achievable rate pair is within 1 bit from the cut-set outer bound which is given by

$$
\begin{aligned}
R_1 &\leq \min\left\{\tfrac{1}{2}\log(1 + P_1), \tfrac{1}{2}\log(1 + P_3)\right\} \\
R_2 &\leq \min\left\{\tfrac{1}{2}\log(1 + P_2), \tfrac{1}{2}\log(1 + P_3)\right\}
\end{aligned}
\tag{14}
$$

Considering (13) and (14), we can conclude that

$$
\begin{aligned}
\frac{1}{2}\log\left(\frac{P_1}{\frac{P_1+P_2}{P_1+P_2+1} + \frac{P_2}{P_2+1}}\right) &> \frac{1}{2}\log\left(\frac{P_1}{\frac{P_1+P_2}{P_1+P_2+1} + \frac{P_1+P_2}{P_1+P_2+1}}\right) \\
&= \frac{1}{2}\log\left(\frac{P_1}{P_1+P_2} + P_1\right) - \frac{1}{2} \\
&> \frac{1}{2}\log(1 + P_1) - 1
\end{aligned}
\tag{15}
$$

where the last inequality is due to the fact $\frac{1}{2}\log\left(\frac{P_1}{P_1+P_2}+P_1\right) > \frac{1}{2}\log\left(1+P_1\right)-\frac{1}{2}$ which has been shown in [6]. Similarly, we have

$$\frac{1}{2}\log\left(\frac{P_2}{\frac{P_1+P_2}{P_1+P_2+1}+\frac{P_1}{P_1+1}}\right) > \frac{1}{2}\log\left(1+P_2\right)-1 \tag{16}$$

$$\frac{1}{2}\log\left(\frac{P_3}{\frac{2P_3}{2P_3+1}+\frac{P_3}{P_3+1}}\right) > \frac{1}{2}\log\left(1+P_3\right)-1 \tag{17}$$

The three inequalities (15)–(17) show that the achievable rate region derived in this paper is within 1 bit from the cut-set outer bound.

### 3.2    Achievable Rate Region When Relay Knows Both $S_1$ and $S_2$

When the relay node knows both interferences $S_1$ and $S_2$, it can subtract the two interferences before decoding since the interferences are additive. Therefore, the uplink (the channel from the two user nodes to the relay node) can be viewed as a clean channel. The downlink (the channel from the relay node to the two user nodes), however, is dirty. The relay node helps to eliminate the interferences with dirty paper coding.

**Theorem 2.** *For the dirty Gaussian two-way relay channel, when relay node 3 knows both the interferences $S_1$ and $S_2$, the rate region which is the closure of the set of all points $(R_1, R_2)$ satisfying*

$$\begin{aligned} R_1 &< \min\left\{\left[\tfrac{1}{2}\log\left(\tfrac{P_1}{P_1+P_2}+P_1\right)\right]^+, \left[\tfrac{1}{2}\log\left(1+P_3\right)\right]^+\right\} \\ R_2 &< \min\left\{\left[\tfrac{1}{2}\log\left(\tfrac{P_2}{P_1+P_2}+P_2\right)\right]^+, \left[\tfrac{1}{2}\log\left(1+P_3\right)\right]^+\right\} \end{aligned} \tag{18}$$

*is achievable and is within 1/2 bit from the cut-set outer bound, where $[x]^+ \triangleq \max\{x, 0\}$.*

*Remark 2.* The achievable rate region derived in Theorem 3 is the same as that derived in the work of Nam [6] in which the two-way relay channel is not corrupted by extra interferences. This means that the interferences can be eliminated completely by the relay node with dirty paper coding when the relay node knows all the interferences in advance.

*Proof.* Again, without loss of generality, we assume $P_1 \geq P_2$ and construct a good nested lattice chain $\Lambda_1 \subset \Lambda_2 \subset \Lambda_c \subset \Lambda_q$ where the second moment of each lattice is constrained to be $\sigma^2\left(\Lambda_1\right) = \min\left(P_1, P_3\right)$, $\sigma^2\left(\Lambda_2\right) = P_2$, $\sigma^2\left(\Lambda_c\right) = \sigma_c^2$ and $\sigma^2\left(\Lambda_q\right) = \sigma_q^2$, $\Lambda_1$, $\Lambda_2$ and $\Lambda_q$ are both Rogers good and Poltyrev good while $\Lambda_c$ is Poltyrev good. Two codebooks $\mathcal{C}_1 = \{\Lambda_c \cap V\left(\Lambda_1\right)\}$ and $\mathcal{C}_2 = \{\Lambda_c \cap V\left(\Lambda_2\right)\}$ are generated.

Since the interferences $S_1$ and $S_2$ are additive and known to the relay node, they can be subtracted from the signals received at the relay node. Therefore, the uplink channel can be viewed as a clean channel. Following the same steps in [6], the relay node can estimate $\hat{\mathbf{T}}_3 = \mathbf{T}_3 = (\mathbf{t}_1 + \mathbf{t}_2 - Q_{\Lambda_2}(\mathbf{t}_2 + \mathbf{U}_2)) \bmod \Lambda_1$ with error probability approaching 0 if the rate pair $(R_1, R_2)$ satisfies (19), where $\mathbf{t}_1 \in \mathcal{C}_1$ and $\mathbf{t}_2 \in \mathcal{C}_2$ are the lattice points associated with the messages transmitted by user node 1 and user node 2 respectively.

$$
\begin{aligned}
R_1 &< \tfrac{1}{2} \log \left( \tfrac{P_1}{P_1 + P_2} + P_1 \right) \\
R_2 &< \tfrac{1}{2} \log \left( \tfrac{P_2}{P_1 + P_2} + P_2 \right)
\end{aligned}
\tag{19}
$$

Having successfully decoded $\hat{\mathbf{T}}_3$, the relay node sends $\hat{\mathbf{T}}_3$ to user node 1 and user node 2 using Gaussian codebooks. Again, we assume $P_1 \geq P_2$, thus $R_1 \geq R_2$ for the uplink. Fix a measure $P_{U,S_1,S_2}$. Generate $2^{n(R_1+R_s)}$ i.i.d. codewords $\{\mathbf{u}^n(t_3, t_s)\}$ each with i.i.d. components drawn according to $P_U$. Randomly and uniformly distribute $2^{n(R_1+R_s)}$ codewords $\{\mathbf{u}^n(t_3, t_s)\}$ into $2^{nR_1}$ bins each with $2^{nR_s}$ codewords. We assume one-to-one correspondence between $\hat{\mathbf{T}}_3 \in \mathcal{C}_1$ and the bin index $t_3$ and denote it as $t_3(\hat{\mathbf{T}}_3)$. It is easy to verify $t_3(\hat{\mathbf{T}}_3)$ is uniformly distributed over $\{1, 2, ..., 2^{nR_1}\}$ since $\hat{\mathbf{T}}_3$ is uniformly distributed over $\mathcal{C}_1$. Knowing the interferences non-causally, the relay node searches the smallest $\tilde{t}_s \in \{1, 2, ..., 2^{nR_s}\}$ from the bin indexed by $t_3(\hat{\mathbf{T}}_3)$ such that $\mathbf{u}^n(t_3(\hat{\mathbf{T}}_3), \tilde{t}_s)$ is jointly typical with $\mathbf{s}_1^n$ and $\mathbf{s}_2^n$. By the covering lemma [14], if $R_s > I(U; S_1, S_2)$, there exists at least one such codeword. The relay node then transmits $\mathbf{x}_3^n = \mathbf{u}^n(t_3(\hat{\mathbf{T}}_3), \tilde{t}_s) - \alpha_r(\mathbf{s}_1^n + \mathbf{s}_2^n)$.

User node 1 estimates $\hat{\mathbf{T}}_3$ according to its received vector $\mathbf{Y}_1$. It chooses one unique codeword $\mathbf{u}^n(t_3(\hat{\mathbf{T}}_{3,1}), \tilde{t}_s) \in \mathcal{C}_{r,1}$ such that $\mathbf{u}^n(t_3(\hat{\mathbf{T}}_{3,1}), \tilde{t}_s)$ and $\mathbf{Y}_1$ are jointly typical, where

$$
\mathcal{C}_{r,1} = \{\mathbf{u}^n(t_3(\mathbf{T}), t_s) : \mathbf{T} = \mathbf{t}_1 + \mathbf{t}'_2 - Q_{\Lambda_2}(\mathbf{t}_2 + \mathbf{U}_2), \mathbf{t}'_2 \in \mathcal{C}_2, t_s \in [1 : 2^{nR_s}]\}
$$

$\mathbf{t}_1$ is the lattice point associated with the message transmitted by itself. Using $\mathbf{t}_1$ as side information, user node 1 estimates the message of user node 2 as

$$
\hat{\mathbf{t}}_2 = (\hat{\mathbf{T}}_{3,1} - \mathbf{t}_1) \bmod \Lambda_2
\tag{20}
$$

If and only if $\hat{\mathbf{T}}_{3,1} = \hat{\mathbf{T}}_3$, the probability that user node 1 successfully estimates the message $\hat{\mathbf{t}}_2 = \mathbf{t}_2$ from user node 2 tends to 1. Notice that the cardinality of $\mathcal{C}_{r,1}$ is $2^{n(R_2+R_s)}$. Thus, from the argument of GP-coding [2], the probability that $\hat{\mathbf{T}}_{3,1} \neq \hat{\mathbf{T}}_3$ tends to 0 as $n \to \infty$ if

$$
R_2 < I(U; Y_1) - I(U; S_1, S_2)
\tag{21}
$$

By dirty paper coding, we choose $\alpha_r = \frac{P_3}{P_3+1}$, the decoding error probability at user node 1 approaches 0 if

$$
R_2 < \frac{1}{2} \log (1 + P_3)
\tag{22}
$$

Taking similar steps, user node 2 can successfully decode message of user node 1 with decoding error probability approaching 0 if

$$
R_1 < \frac{1}{2} \log (1 + P_3)
\tag{23}
$$

Following (19), (22) and (23), the following rate pair is achievable

$$R_1 < \min\left\{\tfrac{1}{2}\log\left(\tfrac{P_1}{P_1+P_2}+P_1\right)^+, \tfrac{1}{2}\log(1+P_3)\right\}$$
$$R_2 < \min\left\{\tfrac{1}{2}\log\left(\tfrac{P_2}{P_1+P_2}+P_2\right)^+, \tfrac{1}{2}\log(1+P_3)\right\} \tag{24}$$

The achievable rate region derived in (24) is the same as that derived in [6] in which the two-way relay channel is not corrupted by extra interferences. Therefore, the rate region derived by (24) is within 1/2 bit from the cut-set outer bound.

## 4   Conclusions

In this paper, we consider a Gaussian dirty two-way relay channel with additive interferences known partially at some of the nodes. Achievable rate regions are derived using nested lattice coding and compute-and-forward relaying for two cases. The nodes which know the interference in advance make use of the structure of the nested lattice codes to pre-cancel part of the interferences. At the relay node, structural gain of computation coding is exploited using nested lattice codes. With the schemes used in this paper, we show that the achievable rate regions are within constant bits from the cut-set outer bound regardless of the interferences.

**Acknowledgments.** This research was supported by National Natural Science Foundation of China (Nos. 61501171, 61271232, 61401146, 61401147).

## References

1. Shannon, C.E.: Channels with side information at the transmitter. IBM J. Res. Dev. **4**, 289–293 (1958)
2. Gelfand, S.I., Pinsker, M.S.: Coding for channel with random parameters. Probl. Control Inf. Theory **1**, 19–31 (1980)
3. Costa, M.H.M.: Writing on dirty paper. IEEE Trans. Inf. Theory **3**, 439–441 (1983)
4. Erez, U., Litsyn, S., Zamir, R.: Lattices which are good for (almost) everything. IEEE Trans. Inf. Theory. **10**, 3401–3416 (2005)
5. Smirani, S., Kamoun, M., Sarkiss, M.: Wyner-Ziv lattice coding for two-way relay channel. In: IEEE International Conference on Advanced Technologies for Communications, pp. 207–212. IEEE Press, New York (2012)
6. Nam, W., Chung, S.Y., Lee, Y.: Capacity of the Gaussian two-way relay channel to within 1/2 bit. IEEE Trans. Inf. Theory **11**, 5488–5494 (2010)
7. Song, Y., Devroye, N., Shao, H.R.: Lattice coding for the two-way two-relay channel. In: IEEE Symposium on Information Theory, pp. 1312–1316. IEEE Press, New York (2013)
8. Sagar, Y.T., Yang, J., Kwon, H.M.: Achievable rate of a two-way relay channel with structured code under Rayleigh Fading. In: IEEE International Conference on Networking and Communications, pp. 644–648. IEEE Press, New York (2014)

9. Zamir, R., Shamai, S., Erez, U.: Nested linear/lattice codes for structured multi-terminal binning. IEEE Trans. Inf. Theory **6**, 1250–1276 (2002)
10. Philoso, T., Zamir, R., Erez, U.: Lattice strategies for the dirty multiple access channel. IEEE Trans. Inf. Theory **8**, 5006–5035 (2011)
11. Song, Y., Devroye, N.: Structured interference-mitigation in two-hop networks. In: IEEE Information Theory and Applications Workshop, pp. 1–6. IEEE Press, New York (2011)
12. Erez, U., Zamir, R.: Achieving 1/2 log(1+SNR) on the AWGN channel with lattice encoding and decoding. IEEE Trans. Inf. Theory **10**, 2293–2314 (2004)
13. Krithivasan, D., Pradhan, S.S.: A proof of the existence of good nested lattices. UM CSPL Technical Reports Series (2011)
14. Gamal El, A., Kim, Y.H.: A Proof of the Existence of Good Nested Lattices. Cambridge University Press, Cambridge (2011)

# Quality-of-Service Driven Resource Allocation via Stochastic Optimization for Wireless Multi-user Relay Networks

Xiao Yin[1,2], Yanbo Ma[1(✉)], Qiang Liu[1], and Wei Su[1]

[1] Shandong University of Finance and Economics, Jinan, China
{yanboma,qiangliu,suwei}@sdufe.edu.cn
[2] Shandong Provincial Key Laboratory of Software Engineering, Jinan, China
yx_018@126.com

**Abstract.** This paper presents a power allocation algorithm for optimizing network resources while considering the delay provisioning in multi-user relay networks. Our aim is to minimize the average power consumed by the relay nodes while satisfying the minimum Qos requirement of all users. Employing the convex optimization theory, we derive an optimal power allocation policy in a quasi-closed form and give two rules of how to select the relay nodes. Furthermore, a stochastic power method is developed to learn the fading state of the channels and carry out the optimal strategy immediately. Moreover, numerical results are provided to demonstrate the performance of the proposed resource allocation policies.

**Keywords:** Resource allocation · Wireless relay networks · QoS · Effective capacity · Stochastic optimization · Convex optimization

## 1 Introduction

Nowadays, green communication is a growing research area which strives for designing energy awareness communication systems so as to enhance energy efficiency [1]. Energy awareness in wireless networks can be achieved by using low-power relays for coverage extension, or improving wireless resource/interference management. Among these approaches, relay based cooperative communication requires minimum modification in the existing network infrastructure, and has been one active research area. By exploiting spatial diversity the cooperative communication schemes [2,3] are well recognized as an effective way to improve the network performance (e.g. capacity, power efficiency, reliability) at the physical layer. Motivated by this, in this paper we consider an effective resource allocation scheme to improve the network capacity for wireless multi-user relay networks.

Many energy-efficient resource allocation schemes addressing this topic have been published recently [4–7]. The framework employed in the cited literatures is mainly based on the information theory. However, it is worth to mention that this

© ICST Institute for Computer Sciences, Social Informatics and Telecommunications Engineering 2018
Q. Chen et al. (Eds.): ChinaCom 2016, Part I, LNICST 209, pp. 316–325, 2018.
DOI: 10.1007/978-3-319-66625-9_31

framework is not suitable for the delay-sensitive multimedia applications, since Shannon theory places no restriction on the delay of the transmission scheme achieving capacity. In order to supply the multimedia applications, in this paper we consider the QoS metric of the statistical delay, which describes a delay-bound violation probability upper-bounded by a certain given value. And the statistical delay related effective capacity [8] is adopted to describe the network capacity for the multimedia applications. It is worth to mention the effective capacity was first introduced by Wu and Negi to describe the maximal arrival rate which can be supported under guaranteed delay QoS requirements. The concept of effective capacity provides us with a degree of freedom to discuss the queueing behaviors at data link layer, such as queue distribution, buffer overflow probabilities, and delay-bound violation probabilities.

As the extended application of effective capacity for wireless networks, in this paper we utilize the concept of effective capacity and provide a general framework for optimizing network resources while considering the delay provisioning in multi-user relay networks. The proposed policy aims to minimize the average power consumed by the relay nodes while satisfying the rate constraints of all users. With the effective capacity theory, the resource allocation policy is cross-layer based and delay QoS oriented jointly. Employing the convex optimization theory, an optimal power allocation policy is derived in a quasi-closed form and two rules of how to select the relay nodes is derived based on the Karush-Kuhn-Tucker (KKT) conditions. Besides, in order to expand the applied range of the proposed scheme, we takes into account the time-varying nature of fading channels without a priori knowledge of the cumulative distribution function (cdf) of the channels. Specifically, we model the channel condition as a stochastic process. Based on the stochastic optimization tools [9–13], the proposed resource allocation schemes can learn the underlying channel distribution. This entails a more systematic and powerful framework for the design and analysis of the stochastic resource allocation schemes in wireless networks.

## 2    System Model and Problem Formulation

### 2.1    System Model

Consider a multiuser relay network, where $M$ source nodes $(S_j, \ j = 1, ..., M)$ transmit data to their respective destination nodes $(D_j, \ j = 1, ..., M)$. There are $N$ relay nodes $(R_i, \ i = 1, ..., N)$ which are employed to assist transmissions from source to destination nodes. Premise that there is no direct link between the source and the destination nodes and a relay can forward data for several users. Moreover, orthogonal transmissions are supposed among different users for simultaneous communications by using different frequency bands. The available channel bandwidth is equally divided into $M$ orthogonal subchannels whose bandwidth is denoted by $B$. Each user is allocated to one subchannel.

At the source, frames from upper layers are put into the queue which is assumed to be infinite-length. Then at the physical layer, frames from the queue are divided into bit-streams. The reverse operations are executed at the receiver.

We assume that the fading processes of all users are jointly stationary and ergodic with continuous joint cumulative distribution. Additionally, the wireless links are assumed to experience different fading from one frame to another, but remain invariant within a frame duration $T_f$.

Let $h_{R_i}^{S_j}$ and $h_{R_i}^{D_j}$ denote the fading channel coefficient for link $S_j$–$R_i$ and $R_i$–$D_j$, respectively. Let $P_{S_j}$ denote the transmit power of $S_j$ and $P_{R_i}^{S_j}$ denote the power transmitted by the relay $R_i$ for assisting the source $S_j$. Let $N_{R_i}$ and $N_{D_j}$ denote the variance of the additive white Gaussian (AWGN) at $R_i$ and $D_j$. We assume that transmission for each source-destination pair via relay nodes is carried out in a time multiplexing manner by Amply-and-forward (AF) protocol. Specifically, each frame duration is equally divided into $N + 1$ intervals. The source $S_j$ broadcasts its signal to all relays at the first interval, and each relay forwards the signal to the destination $D_j$ per interval in orders. Assuming that maximum-ratio-combining is employed at the destination node $D_j$, the signal-to-noise ratio (SNR) at $D_j$ can be written as

$$\gamma_j = \sum_{i=1}^{N} \frac{P_{R_i}^{S_j}}{\alpha_{R_i}^{S_j} P_{R_i}^{S_j} + \beta_{R_i}^{S_j}}, \tag{1}$$

where

$$\alpha_{R_i}^{S_j} = \frac{\frac{N_{R_i}}{N+1}}{|h_{R_i}^{S_j}|^2 P_{S_j}}, \beta_{R_i}^{S_j} = \frac{\frac{N_{D_j}}{N+1}\frac{N_{R_i}}{N+1}}{|h_{R_i}^{S_j}|^2 |h_{R_i}^{D_j}|^2 P_{S_j}} + \frac{\frac{N_{D_j}}{N+1}}{|h_{R_i}^{D_j}|^2}. \tag{2}$$

The data rate from source $S_j$ to destination $D_j$ is given as

$$r_j = \frac{1}{N+1} \log(1 + \gamma_j). \tag{3}$$

The rate function $r_j(\cdot)$ has been proven to be a concave increasing function of $P_{R_i}^{S_j}$ [14]. This convexity property will help us formulate a convex optimization for the problem under consideration as will be shown in the next subsection.

## 2.2   Problem Formulation

Considering the delay provisioning for delay-sensitive traffic, effective capacity is introduced to describe the system throughput with delay QoS guarantees. The effective capacity of link $S_j$–$D_j$ is described as

$$Ec_j = -\frac{1}{\theta} \log(\mathbb{E}[e^{-\theta_j T_f B r_j}]), \tag{4}$$

where $\mathbb{E}[\cdot]$ is the expectation operator and $r_j$ is the data rate from $S_j$ to $D_j$. Note that $Ec_j(\cdot)$ is a monotonically decreasing function of $\theta$, which means a small $\theta$ corresponds to a loose violation probability requirement, while a large $\theta$ matches a strict QoS requirement. Without loss of generality, let $T_f$ and $B$ be equal to 1.

Let $\bar{a}_j$ denote the effective bandwidth of the source traffic flow of the $j$th user. The QoS requirements of link $S_j$–$D_j$ can be guaranteed when $Ec_j \geq \bar{a}_j$ holds, which means that for each source-destination pair, the effective capacity with its required delay QoS exponent is greater or equal to the effective bandwidth of the corresponding source traffic flow. With this delay QoS provisioning, our optimization criteria aims at minimizing the average power consumed by all the relay nodes. Mathematically, we formulate the resource allocation problem considering QoS provisioning as

$$\min_{P_{R_i}^{S_j} \geq 0} \sum_{i=1}^{N} \mathbb{E}_h \left[ \sum_{j=1}^{M} P_{R_i}^{S_j} \right] \quad \text{s.t.} \quad Ec_j \geq \bar{a}_j, \forall j, \tag{5}$$

where $\mathbb{E}_h[\cdot]$ denotes the expectation over all fading realizations. Because $log(\cdot)$ is a monotonically increasing function, the constraints of (5) are equivalent to

$$\mathbb{E}_h \left[ e^{-\theta_j r_j} \right] - e^{-\theta_j \bar{a}_j} \leq 0, \forall j. \tag{6}$$

The objective function of (5) is linear. The constraints (6) are convex since $r_j(\cdot)$ is convex. Therefore, the formulated power allocation problem is a convex optimization problem. It can also be proved that the problem in (5) satisfies Slaters constraint qualification. Thus the strong duality holds and solving the dual problem is equivalent to solving the primal problem.

# 3 Power Allocation and Relay Selection Considering QoS Provisioning

## 3.1 Dual Decomposition Approach

We first introduce $\boldsymbol{\mu} := [\mu_1, \mu_2, ..., \mu_M]^T$ associated with constraints, where $\boldsymbol{\mu} \succeq 0$. The Lagrangian function by relaxing the constraints can be written as

$$L(P_{R_i}^{S_j}, \boldsymbol{\mu}) = \sum_{i=1}^{N} \mathbb{E}_h \left[ \sum_{j=1}^{M} P_{R_i}^{S_j} \right] + \sum_{j=1}^{M} \mu_j \left( \mathbb{E}_h [e^{-\theta_j r_j}] - e^{-\theta_j \bar{a}_j} \right), \tag{7}$$

The dual function is expressed as

$$D(\boldsymbol{\mu}) = \min_{P_{R_i}^{S_j} \geq 0} L(P_{R_i}^{S_j}, \boldsymbol{\mu}), \tag{8}$$

and the dual optimization problem reads as

$$\max_{\boldsymbol{\mu}} D(\boldsymbol{\mu}) \quad \text{s.t.} \quad \mu_j \geq 0, \forall j. \tag{9}$$

Since $D(\boldsymbol{\mu})$ is convex and differentiable, the following gradient iteration algorithm can be used to solve the dual problem (9)

$$\mu_j[t+1] = \left[ \mu_j[t] + s \cdot \left( \mathbb{E}_h \left[ e^{-\theta_j r_j} \right] - e^{-\theta_j \bar{a}_j} \right) \right]^+, \tag{10}$$

where $t$ is the iteration index, $s$ is a sufficiently small positive step size, and $[x]^+ = \max(0, x)$. The dual variables $\mu_j[t]$ will converge to the optimal $\mu_j^*$ as $t \to \infty$, and $P_{R_i}^{S_j}(\mu_j)$ will also converge to the optimal $P_{R_i}^{S_j*}(\mu_j^*)$ owing to the strong duality.

## 3.2  Power Allocation and Relay Selection Policy with Given $\boldsymbol{\mu}$

Here we will derive the optimal power allocation and relay selection policy with given $\boldsymbol{\mu}$. To find the optimal $P_{R_i}^{S_j}$ that minimizes $L(P_{R_i}^{S_j}, \boldsymbol{\mu})$, we need to solve

$$\min_{P_{R_i}^{S_j} \geq 0} \sum_{j=1}^{M} \mathbb{E}_h \left[ \sum_{i=1}^{N} P_{R_i}^{S_j} + \mu_j e^{-\theta_j r_j} \right], \tag{11}$$

which is equivalent to solving the following problem

$$\min \left[ \sum_{i=1}^{N} P_{R_i}^{S_j} + \mu_j e^{-\theta_j r_j} \right] \quad \text{s.t.} \quad P_{R_i}^{S_j} \geq 0, \forall i. \tag{12}$$

Clearly, (12) is a convex optimization problem. Let $\boldsymbol{\lambda} := \lambda_i \geq 0 (i = 1, ..., N)$ be the Lagrange multipliers for the constraints $P_{R_i}^{S_j} \geq 0$. The Lagrangian of (12) is

$$\pounds(P_{R_i}^{S_j}, \boldsymbol{\lambda}) = \sum_{i=1}^{N} P_{R_i}^{S_j} + \mu_j e^{-\theta_j r_j} - \sum_{i=1}^{N} \lambda_i P_{R_i}^{S_j}. \tag{13}$$

Define

$$f(P_{R_i}^{S_j}) = \sum_{i=1}^{N} P_{R_i}^{S_j} + \mu_j e^{-\theta_j r_j}. \tag{14}$$

The Karush-Kuhn-Tucker (KKT) conditions for optimization problem (13) are shown as

$$\lambda_i^* \geqslant 0, \forall i, \tag{15}$$

$$\lambda_i^* P_{R_i}^{S_j*} = 0, \forall i,$$

$$f'(P_{R_i}^{S_j*}) - \lambda_i^* = 0, \forall i.$$

According to the complementary slackness conditions [15] for the optimal solution $P_{R_i}^{S_j*}$ and the dual variables $\lambda_i^*$, we can conclude that

$$\begin{cases} \text{if } f'(P_{R_i}^{S_j*}) > 0, \text{ then } P_{R_i}^{S_j*} = 0, \\ \text{if } P_{R_i}^{S_j*} > 0, \quad \text{then } f'(P_{R_i}^{S_j*}) = 0. \end{cases} \tag{16}$$

From (16), we conclude that the gradient vector of $f'(P_{R_i}^{S_j})$ at the optimum should be equal to 0 when $P_{R_i}^{S_j*} > 0$. Then we can derive the following equation:

$$(1 + \sum_{n=1}^{N} \frac{x_n}{\alpha_n x_n + \beta_n})^{1+\tau\theta_j} = \frac{\tau\mu_j\theta_j\beta_i}{(\alpha_i x_i + \beta_i)^2}, \tag{17}$$

where $\tau = \frac{1}{N+1}$, $\alpha_i = \alpha_{R_i}^{S_j}$, $\beta_i = \beta_{R_i}^{S_j}$, $x_i = P_{R_i}^{S_j*}$. In (17), let $i = 1$, we get

$$\left(1 + \sum_{n=1}^{N} \frac{x_n}{\alpha_n x_n + \beta_n}\right)^{1+\tau\theta_j} = \frac{\tau\mu_j\theta_j\beta_1}{(\alpha_1 x_1 + \beta_1)^2}. \tag{18}$$

Since $x_i$ is assumed larger than 0, we have $\alpha_i x_i + \beta_i > 0$. Then we can get

$$x_i = \frac{\sqrt{\frac{\beta_i}{\beta_1}}(\alpha_1 x_1 + \beta_1) - \beta_i}{\alpha_i}, i > 1. \tag{19}$$

Substituting (19) into (17), we can obtain the following equation with one variable $x_1$

$$\psi_1(\alpha_1 x_1 + \beta_1)^{\frac{2}{\psi_3}} + \psi_2(\alpha_1 x_1 + \beta_1)^{\frac{2}{\psi_3}-1} - \psi_4^{\frac{1}{\psi_3}} = 0, \tag{20}$$

where

$$\psi_1 = 1 + \sum_{i=1}^{N} \frac{1}{\alpha_i}, \quad \psi_2 = -\sum_{i=1}^{N}\left(\frac{\sqrt{\beta_1\beta_i}}{\alpha_i}\right), \quad \psi_3 = 1 + \tau\theta_j, \quad \psi_4 = \tau\mu_j\theta_j\beta_1.$$

It's worth noting that $x_i$ is assumed positive in the foregoing derivations from (17) to (20). But solving function (20) and (19) can not guarantee $x_i > 0$. If there exists $x_i \leq 0$, (17) does not hold and the derivation is wrong. In view of this situation, we divide the index of relays $\{1, ..., N\}$ into two subsets $R_1$ and $R_2$, such that $x_i = 0, \forall i \in R_1$, and $x_i > 0, \forall i \in R_2$. Then, the equation in (17) turn to the following:

$$\left(1 + \sum_{n \in R_2} \frac{x_n}{\alpha_n x_n + \beta_n}\right)^{1+\tau\theta_j} = \frac{\tau\mu_j\theta_j\beta_i}{(\alpha_i x_i + \beta_i)^2}. \tag{21}$$

Based on (21), the relay index set in the derivations from (18) to (20) is also replaced by $R_2$. As a result, our aim is to find out $R_2$ efficiently. From (16), we can infer when $P_{R_i}^{S_j*} = 0$, $f'(P_{R_i}^{S_j*}) \geq 0$. Based on this property, the simplest method is to enumerate all possible pairs of $R_1$ and $R_2$ and checking whether the optimality condition is satisfied. That is, $P_{R_i}^{S_j*} > 0, \forall i \in R_2$ and $f_i'(P_{R_i}^{S_j*}) \geq 0, \forall i \in R_1$. However, the time complexity of enumerating all pairs is exponential. Next, we will improve the algorithm to get $R_1$ and $R_2$ in polynomial time. We proved the following two lemmas where the proofs have been omitted for space.

**Lemma 1.** If $1 - \frac{\tau\mu_j\theta_j}{\beta_i} \geq 0$, then we must have $x_i = 0$.

**Lemma 2.** If $\beta_k \geq \beta_l$ and $x_k > 0$, then we must have $x_l > 0$.

From Lemma 1, we can see that the relay selection policy depends on the channel state and the delay requirement. If the channel state is worse and the delay requirement is loose, $1 - \frac{\tau\mu_j\theta_j}{\beta_i}$ turns out to be nonnegative and the relay node $i$ tends not to supply any power to the $k$-th user. Otherwise, the resource allocation policy will allocate power for the $k$-th user to satisfy its stringent QoS requirements. Through the properties Lemmas 1 and 2 imply, we give the following algorithm to obtain the optimal power solution $P_{R_i}^{S_j*}$.

**Algorithm 1.** Search for Optimal Power Control

---

1: Initialize $R_1 = R_2 = \emptyset$.

2: Compute $\tau\mu_j\theta_j/\beta_i$, for $i = 1, ..., N$.

3: If $1 - \tau\mu_j\theta_j/\beta_i \geq 0$, $R_1 = R_1 \cup \{i\}$, else $R_2 = R_2 \cup \{i\}$.

4: Set $P_{R_k}^{S_j*} = 0$ for $\forall k \in R_1$.

5: Sort the indices in $R_2$ in the decreasing order of $\beta_i$, to obtain the permutation $\pi$.

6: Initialize s=1.

7: For $\forall k \in R_2$, solve Eqs. (19) and (20) to get the optimal solution $P_{R_k}^{S_j*}$. If there exists $k \in R_2$, such that $P_{R_k}^{S_j*} \leq 0$, update $P_{R_{\pi(s)}}^{S_j*} = 0$, $S_1 = R_1 \cup \{\pi(s)\}$, $R_2 = R_2 - \{\pi(s)\}$, $s = s + 1$, and repeat this step.

8: Calculate $f_k'(P_{R_k}^{S_j*})$, $\forall k \in R_1$. If there exists $k \in R_1$, such that $f_k'(P_{R_k}^{S_j*}) < 0$, update $P_{R_{\pi(s)}}^{S_j*} = 0$, $R_1 = R_1 \cup \{\pi(s)\}$, $R_2 = R_2 - \{\pi(s)\}$, $s = s + 1$, goto step 7; else, output the resultant $P_{R_i}^{S_j*}$, $\forall i$.

---

### 3.3 Stochastic Resource Allocation

To implement the gradient iteration (10), we need the explicit knowledge of fading channel cdf to evaluate the expected values. However, in some practical mobile applications, it is infeasible to obtain the channel cdf. As it turns out, the problem without the knowledge of channel cdf can be solved through the stochastic optimization theory [10]. By this theory, $\mathbb{E}_h$ is dropped from (10) and a stochastic gradient iteration algorithm based on per slot fading realization is put forward as follows:

$$\mu_j[t + 1] = \left[\mu_j[t] + s \cdot \left(e^{-\theta_j r_j} - e^{-\theta_j \bar{a}_j}\right)\right]^+, \tag{22}$$

where $t$ is the iteration index and $s$ is a positive step-size. It only requires the fading state of the channels at the current iteration, which can be easily measured.

## 4    Numerical Results

In this section, we provide some numerical results to evaluate the performance of the proposed power allocation policy. Throughout our simulation, we consider a wireless relay network with five users and three relays distributed in a two-dimensional region. The relays are fixed at coordinates (3,1), (3,2) and (3,3). The source and destination nodes are deployed at the lines (0,0)–(0,4) and (6,0)–(6,4), respectively. The average SNR for the link between nodes $i$ and $j$ is given by $\gamma_{ij} = \frac{\bar{\gamma}}{((x_i - x_j)^2 + (y_i - y_j)^2)^{\frac{n}{2}}}$ where the reference SNR $\bar{\gamma}$ is 10 dBW and the loss exponent $n$ is 3.6. The channel fading processes are generated from quasi-static frequency-selective Rayleigh fading channels with $\gamma_{ij}$. The variances of AWGN $N_{R_i}$ and $N_{D_j}$ are assumed to be 1. The transmit power $P_{S_j}$, $j = 1, ..., 5$, are chosen to be 1 W. The unit for the power is Watt in our simulation.

On the premise that the channel fading cdf was unknown in the simulation, the proposed stochastic scheme was used to learn the time varying channel states to approach the optimal resource allocation policy. Figure 1 shows the evolution of Lagrange multiplier $\mu_2$ of each iteration when $\bar{a}_j = 0.1$ and $\theta_j = 0.1$. The curve verifies the stochastic convergence of the iterations algorithm, and we can observe that the Lagrange multiplier $\mu_2$ stochastically converges to its corresponding optimal value $\mu_2^* = 0.5987$. Note that due to the dynamics of per slot fading realization, the value of $\mu_2$ fluctuates around its optimal value within a small neighborhood proportional to the stepsize $s$.

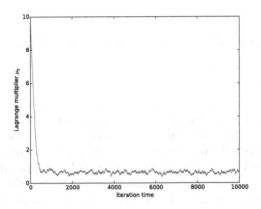

**Fig. 1.** Stochastic convergence of Lagrange multiplier $\mu_2$

To gauge the performance of the proposed algorithm, we compare it with two other power allocation policies. The first scheme named constant power policy, in which each relay use the same transmit-power to transmit signals from source to destination. The second scheme asks to minimize the whole power cost while satisfying a minimum ergodic rate constraints of each source-destination pair, named rate-based policy. The optimal policy proposed in (10), stochastic policy proposed in (22), constant power policy and rate-based policy are compared in terms of the minimum average sum power while satisfying the same delay QoS requirements. We ran the four policy with the constrains of effective capacity $\bar{a}_j = 0.1$ and $\bar{a}_j = 0.5$, $j = 1, ..., 5$. Numerical results are shown in Fig. 2(a) and (b), respectively. Notice that the optimal policy demonstrates the same performance with the stochastic one, which proves that the proposed stochastic scheme can approach the optimal policy via learn the channel fading knowledge on the fly. It is shown that the allocated power of the proposed policy increases with the QoS exponent $\theta$. This illustrates that more power must be consumed in order to guarantee the more strict QoS requirements. Also the proposed policy outperforms the other two policies obviously in power saving. Additionally, the difference value between the two policies increases with the delay QoS exponents.

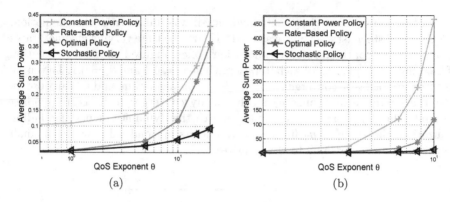

**Fig. 2.** The power allocation policy when $\bar{a}_j = 0.1$ (a) and $\bar{a}_j = 0.5$ (b)

# 5   Conclusion

We have formulated a convex optimization framework for resource allocation by taking the delay QoS requirement into account in wireless relay networks. Based on the framework, we have proposed a power control policy with the objective of minimizing the overall power consumption while fulfilling the minimum Qos requirement. By using the dual decomposition method, we solved the optimization problem and derived a optimal power control policy. Furthermore, we proposed a stochastic method that can learn the fading state of the channels and carry out the optimal strategy immediately. It has been shown that our proposed policy exhibits excellent performance of power saving compared with constant power policy and rate-based policy.

**Acknowledgments.** This work was supported by the National Science Foundation of China (No. 61201269, No. 61571272, No. 61403230), 2014 Shandong housing and urban-rural development soft science research project (No. RK015), the Natural Science Foundation of Shandong Province (Doctoral Foundation)(No. BS0135DX013), and the China Postdoctoral Science Foundation funded project (No. 2015M582104).

# References

1. Bolla, R., Bruschi, R., Davoli, F., Cucchietti, F.: Energy efficiency in the future internet: a survey of existing approaches and trends in energy-aware fixed network infrastructures. IEEE Commun. Surv. Tutorials **13**(2), 223–244 (2011)
2. Nosratinia, A., Hunter, T., Hedayat, A.: Coperative communication in wireless networks. IEEE Commun. Mag. **42**(10), 74–80 (2004). Oct.
3. Hossain, E., Kim, D.I., Bhargava, V.K.: Cooperative Cellular Wireless Networks. Cambridge University Press, Cambridge (2011)
4. He, F., Sun, Y., Xiao, L., Chen, X., Chi, C., Zhou, S.: Capacity region bounds and resource allocation for two-way OFDM relay channels. IEEE Trans. Wireless Commun. **12**(6), 2904–2907 (2013)

5. Zafar, A., Shaqfeh, M., Alouini, M., Alnuweiri, H.: Resource allocation for two source-destination pairs sharing a single relay with a buffer. IEEE Trans. Wireless Commun. **62**(5), 1444–1457 (2014)
6. Jangsher, S., Zhou, H., Li, V.O., Leung, K.C.: Joint allocation of resource blocks, power, and energy-harvesting relays in cellular networks. IEEE J. Selec. Areas Commun. **33**(3), 482–495 (2015)
7. Al-Tous, H., Barhumi, I.: Resource allocation for multiple-sources single-relay cooperative communication OFDMA systems. IEEE Trans. Mob. Comput. **15**(4), 964–981 (2016)
8. Wu, D., Negi, R.: Effective capacity: a wireless link model for support of quality of service. IEEE Trans. Wireless Commun. **2**(4), 630–643 (2003)
9. Rockafellar, R.T., Wets, R.J.-B.: Stochastic convex programming: basic duality. Pacific J. Math. **62**(1), 173–195 (1976)
10. Kall, P., Wallace, S.W.: Stochastic Programming. Wiley, Hoboken (1994)
11. Yang, S., Sheng, Z., McCann, J., Leung, K.: Distributed stochastic cross-layer optimization for multi-hop wireless networks with cooperative communications. IEEE Trans. Mob. Comput. **PP**(99) (2013)
12. Ribeiro, A.: Ergodic stochastic optimization algorithms for wireless communication and networking. IEEE Trans. Sig. Process. **58**(12), 6369–6386 (2010)
13. Wang, D., Wang, X., Cai, X.: Optimal power control for multi-user relay networks over fading channels. IEEE Trans. Wireless Commun. **10**(1), 199–207 (2011)
14. Phan, K., Le, L., Vorobyov, S., Le-Ngoc, T.: Power allocation and admission control in multi-user relay networks via convex programming: centralized and distributed schemes. EURASIP J. Wireless Commun. Netw. **2009** (2009). Article ID 901965
15. Boyd, S., Vandenberghe, L.: Convex optimization. Cambridge University Press, Cambridge (2004)

# System Performance Evaluation and Enhancement

# LTE System Performance Evaluation for High-Speed Railway Environment Under Rician Channel

Lei Xiong[1,2(⊠)], Ru Feng[1], and Ting Zhou[2]

[1] State Key Laboratory of Rail Traffic Control and Safety,
Beijing Jiaotong University, Beijing 100044, China
lxiong@bjtu.edu.cn
[2] Key Laboratory of Wireless Sensor Network and Communication,
Shanghai Institute of Microsystem and Information Technology,
Chinese Academy of Sciences, 865 Changning Road, Shanghai 200050, China

**Abstract.** In high speed railway environment, the LTE system performance evaluation is of vital importance due to complexity of radio propagation scenario and high mobility. In this paper, the Hardware-in-the-Loop (HIL) simulation platform is built, which consists of radio channel emulator, LTE core network and so on. Based on this platform, the LTE system performance is tested under Rician channel with different parameters, such as the K-factor, the angle between the line-of-sight (LOS) and train's velocity. Finally, it is concluded that the LTE system performance degrades with the increase of moving speed, and the degree of degradation is related to the K-factor and the angle between the LOS path and velocity.

**Keywords:** LTE system performance evaluation · Channel emulator · Rician channel

## 1 Introduction

In recent years, with the rapid development of high-speed railway, GSM-R system will no longer meet people's needs of higher speed, higher bandwidth, smaller trans-mission delay and more business requirements. Therefore, the International Union of Railways (UIC) began to consider the evolution of the next generation mobile comm-unication system. At present, the industry has already reached a consensus that we will use Long Term Evolution (LTE) as the next generation mobile communication [1]. As an important application of the current LTE Scenario, high-speed railway has attracted an increasing amount of attention.

In the high-speed railway environment, users generally reflect that the throughput declines rapidly and the quality of transmission deteriorates seriously, which has become an urgent problem to be solved. To solve this problem, first of all, we need to evaluate the LTE system performance accurately, through which to discover the important parameters affecting the performance, and finally to provide support for performance enhancement techniques of high speed railway. As the pioneer of actual network formation, the laboratory simulation for LTE system performance in high-speed environment is of great significance.

© ICST Institute for Computer Sciences, Social Informatics and Telecommunications Engineering 2018
Q. Chen et al. (Eds.): ChinaCom 2016, Part I, LNICST 209, pp. 329–338, 2018.
DOI: 10.1007/978-3-319-66625-9_32

In 3GPP TSG-RAN WG4 Meeting, the Ericsson has simulated the PDSCH performance for EVA channels with a Doppler spread of between 200 and 850 Hz in different SNR, from which we can know the Doppler shift has great influence on the performance. In addition, some channel models such as two paths channel model, leaky cable propagation channel are proposed for the High Speed Scenario and the simulation of them have been done. However, there is little research on the performance of high speed railway under Rician channel. This paper focuses on it.

HIL simulation platform is built to evaluate the LTE system performance, this paper analyzes the performance under Rician channel with different parameters. The impact of K-factor and the angle between LOS path and velocity are the emphasis of our study, which provide an important basis for performance enhancement techniques. The paper is organized as follows: LTE channel model for high speed railway is described in Sect. 2. In Sect. 3, some environment parameters for HIL simulation platform is introduced and the performance evaluation is made. The measurement results are shown in Sect. 4. Finally, in Sect. 5, we draw some conclusions.

## 2   LTE Channel Model for High Speed Railway Scenario

Channel model is of vital importance for a communication system. Due to the signifi-cance of this topic, many researchers have spent much effort on the channel modeling and have got some achievements. Generally, we can divide these channel models into three types. First, the statistical channel model, such as Rician Model and Gaussian Statistical Model. Second, the deterministic channel model, which is based on the actual measurement of the channel circumstance. As to the semi-deterministic channel model, it includes COST 259, COST 273, Spatial channel Model (SCM), Spatial Channel Model Extension (SCME), WINNER Model and so on [2].

The semi-deterministic channel model contains delay and spatial characteristics, which makes the channel so complex that we can't make sure which parameters affect the performance of the system clearly. We choose Rician channel as the emphasis of this paper. On the one hand, in the realistic high-speed railway environment, the running route is linear, so there exists a LOS path and some non-LOS (NLOS) paths which can be describe as a Rician channel. On the other hand, high speed is a major characteristic of the channel, and the Doppler shift caused by high speed is crucial to wireless communication system. During the running way, the train will experience some scenarios, such as open suburb, cutting, viaducts and so on [3], which has different K-factors. What's more, with the relative position of BS and MS changing, the angle between LOS path and velocity differ causing different Doppler shift. Ricia-n channel has some simple but important parameters so that we can make a qualitative analysis of the influence of the angle between LOS path and velocity and K-factor on the system performance. Finally, find out which parameters affect the performance, how they do and what's the degree of the influence.

The Rician channel can be decomposed into a specular component for the LOS path and a scattering component subject to Rayleigh distribution for the NLOS path between the Tx and the Rx, where the K-factor is defined as the power ratio of the two [4].

From the above, the Doppler power density spectrum of Rician channel can be considered as the superposition of that of Rayleigh channel and a single pulse. The Doppler power density spectrum of Rayleigh channel is written as

$$S(f) = \begin{cases} \dfrac{\sigma_0^2}{\pi f_{max} \sqrt{1 - (f/f_{max})}}, & |f| < f_{max} \\ 0, & |f| \geq f_{max} \end{cases} \tag{1}$$

where $\sigma_0^2$ is the power of NLOS path, $f_{max}$ is the maximum Doppler shift of the LOS component. Doppler shift is as follows:

$$f_d = f\frac{v}{c}\cos\theta \tag{2}$$

where $\theta$ is the angle between LOS path and velocity. If $v = 300$ km/h and $f = 2330$ MHz, the maximum Doppler shift shall be 647.2 Hz.

The Doppler shift of the LOS path is changing with $\theta$. When $\theta$ is 180°, the Doppler shift of the LOS path is maximum, while it is minimum for 90°. With $\theta$ equal to 180°, 90° and 45°, the maximum, minimum and median can be achieved, which represents a wider characteristics of Rician channel. Doppler shift of LOS path in different angles is given in Table 1.

Figure 1 shows the superposition of Doppler power density spectrum of Rayleigh channel and a single pulse. Doppler shift of LOS path for different angle is disparate. What's more, different K-factors correspond to different power allocation of LOS path and NLOS path.

Table 1. Doppler shift of LOS path

| $\theta$ | Doppler shift $f_d$ (Hz) |
|---|---|
| 45° | 457.7 |
| 90° | 0 |
| 180° | −647.2 |

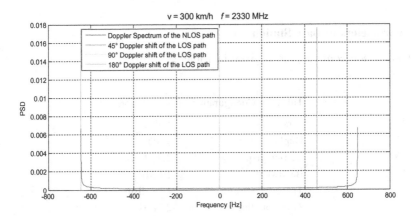

Fig. 1. Doppler power density spectrum in Rician channel

## 3  HIL Simulation Platform

We build the HIL simulation platform in the laboratory shown as Fig. 2, which consists of radio channel emulator, test mobile terminal (MS), base station (BS), LTE core network and Qos test software.

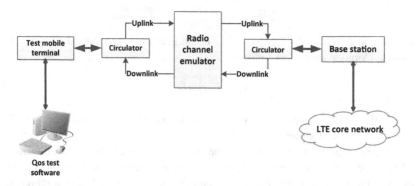

**Fig. 2.** HIL simulation platform for LTE system performance evaluation

The test mobile terminal is ZTE ME3760 supporting the frequency of 2.330 GHz under TDD duplex mode, and it achieves the function of network registration and data reception. The radio channel emulator C8 is used to emulate the radio propagation, which both has the flexibility of software simulation and the accuracy of the hardware emulation. As for the radio channel, the classical channel–Rician channel is used, what's more, the K-factor, the angle between LOS path and velocity and moving speed can be set flexibly on the platform, which provides the feasibility for the evaluation. The Qos software can test the UDP delay and throughput of the system.

In order to evaluate the performance, some environment parameters should be determined, such as configuration of base station, performance indicator, received power.

### 3.1  Parameters of Base Station

The base station configuration is given in Table 2.

**Table 2.** Configuration of base station

| Parameter | Value |
| --- | --- |
| Duplex mode | TDD |
| Carrier frequency | 2.33 GHz |
| Bandwidth | 10 MHz |
| Transmit power | 17.8 dBm |
| Timeslot allocation | 2 [1:3] |
| Special timeslot allocation | 7 [10:2:2] |

## 3.2  Performance Indicator

The performance of a wireless communication system mainly includes effectiveness, reliability and real-time performance. This paper focuses on the two aspects of effectiveness and real-time performance, so the system performance indicators are throughput and UDP delay, from which the throughput can measure the effectiveness of the system, and UDP delay does in real-time performance.

Throughput: It is defined as the amount of data uploaded or downloaded in a unit time, which is significant to a system. There are many factors that affect the throughput, including bandwidth, timeslot allocation, special timeslot allocation, control channel over, service type and so on.

UDP delay: It is defined as the time interval of the data packet transmitting from the user to Gi interface of GGSN.

## 3.3  Receiving Power

In the 3GPP specification, the Signal Receiving Power Reference (RSRP) and Received Signal Strength Indicator (RSSI) are related to the received power.

RSRP is defined as the linear average over the power contributions (in [W]) of the resource elements that carry cell-specific reference signals within the considered measurement frequency bandwidth. The reference point for the RSRP shall be the antenna connector of the UE [5]. It can reflect the useful signal of the cell. Figure 3 is a schematic diagram of the RSRP calculation method. $R_0$ is cell-specific reference signals [6].

RSSI comprises the linear average of the total received power (in [W]) observed only in OFDM symbols containing reference symbols for antenna port 0, in the measurement bandwidth, over N number of resource blocks by the UE from all sources, including co-channel serving and non-serving cells, adjacent channel interference, thermal noise etc. [5]. Although it is also the average value, it contains other interference signals from the outside, which makes the average value of measurement higher than that of the useful signal. As a result, RSRP is used as the indicator of received power.

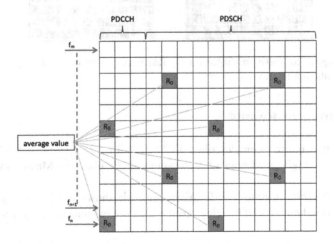

**Fig. 3.** Schematic diagram of the RSRP calculation method

Measure RSRP and RSSI using the base station analyzer. And the corresponding relationship is shown in Table 3.

**Table 3.** Relationship between RSRP and RSSI

| RSSI (dBm) | RSRP (dBm) |
|---|---|
| −50 | −68.28 |
| −51 | −69.48 |
| −52 | −70.41 |
| −53 | −71.29 |
| −56 | −74.28 |
| −66 | −84.92 |
| −71 | −91.43 |
| −72 | −92.51 |
| −73 | −93.11 |
| −74 | −93.75 |

When the RSRP is lower than −93.75 dBm, RS signal constellation is so indistinguishable that it cannot be demodulated correctly shown as Fig. 4. Therefore, this paper uses the RSSI value for −52 dBm and −73 dBm, that is, the corresponding RSRP value for the −70.41 dBm and −93.11 dBm, which makes the evaluation of the system more reasonable.

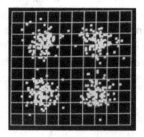 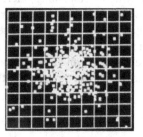

**Fig. 4.** RS signal constellation diagram with RSRP is −96.98 dBm (the right figure) and −92.51 dBm (the left figure)

## 4   Measurement Results

Key parameters haven been described in Sect. 3. In this section, the LTE system performance for high-speed railway is measured on the platform. Measurement results are as follows.

The relationship of system performance and $\theta$ is shown in Figs. 5 and 6 for two aspects of throughput and UDP delay, from which the influence of the received power is apparent.

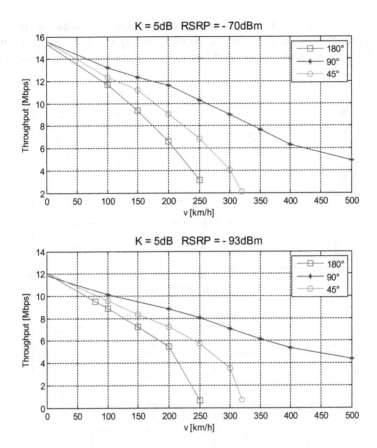

**Fig. 5.** The throughput with $\theta = 180°$, $90°$ and $45°$

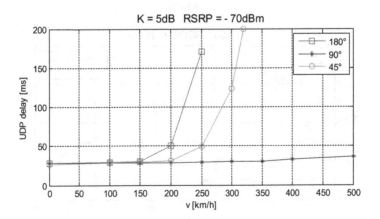

**Fig. 6.** The UDP delay with $\theta$ 180°, 90° and 45°

Shown as above, the LTE system performance degrades with the increase of moving speed. What's more, it deteriorates most rapidly for 180°, and performs well for 90°. To be precise, the system performance is excellent with high throughput and

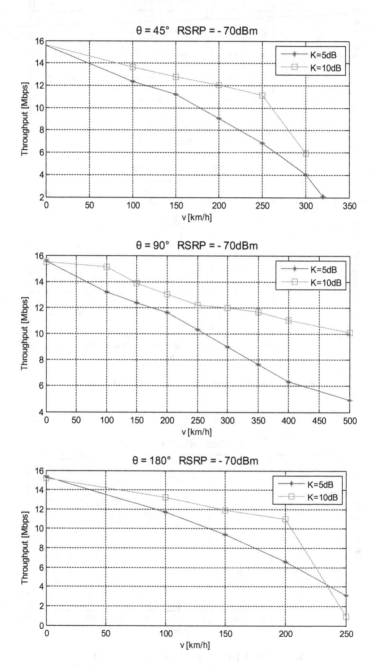

**Fig. 7.** The throughput with K = 5 dB and 10 dB

small UDP delay for low moving speed and $\theta$ has almost no influence on performance. On the contrary, it is poor with low throughput and large UDP delay for high moving speed and $\theta$ has a great influence on performance. When $\theta$ is 180°, the Doppler shift of LOS path is maximum which leads to poor performance that MS cannot attach the network if moving speed is up to 280 km/h. And for $\theta$ equal to 45°, there exists a Doppler shift of LOS path but not large, and when moving speed is up to 330 km/h, MS cannot attach the network. As for 90°, there is only the Doppler shift of NLOS path which obeys rayleigh distribution. The proportion of NLOS path is so small in power that the performance changes little with the increase of moving speed.

In the figures with RSRP covering −93 dBm and −70 dBm, no matter what $\theta$ and K-factor are, the performance is better in higher RSRP. For higher RSRP, in the same environment, we can get higher signal-to-noise ratio (SNR). That is, if possible, we can increase power properly to improve the system performance.

The relationship of system performance and K-factor is shown in Figs. 7 and 8 for two aspects of throughput and UDP delay.

From the figures above, when moving speed is 0, the K-factor has no effect on the system performance. Under the condition of low speed, the greater the K-factor is, the better the performance is. But for high speed, when $\theta$ is 45°and 90°, the performance is better for greater K-factor, while it deteriorates for 180°. To explain this phenomenon, first we know that the power of LOS path is higher for greater K-factor, which makes the performance well. But at the same time, in the condition of high speed for 180°, the higher the power of LOS path is, the higher proportion of the maximum Doppler shift accounts for, it has such a great influence that the performance decreases.

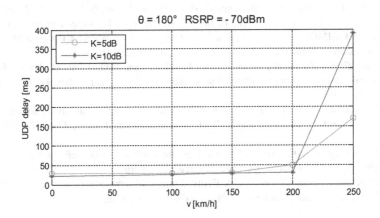

**Fig. 8.** The UDP delay with K = 5 dB and 10 dB

## 5 Conclusion

In the paper, we evaluate the LTE system performance for high-Speed railway environment under Rician channel on the HIL simulation platform. From the simulation results, the conclusions can be made on three aspects. In general, the LTE system performance degrades with the increase of moving speed. More specifically, in the condition of high speed, $\theta$ has a great influence on the performance. When $\theta$ is 180°, the performance is worst that MS can't attach the network for the speed up to 280 km/h. What's more, the performance is better under the Rician channel with greater K-factor in low speed. However, in the case of high speed and $\theta$ of 180°, when moving speed reaches a certain value, which is almost 230 km/h, the greater the K-factor is, the worse the performance is. As for the received power, we can achieve better performance in higher received power. These conclusions can make contributions to performance enhancement techniques.

**Acknowledgment.** This work was supported by the National Natural Science Foundation of China under Grant 61471030, the Fundamental Research Funds for the Central Universities under Grant 2014JBZ021, National Science and Technology Major Project (2015ZX03 001027-003), the Research Fund of Beijing Municipal Science & Technology Commission (No. Z151100002415029), the State Key Laboratory of Rail Traffic Control and Safety under Grant RCS2016ZZ004, the Program for Development of Science and Technology of China Railway Corporation under grant 2015X010-C and 2014X013-A, Key laboratory of wireless sensor network and communication, Chinese Academy of Sciences (NO. 2013005), Key Project of Beijing. Science and Technology Commission Supported under Grant (D151100000115004).

# References

1. Martin-Vega, F.J., Delgado-Luque, I.M., Blanquez-Casado, F., Gomez, G., Aguayo-Torres, M.C., Entrambasaguas, J.T.: LTE performance over high speed railway channel. In: IEEE 78th Vehicular Technology Conference (VTC Fall), Las Vegas, NV, pp. 1–5 (2013)
2. Xiang, X., Wu, M., Zhao, R., Xu, J., Su, X.: Research on high-speed railway model for train-ground MIMO channel. In: International Symposium on Wireless Personal Multimedia Communications (WPMC), Sydney, NSW, pp. 724–728 (2014)
3. Chen, B., Zhong, Z., Ai, B., Guan, K., He, R., Michelson, D.G.: Channel characteristics in high-speed railway: a survey of channel propagation properties. IEEE Veh. Technol. Mag. **10** (2), 67–78 (2015)
4. Fan, W., Kyösti, P., Hentilä, L., Nielsen, J.Ø., Pedersen, G.F.: Rician channel modeling for multiprobe anechoic chamber setups. IEEE Antennas Wirel. Propag. Lett. **13**, 1761–1764 (2014)
5. 3GPP Technical Specification 36.214. Evolved universal terrestrial radio access (E-UTRA); Physical layer; Measurements (Release 10). www.3gpp.org
6. 3GPP Technical Specification 36.211. Evolved universal terrestrial radio access (E-UTRA); Physical channels and Modulation (Release 10). www.3gpp.org

# A First Look at Cellular Network Latency in China

Xinheng Wang$^{(\boxtimes)}$, Chuan Xu, Wenqiang Jin, and Guofeng Zhao

School of Communication and Information Engineering,
Chongqing University of Posts and Telecommunications, Chongqing, China
xhwangcqupt@gmail.com, jinwenqiang6668@gmail.com,
{xuchuan, zhaogf}@cqupt.edu.cn

**Abstract.** The cellular networks in China are growing rapidly, thus various radio complex technologies, from 2G to 4G are deployed to support billions of mobile users. In this paper, we take a first attempt to analyze cellular network latency in China. A mobile app NetSense (The application is available at: https:// github.com/lovesick/NetSense/) was scattered up on several hundred mobile terminals to measure the latency at large. Based on the measured results of 4 months, we find out that: (i) China's cellular network adopts hierarchical structure, with more gateways deployed in capital or major cities for each province; (ii) the latency varies largely across geographical locations, ISPs and is also dependent on the deployed cellular technologies; (iii) Considering end-to-end latency, the last mile delay contributes over 70 percentage for the whole transmission latency.

**Keywords:** Cellular network · Latency · Wireless delay · Last mile delay

## 1 Introduction

With the evolution of cellular technology, the wide deployment of 4G technologies and the rapid adoption of new smartphone devices, the cellular networks are growing explosively in China. The universal coverage of 4G networks enable the mobile devices such as phones and tablets have improved our ability of information accessing, sharing and processing. According to the report, more than 760 million users access the Internet via the cellular networks, nearly three-quarters of all the Internet users in China [1].

Although China is with the largest number of cellular users and the fastest growing market of mobile application [2], however, China's cellular networks have received relatively little attention in the measurement community. Perhaps, in China, researchers lack the infrastructure and resources for large-scale cellular network measurement studies such as those carried out in MobiPerf [3], and large data sharing from cellular carriers such as AT&T, which are essential for comprehensive and in-depth studies of the cellular network performance [4–6].

The popular applications, such as IM, social and E-commerce, have attracted more than 200 million users to use. Users share information through exchanging a large number of small packets via short http connections, the performance of information

© ICST Institute for Computer Sciences, Social Informatics and Telecommunications Engineering 2018
Q. Chen et al. (Eds.): ChinaCom 2016, Part I, LNICST 209, pp. 339–348, 2018.
DOI: 10.1007/978-3-319-66625-9_33

exchange would depend on the cellular network latency. Therefore, carriers in China have widely adopted tree topology to construct their cellular networks, with more gateways deployed to provide more access points to Internet. Furthermore, for serving numerous types of mobile devices, each carrier needs to operate a variety of network technologies from 2G to 4G, for example, China Mobile provides GPRS, EDGE, TD-SCDMA and TD-LTE. These make cellular networks in China more complex, leading to very different network performances from others in US or Europe.

In this paper, we take a first look at latency of cellular networks in China. Our goal is to understand the latency characteristics of cellular network in China. To the best of our knowledge, our study is the first to investigate the characteristics of China's cellular network latency. Key contributions of this paper are presented below.

- We conduct a measurement on cellular network latency through our tool NetSense, which deployed on wide range mobile devices within commercial cellular networks in China.
- We show the topologies of cellular core networks, and found that the tree topology being widely adopted in three main cellular carriers, more gateways deployed in capital or major cities of each province, and 3 to 6 hops in the cellular core network.
- We compare the latencies when crossing different carriers, different areas, different technologies (WiFi, 3G, EDGE, GPRS), particularly the latency produced between different 3G technologies (EVDOA, HSDPA, HSPA); even the latency by the same technology crossing different carriers (TD-HSDPA and HSDPA).
- We provide a comprehensive comparison of our results to previous studies, and found that the latency in China is superior to that in US and in Norwegian. We think it is owing to more gateways being deployed in cellular core network in China; that provides more access points to Internet and shortens the latency.

## 2  Measurements and Data

### 2.1  Cellular Network Architecture

There are three major cellular carriers in China, China Mobile, China Unicom and China Telecom. Despite the difference among cellular technologies, a cellular network is usually divided into two parts, the Radio Access Network (RAN) and the Core Network (CN). The simplified architecture of cellular network is shown in Fig. 1. UEs are essentially mobile handsets carried by end users. The RAN allows connectivity between a UE and the CN. They consist of multiple base stations called BSC of 2G technologies (e.g., GPRS, EDGE, 1xRTT, etc.), Node B of 3G technologies (e.g., EVDOA, HSDPA, HSPA, etc.), and Evolved Node B of 4G technologies (e.g., LTE TDD, LTE FDD, etc.). The centralized CN is the backbone of cellular network, which consist a number of mobility management devices and gateways called SGSN and GGSN in China Mobile and China Unicom, PCF and PDSN in China Telecom, MME and S/P-GW of 4G, but the structure of the CN does not differentiate each other.

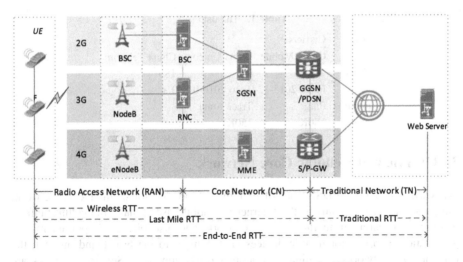

**Fig. 1.** Simplified cellular network structure in China.

## 2.2 Methodology and Data Set

In this study, NetSense, a professional measurement tool was designed and deployed on hundreds smartphones to measure the performance of cellular networks. By doing the tasks embedded in the NetSense, the network performance information can be collected directly from the end users every day, including network type, carriers, location, latency, throughput, trace, HTTP and DNS performance.

We publicly issued the Android version of NetSense application1 in December, 2015, distributed via the major application platform 360's App Store, Baidu's Mobile App Store and 91's Mobile Application Store in China. Till March, 2016 more than 400 users from across the country have installed and run our tool, and more than 300K test records have been collected. Among all records, more than 98% records include complete latency data through ping and trace tools, about 95% of records have GPS readings. According to location information, users from more than 20 provinces were observed.

As shown in Fig. 1, we break down end-to-end RTT into two components: wireless RTT which means the latency between a UE and the NodeB, last mile RTT which is the latency between a UE and the gateway (GGSN/PDSN). The wireless RTT is the latency in the RAN, and last mile RTT is the latency in the cellular core network. We use NetSense to trace route the end to end delay, the partition method is as follows. Since the IP addresses in the cellular network are mostly private address, we use the RTT of first hop with private IP address as the estimation of the wireless RTT in RAN, and RTT of the first hop but with public IP address as the estimation of the last mile RTT in core network. The number of users and records from three carriers are listed in Table 1.

**Table 1.** The data set

| Data | Carriers | | |
|------|--------------|--------------|--------------|
| | China Mobile | China Unicom | China Telecom |
| Users | 126 | 97 | 180 |
| | From 2015-12-01 to 2016-03-30 | | |
| Records | Ping | Trace route | |
| | 180K | 150K | |

## 3  Overview of Cellular Core Network

Gateways (i.e. GGSN/PDSN) are of extreme importance for cellular core network. They provide access points to the Internet for mobile users, make the cellular infrastructures transparent from the external network, and also plan an important role in geolocation mapping for mobile devices [13]. Similar to the broadband internet, the cellular core networks in China also adopt the tree topology. Several gateways are deployed in the capital city or major cities of each province. The packets from a UE are forwarded first to the NodeB, then to aggregation node, and finally to the Internet via one of the gateway.

Figure 2(a) plots the number of gateways for the three ISPs in each province where there are mobile terminals use our NetSense app. Notably, there are at least 3 gateways for each ISP in any province. Note that since the vantage points in our measurement do not cover all regions in China, it is impossible to identify all the gateways in every province. China Mobile deploys more gateways than other two ISPs in each province, since it serves more than 500 million mobile Internet users. In some provinces, there are as many as 11 gateways. Generally, we find more gateways are deployed in more developed provinces, such as Beijing, Guangdong, Shandong and Jiangsu. Compared to the results found in US [13], where there are only 4–6 gateways for each of the four carriers, ISPs in China deploys much more gateways. One possibility is that they need to support much more mobile users than those in US. Another possibility is that these ISPs compete with each other to provide better connectivity to Internet.

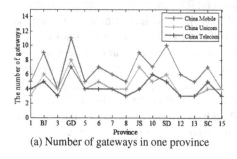

(a) Number of gateways in one province

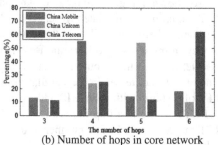

(b) Number of hops in core network

**Fig. 2.** The core network of different carrier.

Figure 2(b) illustrates the number of hops from mobile users to Internet gateways. We can clearly see the difference among three ISPs. For China Mobile, 70% of provincial gateways can be reached within 4 hops, while this percentage is only 40% and for China Unicom and China Telecom. In fact, the number of hops is concentrated around 5 and 6 hops for China Unicom and China Telecom, respectively. This can be explained by the number of gateways as shown in Fig. 2(a). Having more gateways in capital city as well as other big cities in each province could provide users with the close one for connection.

# 4 Cellular Network Latency Characterization

In this section, we first examine characteristics of cellular network latency using. We then proceed to compare our results with measurement studies of cellular network in western countries.

## 4.1 RTT in 4G Network

We focus on comparing cellular network latency performance among the three cellular carriers. For each carrier, given that the evolution of cellular technologies makes it provide several cellular access technologies simultaneously. We further analyze the latency of different cellular network technologies.

Since, 4G networks are widely deployed in Chinese commercial cellular network, and the most data traffics are forwarded by 4G network in mobile wireless network. We use the RTT to measure the network performance from the aspect of latency.

Figure 3(a) plots the CDF of RTT for three carriers. The latency for the 3 carriers exhibit short-tail distributions. Nevertheless, the latency for China Unicom shows a more concentrated effect around 52.9 ms. Indeed, China Telecom has the good performance in terms of latency, followed by China Telecom with average RTT of 63.7 ms and China Mobile with average RTT of 95 ms. Furthermore, Fig. 3(b) shows the transmission latency in terms of jitter, obviously, China Mobile network shows a

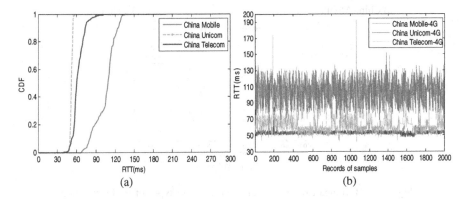

**Fig. 3.** RTT comparison of major carriers.

relative poor performance in transferring data packets stably with RTT values unevenly distributed in the wide range of 80 ms to 148 ms. And the RTT values of the most recorded samples in China Telecom concentrated between 50 ms and 75 ms. However, China Unicom shows an extremely stable data transmission in term of jitter with RTT values covered constantly in the range of 48 ms to 55 ms.

## 4.2    RTT Among Different Types of Accessing Technology

In Fig. 4, we further compare the RTT among different types of cellular networks. As shown in Fig. 4(a), when using 2.75G access technologies, such as GPRS, EDGE, the RTTs are very close to each other, with median RTT of 299.5 ms and 261.7 ms, respectively. Moreover, when considering the 3G access technology TD-HSDPA, the RTT is lower, with median RTT of 195.6 ms. However, the performance of 4G access technology is really astonishing, for TD-LTE, the median RTT is 99 ms.

It is notable that the GPRS networks in China have much better performance in terms of latency than that in US, where the median RTT is 1,000 ms in US [3]. Since GPRS is the main cellular network type of China Mobile, which has been optimized for many years. Its performance is relatively stable and comparable to 3G technology TD-HSDPA.

Figure 4(b) shows latency distribution for the 3G networks used in China Unicom, i.e. UMTS, HSPA and HSDPA. We can see HSDPA has the smallest median RTT of 120.3 ms, and UMTS has the largest median RTT of 156.8 ms. Compared to 3G

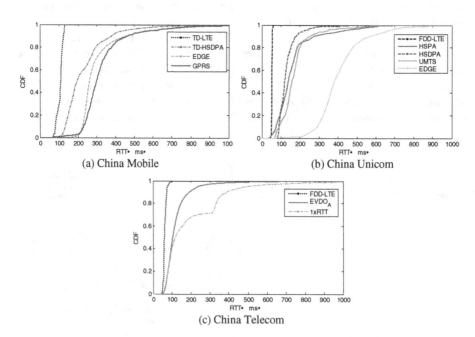

(a) China Mobile                         (b) China Unicom

(c) China Telecom

**Fig. 4.** RTT comparison among different network types of major carriers.

networks, the performance of EDGE is much poor, with the median RTT of 382.2 ms. And the FDD-LTE accessing technology shows an even smaller RTT with 52.9 ms as its median value in China Unicom cellar network. In Fig. 4(c), we observe that EVDOA of China Telecom has better performance than that of 1xRTT, with the median RTT of 105.4 ms compared to 118.8 ms in 1xRTT, which is the earliest CDMA 2.75G access technology. What's more, the 4G FDD-LTE accessing technology applied in China Telecom network shows a better performance as predicted which presents its median RTT value is 60.8 ms.

### 4.3   End-to-End Delay Analysis

We then proceed to analyze the end-to-end delay. Usually the RAN latency dominates the end-to-end delay [12]. In order to quantify the contribution of end-to-end delay, we consider the ratio (r1) of the wireless RTT to the end-to-end RTT, ratio (r2) of the last mile RTT to the end-to-end RTT.

Figure 5 illustrates the CDF of r1 and r2 among main technologies of three carriers. As shown in Fig. 5(a) for China Mobile, the wireless RTT accounts for more than 50% of the end-to-end RTT for 80% of TD-HSDPA measures. We also observe that the differences between r1 and r2 are consistent, and this gap is actually the delay in core network, which is smaller than 5%. We have the same observation for China Unicom and China Telecom, but the difference between r1 and r2 is only 2%.

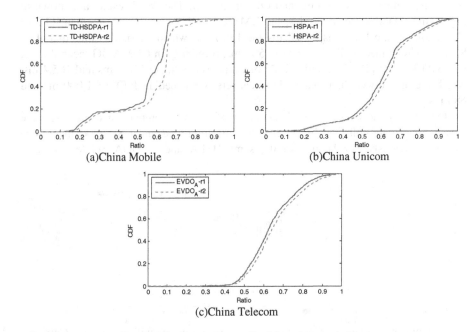

**Fig. 5.** Wireless and last mile delay characteristics.

Our findings suggest that the RAN latency dominates the overall end-to-end delay, independent of ISPs and 3G technologies. We also observe that the median values of r1 are 0.64, 0.63 and 0.62 for China Mobile, China Unicom and China Telecom, respectively. However, with the evolution of cellular technology, the ratio of RAN latency in end-to-end delay becomes constantly smaller, but which is widely distributed.

## 4.4    Comparison with US and EU Cellular Network

We finally compare the latency characteristics of China's cellular networks with those in US and EU. In order to have a fair comparison, we focus on the delay metric with the same network technology. The 3GTest study [3] deployed an app that measures end-to-end delay from the user's handsets to the test server with many 3G tests of four large U.S. cellular carriers in late 2009. After that, they compared network performance among technology types which cover most 3G network types [14]. The recent study [6] conducted an in-depth of 4G LTE network performance using a combination of active and passive measurements. The 3G network study [10] presented a long-term delay measurement from data connections in 3 Norwegian 3G networks.

Figure 6(a) shows the network comparison results of 3G technologies with the measurement data collected by MobiPerf in U.S. Obviously, the latency of UMTS and CDMA 3G technologies deployed in China carriers are much better than those in U.S. carriers, the median RTT of UMTS family and CDMA family are 137.3 ms and 105.4 ms, comparing to 490 ms and 680 ms in U.S. The detail results are shown in Fig. 5, in UMTS 3G technologies, the UMTS, HSDPA and HSPA's median RTT of China Unicom are 156.8 ms, 120.3 ms and 138.7 ms, which are smaller than that of U. S. carriers with median RTT of nearly 500 ms. Similarity in CDMA 3G technologies, the 1xRTT and EVDOA's median RTT of China Telecom are 118.8 ms and 105.4 ms, which are also lower than that of U.S. carriers, with median RTT of 1,000 ms and 680 ms.

Figure 6(b) shows the network latency performance comparison results with the measurement data collected by wireless mobile mini-card and USB modem in Norwegian. Obviously, the latency of the same HSPA and EVDOA 3G technologies

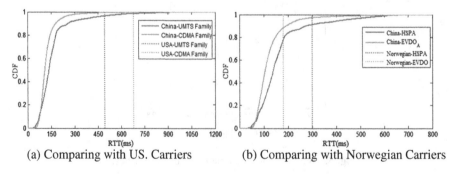

(a) Comparing with US. Carriers          (b) Comparing with Norwegian Carriers

**Fig. 6.** Comparing with previous measurement results.

deployed in China carriers are better than those in Norwegian carriers, with the median RTT of 138.7 ms and 105.4 ms, comparing to 300 ms and 180 ms.

Since carriers in China have to serve huge number of mobile users, they deploy much more gateways in every province than in other counties, which would be the main reason for the better latency performance in China.

## 5 Related Work

The characteristics of cellular networks have been studied for few years. Some existing works have studied the performance on smartphones, which compared 3G and WiFi performance on smartphones [7], compared cellular network performance on different smartphones among carriers [3], profiled diverse usage behaviors of smartphone applications [8] and studied the correlation among IP address, location and network latency for smartphones [7]. Some studies also performed large-scale measurement of cellular networks. Seetharam et al. focused on measuring cellular network parameters such as throughput, latency and packet loss by performing TCP downloads, uploads and others experiments within different wireless services providers' networks. [5] Rusan et al. analyzed the impact of backhaul packet delay on the LTE S1-U interface, which provides user plane transport between the Core Network and the Evolved NodeBs [9]. Elmokashfi et al. studied the cellular network delay characteristics from data connections in 3 Norwegian 3G networks [10]. Arlos et al. studied the influence of the packet size on the delay in 3G networks [11]. Qian et al. performed network-wide measurement studies of cellular periodic transfers [12]. Cellular network infrastructures also have been studied. Xu et al. characterized 3G data network infrastructure, found that the routing of cellular data traffic is quite restricted as traffic traverse through a small number of gateway nodes [13]. Wang et al. unveiled cellular carriers' NAT and firewall policies [4].

## 6 Conclusion

In this paper, we made the efforts to characterize the infrastructure of cellular core network, and the latency of three major cellular carriers in China. Our study was based on four months data collected from widely deployed measurement application Net-Sense. Compared the latency performance under situation of different carriers, technologies and areas, We found that in 2G technologies, GRPS and EDGE of China Mobile has the best performance, but in 3G technologies, the latency with HSPA of China Unicom and EVDOA of China Telecom are much better than TD-HSDPA of China Mobile, which makes China Mobile first deployed the 4G technology TD-LTE in December 2013. Furthermore, the 4G technologies provide a predictable small transmission latency in all three carriers' network, probably because more base stations are installed for functioning 4G mobile network compared with previous networking technologies.

For furthering this research, we are exploring other factors, such as network type, packet size and mobile device, which might have impact on the cellular network latency would be considered. On the other hand, we are exploring the cellular network performance more detailed from the perspective of throughput, DNS lookup and TCP flow of 3G and 4G technology.

**Acknowledgments.** This work is supported by the National Science Foundation of China (NSFC) under grant 61402065, Chongqing key science and technology project (No. cstc2014jcsf70001) and Young Backbone Teacher Funding Program of Chongqing Municipal Education Commission.

# References

1. CNNIC: Statistical Report on Internet Development in China. http://www.cnnic.net.cn/hlwfzyj/
2. Tian, Y., Dey, R., Liu, Y., et al.: Topology mapping and geolocating for China's internet. IEEE Trans. Parallel Distrib. Syst. **24**(9), 1908–1917 (2013)
3. Huang, J., Xu, Q., Tiwana, B., Mao, Z.M., Zhang, M., Bahl, P.: Anatomizing application performance differences on smartphones. In: Proceedings of Mobisys. ACM (2010)
4. Wang, Z., Qian, Z., Xu, Q., Mao, Z.M., Zhang, M.: An untold story of middleboxes in cellular networks. In: Proceedings of the ACM SIGCOMM (2011)
5. Seetharam, A., Walker, P.: An empirical characterization of cellular network performance. In: 2016 International Conference on Computing, Networking and Communications (ICNC). IEEE (2016)
6. Huang, J., et al.: An in-depth study of LTE: effect of network protocol and application behavior on performance. In: Proceedings of the ACM SIGCOMM 2013 Conference on SIGCOMM. ACM (2013)
7. Gass, R., Diot, C.: An experimental performance comparison of 3G and WiFi. In: Proceedings of PAM (2010)
8. Xu, Q., Erman, J., Gerber, A., Mao, Z.M., Pang, J., Venkataraman, S.: Identifying diverse usage behaviors of smartphone apps. In: IMC (2011)
9. Rusan, A., Vasiu, R.: Assessment of packet latency on the 4G LTE S1-U interface: impact on end-user throughput. In: 2015 23rd International Conference on Software, Telecommunications and Computer Networks (SoftCOM). IEEE (2015)
10. Elmokashfi, A., Kvalbein, A., Xiang, J., et al.: Characterizing delays in norwegian 3G networks. In: Proceedings of PAM (2012)
11. Arlos, P., Fiedler, M.: Influence of the packet size on the one-way delay in 3G networks. In: Proceedings of PAM (2010)
12. Qian, F., Wang, Z., Gao, Y., Huang, J., Gerber, A., Mao, Z.M., Sen, S., Spatscheck, O.: Periodic transfers in mobile applications: network-wide origin, impact, and optimization. In: Proceedings of the 21st International Conference on World Wide Web (2012)
13. Xu, Q., Huang, J., Wang, Z., Qian, F., Gerber, A., Mao, Z.M.: Cellular data network infrastructure characterization and implication on mobile content placement. In: Proceedings of ACM SIGMETRICS, San Jose, CA (2011)
14. Balakrishnan, M., Mohomed, I., Ramasubramanian, V.: Where's that phone?: geolocating IP addresses on 3G networks. In: Proceedings of IMC (2009)

# Rate-Splitting Non-orthogonal Multiple Access: Practical Design and Performance Optimization

Xinrui Huang[✉], Kai Niu, Zhongwei Si, Zhiqiang He, and Chao Dong

Key Laboratory of Universal Wireless Communications, Ministry of Education, Beijing University of Posts and Telecommunications, Beijing 100876, China
{hxr728,niukai,sizhongwei,hezq,dongchao}@bupt.edu.cn

**Abstract.** In this paper we propose a novel rate-splitting non-orthogonal multiple access (RS-NOMA) scheme implemented in power-domain for practical scenarios in 5G mobile communication systems. The proposed scheme is exploited to solve the mismatch between Quality-of-Service (QoS) and channel conditions of users via rate-splitting instead of power reallocation as the conventional NOMA does. The RS-NOMA scheme contributes to both system spectrum efficiency and user flexibility on resource allocation. We investigate the signal-to-noise ratio (SNR) region division for the proposed scheme and then a splitting factor optimizing algorithm to enable the system achieving the maximum throughput. Simulation results show that the RS-NOMA scheme significantly improves the user flexibility with almost no loss to the system spectrum efficiency.

**Keywords:** Rate-splitting · Non-orthogonal multiple access · MCS selection · Spectrum efficiency · User flexibility

## 1 Introduction

With the worldwide spread of 4G wireless technology, mobile internet has been developed rapidly. Explosive growth of traffic volume, massive interconnected devices and new diverse services all challenge the future mobile communications technology [1]. The fifth generation (5G) mobile communication has attracted significant focus and research. Facing with the higher requirements in all aspects, the main demand for 5G systems are still the higher capacity and higher quality of user experience [2,3].

Due to the urgent demand for high capacity and massive number of connected devices, non-orthogonal multiple access (NOMA) suggests one candidate technique for future radio access owing to its advantages to orthogonal multiple access (OMA) [4]. One of the NOMA schemes proposed in [5] is implemented by multiplexing users in power-domain at the transmitter side and separating signals at the receiver side based on successive interference cancellation (SIC) [5]. Once the power is allocated for each user, the transmit rate is correspondingly determined no matter whether it is appropriate. We would like to refer to the NOMA scheme applied to the uplink in [5] as the Fixed-NOMA scheme.

© ICST Institute for Computer Sciences, Social Informatics and Telecommunications Engineering 2018
Q. Chen et al. (Eds.): ChinaCom 2016, Part I, LNICST 209, pp. 349–359, 2018.
DOI: 10.1007/978-3-319-66625-9_34

From a theoretical perspective, the Fixed-NOMA scheme can achieve the vertices of the Gaussian multiple-access channel (GMAC) capacity region characterized in [6]. Furthermore, a rate-splitting approach to the GMAC called rate-splitting multiple accessing (RSMA) was presented in [7] to achieve every point of the boundary of the capacity region using only single-user codes. The main idea behind the RSMA technique is to split some original inputs into more virtual inputs so as to split their rates as well. The RSMA technique enables the users achieving any rate partition while the sum rate of system remains maximum. Conceptually, the RSMA technique can efficiently improve the users flexibility on resource allocation depending on different Quality-of-Service (QoS). Some rate-splitting schemes extended from the RSMA technique in [7] have been discussed (see [8,9]) while the practical design is seldom investigated.

In this paper, we propose a RS-NOMA scheme for 5G mobile communication systems to meet the demand for ultra-high data traffic and ultra-high connection ability [1]. The proposed scheme offers an optimal splitting approach to solve the mismatch between QoS and channel conditions of users. The main idea is to make the users whose QoS are lower while the channel conditions are better to assist the ones whose situations are converse. We would like to refer to the former users as the "strong users" and the latter ones as the "weak users". Compared with the Fixed-NOMA scheme, the proposed scheme enables the users adjusting their rates flexibly according to their QoS despite the power has already been assigned and constrained. However, different with the Fixed-NOMA scheme, the proposed scheme requires the cooperative communication between the transmitting nodes since the "strong users" demand for the information from the "weak users". We consider the device-to-device (D2D) communication between the transmitting nodes which has been recognized as an underlay to cellular infrastructures [10]. Simulation results show that the proposed RS-NOMA scheme achieves the maximum throughput during the signal-to-noise ratio (SNR) region where the rates of the "strong users" are higher. It is also verified to be efficient to improve the user flexibility on resource allocation with almost no loss to the system capacity compared with the Fixed-NOMA scheme.

## 2    System Model

We consider the systems illustrated in Fig. 1, where nodes Tx1 and Tx2 denote the transmitting nodes and node Rx denotes the receiving node. We suppose the case of single transmit and receive antenna in this paper.

The initial system is shown in Fig. 1(a). When nodes Tx1 and Tx2 communicate simultaneously with node Rx by transmitting signal $x_1$ and $x_2$ respectively, the received signal at node Rx is given by

$$y = \sqrt{P_1} h_1 x_1 + \sqrt{P_2} h_2 x_2 + n, \tag{1}$$

where $P_i$ is the transmit power allocated for node Tx$i$ and $h_i$ is the channel coefficient between node Tx$i$ and Rx, $i = 1, 2$. We assume the additive white Gaussian noise (AWGN) $n$ with variance $\sigma_n^2$.

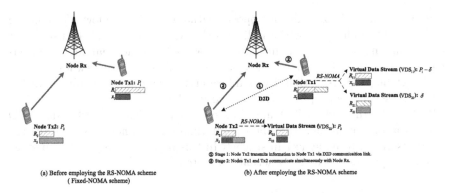

(a) Before employing the RS-NOMA scheme
( Fixed-NOMA scheme)

(b) After employing the RS-NOMA scheme

**Fig. 1.** (a) Communication system with mismatch between QoS and channel conditions. (b) Communication system with RS-NOMA scheme which solving the mismatch between QoS and channel conditions

Assuming $E\left[|x_i|^2\right] = 1$, $i = 1, 2$, where $E\left[\cdot\right]$ stands for the statistical expectation, the received signal-to-interference and noise ratio (SINR) for $x_1$ and $x_2$ can be respectively written as

$$\text{SINR}_1 = \frac{P_1|h_1|^2}{P_2|h_2|^2 + \sigma_n^2}, \text{SINR}_2 = \frac{P_2|h_2|^2}{P_1|h_1|^2 + \sigma_n^2}. \tag{2}$$

In this case, we assume that $\text{SINR}_1 > \text{SINR}_2$, therefore $x_1$ comes first in the decoding order when SIC process is implemented at node Rx [3]. Supposing successful decoding without error propagation, the rate of the data streams from nodes Tx1 and Tx2 can be given by

$$R_1 = \log\left(1 + \frac{P_1|h_1|^2}{P_2|h_2|^2 + \sigma_n^2}\right), \tag{3}$$

$$R_2 = \log\left(1 + \frac{P_2|h_2|^2}{\sigma_n^2}\right). \tag{4}$$

Assuming that $\rho$ represents the SNR at node Rx, we obtain the relation

$$\sigma_n^2 = (P_1 + P_2) \times 10^{\frac{-\rho}{10}}. \tag{5}$$

In Fig. 1, we assume that the channel condition between nodes Tx1 and Rx is good as the short solid arrow indicates while the one between nodes Tx2 and Rx is poor as the long solid arrow represents. Accordingly, the achievable rate of the data stream from node Tx1 is higher than that from Tx2 as the sizes of shadow blocks represent. In the contrary, the QoS of node Tx1 is supposed to be lower than Tx2 as the sizes of filled blocks represent.

Apparently, in Fig. 1(a), the shadow block is longer than the filled one at node Tx1, which means the achievable rate $R_1$ is surplus for transmitting signal

$x_1$. However, node Tx2 is in an opposite situation. The shadow block is too short to load the filled one which indicates the achievable rate $R_2$ is insufficient for transmitting signal $x_2$. A mismatch between QoS and channel conditions appears in Fig. 1(a). To compete against the contradiction, we seek for solution where Tx1 helps transmitting Tx2's information using its extra rate, and the RS-NOMA scheme is proposed as shown in Fig. 1(b).

We assume that nodes Tx1 and Tx2 can communicate directly with D2D communication link in Fig. 1(b), and the information from node Tx2 has already been transmitted to node Tx1 in stage 1. In this paper, we emphasize on stage 2 where the proposed scheme is actually adopted.

## 3    Rate-Splitting Non-orthogonal Multiple Access

To solve the mismatch between QoS and channel conditions, we propose a RS-NOMA scheme for practical system, due to its benefit in adjusting the user rates flexibly. The SNR region division for the proposed scheme is investigated and the algorithm to select the optimal splitting factor is designed.

### 3.1    Introduction of RS-NOMA Scheme

The main idea of the RS-NOMA scheme is to split original data streams into virtual data streams as depicted in Fig. 2. At the transmitter, original data streams from $L$ real users are split into at most $2L-1$ virtual data streams with splitting rates $r_i, i = 1, 2, \ldots, 2L-1$. Transmit power $p_i, i = 1, 2, \ldots, 2L-1$ with splitting factors are assigned to virtual data streams to adjust the splitting rates. At the receiver, each virtual data stream is regarded as a single user and decoded in an SIC manner.

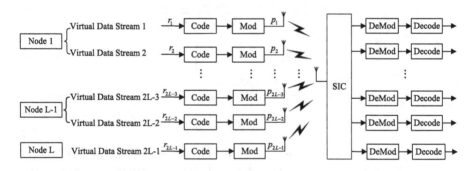

**Fig. 2.** Block diagram of the RS-NOMA scheme.

Taking Fig. 1(b) as an example, we adopt the RS-NOMA scheme to split the rate of original data stream from node Tx1 in stage 2. The long shadow block at node Tx1 is divided into two parts, so one of them can be assigned to carry a short filled block from node Tx2 to help node Tx2 transmitting information.

We define $\delta$ as the splitting factor in power-domain. The received signal at node Rx using the RS-NOMA scheme in system can be written as follows:

$$y = \sqrt{P_1 - \delta} h_1 x_{11} + \sqrt{\delta} h_1 x_{21} + \sqrt{P_2} h_2 x_{22} + n, \tag{6}$$

where $x_{11}$ is the original signal $x_1$ of node Tx1, $x_{21}$ and $x_{22}$ are split from the original signal $x_2$ of node Tx2. Apparently, the whole system has transformed from two original data streams of real nodes to three virtual data streams as $VDS_{11}$, $VDS_{21}$ and $VDS_{22}$. As shown in Fig. 1(b), $VDS_{11}$ and $VDS_{21}$ currently carry $x_{11}$ and $x_{21}$ respectively at node Tx1 while node Tx2 only transmits $x_{22}$ which is part of the original signal $x_2$ via $VDS_{22}$.

In addition, we would like to point out that the modulation and coding scheme (MCS) of the data streams are adaptively chosen via the channel state information as implementation in practical system [11].

### 3.2 SNR Region Division for RS-NOMA Scheme

As introduced earlier, the main idea of the RS-NOMA scheme is to enable the "strong users" assisting the "weak users" by utilizing the extra rates. Therefore, according to the user rates, we can divide the SNR region into general two parts. During the SNR region where the rates of the "strong users" are higher than the "weak users", we employ the RS-NOMA scheme with the optimal splitting factor and we would like to refer to it as the RS-SNR region. While during the SNR region where the situations are converse, we set the splitting factor to be zero which actually turns into the Fixed-NOMA scheme. The SNR region division offers a reference to use the RS-NOMA scheme flexibly.

In Fig. 1(b), we consider the SNR region where the rates of the original data streams from nodes Tx1 and Tx2 satisfy $R_1 \geq R_2$. Substituting (5) back into (3) and (4), the RS-SNR region at receiving node can be written as

$$\rho \leq 10 \log \frac{\left(P_1|h_1|^2 - P_2|h_2|^2\right)(P_1 + P_2)}{P_2^2|h_2|^4}. \tag{7}$$

In different scenarios, the RS-SNR region varies and can be calculated by (7) once the RS-NOMA scheme is employed.

### 3.3 Splitting Factor Optimizing Algorithm

The RS-NOMA scheme is capable to achieve every point of the boundary of the GMAC capacity region by choosing different splitting factors similar to the RSMA technique in [7]. During the RS-SNR region obtained by (7), we develop a splitting factor optimizing algorithm consisting of a series of criteria. The proposed algorithm selects the optimal splitting factor for current system to achieve the maximum throughput.

**Criterion I: Appropriate Detecting Order**

According to the RSMA technique proposed in [7], all virtual data streams are detected based on SIC at receiver, and the detecting order is decided by SINR. Besides, the detecting order of the un-split users must be placed among the split ones to adjust the user rates by altering the splitting factors (see [7]). The SINR of the virtual data streams in Fig. 1(b) are given by

$$\text{SINR}_{11} = \frac{(P_1 - \delta)\,|h_1|^2}{P_2|h_2|^2 + \delta|h_1|^2 + \sigma_n^2},\tag{8}$$

$$\text{SINR}_{21} = \frac{\delta|h_1|^2}{P_2|h_2|^2 + (P_1 - \delta)\,|h_1|^2 + \sigma_n^2},\tag{9}$$

$$\text{SINR}_{22} = \frac{P_2|h_2|^2}{(P_1 - \delta)\,|h_1|^2 + \delta|h_1|^2 + \sigma_n^2}.\tag{10}$$

When $\delta < P_1/2$, we can obviously obtain from (8) and (9) that $\text{SINR}_{21} < \text{SINR}_{11}$. Then the SINR of the three virtual data streams which determines the detecting order should satisfy the follows:

$$\text{SINR}_{21} < \text{SINR}_{22} < \text{SINR}_{11}.\tag{11}$$

Submitting (8)–(10) to (11), we can obtain constraint of splitting factors as

$$\delta < \frac{P_2^2|h_2|^4 + P_1P_2|h_1|^2|h_2|^2 + P_2|h_2|^2\sigma_n^2}{P_1|h_1|^4 + |h_1|^2\sigma_n^2 + P_2|h_1|^2|h_2|^2}$$
$$\text{when } P_1|h_1|^2 > 2P_2|h_2|^2, \text{ or}\tag{12}$$

$$\delta < \frac{P_1^2|h_1|^4 - P_2^2|h_2|^4 + \left(P_1|h_1|^2 - P_2|h_2|^2\right)\sigma_n^2}{P_1|h_1|^4 + |h_1|^2\sigma_n^2 + P_2|h_1|^2|h_2|^2}\tag{13}$$
$$\text{when } P_1|h_1|^2 < 2P_2|h_2|^2.$$

Assuming decoding successfully without error propagation, the rates of the three virtual data streams are given by

$$R_{21} = \log\left(1 + \frac{\delta|h_1|^2}{\sigma_n^2}\right),\tag{14}$$

$$R_{22} = \log\left(1 + \frac{P_2|h_2|^2}{\delta|h_1|^2 + \sigma_n^2}\right),\tag{15}$$

$$R_{11} = \log\left(1 + \frac{(P_1 - \delta)|h_1|^2}{\delta|h_1|^2 + P_2|h_2|^2 + \sigma_n^2}\right),\tag{16}$$

which can be altered by varying $\delta$. When $\delta > P_1/2$, the constraint of splitting factors can be calculated in the same way as described above.

## Criterion II: Appropriate SINR for Successful Decoding

Using the RS-NOMA scheme, we would like to ensure each virtual data stream being decoded successfully. We consider the stream whose detecting order is the last to be on reliable communication [12].

When $\delta < P_1/2$, VDS$_{21}$ is the last one to be detected by comparing (8)–(10). To ensure VDS$_{21}$ on reliable communication, the splitting factors are subject to follows:

$$\frac{E_b}{\sigma_n^2} > \frac{2^{R_{AMC}/W} - 1}{R_{AMC}/W} \Rightarrow \frac{\delta}{R_{AMC} \times \sigma_n^2} > \frac{2^{R_{AMC}} - 1}{R_{AMC}/W}$$
$$\Rightarrow \delta > \sigma_n^2 \times \left(2^{R_{AMC}} - 1\right) \times W, \tag{17}$$

where $E_b$ is the energy per bit, $R_{AMC}$ is the practical rate depending on adaptive MCS level, and $W$ is the system bandwidth. Equation (17) gives another constraint of splitting factors.

When $\delta > P_1/2$, VDS$_{11}$ becomes the last one to be detected and the constraint of splitting factors can be calculated as follows:

$$\delta < P_1 - \sigma_n^2 \times \left(2^{R_{AMC}} - 1\right) \times W. \tag{18}$$

## Criterion III: Appropriate MCS Level

In practical system, the MCS level of signals are adaptive to the channel quality information (CQI). Therefore, the criteria for optimal splitting factor should be jointly designed with the MCS level.

Compared (15) with (4), we can obtain that the rate of un-split node Tx2 is reduced which leads to a drop of MCS level. In addition, we would like to point out that the rate of un-split user in the RS-NOMA scheme always decreases as well as the MCS level. To avoid that the rate of un-split user is too low, we propose a constraint of modulation scheme for the un-split user. Supposing that $m = \log_2 M$ denotes the modulation level, where $M$ is the modulation order, the modulation scheme of the un-split node Tx2 should satisfy:

$$|m_{Tx2} - m_{VDS_{22}}| \leq 2, \tag{19}$$

where $m_{Tx2}$ and $m_{VDS_{22}}$ are adaptively determined by CQI.

The above criteria are organized by their importance. When all splitting factors have been traversed according to the criteria, we can obtain a set of splitting factors $\mathcal{S} = \{\delta_1, \delta_2, \ldots, \delta_k\}$. The optimal splitting factor could be selected based on the practical QoS. We suppose that the system in Fig. 1(b) demands for higher transmission rate for VDS$_{21}$, which means that VDS$_{21}$ is expected to carry more information for node Tx2. Taking (14), (17) and (18) into account, the optimal splitting factor $\delta_{opt}$ should be finally decided by being maximized when ensuring all virtual data streams on reliable communication. As a summary, the proposed algorithm to select the optimal splitting factor during the RS-SNR region is described in Algorithm 1.

---

**Algorithm 1.** Splitting factor optimizing algorithm

---

**Input:** Power assigned to each transmitting node $P_i$, each user's channel coefficient $h_i$, noise variance $\sigma_n^2$ and step of splitting factor $\Delta\delta$;

**Output:** Optimal splitting factor $\delta_{opt}$;

1: Initialize a set $\mathcal{S} = \emptyset$, $\delta = 0$;
2: Calculate the RS-SNR region by (8) for the RS-NOMA scheme;
3: **for** $\delta = \delta + \Delta\delta \to P_i(split\ node)$ **do**
4:     **if** $\delta$ is in the intervals calculated by criterion I **then**
5:         **if** $\delta$ satisfies the constraint in criterion II **then**
6:             **if** the MCS of the virtual data streams determined by $\delta$ satisfies criterion III **then**
7:                 Go to step 17;
8:             **else**
9:                 Go to step 3;
10:             **end if**
11:         **else**
12:             Go to step 3;
13:         **end if**
14:     **else**
15:         Go to step 3;
16:     **end if**
17:     Add current $\delta$ to $\mathcal{S}$;
18: **end for**
19: Select the optimal splitting factor $\delta_{opt}$ by practical QoS from $\mathcal{S} = \{\delta_1, \delta_2, \ldots, \delta_k\}$.

---

# 4  Performance Analyses

In this section, we study the performance of the proposed RS-NOMA scheme through numerical and simulation results. We consider the communication system as illustrated in Fig. 1(b) and we only analyze stage 2. For simplicity, we normalize the transmit power as $P_1 = P_2 = 1$, and we assume that $|h_1| = \sqrt{2}$, $|h_2| = \sqrt{0.4}$.

## 4.1  Theoretical Results

Figure 3 shows the theoretical system capacity region. The legend $\delta = 0$ denotes the achievable sum rate of the Fixed-NOMA scheme based on (3) and (4) which is a vertex of the capacity region. Only by successful SIC process at node Rx can the system in Fig. 1(a) achieve it. The RS-NOMA scheme achieves different points of the boundary of the capacity region when splitting factors vary. The achievable sum rate can be calculated by (14)–(16). The figure demonstrates that the RS-NOMA scheme enables the system flexibly achieving the maximum sum rate with alternative splitting factors from a theoretical perspective.

Figure 4 depicts the theoretical separate rate of original data stream (Fixed-NOMA scheme) and virtual data stream with various splitting factors. To compare the performance between the Fixed-NOMA scheme and the RS-NOMA

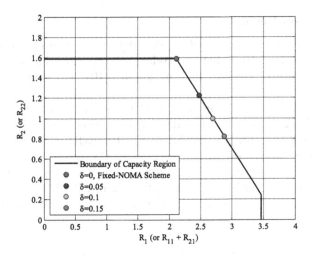

**Fig. 3.** Theoretical achievable system capacity of the Fixed-NOMA scheme and the RS-NOMA scheme with various $\delta$.

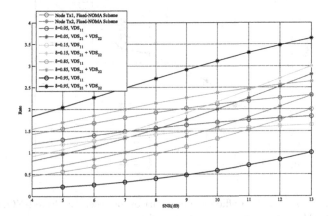

**Fig. 4.** Theoretical separate rate of original data stream (Fixed-NOMA scheme) and virtual data stream with various $\delta$.

scheme, we equally regard the $VDS_{11}$ as one stream from a node and combine the $VDS_{21}$ and $VDS_{22}$ as one stream from another node. From Fig. 4, we observe that the RS-SNR region for the RS-NOMA scheme is $\rho \leq 13\,dB$ which proves to be consistent with the results calculated by (7) using current parameters. Different splitting factors lead to different rate of each VDS and the proposed RS-NOMA scheme is exploited to select the optimal splitting factor from all these available factors.

## 4.2    Simulation Results

The above analyses are based on Gaussian signal model. However, in practical implementation, the modulation and coding scheme will bring some deviations to theoretical results. We use the schemes in 3GPP LTE standard [13] as a reference.

Figure 5 exhibits the system sum spectrum efficiency comparison between the Fixed-NOMA scheme and the RS-NOMA scheme with different splitting factors including the optimal one during the RS-SNR region. The simulation results illustrate that the proposed algorithm selects the optimal splitting factor to achieve the maximum throughput. In addition, it verifies that the proposed RS-NOMA scheme contributes to current system on both spectrum efficiency and user flexibility. We have to point out that the adaptive selection of MCS level leads to the jitters of curves.

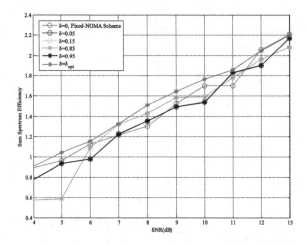

**Fig. 5.** System sum spectrum efficiency comparison between the Fixed-NOMA scheme and the RS-NOMA scheme with various $\delta$ in simulation.

## 5    Conclusion

We propose a practical design and performance optimization method for RS-NOMA scheme. The proposed scheme contributes to a better match between QoS and channel conditions of users by rate-splitting. We investigated the SNR region division for the RS-NOMA scheme and the splitting factor optimizing algorithm. Simulation results show that by appropriately exploiting the optimal slitting factor, the proposed scheme significantly improves the user flexibility with almost no loss to the system spectrum efficiency.

**Acknowledgment.** This work is supported by National High Technology Research and Development Program of China (863 Program 2015AA01A709), and National Natural Science Foundation of China (61401037).

# References

1. IMT-2020(5G) Promotion Group, "5G Vision and Requirements" (2014)
2. Thompson, J., et al.: 5G wireless communication systems: prospects and challenges. IEEE Commun. Mag. **52**(2), 62–64 (2014). (Guest Editorial)
3. Benjebbour, A., Saito, Y., Kishiyama, Y., Li, A., Harada, A., Nakamura, T.: Concept and practical considerations of non-orthogonal multiple access (NOMA) for future radio access. In: International Symposium on Intelligent Signal Processing and Communications Systems (ISPACS), Naha, pp. 770–774 (2013)
4. Saito, Y. Kishiyama, Y., Benjebbour, A., Nakamura, T., Li, A., Higuchi, K.: Non-orthogonal multiple access (NOMA) for cellular future radio access. In: 2013 IEEE 77th Vehicular Technology Conference (VTC Spring), Dresden (2013)
5. Higuchi, K., Benjebbour, A.: Non-orthogonal multiple access (NOMA) with successive interference cancellation for future radio access. IEICE Trans. Commun. **98**(3), 403–414 (2015)
6. Cover, T., Thomas, J.: Elements of Information Theory. Wiley-Interscience, New York (1991)
7. Rimoldi, B., Urbanke, R.: A rate-splitting approach to the Gaussian multiple-access channel. IEEE Trans. Inf. Theory **42**(2), 364–375 (1996)
8. Cao, J., Yeh, E.M: Differential quality-of-service in multiple-access communication via distributed rate splitting. In: Global Telecommunications Conference, GLOBECOM 2005. IEEE (2005)
9. Cao, J., Yeh, E.M.: Asymptotically optimal multiple-access communication via distributed rate splitting. IEEE Trans. Inf. Theory **53**(1), 304–319 (2007)
10. Doppler, K., Rinne, M., Wijting, C., Ribeiro, C.B., Hugl, K.: Device-to-device communication as an underlay to LTE-advanced networks. IEEE Commun. Mag. **47**(12), 42–49 (2009)
11. Hanzaz, Z., Schotten, H.D.: Analysis of effective SINR mapping models for MIMO OFDM in LTE system. In: 9th International Wireless Communications and Mobile Computing Conference (IWCMC), Sardinia, pp. 1509–1515 (2013)
12. Tse, D., Viswanath, P.: Fundamentals of Wireless Communication. Cambridge University Press, Cambridge (2005)
13. 3GPP TS 36.213: Physical layer procedures, Release 12, 2014

# Improved Proportional Fair Scheduling Mechanism with Joint Gray-Mapping Modulation for NOMA

Jing Guo$^{(\boxtimes)}$, Xuehong Lin, and Zhisong Bie

Key Lab of Universal Wireless Communications, Ministry of Education,
Beijing University of Posts and Telecommunications, Beijing, China
guojing_bupt@163.com, {xhlin,zhisongbie}@bupt.edu.cn

**Abstract.** Non-orthogonal multiple access (NOMA) is a promising technique with high spectral efficiency to meet requirements for 5G. This paper mainly introduces key algorithms of NOMA with successive interference cancellation (SIC). Far-UEs and Near-UEs are co-scheduled as a group on the same resource block with different power allocation. To seek a good trade-off between computational complexity and system capacity, an improved method of proportional fair (PF) scheduling with joint Gray-mapping modulation is proposed. The results show that NOMA with SIC significantly enhances the system performance and spectral efficiency compared to conventional orthogonal multiple access (OMA), bringing 22.59% and 21.26% gain in cell average and cell edge throughput respectively. And using the Gray-mapped composite constellation and reducing signalling overhead with the improved pre-fixed power allocation method, which is promote to practical use, brings negligible performance loss.

**Keywords:** Non-orthogonal multiple access · Proportional fair · Power allocation · Successive interference cancellation

## 1 Introduction

With the advent of 5G communication system, the increasing demand of mobile data traffic poses challenging requirements for technological innovation. To address problems such as higher spectral efficiency, massive connectivity and lower latency, several companies in mobile communication industry proposed that non-orthogonal multiple access (NOMA) with successive interference cancellation (SIC) should be widely used in 5G, which achieves better system performance [1, 2].

There have been many related studies on key NOMA techniques. UE selection algorithm in [3] is proposed to reduce interference with certain computational complexity. The fixed power allocation (FPA) algorithm with reducing signalling overhead brings performance loss in [4, 5]. The paper in [6] just gives theoretical formulas to

This work was supported by the Fundamental Research Funds for the Central Universities under Grant 2014ZD03-01, by the National High-Tech R&D Program (863 Program) under Grant 2015 AA01A705, by the Special Youth Science Foundation of Jiangxi under Grant 20133ACB21007.

©·ICST Institute for Computer Sciences, Social Informatics and Telecommunications Engineering 2018
Q. Chen et al. (Eds.): ChinaCom 2016, Part I, LNICST 209, pp. 360–369, 2018.
DOI: 10.1007/978-3-319-66625-9_35

calculate proportional fairness factor in multi-UE transmission. And the paper in [7] introduces the multi-UE proportional fair (PF) scheduling method for uplink NOMA. In order to promote practical use of NOMA, [8–10] mainly tell how to implement SIC with low complexity at receiver side. The paper in [11] gives detailed descriptions of NOMA schemes under various realistic environments.

In this paper, we focus on key downlink NOMA techniques and propose improved schemes to promote better system performance and lower complexity with taking signalling overhead and practical use into consideration. The remainder of this paper is organized as follows. Section 2 introduces NOMA concept with SIC and signal model. Section 3 discusses several key algorithms and proposes improved methods. Section 4 gives the simulation parameters, system-level simulation results and analysis of different schemes. The conclusions are drawn in Sect. 5.

## 2 Descriptions of NOMA with SIC

For simplicity of presentation, we use two-UE system model to introduce the implementation of downlink NOMA. In this paper, we assume a multiple input multiple output (MIMO) system where the number of transmitter antennas is 2 ($N_t = 2$) and the number of receiver antennas is 2 ($N_r = 2$). The final transmitted signal and received signal at $k$-th UE can be described by:

$$\mathbf{x}(k) = \sqrt{\alpha_1}\mathbf{x_1}(k) + \sqrt{\alpha_2}\mathbf{x_2}(k), \mathbf{y}(k) = \mathbf{h_k}\mathbf{x}(k) + \mathbf{n_k} \tag{1}$$

where ($\alpha_1$, $\alpha_2$) denotes the power ratio for Near-UE (i.e. UE1) and Far-UE (i.e. UE2) respectively and $\alpha_1 + \alpha_2 = 1$. $\mathbf{x}(k)$ and $\mathbf{y}(k)$ represent the MIMO transmitted signal and received signal at $k$-th UE. $\mathbf{h_k}$ is the channel coefficient between $k$-th UE and its serving cell, and $\mathbf{n_k}$ is including white Gaussian noise and inter-cell interference.

Without loss of generality, we assume the channel condition of UE1 is better than that of UE2. At receiver side, in order to implement SIC to decode the original signals more effectively, it should be satisfied with $\alpha_1 < \alpha_2$. We first decode and reconstruct the original signal of UE2 with taking UE1 as interference. Then decode UE1 on the basis of knowing UE2 well, which means the signal of UE2 can be completely cancelled at the receiver of UE1. The formulas of SINR in NOMA mode are shown:

$$SINR_{1,NOMA} = \alpha_1 P_0 |h_1|^2 / N_1, SINR_{2,NOMA} = (\alpha_2 P_0 |h_2|^2)/(\alpha_1 P_0 |h_2|^2 + N_2) \tag{2}$$

where $P_0$ is the total transmission power at BS, and ($N_1$, $N_2$) is the noise power for UE1 and UE2 respectively. $SINR_{k,NOMA}$ and $SINR_{k,OMA}$ separately denote SINR in NOMA mode and OMA mode at $k$-th UE, which can be expressed by:

$$SINR_{1,NOMA} = \alpha_1 SINR_{1,OMA}, SINR_{2,NOMA} = \alpha_2/(\alpha_1 + 1/SINR_{2,OMA}) \tag{3}$$

# 3  Practical Scheduling Algorithms for Downlink NOMA

Detailed descriptions of each algorithm in practical scenarios are shown below, such as UE classification, power allocation and PF scheduling.

## 3.1  UE Classification

For NOMA system model of UE classification, we use coupling loss including all power loss between $k$-th UE and its serving BS to divide UE groups with simplicity, which can be represented by $PL_k$. Assuming the threshold of coupling loss is $PL_T$, if $PL_k < PL_T$, the $k$-th UE is Near-UE, otherwise, the $k$-th UE is Far-UE. Then all UEs can be divided into two groups, which is shown in Fig. 1 below:

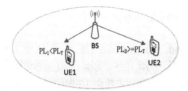

**Fig. 1.** Illustration of UE classification in NOMA system

## 3.2  Power Allocation

For NOMA system, one key is how to allocate power for pairing UEs with better performance and less signalling overhead. The best performance can be achieved by searching all possible UE pairs [4]. And it will inevitably bring high computational complexity and huge resource consumption for granted, which is very difficult to practical use. There are some practical methods of power allocation as below.

### 3.2.1  Pre-fixed Power Ratio Set Method
Considering different channel conditions between UEs and to facilitate the demodulation at receiver, it should be satisfied with $\alpha_1 < \alpha_2$. Pre-fixed power ratio set is one method that can be easy to implement with performance loss and less network signalling overhead which is provided to inform power ratios to the pairing UEs [12].

### 3.2.2  Adaptive Power Ratio Method with Independent Modulation
Based on the pre-fixed power ratio set method, we can get some power ratios as a candidate set. Searching all available ratios and choosing the best one with taking system performance into consideration, in which way, both requirements of resource consumption and system performance could be satisfied to a certain degree.

This adaptive method is proposed on the basis of condition that two UEs are independent in the process of coding, non-Gray mapping and modulating [13], and they are only combined in the power domain without taking other details into consideration, which is shown in Fig. 2.

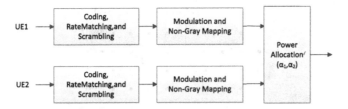

**Fig. 2.** Illustration of transmitter processing of independent modulation of NOMA system

### 3.2.3   Improved Adaptive Power Ratio Method with Joint Modulation

Above two methods do not take the legacy constellation and joint modulation for co-scheduled NOMA UEs into consideration. In order to reduce changes to the existing OMA system and facilitate to practical promotion, this improved adaptive power allocation method with joint Gray-mapping modulation [13] is proposed and shown in Fig. 3.

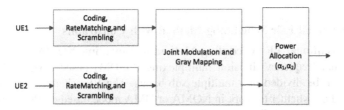

**Fig. 3.** Illustration of transmitter processing of joint modulation of NOMA system

Generally speaking, most Far-UEs with worse channel conditions are modulated by QPSK. Then we can set Far-UEs as QPSK fixedly with less network signalling overhead. To implement joint Gray-mapping modulation, the configuration of power ratios should be altered to applicable use.

- If Near-UE is QPSK, then the power ratio is configured with 2:8, which followed by co-modulated 16QAM perfectly.
- If Near-UE is 16QAM, then the power ratio is configured with 5:16, which followed by co-modulated 64QAM correspondingly.
- If Near-UE is 64QAM, then the power ratio is configured with 21:64, which followed by co-modulated 256QAM with low probability of appearance.

The power ratio is calculated by energy allocation and the composite constellation. Use the traditional constellation to find position $(i_1, q_1)$ for UE1 and position $(i_2, q_2)$ for UE2, and the composite constellation to find $(i, q)$, where $i$ and $q$ denote the real and imaginary parts in the constellation respectively. It is satisfied with:

$$\sqrt{\alpha_1}(i_1, q_1) + \sqrt{\alpha_2}(i_2, q_2) = (i, q) \tag{4}$$

Then the power ratios can be set with evaluating potential system-level gain and complexity under realistic deployment scenarios. Take an example of the composite constellation (64QAM) of Far-UE with QPSK and Near-UE with 16QAM to illustrate details, as shown in Fig. 4.

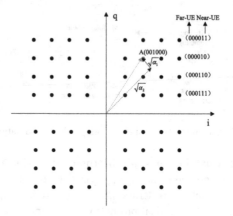

**Fig. 4.** An example of the composite constellation (64QAM) of Far-UE with QPSK and Near-UE with 16QAM

### 3.3   Proportional Fair Scheduling Method with Constraints

### 3.3.1   Conventional PF Scheduling Method in Downlink NOMA

For orthogonal frequency division multiplexing (OFDM) based system, the system bandwidth can be divided into multiple sub-bands. The BS scheduler can decide for each subband on whether to work in NOMA or OMA mode based on PF factor to trade off system capacity and UE fairness. The set of candidate UEs that maximizes PF factor is approximated as follows [4]:

$$PF_U(s) = \sum_{k \in U} (PF_k(s)) = \sum_{k \in U} \left( \frac{R_k(s,t)}{T_k(t)} \right) \tag{5}$$

$$U_s^* = \underset{U}{\mathrm{argmax}}(PF_U(s)) \tag{6}$$

The term $U$ denotes the set of pairing UEs including Far-UEs and Near-UEs. And $PF_s(U)$ is the set of PF factors of candidate UEs. Choose the maximum of PF factors to decide final scheduling UE pairs in subband $s$. The PF factor of $k$-th UE in subband $s$ is represented by $PF_k(s)$. $R_k(s, t)$ denotes the instantaneous throughput of $k$-th UE in subband $s$ at time $t$ and $T_k(t)$ is the already successfully delivered throughput of $k$-th UE at time $t$.

And the throughputs are updated as follows [6]:

$$T_k(t+1) = \begin{cases} (1 - 1/t_c)T_k(t) + 1/t_c R_k(t), & k = k^* \\ (1 - 1/t_c)T_k(t), & k \neq k^* \end{cases} \tag{7}$$

where $k^*$ is the scheduled UE and $t_c$ defines the time horizon in which we want to achieve fairness, generally the value is set to 200 TTI.

### 3.3.2  Improved PF Scheduling Method with MIMO Fusion and Joint Modulation

To further improve potential system gain under practical situations, we propose the improved PF scheduling method with MIMO fusion and joint modulation. We define the coefficient of PF factor to promote NOMA potential gain as below:

$$\beta = PF_{OMA}/PF_{NOMA} \tag{8}$$

where $\beta$ is a parameter for adjusting NOMA and OMA scheduling priority and has influence on the cell average and cell edge throughput with typical values between 1 and 2, which needs to be determined by system-level simulations. In conventional NOMA scheduling method, the value of $\beta$ is 1.

In MIMO transmission system, pairing UEs in NOMA scheduling mode should have the same PMI index [14]. Specifically, if the rank of transmission mode is larger than 1, the same PMI index should be at least guaranteed in one layer. Due to the improved adaptive power ratio method with joint Gray-mapping modulation, it has better system robustness and stability compared to the adaptive power ratio method with independent non-Gray-mapping modulation.

## 4  Simulation Results and Analysis

To evaluate the performance gain of the improved method under realistic scenarios, the system-level simulation for downlink NOMA is conducted. The simulation parameters are listed in Table 1 below.

**Table 1.** System-level simulation parameters

| Cell layout | Hexagonal grid, 19 sites, 3 cells per site |
|---|---|
| ISD | 500 m |
| Carrier frequency | 2 GHz |
| Number of RB | 50 |
| System bandwidth | 10 MHz |
| Traffic mode | Full buffer |
| Receiver mode | MMSE-IRC |
| Number of BS antennas | 2 |
| Number of MS antennas | 2 |
| BS antenna gain | 17 dBi |
| HONET max attenuation | 25 dB |
| BS antenna height | 25 m |
| MS antenna Height | 1.5 m |

(*continued*)

| Antenna tilt angle | 12° |
|---|---|
| Scenario | ITU Urban Macro [15] |
| Thermal noise | −174 dBm/Hz |
| Coupling loss | Path-loss, shadowing, small scale fading, penetration and antenna gain |
| Penetration loss | 9 dB |
| UE speed | 3 km/h |

This part presents the system-level simulation results for downlink NOMA system and detailed analysis of different methods for comparison.

The impact of the threshold of coupling-loss $PL_T$ on UE candidate sets is shown in Table 2. The larger value of $PL_T$ means more UEs are defined as Near-UE. To minimize the different ratios between Near-UEs and Far-UEs, we choose 85 dB as the suitable $PL_T$ to make better potential performance of NOMA scheduling.

**Table 2.** Ratios of UE categories with the different threshold of coupling loss

| $PL_T$ (dB) | Near-UE (%) | Far-UE (%) |
|---|---|---|
| 82 | 41.23 | 58.77 |
| 84 | 47.54 | 52.46 |
| 85 | 50.10 | 49.90 |
| 86 | 52.28 | 47.72 |
| 88 | 58.25 | 41.75 |

The overall cell throughput for different numbers of UEs per cell is summarized in Fig. 5. Take 20 UEs per cell with $\beta = 1.5$ for example, the gains of cell average and cell edge throughput are up to 22.59% and 21.26%. With the increasing number of UEs, the gain is roughly increased with more NOMA scheduling mode into use.

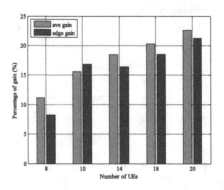

**Fig. 5.** Gain of cell average and cell edge throughput with different numbers of UEs per cell

The NOMA gain for different numbers of subbands is summarized in Fig. 6. The number of subband is 1 means wideband scheduling. With the increasing numbers of subbands, the gains for cell average and cell edge throughput are reduced in general. The reason is that power allocation and scheduling is implemented for subband, while MCS selection remains wideband. In addition, the baseline OMA with more subbands achieves better performance with frequency selective scheduling.

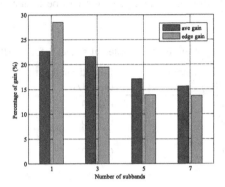

**Fig. 6.** Gain of cell average and cell edge throughput with different numbers of subbands

The improved PF scheduling method makes good use of the coefficient of PF factor to achieve system gain. The figure in Fig. 7 is drawn to evaluate the impact of $\beta$ on the system performance. In general, with the increase of coefficient of PF factor, the cell average throughput has a rising tendency with fully exploiting NOMA superiority, and the gain of cell edge throughput is first up and down later. Taking a good trade-off between cell average and cell edge throughput, we choose 1.5 as the suitable coefficient of PF factor with 15.58% and 16.87% gain respectively in cell average and cell edge throughput with the situation of 10 UEs per cell and 9 subbands. Compared to the conventional NOMA scheduling with $\beta = 1$, the additional achieved gains are 7.54% and 2.9% for cell average and cell edge throughput.

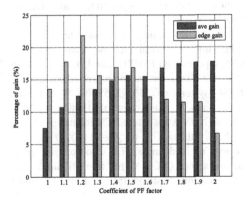

**Fig. 7.** Gain of cell average and cell edge throughput with different coefficients of PF factor

It is obvious that NOMA brings better performance than OMA. Compared the improved PF scheduling method with joint Gray-mapping modulation to the adaptive NOMA scheme with $\beta = 1.5$, there is 1.2% and 3.52% loss for cell average and cell edge throughput respectively as shown in Table 3. For Far-UEs, the ratios of QPSK and 16QAM are 83.36% and 16.64%, giving the convincing evidence to implement the proposed adaptive power ratio method with joint Gray-mapping modulation. The proposed scheduling method brings negligible performance loss with less signalling overhead and implementation complexity, which can be better practical use.

**Table 3.** Comparison between different schemes for 10 UEs per cell

| Schemes | Ave throughput (bps/Hz) | Edge throughput (bps/Hz) | Ave/edge gain (%) |
|---|---|---|---|
| OMA | 1.7868 | 0.0479 | 0/0 |
| Adaptive NOMA | 2.0652 | 0.0560 | 15.58/16.87 |
| Improved NOMA | 2.0405 | 0.0540 | 14.2/12.76 |

## 5   Conclusion

The results show that NOMA with SIC significantly enhances the system performance and spectral efficiency compared to the conventional OMA, even taking practical conditions and joint Gray-mapping modulation into consideration. The proposed PF scheduling method achieves noticeable gain with less signalling overhead and implementation complexity.

## References

1. Dai, L., Wang, B., Yuan, Y., Han, S., Chih-Lin, I., Wang, Z.: Non-orthogonal multiple access for 5G: solutions, challenges, opportunities, and future research trends. IEEE Commun. Mag. **53**(9), 74–81 (2015)
2. Saito, Y., Benjebbour, A., Kishiyama, Y., Nakamura, T.: System-level performance evaluation of downlink non-orthogonal multiple access (NOMA). In: 2013 IEEE 24th Annual International Symposium on PIMRC, London, pp. 611–615 (2013)
3. Liu, S., Zhang, C., Lyu, G.: User selection and power schedule for downlink non-orthogonal multiple access (NOMA) system, pp. 2561–2565. ICCW, London (2015)
4. Benjebbovu, A., Li, A., Saito, Y., Kishiyama, Y., Harada, A., Nakamura, T.: System-level performance of downlink NOMA for future LTE enhancements. In: 2013 IEEE Globecom Workshops (GC Wkshps), Atlanta, GA, pp. 66–70 (2013)
5. Benjebbour, A., Saito, Y., Nakamura, T.: Concept and practical considerations of non-orthogonal multiple access (NOMA) for future radio access. In: Intelligent Signal Processing and Communications Systems (ISPACS), pp. 770–774 (2013)

6. Kountouris, M., Gesbert, D.: Memory-based opportunistic multi-user beamforming. In: Proceeding of IEEE International Symposium on Information Theory (ISIT), September 2005
7. Chen, X., Benjebbour, A., Li, A.: Multi-user Proportional Fair Scheduling for Uplink Non-orthogonal Multiple Access (NOMA), pp. 1–5. VTC Spring, Seoul (2014)
8. Yan, C., Harada, A., Benjebbour, A., Lan, Y., Li, A., Jiang, H.: Receiver Design for Downlink Non-Orthogonal Multiple Access (NOMA), pp. 1–6. VTC Spring, Seoul (2015)
9. Choi, J.: H-ARQ based non-orthogonal multiple access with successive interference cancellation. In: IEEE GLOBECOM, New Orleans, LO, pp. 1–5 (2008)
10. Higuchi, K., Kishiyama, Y.: Non-orthogonal access with random beamforming and intra-beam SIC for cellular MIMO downlink. In: 2013 IEEE 78th Vehicular Technology Conference (VTC Fall), Las Vegas, NV, pp. 1–5 (2013)
11. Saito, Y., Benjebbour, A., Kishiyama, Y., Nakamura, T.: System-level performance of downlink non-orthogonal multiple access (NOMA) under various environments. In: 2015 IEEE 81st Vehicular Technology Conference, Glasgow, pp. 1–5 (2015)
12. Yang, S., Chen, P., Liang, L., Bi, Q., Yang, F.: System design and performance evaluation for power domain non-orthogonal multiple access. In: 2015 IEEE/CIC International Conference on Communications in China, Shenzhen, China, pp. 1–5 (2015)
13. 3GPP TR 36.859 V13.0.0: Study on Downlink Multiuser Superposition Transmission (MUST) for LTE, December 2015
14. Tu, F.: Research on the key technologies of multiple antennas communication between multiple nodes, BUPT (2015)
15. Report ITU-R M.2135: Guidelines for evaluation of radio interface technologies for IMT-Advanced (2008)

# Hybrid Interleaved-PTS Scheme for PAPR Reduction in OFDM Systems

Lingyin Wang[(⊠)]

School of Information Science and Engineering,
University of Jinan, Jinan 250022, China
andrewandpipi@hotmail.com

**Abstract.** As one of the main shortcomings in orthogonal frequency division multiplexing (OFDM) systems, large peak-to-average power ratio (PAPR) induces system performance degradation. To improve this problem, partial transmit sequence (PTS) is one of the most promising PAPR reduction schemes, but it requires a complicated phase weighting process which results in large computational complexity. In this paper, a hybrid interleaved-PTS PAPR reduction scheme in OFDM systems is proposed. In proposed hybrid interleaved-PTS scheme, alternate optimization and block interleaving are employed for reducing computational complexity and improving PAPR reduction performance respectively. With the extensive computer simulations and analysis, the proposed hybrid interleaved-PTS scheme can achieve dramatic reduction in computational complexity and similar PAPR reduction performance compared with conventional PTS (C-PTS).

**Keywords:** OFDM · PAPR reduction · PTS · Interleaving · Computational complexity

## 1  Introduction

As an attractive multicarrier modulation, orthogonal frequency division multiplexing (OFDM) meets the demand of high data rate [1] and has been adopted in many fields of wireless communications [2]. However, OFDM systems suffer from system performance degradation because of its high OFDM signal peaks which is usually described by peak-to-average power ratio (PAPR).

Recently, for the sake of improving PAPR performance of OFDM systems, some PAPR reduction schemes have been presented [3,4], such as precoding [5], companding [6], clipping and filtering [7,8], adaptive all-pass filters [9], selected mapping [10,11], partial transmit sequence [12,13], constellation shaping [14] and so on. Partial transmit sequence (PTS) falls into one category and can be viewed as the linear PAPR reduction scheme with good PAPR property. However, in order to find the optimal OFDM candidate sequence, a complicated phase weighting process for all the subblock sequences must be introduced. To alleviate the computational complexity problem of conventional PTS (C-PTS),

© ICST Institute for Computer Sciences, Social Informatics and Telecommunications Engineering 2018
Q. Chen et al. (Eds.): ChinaCom 2016, Part I, LNICST 209, pp. 370–379, 2018.
DOI: 10.1007/978-3-319-66625-9_36

some extensions of PTS have been presented. In [13], an alternate optimized PTS (AO-PTS) is given for reducing computational complexity. Different from C-PTS, only half of the subblock sequences in AO-PTS are involved in the phase weighting process. By doing this, though the reduction in computational complexity can be obtained, the loss of PAPR reduction performance cannot be avoided due to the fact that the number of generated candidate sequences is decreased compared with C-PTS.

In this paper, a hybrid interleaved-PTS PAPR reduction scheme for OFDM systems is proposed. In proposed hybrid interleaved-PTS scheme, alternate optimization and block interleaving are incorporated, where the use of alternate optimization can achieve significant reduction in computational complexity and the interleaving for the first subblock sequence is employed for improving PAPR reduction performance. After the extensive computer simulations are done, the proposed hybrid interleaved-PTS scheme can achieve dramatic reduction in computational complexity and similar PAPR reduction performance compared with C-PTS.

The rest of this paper is organized as follows. In Sect. 2, the corresponding background is described, including the OFDM system model, the definition of PAPR and the measurement of PAPR reduction performance. Section 3 gives conventional PTS scheme for PAPR reduction in OFDM systems. Section 4 introduces proposed hybrid interleaved-PTS scheme and its computational complexity is discussed. In Sect. 5, massive computer simulation results and the corresponding performance analysis are given. In the end, a brief conclusion is done in Sect. 6.

## 2   Background

The input bit stream is firstly mapped by $M$-ary phase shift keying ($M$-PSK) or $M$-ary quadrature amplitude modulation ($M$-QAM). Then, the obtained complex symbols are combined into a sequence $\boldsymbol{X} = [X_0, X_1, \cdots, X_{N-1}]$ and the OFDM signal can be obtained by transmitting this sequence into an OFDM system with $N$ subcarriers.

For the discrete-time OFDM signal, the $n$th sample $x_n$ can be described by

$$x_n = \frac{1}{\sqrt{N}} \sum_{k=0}^{N-1} X_k e^{j2\pi kn/N}, 0 \leq n \leq N - 1 \tag{1}$$

where $X_k$ denotes complex symbol carried by the $k$th subcarrier and $j = \sqrt{-1}$.

In OFDM systems, PAPR is defined by the ratio of the peak power to the average power of an OFDM signal, given by

$$\text{PAPR}(\boldsymbol{x}) = 10\log_{10} \frac{\max_{0 \leq n \leq N-1}\{|x_n|^2\}}{E\{|\boldsymbol{x}|^2\}} \text{dB} \tag{2}$$

where $max\{\cdot\}$ and $E\{\cdot\}$ represent the maximum operator and the mathematical expectation operator respectively and $\boldsymbol{x} = [x_0, x_1, \cdots, x_{N-1}]$.

By employing complementary cumulative distribution function (CCDF) [15], PAPR reduction performance can be described. The CCDF gives the probability that a number of OFDM signals exceed a given PAPR threshold and can be used for evaluating PAPR reduction performance of any PAPR reduction schemes, expressed as

$$CCDF(N, PAPR_0) = Pr\{PAPR > PAPR_0\} = 1 - (1 - e^{-PAPR_0})^N \quad (3)$$

where $PAPR_0$ denotes a given PAPR threshold.

For a discrete-time OFDM signal given in Eq. (1), it can be realized by employing an $N$-point inverse fast Fourier transform (IFFT), which induces that some peak powers may be lost. To avoid this problem, the oversampling is usually adopted. It is verified that the discrete-time OFDM signal with four times oversampling (i.e., $L = 4$) can approximate the real PAPR results [16], where $L$ denotes the oversampling factor.

## 3    Conventional PTS

Firstly, after the input bit stream is mapped, the obtained complex sequence $X$ is divided into several non-overlapped subblock sequences. Here, it is assumed that $V$ is the number of subblock sequences. After the subblock partition is completed, $V$ subblock sequences can be obtained, given by $X_i, i = 1, 2, \cdots, V$. In this way, the input complex sequence $X$ can be expressed by

$$X = \sum_{i=1}^{V} X_i \quad (4)$$

Then, by employing phase weighting factors for all the subblock sequences, the weighted subblock sequences can be combined to generate a candidate sequence, given by

$$x' = IFFT\left\{\sum_{i=1}^{V} b_i X_i\right\} = \sum_{i=1}^{V} b_i \cdot IFFT\{X_i\} = \sum_{i=1}^{V} b_i x_i \quad (5)$$

where $x'$, $x_i$ and $b_i$ denote a candidate sequence, the $i$th subblock sequence in the time domain and the phase factor for weighting the $i$th subblock sequence respectively.

For C-PTS scheme, the phase weighting factor for the first subblock can be set to be one without any PAPR performance loss. Thus, if $W$ phase weighting factors are allowed for weighting $V$ subblock sequences, $W^{V-1}$ candidate sequences can be achieved. Finally, the minimum PAPR value candidate sequence is chosen for transmitting. The block diagram of C-PTS scheme is shown in Fig. 1.

In the original OFDM system, for one input data sequence, only one candidate sequence is arguably generated and its CCDF can be expressed by Eq. (3). But for PTS scheme, $W^{V-1}$ different candidate sequences can be obtained, then

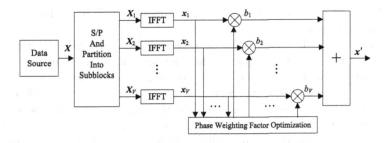

**Fig. 1.** Block diagram of conventional PTS

the CCDF of the chosen candidate sequence with the threshold $PAPR_0$ will become $[\Pr(PAPR > PAPR_0)]^{W^{V-1}}$. Obviously, by employing the PTS scheme, the probability of the PAPR exceeding some threshold $PAPR_0$ is lowered. That is to say, PAPR reduction performance of PTS scheme is decided by the number of generated candidate sequences. Assume that $C$ is the number of candidate sequences, the CCDF of PTS can be given by

$$\begin{aligned}
CCDF_{PTS} &= [\Pr(PAPR > PAPR_0)]^{C} \\
&= \left[1 - (1 - e^{-PAPR_0})^{N}\right]^{C}
\end{aligned} \quad (6)$$

In addition, for the sake of recovering the original input data correctly, the side information is required. By achieving this information, the receiver could know which allowed phase weighting factors has been used for weighting sub-block sequences. In pratical applications, the side information is transmitted accompanying with the selected OFDM candidate sequence.

## 4 Hybrid Interleaved-PTS

### 4.1 Ideas of Proposed Hybrid Interleaved-PTS Scheme

In proposed hybrid interleaved-PTS scheme, the alternate optimization is firstly adopted for simplifying phase weighting process of subblock sequences. As for the alternate optimization, it means that only the even subblock sequences need to be weighted by the allowed phase weighting factors and the odd ones remain unchanged. In this way, compared with C-PTS, the subblock phase weighting process is simplified and the significant reduction in computational complexity can be achieved. It is due to the fact that the number of candidate sequences is decreased when the alternate optimization is adopted. But for the same reason, PAPR reduction performance of proposed scheme is degraded.

After alternate optimization is completed, the number of candidate sequences generated at this stage can be given as follows.

$$\begin{cases} W^{\frac{V}{2}} & V \text{ is even} \\ W^{\frac{V-1}{2}} & V \text{ is odd} \end{cases} \quad (7)$$

where $V$ denotes the number of subblock sequences and $W$ is the number of allowed phase weighting factors.

To improve PAPR reduction performance of proposed hybrid interleaved-PTS, block interleaving is employed for the first subblock sequence. Specifically speaking, the first subblock sequence is partitioned into several blocks and then all the blocks can be permuted by using periodic or random order to generate different sequences. Assume that the original first subblock sequence in the time domain is expressed by $\boldsymbol{x}_1 = [x_{1,0}, x_{1,1}, \cdots, x_{1,i}, \cdots]$, where $x_{1,i}$ denotes the $i$th block in the first subblock sequence. After the permutation of all the blocks is performed, the original first subblock sequence becomes $\boldsymbol{x}_1' = [x_{1,\theta(0)}, x_{1,\theta(1)}, \cdots, x_{1,\theta(i)}, \cdots]$, where $\{i\} \rightarrow \{\theta(i)\}$ is the one-to-one mapping. After the permutation is performed once, the first subblock sequence is changed. Thereupon, all the weighted even subblock sequences can be utilized again to obtain new candidate sequences. By doing this, PAPR reduction performance of proposed hybrid interleaved-PTS can be improved due to the fact that the number of candidate sequences is increased. It is worth mentioning that in the process of generating the new candidate sequences, no complex multiplication is required and only complex additions are needed for obtaining these candidate sequences, given as

$$\boldsymbol{y}' = \boldsymbol{y} - \boldsymbol{x}_1 + \boldsymbol{x}_1' \tag{8}$$

where $\boldsymbol{y}'$, $\boldsymbol{y}$, $\boldsymbol{x}_1$ and $\boldsymbol{x}_1'$ denote a new candidate sequence, the candidate sequence from the stage of alternate optimization, the original first subblock sequence and the interleaved first subblock sequence respectively.

As mentioned above, the candidate sequences in proposed hybrid interleaved-PTS scheme are achieved by two stages, i.e., the alternate optimization and the block interleaving for the first subblock sequence. Finally, the one with the minimum PAPR among all the candidate sequences from two stages is chosen for transmission. The block diagram of proposed hybrid interleaved-PTS scheme is shown in Fig. 2.

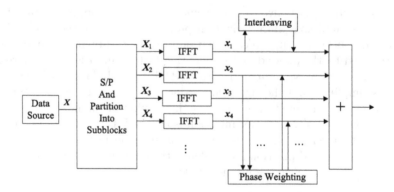

**Fig. 2.** Block diagram of proposed hybrid interleaved-PTS

For easily understanding the proposed hybrid interleaved-PTS scheme, the set of allowed phase weighting factors $\{j, -j\}$ (i.e. $W = 2$) and the number of subblock sequences $V = 4$ are taken as an example. In such conditions, eight candidate sequences cound be obtained in C-PTS. Thus, for proposed hybrid interleaved-PTS scheme, if the similar PAPR reduction performance is expected, the same number of candidate sequences must be achieved. The detailed process of proposed scheme is given as follows. Firstly, the alternate optimization is performed. Because only the even subblock sequences need to be weighted, the phase weighting factors for the odd ones are set to be one. At this stage, four phase weighting sequences can be obtained, given by

$$[1, j, 1, j], [1, -j, 1, j], [1, j, 1, -j], [1, -j, 1, -j]$$

That is to say, at the stage of alternate optimization, four candidate sequences $\boldsymbol{y}_i, i = 1, 2, 3, 4$ can be generated by using the above phase weighting sequences. To obtain the same number of candidate sequences as C-PTS, another four candidate sequences must be generated. Thereupon, the block interleaving for the first subblock sequence is employed. Here, two blocks obtained by partitioning the first subblock sequence are sufficient, i.e. $\boldsymbol{x}_1 = [\boldsymbol{x}_{1,1}, \boldsymbol{x}_{1,2}]$. Then, by permuting these two blocks in the first subblock sequence one time and utilizing all the weighted even subblock sequences again, four new candidate sequences can be obtained on the basis of Eq. (8), given by

$$\boldsymbol{y}_i = \boldsymbol{y}_{i-4} - \boldsymbol{x}_1 + \boldsymbol{x}_1', i = 5, 6, 7, 8 \tag{9}$$

where $\boldsymbol{x}_1' = [\boldsymbol{x}_{1,2}, \boldsymbol{x}_{1,1}]$ denotes the permuted first subblock sequence.

Thus, for proposed hybrid interleaved-PTS scheme, eight candidate sequences can be achieved by two stages. Since the proposed hybrid interleave-PTS scheme gets the same number of candidate sequences as C-PTS, these two schemes have similar PAPR reduction performance.

Moreover, in order to recovery the original input data successfully, the side information is also required in proposed hybrid interleaved-PTS scheme. Just as C-PTS, the same side information transmission method is adopted in proposed scheme.

## 4.2   Computational Complexity Analysis

Compared with C-PTS scheme, the subblock phase weighting process and the generation of parts of candidate sequences in proposed hybrid interleaved-PTS are different. For a fair comparison, it is assumed that the same number of candidate sequences is generated in both proposed hybrid interleaved-PTS and C-PTS. For these two schemes, if the number of subblock sequences is same, the same number of IFFT operations will be required. Therefore, in this section, the number of operations adopted in the subblock phase weighting process and the generation of candidate sequences is only taken into account. For OFDM systems, assume that $L$ times oversampling is adopted, where $L$ is the oversampling factor.

As mentioned above, for the given the number of subblocks sequences $V$ and the number of allowed phase weighting factors $W$, $W^{V-1}$ candidate sequences can be obtained in C-PTS. For C-PTS, $LN(V-1)$ complex additions and $LN(V-1)$ complex multiplications are required for generating each candidate sequence. Thus, in order to obtain all the $W^{V-1}$ candidate sequences, $LN(V-1)W^{V-1}$ complex multiplications and $LN(V-1)W^{V-1}$ complex additions are required in C-PTS.

For proposed hybrid interleaved-PTS scheme, the candidate sequences involve two parts. The first part is achieved at the stage of alternate optimization and the number of candidate sequences in this part can be seen according to Eq. (7). The second part is achieved at the stage of the block interleaving for the first subblock sequence and it should be noted that only complex additions are required for obtaining the candidate sequences in this part. It is due to the fact that for the candidate sequences in the second part, no phase weighting process is involved.

As for the candidate sequences from the first part, because only the even subblock sequences need to be weighted by the allowed phase weighting factors, the number of complex multiplications needed for generating each candidate sequence can be given by

$$\begin{cases} \frac{V}{2}LN & V \text{ is even} \\ \frac{V-1}{2}LN & V \text{ is odd} \end{cases} \tag{10}$$

At the stage of the block interleaving for the first subblock sequence, because no complex multiplication is involved, only complex additions are needed for generating candidate sequences. In terms of Eq. (9), each candidate sequence in the second part requires $2LN$ complex additions.

Thus, computational complexity of proposed hybrid interleaved-PTS can be given as follows.

$$\text{Complex Mul.} : \begin{cases} \frac{V}{2}LNW^{\frac{V}{2}} & V \text{ is even} \\ \frac{V-1}{2}LNW^{\frac{V-1}{2}} & V \text{ is odd} \end{cases} \tag{11}$$

$$\text{Complex Add.} : \begin{cases} \left[(V-3)W^{\frac{V}{2}} + 2W^{V-1}\right]LN & V \text{ is even} \\ \left[(V-3)W^{\frac{V-1}{2}} + 2W^{V-1}\right]LN & V \text{ is odd} \end{cases} \tag{12}$$

## 5    Simulation Results and Analysis

To show the PAPR reduction performance of proposed hybrid interleaved-PTS scheme, the corresponding computer simulations are done. An OFDM system with 256 subcarriers (i.e., $N = 256$) is adopted. In simulations, the set of phase weighting factors $\{j, -j\}$ (i.e., $W = 2$) is used for performing the subblock phase weighting process. Moreover, to approach the real PAPR reduction performance, the oversampling factor $L = 4$ is employed.

Figure 3 gives PAPR reduction performance of proposed hybrid interleaved-PTS employing QPSK modulation with the number of subblock sequences $V = 4, 8$. For a comparison, PAPR reduction performances of AO-PTS and C-PTS are also given in Fig. 3. For each value of $V$, the number of candidate sequences in proposed hybrid interleaved-PTS is the same as that in C-PTS.

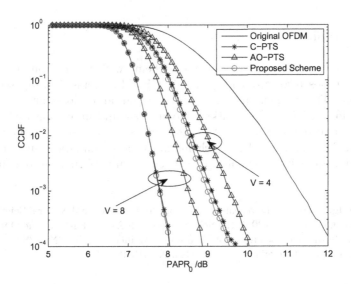

**Fig. 3.** CCDFs of proposed hybrid interleaved-PTS, AO-PTS and C-PTS

It is shown in Fig. 3 that the CCDF curves of the proposed hybrid interleaved-PTS scheme and C-PTS scheme are almost overlapped, which means that these two schemes have similar PAPR reduction performance. But for AO-PTS scheme, its PAPR reduction performance is much worse than those of C-PTS scheme and proposed hybrid interleaved-PTS scheme, which is due to the fact that among these three schemes, the number of candidate sequences generated in AO-PTS is the least.

As to computational complexity, a comparison between proposed hybrid interleaved-PTS and C-PTS in terms of complex multiplication and complex addition is shown in Table 1.

**Table 1.** Comparison of complexity between proposed hybrid interleaved-PTS and C-PTS

| $W$ | $V$ | Complex Mul. (%) | Complex Add. (%) |
|---|---|---|---|
| 2 | 4 | 66.7 | 16.7 |
| 2 | 8 | 92.9 | 62.5 |

As we can see in Table 1, proposed hybrid interleaved-PTS gains lower computational complexity than C-PTS. For instance, if $W = 2$ and $V = 8$, 92.9% complex multiplication reduction and 62.5% complex addition reduction can be achieved. Moreover, if an increase in the number of subblock sequences is shown, proposed hybrid interleaved-PTS could gain more reduction in computational complexity.

# 6   Conclusion

In this paper, a hybrid interleaved-PTS scheme with low computational complexity is proposed for reducing PAPR in OFDM systems. In proposed hybrid interleaved-PTS scheme, alternate optimization and block interleaving are employed for reducing computational complexity and improving PAPR reduction performance respectively. With the extensive computer simulations, the proposed hybrid interleaved-PTS scheme can achieve dramatic reduction in computational complexity and similar PAPR reduction performance compared with C-PTS.

**Acknowledgements.** The research was supported by National Natural Science Foundation of China (No. 61501204), the Science Research Award Fund for the Outstanding Young and Middle-aged Scientists of Shandong Province of China (No. BS2013DX014), the Doctor Fund of University of Jinan (No. XBS1309).

# References

1. Prasad, R.: OFDM for Wireless Multimedia Communications. Artech House, Boston (2004)
2. Hwang, T., Yang, C., Wu, G., Li, S., Lee, G.Y.: OFDM and its wireless application: a survey. IEEE Trans. Veh. Technol. **58**(4), 1673–1694 (2009)
3. Han, S.H., Lee, J.H.: An overview of peak-to-average power ratio reduction techniques for multicarrier transmission. IEEE Wirel. Commun. **12**(2), 56–65 (2005)
4. Jiang, T., Wu, Y.: An overview: peak-to-average power ratio reduction techniques for OFDM signals. IEEE Trans. Broadcast. **54**(2), 257–268 (2008)
5. Hao, M.-J., Lai, C.-H.: Precoding for PAPR reduction of OFDM signals with minimum error probability. IEEE Trans. Broadcast. **56**(1), 120–128 (2010)
6. Mazahir, S., Sheikh, S.A.: An adaptive companding scheme for peak-to-average power ratio reduction in OFDM systems. KSII Trans. Internet Inf. Syst. **9**(12), 4872–4891 (2015)
7. Zhu, X., Pan, W., Li, H., Tang, Y.: Simplified approach to optimized iterative clipping and filtering for PAPR reduction of OFDM signals. IEEE Trans. Commun. **61**(5), 1891–1901 (2013)
8. Sohn, I., Kim, S.C.: Neural network based simplified clipping and filtering technique for PAPR reduction of OFDM signals. IEEE Commun. Lett. **19**(8), 1438–1441 (2015)
9. Hong, E., Har, D.: Peak-to-average power ratio reduction for MISO OFDM systems with adaptive all-pass filters. IEEE Trans. Wirel. Commun. **10**(10), 3163–3167 (2011)

10. Bauml, R.W., Fischer, R.F.H., Huber, J.B.: Reducing the peak-to-average power ratio of multicarrier modulation by selective mapping. Electron. Lett. **32**(22), 2056–2057 (1996)

11. Wang, L., Liu, J.: Partial phase weighting selected mapping scheme for peak-to-average power ratio reduction in orthogonal frequency division multiplexing system. IET Commun. **9**(2), 147–155 (2015)

12. Muller, S.H., Huber, J.B.: OFDM with reduced peak-to-average power ratio by optimum combination of partial transmit sequences. Electron. Lett. **33**(5), 368–369 (1997)

13. Jayalath, A.D.S., Tellambura, C., Wu, H.: Reduced complexity PTS and new phase sequences for SLM to reduce PAP of an OFDM signal. In: Vehicular Technology Conference (VTC), Tokyo, Japan, vol. 3, pp. 1914–1917 (2000)

14. Laroia, R., Farnardin, N., Tretter, S.: On optimal shaping of multidimensional constellations. IEEE Trans. Inf. Theory **40**(4), 1044–1056 (1994)

15. Jiang, T., Guizani, M., Chen, H.-H., Xiang, W., Wu, Y.: Derivation of PAPR distribution for OFDM wireless systems based on extreme value theory. IEEE Trans. Wirel. Commun. **7**(4), 1298–1305 (2008)

16. Tellambura, C.: Computation of the continuous-time PAR of an OFDM signal with BPSK subcarriers. IEEE Commun. Lett. **5**(5), 185–187 (2001)

# Coverage Probability and Data Rate of D2D Communication Under Cellular Networks by Sharing Uplink Channel

Tianyu Zhang, Jian Sun, Xianxian Wang, and Zhongshan Zhang[(✉)]

University of Science and Technology Beijing, Beijing 100083, China
ztyvip@126.com, sj103063@163.com, zhangzs@ustb.edu.cn

**Abstract.** The device-to-device (D2D) communication has been regarded as a promising technique to effectively upgrade the existing cellular network. Despite the intriguing perspectives of D2D technique, the performance of D2D-aided cellular network may degrade owing to the severe interference imposed by newly introduced D2D links. With a motive to deal with this problem, the key performance parameters of D2D-aided underlaying cellular networks, including the coverage probability and total data rate have been investigated. Firstly, we analyze the expressions of coverage probability for both the conventional cellular links and the D2D links, and then we give out the approximate expression of the ergodic rate for both individual links and that of the whole underlaying system. After that, in order to optimize the performance of the system in terms of throughput, more parameters closely related to the channel capacity are studied. Finally, the simulation results revealed that the best values for key parameters (e.g. the density of D2D users) are attainable, and the total data rate can been greatly improved according to our proposed strategies.

## 1 Introduction

With the booming of smart devices, the mobile traffics have been through a tremendous growing trend. Since the existing standards and mechanisms can no longer efficiently support the ever-growing traffic demands of customers, buttons for effective countermeasures need to be pressing imminently. Meanwhile, heavy burden of base stations (BSs) should be relieved substantially by offloading the mobile traffics from BS side to the terminal side [1,2].

Device-to-device (D2D) communication has been regarded as a newly introduced supplementary technique for cellular communication owing to its great capabilities of significantly improving the spectral efficiency of wireless networks [3,4]. Since a so called "D2D pair" has plenty of merits over the conventional cellular networks (CNs), including extending the radio coverage and supporting a variety of proximity mobile services [5,6]. However, since the same licensed spectrum is shared by the D2D users (DUs) and conventional Cellular Users (CUs) during D2D transmission, a severe interference to the CUs may affect the transmitting performance when the D2D transmitter (DT) and CUs are coexisting [7,8].

© ICST Institute for Computer Sciences, Social Informatics and Telecommunications Engineering 2018
Q. Chen et al. (Eds.): ChinaCom 2016, Part I, LNICST 209, pp. 380–389, 2018.
DOI: 10.1007/978-3-319-66625-9_37

To address the above-mentioned issues, interference-management schemes and power control policy should be studied [8–10]. In particular, it is also necessary to take the other important factors (for example, the location and number of D2D pairs) into account when we implement D2D-aided underlaying CNs.

In [11], the author proposed an expression for the coverage probability of the CUs based on the Poisson point process (PPP). Besides, in [12], the authors introduced a model concerning signal-to-interference-plus-noise ratio (SINR) in multi-cell systems. However, both the authors of [11,12] did not analyze the impact on the distribution of co-cell CUs, which is critical for a constantly changing network.

In this paper, we studied the coverage probability and the total data rate of the D2D aided cellular systems. We assume that $K$ D2D pairs share the same radio resource with $M$ CUs according to PPP model. The main contributions of this paper include the following: (1) analyzing the approximate expressions for the average coverage probabilities and the total data rate of both the CUs and the D2D pairs; (2) investigating the best performance of the hybrid network; and (3) optimizing the total data rate of the D2D-aided underlaying CNs through simulations by fine-tuning the crucial parameters, including the density of DUs, the scaling factor (between D2D and cellular links) and the total number of users and the maximum number of users (including CUs and DUs).

The framework of the paper is as follows. Section 2 introduces the system model of D2D aided cellular system. In Sect. 3, we derived the expressions of coverage probability for the cellular and D2D links. And the total data rate is studied in Sect. 4. And then, the numerical results are analyzed in Sect. 5. Finally, Sect. 6 draws the conclusion of the paper.

## 2    System Model

In Fig. 1, we consider a single cell in which the BS located at the center with a radius of $R$. We assume that there are $M$ CUs and $K$ D2D pairs in the system model, and D2D pairs will share the same licensed uplink spectrum resources with CUs. Moreover, within the cell coverage, we assume that all the $M$ CUs are distributed according to a homogeneous PPP $\Phi_1$ model with the density of $\lambda_c$. Similarly, all the $K$ DTs are set to be placed according to a homogeneous PPP $\Phi_2$ model with the density of $\lambda_d$ in the cell. In addition, the DT-DR interval (i.e. $d_{TR}$) is set to be time-invariant. Finally, each D2D pair is perceived as a single point under a large-cellular-coverage environment. The number of CUs (or DTs) in a cell can be modelled as a Poisson distributed random variable, and with the mean of $\mathbb{E}[K] = \lambda_d \pi R^2$ ($\mathbb{E}[M] = \lambda_c \pi R^2$).

In the following, a normal situation is considered, i.e. both the inter-CU and inter-DU interference exist, with non-zero the interference of CU-DU observed at the same time. All the above-mentioned interferences are illustrated in Fig. 1. Under this circumstance, three primary interference sources exist, including the interference applied on the DR by CUs, the interference applied on the DR by the geographically close-by DTs, and the interference applied on the BS by the DTs.

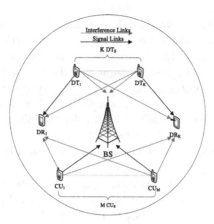

**Fig. 1.** The system model of the D2D aided cellular system, and each cell provided the services to all users (i.e. CUs and DUs), and DUs share the same uplink resource with CUs.

For a given cell, the received signal at the BS can be rewritten as

$$y_{BS_0} = \sum_{k=1}^{M} \sqrt{cd_{C_k,BS}^{-\alpha} P_{C_k}} \cdot h_{C_k,BS} \cdot s_{C_k}$$

$$+ \sum_{i=1}^{K} \sqrt{cd_{DT_i,BS}^{-\alpha} P_{DT_i}} \cdot h_{DT_i,BS} \cdot s_{DT_i} + N, \tag{1}$$

where we let $P_{C_k}$ denote the transmit power of the $k$-th CU, and $P_{DT_i}$ denote the transmit power of the $i$-th DT, and $d_{C_k,BS}$ ($d_{DT_i,BS}$) represents the interval between the $k$-th CU (the $i$-th DT) and the BS. Furthermore, $h_{C_k,BS}$ ($h_{DT_i,BS}$) denotes the channel coefficient of the $k$-th CU (the $i$-th DT) to the BS with a distribution of $\mathcal{CN}(0,\mu)$. Besides, $c$ and $\alpha$ denote the path loss constant and the path loss exponent, respectively, and $s_{C_k}$ and $s_{DT_i}$ denote the transmit signals of the $k$-th CU and the $i$-th DT, respectively. Moreover, $E\left\{|s|^2\right\} = 1$ is satisfied, and, $N$ denotes the variance of the additive white Gaussian noise (AWGN) at the receiver with a distribution of $\mathcal{CN}(0,\sigma^2)$.

As a result, the received signals at the $j$-DR can be rewritten as

$$y_{DR_j} = \sum_{k=1}^{M} \sqrt{cd_{C_k,DR_j}^{-\alpha} P_{C_k}} \cdot h_{C_k,DR_j} \cdot s_{C_k}$$

$$+ \sum_{i=1}^{K} \sqrt{cd_{DT_i,DR_j}^{-\alpha} P_{DT_i}} \cdot h_{DT_i,DR_j} \cdot s_{DT_i} + N, \tag{2}$$

where $d_{C_k,DR_j}$ denotes the interval between the $j$-th DR and the $k$-th CU, $d_{DT_i,DR_j}$ denotes the interval between the $j$-th DR and the $i$-th DT, respectively.

Moreover, $h_{C_k,DR_j}$ represents the channel coefficients of the $k$-th CU to the $j$-th DR, $h_{DT_i,DR_j}$ represents the channel coefficients of the $j$-th DR to the $i$-th DT, respectively, under the distribution following $\mathcal{CN}(0,\mu)$.

We apply subscript 0 and $k(l)$ represent the BS and the $k(l)$-th CU, and we apply subscript $i(j)$ denote the $i$-th DT (the $j$-th DR). For instance, we let $d_{i,j}$ instead of $d_{DT_i,DR_j}$ denote the interval between the $i$-th DT and the $j$-th DR. According to the above-mentioned models, the SINR of the CU and the $j$-th DR can be expressed as

$$\text{SINR}_k = \frac{P_k d_{k,0}^{-\alpha}|h_{k,0}|^2}{\sum\limits_{i=1}^{K} P_i d_{i,0}^{-\alpha}|h_{i,0}|^2 + \sum\limits_{\substack{l=1 \\ l \neq k}}^{M} P_l d_{l,0}^{-\alpha}|h_{l,0}|^2 + \sigma^2},$$

$$\text{at the BS} \qquad (3a)$$

$$\text{SINR}_j = \frac{P_i d_{i,j}^{-\alpha}|h_{i,j}|^2}{\sum\limits_{k=1}^{M} P_k d_{k,j}^{-\alpha}|h_{k,j}|^2 + \sum\limits_{\substack{i=1 \\ i \neq j}}^{K} P_i d_{i,j}^{-\alpha}|h_{i,j}|^2 + \sigma^2},$$

$$\text{at the DR.} \qquad (3b)$$

## 3    Analysis of Coverage Probability

In this section, we will discuss the coverage probability of the cellular links and the D2D links, and derive the approximate expression of each link, where all CUs and D2D pairs are functioning synchronously. Without loss of generality, the DT-DR interval (i.e. $d_{TR}$) is set to be time-invariant.

### 3.1    Coverage Probability for Cellular Links

According to the aforementioned assumptions and the realizations of the PPP $\Phi_1$ and $\Phi_2$, for a established SINR threshold (at BS) at the $k$-th CU (i.e. $\beta_c$), the average uplink coverage probability can then be written as

$$P_{\text{cov}}^{\text{CU}}(\beta_c, \lambda, \alpha) = \mathbb{E}\left[\mathbb{P}\left\{\text{SINR}_k > \beta_c\right\}\right], \qquad (4)$$

with

$$\mathbb{P}\{d_{TR} > \beta_c\}$$

$$= \mathbb{P}\left\{\frac{P_k d_{k,0}^{-\alpha}|h_{k,0}|^2}{\sum\limits_{i \in \phi_2} P_i d_{i,0}^{-\alpha}|h_{i,0}|^2 + \sum\limits_{l \in \phi_1 \setminus \{k\}} P_l d_{l,0}^{-\alpha}|h_{l,0}|^2 + \sigma^2} > \beta_c\right\}$$

$$= \exp\left(-\frac{\mu \beta_c d_{k,0}^{\alpha} \sigma^2}{P_k}\right) L_{I_d}\left(\frac{\mu \beta_c d_{k,0}^{\alpha}}{P_k}\right) L_{I_c}\left(\frac{\mu \beta_c d_{k,0}^{\alpha}}{P_k}\right), \qquad (5)$$

where $I_d = \sum\limits_{i \in \phi_2} P_i d_{i,0}^{-\alpha} |h_{i,0}|^2$, $I_c = \sum\limits_{l \in \phi_1 \backslash \{k\}}^{M} P_l d_{l,0}^{-\alpha} |h_{l,0}|^2$, $s = \dfrac{\mu \beta_c d_{k,0}^\alpha}{P_k}$, and $\mathcal{L}_{I_d}(s)$

and $\mathcal{L}_{I_c}(s)$ denote the Laplace transformation of random variables(i.e. $I_d$ and $I_c$ evaluated at $s$, respectively). Moreover, the expression $\mathcal{L}_{I_d}(s)$ is shown to be

$$
\begin{aligned}
\mathcal{L}_{I_d}(s) &= \mathbb{E}\left[\exp\left(-s \sum_{i \in \phi_2} P_i d_{i,0}^{-\alpha} |h_{i,0}|^2\right)\right] \\
&= \exp\left[-\frac{2\pi \lambda_d}{\alpha}\left(\frac{\mu \beta_c P_i}{P_k}\right)^{\frac{2}{\alpha}} \Gamma\left(\frac{2}{\alpha}\right)\Gamma\left(1-\frac{2}{\alpha}\right) d_{k,0}^2\right],
\end{aligned} \tag{6}
$$

where $\Gamma(x)$ denotes the Gamma function with $\Gamma(x) = \int_0^\infty t^{x-1} e^{-t} dt$.

Similarly, we can derive

$$
\mathcal{L}_{I_c}(s) = \exp\left[-\frac{2\pi \lambda_c}{\alpha}\left(\frac{\mu \beta_c P_l}{P_k}\right)^{\frac{2}{\alpha}} \Gamma\left(\frac{2}{\alpha}\right)\Gamma\left(1-\frac{2}{\alpha}\right) d_{k,0}^2\right]. \tag{7}
$$

By substituting (6) and (7) into (5) and using the Euler's Formula $\Gamma(1-x)\Gamma(x) = \dfrac{\pi}{\sin \pi x}$, the cellular links' coverage probability can be written as

$$
P_{\text{cov}}^{\text{CUE}}(\beta_c, \lambda, \alpha) = \int_0^R e^{-ar^\alpha - br^2 - cr^2} f_r(r) dr, \tag{8}
$$

where $a = \dfrac{\beta_c \sigma^2}{P_k}$, $b = \dfrac{2\pi^2 \lambda_d}{\alpha \sin(2\pi/\alpha)}\left(\dfrac{\mu \beta_c P_i}{P_k}\right)^{\frac{2}{\alpha}}$, $c = \dfrac{2\pi^2 \lambda_c}{\alpha \sin(2\pi/\alpha)}\left(\dfrac{\mu \beta_c P_l}{P_k}\right)^{\frac{2}{\alpha}}$ and $r = d_{k,0}$.

## 3.2   Coverage Probability for D2D Links

Now we consider a D2D pair and assume that its DR is located at the origin place. We can define that the threshold at the $j$-th DR is $\beta_d$, and then the average coverage probability over the plane can be written as

$$
P_{\text{cov}}^{\text{D2D}}(\beta_d, \lambda, \alpha) = \mathbb{E}\left[\mathbb{P}\{\text{SINR}_j > \beta_d\}\right], \tag{9}
$$

where

$$
\begin{aligned}
\mathbb{P}\{\text{SINR}_j > \beta_d\} &= \mathbb{P}\left\{\frac{P_j d_{TR}^{-\alpha} |h_{i,i}|^2}{I_c + I'_d + \sigma^2} > \beta_d\right\} \\
&= \exp\left(-\frac{\mu \beta_d d_{TR}^\alpha \sigma^2}{P_j}\right) L_{I'_c}(s') L_{I'_d}(s'), 
\end{aligned} \tag{10}
$$

with $I'_c = \sum_{k \in \phi_1} P_k d^{-\alpha}_{k,j} |h_{k,j}|^2$, $I'_d = \sum_{i \in \phi_2 \setminus \{j\}}^{N} P_i d^{-\alpha}_{i,j} |h_{i,j}|^2$ and $s' = \dfrac{\mu \beta_d d^{\alpha}_{TR}}{P_j}$.

Similar to (6), the expressions of $\mathcal{L}_{I'_c}(s')$ and $\mathcal{L}_{I'_d}(s')$ can be given by

$$\mathcal{L}_{I'_c}(s') = \exp \left[ -\frac{2\pi \lambda_c}{\alpha} \left( \frac{\mu \beta_d d^{\alpha}_{TR} P_k}{P_j} \right)^{\frac{2}{\alpha}} \Gamma \left( \frac{2}{\alpha} \right) \Gamma \left( 1 - \frac{2}{\alpha} \right) \right]$$

$$= \exp \left[ \frac{2\mu \pi^2 \lambda_c}{\alpha \sin(2\pi/\alpha)} \left( \frac{\beta_d P_k}{P_i} \right)^{\frac{2}{\alpha}} \right] \tag{11}$$

and

$$\mathcal{L}_{I'_d}(s') = \exp \left[ -\frac{2\pi \lambda_d}{\alpha} \left( \frac{\mu \beta_d d^{\alpha}_{TR} P_i}{P_j} \right)^{\frac{2}{\alpha}} \Gamma \left( \frac{2}{\alpha} \right) \Gamma \left( 1 - \frac{2}{\alpha} \right) \right]$$

$$= \exp \left[ \frac{2\mu \pi^2 \lambda_d}{\alpha \sin(2\pi/\alpha)} (\beta_d)^{\frac{2}{\alpha}} \right] \tag{12}$$

where $P_j$ denotes the transmit power of the $j$-th DT.

Let us consider the case in which a time-invariant transmit power is assumed in either the DTs ($P_D$) or the CUs ($P_C$), thus the expression of the coverage probability of the typical D2D links can then be derived as

$$P^{\mathrm{D2D}}_{\mathrm{cov}} (\beta_d, \lambda, \alpha) = \mathbb{E} \left[ \mathbb{P} \left\{ \mathrm{SINR}_{DR} > \beta_d \right\} \right]$$

$$= \exp \left( -a' d^{\alpha}_{TR} - b' d^2_{TR} - c' d^2_{TR} \right), \tag{13}$$

where $a' = \left( \dfrac{\beta_d \sigma^2}{P_D} \right)$, $b' = \dfrac{2\mu \pi^2 \lambda_d}{\alpha \sin(2\pi/\alpha)} (\beta_d)^{\frac{2}{\alpha}}$, and $c' = \dfrac{2\mu \pi^2 \lambda_c}{\alpha \sin(2\pi/\alpha)} \left( \dfrac{\beta_d P_k}{P_i} \right)^{\frac{2}{\alpha}}$.

## 4    Analysis of Sum Rate

Now we give out the ergodic rate of each part in the system. And then, the total rate of system is discussed. Finally, we propose an optimization constraint to enhance the system performance by fine-tuning one important index: scale factor for the D2D pairs and controlling the number of all users at the same time.

### 4.1    Ergodic Rate of D2D and Cellular Links

From (29) in [13], the ergodic rate of D2D links can then be derived relying on the SINR distribution of the typical D2D links:

$$\bar{R}^{\mathrm{D2D}} = \int_0^{\infty} \log_2(1 + \beta_d) f_{\mathrm{SINR}}(\beta_d) d\beta_d. \tag{14}$$

Similar to (14), the ergodic rate of cellular links can be given by

$$\bar{R}^{\mathrm{CU}} = \frac{1}{\ln 2} \int_0^\infty \frac{P_{\mathrm{cov}}^{\mathrm{CU}}}{1 + \beta_c} d\beta_c. \tag{15}$$

## 4.2  Sum Rate of Hybrid Network

And according to the Shannon's theorem [14], the total rate of D2D links can be expressed as

$$
\begin{aligned}
R^{\mathrm{D2D}} &= \mathbb{E}\left[\sum_{i=1}^K \log_2\left(1 + \mathrm{SINR}_{DR}\right)\right] \\
&= \lambda_d \pi R^2 \cdot \bar{R}^{\mathrm{D2D}}.
\end{aligned} \tag{16}
$$

In the same approach, we get the total rate of cellular links as

$$R^{\mathrm{CU}} = \lambda_c \pi R^2 \cdot \bar{R}^{\mathrm{CU}}. \tag{17}$$

Based on (16) and (17),the total rate of Hybrid Network can be expressed as

$$R^{\mathrm{SUM}} = \lambda_d \pi R^2 \bar{R}^{\mathrm{D2D}} + \lambda_c \pi R^2 \bar{R}^{\mathrm{CU}}. \tag{18}$$

## 4.3  Best Model of Allocation Schemes for Hybrid Network

Based on previous analysis, the system performance cannot keep getting better unlimitedly with the increase of the number of D2D links sharing the same resources with cellular links. In order to obtain the best ratio of D2D pairs compared to total users, we define a density factor $\lambda$ for all the users sharing the same resource (i.e. there are totally $N$ users, $N = \lambda \pi R^2$), and a scale factor $\eta$ for all D2D users, indicating the proportion of D2D users out of total users (i.e. the density of D2D pairs can then be expressed as $\lambda_d = \eta\lambda$ and that of CUs can be expressed as $\lambda_c = (1 - \eta)\lambda$). In this case, the sum data rate can be rewritten as

$$R^{\mathrm{SUM}} = \eta\lambda \pi R^2 \bar{R}^{\mathrm{D2D}} + (1 - \eta)\lambda \pi R^2 \bar{R}^{\mathrm{CU}}. \tag{19}$$

When the number of CUs or D2D pairs increases, the interference applied by these additional users will be increased consequently. Based on the previous analysis, the sum data rate of hybrid network is determined by the factors $\eta$ and $\lambda$. Furthermore, in order to maximize the performance of hybrid system, the optimization functions can then be formulated as:

$$
\begin{aligned}
\max_{(\lambda, \eta)} \quad & \eta\lambda \pi R^2 \bar{R}^{\mathrm{D2D}} + (1 - \eta)\lambda \pi R^2 \bar{R}^{\mathrm{CU}} \\
s.t. \quad & P_{\mathrm{cov}}^{\mathrm{CU}} > 1 - \gamma_c \\
& P_{\mathrm{cov}}^{\mathrm{D2D}} > 1 - \gamma_d,
\end{aligned} \tag{20}
$$

where $\gamma_c$ and $\gamma_d$ denote the outage probability for cellular link and D2D link, respectively.

# 5    Numerical Analysis

In this section, we assume that there are totally $N$ user (i.e. equals $\lambda\pi R^2$), which contains $M$ (i.e. equals $(1-\eta)\lambda\pi R^2$) CUs and $K$ (i.e. equals $\eta\lambda\pi R^2$) D2D pairs. Now, we can conclude that the scale factor $\eta$ is equal to $K/N$ or $\lambda_d/\lambda$. The BS is located at the center of the cell, and the simulation parameters are set as follows. The cell radius is set to be $500\,\text{m}$, the power of cellular and that of DT are set to be $100\,\text{mw}$ and $1\,\text{mw}$, respectively (i.e.:$P_c = 100\,\text{mw}$, $P_d = 1\,\text{mw}$). We assume the interval between DT and corresponding DR is established at $50\,\text{m}$. And the $\mu = 1$; $\alpha = 4$.

In Fig. 2, the interrelationship between the total data rate $R^{\text{TOTAL}}$ and the density of DUs (i.e. $\lambda_d$) with varying CUs (i.e. $M = 2, 6, 10$) is depicted. In spite of the number of CUs/DUs, the interference will always be applied along with the increase of system capacity. For a given number of CUs, an best total rate does exist and shows with the increase of the density of DUs. Note that when the density of DUs is set to be a certain constant, the total data rate of the system will fall off as the raising of CUs. We may then draw a conclusion that the total rate can be improved by employing D2D mode, but it has a maximum limit. And when a single sub-channel is allocated only to an individual CU, the system performance is inclined to ameliorate. Therefore, by properly adjusting the density of DUs we can optimize the sum system rate effectively.

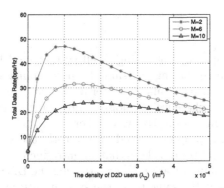

**Fig. 2.** Curves of total data rate of the system as functions of the density of DUs ($\lambda_d$) when the number of CUs ($M$) equals 2, 6 and 10, respectively.

In Fig. 3, the interrelationship between the total rate and the total number of users (i.e. $N$) is presented, provided that $\eta = 0.4, 0.8$. As is shown in the figure, for an established $\eta$, an best total rate does exist with the increase of users' density (a higher $\eta$ implying a higher total rate). Furthermore, when the condition $\bar{R}^{\text{D2D}} > \bar{R}^{\text{CU}}$ is satisfied, the total rate will then be elevated. Otherwise, if $\bar{R}^{\text{D2D}} < \bar{R}^{\text{CU}}$, the employment of D2D mode may not benefit the system, but, on the contrary, will degrade the total rate. The point of intersection A denotes the best user density for total data rate, implying that more mobile

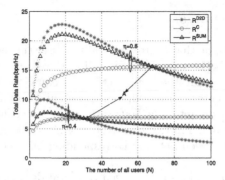

**Fig. 3.** Curves of total data rate as functions of the total number of users ($N$) when the scale factor $\eta$ equals 0.4 and 0.8, respectively.

users can be managed and served for a higher $\eta$, the reason is that the interference applied by the D2D links is much lower than that applied by the CUs. Note that when $\eta = 0.8$, the best number of users is 1.5 times that of $\eta = 0.4$. Consequently, we can ameliorate the system performance in terms of total rate can be obtained by increasing $\eta$, and the total rate can be optimized by fitly fine-tuning $\eta$ (i.e. the proportion of D2D users out of total users) in the presence of a certain given number of total users.

## 6    Conclusions

In this paper, we proposed a new single cell system model where all $M$ CUs and $N$ D2D pairs are co-sharing the same licensed uplink spectrum resources. We analyzed the system performance in terms of coverage probability and the total system rate (when there was no noise), and then gave out the approximate expressions for each link, respectively. Furthermore, the optimization strategy for hybrid network was proposed based on the total users and the scale factor of D2D pairs. Numerical results show that by introducing D2D communication underlaying cellular communication and controlling the D2D proportion and the total number of users at the same time, the system performance can be greatly improved.

**Acknowledgments.** This work was supported by the key project of the National Natural Science Foundation of China (No. 61431001) and the 5G research program of China Mobile Research Institute (Grant No. [2015] 0615). The corresponding author is Dr. Zhongshan Zhang.

## References

1. Zhang, Z., Long, K., Wang, J.: Self-organization paradigms and optimization approaches for cognitive radio technologies: a survey. IEEE Trans. Wirel. Commun. **20**(2), 36–42 (2013)

2. Zhang, Z., Long, K., Vasilakos, A.V., Hanzo, L.: Full duplex wireless communications: challenges, solutions and future research directions. Proc. IEEE **104**(7), 1369–1409 (2016)
3. Andreev, S., Pyattaev, A., Johnsson, K., Galinina, O., Koucheryavy, Y.: Cellular traffic offloading onto network-assisted device-to-device connections. IEEE Commun. Mag. **52**(4), 20–31 (2014)
4. Doppler, K., Rinne, M., Wijting, C., Ribeiro, C.B., Hugl, K.: Device-to-device communication as an underlay to LTE-advanced networks. IEEE Commun. Mag. **47**(12), 42–49 (2009)
5. Lin, X., Andrews, J., Ghosh, A., Ratasuk, R.: An overview of 3GPP device-to-device proximity services. IEEE Commun. Mag. **52**(4), 40–48 (2014)
6. Min, H., Seo, W., Lee, J., Park, S., Hong, D.: Reliability improvement using receive mode selection in the device-to-device uplink period underlaying cellular networks. IEEE Trans. Wirel. Commun. **10**(2), 413–418 (2011)
7. Min, H., Lee, J., Park, S., Hong, D.: Capacity enhancement using an interference limited area for device-to-device uplink underlaying cellular networks. IEEE Trans. Wirel. Commun. **10**(12), 3995–4000 (2011)
8. Yin, R., Yu, G., Zhang, H., Zhang, Z., Li, G.Y.: Pricing-based interference coordination for D2D communications in cellular networks. IEEE Trans. Wirel. Commun. **14**(3), 1519–1532 (2015)
9. Mumtaz, S., Huq, S., Mohammed, K., Radwan, A., Rodriguez, J., Aguiar, R.L.: Energy efficient interference-aware resource allocation in LTE-D2D communication. In: Proceedings of the IEEE International Conference on Communications (ICC), pp. 282–287. IEEE (2014)
10. Oduola, W.O., Li, X., Qian, L., Han, Z.: Power control for device-to-device communications as an underlay to cellular system. In: Proceedings of the IEEE International Conference on Communications (ICC), pp. 5257–5262. IEEE (2014)
11. Mustafa, H.A., Shakir, M.Z., Imran, M.A., Imran, A., Tafazolli, R.: Coverage gain and device-to-device user density: stochastic geometry modeling and analysis. IEEE Commun. Lett. **19**(10), 1742–1745 (2015)
12. Andrews, J.G., Baccelli, F., Ganti, R.K.: A tractable approach to coverage and rate in cellular networks. IEEE Trans. Commun. **59**(11), 3122–3134 (2011)
13. Lee, N., Lin, X., Andrews, J.G., Heath, R.: Power control for D2D underlaid cellular networks: modeling, algorithms, and analysis. IEEE J. Select. Areas Commun. **33**(1), 1–13 (2015)
14. Cover, T.M., Thomas, J.A.: Elements of Information Theory. Wiley, New York (1991)

# Optical Systems and Networks

# A Novel OFDM Scheme for VLC Systems Under LED Nonlinear Constraints

Lingkai Kong, Congcong Cao, Siyuan Zhang, Mengchao Li, Liang Wu[✉],
Zaichen Zhang, and Jian Dang

National Mobile Communications Research Laboratory, Southeast University,
Nanjing 210096, China
{konglingkai,caocongcong,zhangsiyuan,limengchao,wuliang,
zczhang,newwanda}@seu.edu.cn

**Abstract.** In this paper, a novel optical orthogonal frequency division multiplexing (O-OFDM) scheme based on real-imaginary coefficients separation is proposed for visible light communications (VLCs) to mitigate nonlinear distortion of light-emitting diodes (LEDs). In the proposed scheme, the transmitted signal in the frequency domain does not need to be Hermitian symmetric, and real and imaginary parts are separated. Signals are introduced to keep the clipped information due to the high peak to average power ratio of OFDM, and a procedure to recover the clipped information is proposed. The transmit strategy and receive algorithm of the proposed scheme are presented in detail. Simulation results show that compared with traditional O-OFDM schemes, the proposed scheme can achieve better bit error rate performance under LED nonlinear constraints and reduce the requirement for the linear dynamic range of LEDs.

**Keywords:** Optical orthogonal frequency division multiplexing (O-OFDM) · Clipped infomation · Coefficients separation · Nonlinear distortion · Light-emitting diodes (LEDs)

## 1 Introduction

Optical wireless communications which employ light-emitting diodes (LEDs) as transmitters and photodiodes (PDs) as receivers have received increasing attention in both academia and industry due to its inherent high efficiency and security [1]. Intensity modulation and direct detection (IM/DD) is the most commonly used scheme in optical wireless communications [2,3]. In IM/DD systems, the transmitted signals must be nonnegative, and most radio frequency (RF) modulation schemes cannot be directly used.

Recently, orthogonal frequency division multiplexing (OFDM) has been employed in visible light communication (VLC) systems to compat inter-symbol interference (ISI) and achieve high spectral efficiency. To statisfy the requirement in IM/DD system, a number of O-OFDM schemes have been proposed. The simplest method is direct-current biased optical orthogonal frequency division

© ICST Institute for Computer Sciences, Social Informatics and Telecommunications Engineering 2018
Q. Chen et al. (Eds.): ChinaCom 2016, Part I, LNICST 209, pp. 393–402, 2018.
DOI: 10.1007/978-3-319-66625-9_38

multiplexing (DCO-OFDM) [4]. Asymmetrically clipped optical OFDM (ACO-OFDM) [5], unipolar OFDM (U-OFDM) [6] and flip OFDM [7] can achieve higher power efficiency than the conventional DCO-OFDM at the expense of losing half of the spectral efficiency. In [8], a real and imaginary coefficients separation OFDM (RIS-OFDM) scheme, which is based on real and imaginary coefficients separation, is proposed in multiple-input multiple-output (MIMO) systems with better performance and lower complexity.

However, there is one common in all of the above schemes that they did not consider the nonlinear distortion by LEDs [9]. By applying a digital predistortion [10], the nonlinear transfer characteristic of LEDs can be modeled as double-side clipping. Unfortunately, the linear region of LEDs is still not large enough in a practical scenario and the nonlinear distortion is still a serious problem which degrades the system performance due to the high peak-to-average-power ratio (PAPR) of O-OFDM. ACO-OFDM specified recoverable upper clipping system is introduced in [11], which fully utilizes the structure of ACO-OFDM to mitigate the nonlinear distortion at the expense of increasing the receiver complexity. Also, its spectral efficiency is low due to the inherent characteristics of ACO-OFDM. In polar OFDM (P-OFDM) [12], a polar coordinate transformation is conducted with abilities to acheive relatively high spectral efficiency and better bit error rate (BER) performance under practical conditions of fixed power and LED nonlinear constraints.

In this paper, we develop a novel O-OFDM system based on real-imaginary coefficients separation and recoverable clipping to mitigate the nonlinear distortion due to LEDs. The proposed system fully utilizes the structure of coefficients separation and dynamic range of LEDs. Simulation results show that the proposed scheme achieves better BER performance under LED nonlinear constraints and reduces the requirement for the linear dynamic range of LEDs compared with DCO-OFDM, ACO-OFDM and P-OFDM.

The rest of the paper is organized as follows. In Sect. 2, the simplified LED nonlinear model is given. The transmit strategy and receive algorithm of the proposed scheme are described in detail in Sect. 3. Then simulation results are presented and discussed in Sect. 4. Finally, Sect. 5 concludes this paper.

## 2    Nonlinear Model of LED

Because of the p-n junction and the saturation effect of the LEDs, there is a nonlinear relation between the input and the output of the LEDs. However, by applying predistortion techniques [10], The nonlinear transfer characteristic of LEDs can be modeled as double-sided clipping. The simplified LED model in [13] is employed in this paper, and can be expressed as

$$G[x] = \begin{cases} I_L, & x < I_L \\ x, & I_L < x < I_H \\ I_H, & x < I_H \end{cases}, \tag{1}$$

where $G[\cdot]$ denotes the simplified LED nonlinear model, and $[I_L, I_H]$ is the linear region of LED.

To quantify the dynamic range of LEDs, the clipping ratio (CR) is defined as [12]

$$\text{CR}\,(\text{dB}) = 10\log_{10}\frac{I_H - I_L}{P_{\text{opt}}} = 10\log_{10}\frac{DR_{\text{LED}}}{P_{\text{opt}}}, \tag{2}$$

where $P_{\text{opt}}$ is the transmitted optical power and $DR_{\text{LED}}$ denotes the dynamic range of the LEDs.

## 3   Proposed O-OFDM Scheme

In this section, a novel O-OFDM system based on real-imaginary coefficients separation and recoverable clipping is proposed to improve BER performance when the linear region of LED is constrained.

### 3.1   Transmitter

The block diagram of the proposed system is illustrated in Fig. 1. At the transmitter, the modulated information symbols are only mapped onto the odd subcarriers and the even subcarriers are set to zero. Then, the complex data signal in the frequencey domain $\mathbf{X} = [0, X(1), 0, X(3) \cdots, 0, X(N-1)]$ is input into the inverse fast Fourier transform (IFFT) module, where $N$ is the size of IFFT. In contrast to schemes such as ACO-OFDM, $\mathbf{X}$ dose not need to be Hermitian symmetric. After IFFT, the time domain signal $x(n)$ has odd symmetry property, that is

$$x(n) = -x(n + \frac{N}{2}); \; n = 0, 1, 2, \cdots, \frac{N}{2} - 1, \tag{3}$$

where $x(n)$ is complex.

Due to the odd symmetry, half of the output signals can be considered as redundant information which can be employed to separate the real and imaginary

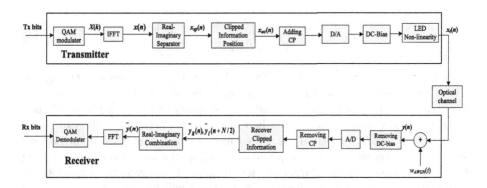

**Fig. 1.** Block diagram of the proposed system

parts of $x(n) = x_R(n) + jx_I(n)$, where $x_R(n)$ and $x_I(n)$ are real, and the real and imaginary parts of $x(n)$, respectively. The process is described as

$$x_{sp}(n) = \begin{cases} x_R(n), 0 \le n \le \frac{N}{2} - 1 \\ x_I(n), \frac{N}{2} \le n \le N - 1 \end{cases}, \tag{4}$$

where $x_{sp}(n)$ is the $n$-th time-domain sample after the real-imaginary separator.

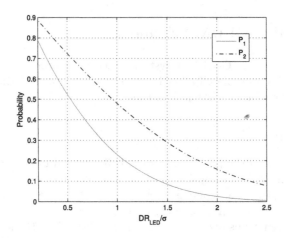

**Fig. 2.** $P_1$ and $P_2$ versus $DR_{\mathrm{LED}}/\sigma$ when $DC = (I_H + I_L)/2$

Although the signals $x_{sp}(n)$ can be transmitted after adding the DC bias, it will suffer severe clipping distortion due to the dynamic range of LEDs. Therefore, we introduce $x_c(n)$ to make the clipped information recoverable. However, if we keep all clipped information, $x_c(n)$ will be as long as $x_{sp}(n)$, which will cost too much. Fortunately, the structure of real-imaginary coefficients separation provides us a better solution. Note that the possibility of $x_R(n)$ and $x_I(n + \frac{N}{2})$ being clipped at the same time follows

$$P_1 = \left(1 - \frac{1}{\sqrt{\pi}\sigma} \int_{I_L - DC}^{I_H - DC} e^{-\frac{x^2}{\sigma^2}} dx\right)^2, \tag{5}$$

where $\sigma^2$ is the variance of $X(k)$. Figure 2 plots $P_1$ and $P_2$ versus $DR_{\mathrm{LED}}/\sigma$, where $DC$ is set to the middle of the linear range of the LEDs, $P_2$ denotes the possibility of $x_R(n)$ being clipped, and the possibility of $x_I(n + \frac{N}{2})$ being clipped is equal to $P_2$. It can be seen that when $DR_{\mathrm{LED}}/\sigma > 2$, the possibility of $x_R(n)$ and $x_I(n + \frac{N}{2})$ being clipped at the same time is smaller than 0.025, which is very small. Therefore, we can just keep one of the clipped information by comparing the absolute value, and the larger one will be kept. To recover the original signal successfully at the receiver, the polarity of $x_c(n)$ will be determined by which part was clipped from, e.g. when it is clipped from $x_R(n)$, $x_c(n)$ will be positive, otherwise, when it is clipped from $x_I(n + \frac{N}{2})$, $x_c(n)$ will be negative. As can be seen that the length of $x_c(n)$ only need to be $\frac{N}{2}$ since the structure of coefficients separation is fully utilized. The recoverable clipping reposition process is illustrated as Fig. 3, which can be mathematically expressed as

$$x_c(n) = \begin{cases} |e_R(n)|, & |e_R(n)| \geq |e_I(n)| \\ -|e_I(n)|, & |e_R(n)| < |e_I(n)| \end{cases}, \tag{6}$$

where $n = 0, 1, 2, \cdots, \frac{N}{2} - 1$, $e_R(n)$ and $e_I(n)$ denotes the clipped information of $x_R(n)$ and $x_I(n)$ respectively, which follow

$$e_R(n) = \begin{cases} x_R(n) - \lambda_{\max}, & x_R(n) > \lambda_{\max} \\ 0, & \lambda_{\min} \leq x_R(n) \leq \lambda_{\max} \\ x_R(n) - \lambda_{\min}, & x_R(n) < \lambda_{\min} \end{cases} \tag{7}$$

$$e_I(n) = \begin{cases} x_I(n + \frac{N}{2}) - \lambda_{\max}, & x_I(n + \frac{N}{2}) > \lambda_{\max} \\ 0, & \lambda_{\min} \leq x_I(n + \frac{N}{2}) \leq \lambda_{\max} \\ x_I(n + \frac{N}{2}) - \lambda_{\min}, & x_I(n + \frac{N}{2}) < \lambda_{\min} \end{cases}, \tag{8}$$

where $\lambda_{\max} = I_H - DC$, $\lambda_{\min} = I_L - DC$ and $n = 0, 1, \cdots, \frac{N}{2} - 1$. After the recoverable clipping procedure, the signals transmitted by LED can be expressed as

$$x_t(n) = \begin{cases} G[x_{sp}(n) + DC], & 0 \leq n \leq N - 1 \\ G[x_c(n - N) + DC]. & N \leq n \leq \frac{3N}{2} - 1 \end{cases}. \tag{9}$$

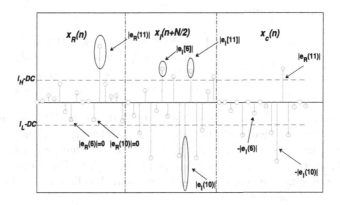

**Fig. 3.** Example of recoverable clipping procedure

Due to the property of $x_c(n)$, the optical transmitted power of the system do not change and appoximately equals to $DC$, which is the same as that of DCO-OFDM [14].

## 3.2  Receiver

Additive white Gaussian noise (AWGN) channel is assumed in this paper, and the received signal $y(n)$ is expressed as

$$y(n) = x_t(n) + w(n), \tag{10}$$

where $w(n)$ is the Gaussian noise component. After removing the DC-bias, define the corresponding received sample group as

$$\gamma(n) = (y_1(n), y_2(n), y_c(n)), \tag{11}$$

where $y_1(n) = y(n) - DC$, $y_2(n) = y(n + \frac{N}{2}) - DC$, $y_c(n) = y(n + N) - DC$ and $n = 0, 1, 2, \cdots, \frac{N}{2} - 1$.

According to $y_c(n)$ and (6), it can be determined where the clipped signal comes from, for example, from $x_R(n)$, or from $x_I(n + \frac{N}{2})$ or neither of them are clipped. Then, whether $y_c(n)$ should be added or subtracted is determined by the polarity of its corresponding part. Therefore, for a given corresponding sample group $\gamma(n)$, there are four decision regions, which can be described as

$$D_1 : \begin{cases} y_c(n) \geq 0, \\ y_1(n) \geq 0; \end{cases} D_3 : \begin{cases} y_c(n) < 0, \\ y_2(n) \geq 0; \end{cases}$$

$$D_2 : \begin{cases} y_c(n) \geq 0, \\ y_1(n) < 0; \end{cases} D_4 : \begin{cases} y_c(n) < 0, \\ y_2(n) < 0. \end{cases} \tag{12}$$

After the decision region of $\gamma(n)$ has been determined according to (12), the corresponding recovery procedure is

$$(\tilde{y}_R(n), \tilde{y}_I(n + \frac{N}{2})) = \begin{cases} (y_1(n) + y_c(n), y_2(n)), \gamma(n) \in D_1 \\ (y_1(n) - y_c(n), y_2(n)), \gamma(n) \in D_2 \\ (y_1(n), y_2(n) + y_c(n)), \gamma(n) \in D_3 \\ (y_1(n), y_2(n) - y_c(n)), \gamma(n) \in D_4 \end{cases}, \tag{13}$$

where $n = 0, 1, 2, \cdots, \frac{N}{2} - 1$. It should be noted that, due to AWGN, the polarity of $x_c(n)$ may be changed and thus lead to error detection when determining which part it belongs to. However, this situation only happens when $x_c(n)$ is very small or zero thus carrying few clipped information. Therefore, the system performance may not be significantly affected, and the effect is also investigated further in the next section.

Then the real-imaginary combination block will be performed according to (3) and (4), the output is

$$\tilde{y}(n) = \begin{cases} \tilde{y}_R(n) - j\tilde{y}_I(n + \frac{N}{2}), 0 \leq n \leq \frac{N}{2} - 1 \\ -\tilde{y}(n - \frac{N}{2}), \qquad \frac{N}{2} \leq n \leq N - 1 \end{cases}. \tag{14}$$

After that, the receiver applies FFT, and signals can be demodulated.

The spectral efficiency of the proposed scheme is given by

$$\eta_{\text{proposed}} = \frac{\frac{N}{2}}{N + \frac{N}{2} + N_{\text{cp}}} \log_2(M)$$
$$= \frac{N}{3N + 2N_{\text{cp}}} \log_2(M), \tag{15}$$

where $M$ is the modulation order of the modulated subcarriers, and $N_{\text{cp}}$ is the length of cyclic prefix (CP). The spectral efficiency of DCO-OFDM is shown as [15]

$$\eta_{\text{DCO-OFDM}} = \frac{N - 2}{2(N + N_{\text{cp}})} \log_2(M). \tag{16}$$

Campared with DCO-OFDM, half of the spectral efficiency is lost in ACO-OFDM [14]. Since no Hermitian symmetry is needed in P-OFDM, its spectral efficiency is expressed as [15]

$$\eta_{\text{P-OFDM}} = \frac{N}{2(N + N_{\text{cp}})} \log_2(M). \tag{17}$$

When $N$ is great, we can get

$$\eta_{\text{proposed}} \approx \frac{4}{3} \eta_{\text{ACO-OFDM}}$$
$$\approx \frac{2}{3} \eta_{\text{DCO-OFDM}} \approx \frac{2}{3} \eta_{\text{P-OFDM}}. \tag{18}$$

## 4    Simulation Results

The performances of the proposed scheme, DCO-OFDM, ACO-OFDM, and P-OFDM are campared in this section. In the simulations, $N = 128$, $P_{\text{elec}} = E[X^2(k)]$ is normalized to 1, and $P_{\text{opt}}$ is equal to 30 dBm, i.e. $DC = 1$, to satisfy the illumination requirement. $I_L$ is set to zero. The AWGN channel is considered, and $N_{\text{cp}} = 0$. To achieve the same data rate, 4-QAM is used in DCO-OFDM and P-OFDM, and 8-QAM and 16-QAM are employed in the proposed system and ACO-OFDM, respectively. A scaling factor is used for ACO-OFDM and P-OFDM to achieve the required optical power level [13].

The BER performances of the four O-OFDM scheme are shown in Fig. 4, where $CR = 3$ dB. At the BER of $10^{-3}$, the proposed system achieves significant performance gain of about 5.2 dB and 3.2 dB over DCO-OFDM and P-OFDM, respectively. For ACO-OFDM, it even cannot work under this circumstance because of the severe nonlinear distortion. It can be seen that when SNR is relatively low, the proposed system achieves no performance gain compared with DCO-OFDM, while for high SNR, the proposed system outperforms DCO-OFDM. The reason is that, when SNR is low, the AWGN is the dominant element to affect the system performance instead of nonlinear distortion.

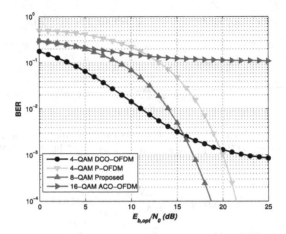

**Fig. 4.** BER performance comparison among different schemes when CR = 3 dB

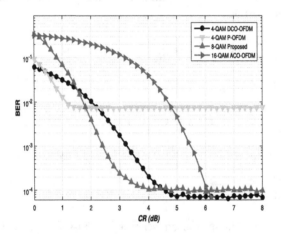

**Fig. 5.** BER performance versus CR

When SNR increases, which is also the working region for practical systems, the nonlinear distortion is the dominant and the proposed scheme achieves better performance. Besides, there is no error floor in the Proposed scheme.

Figure 5 plots the BER performance of the four schemes versus the CR when $E_{b,opt}/N_0 = 18$ dB. As shown in Fig. 5, for the proposed scheme, P-OFDM and DCO-OFDM, the BER performance degrades dramatically with the decrease of the CR when the CR is smaller than a threshold due to the insufficient dynamic range. But all of the curves will converge to a BER floor when the CR is large enough. The observed BER floor is mainly determined by the level of the noise. For a target BER of $10^{-3}$, the requirement for the CR of the proposed system is approximately 2.4 dB, while that of DCO-OFDM is 3.3 dB. For ACO-OFDM, CR should be greater than 5.5 dB. Therefore, the requirement for CR of the proposed scheme is successfully reduced by 0.9 dB and 3.1 dB compared with DCO-OFDM and ACO-OFDM, respectively. Note that even when CR is large enough, P-OFDM still cannot achieve the target BER in this environment due to the influence of the high noise power. It is also shown that ACO-OFDM is the most susceptible to the impact of the low dynamic range of the LEDs.

It is mentioned that there are two cases when the receiver will detect incorrectly: (1) $x_c(n)$ is zero and thus $y_c(n)$ belongs to neither $y_1(n)$ nor $y_2(n)$; (2) the polarity of $x_c(n)$ is reversed due to the Gaussian noise. A genie detector which always makes the perfect decisions is simulated in Fig. 6, where CR = 3 dB. It is indicated that, with a genie receiver, there would be a 1 dB BER performance gain. Therefore, the proposed scheme can work well, and is not sensitive to the incorectness of the polarity of $x_c(n)$.

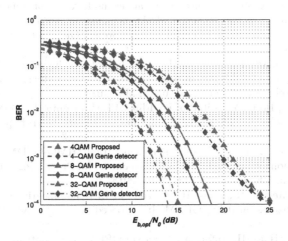

**Fig. 6.** BER performance comparison with a genie detector under CR = 3 dB

## 5  Conclusion

A novel O-OFDM scheme based on real-imaginary coefficients separation and recoverable clipping procedure has been proposed in this paper to mitigate the nonlinear distortion due to LEDs. The proposed scheme fully makes use of the structure of coefficients separation and considers the dynamic range of LEDs. In the proposed scheme, the transmitted signal in the frequency domain dose not need to be Hermitian symmetric, and real and imaginary parts of the time domain signal are separated. Compared with DCO-OFDM, ACO-OFDM, and P-OFDM, the proposed scheme can achieve better BER performance under LED nonlinear constraints and reduce the requirement for the linear dynamic range of LEDs The proposed O-OFDM is a promising scheme to be implemented in practical VLC systems.

**Acknowledgments.** This work is supported by NSFC projects (61501109, 61571105, and 61223001), 863 project (No. 2013AA013601), and Jiangsu NSF project (No. BK20140646).

# References

1. Komine, T., Nakagawa, M.: Fundamental analysis for visible-light communication system using LED lights. IEEE Trans. Consum. Electron. **50**(1), 100–107 (2004)
2. Elgala, H., Mesleh, R., Haas, H.: Indoor optical wireless communication: potential and state-of-art. IEEE Commun. Mag. **49**(9), 56–62 (2011)
3. Wu, L., Zhang, Z., Liu, H.: Modulation scheme based on precoder matrix for MIMO optical wireless communication systems. IEEE Commun. Lett. **16**(9), 1516–1519 (2012)
4. Carruthers, J., Kahn, J.: Multiple-subcarrier modulation for nondirected wireless infrared communication. IEEE J. Sel. Areas Commun. **14**(3), 538–546 (1996)
5. Armstrong, J., Lowery, A.J.: Power efficient optical OFDM. Electron. Lett. **42**(6), 370–372 (2006)
6. Tsonev, D., Sinanovic, S., Haas, H.: Novel unipolar orthogonal frequency division multiplexing (U-OFDM) for optical wireless. In: Proceedings of the IEEE 75th Vehicular Technology Conference, p. 15, May 2012
7. Fernando, N., Hong, Y., Viterbo, E.: Flip-OFDM for optical wireless communications. In: Proceedings of the IEEE Information Theory Workshop, p. 59, October 2011
8. Wu, L., Zhang, Z., Liu, H.: Coefficients separation MIMO-OFDM optical wireless communication system in diffuse fading channels. In: Proceedings of the IEEE ICC 2015, London, UK, pp. 5132–5137, June 2015
9. Elgala, H., Mesleh, R., Haas, H.: A study of LED nonlinearity effects on optical wireless transmission using OFDM. In: Proceedings of the WOCN, p. 15, April 2009
10. Dimitrov, S., Haas, H.: Information rate of OFDM-based optical wireless communication systems with nonlinear distortion. J. Lightwave Technol. **31**(6), 918–929 (2013)
11. Xu, W., Wu, M., Zhang, H.: ACO-OFDM-specified recoverable upper clipping with efficient detection for optical wireless communications. IEEE. Photon. **6**(5), 1–17 (2014)
12. Elgala, H., Little, T.D.C.: Polar-based OFDM and SC-FDE links toward energy-efficient Gbps transmission under IM-DD optical system constraints. IEEE/OSA J. Opt. Commun. Netw. **7**(2), A277–284 (2015)
13. Zhang, H., Yuan, Y., Xu, W.: PAPR reduction for DCO-OFDM visible light communications via semidefinite relaxation. IEEE Photon. Technol. Lett. **26**(17), 1718–1721 (2014)
14. Armstrong, J., Schmidt, B.J.C.: Comparison of asymmetrically clipped optical OFDM and DC-biased optical OFDM in AWGN. IEEE Commun. Lett. **12**, 343–345 (2008)
15. Yang, Y., Zeng, Z., Feng, S.: A simple OFDM scheme for VLC systems based on $\mu$-law mapping. IEEE Photon. Technol. Lett. **28**(6), 641–644 (2016)

# Design and Implementation of Link Loss Forwarding in 100G Optical Transmission System

Zhenzhen Jia[1], Wen He[1], Chaoxiang Shi[1(✉)], Jianxin Chang[2], and Meng Gao[2]

[1] School of Communication and Information Engineering, Chongqing University of Posts and Telecommunications, Chongqing 400065, China
`jiazhenzhen343@163.com, wenhcqupt@163.com, shicx@cqupt.edu.cn`
[2] CNMP Networks INC., Beijing, China
`{jxchang,mgao}@cnmpnetworks.net`

**Abstract.** We have previously proposed and implemented a novel low cost 100G transmission system which has the 1 RU only size and a small form factor [1]. In this paper we further develop a LLF (Link Loss Forward) feature which can monitor the health of this 100G system and make a necessary link failure management. The mechanism is based on the fast FPGA insertion/desertion processing and the usage of un-used overheads of OTN digital wrapper as an in-band tunneling, so that the remote link failure relay, link failure isolation, and alarm report can be done properly. Finally, when the link failure is re-covered, the system will detect it and do automatic recovery as well as alarm clearance accordingly.

**Keywords:** 100G · Link loss forwarding · FPGA

## 1 Introduction

Todays communication is entering the data centralized Internet+ era, applications such as cloud computing, mobile internet, 4G/5G wireless, internet video stream, social network and E-commerce, etc., are creating a lot of business opportunities and therefore driving network capacity demand rapidly. The traditional 10G network is facing enormous challenges due to its limited capacity. As a result, large data center switch and router are being upgraded to 100 GbE or 100G OTN interface, which is driving the optical transmission network have be compatible in term of 100G transmission capability [1,2].

On the other hand, Optical network has become increasingly complex, and the importance of the optical network management has also become an increasing predominantly necessary. The presence of a network management system is essential to ensure efficient, secure, and continuous operation of any network. Specifically, a network management implementation should be capable of handling the configuration, fault, performance, security, accounting, and safety in the network [2].

© ICST Institute for Computer Sciences, Social Informatics and Telecommunications Engineering 2018
Q. Chen et al. (Eds.): ChinaCom 2016, Part I, LNICST 209, pp. 403–411, 2018.
DOI: 10.1007/978-3-319-66625-9_39

We have proposed and implemented a novel low-cost 100G transmission platform which is based on Inverse-Multiplexing Technology and MLD (Multiplex-
lane Distribution) mechanism [1]. In this paper, in order to do necessary link
failure and OAM management, we further proposes a scheme to implement the
network management feature of link loss forwarding (LLF) [3]. In the 100G
transmission system, when there is a sudden link failure occurring on either
client side or long haul transmission side, the alarm signal must be delivered to
remote equipment instantly, otherwise, the remote equipment will still think the
transmission line is in normal situation, and continually transmit data to 100G
switch or router, but these data information are really garbage [4]. To solve
this problem, we propose to use 2 bytes RES of Optical Transport Network-
OTN (the ITU-T G.709 [5]) overhead to transport link loss information. This
is implemented by insertion/desertion of link loss message via the high speed
FPGA (i.e., Field-Programmable Gate Array), from the on-used overhead of
OTN framer. When the link loss message is embedded and transmitted to the
remote device together with the 100G real traffic, the receiving alarm signals will
make the remote device stop sending the optical signal to its associated 100G
switch or router to prevent garbage data or spam.

## 2    Experiment Setup

### 2.1    Introduction of 100G Transmission System

The system block diagram of 100G transmission and the prototype picture are
shown in Fig. 1(a) and (b) respectively. CFP module coverts 100 GE traffic to
10-lane10.3125 Gb/s electrical CAUI interface which is defined by IEEE802.3ba
standard [6]. For better performance, ten 10G OTN frames are designed in 100G
transmission system to provide FEC and performance function. Every lane of
CAUI signal is transparently mapped into 10G OTN frame. And then send to
DWDM SFP+ for long haul transmission. In the design, we chose OTN frame

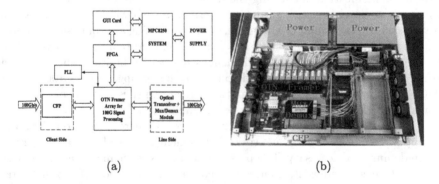

(a)                              (b)

**Fig. 1.** (a) 100G transmission system block diagram; (b) prototype picture of a 100G
optical transmission device

chip to do digital wrapper technology, the MPC8250 is used as a system central controller, and FPGA can insert and drop the link loss signal.

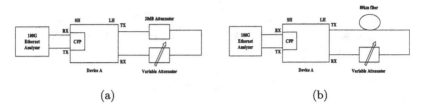

(a)                                                    (b)

**Fig. 2.** (a) Line side test diagram with 20 dB attenuator; (b) Line side test diagram with 80 km fiber

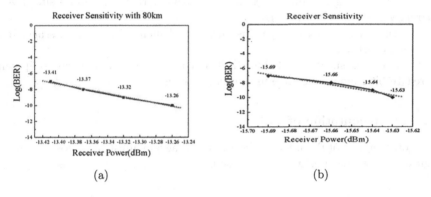

(a)                                                    (b)

**Fig. 3.** (a) LH receiver sensitivity with 20 dB attenuator; (b) LH receiver sensitivity with 80 km SM fiber

The most important parameters of above test in Fig. 2 are receiver sensitivity and dispersion penalty. The difference between Fig. 2(a) and (b) is that (a) uses 20 dB attenuator, (b) uses 80 km SM fiber, which all can get receive optical power through adjusting the variable attenuator. We should note that the receiving power is the total power of 10 lanes. The receiver sensitivity of Fig. 3(a) and (b) is −15.46 dBm and −12.86 dBm respectively around the BER at $10^{-}12$. By comparison, the receiver sensitivity of 80 km SM fiber is bigger because of the system performance degradation which is caused by degradation. The dispersion penalty is about 2.7 dB.

## 3   Link Loss Forward for 100G Optical Transmission System

### 3.1   Design of LLF (Link Loss Forward)

In order to transport urgent information between two peer equipment in remote sites, express tunneling is designed by means of RES bytes of OTN frame.

Successive four RES are used as one express package to transmit remote message. The package is defined as Fig. 4.

| Sync_head | Sync_check | Remote_message | Message_check |

**Fig. 4.** Urgent LOS frame

Sync_head: Sync_head is used for synchronizing the package between the byte stream.

Sync_check: Sync_check is used to verify that sync head is correct.

Remote_message: Remote_message is a 16 bit data from remote site. Every bit represents different LOS emergency.

Message_check: Message_check is ones complement of remote message. It is used as a checksum.

If these four successive 16 bit RES0 is correctly received, local equipment stored 16 bit Remote_message in internal register.

### 3.2  Implementation of LLF

As shown in Fig. 5(a) and (b), the system diagram illustrates how the OTN digital wrapper technology is being used.

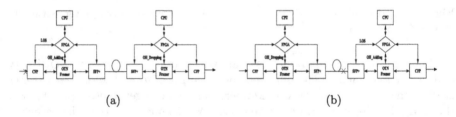

(a)                               (b)

**Fig. 5.** (a) Processing system block diagram of client side link failure; (b) Processing system block diagram of line side link failure

Figure 5(a) and (b) show the implementation principle of link loss forwarding when link failures happen on client side and long haul transmission side, respectively. The main steps to implement link loss forwarding of client side are as follows:

- The link loss occurs at the client side in local device A, or the link loss occurs at the line side in remote device B.

- Let us first look at the local device. The CFP and SFP+ modules have control signal pins which are connected to the FPGA. The CFP module or the SFP+ module detects the loss of signal (LOS) and sends a LOS which represents the link failure of device A or B, once the FPGA get the LOS it will send the signal and transmit in two directions. In the one direction, the local device will receive the LOS and disable the TX of 100G CFP module, so that local device will stop sending garbage data to its connected 100G switch or router to prevent the spam. In the other direction for the remote device, FPGA will insert the LOS signal into the un-used overhead of OTN famer, and then send this link failure message to the remote site device through SFP+ module and long distance transmission.

- On the other hand, the remote side device receives the signal and detects LOS through the received overhead of OTN frame. As a next step, FPGA will process this LOS signal and start the action to disable its client side 100G CFPTX, so that the remote side device 100G CFP will also stop transmitting garbage data to its connected 100G switch or router.

- Based on the above processes, whence link failure occurs at either client side or long link transmission side, both the local device or remote deice will start instant action to disable the 100G CFP TX and cut the connection, so that no more garbage data will continuously be sent to the associated 100G switch or router to prevent the spam. This process is so called link loss forward, or LLF.

- Another scenario is the automatic link recovery process. Once the link becomes normal, FPGA will detect the link status by polling CFP and SFP+ with the 200 ms interval. Once the link LOS disappears, the link recovery to normal signal will be transferred in two directions. In the one direction, local device will turn on the TX and make the 100G CFP working normally; In the other direction, remote device will receive the link normal signal through the express tunneling of OTN framer overhead and also make the 100G CFP working properly.

### 3.3   Experiment Results of Link Loss Forward

The test results for link loss forwarding have been presented in Fig. 6(a) and (b) respectively. We can un-plug the RX fiber of CFP or SFP+ modules to produce

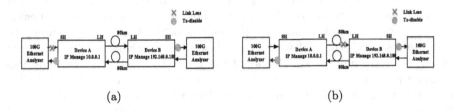

(a)                                      (b)

**Fig. 6.** (a) Link failure test of client side; (b) Link failure test of line side

```
*10.0.0.1:> show power-m
  Idx        WaveLength  TX Power     RX Power     Bias        Temperature
==========================================================================
 LH 1/1/1   -                -            -          -           -
     Lane1   1560 nm        0.6 dBm    -23.8 dBm    88.6 mA    42.3 C
     Lane2   1559 nm        0.7 dBm    -23.4 dBm    96.0 mA    39.1 C
     Lane3   1558 nm        0.8 dBm    -23.0 dBm    97.9 mA    46.1 C
     Lane4   1558 nm        1.0 dBm    -23.6 dBm    86.5 mA    45.4 C
     Lane5   1557 nm        0.8 dBm    -22.3 dBm    80.1 mA    47.4 C
     Lane6   1556 nm        1.4 dBm    -23.1 dBm    93.3 mA    47.8 C
     Lane7   1555 nm        1.1 dBm    -23.3 dBm    91.3 mA    47.4 C
     Lane8   1554 nm        0.8 dBm    -23.7 dBm    82.1 mA    49.2 C
     Lane9   1554 nm        1.4 dBm    -23.1 dBm    91.3 mA    43.6 C
     Lane10  1553 nm        1.6 dBm    -22.4 dBm    95.4 mA    45.8 C
 SH 1/1/1   -                -            -          -           -
     Lane1   -              0.9 dBm     -0.3 dBm    76.7 mA    44.9 C
     Lane2   -              0.6 dBm     -0.5 dBm    76.0 mA    45.0 C
     Lane3   -              0.6 dBm     -0.7 dBm    75.4 mA    44.9 C
     Lane4   -              0.4 dBm     -0.7 dBm    76.5 mA    45.0 C
```

(a)

```
*192.168.0.188:> show power-m
  Idx        WaveLength  TX Power     RX Power     Bias        Temperature
==========================================================================
 LH 1/1/1   -                -            -          -           -
     Lane1   1560 nm        0.7 dBm    -22.4 dBm    92.5 mA    46.5 C
     Lane2   1559 nm        1.3 dBm    -22.5 dBm    75.0 mA    43.0 C
     Lane3   1558 nm        0.7 dBm    -22.4 dBm    87.6 mA    52.2 C
     Lane4   1558 nm        1.0 dBm    -22.2 dBm    64.3 mA    49.0 C
     Lane5   1557 nm        0.7 dBm    -22.7 dBm    88.5 mA    53.0 C
     Lane6   1556 nm        0.7 dBm    -20.7 dBm    93.4 mA    53.2 C
     Lane7   1555 nm        1.4 dBm    -21.4 dBm    83.6 mA    51.2 C
     Lane8   1554 nm        0.8 dBm    -21.8 dBm    90.5 mA    53.0 C
     Lane9   1554 nm        0.5 dBm    -21.0 dBm    94.7 mA    47.8 C
     Lane10  1553 nm        1.1 dBm    -21.4 dBm    89.7 mA    51.0 C
 SH 1/1/1   -                -            -          -           -
     Lane1   -              1.1 dBm      0.3 dBm    75.6 mA    45.0 C
     Lane2   -              0.6 dBm     -0.6 dBm    76.0 mA    44.9 C
     Lane3   -              0.8 dBm     -0.1 dBm    76.2 mA    44.9 C
     Lane4   -              0.8 dBm     -0.4 dBm    77.5 mA    44.9 C
```

(b)

**Fig. 7.** (a) The power-m of the device A; (b) The power-m of the device B

the link loss situation, as a consequence TX-disable of 100G CFP modules is our expected result. We do the IP configuration to simulate the connection between the local and remote device. The most important parameters are the power-monitor, whose variation indicates the success of the link loss forwarding. In other words, in the normal working condition, the receiving and transmitting power of optical module are in normal range. On the contrary, when link loss occurs, the receiving power is -50 dBm. Also, when we do the Tx-disable of CFP or SFP+, their transmitting power is -50 dBm, which indicates that there is no light output from CFP or SFP+. On the client side, 100 GbE signal are divided into 4 lanes to be handled. Figure 7($a$) and ($b$) show the power-monitor of device

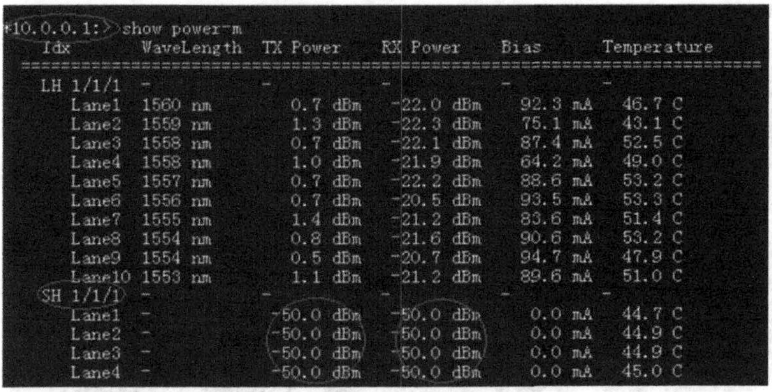

(a)

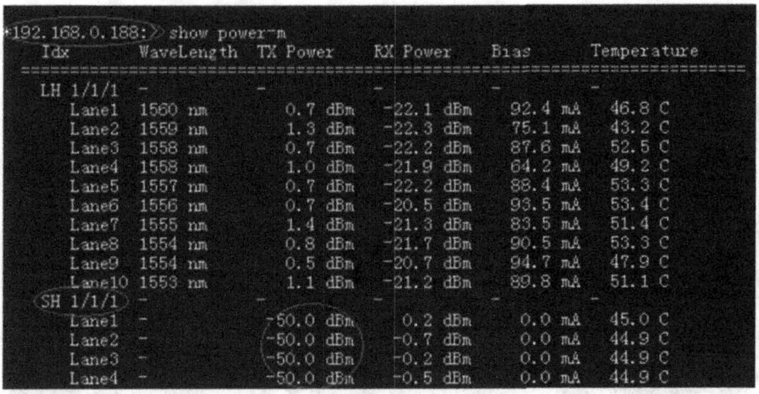

(b)

**Fig. 8.** (a) The power-m of local devices; (b) The power-m of remote devices

A and B before the link failure. Figure 8(a) and (b) show the power-monitor of device A and B after the link failure of client side happens . Figure 9(a) and (b) show the power-monitor of device A and B after the link failure of line side happens . All of the testing data are collected from the network management system via command line or CLI.

In the Fig. 7(a) and (b), without link failure, the TX and RX power of CFP or SFP+ modules are in normal range, no link failure occurs.

From the Fig. 8, we can know that the RX power of CFP module will change to −50 dBm when the link failure occurs at the client side of device A. At the

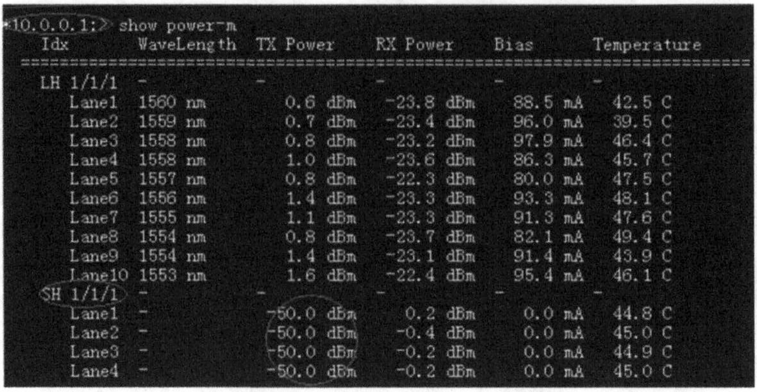

```
*10.0.0.1:> show power-m
  Idx        WaveLength  TX Power    RX Power    Bias      Temperature
==========================================================================
 LH 1/1/1   -            -           -           -         -
   Lane1    1560 nm      0.6 dBm     -23.8 dBm   88.5 mA   42.5 C
   Lane2    1559 nm      0.7 dBm     -23.4 dBm   96.0 mA   39.5 C
   Lane3    1558 nm      0.8 dBm     -23.2 dBm   97.9 mA   46.4 C
   Lane4    1558 nm      1.0 dBm     -23.6 dBm   86.3 mA   45.7 C
   Lane5    1557 nm      0.8 dBm     -22.3 dBm   80.0 mA   47.5 C
   Lane6    1556 nm      1.4 dBm     -23.3 dBm   93.3 mA   48.1 C
   Lane7    1555 nm      1.1 dBm     -23.3 dBm   91.3 mA   47.6 C
   Lane8    1554 nm      0.8 dBm     -23.7 dBm   82.1 mA   49.4 C
   Lane9    1554 nm      1.4 dBm     -23.1 dBm   91.4 mA   43.9 C
   Lane10   1553 nm      1.6 dBm     -22.4 dBm   95.4 mA   46.1 C
 SH 1/1/1   -            -           -           -         -
   Lane1    -            -50.0 dBm   0.2 dBm     0.0 mA    44.8 C
   Lane2    -            -50.0 dBm   -0.4 dBm    0.0 mA    45.0 C
   Lane3    -            -50.0 dBm   -0.2 dBm    0.0 mA    44.9 C
   Lane4    -            -50.0 dBm   -0.2 dBm    0.0 mA    45.0 C
```

(a)

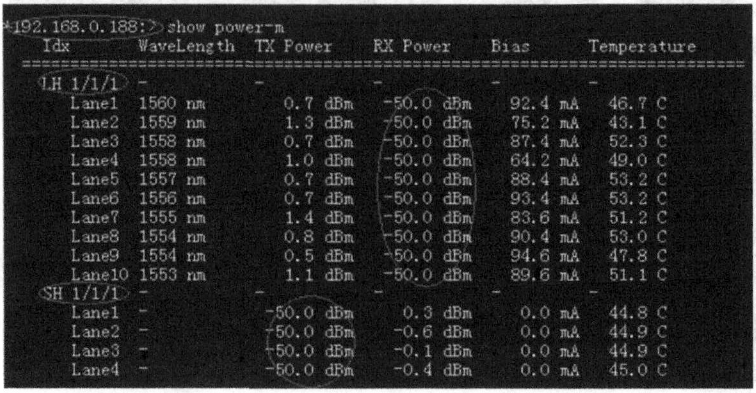

```
*192.168.0.188:> show power-m
  Idx        WaveLength  TX Power    RX Power    Bias      Temperature
==========================================================================
 LH 1/1/1   -            -           -           -         -
   Lane1    1560 nm      0.7 dBm     -50.0 dBm   92.4 mA   46.7 C
   Lane2    1559 nm      1.3 dBm     -50.0 dBm   75.2 mA   43.1 C
   Lane3    1558 nm      0.7 dBm     -50.0 dBm   87.4 mA   52.3 C
   Lane4    1558 nm      1.0 dBm     -50.0 dBm   64.2 mA   49.0 C
   Lane5    1557 nm      0.7 dBm     -50.0 dBm   88.4 mA   53.2 C
   Lane6    1556 nm      0.7 dBm     -50.0 dBm   93.4 mA   53.2 C
   Lane7    1555 nm      1.4 dBm     -50.0 dBm   83.6 mA   51.2 C
   Lane8    1554 nm      0.8 dBm     -50.0 dBm   90.4 mA   53.0 C
   Lane9    1554 nm      0.5 dBm     -50.0 dBm   94.6 mA   47.8 C
   Lane10   1553 nm      1.1 dBm     -50.0 dBm   89.6 mA   51.1 C
 SH 1/1/1   -            -           -           -         -
   Lane1    -            -50.0 dBm   0.3 dBm     0.0 mA    44.8 C
   Lane2    -            -50.0 dBm   -0.6 dBm    0.0 mA    44.9 C
   Lane3    -            -50.0 dBm   -0.1 dBm    0.0 mA    44.9 C
   Lane4    -            -50.0 dBm   -0.4 dBm    0.0 mA    45.0 C
```

(b)

**Fig. 9.** (a) The power-m of local devices; (b) The power-m of remote devices

same time, the LOS signal will be transmitted through express tunneling of OTN overhead. After a few seconds, link loss forwarding become effective, as a result the CFP modules of both devices will make the TX disable which shows that the TX power of both devices CFP are $-50$ dBm, this verifies the effectiveness of client side link loss forwarding.

From the Fig. 9, we can know that the RX power of SFP+ module will change to $-50$ dBm when the link loss occurs at the line side of device B. At the same time, the LOS signal will be transmitted through express channel by

OTN framer. Thereafter, link loss forwarding starts to action, as a result the CFP modules of both devices will make the TX disable that is the TX power of both devices are −50 dBm, which verify the effectiveness of line side link loss forwarding.

## 4    Conclusions

Based on our proposed novel low-cost 100G transmission platform, we have further proposed a scheme to implement Link Loss Forwarding-LLF. The mechanism is based on the fast FPGA processing and the usage of un-used overheads of OTN digital wrapper. Our testing results show that when link failures occur, our system can do accordingly link failure management and stopping send garbage data to the connected 100G switch or router to prevent the spam. When the link failure is re-covered, the system will do automatic recovery and return to the good working condition.

## References

1. Yang, O., Dong, C., Liu, Q.C., Shi, C.X.: A small form factor and low cost 100 Gb/s optical transmission system based on inver-multiplexing technology. In: International Conference on Communications and Networking in China, pp. 85–89. IEEE (2015)
2. Shi, H.W., Zhang, P.T.: Advanced Technologies for 100G Optical Networking. In: Applied Mechanics and Materials, pp. 303–306 (2013)
3. Miller, G.M., Corp, D.O.: System and method for enhancement of Ethernet link loss forwarding. In: US, US 8687504 B2 (2014)
4. Zhang, X., Xu, J., Liu, W., et al.: The application scheme of 40G and 100G ethernet. In: International Conference on Optical Communications and Networks, p. 41 (2011)
5. ITU-T Recommendation G.709, Interface for the Optical Transport Networks (2009)
6. Fu, K., Ma, Z.Q., Li, X.S.: Standard research of IEEE P802.3ba in 40 Gb/s,100 Gb/sEthernet. Opt. Commun. Technol. **33**, 11 (2009)

# 4×25-Gb/s Duo-Binary System over 20-km SSMF Transmission with LMS Algorithm

Mengqi Guo, Ji Zhou, Xizi Tang, and Yaojun Qiao[✉]

State Key Laboratory of Information Photonics and Optical Communications,
School of Information and Communication Engineering, Beijing University of Posts
and Telecommunications (BUPT), Beijing 100876, China
qiao@bupt.edu.cn

**Abstract.** We propose a 4×25-Gb/s intensity-modulated direct detection (IM/DD) duo-binary system with 50-GHz channel spacing. Both of the modulator and photodetector (PD) have 10-GHz 3-dB electrical bandwidth. At receiver, least mean square (LMS) algorithm is used to compensate the signal distortion after transmission. After 20-km standard single mode fiber (SSMF) transmission, LMS algorithm improves about 2-dB receive sensitivity at forward error correction (FEC) limit (BER = $10^{-3}$) in duo-binary system. With LMS algorithm, duo-binary system has about 5-dB receive sensitivity improvement at FEC limit compared to on-off keying (OOK) system over 20-km SSMF transmission. This paper proposes a feasible scheme for future high-speed passive optical network (PON).

**Keywords:** Duo-binary system · Intensity-modulated direct detection (IM/DD) · Least mean square (LMS) algorithm · Passive optical network (PON)

## 1 Introduction

100G passive optical network (PON) has been investigated to meet the demand of high-speed and low cost access network [1,2]. With the increase of data rate, the electrical bandwidth of devices and chromatic dispersion become limitation factors of transmission system. Duo-binary modulation technique was proposed as a high-speed transmission scheme in band-limiting system [3]. It attracts lots of attention due to its resistance to intersymbol interference caused by chromatic dispersion [4]. Orthogonal frequency-division multiplexing (OFDM) also has been applied in high-speed access network, its superiority in high spectral efficiency can reduce the required bandwidth, and it also has robustness against chromatic dispersion [5]. However, as a multi-carrier modulation technique, OFDM has high computational complexity and high peak-to-average power ratio (PAPR) [6], which make duo-binary system more likely to be chosen. Intensity-modulated direct detection (IM/DD) optical transmission system has been used in short-haul optical transmission system due to its simple structure

© ICST Institute for Computer Sciences, Social Informatics and Telecommunications Engineering 2018
Q. Chen et al. (Eds.): ChinaCom 2016, Part I, LNICST 209, pp. 412–422, 2018.
DOI: 10.1007/978-3-319-66625-9_40

and low cost [7]. So the high-speed and low cost duo-binary IM/DD system can be a feasible scheme for PON.

Varies duo-binary signal generating methods such as delay-and-add filter or low pass filter have been put forward and varies improved duo-binary schemes to increase system performance or decrease complexity and cost have been developed [8–10]. Differential precoding and electrical filter are used to generate three-level duo-binary signal in general. Precoding at transmitter makes it easier to decode at receiver because without precoding a more complex decoding process is required, which is likely to cause error propagation [8]. The precoded binary signal can convert to three-level duo-binary signal by delay-and-add method [8], this delay-and-add method can be approximated by using a low pass filter with about a quarter of data rate 3-dB bandwidth in electrical domain [9]. The methods to modulate the three-level electrical duo-binary to optical carrier are commonly classified into two categories. The three-level electrical signal can be directly modulated to three-level optical signal [8,10]. Another method is using Mach-Zehnder modulator (MZM) to modulate both amplitude and phase, so three-level electrical signal is modulated to two-level optical signal [9].

As we known, it is impossible to ignore the signal distortion after transmission, especially when the data capacity is increased to meet the transmission demand. Adding linear equalization algorithm is a feasible method to compensate the distortion and it does not require much cost. Least mean square (LMS) algorithm is a widely used simple linear equalization algorithm, its implementation only requires two multiplications and two additions per filter coefficient [11]. LMS algorithm can be used in different types of optical communication systems such as high speed OFDM system [12] and Nyquist single carrier visible light communication (VLC) system [13]. With LMS algorithm the distortion can be significantly compensated by updating tap-weight vector, so the bit error rate (BER) performance is improved.

In this paper, we propose a 4×25-Gb/s IM/DD duo-binary system with 50-GHz channel spacing. LMS algorithm can be employed to compensate the signal distortion after 20-km standard single mode fiber (SSMF) transmission. Both of the modulator and photodetector (PD) have 10-GHz 3-dB electrical bandwidth. The effect of LMS algorithm is analyzed and system performance of duo-binary system is compared with on-off keying (OOK) system.

## 2 Principle

### 2.1 Duo-Binary System

Figure 1 shows the duo-binary IM/DD system scheme for single wavelength transmission. At first, the 25-Gb/s digital OOK data sequence should conduct precoding, which is demonstrated in Fig. 2. The precoding process is needed at transmitter because without precoding a more complex decoding process is required at receiver, which is likely to cause error propagation due to the previous signal is useful to decode signal at the present time. We get inverse of the original signal, then add a zero at the front to perform differential encoding. After achieving the precoded signal, as shown in Fig. 3, the signal period is 0.04-ns, the first fourteen signals are the same as the corresponding signals in Fig. 2. Then the precoded signals pass through a low pass band-limiting filter with 6-GHz 3-dB bandwidth. The bandwidth of precoded signal is 25-GHz so that high-frequency components are attenuated by this filter. As shown in Fig. 3, if the precoded signal changes between "1" and "0" quickly, the low pass band-limiting filter causes the signal unable to achieve its original value, it only can achieve the value of about 0.5. Therefore, the three-level signal can be generated by this low pass band-limiting filter. Figure 4 reveals the electrical spectrum and eye diagram of the generated duo-binary signal. We can find the high-frequency components of 25-GHz bandwidth transmitted signal are attenuated by the 6-GHz 3-dB bandwidth filter seriously, and the eye diagram demonstrates the duo-binary signal with three levels. Then, we can adjust amplitude and bias to make all the signal positive. The three-level electrical signal is directly modulated to three-level optical signal by MZM. Therefore, the amplitude range of duo-binary signal and OOK signal are the same.

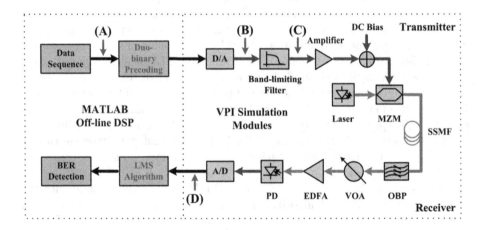

**Fig. 1.** Duo-binary IM/DD system scheme for single wavelength transmission.

At receiver side, we get the positive three-level duo-binary signal, decrease the amplitude of the signals by the mean value of them, and then adjust the amplitude of the signals by multiplying a proper number so that all the signal values are nearby "1", "0" or "−1", two thresholds are needed to make decision. LMS algorithm has significant effect to compensate the signal distortion. After getting the absolute value of the received signal, we can perform BER detection to obtain the system performance.

## 2.2 LMS Algorithm

LMS algorithm is one of the most widely used linear equalization algorithms, it can be considered as a stochastic implementation of steepest descent method [11].

| Original signal (A): | 1 1 1 1 0 1 1 1 0 0 1 1 0 1 |
|---|---|
| Inverse of original signal: | 0 0 0 0 1 0 0 0 1 1 0 0 1 0 |
| Differential encoding: | 0 0 0 0 0 1 1 1 1 0 1 1 1 0 0 |
| Precoded signal (B): | 0 0 0 0 1 1 1 1 0 1 1 1 0 0 |
| Duo-binary signal (C): | 0 0 0 0 $\frac{1}{2}$ 1 1 1 $\frac{1}{2}$ $\frac{1}{2}$ 1 1 $\frac{1}{2}$ 0 |
| Received signal (D): | -1 -1 -1 -1 0 1 1 1 0 0 1 1 0 -1 |
| Absolute value for BER detection: | 1 1 1 1 0 1 1 1 0 0 1 1 0 1 |

**Fig. 2.** Transformation of data in duo-binary system.

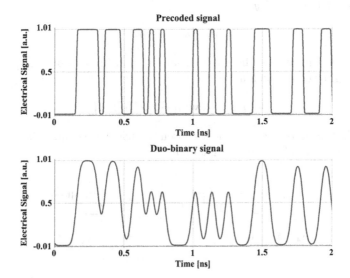

**Fig. 3.** The inputs and outputs of band-limiting filter corresponding to (B) and (C) in duo-binary system scheme.

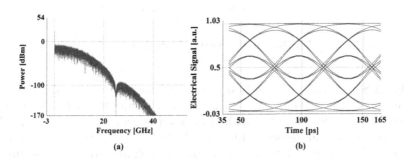

**Fig. 4.** (a) Electrical spectrum of duo-binary signal in (C); (b) eye diagram of duo-binary signal in (C).

Figure 5 reveals the structure of LMS algorithm with $N+1$ taps, the objective is achieving proper tap-weight vector $\mathbf{w}[n]$ so as to compensate the signal influence at other times to the signal at the present time. Three steps for each iteration are presented as follows.

The output signal $y[n]$ can be calculated by

$$y[n] = \mathbf{w}^H[n]\mathbf{x}[n] \tag{1}$$

where the tap-weight vector $\mathbf{w}[n] = [w_0[n], w_1[n], \ldots, w_N[n]]^T$ and the input signal $\mathbf{x}[n] = [x[n], x[n-1], \ldots, x[n-N]]^T$, $\mathbf{w}^H[n]$ means the complex conjugate of tap-weight vector $\mathbf{w}[n]$.

Then the error signal $e[n]$ is the difference between desired output signal $d[n]$ and actual output signal $y[n]$,

$$e[n] = d[n] - y[n] \tag{2}$$

Finally, we can utilize the error signal $e[n]$ and input signal $\mathbf{x}[n]$ to update the tap-weight vector, such as

$$\mathbf{w}[n+1] = \mathbf{w}[n] + 2\mu e^*[n]\mathbf{x}[n] \tag{3}$$

where $\mu$ is the step size, which is chosen sufficiently small, $e^*[n]$ means the complex conjugate of the error signal $e[n]$.

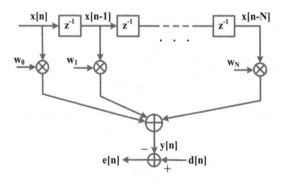

**Fig. 5.** The structure of LMS algorithm.

By LMS algorithm, the received signal can converge to desired signal so as to compensate the signal distortion. However, we should have the desired signal to converge to. From Fig. 2 we can find the received signal is nearby "1", "0" or "−1", these signals are generated by band-limiting filter at the transmitter. We only have the precoded signal saved in MATLAB off-line processing, so that we should encode the precoded signal at receiver to imitate the function of band-limiting filter to get desired three-level received signal. The encoding process is demonstrated in Fig. 6.

| n : | 0 | 1 | 2 | 3 | 4 | 5 | 6 | 7 | 8 | 9 | 10 | 11 | 12 | 13 | 14 |
|---|---|---|---|---|---|---|---|---|---|---|---|---|---|---|---|
| Precoded signal : | 0 | 0 | 0 | 0 | 1 | 1 | 1 | 1 | 0 | 1 | 1 | 1 | 0 | 0 | |
| Bit to amplitude mapping m(n): | -1 | -1 | -1 | -1 | -1 | 1 | 1 | 1 | 1 | -1 | 1 | 1 | 1 | -1 | -1 |
| Desired signal d(n): | -1 | -1 | -1 | -1 | 0 | 1 | 1 | 1 | 0 | 0 | 1 | 1 | 0 | -1 | |

**Fig. 6.** Encoding process to get the desired signal.

The precoded signal is consisted of "0" and "1", if the original precoded signal is "0", the corresponding bit to amplitude mapping signal $m(n)$ is set to "−1", if the original precoded signal is "1", the corresponding bit to amplitude mapping signal $m(n)$ is still set to "1". Then add a "−1" at the front of $m(n)$. Equation (4) shows how to get the desired signal $d(n)$,

$$d(n) = \frac{m(n-1) + m(n)}{2}, \qquad n = 1, 2, \ldots \qquad (4)$$

After obtaining the desired signal $d(n)$, LMS algorithm can be applied to compensate the signal distortion.

## 3  Simulation System and Results Discussion

### 3.1  Simulation System

Figure 1 reveals the duo-binary IM/DD simulation system for single wavelength transmission. We use MATLAB to perform off-line digital signal processing, the electrical and optical devices are VPItransmissionMaker (VPI) simulation modules. Data rate for each channel is 25-Gb/s, four channels are used to carry signal and seeds for data sequence of each channel are different. The center frequencies of four channels are set to 193.5-THz, 193.45-THz, 193.4-THz and 193.35-THz with 50-GHz channel spacing.

The simulation system is set up according to the actual experimental system. The OOK data sequence performs precoding, digital to analog conversion, and passes through a low pass band-limiting filter. After adjusting amplitude and bias, the duo-binary signal is modulated to the optical carrier by MZM with 10-GHz 3-dB electrical bandwidth, and four channels are multiplexed by optical multiplexer. The launching optical power is set to 0-dBm.

After 20-km SSMF transmission, the center frequency of optical band pass filter is set according to the center frequency of each channel, the bandwidth is set to 2.5 times of bit rate, that is 62.5-GHz, so all the signal of this channel can pass through the band pass filter. Then, a variable optical attenuator (VOA) is used to change the received optical power, and an Erbium doped fiber amplifier (EDFA) with power-controlled status can keep a constant input power of PD. The optical signal is converted to electrical signal by PD with 10-GHz 3-dB electrical bandwidth. After analog to digital conversion, the digital signal is handled by MATLAB off-line processing. We use LMS algorithm to compensate the signal distortion, and conduct BER detection at last.

To highlight the advantage of duo-binary system with LMS algorithm, we also compare it with the 4×25-Gb/s OOK system. Both the two systems have the same data rate and transmission distance. OOK system also use 10-GHz 3-dB electrical bandwidth devices and LMS algorithm is also applied.

## 3.2   Results Discussion

Figure 7 demonstrates the optical spectrum and BER performance of four channels for duo-binary system with LMS algorithm, the center frequency of four-channel signal is 193.425-THz and channel spacing is 50-GHz. After 20-km SSMF transmission, the BER performances of four channels are almost the same, because channel spacing is enough for the band-limiting duo-binary signal. The first channel with 193.5-THz center frequency is tested for performance evaluation.

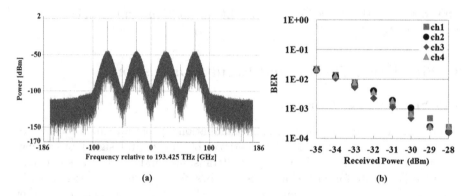

(a)                          (b)

**Fig. 7.** (a) Optical spectrum of four channels; (b) BER performance of four channels after 20-km SSMF transmission.

BER performance for duo-binary system and OOK system before and after using LMS algorithm of the first channel is compared. Figure 8 reveals for duo-binary system, LMS algorithm has effect of converging the received signal to its original signal to compensate the distortion, especially when the received optical power is not too small. Figure 8(a) reveals the required received power for duo-binary system with LMS algorithm is about 2-dB less than duo-binary system without LMS algorithm for both back-to-back (BTB) and 20-km SSMF transmission at forward error correction (FEC) limit (BER=$10^{-3}$). Figure 8(b) and 8(c) depict the constellations before and after using LMS algorithm for 20-km SSMF transmission, respectively. The color bar represents numbers of received data as different colors. The constellation points with LMS algorithm are closer to "1", "0" or "−1" than the constellation points without LMS algorithm. The constellation points around "1" is not as close as the constellation points

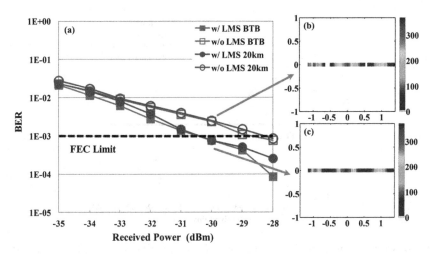

**Fig. 8.** (a) BER performance of the first channel for duo-binary system with or without LMS algorithm; (b) duo-binary constellation before using LMS algorithm for 20-km SSMF transmission; (c) duo-binary constellation after using LMS algorithm for 20-km SSMF transmission. (Color figure online)

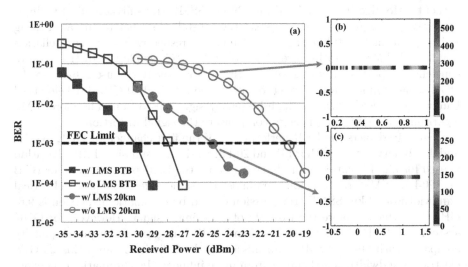

**Fig. 9.** (a) BER performance of the first channel for OOK system with or without LMS algorithm; (b) OOK constellation before using LMS algorithm for 20-km SSMF transmission; (c) OOK constellation after using LMS algorithm for 20-km SSMF transmission.

around "−1" because the signal with high amplitude is easier to be affected by amplified spontaneous emission (ASE) noise in the process of transmission.

The effect of LMS algorithm is more apparent in Fig. 9, especially for 20-km SSMF transmission due to LMS algorithm has the function of compensating

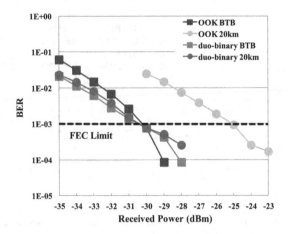

**Fig. 10.** Comparison of BER performance of the first channel between OOK system and duo-binary system for BTB and 20-km SSMF transmission.

chromatic dispersion. Figure 9(a) reveals the required received power for OOK system with LMS algorithm is about 2-dB and 5-dB less than OOK system without LMS algorithm for BTB and 20-km SSMF transmission at FEC limit, respectively. Figure 9(b) and (c) depict the constellations before and after using LMS algorithm for 20-km SSMF transmission, respectively. The constellation points with LMS algorithm are closer to "1" or "0", while the distribution of constellation points without LMS algorithm is relatively confused, because the OOK signal is more sensitive to chromatic dispersion and 10-GHz 3-dB electrical bandwidth devices cause the high-frequency signal distortion. Therefore, LMS algorithm has significant effect to compensate the signal distortion.

Figure 10 depicts the BER performance of the first channel for OOK system and duo-binary system with BTB and 20-km SSMF transmission. LMS algorithm is used for all of them. For duo-binary system, the BER performances for BTB and 20-km SSMF transmission are almost the same, due to the 3-dB electrical bandwidth of 20-km SSMF transmission caused by chromatic dispersion is 9.6-GHz [14], which is more than 6-GHz of duo-binary signal. However, for OOK system, the BTB transmission has about 5-dB improvement in power penalty compared with 20-km SSMF transmission at FEC limit, because this 25-GHz electrical bandwidth signal suffers from more influence by chromatic dispersion. The BER performance of duo-binary system with 20-km SSMF transmission has about 5-dB improvement in power penalty compared with OOK system with 20-km SSMF transmission at FEC limit. Consequently, duo-binary system has advantage over OOK system in its resistance to chromatic dispersion due to the low spectral bandwidth, and LMS algorithm has effect to compensate the signal distortion.

# 4  Conclusion

In this paper, a 4×25-Gb/s IM/DD duo-binary system with 50-GHz channel spacing is demonstrated. Both of the modulator and PD have 10-GHz 3-dB electrical bandwidth, and the system performance is improved by LMS algorithm. LMS algorithm can converge received signal to its original value, so the signal distortion is compensated after transmission. For duo-binary system, LMS algorithm improves about 2-dB receive sensitivity at FEC limit for both BTB and 20-km SSMF transmission. For OOK system, LMS algorithm improves about 2-dB and 5-dB receive sensitivity at FEC limit for BTB and 20-km SSMF transmission, respectively. After using LMS algorithm, duo-binary system has about 5-dB improvement of receive sensitivity at FEC limit compared to OOK system for 20-km SSMF transmission. This paper proposes a feasible scheme for future high-speed passive optical network.

**Acknowledgments.** This work was supported in part by National Natural Science Foundation of China (61271192, 61427813, 61331010); National 863 Program of China (2013AA013401); Research Fund of ZTE Corporation.

# References

1. Van Veen, D., Houtsma, V., Winzer, P., Vetter, P.: 26-Gbps PON transmission over 40-km using duobinary detection with a low cost 7-GHz APD-based receiver. Paper Tu.3.B.1, European Conference and Exhibition on Optical Communications (2012)
2. Zhou, J., Qiao, Y.: Low-peak-to-average power ratio and low-complexity asymmetrically clipped optical orthogonal frequency-division multiplexing uplink transmission scheme for long-reach passive optical network. Opt. Lett. **40**, 4034–4037 (2015)
3. Lender, A.: The duobinary technique for high-speed data transmission. IEEE Trans. Commun. Electron. **82**, 214–218 (1963)
4. Yonenaga, K., Kuwano, S.: Dispersion-tolerant optical transmission system using duobinary transmitter and binary receiver. J. Lightwave Technol. **15**, 1530–1537 (1997)
5. Zhou, J., Qiao, Y., Cai, Z., Ji, Y.: Asymmetrically clipped optical fast OFDM based on discrete cosine transform for IM/DD systems. J. Lightwave Technol. **33**, 1920–1927 (2015)
6. Cvijetic, N.: OFDM for next-generation optical access networks. J. Lightwave Technol. **30**, 384–398 (2012)
7. Zhou, J., Yan, Y., Cai, Z., Qiao, Y., Ji, Y.: A cost-effective and efficient scheme for optical OFDM in short-range IM/DD systems. IEEE Photon. Technol. Lett. **26**, 1372–1374 (2014)
8. Van Veen, D.T., Houtsma, V.E.: Symmetrical 25-Gb/s TDM-PON with 31.5-dB optical power budget using only off-the-shelf 10-Gb/s optical components. J. Lightwave Technol. **34**, 1636–1642 (2016)
9. Ono, T., Yano, Y., Fukuchi, K., Ito, T., Yamazaki, H., Yamaguchi, M., Emura, K.: Characteristics of optical duobinary signals in terabit/s capacity, high-spectral efficiency WDM systems. J. Lightwave Technol. **16**, 788–797 (1998)

10. Gu, X., Dodds, S.J., Blank, L.C., Spirit, D.M., Pycock, S.J., Ellis, A.D.: Duobinary technique for dispersion reduction in high capacity optical systems-modelling, experiment and field trial. IEEE Proc. Optoelectron. **143**, 228–236 (1996)
11. Farhang-Boroujeny, B.: Signal Processing Techniques for Software Radios. Lulu Publishing House, Raleigh (2008)
12. Wang, Y., Yu, J., Chi, N.: Demonstration of 4 128-Gb/s DFT-S OFDM signal transmission over 320-km SMF with IM/DD. IEEE Photon. J. **8**, 1–9 (2016)
13. Wang, Y., Huang, X., Zhang, J., Wang, Y., Chi, N.: Enhanced performance of visible light communication employing 512-QAM N-SC-FDE and DD-LMS. Opt. Express **22**, 15328–15334 (2014)
14. Hsu, D.Z., Wei, C.C., Chen, H.Y., Chen, J., Yuang, M.C., Lin, S.H., Li, W.Y.: 21-Gb/s after 100-km OFDM long-reach PON transmission using a cost-effective electro-absorption modulator. Opt. Express **18**, 27758–27763 (2010)

# Self-homodyne Spatial Super-Channel Based Spectrum and Core Assignment in Spatial Division Multiplexing Optical Networks

Ye Zhu, Yongli Zhao, Wei Wang, Xiaosong Yu[✉],
Guanjun Gao, and Jie Zhang

State Key Laboratory of Information Photonics and Optical Communications,
Beijing University of Posts and Telecommunications, Beijing 100876, China
{zhuye,yonglizhao,weiw,xiaosongyu,ggj,
lgr24}@bupt.edu.cn

**Abstract.** Space Division Multiplexing (SDM) has been introduced as a promising technique to improve the capacity of optical transport networks. In SDM optical networks, Multi-Core Fiber (MCF) is taken as the infrastructure, and the spectrum resources of one MCF are distributed in multiple cores. According to such features, self-homodyne spatial super-channel has been introduced to support setting up super-channels across multiple cores in one MCF, and it relaxes the contiguous constraint in traditional Elastic Optical Networks (EON). Based on self-homodyne spatial super-channel, this paper focuses on the problem of Spectrum and Core Assignment (SCA) in SDM networks. We set up a self-homodyne spatial super-channel based resource model, including several types of MCF with certain inter-core crosstalk. Accordingly, we proposed a Self-homodyne Spatial Super-channel based Spectrum and Core Assignment scheme. Simulation results show that the proposed scheme can improve the spectrum consumption ratio and reduce blocking probability significantly.

**Keywords:** Spatial Division Multiplexing · Spatial super-channel · Spectrum and Core Assignment

## 1 Introduction

With the development of flexible and dynamic network based applications (e.g., cloud computing, video on demand and time varying services), the demand for network bandwidth has been increasing significantly during the past several years, and this trend will continue. As an effective approach, which can support high-speed optical channels beyond 100 GB/s, Elastic Optical Networks (EON) has been proposed to improve the spectrum efficiency of current optical networks. Nevertheless, the transmission capacity of Single-Core Fiber (SCF) will reach the physical limitation soon [1]. To meet the increasing demands for network bandwidth, Spatial Division Multiplexing (SDM) has been investigated as an infrastructural technique, which can improve the capacity of single fiber link up to 1 Pbps, by using Multi-Core Fiber (MCF) [2] or Multi-Mode Fiber

© ICST Institute for Computer Sciences, Social Informatics and Telecommunications Engineering 2018
Q. Chen et al. (Eds.): ChinaCom 2016, Part I, LNICST 209, pp. 423–430, 2018.
DOI: 10.1007/978-3-319-66625-9_41

(MMF). Then, spatial division multiplexing enabled elastic optical networks (SDM-EONs) will become the most important form of future optical transport networks.

MCF is mainly considered in the paper because it is more practical compared with MMF, which also brings some new features and challenges for optical networks. On the one hand, spectrum continuous constraint has been alleviated, which means that the signal can interchange between different cores freely while maintaining the same spectrum slice On the other hand, inter-core crosstalk may occur when the same spectrum slice overlaps in neighbor cores. Some methods has been proposed for measuring the crosstalk statistically in MCF. At networking level, some schemes were proposed to avoid inter-core crosstalk in Routing, Spectrum and Core Assignment (RSCA) process, such as a first-fit scheme and ILP-based scheme [3]. First-fit scheme is generally used to ensuring both slot consistency and continuity constraints along the path. Based on first-fit, ILP-based scheme was proposed to minimize the maximum number of spectrum slices required on any core of MCF. However, the proposed first-fit and ILP schemes do not consider the dynamic traffic and would result in higher blocking probability and spectrum fragments. Taking fragmentation into account, a pre-defined core classification scheme [4] was proposed to reduce the fragmentation of each core. In general, all the works above take cross-talk into account and aim to provision light-paths under the consistent and contiguous constraint of subcarriers in EON. Meanwhile, spatial super channel has been investigated from hardware perspective to relax the traditional contiguous constraint in spectrum dimension. By exploiting the highly correlated properties of different cores in one single MCF, Puttnam et al. show that spatial super channel and Self-Homodyne Detection (SHD) are available in MCF [5, 6]. To support self-homodyne spatial super-channel switching in SDM networks, a hybrid add-drop node that can realize low Optical Signal Noise Ratio (OSNR) is presented in [7]. However, all the above RSCA schemes, which are limited by traditional contiguous constraint, have not considered the self-homodyne spatial super-channel, especially under crosstalk-aware condition, thus they cannot achieve optimal resource efficiency in self-homodyne spatial super-channel enabled SDM networks. This paper focuses on the Spectrum and Core Assignment (SCA) problem in self-homodyne spatial super-channel enabled SDM networks.

This paper discusses the SCA problem based on self-homodyne spatial super channel. We set up a resource model for SDM optical networks to address the relationship between fiber, core and wavelength. According to the resource model, we also propose a self-homodyne spatial super-channel based spectrum and core assignment (SSS-SCA) scheme under the limitation of inter-core cross-talk (XT). Simulation results show that the proposed SCA scheme can reduce the blocking probability and improve the efficiency of resource network significantly.

## 2    Self-homodyne Spatial Super-Channel Based Resource Model and Crosstalk Analysis

In this paper, we consider the problem of SCA in the scenario of SDM enabled EONs, where the spectrum resource can be simplified as Frequency Slot (FS) in each MCF. We formulate the physical network as a graph $G(V, E)$, where $V$ is a set of network nodes, and $E$ is a set of MCF links. In SDM networks, each link $L(L \in E)$ is composed of a core set $C$, and each core has a set of FSs. In order to express the network resource occupation status more clearly, a matrix $A_l$ is defined to denote the FS occupation status of fiber link $l$ as (1).

$$A_l = \begin{bmatrix} O_{1,1} & O_{1,2} & \dots & O_{1,c} \\ O_{2,1} & O_{2,2} & \dots & O_{2,c} \\ \dots & \dots & \dots & \dots \\ O_{f,1} & O_{f,2} & \dots & O_{f,c} \end{bmatrix} \tag{1}$$

As is shown above, $A_l$ is composed of $c$ columns and $f$ rows, which represents $c$ cores in link L and $f$ FSs in each core. The matrix element $O_{i,j}$ is a binary value, which is used to denote the occupation status of slot $i$ in core $j$. For example, $O_{i,j} = 1$ means the corresponding FS is available, while $O_{i,j} = 0$ means occupied. For a pending end-to-end connection request, we formulate it as $R(s, d, b)$, where s and $d$ are the source-destination node pair, and $b$ is the required bitrates of this request. Once a request arrives, the network operator needs to select spectral modulation format [8] according to the Signal-to-Noise Ratio (SNR) in the selected path.

Trench-assisted MCFs [9] are the mostly preferred in SDM transmission due to crosstalk interference. This paper focuses the SCA problem under inter-core XT in 3 types of MCFs, including 7, 12, 19 core fibers as shown in Fig. 1.

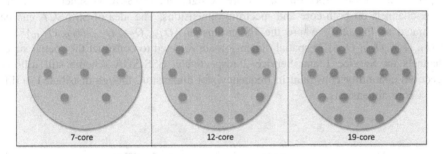

**Fig. 1.** MCFs with 7-core, 12-core, 19-core

In addition, inter-core crosstalk is a key constraint in SDM optical networks, and it would occur when the same frequency slot in adjacent cores is used simultaneously. Equations (2) and (3) is defined to evaluate the mean crosstalk XT for MCF [10].

$$h = (2 \cdot k^2 \cdot r)/(\beta \cdot wth). \tag{2}$$

$$XT = \{n - n \cdot \exp[-(n+1) \cdot 2hL]\}/\{1 + n \cdot \exp[-(n+1) \cdot 2hL]\}. \tag{3}$$

In Eq. (2), $h$ denotes the mean increase in crosstalk per unit length. $k$, $r$, $\beta$, and $wth$ are the relevant fiber parameters, representing the coupling coefficient, bend radius, propagation constant, and core-pitch, respectively. In Eq. (3), $n$ is the number of the adjacent cores and $L$ represents the fiber length. For the centered core of 7-core MCF in Fig. 1, $n$ equals to six, while for other marginal cores, $n$ equals to three, which determinate the inter-core crosstalk policy to some extent. From the crosstalk calculation equations, we note that the crosstalk is affected by the number of adjacent cores and the length of the fiber.

## 3    Self-homodyne Spatial Super-Channel Based Spectrum and Core Assignment Scheme

In spatial super channel, high bitrates data streams are transported as groups of sub-channels occupying the same wavelength in separate cores. To simplify, in this case we assume that the optical nodes have the wavelength conversion ability, so that the spatial super channel can be constructed with different wavelengths in separated cores. This paper discusses the problem of SCA in spatial super channel enabled SDM networks. Traditionally, continuity is one of the most important constraints for building super channels in EONs, and many discontinuous FSs cannot be used to carry high bitrates requests. Taking Fig. 2(a) as an example, most FSs are unavailable which is due to higher inter-core crosstalk in the resource map except several free spectrum fragments. When a new service request arrives with the requirement of 5 FSs, no core has enough vacant continuous frequency slots and this request will be blocked. To handle this kind of un-optimal condition, we propose a Self-homodyne Spatial Super-channel based Spectrum and Core Assignment (SSS-SCA) scheme to build super channels on both core and spectrum dimensions. The idea of SSS-SCA can be illustrated as Fig. 2(b), where the FS groups of $\{O_{1,6}, O_{2,7}, O_{2,8}, O_{1,9}, O_{1,10}\}$ and $\{O_{3,1}, O_{3,2}, O_{4,3}, O_{3,4}\}$ in spatial dimension are selected to construct the spatial super channels for Service 1 and Service 2 respectively. SSS-SCA scheme still follows spectrum continuity constraint in frequency slot dimension, though distributed in different core dimensions.

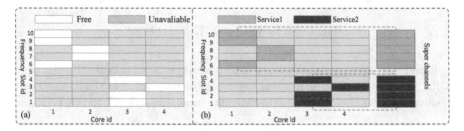

**Fig. 2.** (a) Common network occupation status one single link before using spatial super channel; (b) SCA with spatial super channels

The SSS-SCA scheme is described as follows.

---

**Self-homodyne Spatial Super-channel based Spectrum and Core Assignment Scheme**

---

1:   **for** a pending service request $R(s, d, b)$;
2:   calculate routing path with KSP algorithm and get $k$ shortest paths as a set $\{P\}$;
3:   **if** there is no candidate path in $\{P\}$, **then**
4:      block this request $R(s, d, b)$;
5:   **else**
6:      **for** each path $p_0 \in \{P\}$, **do**
7:         decide the appropriate modulation format, get crosstalk threshold $XT_{TH}$ and calculate the number of required FS $n$;
8:         **for** each core $c$ on path $p_0$, **do**
9:            calculate all the available FS segments as a set $\{F\}_c$,
10:           **if** there exists a FS segment whose length $m \geqslant n$, **then**
11:              calculate the crosstalk $XT$;
12:              **if** $XT \leqslant XT_{TH}$, **then**
13:                 allocate the required FS;
14:              **else if** $m < n$ or $XT \geqslant XT_{TH}$, **then**
13:                 iterate over all core dimensions to construct spatial superchannel with available FSs, get $\{M\}$;
16:                 **if** there is a candidate $m_k$ in $\{M\}$ whose length $l \geqslant n$ in $\{M\}$ which satisfies $XT \leqslant XT_{TH}$, **then**
17:                    allocate the required FS;
18:                 **else**
19:                    block the service request;
20:                 **end if**;
21:              **end if**;
22:           **end if**
23:        **end for**
24:     **end for**
25: **end if**

---

The SSS-SCA algorithm above provides the overall procedure for achieving dynamic service provisioning. Lines 1–4 are for calculating an optimal path candidate $p_0$, using KSP algorithm. Line 5–25 show the details of allocating FSs. Specifically, we first calculate the unoccupied FSs of the whole $p_0$ according to the consistency constraint, and get all the available FSs segments as a set $\{F\}_c$ for each core $c$ on this path. From all the available FS segments of path $p_0$, find a FSs segment $f$ which contains more than $n$ continuous slots, and allocate the required FSs from it directly. If no available FSs segment, a spatial super-channel should be constructed as following procedures. Integrating all the FS segment of path $p_0$ to construct a new spatial super-channel segment group $\{M\}$ where each element $m \in \{M\}$ is selected as the policy of being continuous in spectral dimension (whether continuous in spatial dimension or not). If there is an appropriate $m_k$ which can afford more than $n$ slots for which the inter-core crosstalk is below $XT_{TH}$, then the required FSs are allocated. Else, block the service request.

## 4    Performance Evaluation

We evaluate the performance of the proposed SCA scheme through simulations on NSFNET topology with14 nodes and 21 links, where each node is configured as optical nodes with the ability of wavelength conversion, and each link is configured as MCF. The number of frequency slots per core is set to 300. Under each traffic load, the simulator generates 5000 end-to-end requests following Poisson model with the fixed departing rate 0.04. The source and destination $n$ nodes of each request are generated randomly. In this simulation, the bitrate request is simplified as the number of FSs by assuming that the modulation format is fixed as BPSK. Taking the Random SCA scheme as the benchmark, we evaluate the performance of SSS-SCA in terms of blocking probability and Resource Consumption Ratio in two conditions. (1) The traffic load is fixed to 2000 Erlang, and the number of required FSs of each request is generated randomly between 10 and 15. We evaluate the performance of the proposed scheme under 3 types of MCFs in this condition. (2) The core number of each MCF link is fixed to be 7, and the number of required FSs are evenly distributed in following two intervals: from 5 to 10 and from 10 to 15. We evaluate the performance of SSS-SCA under different traffic loads.

The figures shown above indicate that the blocking probability of SSS-SCA scheme is lower than that of random SCA scheme, while the Resource Consumption Ratio of SSS-SCA scheme is higher than that of random-SCA scheme both in experimental MCFs and traffic load. Both advantages are due to the characteristics of SSS-SCA scheme of utilizing distributed FSs to configure spatial super channel. Therefore, less spectrum fragments will result in higher Resource Consumption Ratio and lower blocking probability eventually.

Figures 3 and 4 compare the performances of random SCA scheme and SSS-SCA scheme in multi-core MCFs, and it is notable that SSS-SCA performs better in the conditions of 7-core, 12-core and 19-core MCF.

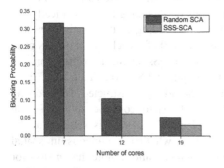
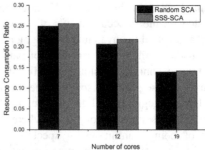

**Fig. 3.** Blocking probability of various core number (Erlang = 2000).

**Fig. 4.** Resource consumption ratio of various core number (Erlang = 2000).

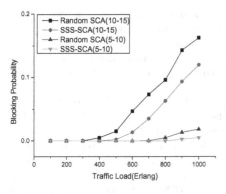

**Fig. 5.** Blocking probability of various traffic load (Core = 7).

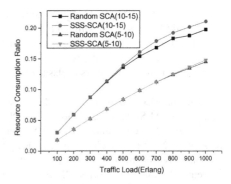

**Fig. 6.** Resource consumption ratio of various traffic load (Core = 7).

Figures 5 and 6 show that both blocking probability and spectrum Resource Consumption Ratio grow constantly as the traffic load increasing from 100 to 1000 Erlang. In the comparison between the two conditions where the required FSs are distributed in different ranges, it is notable that the advantages of the proposed SSS-SCA scheme are more significant in the condition with more FS requirement, especially when traffic load is beyond 500 Erlang. Under the random SCA scheme, the more FSs a request required, the more likely it is blocked for lacking enough contiguous FSs in one single core. Hence, there are few blocked requests which need the optimization of SSS-SCA in the condition where the requests require fewer FSs.

## 5 Conclusion

In this paper, spatial super-channel based SCA scheme is introduced in SDM optical networks. Simulation results show that the proposed SCA scheme is a promising scheme, which can reduce blocking probability and improve Resource Consumption Ratio all in 9-core, 12-core, 19-core MCFs.

**Acknowledgments.** This work has been supported in part by NSFC project (61601052, 61271189, 61571058, 61302085), and the Fund of State Key Laboratory of Information Photonics and Optical Communications (BUPT).

## References

1. Morioka, T.: New generation optical infrastructure technologies: 'EXAT initiative' towards 2020 and beyond. In: OECC 2009, FT4, Hong Kong SAR, China (2009)
2. Takara, H., Sano, A., et al.: 1.01-Pb/s (12 SDM/222 WDM/456 Gb/s) crosstalk-managed transmission with 91.4-b/s/Hz aggregate spectral efficiency. In: European Conference and Exhibition on Optical Communication. Optical Society of America, Th. 3. C. 1 (2012)

3. Muhammad, A., Zervas, G., Simeonidou, D., et al.: Routing, spectrum and core allocation in flexgrid SDM networks with multi-core fibers. In: 2014 International Conference on Optical Network Design and Modeling, pp. 192–197. IEEE (2014)

4. Fujii, S., Hirota, Y., Tode, H., et al.: On-demand spectrum and core allocation for reducing crosstalk in multicore fibers in elastic optical networks. J. Opt. Commun. Netw. **6**(12), 1059–1071 (2014)

5. Puttnam, B.J., Mendinueta, J.M.D., Sakaguchi, J., et al.: 210 Tb/s self-homodyne PDM-WDM-SDM transmission with DFB lasers in a 19-core fiber. In: 2013 IEEE Photonics Society Summer Topical Meeting Series, PSSTMS 2013 (2013)

6. Amaya, N., Yan, S., Channegowda, M., et al.: Software defined networking (SDN) over space division multiplexing (SDM) optical networks: features, benefits and experimental demonstration. Opt. Express **22**(3), 3638–3647 (2014)

7. Sakaguchi, J., Klaus, W., Puttnam, B.J., et al.: SDM-WDM hybrid reconfigurable add-drop nodes for self-homodyne photonic networks. In: 2013 IEEE Photonics Society Summer Topical Meeting Series (2013)

8. Nelson, L.E., Feuer, M.D., Abedin, K., et al.: Spatial superchannel routing in a two-span ROADM system for space division multiplexing. J. Lightwave Technol. **32**(4), 783–789 (2014)

9. Sakaguchi, J., Puttnam, B.J., et al.: 305 Tb/s space division multiplexed transmission using homogeneous 19-core fiber. J. Lightwave Technol. **31**(4), 554–562 (2013)

10. Saridis, G.M., Alexandropoulos, D., Zervas, G., et al.: Survey and evaluation of space division multiplexing: from technologies to optical networks. IEEE Commun. Surv. Tutor. **17**(4), 2136–2156 (2015)

# Management of a Hub-Spoken Optical Transmission Network with the Point to Multi Point (P2MP) Topology

Wen He[1,2(✉)], Zhenzhen Jia[1,2], Chaoxiang Shi[1], Jianxin Chang[1,2], and Meng Gao[2]

[1] School of Communication and Information Engineering, Chongqing University of Posts and Telecommunications, Chongqing 400065, China
wenhcqupt@163.com, jiazhenzhen343@163.com, shicx@cqupt.edu.cn
[2] CNMP Networks, INC Beijing, China
{jxchang,mgao}@cnmpnetworks.net

**Abstract.** We have previously proposed and implemented a low cost and small form factor 8x10G optical transmission system based on digital-wrapper technology, which can be used as a Hub node device in the Point to Multi Point (P2MP) or Hub-spoken network application [1]. In this paper, we further develop a small remote edge node device which can complete the full scope work for the Hub-spoken network. Especially, we develop software for the control plane and network management system. This P2MP network management system is based on the fast FPGA processing and the OTN digital wrapper (ITU-T G.709) to provide in-band communication. Our test results show that we can simultaneously do network management from the Hub node to up to 8 remote small edge nodes, which has the great advantage comparing with using multiple OSC (optical supervising channel) of the traditional optical network.

**Keywords:** Hub-spoken · P2MP · FPGA · OTN digital wrapper

## 1 Introduction

It is well know that optical network can provide high-capacity, long-distance, high reliable transmission for almost all kinds of different networks for telecom service providers such as metro, access, and long haul. The other applications include enterprise, LAN as well as data center interconnection. In the mean time, optical network has become increasingly complex, so that the importance of the optical network management has also become predominantly necessary, which can ensure efficient, secure, and continuous operation of any network. Specifically, a network management such as OAM implementation should be capable of handling the configuration, fault, performance, security, accounting, and safety in the network [2].

© ICST Institute for Computer Sciences, Social Informatics and Telecommunications Engineering 2018
Q. Chen et al. (Eds.): ChinaCom 2016, Part I, LNICST 209, pp. 431–439, 2018.
DOI: 10.1007/978-3-319-66625-9_42

On the other hand, recently, traditional and new service providers all tend to migrate their role to do not only the network service but also the content providing service. As a result, the demand for Point to Multipoint (P2MP) traffic is quickly increasing due to explosive growth of large amounts of new services such as video content distribution, IP-TV, and other on-demand services. It should be also noted that P2MP application also drives the special requirement in term of network management as it has a typical Hub-spoken traffic pattern or star network topology. To do the optical network management, there are three methods which are (1) digital wrapper technology, (2) subcarrier modulation technology, and (3) optical supervisory channel technology (OSC). Since the sub-carrier modulation technique modulates a low-frequency signal on an existing optical signal, which is essentially increasing the optical channel layer noise to the client signal, and there is also a conflict between the sub-carrier low frequency portion of modulated light and the client signals. On the other hand, OSC is used to transform the management information for point to point transmission application between two NEs (network equipment). However, for P2MP network application multiple OSC should be needed to perform the network management function from HUB to each remote nodes, which will add a lot of cost [3]. In addition, the OSC requires an additional wavelength to transmit the network management information and will be a waste of a wavelength resource. Digital wrapper technology can provide a good optical network concept as it can always combine with standard OTN and FEC (forward error correction), as well as provides the in-band capability for the network management system.

We have previously proposed a small form factor and low cost 8x10G trans-mission system as Fig. 1. There are 8 channels. Each short haul SFP+ module coverts 10GE traffic to SFI interface. For better performance, 10G OTN framer is applied in system. Each signals can be mapped to 10G OTN framer with FEC by OTN framer and then send to long haul SFP+ for long haul transmission.

**Fig. 1.** 8x10G transmission system

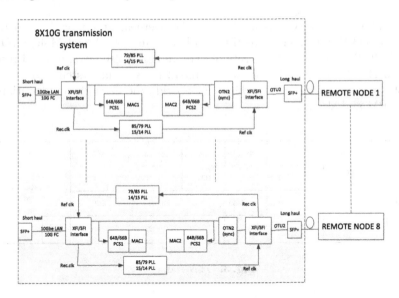

**Fig. 2.** Hub-spoken network architecture

It can do many flexible network applications, such as point to point WDM transmission or Metro WDM ring application. In addition, the device can also be configured to do the point to multi point (P2MP) application at the Hub node. In this paper, in order to complete the full picture of Hub-spoken network architecture as Fig. 2, we further develop a small remote edge node device which has only 1/4 size of Hub device, and has two slots which can be configured as with one dual-channel 10G card and one management card or both as dual-channel 10G card. In addition, we further do the software development for the control plane and network management system for this P2MP network. It should be noted that we do not use the OSC in optical network, since it will be too much expensive to have 8 OSC links for a Hub to 8 different remote edge nodes. In stead, 2 bytes GCC0 of OTN overhead are used to transparently transport network management message for each in-band communication channel. High speed FPGA is used to insert or drop the overhead to/from the actual OTN frame. The advantage is that at a HUB node up to 8 links OTN overhead can be processed by one FPGA simultaneously. This design has an innovation which can simultaneously do multiple network management, and it can support up to 8 in-band management channels communication from Hub location to 8 different remote nodes through long haul transmission.

The system is based on standard of ITU-T G.709 [4], where the client signal will be encapsulated by a digital wrapper framer. Figure 3 shows the structure of OTN frame, there are many OH (overhead) and it can also provide FEC function which can improve the transmission performance as well as to do the fault monitoring. 2 bytes GCC0 of OTN overhead are used to transparently transport network management message for each in-band communication channel. In our system, high speed FPGA is used to do the overhead insert or drop to/from the actual OTN frame. The rate of the In-band can reach 1.3549 Mbit/s. (OTN frame is $4080 \times 4$ byte, and the rate of OTU1e is 11.049 Gbit/s, in-band rate is equal to $11.049 * 10^6 * (2/(4080 * 4)) = 1354.9$ bit/s). Hub system can simultaneously access multiple nodes which can provide the network configuration as well as PM and alarm.

| FAS | | | MAFS | SM | GCC0 | RES | Mapping and cascading | |
|---|---|---|---|---|---|---|---|---|
| RES | TCM ACT | TCM6 | | TCM5 | TCM4 | FTFL | | |
| TCM3 | TCM2 | | TCM1 | | PM | EXP | | |
| GCC1 | GCC2 | APS/PCC | | RES | | | PSI | |

**Fig. 3.** OTN frame

## 2    Experiment Set-Up

Figure 4 shows experiment set up for point to multi point or P2MP application. It is a typical structure of HUB-SPOKEN, i.e., a central hub node device is connecting to multiple remote edge nodes. The Hub node usually located at the service provider central office and provided optical connection between their

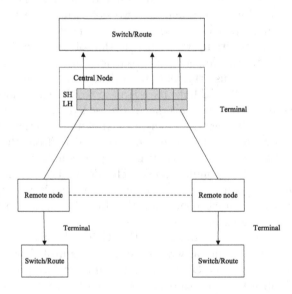

**Fig. 4.** Star application (central node as terminal)

switch/router and remote edge node. As shown in Fig. 4 up to 8 remote nodes can be supported by this P2MP network.

In addition, remote node can be customer premise, where the original data service is connected to the central node. Our device play the important role to connect the service from Hub node to each remote node, i.e., transmitting traffic from central Hub node to each remote node and also doing some important network OAM management. There is a transmission link between Hub node and each remote node. The details of our hub node transmission device can be referred by reference [1].

The remote edge node device is illustrated by Fig. 5 which is small box with two slots of one management card and one dual-channel 10G card.

**Fig. 5.** Remote node device

## 3   OAM SW Implementation

We design a protocol to efficiently transmit the management information transparently, which is responsible to collect and maintain the information about remote node device. 2 bytes GCC0 of OTN OH is used to transparently transport network management information. Frame of In-Band information is listed as the following Fig. 6.

| SFD(2byte) | TYP | RES | Length(2byte) | Playload | CRC |
|---|---|---|---|---|---|

**Fig. 6.** Inband frame

SFD: "0xABAB"; two byte start frame delimiter, which denotes one frame start
TYP: define the type of frame.

"0x01" means networks management package.

"0x02" means remote command for Simple Management use

"0x03" means remote register read and write for register mapping mode

RES: reserved for future use

Length: length of payload to be transmitted. This length is only included the payload.

Payload: Data need to be sent to remote site

CRC: Checksum of even BIP8 check.

In addition, we also develop a private Protocol of LLH (Low Level Shake Hands), which is used to identify the device type include the bit rate and protocol. As an example, if customer put one site device with OTU2(10.709 Gb/s), while the peer site with in OTU1e (11.049 Gb/s). In this case, traffic will not be OK, and in-band OSC channel can also not be built up. Low level shake hands (LLH) protocol is designed to solve this kind of mismatch problem. LLH is implemented by periodically turn on/of long haul laser to generate a low speed optical pules which carries the shake hands information. Frame of LLH: LLH frame is defined as Fig. 7. BYTE1 is LLH sync and LLH Command, BYTE2 is the bit negation of BYTE1 to check if BYTE1 is correct.

SOF0 – SOF2: Start of Frame indicator. "010" means frame start

C/S: Command or Status indicator. "1" C Command; "0" C Status information

D0– D3: Data to transmit.

When D0 = "0", following 3 bit defines the Rate mode of LH

"001" LH Rate is OTU2 (10.709 Gb/s)

"010" LH Rate is OTU1e (11.049 Gb/s)

"011" LH Rate is OTU2e (11.1 Gb/s)

"100" LH Rate is OTU2f

When D0 = "1", following 3 bit defined as other command or information

"0101100" is defined as remote reset command.

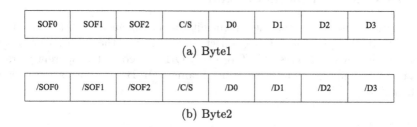

(a) Byte1

(b) Byte2

**Fig. 7.** LLH frame

## 4 Remote Node Device

Remote node device is a small and only 1/4 size of hub device which consists of Management card, dual-channel 10G card and power module as show in Fig. 5. Dual-channel 10G card is also show by the Fig. 8, which is constructed by 4

SFP+ module, a digital wrapper chip of VSC8492, FPGA, MCU, RAM, FLASH, etc. Client 10G switch or router sends 10G Signal to SFP+ module. It is then encapsulated into a 10G OTN frame signal by OTN Framer. 10G OTN framer, which is designed to provide FEC function and in-band network OAM management capability. Signal is transparently mapped into 10G OTN frame with FEC. After digital wrapper OTN frame process, signal will be sent to long haul SFP+ module for long distance transmission.

**Fig. 8.** Management card and dual-channel 10G card for remote device

The software architecture for management card is based on FreeRTOS running on 32 bit-MCU (STM32F103VET6) [5]. The structure of software is shown as Fig. 9 which includes 4 layers. The lowest layer is Hardware layer. The upper layer includes OS software which is designed based the on FreeRTOS (Real-time operating system), software drivers includes Console driver, SFP+ driver, CAN driver, FPGA driver, etc. The second layer including HWM (hardware monitor), DB, alarm, etc. The top of the structure is CLI (command line interface) which receives message including in-band message.

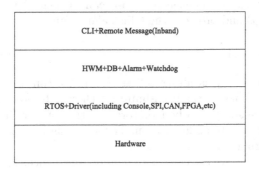

**Fig. 9.** Software structure based on MCU

After storing information in ping-pong RAM by FPGA, MCU can read the information form buffer through verifying header continually. In order to do priority process with the receiving information. We set a interrupt generated by EXTI and send to MCU. And the Fig. 10 is flow chart about Inband information process.

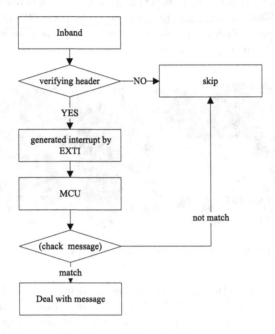

**Fig. 10.** Flow chart of Inband information process

Management card is designed based on a MCU of control devices which is show by Fig. 8, which can control and manage the management card through CAN bus by UART/USB/LAN interface. It consists of MCU, DDR, FLASH, RAM, etc. In our design, management card can manage the 10G card through LAN/Console/USB and provides the Office alarm functions.

## 5    Testing Result

P2MP experiment set up is illustrated as Fig. 4. We can use a PC to monitor and manage multi links status from hub to each remote node. All the PM and remote node device status can be monitored by the software from both the hub node location and remote node location. The following Fig. 11 shows the testing results for comparing.

In this experiment, we use console to monitor the device. The Hub equipment can get each remote node equipment status information through digital wrapper in-band management channel. It can be seen that the monitoring status of the remote equipment by hub node is the same as the result which is got directly from the remote node, which proves that P2MP method is implemented correctly and can monitors the multi remote devices efficiently.

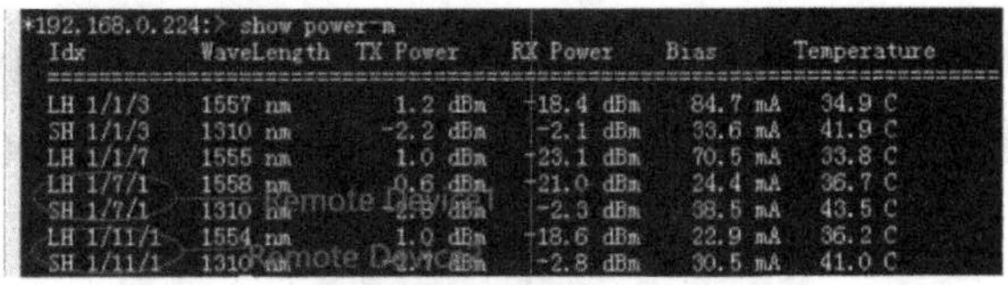

(a) local device

(b) remote device1

(c) remote device2

**Fig. 11.** Local and remote device status

**Acknowledgment.** We have built an experimental set up for point to multi point (P2MP) optical network by using a low cost 8x10G device of hub node and a small remote node device, which are both developed by ourselves. We also define and develop a software for the control plane and network management system. This P2MP network management system is based on the fast FPGA processing and the OTN digital wrapper (ITU-T G.709) to provide in-band communication. Our test results have shown that we can simultaneously monitor up to 8 remote nodes status from the hub node through the OTN digital wrapper in-band channel, which has the great advantage comparing with using multiple OSC of the traditional optical network.

# References

1. Liu, Q., Ouyang, C., Shi, C.: A small form factor and low cost 810 Gb/s optical transmission system based on digital-wrapper technology. In: 2015 Eighth International Symposium on Computational Intelligence and Design, (ISCID), pp. 275–280. IEEE Computer Society (2015)
2. Sul, D.M., Kim, S.M., Lee, J.H.: LSP merge in point to multipoint in-band OAM. In: 12th International Conference on Optical Internet (COIN) (2014)
3. Zhen, C., Yingjin, L.: Hub-spoken major appliance logistics net work building and practice. In: Computational and Information Sciences, (ICCIS), pp. 383–387 (2013)
4. ITU-T Recommendation G.709. Interface for the Optical Transport NetWorks (2009)
5. Hou, S., Wu, S.: Design and realization of family intelligent interactive terminal based on STM32. In: 9th International Conference on Fuzzy Systems and Knowledge Discovery (2012)

# Optimal Power Allocations for Full-Duplex Enhanced Visible Light Communications

Liping Liang, Wenchi Cheng[✉], and Hailin Zhang

State Key Laboratory of Integrated Services Networks,
Xidian University, Xi'an, China
lpliang@stu.xidian.edu.cn,
{wccheng,hlzhang}@xidian.edu.cn

**Abstract.** We consider the two nodes indoor full-duplex transmission over bidirectional channels with imperfect self-interference cancellation in visible light communications (VLCs). The light emitting diodes (LEDs) are used for illumination and data transmission while the photo diodes (PDs) are used for reception. In this paper, we first formulate the sum-capacity maximization problem for the full-duplex bidirectional VLCs. Then, we develop an optimal power allocation scheme, which has the closed-form expression, to achieve the maximum sum-capacity for two nodes indoor full-duplex bidirectional VLCs. The obtained numerical results verify our developed optimal power allocation scheme and show that the full-duplex transmission can significantly increase the sum-capacity than the traditional half-duplex transmission.

**Keywords:** Visible light communications · Full-duplex · Bidirectional transmission · Power allocations · Self-interference · Sum-capacity

## 1 Introduction

The optical wireless communication, which can efficiently overcome the spectrum deficiency problem in radio communications, has attracted a lot of attention in past few years. It has been shown that the optical wireless communications can be applied in transdermal communications, transports, mobile medical body area networks, underwater communications, and indoor optical wireless communications [1–4]. Among various optical wireless communications, the VLC rapidly emerges as an attractive communication technology [1]. Visible light communication uses visible light spectrum in the range of wavelength 380–780 nm, which is license-free and does not generate the electromagnetic interference to the existing radio frequency (RF) systems. In VLC systems, white light emitting diodes (LEDs) are used for illumination as well as the signal transmitter while photo diodes (PDs) are used as the receiver. The LEDs

This work was supported in part by the National Natural Science Foundation of China (No. 61401330), the 111 Project of China (B08038), and the Natural Science Foundation of Shaanxi Province (No. 2016JQ6027).

can support cable free communications as high as several tens Mbps between the LEDs and the PDs [5].

In half-duplex VLC systems, we need two time-slots to communicate between the two nodes, resulting in low network throughput. To deal with this issue, we propose to use full-duplex VLCs in this paper. The full-duplex wireless communication holds the promise of double spectral efficiency, compared with the traditional half-duplex wireless communication [6, 7], through simultaneous transmission and reception using the same frequency band at the same time. The wireless full-duplex communication mode was thought to be unfeasible because of the very large self-interference leaked from the local transmitter to the local receiver, thus making it difficult to extract the useful receive signal transmitted from the other node. Therefore, it is critical to be able to limit the power of the self-interference to implement full-duplex communications in practice. Recently, a great number of research works have shown the possibility of using full-duplex transmission in wireless communications using advanced propagation-domain interference suppression, analog-domain interference cancelation, and digital-domain interference cancelation [8–12]. Taking the self-interference as a part of useful information, the authors of [13] applied the full-duplex relay VLC based system to mitigate the self-interference. Some researchers proposed a self-adaptive minimum contention window full-duplex MAC protocol to mitigate channel collisions for VLCs [14]. To employ the full-duplex capacity efficiently, the paper [15] proposed two contention protocols, named UALOHA and FD-CSMA. The authors of [16] proved that the average electrical SNR per transmit antenna is considerably high in indoor MIMO optical wireless communications.

In this paper, we consider the two nodes full-duplex bidirectional transmission under imperfect self-interference cancelation in VLCs. We develop an optimal power allocation scheme to maximize the sum-capacity of two nodes visible light full-duplex bidirectional transmission for VLCs. For visible light full-duplex transmission in high signal-to-interference-noise rate (SINR) region, we derive the closed-form expression of optimal power allocation scheme.

The rest of this paper is organized as follows. Section 2 describes the system model. Section 3 formulates sum-capacity maximization problem for the full-duplex VLCs. Section 4 develops the optimal power allocation scheme in the high SINR region for visible light full-duplex bidirectional transmission. Section 5 carries out the numerical results to evaluate our developed optimal power allocation scheme and the achieved sum-capacity for two nodes visible light full-duplex bidirectional transmission compared with the traditional half-duplex transmission. Section 6 concludes the paper.

## 2 The System Model

In this paper, we consider the two nodes wireless full-duplex bidirectional visible light communications, as illustrated in Fig. 1, where node A and node B transmit their data to node B and node A, respectively. Each node is equipped with LEDs and PDs. The LEDs are used for both illumination and transmission while the PDs are used for reception. The optical modulation and demodulation schemes are set as intensity

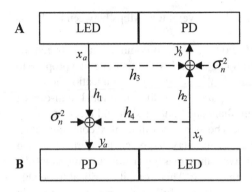

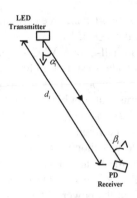

**Fig. 1.** The two nodes full-duplex bidirectional transmission in VLCs.

**Fig. 2.** The geometry of a transmitter-receiver pair.

modulation (IM) and direct detection (DD). The channels from node A to node B and from node B to node A use the same frequency band at the same time.

The shot and thermal noise in the receiver are modeled as additive white Gaussian noise (AWGN) and are added to the signal in the electrical domain. Thus, we have the total noise variance as $\sigma_n^2 = \sigma_{shot}^2 + \sigma_{thermal}^2$, where $\sigma_{shot}^2$ is the shot noise variance and $\sigma_{thermal}^2$ is the thermal noise variance [17]. We assume that all total noise variances are the same and uniformly denoted by $\sigma_n^2$ for mathematical simplification. We assume that the optical signal propagates from the transmitter to the receiver directly (Light of Sight) and the reflections are ignored [16]. We denote by $h_1^2$ and $h_2^2$ the channel gains from node A to node B and from node B to node A, respectively. We denote by $h_3^2$ and $h_4^2$ the self-interference channel gains from local transmitter to local receiver at nodes A and B, respectively. For one transmitter-receiver pair as shown in Fig. 2, the $h_i$ ($i = 1, 2, 3, 4$) is given by

$$h_i = \begin{cases} \frac{(m+1)A}{2\pi d_i^2} \cos^m(\alpha_i) \cos^\gamma(\beta_i) & \text{if } \alpha_i, \beta_i \in \left(0, \frac{\pi}{2}\right); \\ 0 & \text{others,} \end{cases} \tag{1}$$

where $m$ is the Lambertian emission order and given as follow (We assume that there is only one Lambertian emitting mode for LED):

$$m = \frac{-\ln 2}{\ln(\cos \psi_{1/2})}. \tag{2}$$

The parameter $\psi_{1/2}$ is the semi-angle of the LED at half-power. In Eq. (1), $A$ is the active area of PD and $\gamma$ is the filed-of-view (FoV) coefficient of the PD receiver [18]. For the *ith* channel ($h_i$), $d_i$, $\alpha_i$ and $\beta_i$ ($i = 1, 2, 3, 4$) are the distance from LED to PD, the irradiance angle at LED, and the incident angle at PD, respectively. We denote by $P_a$ and $P_b$ the transmitter power at nodes A and B, respectively.

To evaluate the performance of visible light full-duplex bidirectional transmission, we employ the concept of capacity region [19]. The capacity region for two nodes visible light full-duplex transmission is defined as the set of rate pairs $(R_A, R_B)$ such that the transmitters of node A and node B can reliably transmit data to the receivers of node B and node A simultaneously, where $R_A$ and $R_B$ denote the channel rates from node A to node B and from node B to node A, respectively. Because node A and node B share the same bandwidth, there is a tradeoff between the reliable communication rates $R_A$ and $R_B \cdot R_A(R_B)$ increases as $R_B(R_A)$ decreases. The received signal at nodes A and B, denoted by $\mathbf{y}_b$ and $\mathbf{y}_a$, respectively, can be derived as follows:

$$\begin{cases} \mathbf{y}_a = \sqrt{P_a}h_1\mathbf{x}_a + \sqrt{P_b}h_4\mathbf{x}_b + \sigma_n^2; \\ \mathbf{y}_b = \sqrt{P_b}h_3\mathbf{x}_a + \sqrt{P_a}h_2\mathbf{x}_b + \sigma_n^2, \end{cases} \tag{3}$$

where $\mathbf{x}_a$ and $\mathbf{x}_b$ represent the transmitted signal at nodes A and B, respectively, as illustrated in Fig. 1. Then, we define the sum-capacity as the scalar performance measure to evaluate the two nodes visible light full-duplex bidirectional transmission. The sum-capacity for two nodes visible light full-duplex bidirectional transmission, denoted by $\mathbf{s}_b$, is formulated as follows:

$$\mathbf{s}_b = \mathbf{y}_a + \mathbf{y}_b. \tag{4}$$

## 3   The Sum-Capacity Maximization Problem Formulation

For the wireless full-duplex bidirectional transmission, there still exists the residue self-interference even the advanced self-interference mitigation schemes are applied [8–12]. To characterize self-interference in visible light full-duplex bidirectional transmission, this section introduces a parameter $\kappa$ ($0 \leq \kappa \leq 1$), which is defined as the self-interference mitigation coefficient. Then based on self-interference mitigation coefficient, we can build up the received residue self-interference model, denoted by $f(P_t, h, x_t)$ as follows:

$$f(P_t, h, x_t) = \sqrt{\kappa P_t}hx_t, \tag{5}$$

where $x_t$, $h$, and $P_t$ represent the local transmit signal, the channel gain from the local transmitter to the local receiver, and the transmit power, respectively. Based on Eq. (5), it is clear that self-interference decreases with self-interference mitigation coefficient $\kappa$ decreases. When $\kappa = 1$, self-interference mitigation technique does not work. When $\kappa = 0$, it indicates that self-interference between the local transmitter and the local receiver can be completely canceled. In fact, $\kappa = 0$ is impossible using the current techniques.

We assume that all self-interference mitigation coefficients are the same and uniformly denoted by $\kappa$ for mathematical simplification. Then, the received signal at nodes A and B, denoted by $\mathbf{y}_b$ and $\mathbf{y}_a$, respectively, can be formulated as follows:

$$\begin{cases} \mathbf{Y}_a = \sqrt{P_a}h_1\mathbf{x}_a + f(\sqrt{P_b}, h_4, \mathbf{x}_b) + \sigma_n^2 = \sqrt{P_a}h_1\mathbf{x}_a + \sqrt{\kappa P_b}h_4\mathbf{x}_b + \sigma_n^2; \\ \mathbf{Y}_b = \sqrt{P_b}h_2\mathbf{x}_b + f(\sqrt{P_a}, h_3, \mathbf{x}_a) + \sigma_n^2 = \sqrt{P_b}h_2\mathbf{x}_b + \sqrt{\kappa P_a}h_3\mathbf{x}_a + \sigma_n^2. \end{cases} \quad (6)$$

We denote by $SINR_a$ and $SINR_b$ the SINRs of the received signal $Y_a$ and $Y_b$. Then, based on the analyses above, $SINR_a$ and $SINR_b$ can be expressed as follows:

$$\begin{cases} SINR_a = \frac{P_a h_1^2}{\sigma_n^2 + \kappa P_b h_4^2}; \\ SINR_b = \frac{P_b h_2^2}{\sigma_n^2 + \kappa P_a h_3^2}. \end{cases} \quad (7)$$

The capacity from node A to node B and from node B to node A, denoted by $C_{ab}(P_a, P_b)$ and $C_{ba}(P_a, P_b)$, respectively, can be derived as follows:

$$\begin{cases} C_{ab} = \log(1 + SINR_a); \\ C_{ba} = \log(1 + SINR_b). \end{cases} \quad (8)$$

Thus, we can derive the achievable sum-capacity of two nodes optical wireless full-duplex bidirectional transmission, denoted by $C_B(P_a, P_b)$, as follows:

$$C_B(P_a, P_b) = C_{ab}(P_a, P_b) + C_{ba}(P_a, P_b) = \log(1 + SINR_a) + \log(1 + SINR_b). \quad (9)$$

Our goal aims at allocating the transmit power to achieve the maximum sum-capacity for two nodes optical wireless full-duplex bidirectional transmission. Then, we can formulate the sum-capacity maximization problem, denoted by **P1**, as follows:

$$\textbf{P1} : \arg \max_{(P_a, P_b)} \{C_B(P_a, P_b)\} \quad (10)$$

$$\text{s.t.}: \quad (1)\ P_a > 0, P_b > 0; \quad (11)$$

$$(2)\ P_a + P_b \leq \overline{P}, \quad (12)$$

where $\overline{P}$ represents the average power constraint. Observing $C_B(P_a, P_b)$ specified in Eq. (9), we know that the capacity $C_B(P_a, P_b)$ is a nonconcave function over the space spanned by $(P_a, P_b)$. Thus, **P1** is not a strictly convex optimization problem. To obtain the maximum capacity $C_B(P_a, P_b)$, it is desirable that **P1** is a strictly convex optimization problem. In the following section, we convert **P1** to convex optimization problem and develop the optimal power allocation scheme to obtain the global optimal solution for **P1**.

## 4 The Optimal Power Allocation Scheme in the High SINR Region

In the high SINR region, $C_B(P_a, P_b)$ can be re-written as follows:

$$C_B(P_a, P_b) = \log\left(\frac{P_a h_1^2}{\sigma_n^2 + \kappa P_b h_4^2}\right) + \log\left(\frac{P_b h_2^2}{\sigma_n^2 + \kappa P_a h_3^2}\right)$$

$$= \log\left(\frac{P_a P_b h_1^2 h_2^2}{\sigma_n^4 + \sigma_n^2 \kappa P_a h_3^2 + \sigma_n^2 \kappa P_b h_4^2 + \kappa^2 P_a P_b h_3^2 h_4^2}\right). \tag{13}$$

Because log ($\bullet$) is a monotonically increasing function as the independent variables increase, we can convert the problem *P1* to a new problem *P2*, which is an equivalent problem as *P1* and can be expressed as follows:

$$P2: \quad \max_{(P_a, P_b)} \left(\frac{P_a P_b h_1^2 h_2^2}{\sigma_n^4 + \sigma_n^2 \kappa P_a h_3^2 + \sigma_n^2 \kappa P_b h_4^2 + \kappa^2 P_a P_b h_3^2 h_4^2}\right) \tag{14}$$

subject to the constraints given in Eqs. (11) and (12). Then we have the Lemma 1 as follows:

*Lemma 1:* The problem *P2* is a strictly convex optimization problem.

*Proof:* We define the function $f(P_a, P_b)$ as follows:

$$f(P_a, P_b) = \frac{h_1^2 h_2^2}{\frac{\sigma_n^4}{P_a P_b} + \frac{\sigma_n^2 \kappa h_3^2}{P_b} + \frac{\sigma_n^2 \kappa h_4^2}{P_a} + \kappa^2 h_3^2 h_4^2}. \tag{15}$$

Since $(\sigma_n^4/P_a P_b + \sigma_n^2 \kappa h_3^2/P_b + \sigma_n^2 \kappa h_4^2/P_a + \kappa^2 h_3^2 h_4^2)$ decreases as $P_a$ and $P_b$ increase, $(\sigma_n^4/P_a P_b + \sigma_n^2 \kappa h_3^2/P_b + \sigma_n^2 \kappa h_4^2/P_a + \kappa^2 h_3^2 h_4^2)$ is strictly convex on the space spanned by $(P_a, P_b)$ when $P_a$ and $P_b$ are subject to the constraints given in Eqs. (11) and (12). Thus, $f(P_a, P_b)$ is a strictly concave function on the space spanned by $(P_a, P_b)$. On the other hand, it is clear to verify that all inequalities constraints (Eqs. (11) and (12)) are linear on the space spanned by $(P_a, P_b)$. Therefore, the problem *P2* is a strictly convex optimization problem. To derive the optimal solutions of the problem *P2*, we have the following Theorem 1.

*Theorem 1:* The optimal solutions to the problem *P2*, denoted by $P_a^*$ and $P_b^*$, are determined by

$$\begin{cases} P_a^* = \frac{\sigma_n^2 + \kappa \bar{P} h_4^2 - \sqrt{(\sigma_n^2 + \kappa \bar{P} h_4^2)^2 - \kappa(h_4^2 - h_3^2)(\bar{P}\sigma_n^2 + \kappa \bar{P}^2 h_4^2)}}{\kappa(h_4^2 - h_3^2)}; \\ P_b^* = \frac{-\sigma_n^2 - \kappa \bar{P} h_3^2 + \sqrt{(\sigma_n^2 + \kappa \bar{P} h_4^2)^2 - \kappa(h_4^2 - h_3^2)(\bar{P}\sigma_n^2 + \kappa \bar{P}^2 h_4^2)}}{\kappa(h_4^2 - h_3^2)}. \end{cases} \tag{16}$$

*Proof:* Because problem *P2* is a strictly convex optimization problem, it has the unique optimal solution. It is easy to know that the optimal solutions to problem *P2* need to satisfy $P_a^* + P_b^* = \bar{P}$. Thus, the optimal solution $P_a^*$ and $P_b^*$ need to satisfy

$$
\begin{cases}
\dfrac{\partial f(P_a,P_b)}{\partial P_a} = \dfrac{\sigma_n^4(\bar{P}-2P_a)h_1^2 h_2^2 - \sigma_n^2 P_a^2 \kappa h_1^2 h_2^2 h_3^2 + \sigma_n^2(\bar{P}-P_a)^2 \kappa h_1^2 h_2^2 h_4^2}{(\sigma_n^4 + \sigma_n^2 \kappa P_a h_3^2 + \sigma_n^2 \kappa P_b h_4^2 + \kappa^2 P_a P_b h_3^2 h_4^2)^2}; \\[4mm]
\dfrac{\partial f(P_a,P_b)}{\partial P_b} = \dfrac{\sigma_n^4(\bar{P}-2P_b)h_1^2 h_2^2 - \sigma_n^2 P_b^2 \kappa h_1^2 h_2^2 h_4^2 + \sigma_n^2(\bar{P}-P_b)^2 \kappa h_1^2 h_2^2 h_3^2}{(\sigma_n^4 + \sigma_n^2 \kappa P_a h_3^2 + \sigma_n^2 \kappa P_b h_4^2 + \kappa^2 P_a P_b h_3^2 h_4^2)^2}; \\[4mm]
(P_a^* + P_b^*) - \bar{P} = 0; \\[2mm]
P_j^* > 0, j \in \{a,b\}.
\end{cases}
\tag{17}
$$

Solving Eq. (17), we can derive the optimal solution expressed as shown in Eq. (16). Thus, Theorem 1 follows.

Theorem 1 gives the expression of the optimal solutions $P_a^*$ and $P_b^*$ in the high SINR region. The solutions are very accurate in the high SINR region and have the simple closed-form expression.

## 5  Numerical Results

In this section, we conduct numerical results to evaluate the performance of our developed optimal power allocation scheme for the visible light full-duplex bidirectional transmission. We consider a 4 m × 4 m × 3 m space. We assume that the LEDs are Lambertian sources with the semi-angle at half power $\psi_{1/2} = 60°$ (which determines $m = 1$). We further assume that the average power constraint $\bar{P}$ is set as 70 W. We set $A = 15$ mm$^2$ smaller than 1 cm$^2$ and $\gamma = 1.4738$ [16].

Figure 3 depicts the developed power allocation scheme for the two nodes visible light full-duplex transmission, where we set the irradiance angle at LED ($\alpha_i$) as 15° and the incident angle at PD ($\beta_i$) as 30° ($i = 1, 2, 3, 4$). As shown in Fig. 3, when the distance ($h_3$) from the local transmitter to the local receiver at node A is very closed to distance ($h_4$) from the local transmitter to the local receiver at node B, the optimal power $P_a^*$ and $P_b^*$ are almost half of the average power. The optimal power of node A increases as $h_3$ decreases and $h_4$ increases. The optimal power of node B increases as $h_3$

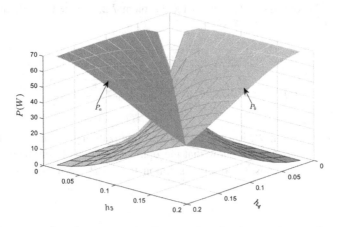

**Fig. 3.** The power allocations versus the distances from local transmitters to local receivers.

increases and $h_4$ decreases. This result proves that the visible light full-duplex transmission can be well applied because the large self-interference has been efficiently mitigated in the high SINR region.

Figure 4 evaluates the sum-capacity of using our developed optimal full-duplex power allocation scheme and the half-duplex scheme with different irradiance angle at LEDs and different incident angle at PDs, where we set distances from the transmitter of node A to the receiver of node B and from the transmitter of node B to the receiver of node A as 0.9 m and 0.5 m, respectively. We assume that the irradiance angle at LEDs and the incident angle at PDs from local LEDs to local PDs for node A and node B are set as 15° and 30°, respectively. The irradiance angle at LEDs and the incident angle at PDs from node A to node B and from node B to node A are set as the same size, i.e., $\alpha_1 = \alpha_2$ and $\beta_1 = \beta_2$. Thus, we can obtain the result that the sum-capacity decreases as irradiance angle at LEDs and incident angle at PDs increase. As we expected, the sum-capacity of using our optimal full-duplex power allocation scheme is much larger than the traditional half-duplex scheme except the scenario that both irradiance angle at LEDs and incident angle at PDs are very closed to 90°. The ideal case is that the LEDs are always oriented to the PDs, i.e., $\alpha_i = 0°$ and $\beta_i = 0°$ ($i = 1, 2$). Under this case, we have the maximum sum-capacity for the full-duplex VLCs.

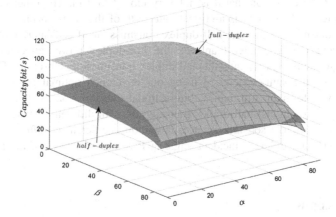

**Fig. 4.** The sum-capacity of using our developed optimal full-duplex power allocation scheme and the half-duplex scheme versus different irradiance angle at LEDs and different incident angle at PDs.

Figure 5 depicts the sum-capacity of using our optimal full-duplex power scheme and the half-duplex scheme with different and different $d$. The distances from the local transmitter to the local receiver at nodes A and B are set as 0.08 m and 0.1 m, respectively. The irradiance angle at LED ($\alpha_i$) and the incident angle at PD ($\beta_i$) are set as the same as those in Fig. 3 ($i = 1, 2, 3, 4$). As shown in Fig. 5, we obtain that the sum-capacity of both visible light full-duplex and half-duplex transmission decreases as $d$ and $\kappa$ increases. The sum-capacity of using our optimal full-duplex power allocation scheme is nearly twice compared with that of the half-duplex scheme except the case that the distance between the two nodes is closed to 4 m and $\kappa$ is considerably small.

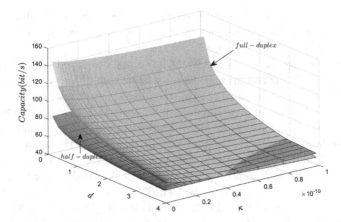

**Fig. 5.** The sum-capacity of using our developed optimal full-duplex power allocation scheme and the half-duplex scheme versus κ and $d$.

As self-interference mitigation coefficient (κ) increases, the sum-capacity of using the optimal visible light full-duplex power allocation scheme is larger than the half-duplex scheme under the condition that $d$ is not very closed to 4 m. The other case is that $d$ approximates to 4 m, there is a critical value κth of the sum-capacity between the full-duplex transmission and the half-duplex transmission. If self-interference mitigation coefficient (κ) is smaller than κth, the full-duplex power allocation scheme achieves larger sum-capacity than the half-duplex transmission. Observing Figs. 4 and 5, we find that the sum-capacity of using our developed optimal power allocation scheme in visible light full-duplex bidirectional transmission is larger than the sum-capacity in traditional half-duplex transmission with different distance d between the two nodes, different self-interference mitigation coefficient κ, different irradiance angle at LEDs, and different incident angle at PDs in most cases in the high SINR region.

## 6 Conclusions

In this paper, we built up the model to analyze the two nodes full-duplex bidirectional transmission in VLCs. Based on this model, we developed the optimal power allocation scheme to maximize the sum-capacity of two nodes visible light full-duplex bidirectional transmission. In high SINR region, we obtained the maximum sum-capacity of two nodes with different distance from the local transmitter to the local receiver, different distance between the two nodes, different self-interference mitigation coefficient, different irradiance angle at LEDs, and different incident angle at PDs. The numerical results show that visible light full-duplex transmission can significantly increase the sum-capacity than the traditional half-duplex transmission.

# References

1. Arnon, S., Uysal, M., Ghassemlooy, Z., Xu, Z., Cheng, J.: Guest editorial optical wireless communications. IEEE J. **33**, 1733–1737 (2015)
2. Sanz, M.G.: Visible light data communications. Project, Dept. of Electronics and Electrical Engineering, University of Glasgow, UK (2011–2012), http://www.glasgow.ac.uk/engineering
3. Elgala, H., Mesleh, R., Haas, H.: Indoor optical wireless communications: potential and State-of-the-art. IEEE Commun. Mag. **49**(9), 56–62 (2011)
4. Tsonev, D., Sinaovic, S., Hass, H.: Practical MIMO capacity for indoor optical wireless communication with white LEDs. In: Proceedings of IEEE VTC-Spring, New York, pp. 1–5 (2013)
5. Bouchet, O.: Visible-light communication system enabling 73 Mb/s data streaming. In: IEEE GLOBECOM 2010 Workshop on Optical Wireless Communications, Miami, Florida (2010)
6. Bliss, D.W., Parker, P.A., Margetts, A.R.: Simultaneous transmission and reception for improved wireless network performance. In: IEEE Workshop Statistics and Signal Process, pp. 478–482 (2007)
7. Riihonen, T., Werner, S., Wichman, R.: Comparison of full-duplex and half-duplex modes with a fixed amplify-and-forward relay. In: IEEE Wireless Communications and Networking Conference, pp. 1–5 (2009)
8. Choi, J.I., Jain, M., Srinivasan, K., Levis, P., Katti, S.: Achieving single channel, full duplex wireless communication. In: Proceedings of 16th ACM MOBICOM, Chicago, Illinois, USA (2010)
9. Jain, M., Chio, J.I., Kim, T.M., Bharadia, D., Seth, S., Srinivasan, K., Levis, P., Katti, S., Sinha, P.: Practical, real-time, full duplex wireless. In: Proceedings of 17th ACM MOBICOM, Las Vegas, Nevada, USA (2011)
10. Duarte, M., Sabharwal, A.: Full-duplex wireless communications using off-the-shelf radios: feasibility and first results. In: Proceedings of Annual Asilomar Conference on Signals, Systems and Computers, pp. 1558–1562 (2011)
11. Bozidar, R., Dinan, R., Peter, K., Alexandre, P., Nikhil, S., Vlad, B., Gerald, D.: Rethinking indoor wireless mesh design: low power, low frequency, full-duplex. In: 5th IEEE Workshop on Wireless Mesh Networks (WIMESH 2010), pp. 1–6 (2010)
12. Everett, E., Duarte, M., Dick, C., Sabharwal, A.: Empowering full-duplex wireless communication by exploiting directional diversity. In: 45th Asilomar Conference on Signals, Systems and Computers, pp. 2002–2006 (2011)
13. Yang, H., Pandharipande, A.: Full-duplex relay VLC in LED lighting linear system topology. In: IECON 39th Annual Conference of the IEEE, pp. 6075–6080 (2013)
14. Wang, Z., Liu, Y., Lin, Y., Huang, S.: Full-duplex MAC protocol based on adaptive contention window for visible light communication. IEEE/OSA J. Opt. Commun. Netw. **7**, 164–171 (2015)
15. Zhang, Z., Yu, X., Wu, L., Dang, J., Li, V.O.K.: Performance analysis of full-duplex visible light communication networks. In: ICC, pp. 3933–3938 (2015)
16. Nuwanpriya, A., Ho, S., Chen, C.S.: Indoor MIMO visible light communications: novel angle diversity receivers for mobile users. IEEE J. **33**, 1780–1792 (2015)
17. Fath, T., Haas, H.: Performance comparison of MIMO techniques for optical wireless communications in indoor environments. IEEE Trans. Commun. **61**(2), 733–742 (2013)

18. Yang, S.-H., Jung, E.-M., Han, S.-K.: Indoor location estimation based on LED visible light communication using multiple optical receivers. IEEE Commun. Lett. **17**(9), 1834–1837 (2013)
19. Cheng, W., Zhang, X., Zhang, H.: Optical dynamic power control for full-duplex bidirectional-channel based wireless networks. In: Proceedings of IEEE INFOCOM, pp. 3120–3128 (2013)

# Signal Detection and Estimation

# A Novel Bitwise Factor Graph Belief Propagation Detection Algorithm for Massive MIMO System

Lin Li[1,2] and Weixiao Meng[1,2(✉)]

[1] Communications Research Center, Harbin Institute of Technology, Harbin, China
[2] Key Laboratory of Police Wireless Digital Communication,
Ministry of Public Security, Harbin, China
wxmeng@hit.edu.cn

**Abstract.** As a low computational complexity detection algorithm for Massive Multi-Input-Multi-Output (MIMO) system, the well known factor graph belief propagation (BP) detection algorithm is effective for binary phase shift keying (BPSK) signal, but not appropriate for quadrature amplitude modulation (QAM) signal. In this paper, the complex transmitted signal vector modulated by QAM is transformed into the real valued bitwise vector which can be viewed as a transmitting signal vector modulated by BPSK. With the real valued bitwise vector and transformed channel gain matrix, an improved bitwise factor graph (BFG) graphic model is developed, and a BFG-BP algorithm is proposed to detect QAM signals in Massive MIMO system. Over a finite time of polynomial computational complexity of $O(N_T)$ per symbol, where $N_T$ denotes the number of transmitted antennas, the proposed BFG-BP detection algorithm obtains the approximate optimum BER performance of maximum likelihood detection algorithm with rapid convergence rate, and also achieves the theoretical spectral efficiency at medium high average received signal-to-noise ratio. Simulation results prove the effeteness of the proposed BFG-BP for detecting QAM signals in Massive MIMO system.

**Keywords:** Massive MIMO · Detection algorithm · Bitwise factor graph · Belief propagation · Bit error rate (BER) · Computational complexity

## 1 Introduction

The detection algorithm for Massive Multi Input Multi Output (MIMO) system captured much attention in recent years [1,2]. Due to the large scale antennas in Massive MIMO system, the problem of obtaining optimum bit error rate (BER)

---

W. Meng—This work is supported by National Natural Science Foundation of China: No. 61471143.

© ICST Institute for Computer Sciences, Social Informatics and Telecommunications Engineering 2018
Q. Chen et al. (Eds.): ChinaCom 2016, Part I, LNICST 209, pp. 453–462, 2018.
DOI: 10.1007/978-3-319-66625-9_44

along with lower computational complexity is non-deterministic polynomial-time hard (NP-hard), and is difficult to be solved.

The maximum likelihood (ML) detection algorithm obtains the optimum BER performance for MIMO system [3]. However, the computational complexity of ML increases exponentially with the number of transmitting antennas, which is too high for ML to be employed in Massive MIMO system. The traditional linear detection algorithms, such as minimum mean square error (MMSE), have much lower polynomial computational complexity than ML. But the BER performance of MMSE is poor, and is required to be improved for Massive MIMO system.

Recently, many detection algorithms for Massive MIMO system have been investigated, such as the likelihood ascent search (LAS) algorithm [4], the Markov Chain Monte Carlo (MCMC) algorithm [5], the Probabilistic Data Association (PDA) algorithm [6], the Markov random field (MRF) and the factor graph (FG) based belief propagation (BP) detection algorithms [7,8], etc. They obtain approximate optimum BER performance with polynomial computational complexity. Particularly, the FG-BP detection algorithm has a relative low computational complexity, and has a considerable potential of application in Massive MIMO system. Though the FG-BP is effective for Binary Phase Shift Keying (BPSK) signals, it is not appropriate for quadrature amplitude modulation (QAM) signals.

In this paper, the complex transmitted signal vector modulated by QAM is transformed into the real valued bitwise vector which can be viewed as a transmitting signal vector modulated by BPSK. With the real valued bitwise vector and transformed channel gain matrix, we develop an improved bitwise factor graph (BFG) graphic model, and propose a novel BFG-BP algorithm to detect QAM signals in Massive MIMO system. With one order polynomial computational complexity, the proposed BFG-BP obtains an approximate optimum BER performance of ML, and achieves the theory spectral efficiency at a medium high average received signal-to-noise (SNR) as well.

The rest of the paper is organized as follows. The detection model for Massive MIMO system is presented in Sect. 2. Section 3 deduces the proposed BFG-BP algorithm. Section 4 gives the corresponding computational complexity. The simulation is introduced in Sect. 5. Finally, Sect. 6 draws the conclusion.

**Notation.** In this paper, a vector and a matrix are represented with lower-case and uppercase boldface letters. $(\cdot)^T$, $(\cdot)^{-1}$, $(\cdot)^H$, $\|\cdot\|$, $\otimes$, $E\{\cdot\}$, $\Re(\cdot)$ and $\Im(\cdot)$ denote transpose, inverse, complex conjugate transpose, 2-norm, Kronecker product, statistical expectation, real part and imaginary part of a matrix, respectively. $\mathbb{C}$ and $\mathbb{R}$ refer to the complex and real domain, respectively.

## 2   System Model

For both the point to point and the up-link multiuser Massive MIMO system in single cell or non-cooperative multi cell, we employ the vertical Bell Layered space-time (VBLAST) system as the uncoded detection model [10]. For the Massive MIMO system, hundreds and thousands of antennas are considered, and the number of transmitted and received antennas are denoted as $N_T$ and $N_R$, respectively. The channel gain matrix can be written as

$$\mathbf{H}' = \begin{bmatrix} h'_{11} & h'_{12} & \cdots & h'_{1N_T} \\ h'_{21} & h'_{22} & \cdots & h'_{2N_T} \\ \vdots & \vdots & \ddots & \vdots \\ h'_{N_R1} & h'_{N_R2} & \cdots & h'_{N_RN_T} \end{bmatrix} \tag{1}$$

where $\mathbf{H}' \in \mathbb{C}^{N_R \times N_T}$ and $N_R \geq N_T$. $h'_{ln}$ denotes the channel gain from the $n$th transmitted antenna to the $l$th received antenna, $l \in \{1, 2, \cdots, N_R\}$, $n \in \{1, 2, \cdots, N_T\}$. In quasi-static environment, the channel is assumed to be flat fading. $\mathbf{H}'$ is invariant during a frame, but it changes independently from frame to frame. $h'_{ln}$ is a zero mean, independent, and identically distributed complex Gaussian random variable with variance 1. In addition, the channel state is assumed to be known at the receiver.

During a symbol time, the $N_T \times 1$ transmitted signal vector can be denoted as

$$\mathbf{x}' = [x'_1, \cdots, x'_n, \cdots, x'_{N_T}]^T \tag{2}$$

where $x'_n \in \mathbb{S}$ is modulated from bits stream into a symbol according to the modulation alphabet. $\mathbb{S} = \mathbb{A} + j\mathbb{A}$ is referred to as the complex alphabet of M-QAM modulation, and

$$\mathbb{A} = \left[-(\sqrt{M} - 1), \cdots, -3, -1, 1, 3, \cdots, (\sqrt{M} - 1)\right] \tag{3}$$

where $M$ denotes the modulation order.

The received signal can be denoted as $\mathbf{y}' = [y'_1, \cdots, y'_l, \cdots, y'_{N_R}]^T \in \mathbb{C}^{N_R \times 1}$, and is given by

$$\mathbf{y}' = \mathbf{H}'\mathbf{x}' + \mathbf{w}' \tag{4}$$

where $\mathbf{w}' = [w'_1, \cdots, w'_l, \cdots, w'_{N_R}]^T \in \mathbb{C}^{N_R \times 1}$ refers to the complex additive white Gaussian noise (AWGN), and $E\left\{\mathbf{w}'\mathbf{w}'^H\right\} = \sigma^2 \mathbf{I}_{N_R}$. The $\sigma^2$ is the noise variance, and $\mathbf{I}_{N_R}$ signifies a $N_R \times N_R$ identity matrix.

## 3 Proposed BFG-BP Detection Algorithm

Consider the real-valued system model corresponding to (4), i.e.,

$$\mathbf{y} = \mathbf{H}\mathbf{x} + \mathbf{w} \tag{5}$$

where

$$\mathbf{y} \triangleq \begin{bmatrix} \Re(\mathbf{y}') \\ \Im(\mathbf{y}') \end{bmatrix}, \ \mathbf{H} \triangleq \begin{bmatrix} \Re(\mathbf{H}') & -\Im(\mathbf{H}') \\ \Im(\mathbf{H}') & \Re(\mathbf{H}') \end{bmatrix}, \ \mathbf{x} \triangleq \begin{bmatrix} \Re(\mathbf{x}') \\ \Im(\mathbf{x}') \end{bmatrix}, \ \mathbf{w} \triangleq \begin{bmatrix} \Re(\mathbf{w}') \\ \Im(\mathbf{w}') \end{bmatrix}. \tag{6}$$

Herein, $\mathbf{y}$, $\mathbf{H}$, $\mathbf{x}$ and $\mathbf{w}$ signify the real valued received signal vector, channel gain matrix, transmitted signal vector and noise vector, respectively. For the sake of convenience, $\mathbf{y}$, $\mathbf{x}$ and $\mathbf{w}$ are rewritten as follows:

$$\mathbf{y} = [y_1, \cdots, y_{n_r}, \cdots, y_{2N_R}]^T \tag{7}$$

$$\mathbf{x} = [x_1, \cdots, x_{n_t}, \cdots, x_{2N_T}]^T \tag{8}$$

$$\mathbf{w} = [w_1, \cdots, w_{n_r}, \cdots, w_{2N_R}]^T \tag{9}$$

where $n_t = 1, 2, \cdots, 2N_T$, $n_r = 1, 2, \cdots, 2N_R$.

In the context of M-QAM, the real valued symbol $x_{n_t}$ is expanded to the bit domain and written as

$$x_{n_t} = \sum_{k=0}^{K-1} 2^k b_{n_t}^k = \mathbf{c}\,\mathbf{b}_{n_t} \tag{10}$$

where $K = \log_2(\sqrt{M})$ refers to the total number of bits for each real valued symbol, and

$$\mathbf{c} = [2^0, 2^1, \cdots, 2^k, \cdots, 2^{K-1}] \tag{11}$$

$$\mathbf{b}_{n_t} = [b_{n_t}^{(0)}, b_{n_t}^{(1)}, \cdots, b_{n_t}^{(k)}, \cdots, b_{n_t}^{(K-1)}]^T \tag{12}$$

where $\mathbf{b}_{n_t}$ can be interpreted as the $n_t$th bitwise transmitted vector. $b_{n_t}^{(k)} \in \mathbb{B}$ represents the $k$th bit value from the $n_t$th transmitted antenna. $\mathbb{B} = \{1, -1\}$ signifies the bitwise alphabet. $k = 0, 1, \cdots, K-1$.

Denote

$$\mathbf{b} = [\mathbf{b}_1^T, \mathbf{b}_2^T, \cdots, \mathbf{b}_{n_t}^T, \cdots, \mathbf{b}_{2N_T}^T]^T \tag{13}$$

as a collection of the bitwise transmitted vector. According to (8) and (10), the transmitted signal vector $\mathbf{x}$ can be rewritten as

$$\mathbf{x} = (\mathbf{I}_{2N_T} \otimes \mathbf{c})\mathbf{b}. \tag{14}$$

It follows from (5) and (14) that

$$\mathbf{y} = \mathbf{H}(\mathbf{I}_{2N_T} \otimes \mathbf{c})\mathbf{b} + \mathbf{w} = \tilde{\mathbf{H}}\mathbf{b} + \mathbf{w} \tag{15}$$

where $\tilde{\mathbf{H}} = \mathbf{H}(\mathbf{I}_{2N_T} \otimes \mathbf{c}) \in \mathbb{R}^{(2N_R) \times (2KN_T)}$ can be regarded as the equivalent channel gain matrix.

It can be seen that the bitwise alphabet $\mathbb{B}$ is the same with the modulation alphabet of BPSK. The bitwise transmitted vector $\mathbf{b}$ can be viewed as the signal which is modulated by BPSK.

According to (15), the maximum a posteriori probability (MAP) detection of $\mathbf{b}$ can be given by [11]

$$\hat{b}_{n_t}^{(k)} = \arg\max_{b_{n_t}^{(k)} \in \mathbb{B}} p(b_{n_t}^{(k)}|\mathbf{y}, \tilde{\mathbf{H}}) \tag{16}$$

where $p(b_{n_t}^{(k)}|\mathbf{y}, \tilde{\mathbf{H}})$ denotes the posteriori probability (APP) of the $b_{n_t}^{(k)}$. According to the above derivation, we develop a bitwise FG (BFG) graphic model. Its modeling process is illustrated in Fig. 1(a).

Based on the BFG graphic model, a novel BFG-BP detection algorithm is proposed. Figure 1(b) and (c) briefly shows message passing of the proposed BFG-BP, where the observation node and the bitwise variable node signify the real valued received symbol and transmitted bit, respectively.

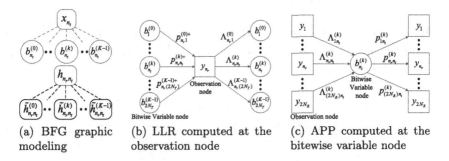

(a) BFG graphic modeling

(b) LLR computed at the observation node

(c) APP computed at the bitewise variable node

**Fig. 1.** Graphic modeling and message passing of the proposed BFG-BP

Consider the message which passes from the $n_t^{(k)}$th bitwise variable node to the $n_r$th observation node. It follows from (7) and (15) that

$$y_{n_r} = \tilde{h}_{n_r n_t}^{(k)} b_{n_t}^{(k)} + \sum_{j=1,j\neq n_t}^{2N_T} \sum_{i=0,i\neq k}^{K-1} \tilde{h}_{n_r j}^{(i)} b_j^{(i)} + w_{n_r} = \tilde{h}_{n_r n_t}^{(k)} b_{n_t}^{(k)} + z_{n_r n_t}^{(k)} \quad (17)$$

where $\tilde{h}_{n_r n_t}^{(k)}$ denotes the $(n_r, n_t^{(k)})$th entry of $\tilde{\mathbf{H}}$, and

$$z_{n_r n_t}^{(k)} = \sum_{j=1,j\neq n_t}^{2N_T} \sum_{i=0,i\neq k}^{K-1} \tilde{h}_{n_r j}^{(i)} b_j^{(i)} + w_{n_r} \quad (18)$$

represents the Gaussian approximate interference (GAI) to the bit variable $b_{n_t}^{(k)}$, which is coming from the $n_t^{(k)}$ transmitted bitwise node and received by the $n_r$th observation node. In addition, $z_{n_r n_t}^{(k)}$ approximately follows the Gaussian distribution [9], i.e., $z_{n_r n_t}^{(k)} \sim \mathcal{CN}(\mu_{z_{n_r n_t}^{(k)}}, \sigma^2_{z_{n_r n_t}^{(k)}})$, where

$$\mu_{z_{n_r n_t}^{(k)}} = \sum_{j=1,j\neq n_t}^{2N_T} \sum_{i=0,i\neq k}^{K-1} \tilde{h}_{n_r j}^{(i)} \mathbb{E}(b_j^{(i)}) \quad (19)$$

$$\sigma^2_{z_{n_r n_t}^{(k)}} = \sum_{j=1,j\neq n_t}^{2N_T} \sum_{i=0,i\neq k}^{K-1} (\tilde{h}_{n_r j}^{(i)})^2 Var(b_j^{(i)}) + \sigma^2/2. \quad (20)$$

$\mathbb{E}(b_j^{(i)})$ and $Var(b_j^{(i)})$ denote the mean and variance of the bitwise variable $b_j^{(i)}$, respectively.

The log-likelihood ratio (LLR) of $b_j^{(i)}$ at the $n_r$th observation node is denoted by $\Lambda_{n_r n_t}^{(k)}$, and can be written as

$$\Lambda_{n_r n_t}^{(k)} = \log \frac{p(y_{n_r}|\tilde{\mathbf{H}}, b_{n_t}^{(k)} = +1)}{p(y_{n_r}|\tilde{\mathbf{H}}, b_{n_t}^{(k)} = -1)} = \frac{2}{\sigma_{z_{n_r n_t}^{(k)}}^2} \tilde{h}_{n_r n_t}^{(k)} (y_{n_r} - \mu_{z_{n_r n_t}^{(k)}}). \tag{21}$$

After passing the message of LLR from observation nodes to the $n_t^{(k)}$th bit-wise variable node, the posterior probability of $\{b_{n_t}^{(k)} = +1\}$ is denoted by $p_{n_r n_t}^{(k)+}$, and computed as

$$p_{n_r n_t}^{(k)+} \triangleq p_{n_r n_t}^{(k)}(b_{n_t}^{(k)} = +1|\mathbf{y}) = \frac{\exp\left(\sum_{m=1, m \neq n_r}^{2N_R} \Lambda_{m n_t}^{(k)}\right)}{1 + \exp\left(\sum_{m=1, m \neq n_r}^{2N_R} \Lambda_{m n_t}^{(k)}\right)}. \tag{22}$$

After a certain number of iterations, $b_{n_t}^{(k)}$ is detected as the one which has the sign of the sum of LLR for all the receiving antennas, i.e.,

$$\hat{b}_{n_t}^{(k)} = \text{sign}\left(\sum_{n_r=1}^{2N_R} \Lambda_{n_r n_t}^{(k)}\right). \tag{23}$$

## 4  Computational Complexity Analysis

As shown in Table 1, the computational complexity of the proposed BFG-BP detection algorithm mainly comes from three parts. Firstly, the LLR computation at the observation node given in (21) requires roughly $O(N^2)$. Secondly, the posterior probability computation at the bitwise variable node given in (22) takes about $O(N^2)$. Finally, the BFG graphic modeling described in (15) requires nearly $O(N)$. Considering that there exists $N$ transmitted symbols, the total computational complexity of the proposed BFG-BP algorithm for each symbol is $O(N^2 + N^2 + N)/N \approx O(N)$.

**Table 1.** The computational complexity of the proposed BFG-BP detection algorithm

| Main computational part | Computational complexity |
| --- | --- |
| LLR calculation | $O(N^2)$ |
| APP calculation | $O(N^2)$ |
| BFG graphic modeling | $O(N)$ |

## 5   Simulation Results

In the simulations, $N_T \times N_R$ is used to denote the number of transmitting and receiving antennas of the Massive MIMO system, where $N_T$ and $N_R$ are varied from 64 to 1024, unless otherwise stated. In addition, the detection of M-QAM signals is investigated to examine the advantages of the proposed BFG-BP detection algorithm, and $M = 4$. The average received SNR (dB) per received antenna ranges from 0 dB to 12 dB.

### 5.1   BER

In this simulation, the BER performance of the proposed BFG-BP detection algorithm is compared with that of the MMSE in [4]. Due to the high computational complexity of ML in Massive MIMO system, the single-input-single-output (SISO) AWGN performance is employed as a lower bound to evaluate our detection performance, where the theory BER for M-QAM of SISO AWGN is given by [12]

$$P_{theory} = a \cdot Q\left(\sqrt{b \cdot (\text{SNR}/\log2(M))}\right) \tag{24}$$

where $a = 2(1 - 1\big/\sqrt{M})\big/\log_2(\sqrt{M})$, $b = (6\log_2(\sqrt{M})\big/(M-1))$. $Q(x)$ signifies a function of $x$, where $Q(x) = \frac{1}{2}\text{erfc}(\frac{x}{\sqrt{2}})$ and $\text{erfc}(\cdot)$ denotes the complementary error function [12].

Figure 2(a) illustrates the BER performance of the proposed BFG-BP detection algorithm. It can be seen that when the average received SNR is 12 dB, the proposed BFG-BP reaches an average BER of $10^{-5}$ and approximates the BER of ML. Under the same condition, however, the MMSE only reaches an average BER of $10^{-2}$. The BER of the proposed BFG-BP decreases rapidly and approximates to the optimum performance of ML, and is much better than that of MMSE, when the average received SNR increases.

Figure 2(b) shows the convergence rate of the proposed BFG-BP. In this simulation, $N_T = N_R = 128$, the average received SNR is 12 dB. The simulation result shows that the BER of the proposed BFG-BP converges to a stable scope of $10^{-5}$, when the number of iteration is larger than 14. Moreover, the BER of the proposed BFG-BP reaches the optimum performance of ML.

Figure 2(c) illustrates the BER of the proposed BFG-BP versus the number of antennas. The average received SNR is fixed at 12 dB. $N_T = N_R$, and they range from 64 to 512. Evidently, the simulation result shows that the BER of the proposed BFG-BP reaches $10^{-5}$, and approximates to the optimum one of ML, when $N_R$ and $N_T$ are larger than 64. The BER of the MMSE is roughly $10^{-2}$, and almost remains unchanged even if the number of antennas goes very large. Therefore, the proposed BFG-BP is better for Massive MIMO system.

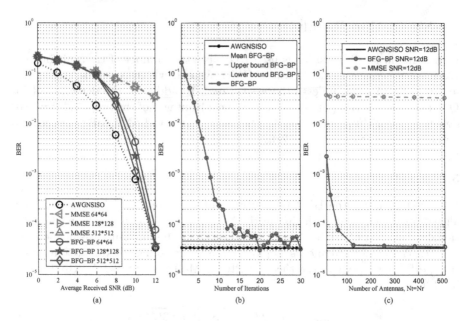

**Fig. 2.** The BER performance of the proposed BFG-BP detection algorithm for Massive MIMO system at 4QAM. (a) The BER versus the average received SNR (b) the convergent rate of the proposed BFG-BP, where $N_T = N_R = 128$ and the average received SNR is fixed at $12\,\mathrm{dB}$ (c) the BER versus the number of antennas, where $N_T = N_R$.

## 5.2    Spectral Efficiency

For VBLAST detection model, the theoretical spectral efficiency is denoted as $\mathrm{SE}_{theory}$ and given by [13]

$$\mathrm{SE}_{theory} = N_T \log_2(M). \tag{25}$$

In the simulations, we compare the spectral efficiency of the proposed BFG-BP with the above mentioned theoretical spectral efficiency.

Figure 3(a) shows the normalized spectral efficiency per transmitted antenna of the proposed BFG-BP with the average received SNR. The results indicate that the spectral efficiency of the proposed BFG-BP increases when the average received SNR goes large, and it converges to the theoretical spectral efficiency when the average received SNR is larger than $10\,\mathrm{dB}$. The least average received SNR required for the proposed BFG-BP to reach the theoretical spectral efficiency is around $12\,\mathrm{dB}$, which is less than that required for MMSE.

Figure 3(b) depicts the normalized spectral efficiency per transmitted antenna of the proposed BFG-BP for increasing number of antennas, where $N_T = N_R$. It can be seen that the normalized spectral efficiency of the proposed BFG-BP increases with the number of antennas, until it converges to the normalized theory one. However, the spectral efficiency of MMSE is much lower than that of the proposed BFG-BP, and remains invariable regardless the number of antennas.

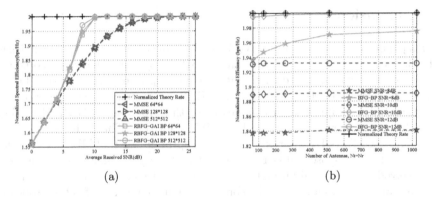

(a)                                    (b)

**Fig. 3.** The normalized spectral efficiency of Massive MIMO system by means of the proposed BFG-BP detection algorithm at 4QAM

### 5.3 Computational Complexity

Figure 4 illustrates the comparison of the computational complexity in the number of floating point operations (flops) among the proposed BFG-BP algorithm, the MMSE in [4] and the ML in [4]. Both BFG-BP and MMSE have a polynomially increasing computational complexity, whereas the computational complexity of ML increases exponentially with the number of antennas. Compared with MMSE and ML, the results clearly show that the computational complexity of the proposed BFG-BP is the lowest and is more applicable for Massive MIMO system.

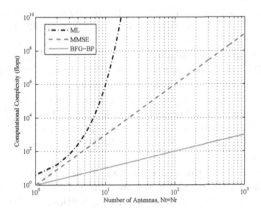

**Fig. 4.** The computational complexity of the proposed BFG-BP versus the number of antennas, where $N_t = N_r$.

# 6    Conclusion

In this paper, an improved BFG graphic model is developed, and a new BFG-BP detection algorithm is proposed for Massive MIMO system. The proposed BFG-BP detection algorithm is demonstrated to be applicable for detecting QAM signals. For Massive MIMO system, the BER performance, the spectral efficiency and the computational complexity of the proposed BFG-BP detection algorithm are better than those of the MMSE algorithm. The BER performance of the proposed BFG-BP approximates to the optimum BER of ML. The spectral efficiency of the proposed BFG-BP reaches the theoretical value, when the average received SNR is medium high or the number of transmitting and receiving antennas are large. In addition, the computational complexity of is the proposed BFG-BP is $O(N_T)$ per symbol, which increases linearly with number of antenna.

# References

1. Andrews, J.G., Buzzi, S., Choi, W., et al.: What will 5G be? IEEE J. Sel. Areas Commun. **32**, 1065–1082 (2014)
2. Larsson, E.G., Edfors, O., Tufvesson, F., et al.: Massive MIMO for next generation wireless systems. IEEE Commun. Mag. **52**, 186–195 (2014)
3. Yang, S., Hanzo, L.: Fifty years of MIMO detection: the road to large-scale MIMOs. Commun. Surv. Tutor. **17**, 1941–1988 (2015)
4. Larsson, E.G.: MIMO detection methods: how they work. IEEE Sig. Process. Mag. **26**, 91–95 (2009)
5. Vardhan, K.V., Mohammed, S.K., Chockalingam, A., et al.: A low-complexity detector for large MIMO systems and multicarrier CDMA systems. IEEE J. Sel. Areas Commun. **26**, 473–485 (2008)
6. Chen, J., Hu, J., Sobelman, G.E.: Stochastic MIMO detector based on the Markov chain Monte Carlo algorithm. IEEE Trans. Sig. Process. **62**, 1454–1463 (2014)
7. Yang, S., Lv, T., Maunder, R.G., et al.: From nominal to true a posteriori probabilities: an exact Bayesian theorem based probabilistic data association approach for iterative MIMO detection and decoding. IEEE Trans. Commun. **61**, 2782–2793 (2013)
8. Yoon, S., Chae, C.B.: Low-complexity MIMO detection based on belief propagation over pairwise graphs. IEEE Trans. Veh. Technol. **63**, 2363–2377 (2014)
9. Som, P., Datta, T., Srinidhi, N., et al.: Low-complexity detection in large-dimension MIMO-ISI channels using graphical models. IEEE J. Sel. Top. Sig. Process. **5**, 1497–1511 (2011)
10. Loyka, S., Gagnon, F.: Performance analysis of the V-BLAST algorithm: an analytical approach. IEEE Trans. Wirel. Commun. **3**, 1326–1337 (2004)
11. Choi, J.: On the partial MAP detection with applications to MIMO channels. IEEE Trans. Sig. Process. **53**, 158–167 (2005)
12. Cho, K., Yoon, D.: On the general BER expression of one- and two-dimensional amplitude modulations. IEEE Trans. Commun. **50**, 1074–1080 (2002)
13. Mesleh, R.Y., Haas, H., Sinanovic, S., et al.: Spatial modulation. IEEE Trans. Veh. Technol. **57**, 2228–2241 (2008)

# Development of 4 × 4 Parallel MIMO Channel Sounder for High-Speed Scenarios

Dan Fei[1,2(✉)], Bei Zhang[2], Ruisi He[1,2], and Lei Xiong[1,2]

[1] Beijing Engineering Research Center of High-speed Railway, Broadband Mobile
Communications, Beijing Jiaotong University, Beijing, China
[2] State Key Laboratory of Rail Traffic Control and Safety,
Beijing Jiaotong University, Beijing, China
{dfei,13111010,ruisi.he,lxiong}@bjtu.edu.cn

**Abstract.** High reliable wireless communication with big data rate in high-speed moving scenarios is currently a hot topic, and channel sounding plays an very important role in the related research as a basic tool to know the channel characteristics. For MIMO channel sounding in high-speed moving scenarios, to meet the requirement of CIR measurement speed is a big challenge so that the fully parallel MIMO structure has to be used, which will induce severe crosstalk at the receiver and usually, the problem can be solved by CDM and FDM methods. But until now, which solution is better, there is no conclusion. So, in this paper we aim at developing a channel sounder that can support 4 × 4 MIMO sounding at the speed of above 1000 km/h after the performance comparison of FDM and CDM. Based on the autocorrelation and orthogonal properties analysis of common used signal for CDM, including m, ZC and LS sequence, we choose the FDM solution utilizing the multi-carrier technique, because of its higher measurement dynamic range. And finally, we complete the implementation and validation of the hardware.

**Keywords:** Channel sounding · MIMO · High-speed · CDM · FDM

## 1 Introduction

Currently, the Internet of Vehicle (IoV), High-Speed Train (HST), and autopilot technologies have become the focus of attention, it drives the wireless communication technology in moving environment to face new challenging requirements. As the basis of wireless communications technologies research, wireless channel research is of great significance to the signal processing algorithm study, network design and system optimization. Wireless channel research relies on an important tool, channel sounder. Unfortunately, commercial channel sounder is monopolized by a few companies like MEDAV and Keysight (after it bought Anite), which led directly to the extremely high cost of channel sounder. Furthermore, limited by the dedicated hardware and software structure, the hardware using efficiency and flexibility are very poor, compared with their price.

© ICST Institute for Computer Sciences, Social Informatics and Telecommunications Engineering 2018
Q. Chen et al. (Eds.): ChinaCom 2016, Part I, LNICST 209, pp. 463–471, 2018.
DOI: 10.1007/978-3-319-66625-9_45

For MIMO channel sounding, especially for high-speed moving scenarios, the impulse response (CIR) measure speed must be fast enough to effectively capture the fast fading characteristics of high-speed mobile channel. And currently, most of the MIMO channel sounders are based on time division multiplexing (TDM) structure which measure the subchannels sequently by electronic switching. According to how the switches are used, the channel sounder can be further divided into fully switched structure [1,2] and semi-switched structure [3,4], as shown in Fig. 1(a) and (b). The TDM structure requires only a single transmitter or receiver, which can effectively reduce the system cost, and effectively eliminate crosstalk between different transmitting antennas. So it is suited to static or lower speed moving scenarios channel sounding, but for high-speed moving scenarios, it will lose much channel information during the switching duration. So, the fully parallel structure has to be used as shown in Fig. 1(c).

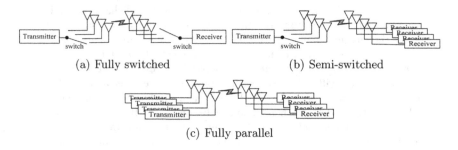

(a) Fully switched               (b) Semi-switched

(c) Fully parallel

**Fig. 1.** MIMO channel sounding structures

In fully parallel structure, the crosstalk cancellation between different transmitting antennas is the first thing and usually we can choose to use frequency division multiplexing (FDM) [5,6] or code division multiplexing (CDM) [7,8]. But which solution is better for the $4 \times 4$ MIMO channel sounding in high-speed scenarios, there is no final conclusion. So, in this paper, we will compare the performance of CDM and FDM structure and choose the best way to design the sounder by analyzing the autocorrelation and orthogonal property of the common used sounding signal, including m sequence, Zadoff-Chu (ZC), and Loosely Synchronous (LS).

The rest of the paper is organized as follows. Section 2 analyzes the autocorrelation and orthogonal property of common used sounding signal for CDM and chooses the multiplexing structure. Section 3 describes the $4 \times 4$ MIMO channel sounder hardware implementation and verification. Section 4 gives the conclusions of the paper.

## 2    CDM or FDM

The performance of channel sounding mainly depends on two features of the sounding signal, the power continuity and measurement dynamic range, the former determines the measurement validity which means not losing channel information of time and frequency domain, and the latter determines the measurement range of distance and delay. Compared to FDM, the CDM signal has consecutive power in both time and frequency domain, but FDM signal only consecutive in time domain. So, from the aspect of power continuity, CDM is better. Then, we will focus on the performance of measurement dynamic range for CDM and FDM.

For CDM, the measurement dynamic range mainly depends on the autocorrelation and orthogonal property of the sounding signal for which the m sequence, ZC, and LS are common used.

### 2.1  Autocorrelation Property

Figure 2 shows the autocorrelation property of the sequences with the maximal amplitude of 1 and the length of 2048 samples. The Y axis is the logarithmic amplitude, and the X axis is the relative time. As we can see, each sequence has a good autocorrelation peak more than 40 dB. So, the dynamic range is big enough for channel sounding. Especially, compared to m sequence, the ZC sequence has a much weaker sideband, which means it has better autocorrelation property.

For the LS sequence, there are strong autocorrelation values in some parts of the sideband, slightly higher than the first two sequences, but in the other parts, the autocorrelation values are extremely weak, close to −300 dB, as shown in the sequence Fig. 1(c). The part marked by red line is called Interference Free Window (IFW). Therefore, according to the principle of channel sounding, if the length of IFW is greater than the maximal channel delay, it can be used for effective channel sounding and the perfect autocorrelation property will greatly increase the measurement dynamic range. But we can also find that, the length of IFW is only one-fourth the whole signal length, which will reduce the CIR measurement speed.

### 2.2  Orthogonal Property

Figures 3 shows the orthogonal property of the sequence pairs. And we can see that the orthogonality of the m and ZC sequence are relatively poor, the cross-correlation value approaching 40 dB, which will introduce large crosstalk in parallel MIMO structure, especially with the increasing of the antenna number. So, it will reduce the measurement dynamic range significantly. Compared to m and ZC sequence, LS sequence shows a perfect orthogonal property, because it doesn't introduce additional crosstalk compared with the autocorrelation, the cross-correlation value approaching −300 dB. So, it seems like the LS sequence is an ideal candidate sounding signal for CDM structure.

In our system, we want to build a 4 × 4 MIMO sounding system, so we need 4 LS sequences with each sequence orthogonal to the others. It's worth noting that, in the 6 ($C_4^2$) LS sequences pairs, there are only two mate pairs [7], for example Nos. 1 and 2, 3 and 4 in our situation, and the others are not mate pairs. Figure 3(c) and (d) show respectively the orthogonal property of

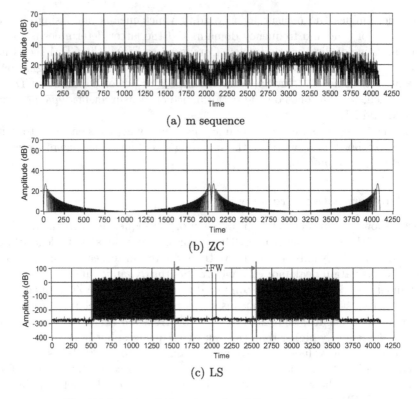

**Fig. 2.** Autocorrelation property of the sounding signals

LS mate pairs and not mate pairs. And we can see that, for the LS sequences which are not mate pairs, the achievable IFW length is the half of the case of mate pairs. That's to say, when we want to use LS sequence for $4 \times 4$ MIMO channel sounding, only one-eighth of the total sequence length is effective, thus decreasing the CIR measurement speed greatly. And this problem will be further exacerbated if we want to expand the system channels. So, in this paper, we will choose FDM structure for the system to increase the measurement dynamic range because there is little crosstalk among the Tx antennas when the signals are frequency divided.

### 2.3  FDM Solution

There are two solutions usually used for channel sounding, as shown in Fig. 4. In solution 1, all the Tx antennas are enabled concurrently to transmit specific sub-band of signals. So, when the total measurement bandwidth is B and the number of Tx antennas is N, the bandwidth of each sub-band is B/N. In the time domain, each Tx antenna change the transmitting signal to other sub-band in the next symbol duration to traverse all the sub-bands. This solution can be used for channel sounding in static scenario, but not for high-speed moving scenarios

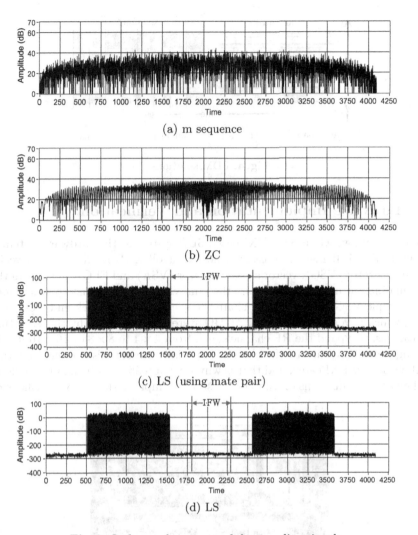

(a) m sequence

(b) ZC

(c) LS (using mate pair)

(d) LS

**Fig. 3.** Orthogonal property of the sounding signals

because at the definite time or place, the antennas are transmitting signals very different from each other in frequency domain, which will cause measurement error for MIMO system.

So, in our system, we choose the solution 2, in which, each Tx antenna utilizing multiple carriers by allocating sub-carriers that are orthogonal among them with comb type as shown in Fig. 4. This methods has a big advantage that it can measure all Tx signals simultaneously and there is no big difference among the Tx signals because the sub-carrier spacing can be designed bo be much smaller than the coherent bandwidth.

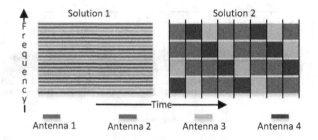

**Fig. 4.** FDM solutions

## 3  Hardware Implementation and Verification

In our system, we will use the PXI based SDR system as the hardware system as shown in Fig. 5. It mainly consists of host controller, PXI/PXIe chassis, vector signal generator (VSG), vector signal analyzer (VSA) and FPGA models. In this system different hardware can share the same chassis, so it is easy to synchronize the multiple VSGs and VSAs by share the same reference clock and local oscillator, which is very important for MIMO system. In addition, by this structure, we can easily expand the RF channels, e.g. from $4 \times 4$ to $8 \times 8$ or $16 \times 16$ just by adding more hardware to the chassis. Especially we can also connect multiple PXI chassis by PXI cable, and that is why we can realize both channel sounding and emulation functions on the same system to improve the hardware efficiency.

**Fig. 5.** The hardware equipment

The principle block diagram is shown as Fig. 6. The VSGs are used as transmitter and the VSAs are used as receiver. At the transmitter, all the VSGs share the same local oscillator (LO) and reference clock which is disciplined to GPS

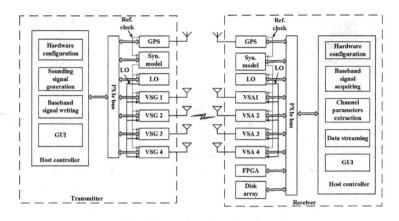

**Fig. 6.** The hardware block diagram

PPS clock, as well as the VSAs at the receiver. So the synchronization performance can be guaranteed and it is a basic requirement for MIMO measurement system. The system parameters are shown in Table 1.

**Table 1.** System parameters of the 4 × 4 MIMO sounder

| Parameters | Value |
|---|---|
| Frequency range | 85 MHz to 6.6 GHz |
| Maximal RF bandwidth | 50 MHz |
| Maximal output power | 40 dBm |
| Input dynamic range | −120 to 20 dBm |
| Data streaming | 3.6 GB/s, capacity: 3.5 TB |
| Channel parameter extraction | CIR, PDP, AoA, AoD, DS, AS |
| Support moving speed | >1000 km/h |

To verify the measurement capability of the sounding system, we build a closed-loop test system with commercial channel emulator as shown in Fig. 7. The channel emulator supports up to 16 sub-channels emulation with the maximal bandwidth of 75 MHz and the frequency range from 85 MHz to 3 GHZ. In the test system, a 4 × 4 MIMO channel model with customized multi-path is used. The simulated and measured CIR of sub-channels at receive antenna 1 is shown in Fig. 8, and we can see that they have good consistency, including the amplitude and delay. So, it verifies the measurement ability of this system because many other channel parameters can be derived by CIR.

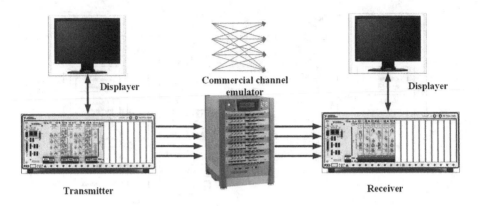

**Fig. 7.** The verification system

Simulated CIR                                  Measured CIR

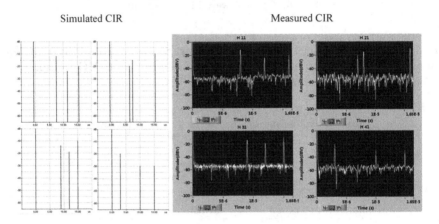

**Fig. 8.** The simulated and measurement result

## 4 Conclusion

In this paper, we compared the CDM and FDM methods for the sounding structure based on the analysis of autocorrelation and orthogonal properties for the common used sounding signals, including m sequence, ZC and LS sequence. Based on the results, we chose the FDM for the system design because of its high measurement dynamic range. And finally, we build a broadband wireless channel sounder that can support $4 \times 4$ MIMO wireless channel sounding in high-speed moving scenarios based on PXI software defined radio system with many special features, including fully parallel MIMO channel sounding structure with high-speed data streaming up to 3.6 GB/s and supporting high-speed moving scenarios above 1000 km/h. And because of the PXI module based hardware structure, it is easy to expand to $8 \times 8$, $16 \times 16$, and even $32 \times 32$ MIMO system. Especially, it also supports MIMO prototype system development since the SDR structure, which is on-going in our future works and in the next few months, we will use the system for the channel sounding in Datong to Xian high-speed railway.

**Acknowledgment.** This work has been funded by the Research Fund of Beijing Municipal Science & Technology Commission (Nos. Z151100001615078, D151100000115004, and Z151100002415029), the National Natural Science Foundation of China under Grant 61471030, National Science and Technology Major Project (2015ZX03001027-003), the Program for Development of Science and Technology of China Railway Corporation under grant 2015X010-C, the Program for Development of Science and Technology of China Railway Corporation under grant 2014X013-A, China Postdoctoral Science Foundation under Grant 2016M591355, National Natural Science Foundation of China under Grant 61501020, and State Key Laboratory of Rail Traffic Control and Safety under Grant RCS2016ZJ005.

# References

1. Kivinen, J., Korhonen, T.O., Aikio, P., Gruber, R., Vainikainen, P.: Wideband radio channel measurement system at 2 GHz. IEEE Trans. Instrum. Meas. **48**, 39–44 (1999)
2. Trautwein, U., Schneider, C., Sommerkorn, G., Hampicke, D., Thoma, R., Wirnitzer, W.: Measurement data for propagation modeling and wireless system evaluation. In: COST 273 Meeting, Barcelona, Spain, TD(03) 021, 15–17 January 2003
3. Salous, S., Lewenz, R., Hawkins, I., Razavi-Ghods, N., Abdallah, M.: Parallel receiver channel sounder for spatial and MIMO characterisation of the mobile radio channel. In: IEE Proceedings on Communications, vol. 152, no. 6, pp. 912–918, December 2005
4. Feeney, S.M., Filippidis, P., Lewenz, R., Salous, S.: Multi-band channel sounder in the 2–6 GHz band. In: Proceedings of BWA, Cambridge, pp. 1–4 (2004)
5. Takada, J., Sakaguchi, K., Araki, K.: Development of high resolution MIMO channel sounder for the advanced modeling of wireless channels. In: Proceedings of 2001 Asia-Pacific Microwave Conference, APMC 2001, Taipei, Taiwan, Republic of China, vol. 2, pp. 563–568, 3–6 December 2001
6. Sakaguchi, K., Takada, J., Araki, K.: A novel architecture for MIMO spatio-temporal channel sounder. IEICE Trans. Electron. **85**(3), 436–441 (2002)
7. Chung, H.K., Vloeberghs, N., Kwon, H.K., et al.: MIMO channel sounder implementation and effects of sounder impairment on statistics of multipath delay spread. In: IEEE 62nd Vehicular Technology Conference, VTC-2005-Fall, vol. 1, pp. 349–353. IEEE (2005)
8. Kim, W., Park, J.J., Kim, M.D., et al.: Time-division multiplexing based MIMO channel sounder using loosely synchronous codes. In: 2007 IEEE 66th Vehicular Technology Conference, VTC-2007 Fall, pp. 897–901. IEEE (2007)

# Blind Spectrum Sensing Based on Unilateral Goodness of Fit Testing for Multi-antenna Cognitive Radio System

Yinghui Ye[1,2] and Guangyue Lu[2(✉)]

[1] State Key Laboratory of Integrated Services Networks,
Xidian University, Xi'an, China
connectyyh@126.com
[2] National Engineering Laboratory for Wireless Security,
Xi'an University of Posts and Telecommunications, Xi'an, China
tonylugy@163.com

**Abstract.** Goodness of fit tests have been used to find available spectrum in cognitive radio system. In this paper, a unilateral Right-tail Anderson-Darling (URAD) criterion, one of goodness of fit test, is introduced and a blind spectrum sensing scheme based on URAD criterion by using Student's distribution is proposed for multiple antennas cognitive radio system. The spectrum sensing is reformulated as a unilateral Student's testing problem, and the URAD criterion is employed to sense the available spectrum. Numerical simulations verify that the proposed spectrum scheme is robust to noise uncertainty, and greatly outperforms five classical spectrum sensing schemes.

**Keywords:** Cognitive radio · Blind spectrum sensing · A unilateral Right-tail Anderson-Darling criterion · Noise uncertainty · Multiple antennas

## 1 Introduction

In wireless communication, Cognitive Radio (CR) is a promising technology to solve the problem of spectrum scarcity owing to the increase of wireless applications and services. The main purpose of CR system is to detect the presence of primary user (PU) within the desired frequency band and then enable secondary users (SU) to access the vacant channel rapidly without causing interference to PU [1]. Therefore, spectrum sensing is a fundamental task in CR.

Recently, goodness of fit (GOF) test is utilized in spectrum sensing and several spectrum sensing schemes based on GOF test, with different criteria and different statistics, are proposed in [2–6,8]. For examples, an Anderson-Darling (AD) sensing in [2] using AD criterion is proposed; spectrum sensing based on Order-Statistics is illustrated in [3]. Both [2,3] show that the spectrum sensing scheme based on GOF test is superior to energy detection (ED) scheme in Additive White Gaussian Noise (AWGN) Channels; however, those schemes also

© ICST Institute for Computer Sciences, Social Informatics and Telecommunications Engineering 2018
Q. Chen et al. (Eds.): ChinaCom 2016, Part I, LNICST 209, pp. 472–479, 2018.
DOI: 10.1007/978-3-319-66625-9_46

suffer from the noise uncertainty and the noise variance must be known as prior information. Subsequently, to circumvent the weakness in [2,3], several schemes are given in [2]. In [4], a multiple antennas assisted and empirical characteristic function (MECF) based blind spectrum sensing is proposed via calculating the distance between the empirical characteristic function and assumed characteristic function. In [5], a new statistics is constructed via sample feature and the AD criterion is used. In [6], a censored AD (CAD) criterion is given. All proposed schemes in [4–6] are better than ED.

However, all schemes in [2–6] are only effective for static PU signal, which means the PU signal are unchangeable during the sensing period, according to [7], and this is not common situation in CR system. Meanwhile, [7] shows that the performance of AD sensing [3] is worse than ED scheme when the PU signal is dynamic during the sensing period (the detailed simulation can be found in [7]). The essential reason is that AD criterion is sensitive to mean rather than variance. To apply the GOF tests into spectrum sensing for dynamic PU signal and improve the performance of AD sensing, Jin in [8] propose a spectrum sensing scheme based on a modified AD criterion using chi2-distribution (MADC). Even though MADC scheme is effective, the work [8] did not fully exploit the inherent signal property, especially, in multi-antenna system.

It is widely known that multiple antennas can offer extra space-dimension information which can be employed to improve the spectrum sensing performance and beneficial to achieve blind spectrum sensing. For example, Zeng utilizes the multiple antennas and proposes two famous spectrum sensing methods including Covariance Absolute Value (CAV) detection and Maximum-Minimum Eigenvalue (MME) detection. However, the existing methods has poor detection performance with small samples.

For improving detection performance with small samples, in this paper, we apply the GOF tests into the multi-antenna CR scenarios. Firstly, we introduce a new kind of statistic via utilizing the dimension information and reformulate the spectrum sensing problem as a unilateral GOF test problem. To examine the above GOF test, we deduce a new GOF criterion called unilateral Right-tail Anderson-Darling criterion (URAD); and then a new blind spectrum sensing scheme based on URAD criterion using this statistic is proposed, which is called URAD sensing. Our analyses and simulations show that the URAD sensing does not need noise variance and be free of noise uncertainty. Moreover, the URAD sensing is superior to ED no matter when there is noise uncertainty or not.

The rest of this paper is organized as follows: URAD sensing is introduced in Sect. 2; the simulation results are given in Sect. 3; finally, the conclusion is drawn.

## 2   System Model

Suppose that each of $P$ antennas in SU receives $N$ samples during the sensing period. The received sample for the $p_{th}$ antenna at $n$ instance is denoted as $X_p(n)$ $(p = 1, 2, \cdots, P; n = 1, 2, \cdots, N)$. For spectrum sensing, there are two hypothesizes $H_0$ and $H_1$, where $H_0$ denotes the PU is absent and $H_1$ denotes the PU is present. Therefore, the spectrum sensing problem can be formulated as a binary hypothesis test [1], such that

$$X_p(n) = \begin{cases} W_p(n) & , H_0 \\ S_p(n) + W_p(n) & , H_1 \end{cases} \tag{1}$$

where $S_p(n)$ and $W_p(n)$ are the samples of the transmitted PU signal and the Gaussian noise, respectively. Without loss of generality and for simplify, we assume that $X_p(n)$ and $W_p(n)$ are completely independent; at the same time, we also assume $X_p(n)$ is real-valued; otherwise, simply replace $X_p(n)$ by its real or imaginary parts.

## 3    URAD Sensing

### 3.1    Spectrum Sensing as a Unilateral GOF Test Problem

Denote the correlation coefficient between $X_p(n)$ and $X_q(n)$ $(p \neq q)$ as following

$$\rho_{p,q} = \frac{\sum\limits_{n=1}^{N} X_p(n)X_q(n) - N\bar{X}_p\bar{X}_q}{\sqrt{\sum\limits_{n=1}^{N} X_p^2(n) - N\bar{X}_p^2}\sqrt{\sum\limits_{n=1}^{N} X_q^2(n) - N\bar{X}_q^2}} \tag{2}$$

where $\bar{X}_p = \frac{1}{N} \sum\limits_{n=1}^{N} X_p(n)$.

In terms of (2), it is easily to find that $\rho_{p,q} = \rho_{q,p}$, thus, for a given $P$ antennas, we can get $M = P(P-1)/2$ different correlation coefficients. For simplicity, let $\rho_m$ $(m = 1, 2, \ldots, M)$ denote the $M_{th}$ different correlation coefficients. Define variable $\eta_m$ as

$$\eta_m \triangleq \sqrt{N-2}\rho_m \Big/ \sqrt{1 - \rho_m^2} \tag{3}$$

When the PU is absent, $X_p(n)$ is the Gaussian noise $W_p(n)$, the received signal between $p_{th}$ and $q_{th}$ are independent and identically distributed, thus, the $\rho_m$ and $\eta_m$ are equal to zero. Actually, since the number of samples is limited in real situation, $\eta_m$ is not always equal to zero and obeys a certain distribution. According to [10] in page 121, in this case, the variable $\eta_m$ obeys a Student's distribution with $N-2$ degrees and its cumulative distribution function (CDF) is denoted as $F_0(\eta)$ in this paper. Let $F_M(\eta)$ denote the empirical CDF of the variable $\eta_m$, that is,

$$F_M(\eta) \triangleq |\{m : \eta_m < \eta, 1 \leq m \leq M\}| / M \tag{4}$$

where $|\bullet|$ is the cardinality function. According to the Glivenko-Cantelli theorem, in $H_0$ case, $F_0(\eta) = F_M(\eta)$.

When the PU is present, the received signal between $p_{th}$ and $q_{th}$ are correlated. $\rho_m$ is the positive correlation coefficient $(0 < \rho_m < 1)$ and is increased with the growth of signal to noise ratio (SNR). In terms of (2), it can be found that $\eta_m$ also increases as $\rho_m$ grows when $0 < \rho_m < 1$. In this situation, the probability density function (PDF) of $\eta_m$ deviates rightward from the PDF of the Student's distribution with $N - 2$ degrees, leading to $F_0(\eta) > F_M(\eta)$.

Hence, the spectrum sensing problem can be reformulated as a unilateral Student's distribution testing problem, that is,

$$\begin{cases} F_0(\eta) = F_M(\eta), \ H_0 \\ F_0(\eta) > F_M(\eta), \ H_1 \end{cases} \tag{5}$$

### 3.2   URAD Criterion

Based on the above analysis, we employ $\eta_m$ as a new statistic for the proposed scheme. In the following, different from existing works [2–6], we propose a new GOF criterion and apply it to test formula (5).

Two modified AD criteria are introduced in [11] such as Right-tail Anderson-Darling (RAD) criterion and Left-tail Anderson-Darling (LAD) criterion, respectively, which emphasizes the right-tail test and the left-tail test, respectively. The test statistics of RAD criterion can be defined as [11]

$$T_{RAD} = M \int_{-\infty}^{+\infty} [F_0(\eta) - F_M(\eta)]^2 \frac{dF_0(\eta)}{1 - F_0(\eta)} \tag{6}$$

For testing the unilateral alternative hypothesis, the square of $F_0(\eta) - F_M(\eta)$ should not be considered because $F_0(\eta) - F_M(\eta) \geq 0$ is always contented (see (5)). Therefore, based on RAD criterion, we propose a unilateral RAD (URAD) criterion, and then the test statistic of URAD criterion is defined as

$$T_{URAD} = M \int_{-\infty}^{+\infty} [F_0(\eta) - F_M(\eta)] \frac{dF_0(\eta)}{1 - F_0(\eta)} \tag{7}$$

For given $\eta_m$ $(m = 1, 2, \ldots, M)$, we assume $\eta_1 \leq \eta_2 \leq \cdots \leq \eta_M$, then formula (6) can be rewritten as

$$\begin{aligned} T_{URAD} &= M \int_{-\infty}^{+\infty} [F_0(\eta) - F_M(\eta)] \frac{dF_0(\eta)}{1 - F_0(\eta)} \\ &= M \int_{-\infty}^{\eta_1} [F_0(\eta) - 0] \frac{dF_0(\eta)}{1 - F_0(\eta)} \\ &\quad + M \int_{\eta_1}^{\eta_2} [F_0(\eta) - \frac{1}{M}] \frac{dF_0(\eta)}{1 - F_0(\eta)} \\ &\quad + \cdots \\ &\quad + M \int_{\eta_M}^{+\infty} [F_0(\eta) - 1] \frac{dF_0(\eta)}{1 - F_0(\eta)} \\ &= - \sum_{m=1}^{M} \ln(1 - F_0(\eta_m)) - M \\ &= - \sum_{m=1}^{M} \ln(1 - Z_m) - M \end{aligned} \tag{8}$$

where $Z_m = F_0(\eta_m)$. In the URAD criterion, the hypothesis $H_0$ is accepted if $T_{URAD} < \gamma$, where $\gamma$ is a decision threshold; otherwise, the hypothesis $H_0$ is rejected. Denote the false alarm probability $P_f$ and detection probability $P_d$, respectively, as

$$P_f = prob\{T_{URAD} \geq \gamma | H_0\} \tag{9}$$

$$P_d = prob\{T_{URAD} \geq \gamma | H_1\} \tag{10}$$

According to (9), the $\gamma$ can be determined for the pre-given $P_f$ through Monte Carlo simulations. Table 1 presents some simulation results using more than $10^5$ Monte Carlo simulations. Note that the detection threshold keeps unchangeable when the $N \geq 50$.

**Table 1.** The threshold versus samples in urad sensing with $P_f = 0.05$

| $N$ | 10 | 20 | 30 | 40 | $N \geq 50$ |
|---|---|---|---|---|---|
| $P = 4$ | 3.637 | 3.156 | 3.017 | 2.990 | 2.818 |

Hence, the proposed URAD sensing can be summarized in the following steps:

Step1: selecting a detection threshold $\gamma$ for a given $P_f$;

Step2: calculating the $M$ different correlation coefficients according to (2) using the received samples;

Step3: calculating the $\eta_m (m = 1, 2, \ldots, M)$ and calculating $T_{URAD}$;

Step4: accepting $H_0$ if $T_{URAD} < \gamma$; otherwise, accept $H_1$.

Remark: In the real CR system, the noise uncertainty $\beta$ always exists [9]. When the noise uncertainty is considered in spectrum sensing, the real noise variance is evenly distributed in an interval $[c^{-1}\sigma^2, c\sigma^2]$, where $c = 10^{(0.1\beta)}$ [9]. Hence, if spectrum sensing scheme needs noise variance, the spectrum sensing scheme must be affected by noise uncertainty. From (3), (8) and Table 1, it can be readily seen that the $\eta_m (m = 1, 2, \ldots, M)$, $T_{URAD}$ and detection threshold are independent of the noise variance, which make the URAD sensing be free of the noise uncertainty. Meanwhile, all that the URAD sensing needs is the received samples, that is, no other prior information is required.

## 4    Simulation Results

In this section, the detailed detection performance comparisons among the URAD sensing, the ED scheme [1], AD scheme [2], MADC scheme [8], MME scheme and CAV scheme [9] are illustrated.

Suppose the noise variance $\sigma^2 = 1$ for the ED, AD and MADC schemes. Meanwhile the noise variance is assumed to be unknown for MME and URAD sensing. Two types of PU signal are illustrated as in [7]. One type of PU signal is Gaussian variable with zero mean and $\alpha^2$ signal variance, which is utilized for all of radio frequency (RF), intermediate frequency (IF) and baseband sensing;

another type of PU signal is $S_p(n) = sin[(2\pi n)/K + \varphi]$, which is considered in RF/IF sensing (see [7]). For two types of PU signal, only simulations using Gaussian PU signal with $\alpha^2$ are provided owing to the similar simulation results for the proposed scheme and the wider application fields for Gaussian PU signal.

Figure 1 presents the detection probabilities, $P_d$, of six schemes with respect to different SNR scenarios at $P_f = 0.05, N = 50, P = 4$ over AWGN channels. It can be seen that the proposed scheme is much better than other schemes for the same number of samples at different $SNRs$, i.e., the URAD sensing outperforms ED almost 2 dB. For example, at SNR $= -7$ dB, $P_d$ of the URAD sensing, ED, MADC, MME, AD and CAV respectively, is 0.88, 0.57, 0.50, 0.36, 0.16, 0.53.

To further prove the performance of the proposed scheme, Fig. 2 shows Receiver Operating Characteristic (ROC) curves of five schemes at SNR $= -6$ dB, $N = 50, P = 4$. It is clear that the performance of the URAD sensing is superior to ED, MADC, MME and AD whatever the $P_f$ is.

In the real CR system, it is necessary to verify the effect of noise uncertainty for the proposed scheme due to the fact that the noise uncertainty $\beta$ always exists. Note that the noise uncertainty is normally below 1 dB to 2 dB. Figure 3 presents the ROC curves of five schemes over AWGN channels with $\beta=1$ dB, SNR $= -6$ dB, $N = 50, P = 4$.

An examination of the Figs. 2 and 3 reveals that the URAD sensing and MME are free of noise uncertainty, and the MADC, ED, AD are affected by noise uncertainty. Meanwhile, it is not hardly to find ED scheme is the most sensitive to noise uncertainty among five schemes. For example, when there is no noise uncertainty at $P_f = 0.05$, $SNR = -6$ dB, $P_d$ of the URAD sensing, ED, MADC, MME, AD respectively, is 0.91, 0.73, 0.65, 0.49, 0.23 (see Figs. 1 or 2); when $= 1$ dB and $P_f = 0.05$, $P_d$ of the URAD sensing, ED, MADC, MME, AD respectively, is 0.90, 0.41, 0.39, 0.49, 0.24 (see Fig. 3).

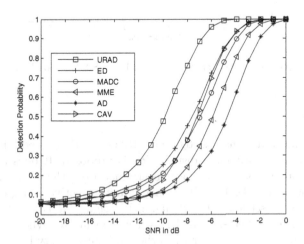

**Fig. 1.** $P_d$ against $SNRs$ for six schemes with $P_f = 0.05$, $N = 50$, $P = 4$

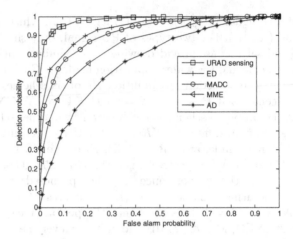

**Fig. 2.** ROC curves of five schemes when $SNR = -6\,\mathrm{dB}$, $N = 50, P = 4$

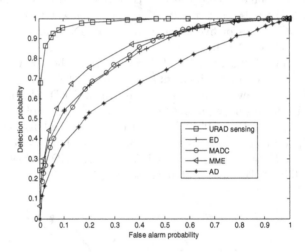

**Fig. 3.** ROC curves of five schemes when $\beta = 1\,\mathrm{dB}$, $SNR = -6\,\mathrm{dB}$, $N = 50, P = 4$

## 5    Conclusion

In this paper, multi-antenna assisted and URAD criterion based blind spectrum sensing scheme using Student's distribution is proposed. It does not need any prior information and be free of noise uncertainty. Both theoretical analysis and simulations show that the URAD sensing is more effective and greatly outperforms four existing schemes. For dynamic PU signal, it is worth noting that the URAD sensing is better than ED scheme no matter when there is noise uncertainty or not and no matter what the noise uncertainty is.

**Acknowledgement.** This work was supported by Natural Science Foundation of China (61271276, 61301091), and Natural Science Foundation of Shaanxi Province (2014JM8299).

# References

1. Masonta, M.T., Mzyece, M., Ntlatlapa, N.: Spectrum decision in cognitive radio networks: a survey. IEEE Commun. Surv. Tutor. **15**(3), 1088–1107 (2013)
2. Wang, H., Yang, E.H., Zhao, Z., et al.: Spectrum sensing in cognitive radio using goodness of fit testing. IEEE Trans. Wirel. Commun. **8**(11), 5427–5430 (2009)
3. Rostami, S., Arshad, K., Moessner, K.: Order-statistic based spectrum sensing for cognitive radio. IEEE Trans. Wirel. Commun. **16**(5), 592–595 (2012)
4. Shen, L., Wang, H., Zhang, W., et al.: Multiple antennas assisted blind spectrum sensing in cognitive radio channels. IEEE Commun. Lett. **16**(1), 92–94 (2012)
5. Shen, L., Wang, H., Zhang, W., et al.: Blind spectrum sensing for cognitive radio channels with noise uncertainty. IEEE Trans. Wirel. Commun. **10**(6), 1721–1724 (2011)
6. Patel, D.K., Trivedi, Y.N.: Non-parametric blind spectrum sensing based on censored observations for cognitive radio. J. Sig. Process. Syst. **78**(3), 275–281 (2015)
7. Nguyen-Thanh, N., Kieu-Xuan, T., Koo, I.: Comments on spectrum sensing in cognitive radio using goodness-of-fit testing. IEEE Trans. Wirel. Commun. **10**(11), 3409–3411 (2012)
8. Jin, M., Guo, Q., Xi, J.: Spectrum sensing based on goodness of fit test with unilateral alternative hypothesis. Electron. Lett. **50**(22), 1645–1646 (2014)
9. Zeng, Y., Liang, Y.C., Hoang, A.T., et al.: A review on spectrum sensing for cognitive radio: challenges and solutions. EURASIP J. Adv. Sig. Process. **2010**(1), 1–15 (2010)
10. Anderson, T.W.: An Introduction to Multivariate Statistical Analysis, 3rd edn. Wiley-Interscience, Hoboken (2003)
11. Sinclair, C.D., Spurr, B.D., Ahmad, M.I.: Modified Anderson darling test. Commun. Stat. Theory Methods **19**(10), 3677–3686 (1990)

# Frequency Detection of Weak Signal in Narrowband Noise Based on Duffing Oscillator

Shuo Shi, Qianyao Ren[✉], Dezhi Li, and Xuemai Gu

Communication Research Center, Harbin Institute of Technology, Harbin, China
{crcss,lidezhi,guxuemai}@hit.edu.cn,
renqianyao@163.com

**Abstract.** Duffing oscillator is used to detect weak signal in strong noise because traditional linear methods cannot work correctly in this situation. Normal Duffing oscillator is used under broadband noise because it is immune to broadband noise. But it is not suitable in narrowband noise because zero expectation of noise is damaged in narrowband noise. In this paper, the difference influence to Duffing oscillator between broadband noise and narrowband noise is analyzed and the resistance of Duffing oscillator to narrowband noise is proved. Then a new frequency detection method based on higher initial driving force amplitude and duration of cycle state is developed. Finally, the appropriate initial amplitude needed in this method is confirmed and the method is verified that it can detect frequency in narrowband noise by simulation.

**Keywords:** Duffing oscillator · Narrowband noise · Signal frequency detection · Initial driving force

## 1 Introduction

In modern communication, weak signal detection is more and more important because weak signal is usually used or emergent in communication to economize transmitting power or just be restricted by channel which is normal in both signal reception and signal detection. The comprehension of weak signal can be divided into two parts. On the one hand, signal transmitting power is weak, and noise maybe not very strong or even can be ignored. Due to low signal power, the SNR is very low. On the other hand, signal power is not weak, but noise is strong enough to submerge signal. So the SNR is also very low. In other words, one cause is low signal power, the other cause is strong noise.

In complex channel with strong noise, weak signal mostly refers to the second kind that signal power is not very weak but noise is really strong. The traditional linear methods such as coherent method cannot detect weak signal when SNR is very low because strong noise can make judgment threshold value inaccurate. So the nonlinear method such as Duffing oscillator has been put forward to detect this kind of weak signal. Duffing oscillator is a kind of chaos system that is immune to noise and sensitive to signal [1]. Since Holmes found out that Duffing function contains strange

© ICST Institute for Computer Sciences, Social Informatics and Telecommunications Engineering 2018
Q. Chen et al. (Eds.): ChinaCom 2016, Part I, LNICST 209, pp. 480–488, 2018.
DOI: 10.1007/978-3-319-66625-9_47

attractor and seeming random process can be generated by deterministic Duffing oscillator [2], many signal detection methods have been provided such as Lyapunov exponent [3] and intermittent chaos theory [4].

However, these methods to detect weak signal are almost studied in broadband noise because noise band is extended by scale transformation when it turns to communication signal with high frequency from original mathematic model. The band of noise in these methods is much wider than signal band, so noise that can really influence signal is weaker than the value used in calculating SNR. Therefore, the detection of weak signal in communication field should be studied under narrowband noise that is suitable for more communication environments.

Frequency detection is the first step of signal detection with which other signal parameters can be detected. Therefore, in this paper, frequency detection of weak signal in narrowband noise is studied and analyzed. First, the basic property of Duffing oscillator and method to detect signal frequency based on Duffing oscillator are introduced. Then, the influence of narrowband noise to Duffing oscillator is analyzed and compared with the influence in broadband noise. And an improved method based on the analysis is raised to detect signal frequency in narrowband noise. Finally, the method is verified and its parameter is set through simulation.

## 2 Basic Property of Duffing Oscillator

Duffing oscillator is the application of Duffing function. In many kinds of Duffing oscillators, the most common one is Holmes-Duffing oscillator whose function is:

$$\ddot{x} + k\dot{x} - x + x^3 = \gamma \cos(t) \tag{1}$$

where, $\gamma \cos(t)$ is driving force, $\gamma$ is its amplitude and $k$ is damping factor. There are two important characteristics of Duffing oscillator, one is the sensibility to initial value and the other one is immunity to noise.

### 2.1 Sensibility to Initial Value and Frequency Detection Method

There are two main states of Duffing oscillator that one is large scale cycle state and the other is chaos state and they are decided by initial value of driving force amplitude. To driving force $\gamma \cos(t)$, there is a critical amplitude of driving force $\gamma_c$. The state of oscillator will change with increasing of actual amplitude of driving force. It stays in chaos state when $\gamma < \gamma_c$ and turns into large scale cycle when $\gamma > \gamma_c$ and there is explicit difference between the two states, so the small change of driving force amplitude is converted to explicit change of oscillator state, that make Duffing oscillator is sensitive to initial value.

Therefore, signal frequency can be detected by Duffing oscillator array with difference frequency. The initial driving force value of each oscillator is set as critical value $\gamma_c$. When there is signal with the same frequency as some oscillator input, the corresponding oscillator will turn into large scale cycle state and other oscillators will keep in chaos state.

## 2.2   Immunity to Gaussian White Noise

When there is noise in Duffing oscillator, the variable $x$ of Duffing oscillator will be interfered by $\Delta x$. So the function will turn into:

$$(\ddot{x} + \Delta\ddot{x}) + k(\dot{x} + \Delta\dot{x}) - (x + \Delta x) + (x + \Delta x)^3 = \gamma\cos(t) + n(t) \tag{2}$$

The result of subtraction between (1) and (2) is (3), where the higher order of $\Delta x$ is ignored because $\Delta x$ is very small.

$$\Delta\ddot{x} + k\Delta\dot{x} - \Delta x + 3x^2\Delta x = n(t) \tag{3}$$

The vector term of (3) is shown as (4)

$$\dot{X}(t) = A(t)X(t) + N(t) \tag{4}$$

where $X(t) = \begin{bmatrix} x_1 \\ x_2 \end{bmatrix} = \begin{bmatrix} \Delta x(t) \\ \Delta\dot{x}(t) \end{bmatrix}$, $A(t) = \begin{bmatrix} 0 & 1 \\ 1 - 3x^2 & -k \end{bmatrix}$, $N(t) = \begin{bmatrix} 0 \\ n(t) \end{bmatrix}$

The result of (4) is

$$X(t) = \phi(t, t_0)X_0 + \int \phi(t, u)N(u)du \tag{5}$$

It can be considered as $X(t) = \int \phi(t, u)N(u)du$ because $\phi(t, t_0) X_0$ is transient solution. The expectation of $X(t)$ is $E\{X(t)\} = \int \phi(t, u)E\{N(u)\}du = 0$.

According to the analysis above, the expectation of $\Delta x$ and its derivative is zero. Therefore, Duffing oscillator will be immune to noise as long as the expectation of noise or interference is zero. Noise will not change the state of Duffing oscillator but make its image rough.

# 3   Frequency Detection Method in Narrowband Noise

## 3.1   The Difference of Duffing Oscillator in Narrowband and Broadband Noise

According the analysis above, the immunity of Duffing oscillator to noise is on the base of Gaussian white noise whose expectation is zero. When noise band is not infinity, noise expectation is nonzero and the expectation of $\Delta x$ is nonzero either. So Duffing oscillator is not completely immune to narrowband noise.

This conclusion can also be raised through analysis of noise frequency spectrum. Duffing oscillator is firstly applied in dynamics system where driving force frequency is 1–10 Hz. When it is used in communication system where driving force frequency is much more than the one in dynamics system, scale transformation has to be used. But noise band will be extended by scale transformation at the same time. So the noise power is very strong while real noise whose frequency range is similar to signal that can influence signal is not strong. So the conclusion of Duffing oscillator that it is immune to noise is suitable in broadband noise but not in narrowband noise.

Due to the influence of strong narrowband noise, phase diagram of Duffing oscillator is so rough that cycle and chaos state cannot be distinguished. Taking large scale cycle state as an example, its phase diagram in broadband noise and narrowband noise is different as shown in Figs. 1 and 2.

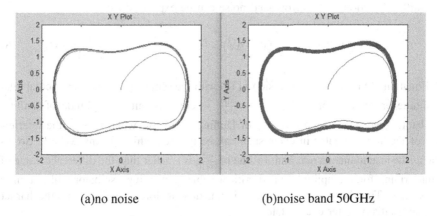

(a)no noise                    (b)noise band 50GHz

**Fig. 1.** Phase diagram of Duffing oscillator when there is no noise and there is noise whose band is 50 GHz.

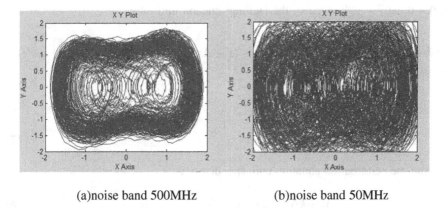

(a)noise band 500MHz            (b)noise band 50MHz

**Fig. 2.** Phase diagram of Duffing oscillator when noise band is 500 MHz and 50 MHz.

In Figs. 1 and 2, initial amplitude of driving force is 0.8261, and signal amplitude is 0.1. SNR is −10 dB and noise band is different in each figure. According to the result. The large-scale cycle state is clear when noise band is 50 GHz that it is similar to phase diagram without noise. With the reduce of noise band, phase diagram of Duffing oscillator does not show the proper state that it displays like phase diagram of chaos.

That is to say, under strong narrowband noise, oscillator will not be periodic or chaotic as usual, and the conclusion that is obtained without noise is incorrect.

## 3.2    Improvement of Duffing Oscillator's Resistance to Narrowband Noise

According to the analysis above, under strong narrowband noise, Duffing oscillator is not immune to noise, but it can still resist the influence of noise.

Duffing function with narrowband noise can be expressed as:

$$(\ddot{x} + \Delta\ddot{x}) + k(\dot{x} + \Delta\dot{x}) - (x' + \Delta x') + (x' + \Delta x')^3 = (\gamma + \frac{n(t)}{\cos(t)})\cos(t) \qquad (6)$$

Equation (6) is another expression of (2) with the same style as (1). The actual total amplitude of driving force is $\gamma' = \gamma + \frac{n(t)}{\cos(t)}$ where $\gamma$ is initial amplitude of Duffing oscillator. According to the property of Duffing oscillator, when $\gamma' > \gamma_c$, the interference of Duffing oscillator in cycle state can be ignored which means $\Delta x' = 0$. So, as long as the instantaneous maximum value of $\frac{n(t)}{\cos(t)}$ is smaller than the difference value of initial driving force amplitude $\gamma$ and critical value $\gamma_c$, Duffing oscillator will not enter chaos state. That is to say, the higher initial driving force amplitude is, the harder Duffing oscillator enter chaos state.

If $\gamma' < \gamma_c$, Duffing oscillator will be influenced by narrowband noise seriously. Assuming $\cos(t) > 0$, because $\gamma > \gamma_c$, the instantaneous value of noise is lower than zero. Noise can be divided into two parts as $n(t) = n_1(t) + n_2(t)$, where $n_1(t) < 0$, $n_2(t) < 0$, let $\gamma + \frac{n_1(t)}{\cos(t)} = \gamma_c$, so the Duffing function turn into:

$$
\begin{aligned}
(\ddot{x} + \Delta\ddot{x}) + k(\dot{x} + \Delta\dot{x}) - (x' + \Delta x') + (x' + \Delta x')^3 &= \left[\gamma + \frac{n_1(t)}{\cos(t)} + \frac{n_2(t)}{\cos(t)}\right]\cos(t) \\
&= \left[\gamma_c + \frac{n_2(t)}{\cos(t)}\right]\cos(t) \\
&= \gamma_c \cos(t) + n_2(t)
\end{aligned}
$$
$$(7)$$

And the perturbation equation correspondingly is

$$\Delta\ddot{x} + k\Delta\dot{x} - \Delta x + (x + \Delta x)^3 - x^3 = n_2(t) \qquad (8)$$

$n_2(t)$ is divided from n(t), and they have the same sign, so the instantaneous absolute value of $n_2(t)$ is smaller than the one of $n(t)$, and the same result can be reached when $\cos(t) < 0$. So the influence of $n_2(t)$ is less than n(t). That is to say, narrowband noise to Duffing oscillator has been reduced.

Above all, when the total amplitude of driving force $\gamma'$ that is the combination of initial amplitude $\gamma$ and amplitude of signal input is higher than instantaneous value of $\gamma_c + \frac{n(t)}{\cos(t)}$, Duffing oscillator will always be in large scale cycle state, which is similar to the state without noise. And the difference is the size of cycle orbit. When the total amplitude of driving force $\gamma'$ is lower than the instantaneous value of $\gamma_c + \frac{n(t)}{\cos(t)}$, the influence of narrowband noise still exists. The higher the total amplitude of driving force is, the smaller the influence is. Therefore, the increasing of initial driving force $\gamma$ can improve the resistance of Duffing oscillator to narrow noise.

### 3.3    New Method to Detect Signal Frequency Based on the Improvement

According to analysis above, increase of initial driving force amplitude can improve the resistance of Duffing oscillator to noise, but the influence of narrowband noise still exists.

The zero expectation of noise is used in proof of immunity to noise, so it will need enough time to reflect that the mean value of noise is zero. That is to say, if Duffing oscillator can run for a long time, it will reach the state that is immune to noise in broadband noise. It is also suitable to narrowband noise that the resistance of Duffing oscillator will be displayed to maximum when Duffing oscillator runs for a longer time. When the time is not enough long, the roughness of phase diagram or sequence diagram will make the state of Duffing oscillator not clear which will influence the judgment of state.

Therefore, the state of Duffing oscillator can be reached by detecting the total duration of cycle state in narrowband noise. Even if there is still influence of narrowband noise in sequence diagram, total duration of cycle state is longer when oscillator is in cycle state theoretically than the one when oscillator is in chaos state theoretically. So the relationship between the frequency of signal and Duffing oscillator can be reached by detecting the total duration of cycle state. When the frequency of signal is the same as Duffing oscillator, it is the equivalent to add the total amplitude of driving force. That is to say, its duration of cycle state will be longer than the one without signal.

Above all, there are two important steps in frequency detection under strong narrowband noise. The first step is increasing initial driving force amplitude to an appropriate value and the second one is judging Duffing oscillator state by duration of cycle state instead of choice just between chaos state and cycle state.

## 4    Simulation

### 4.1    The Appropriate Initial Driving Force Amplitude

According to analysis above, initial driving force amplitude is critical value under broadband noise, while it is higher than critical value under narrowband noise. So it should be confirmed first before signal frequency detection.

Variation tendency of cycle time duration and driving force amplitude is reached to confirmed appropriate initial driving force amplitude. It is shown as Fig. 3 and the driving force amplitude whose duration of cycle state is long and next variation tendency is increasing should be the appropriate one.

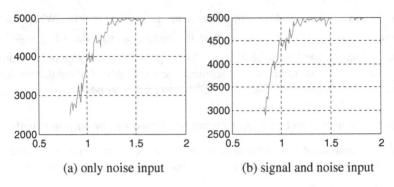

(a) only noise input                    (b) signal and noise input

**Fig. 3.** The variation tendency of cycle time duration and driving force amplitude. The abscissa is driving force amplitude and ordinate is number of cycle point in simulation.

According to Fig. 3, the variation tendency is the same as analysis result above. To find out the appropriate initial value, the difference value is calculated and shown in Fig. 4. The smallest difference that is not changing slowly is corresponding to the appropriate value. From Fig. 4, it can be found that the appropriate value is between 1.0 and 1.2 in driving force amplitude. The accurate value of this part is shown in Table 1. So the critical value of driving force in narrowband noise can be set as 1.0961 according to the result.

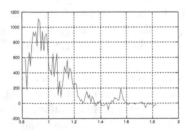

**Fig. 4.** The partial difference of two variation tendency. The abscissa is driving force amplitude and ordinate is difference number of cycle point in simulation between two situations above.

### 4.2    Verification of the New Method

Let the band of narrowband noise is 50 MHz, and the frequency of driving force is 60 MHz, and sample frequency is 6 GHz, so SNR = 0 dB means $N_0 = 10^{-10}$, SNR = $-10$ dB means $N_0 = 10^{-9}$, where the amplitude of signal is 0.1. The frequency spectrum of signal and noise with this two SNR is shown as Fig. 5.

As what is shown in Fig. 5, when SNR is 0 dB, signal is obvious in noise which is the same as in broadband noise. but when SNR is $-10$ dB, signal is covered by noise even if it is still obvious in broadband noise. The result of this two situation is shown in Fig. 6.

**Table 1.** The difference of two variation tendency.

| Amplitude | Noise | Signal | Difference |
|-----------|-------|--------|------------|
| 1.0661 | 3881 | 4538 | 657 |
| 1.0761 | 4341 | 4447 | 106 |
| 1.0861 | 4473 | 4766 | 293 |
| 1.0961 | 4542 | 4633 | 91 |
| 1.1061 | 4350 | 4550 | 200 |
| 1.1161 | 4359 | 4693 | 334 |
| 1.1261 | 4420 | 4900 | 480 |
| 1.1361 | 4420 | 4825 | 405 |
| 1.1461 | 4283 | 4850 | 576 |
| 1.1561 | 4558 | 4887 | 329 |
| 1.1661 | 4513 | 4973 | 460 |
| 1.1761 | 4479 | 4907 | 428 |
| 1.1861 | 4561 | 4851 | 290 |
| 1.1961 | 4624 | 4820 | 196 |

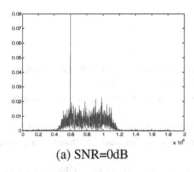
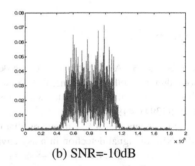

(a) SNR=0dB                     (b) SNR=-10dB

**Fig. 5.** The frequency spectrum of signal and noise with two SNR. The abscissa is time and ordinate is amplitude.

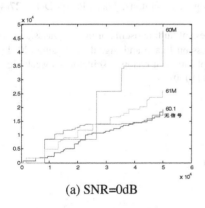
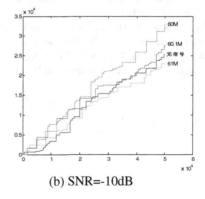

(a) SNR=0dB                     (b) SNR=-10dB

**Fig. 6.** The result of frequency detection mentioned in this paper. The abscissa is time and ordinate is number of cycle point.

According to Fig. 6, number of cycle point is on behalf of cycle state duration. When the frequency of signal and oscillator is the same, the duration of cycle state is obviously longer than others including the signal in wrong frequency and noise only. When the SNR is 0 dB, the disparity is very obvious. With the reduction of SNR, the disparity is reducing too. But the result is still able to be detected.

## 5    Conclusion

In the paper, the difference of Duffing oscillator in broadband noise and narrowband noise is analyzed. It is raised that Duffing oscillator is not immune to noise in narrowband noise like in broadband noise. But the resistance of Duffing oscillator to narrowband noise can be improved by increasing initial driving force amplitude to an appropriate value and the judgment of oscillator state can be more accurate by calculating and comparing total duration of cycle time instead of choice between chaos and cycle state. With this two ways, a new method to detect signal frequency is put forward. Its appropriate driving force value is found out by variation tendency of cycle time duration and driving force amplitude and its correctness is verified by simulation.

## References

1. Wang, G., He, S.: A quantitative study on detection and estimation of weak signals by using chaotic duffing oscillators. Trans. Circ. Syst. **50**(7), 945–953 (2003)
2. Holmes, P.: A nonlinear oscillator with a strange attractor. Philos. Trans. Roy. Soc. B Biol. Sci. **292**(1394), 419–448 (1979)
3. Birx, D.L., Pipenberg, S.J.: Chaotic oscillators and complex mapping feed forward networks (CMFFNS) for signal detection in noisy environments. In: International Joint Conference on Neural Networks, IJCNN, pp. 881–888, (1992)
4. Haykin, S., Puthusserypady, S.: Chaotic dynamics of sea clutter. Chaos: Interdiscipl. J. Nonlinear Sci. **7**(4), 777–802 (1997)
5. Vahedi, H., Gharehpetian, G.B., Karrari, M.: Application of duffing oscillators for passive islanding detection of inverter-based distributed generation units. Trans. Power Deliv. **27**(4), 1973–1983 (2012)
6. Yi, W., Song, J.: The analysis of Melnikov process of duffing oscillator in non-Gaussian color noise environment. In: 4th International Congress on Image and Signal Processing (2011)
7. Wang, G., Chen, D., Lin, J., Chen, X.: The application of chaotic oscillators to weak signal detection. Trans. Ind. Electron. **46**(2), 440–444 (1999)

# Basis Expansion Model for Fast Time-Varying Channel Estimation in High Mobility Scenarios

Xinlin Lai, Zhonghui Chen[✉], and Yisheng Zhao

College of Physics and Information Engineering, Fuzhou University, Fuzhou, China
xinlinlaifzu@163.com, {czh,zhaoys}@fzu.edu.cn

**Abstract.** In order to provide the users with reliable wireless communication service in high-speed mobility scenarios, we need to obtain channel state information by channel estimation. However, the wireless channel presents a characteristic of dynamic change in high-speed mobility environments. It will bring great challenge to channel estimation. Aiming at the high-speed railway communication system, the issue of the fast time-varying channel estimation is investigated in this paper. The impulse response of the fast time-varying channel is modeled as the product of the basis functions and the coefficients by introducing a basis expansion model (BEM). Meanwhile, the comb pilot clusters are inserted in frequency domain. The coefficients of basis functions are derived by the least-square estimation criterion so as to realize the estimation of the channel impulse response. Simulation results show that optimization generalized complex exponential BEM (OGCE-BEM) has the smallest normalized mean square error among the various types of BEMs.

**Keywords:** Fast time-varying channel · Channel estimation · Basis expansion model

## 1 Introduction

It is well known that the wireless channel is complex and variable. If the mobile terminal has high-speed mobility, it is more difficult to obtain the channel state information (CSI). For the long term evolution for railway (LTE-R) system [1], the speed of a train is more than 300 km per hour (km/h). The wireless channel is a frequency-time doubly selective fading channel, which presents a fast time-varying characteristic [2]. It will bring about serious inter-carrier interference, so the system performance will deteriorate severely. The communication system performance can be improved greatly if we obtain the CSI by channel estimation. Therefore, it is of great significance to conduct the research on channel estimation in LTE-R system.

Recently, the channel estimation issue has attracted extensive research attention. In [3], the authors present a blind channel estimation method by zero filling on the receiving data within a time block. It has high spectrum utilization and high data transmission efficiency. The authors of [4] propose that the sender

© ICST Institute for Computer Sciences, Social Informatics and Telecommunications Engineering 2018
Q. Chen et al. (Eds.): ChinaCom 2016, Part I, LNICST 209, pp. 489–501, 2018.
DOI: 10.1007/978-3-319-66625-9_48

transmits a training sequence to update the current CSI at a periodic interval. Data symbols and training sequences are sent separately, and the training sequences are used to estimate the time-varying channel. Coleri et al. [5] compare the channel estimation schemes based on block pilot and comb pilot in orthogonal frequency division multiplexing (OFDM) system. According to the low-pass interpolation, a channel estimation strategy based on comb pilot is developed, which can acquire a high estimation precision. Both the cross correlation in time and frequency domains and the statistical characteristic of the fast fading diffuse wireless channel are fully taken into account in [6]. A channel estimation algorithm based on minimum mean square error is proposed, which can improve the estimation precision.

However, the blind channel estimation method need to use the statistics of the wireless channel. Therefore, it has a high computational complexity and a poor practicability. The channel estimation algorithm based on training sequence wastes a lot of bandwidth, which is suitable for slow changing channels only. Pilot-aided channel estimation strategy has the advantages of low complexity and high accuracy, and is fit to the fast time-varying channel [7]. Among various kinds of pilot-aided channel estimation strategies, the channel estimation strategy based on a basis expansion model (BEM) can well approximate the time-varying channel [8], which has drawn great attention. The representative BEMs are complex-exponential BEM (CE-BEM), generalized complex-exponential BEM (GCE-BEM), polynomial BEM (P-BEM), and so on. In [9], an oversampling technology is adopted to improve the performance of CE-BEM, which can increase the frequency resolution and reduce the estimation error on the edge of spectrum. The authors of [10] present a channel estimation algorithm by inserting the training sequence in the time domain. The channel impulse response of the training sequence is obtained first. Then, the channel impulse response of the useful data is fitted by using the P-BEM. In consequence, there is a strong motivation to investigate the fast time-varying channel estimation via the BEM in high-speed mobility scenarios.

In this paper, we employ BEM to discuss the dynamic changing channel estimation problem in the LTE-R system. Fast time-varying channel model is established by utilizing the BEM. The channel impulse response is expressed as the summation of several basis functions multiplied by the corresponding coefficients. Then we insert isometric comb pilot clusters in the frequency domain. The BEM coefficients are estimated based on the least-square (LS) estimation criterion with low computational complexity. Thus, the fast time-varying channel in high-speed mobility scenarios can be achieved approximately. In addition, we compare different BEMs by simulation in terms of the normalized mean square error (NMSE).

The remainder of this paper is arranged as follows. Section 2 describes the system model of high-speed railway communication scenarios. In Sect. 3, the fast time-varying channel estimation strategy based on BEM is presented. Some simulation results and discussions are shown in Sect. 4. In the end, conclusion and future work are given in Sect. 5.

## 2  System Model

The network architecture of the LTE-R communication system is shown in Fig 1. The coverage area of traditional mobile communication system is usually plane shape, while the coverage area of the high-speed railway communication system is belt shape. The dedicated network topology of LTE-R system is composed of building baseband unit (BBU) and radio remote unit (RRU). A BBU is connected to multiple RRUs by optical fiber, which is used to process baseband signal. Multiple RRUs are continuously and equidistantly deployed along the railway line, which are used to process radio frequency signal. A vehicular station (VS) is installed on the top of the first carriage, which is used to receive radio frequency signals from RRU. By using the cable and the repeater (R) in each carriage, the signals received by VS are sent to a user equipment (UE) in a certain carriage. It should be noted that the wireless channel between RRU and VS is estimated in the paper. In high-speed mobility scenarios, the wireless channel is frequency-time doubly selective fading channel, which will bring challenges to the channel estimation.

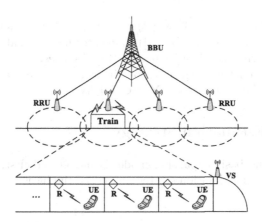

**Fig. 1.** Network architecture of high-speed railway communication system.

We assume that the RRU is sender, and the VS is the receiver. For the discrete time-varying multipath channel, the input signal and output signal in time-domain can be described as [11]: $y[n] = \sum_l h[n, l]x[n - l] + w[n]$, where $h[n, l]$ denotes the channel impulse response at the $n$-th moment on the $l$-th path, $x[n-l]$ is the sending signal at the $(n-l)$-th moment, and $w[n]$ indicates additive white Gaussian noise at the $n$-th moment.

For the LTE-R system, OFDM is one of key technologies. One OFDM symbol need to use $N$ subcarriers. The signals carried by $N$ subcarriers can be written as: $\mathbf{X} \triangleq (X[0], X[1], \cdots X[N - 1])^T$, which represents the sending signal in frequency domain. Before sending the signal, we let the $N$ subcarriers do $N$ point fast Fourier inverse transformation (IFFT). Then we get the time domain signal: $\mathbf{x} = (x[0], \cdots x[N-1])^T$. In order to suppress inter-symbol interference (ISI) of multipath channel effectively, we need to add cyclic prefix to the time domain signal at the sender, and remove the cyclic prefix at the receiver. Therefore, the received signal in time domain can be expressed as:

$$\mathbf{y} = \mathbf{H}\mathbf{x} + \mathbf{w} = (y[0], y[1], \cdots, y[N-1])^T, \tag{1}$$

where $\mathbf{H}$ is an $N \times N$ channel transfer matrix and similar to cyclic shift matrix [8]. The element of the $i$-th row and $j$-th column ($0 \leq i, j \leq N-1$) in the matrix is defined as:

$$\mathbf{H}[i,j] = \begin{cases} h[i, i-j] & (i \geq j) \cap (i-j < L) \\ h[i, i+N-j] & (i < j) \cap (i+N-j < L) \\ 0 & else \end{cases}. \tag{2}$$

At the receiver, the received signal in frequency domain can be expressed as:

$$\mathbf{Y} = \mathbf{F}\mathbf{y} = \mathbf{F}\mathbf{H}\mathbf{F}^H \mathbf{X} + \mathbf{F}\mathbf{w}, \tag{3}$$

where $\mathbf{Y} = (Y[0], Y[1], \cdots, Y[N-1])^T$ denote output signal in frequency domain. $\mathbf{w} = (w[0], w[1], \cdots, w[N-1])^T$ indicates noise signal in time domain. $\mathbf{F}$ is a standard normalized Fourier matrix [12]. As a result, the transfer matrix of the wireless channel in frequency domain can be written as: $\mathbf{G} = \mathbf{F}\mathbf{H}\mathbf{F}^H$. Thus, Eq. (3) can be simplified as: $\mathbf{Y} = \mathbf{G}\mathbf{X} + \mathbf{W}$.

## 3    Channel Estimation Strategy

In this section, the basis expansion model is introduced first. Then, the fast time-varying channel estimation strategy based on the basis expansion model is presented.

### 3.1    Basis Expansion Model (BEM)

For the multipath channel, the channel parameters in each path are changing all the time during an OFDM symbol. The number of channel parameters needed to be estimated is $NL$ [5], which is usually very large. Here, $N$ is the number of sampling points in an OFDM symbol and $L$ represents the number of multipath. Therefore, the estimation of multipath channel cannot be realized directly.

BEM uses $Q$ orthogonal basis functions to approximate the dynamic changes of the channel environment [7]. Then, the channel impulse response for the $l$-th path can be represented as: $\mathbf{h}_l = [h[0,l], h[1,l], \cdots, h[N-1,l]](0 \leq l \leq L-1)$, $L \geq \lceil \tau_{max}/T_s \rceil + 1$, where $\tau_{max}$ denotes the maximum multipath delay and $T_s$ is the sampling period. The $q$-th basis function vector is expressed as: $\mathbf{b}_q = (b[0,q], b[1,q], \cdots, b[N-1,q])^T(0 \leq q \leq Q-1)$, $Q \geq \lceil 2f_{max}NT_s \rceil + 1$, where

$f_{\max}$ is the maximum Doppler frequency shift. Then, we use BEM to match the channel impulse response of the $l$-th path:

$$\mathbf{h}_l = \sum_{q=0}^{Q-1} c_q^l \mathbf{b}_q, \tag{4}$$

where $\mathbf{h}_l$ and $\mathbf{b}_q$ are both $N \times 1$ column vectors, and $c_q^l$ denotes the coefficient of the $l$-th path and the $q$-th basis function. We rewrite Eq. (4) as matrix form: $\mathbf{h}_l = \mathbf{B}\mathbf{c}^l$. Here, $\mathbf{B}$ is an $N \times Q$ matrix. It consists of $Q$ basis functions, which can be written as: $\mathbf{B} = [\mathbf{b}_0, \mathbf{b}_1, \cdots, \mathbf{b}_{Q-1}]$. Moreover, $\mathbf{c}^l$ is a $Q \times 1$ column vector. It consists of $Q$ basis function coefficients of the $l$-th path, which is defined as: $\mathbf{c}^l = \left(c_0^l, c_1^l, \cdots, c_{Q-1}^l\right)^T$. According to BEM, the estimation of the time-varying channel impulse response is transformed into the estimation of the basis function coefficients. Therefore, the number of channel estimation is reduced from $NL$ to $QL$.

Classical complex exponential BEM (CE-BEM) adopts Fourier basis as the basis functions [13]. The resolution of CE-BEM can not meet the requirements while modeling. Therefore, the estimation error on the edge of the spectrum is large. Moreover, discrete Fourier transform leads to spectrum leakage, so the estimation error of CE-BEM is not small enough.

GCE-BEM is an improvement of CE-BEM by using oversampling technique to reduce the sampling interval [9], which can effectively reduce the estimation error on the edge of spectrum caused by insufficient sampling points. The basis functions are defined as:

$$b_q(n) = e^{j2\pi \frac{q-\frac{Q-1}{2}}{KN} n}, \tag{5}$$

where $Q$ meets the condition: $Q \geq \lceil 2f_{\max}KNT_s \rceil + 1$, and we set $K = 2$ generally. The frequency of basis functions is $f_q = (q - (Q-1)/2)/KNT_s$. The maximum frequency of GCE-BEM basis functions is $f_Q = (Q-1)/2KNT_s \geq \lceil f_{\max} \rceil$. Compared with CE-BEM, GCE-BEM has more high-frequency basis functions, whose frequencies are higher than $f_{\max}$. So it will be more susceptible to the effects of high frequency noise. As a result, the modeling error will be more obvious.

Optimization generalized complex exponential BEM (OGCE-BEM) is the result of a correction processing for the frequency of GCE-BEM basis functions. The basis functions are constructed as:

$$b_q(n) = e^{j2\pi g \frac{q-\frac{Q-1}{2}}{KN} n}, \tag{6}$$

where $g = 2Kf_{\max}N/(Q-1)$. The maximum frequency of the basis functions is $g \times (Q-1)/(2KN) = f_{\max}$. OGCE-BEM can remove the basis functions whose frequencies are higher than $f_{\max}$, which can effectively reduces the influence of Gaussian white noise and overcomes the problem of spectrum leakage in CE-BEM. Therefore, OGCE-BEM can approximate the real channel more accurately.

## 3.2  Fast Time-Varying Channel Estimation Strategy

We need to estimate the basis function coefficients of BEM. The main idea is: Firstly, we put the expression of BEM into the channel transfer function in time domain, and then transfer the channel transfer function to the frequency domain. Next, in order to solve the basis function coefficients simply, we separate the BEM coefficients completely. In the end, we can obtain the channel impulse response in time domain [8].

According to the Eq. (4), the channel impulse response for the $l$-th path and the $q$-th basis function can be seen as the linear superposition of $Q$ basis functions at the $n$-th sampling moment, which can be written as: $h[n,l] = \sum\limits_{q=0}^{Q-1} c_q^l b[n,q]$. Then, we put this expression into the channel transfer function in time domain:

$$
\begin{aligned}
y[n] &= \sum_{l=0}^{L-1} \sum_{q=0}^{Q-1} c_q^l b[n,q] x[n-l] + w[n] \\
&= \sum_{q=0}^{Q-1} b[n,q] \left\{ \sum_{l=0}^{L-1} c_q^l x[n-l] \right\} + w[n]
\end{aligned}
\tag{7}
$$

We rewrite the second accumulator of the second row in Eq. (7):

$$
\sum_{l=0}^{L-1} c_q^l x[n-l] = \left( c_q^{L-1}, \cdots, c_q^0 \right) \begin{pmatrix} x[n-L+1] \\ \vdots \\ x[n] \end{pmatrix}.
\tag{8}
$$

In order to facilitate the transformation, we define a matrix: $\Lambda_q^b = diag\{b_q\}$. $\Lambda_q^b$ is an $N \times N$ diagonal matrix, which consists of $N$ elements of column vector $b_q$. We can write Eq. (7) as vector form:

$$
\mathbf{y} = \sum_{q=0}^{Q-1} \Lambda_q^b \mathbf{C}_q \mathbf{x} + \mathbf{w},
\tag{9}
$$

where $\mathbf{C}_q$ is an $N \times N$ standard cyclic matrix. Each column of $\mathbf{C}_q$ consists of $L$ BEM coefficients of the $q$-th basis function, which can be written as:

$$
\mathbf{C}_q = \begin{pmatrix}
c_q^0 & 0 & \cdots & c_q^{L-1} & \cdots & c_q^1 \\
c_q^1 & c_q^0 & \cdots & & c_q^3 & c_q^2 \\
c_q^2 & c_q^1 & c_q^0 & \ddots & \ddots & \vdots \\
\vdots & \ddots & \ddots & \ddots & \vdots & \vdots \\
0 & \cdots & \ddots & \ddots & c_q^0 & 0 \\
0 & \cdots & c_q^{L-1} & \cdots & c_q^1 & c_q^0
\end{pmatrix}.
\tag{10}
$$

The distribution of $\mathbf{C}_q$ is consistent with the channel transfer matrix $\mathbf{H}$. Then we apply Fourier transform to both sides of Eq. (9). For the purpose of facilitating the extraction of the basis functions coefficients, we define a column vector: $\mathbf{c}_q = \left(c_q^0, c_q^1, \cdots, c_q^{L-1}\right)^T$. Therefore, the wireless channel model is transferred to the frequency domain:

$$
\begin{aligned}
\mathbf{Y} = \mathbf{F}\mathbf{y} &= \sum_{q=0}^{Q-1} \mathbf{F}\Lambda_q^b \mathbf{F}^H \mathbf{F}\mathbf{C}_q \mathbf{F}^H \mathbf{F}\mathbf{x} + \mathbf{F}\mathbf{w} \\
&= \sum_{q=0}^{Q-1} \mathbf{D}_q \Delta_q \mathbf{X} + \mathbf{W} = \mathbf{H}^\nabla \mathbf{X} + \mathbf{W}
\end{aligned}
\tag{11}
$$

where $\mathbf{D}_q = \mathbf{F}\Lambda_q^b \mathbf{F}^H = \mathbf{F}diag\left\{\mathbf{b}_q\right\}\mathbf{F}^H$ and $\Delta_q = \mathbf{F}\mathbf{C}_q \mathbf{F}^H = \sqrt{N}diag\left\{\mathbf{F}^L \mathbf{c}_q\right\}$. To observe the Eq. (11), we can find that: $\mathbf{D}_q$ is an $N \times N$ matrix but not a diagonal matrix. The distribution shape of nonzero elements in the matrix is banded and along with the diagonal. Then we transfer $\mathbf{C}_q$ into the frequency domain. And then, we obtain $\Delta_q$, which is an $N \times N$ diagonal matrix. $\mathbf{F}^L$ is an $N \times L$ matrix, which consists of the first $L$ columns of the standard normalized Fourier matrix. Next, we use matrix switching law to realize the following conversion:

$$
\Delta_q \mathbf{X} = \sqrt{N}diag\left\{\mathbf{F}^L \mathbf{c}_q\right\}\mathbf{X} = \sqrt{N}diag\left\{\mathbf{X}\right\}\mathbf{F}^L \mathbf{c}_q = \hat{\mathbf{X}}\mathbf{c}_q,
\tag{12}
$$

where $\mathbf{X}$ and $\mathbf{F}^L \mathbf{c}_q$ are both $N \times 1$ column vectors. We define $\hat{\mathbf{X}} = \sqrt{N}diag\left\{\mathbf{X}\right\}\mathbf{F}^L$, which is an $N \times L$ matrix. Therefore, we separate the BEM coefficients out successfully. Thus, we obtain:

$$
\mathbf{Y} = \sum_{q=0}^{Q-1} \mathbf{D}_q \Delta_q \mathbf{X} + \mathbf{W} = \sum_{q=0}^{Q-1} \mathbf{D}_q \hat{\mathbf{X}}\mathbf{c}_q + \mathbf{W}.
\tag{13}
$$

And we set:

$$
\mathbf{D} = \left[\mathbf{D}_0 \hat{\mathbf{X}}, \cdots, \mathbf{D}_{Q-1}\hat{\mathbf{X}}\right] = [\mathbf{D}_0, \cdots, \mathbf{D}_{Q-1}]\left[I_Q \otimes \hat{\mathbf{X}}\right],
\tag{14}
$$

where $\mathbf{D}$ is an $N \times LQ$ matrix, and $\otimes$ denotes Kronecker product. Then, we define $\bar{\mathbf{c}} = \left[\mathbf{c}_0^T, \mathbf{c}_1^T, \cdots, \mathbf{c}_{Q-1}^T\right]^T$, which is a $LQ \times 1$ column vector. Consequently, we get the basic equation, which can solve the $QL$ BEM coefficients:

$$
\mathbf{Y} = \mathbf{D}\bar{\mathbf{c}} + \mathbf{W}.
\tag{15}
$$

In order to track fast time-varying channel, we need to insert comb pilot in frequency domain. We arrange $M$ pilot clusters in $N$ subcarriers of OFDM system as shown in Fig. 2. The length of each pilot cluster is $L_p + 2L_z$, where $L_p$ is the number of non-zero pilot subcarriers, $L_z$ represents the number of the pilot subcarriers whose value are zero, and we set $L_z$ is an even number. Then we assume that the length of each data cluster is $L_d$. And we set $L_p = 1$. We suppose that the ICI comes mainly from a few adjacent subcarriers. In order to avoid the interference between the pilot information and data information, we arrange guard intervals on both sides to protect the non-zero pilots in comb pilot clusters.

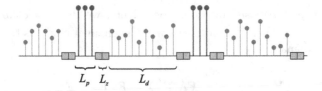

**Fig. 2.** Comb pilot pattern.

We set $\mathbf{X}_m^{(\mathbf{P})}$ $(m = 0, 1, \cdots, M - 1)$ as the $m$-th pilot cluster. Then, we need to select the appropriate received samples. We can find the corresponding pilot-received signal according to the index value of the pilot directly. Considering that the energy of non-zero pilot subcarriers will spread to a few adjacent subcarriers, we set both the received signal in non-zero pilot subcarriers and half of the received signal in the corresponding guard pilot subcarriers which are more close to non-zero pilot as the received samples. And we assume that $L_z$ is an even number. So, we consider the corresponding pilot-received signal of the $m$-th sample cluster $\mathbf{Y}_m^{(p)}$ is a $(L_p + L_z) \times 1$ column vector, which can be written as:

$$
\begin{aligned}
\mathbf{Y}_m^{(p)} &= \sum_{q=0}^{Q-1} \mathbf{D}_{q,m}^{(p)} \hat{\mathbf{X}}^{(p)} \mathbf{c}_q + \sum_{q=0}^{Q-1} \mathbf{D}_{q,m}^{(d)} \hat{\mathbf{X}}^{(d)} \mathbf{c}_q + \mathbf{W}_m \\
&= \sum_{q=0}^{Q-1} \mathbf{D}_{q,m}^{(p)} \hat{\mathbf{X}}^{(p)} \mathbf{c}_q + \mathbf{W}_{d,m} + \mathbf{W}_m^{(p)}
\end{aligned}
, \qquad (16)
$$

where $\mathbf{W}_m^{(p)}$ denotes the Gaussian white noise in frequency domain for the $m$-th sample cluster, and $\mathbf{W}_{d,m}$ indicates the interference between the data subcarriers and the pilot subcarriers. $\mathbf{D}_q^{(p)}$ is an $M(L_p + L_z) \times M(L_p + L_z)$ matrix, which is separated from the corresponding position of the sample subcarriers of $\mathbf{D}_q$. $\mathbf{D}_{q,m}^{(p)}$ is a $(L_p + L_z) \times M(L_p + L_z)$ matrix, which is separated from the corresponding position of the $m$-th sample cluster of $\mathbf{D}_q^{(p)}$.

Then, we define an $M(L_p + L_z) \times L$ matrix: $\hat{\mathbf{X}}^{(p)}$, which is separated from the corresponding position of the sample subcarriers of $\hat{\mathbf{X}}$. Then, we define two matries:

$$
\mathbf{D}_m^{(p)} = \left[ \mathbf{D}_{0,m}^{(p)}, \mathbf{D}_{1,m}^{(p)}, \cdots, \mathbf{D}_{Q-1,m}^{(p)} \right], \qquad (17)
$$

$$
\hat{\mathbf{X}}_Q^{(p)} = I_Q \otimes \hat{\mathbf{X}}^{(p)}, \qquad (18)
$$

where $\mathbf{D}_m^{(p)}$ is a $(L_p + L_z) \times M(L_p + L_z)Q$ matrix, and $\hat{\mathbf{X}}_Q^{(p)}$ is an $M(L_p + L_z)Q \times LQ$ matrix. Therefore, Eq. (16) can be rewritten as: $\mathbf{Y}_m^{(p)} = \mathbf{D}_m^{(p)} \hat{\mathbf{X}}_Q^{(p)} \bar{\mathbf{c}} + \mathbf{W}_{d,m} + \mathbf{W}_m^{(p)}$. Taking all of the sample clusters into account, we define a $(L_p + L_z)M \times M(L_p + L_z)Q$ matrix :

$$
\mathbf{D}^{(p)} = \left[ \mathbf{D}_0^{(p)T}, \mathbf{D}_1^{(p)T}, \cdots, \mathbf{D}_{M-1}^{(p)T} \right]^T . \qquad (19)
$$

Finally, we obtain the received signal of the corresponding sample position $\mathbf{Y}^{(p)}$, which can be derived by: $\mathbf{Y}^{(p)} = \mathbf{D}^{(p)}\hat{\mathbf{X}}_Q^{(p)}\bar{\mathbf{c}} + \mathbf{W}_d + \mathbf{W}^{(p)}$, where $\mathbf{W}_d$ indicates the interference between the data subcarriers and the pilot subcarriers, $\mathbf{W}^{(p)}$ represents the Gaussian white noise in frequency domain, and $\mathbf{Y}^{(p)}$ is a $(L_p + L_z)\,M \times 1$ column vector. Therefore, we obtain the basic equation of pilot-assisted channel estimation strategy. Then, we set a $(L_p + L_z)\,M \times LQ$ matrix: $\boldsymbol{\Omega}^{(p)} = \mathbf{D}^{(p)}\hat{\mathbf{X}}_Q^{(p)}$. Thus, based on LS criterion, we get the estimation of BEM coefficients:

$$\bar{\mathbf{c}} = \left(\boldsymbol{\Omega}^{(p)}\right)^{-\dagger}\mathbf{Y}^{(p)}, \tag{20}$$

where $\left(\boldsymbol{\Omega}^{(p)}\right)^{-\dagger}$ denotes the pseudo inverse matrix of $\boldsymbol{\Omega}^{(p)}$.

## 4   Simulation Results and Discussions

In this section, we evaluate the performance of P-BEM, DCT-BEM, CE-BEM, GCE-BEM, and OGCE-BEM by simulation. The related simulation parameters are set to $N = 256$, $T_s = 0.5$ μs, $f_c = 2.6$ GHz, and $L = 4$.

According to the system model in this paper, we can find that the propagation path of radio wave contains a line-of-sight (LOS) path and multiple non line-of-sight (NLOS) paths. Thus, we can adopt Rician fading channel model to describe the real channel [14]. We use NMSE to measure the estimation precision of various BEMs. NMSE is defined as:

$$NMSE = \frac{\frac{1}{N}\sum_{n=0}^{N-1}\left|h\,[n] - \hat{h}\,[n]\right|^2}{\frac{1}{N}\sum_{n=0}^{N-1}\left|h\,[n]\right|^2}, \tag{21}$$

where $h(n)$ denotes the impulse response value at the $n$-th moment of the real channel, $\hat{h}(n)$ is the estimation of the impulse response at the $n$-th moment. The impulse response of the wireless channel is the sum of $L$ paths at the receiver, so $\hat{h}(n)$ can be represented as $\hat{h}(n) = \sum_{l=0}^{L-1}\hat{h}[n, l]$.

As shown in Figs. 3 and 4, we model the wireless channel by BEMs ($Q = 4$). Then, we adopt the estimation strategy of fast time-varying channel. Next, we regard signal-to-noise ratio (SNR) as a variable in the simulation and set the value range of SNR is $[0, 30]$ dB. It can be seen that the ability of model fitting is getting better as SNR increases. In Fig. 4, the normalized Doppler frequency shift $f_d$ is about 0.12, while the speed of mobile terminal $v$ is 400 km/h. Apart from the similar changing trend of NMSE and SNR, we can observe that the performance of OGCE-BEM is superior to the GCE-BEM on a certain extent. It can be explained that OGCE-BEM effectively reduces the influence of Gaussian white noise and overcomes the problem of spectrum leakage in CE-BEM. In addition, the performance of OGCE-BEM and GCE-BEM are better than DCT-BEM, CE-BEM, and P-BEM obviously while $v = 400$ km/h. In Fig. 3, the speed

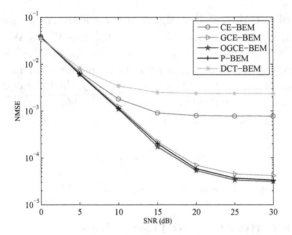

**Fig. 3.** NMSE versus SNR with $v = 50$ km/h.

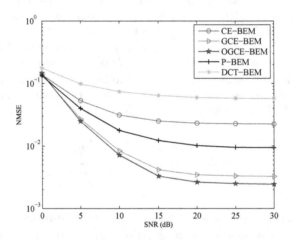

**Fig. 4.** NMSE versus SNR with $v = 400$ km/h.

of mobile terminal $v$ is 50 km/h, the performance of OGCE-BEM is a little better than GCE-BEM and P-BEM, and is much better than CE-BEM and DCT-BEM.

Figure 5 illustrates the relationship between NMSE and the speed of mobile terminal. We set SNR = 20 dB and $Q = 4$. From the figure, we can find that as the speed of mobile terminal increases, the performance of BEMs deteriorates gradually. That is because the speed of mobile terminal is increased continually, which results in an increase in ICI power. Additionally, the capacity of OGCE-BEM and GCE-BEM against the influence of Doppler shift is stronger than P-BEM, DCT-BEM, and CE-BEM visibly. Moreover, the ability of model fitting gets distinctly worse while Doppler shift becomes more and more serious, the reason is that P-BEM and DCT-BEM are sensitive to Doppler shift.

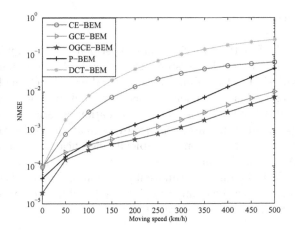

**Fig. 5.** NMSE versus moving speed with SNR = 20 dB.

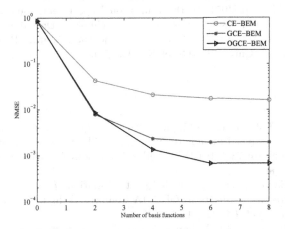

**Fig. 6.** NMSE versus number of basis functions with SNR = 20 dB and $v = 400$ km/h.

Figure 6 depicts the relationship between NMSE and model order $Q$ while $v = 400$ km/h. We know that the performance of OGCE-BEM and GCE-BEM is better than other BEMs in high speed scenarios, so we focus on OGCE-BEM and GCE-BEM. Observing the similar changing tendency between NMSE and model order, we can find that NMSE decreases as the model order grows from 0 to 8. This is because the BEMs can approximate the real channel more accurately as model order becomes higher. Furthermore, estimation precision of various BEMs has reached a relatively ideal order of magnitude while model order is 6, especially OGCE-BEM. It can be explained that a smaller amounts of BEM basis functions are just enough to match the fast time-varying channel.

## 5   Conclusion

We investigated the fast time-varying channel estimation strategy in high-speed railway LTE-R communication system. By using BEM, the channel impulse response was expressed as the summation of several basis functions multiplied by the corresponding coefficients. Then, we inserted comb pilot clusters in the frequency domain. Based on the least-square estimation criterion, we achieved the estimation of the channel impulse response by estimating the BEM coefficients, which can reduce the computational complexity significantly. Simulation results verify that BEM can well approximate the fast time-varying channel. Furthermore, OGCE-BEM has a higher estimation precision in different types of BEMs. In order to further reduce the number of pilots, a distributed compressed sensing method will be considered in the future work.

**Acknowledgments.** This work is supported in part by the National Natural Science Foundation of China (Grant No. U1405251), the Natural Science Foundation of Fujian Province (Grant No. 2015J05122), the Education Department Foundation of Fujian Province (Grant No. JA15089), the Science and Technology Development Foundation of Fuzhou University (Grant No. 2014-XY-30), and the Scientific Research Starting Foundation of Fuzhou University (Grant No. 022572).

## References

1. Martin-Vega, F.J., Delgado-Luque, I.M., Blanquez-Casado, F., Gomez, G., Aguayo-Torres, M.C., Entrambasaguas, J.T.: LTE performance over high speed railway channel. In: 78th IEEE Vehicular Technology Conference, pp. 1–5. IEEE Press, Las Vegas (2013)
2. Muneer, P., Sameer, S.M.: Pilot-aided joint estimation of doubly selective channel and carrier frequency offsets in OFDMA uplink with high-mobility users. IEEE Trans. Veh. Technol. **64**, 411–417 (2015)
3. Wang, S., Hu, J.K.: Blind channel estimation for single-input multiple-output OFDM systems: zero padding based or cyclic prefix based? Wirel. Commun. Mob. Comput. **12**, 204–210 (2013)
4. Cagatay, C.: An accurate and efficient two-stage channel estimation method utilizing training sequences with closed form expressions. IEEE Trans. Commun. **59**, 3259–3264 (2011)
5. Coleri, S., Ergen, M., Puri, A., Bahai, A.: Channel estimation techniques based on pilot arrangement in OFDM systems. IEEE Trans. Broadcast. **48**, 223–229 (2002)
6. Mousa, A., Mahmoud, H.: Channels estimation in OFDM system over Rician fading channel based on comb-type pilots arrangement. IET Sig. Proc. **4**, 598–602 (2010)
7. Zhong, K., Lei, X., Li, S.Q.: Wiener filter for basis expansion model based channel estimation. IEEE Commun. Lett. **15**, 813–815 (2011)
8. Tang, Z.J., Cannizzaro, R.C., Leus, G., Banelli, P.: Pilot-assisted time-varying channel estimation for OFDM systems. IEEE Trans. Signal Process. **55**, 2226–2238 (2007)
9. Leus, G.: On the estimation of rapidly time varying channels. In: 12th European Signal Processing Conference, pp. 2227–2230. IEEE Press, Vienna (2004)

10. Huang, C.L., Chen, C.W., Wei, S.W.: Channel estimation for OFDM system with two training symbols aided and polynomial fitting. IEEE Trans. Commun. **58**, 733–736 (2010)

11. Tse, D., Viswanath, P.: Fundamentals of wireless communication. IEEE Trans. Inf. Theory **52**, 919–920 (2009)

12. Stamoulis, A., Diggavi, S.N., Al-Dhahir, N.: Intercarrier interference in MIMO-OFDM. IEEE Trans. Sig. Process. **50**, 2451–2464 (2002)

13. Chiong, C.W.R., Rong, Y., Xiang, Y.: Channel estimation for time-varying MIMO relay systems. IEEE Trans. Wirel. Commun. **14**, 6752–6762 (2015)

14. Beaulieu, N.C., Chen, Y.: Maximum likelihood estimation of local average SNR in ricean fading channels. IEEE Commun. Lett. **9**, 219–221 (2005)

# Robust Power Allocation Scheme in Cognitive Radio Networks

Hongzhi Wang, Meng Zhu, and Mingyue Zhou[✉]

College of Computer Science and Technology,
Changchun University of Technology,
Yan'an Street 2055, Changchun 130012, China
{hzwang, zmyjlu}@ccut.edu.cn, zhumengvipzm@163.com

**Abstract.** Considering that the spectrum resources are becoming increasingly demand, maximum channel capacity is very crucial for future wireless communication systems, especially for cognitive radio networks (CRNs). However, most existing works usually assume that channel parameter estimation is perfect, which is often damped in practical systems. In this paper, we investigate the robust maximum channel capacity problem in the CRNs. Then assuming that channel parameter uncertainty is bounded, we consider that all channel parameter uncertainties are described by ellipsoid sets. From the perspective of worst-case optimization, we formulate it as a semi-infinite programming (SIP) problem. Furthermore, an optimal iterative algorithm based on the dual decomposition theory and Lagrange multiplier algorithm is applied. Simulation results validate that our robust scheme can achieve the channel capacity maximization considering the worst-case and strictly guarantee the power interference requirement of second users (SUs) under all parameters' uncertainties.

**Keywords:** Capacity maximization · CRNs · Ellipsoidal set · Distributed algorithm · Robust optimization

## 1 Introduction

In recent years, with the rapid development and the wide application of radio communication technology, the demand for wireless spectrum resources becomes exceedingly urgent. According to the report by Federal Communication Commission (FCC), the authorized spectrum utilization is obviously inefficient since the fixed spectrum allocation approach [1]. Dr. Mitola first proposed the concept of cognitive radio technology [2], which is to establish communication among unauthorized users without exceeding the interference that primary users (PUs) can tolerate.

The problem of assigning power to different SUs has recently been an area of active research. There are many papers [3, 4] addressing the problem of channel capacity maximization under the assumption that the parameters and constraints are perfect. However, this information is subject to errors due to measurement uncertainties in practical systems. We often call the corresponding problems for the "nominal" problem [5]. However, these parameters are time-varying, imperfect or uncertainty. Several researches on the problem of parameter uncertainties have been investigated in the

© ICST Institute for Computer Sciences, Social Informatics and Telecommunications Engineering 2018
Q. Chen et al. (Eds.): ChinaCom 2016, Part I, LNICST 209, pp. 502–511, 2018.
DOI: 10.1007/978-3-319-66625-9_49

CRNs. The authors investigate state estimation problems for nonlinear systems with parameter uncertainties. A new robust unscented Kalman filter is devised by analyzing the influence which parameter uncertainties give to covariance matrix [6]. Robust power control strategies for cognitive radios in the presence of sensing delay and model parameter uncertainty is investigated [7]. The authors use a discrete-time Markov chain (DTMC) to characterize the primary users' dynamics as well as the fading channel. Furthermore, most of existing algorithms for power control mechanism problem are centralized [8, 9], where the parameter control and transmission is completed by the base station. Nevertheless, the centralized scheme has obvious computation and transmission overhead that is a shortcoming of the centralized way. Orthogonal frequency division multiplexing (OFDM) has been considered a potential transmission technology for CR systems. We investigated robust power allocation by considering an OFDM framework with transmit power budget and interference threshold into account [10]. In this paper, we investigate the worst case robust formulation under distributed way [11] in cognitive radio wireless ad-hoc networks to maximize channel capacity while keeping the SINR amount of SU within relatively high range.

Considering the above problems, robust optimization techniques are more appropriate obviously. Firstly, we define an uncertainty set, which is an ellipsoid set that captures the parameter uncertainty. Secondly, the robust capacity maximization problem can be converted into a SIP problem, which is transformed into a second order cone programming (SOCP) problem [12] under the worst-case. Thirdly, a distributed algorithm is proposed based on dual decomposition theory and Lagrange multiplier algorithm [13] is proposed to achieve an optimal solution. Finally, the equivalent constraint and the iterative algorithm derived from parameter uncertainty are proposed to acquire optimal solution [14], and the theoretical discussions between robust algorithm and non-robust algorithm are demonstrated by simulation results.

## 2  System Model and Robust Distributed Formulation

### 2.1  System Model

We consider an ad-hoc cognitive radio network as Ref. [15], i.e., each link consists of a transmitter node and a receiver node. Assume that there are $\mathbf{K} = \{1, 2, 3, ..., K\}$ cognitive links and only one primary link in the region of interest.

In this paper, we pay attention to the underlay paradigm in CRNs. In this model, SUs can always access the channel that is assigned to PUs, in which the total interference introduced to PUs is strictly less than a predefined threshold which PUs can tolerate as follows, i.e.,

$$\sum_{i=1}^{k} g_i p_i \leq I_{th}. \tag{1}$$

where $g_i$ denotes the channel gain between the cognitive transmitter (CR-Tx) of link $i$ to the PU receiver (PU-Rx). $p_i$ denotes the transmission power of the CR-Tx for link $i$. $I_{th}$ represents the permissible interference threshold for PU-Rx.

To guarantee the normal work of the system, the transmission power of each SU should not exceed its power budget. We have

$$p_i \leq p_i^{\max}, \ \forall i \in \mathbf{K}. \tag{2}$$

where $p_i^{\max}$ is the maximum transmission power cognitive receiver $i$.

The signal to interference ratio plus noise (SINR) at the cognitive receiver $i$ is

$$SINR_i = \frac{h_{ii}p_i}{\sum\limits_{j \neq i} h_{ij}p_j + \sigma_i}, \ \forall i \in \mathbf{K}. \tag{3}$$

where $h_{ij}$ denotes the channel gain from cognitive transmitter $j$ to receiver $i$. $\sigma_i$ is the background noise at cognitive receiver $i$ which includes both the thermal noise and interference caused by the primary transmission.

The utility function chosen by each SU to be maximized is the data capacity since spectrum efficiency is the main target of cognitive radio. While guaranteeing constraints both (1) and (3), the problem is formulated as

$$\max \sum_{i=1}^{k} \log\left(1 + \frac{h_{ii}p_i}{\sum\limits_{j \neq i} h_{ij}p_j + \sigma_i}\right)$$

$$s.t. \quad C1: \sum_{i=1}^{k} g_i p_i \leq I_{th}, \quad C2: p_i \leq p_i^{\max}, \ \forall i \in \mathbf{K}. \tag{4}$$

where the variable $p_i \geq 0$ for all $i$. Moreover, $\alpha = [\alpha_{ij}]$ can be denoted by the formula as follows

$$\alpha_{ij} = \begin{cases} 0, & if \ i = j, \\ \dfrac{h_{ij}}{h_{ii}}, & if \ i \neq j. \end{cases} \tag{5}$$

Then, objective function in (4) can translate to as follows

$$\max \sum_{i=1}^{k} \log\left(1 + \frac{p_i}{\sum\limits_{j \neq i} \alpha_{ij}p_j + \sigma_i/h_{ii}}\right)$$

$$s.t. \quad C1: \sum_{i=1}^{k} g_i p_i \leq I_{th}, \quad C2: p_i \leq p_i^{\max}, \ \forall i \in \mathbf{K}. \tag{6}$$

In the rest of the section, we will formulate the robust optimization problems considering uncertainties which include both the channel coefficient $\alpha$ and channel gain $g$.

## 2.2  Robust Distributed Formulation Under Ellipsoid Uncertainty Set

We firstly consider the uncertainties of channel parameter matrix $\alpha$ and channel gain $g_i$, and use the ellipsoid set to depict the corresponding parameter uncertainty.

Let $\alpha_i$ denote the uncertainty set of the *ith* row for matrix $\alpha$, which can capture the perturbation of interfering channel gains relative to the main channel gain of link $i$. Denote the actual standardized channel gain between user $j$'s transmitter and user $i$'s receiver as $\bar{\alpha}_{ij} + \Delta\alpha_{ij}$, where $\bar{\alpha}_{ij}$ is the nominal value, and $\Delta\alpha_{ij}$ is the corresponding uncertainty part. Hence, the uncertainty set of $\alpha_i$ for $\bar{\alpha}_{ij}$ under ellipsoid approximation can be expressed as:

$$\alpha_i = \left\{ \bar{\alpha}_i + \Delta\alpha_i : \left\| \Delta\alpha_{ij} \right\|_2^2 \leq \varepsilon_0^2, \ \forall j \neq i, \ i \in \mathbf{K} \right\}. \tag{7}$$

where $\|x\|_2$ refers to the Euclidean norm [16], and $\varepsilon_0$ is the positive upper bound on the uncertainty region.

Let $g_i$ denote the uncertainty set of the *ith* row of matrix $g$, $g_i$ describes the channel gain between cognitive transmitter $i$ and PU receiver, and $g_i = \bar{g}_i + \Delta g_i$, where $\bar{g}_i$ is the nominal value, and the corresponding uncertainty part is $\Delta g_i$. Then the certainty set $g_i$ under ellipsoid approximation is formulated as:

$$g_i = \left\{ \bar{g}_i + \Delta g_i : \left\| \Delta g_i \right\|_2^2 \leq \varepsilon_i^2, \ \forall i \in \mathbf{K} \right\}. \tag{8}$$

where $\varepsilon_i$ is the upper bound on the uncertainty region.

The robust power allocation algorithm with capacity maximization under ellipsoid set can be represented by

$$\max \sum_{i=1}^{k} \log\left(1 + \frac{p_i}{\sum_{j \neq i} (\bar{\alpha}_{ij} + \Delta\alpha_{ij})p_j + \sigma_i/h_{ii}}\right)$$

$$s.t. \quad C1 : \sum_{i=1}^{k} (\bar{g}_i + \Delta g_i)p_i \leq Ith, \ C3 : \left\| \Delta\alpha_{ij} \right\|_2^2 \leq \varepsilon_0^2, \quad \forall j \neq i, i \in \mathbf{K},$$

$$C2 : p_i \leq p_i^{\max}, \ \forall i \in K, \ C4 : \left\| \Delta g_i \right\|_2^2 \leq \varepsilon_i^2, \quad \forall i \in \mathbf{K}. \tag{9}$$

The robust capacity maximization problem (9) is an infinite number of constraints relative to the sets $\alpha_i$ and $g_i$, i.e., it is a SIP problem. We can transform the SIP problem into an equivalent problem with finite constraints under the worst-case. Considering Cauchy–Schwartz inequality, the equivalent problem as follows

$$\max_{\alpha_i \in \alpha}\left\{\sum_{j \neq i} \Delta\alpha_{ij}p_j\right\} = \varepsilon_o \sqrt{\sum_{j \neq i} p_j^2}, \ \max_{g_i \in g}\left\{\sum_i \Delta g_i p_i\right\} = \varepsilon_i \|p_i\|_2, \ \forall i \in \mathbf{K}. \tag{10}$$

Then, the problem (9) is transformed into an equivalent problem under the worst-case.

## 3  The Distributed Capacity Maximization Algorithm

In this section, we develop a worst-case distributed capacity maximization problem by dual decomposition theory. Hence, in this case, we transform constraint C1 in (9) into an equivalent problem as follows

$$\varepsilon_i \|p\|_2 \leq -\bar{g}^T p + I_{th}, \quad \forall i \in \mathbf{K}. \tag{11}$$

However, it is difficult to decompose the coupled part $\varepsilon_i \|p\|_2$. Therefore, we propose a worst-case distributed capacity maximization algorithm along with the convergence, i.e., this constraint can be represented by

$$\sum_i (\bar{g}_i + \varepsilon_i)p_i \leq I_{th}, \quad \forall i \in \mathbf{K}. \tag{12}$$

Taking into account the all parameters uncertainties, where the uncertainties is the worst-case level that is the upper bound of ellipsoid sets, the worst-case distributed capacity maximization problem can be expressed as

$$\max \sum_{i=1}^{k} \log(1 + \frac{p_i}{\sum_{j \neq i} \bar{\alpha}_{ij}p_j + \varepsilon_o \sqrt{\sum_{j \neq i} p_j^2} + \sigma_i/h_{ii}}) \tag{13}$$

$$s.t \quad C1 : \sum_{i=1}^{k} (\bar{g}_i + \varepsilon_i)p_i \leq I_{th}, \quad C2 : p_i \leq p_i^{\max}, \quad \forall i \in \mathbf{K}.$$

Therefore, robust distributed algorithm take more conservative protection into account of the cognitive radio system. The problem (13) is not convex optimization problem. We may rewrite (13) as follows

$$-\min \sum_{i=1}^{k} \log(1 + \frac{p_i}{\sum_{j \neq i} \bar{\alpha}_{ij}p_j + \varepsilon_o \sqrt{\sum_{j \neq i} p_j^2} + \sigma_i/h_{ii}}) \tag{14}$$

$$s.t. \quad C1 : \sum_{i=1}^{k} (\bar{g}_i + \varepsilon_i)p_i \leq I_{th}, \quad C2 : p_i \leq p_i^{\max}, \quad \forall i \in \mathbf{K}.$$

By using the Lagrange multiplier algorithm, a new objective Lagrange function is defined as

$$L(\{p_i\}, u_i, v_i) =$$

$$-\sum_{i=1}^{k} \log(1 + \frac{p_i}{\sum_{j \neq i} \bar{\alpha}_{ij}p_j + \varepsilon_o \sqrt{\sum_{j \neq i} p_j^2} + \sigma_i/h_{ii}}) + u_i(\sum_i (\bar{g}_i + \varepsilon_i)p_i/I_{th} - 1) + v_i(p_i/p_i^{\max} - 1).$$

$$\tag{15}$$

where $u_i \geq 0$ and $v_i \geq 0$ are Lagrange multipliers for the two constraints in (14), respectively. Furthermore, the updating function is defined as        .

$$u_i(t+1) = \max(u_i(t) + \alpha L\_u_i(t), 0), \ \forall i \in \mathbf{K}. \tag{16}$$

$$v_i(t+1) = \max(v_i(t) + \beta L\_v_i(t), 0), \ \forall i \in \mathbf{K}. \tag{17}$$

where $\alpha$ and $\beta$ are the step size which are positive, and t is the iteration times. Moreover, the corresponding gradient $L\_u_i$ and $L\_v_i$ updating function is given by

$$L\_u_i = \sum_i (\bar{g}_i + \varepsilon_i)p_i - I_{th}, \ L\_v_i = p_i - p_i^{\max}, \ \forall i \in \mathbf{K}. \tag{18}$$

To achieve the optimal solution of each SU in the robust formulation, the optimal solution $p_i^*$ for (14) by considering the Karush-Kuhn-Tucker (KKT) conditions can be calculated through the following equality

$$\frac{\partial L(\{p_i\}, u_i, v_i)}{\partial p_i} = 0, \ \forall i \in \mathbf{K}. \tag{19}$$

Therefore, we can get the optimal solution $p_i^*$ for each SU as follows

$$p_i^* = \frac{1}{(u_i \sum_i (\bar{g}_i + \varepsilon_i)/I_{th} + v_i/p_i^{\max}) \ln 2} - (\sum_{j \neq i} \bar{a}_{ij}p_j + \sigma_i/h_{ii} + \varepsilon_0 \sqrt{\sum_{j \neq i} p_j^2}). \tag{20}$$

Different form the traditional water filling solution, the cognitive radio system will strictly converge to the optimal solution in (20). Hence, the robust distributed algorithm can tackle above formulation [10].

# 4 Performance Evaluation

## 4.1 Simulation Settings

In this section, we describe the detail of parameters setting and the channel model for SUs and PUs in our simulations. Firstly, the related parameters and their typical value are provided in Table 1. And, the Euclidean norm is adopted for all parameters' uncertainty regions in our simulations.

## 4.2 Simulation Results

Simulation results are provided to compare the performance of robust algorithm with the non-robust algorithm under the underlay network scenario. Here, the non-robust method refers to the algorithm that does not take channel uncertainties into account and directly utilizes the parameters all channels as if they were perfect. However, we consider the channel parameter uncertainties in robust algorithm.

**Table 1.** Simulation parameters setting

| Related parameters | Typical valves |
|---|---|
| Number of PUs | 1 |
| Number of SUs | 3 |
| PU maximum interference threshold | $3.5 \times 10^{-10}$ mw |
| Perturbation rang of uncertainty parameters $\varepsilon_0$ | 10% |
| Perturbation rang of uncertainty parameters $\varepsilon_i$ | 10% |
| SU maximum transmit power $P$ | $[1.1, 1.2, 1.3]$ mw |
| Average additive noise power $\sigma_i$ at SU receiver | 0.0001 mw |

In Fig. 1, we compare the power allocation algorithms with iteration times in the non-robust scheme and the robust scheme. With the increasing number of iterations, robust algorithm and non-robust algorithm quickly tend to a stable value that not exceed its power budget, i.e., establish a balance. Simulation results show that the optimal power of robust algorithm is slightly less than the non-robust algorithm. That's because the robust algorithm guarantees an acceptable level of performance under worst case conditions.

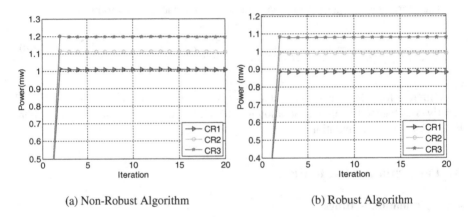

(a) Non-Robust Algorithm          (b) Robust Algorithm

**Fig. 1.** Convergence of robust algorithm and non-robust algorithm

In Fig. 2a, we show the performance of channel capacity for the non-robust scheme and the robust scheme, which characterize the trade-off between uncertainty and networks throughout. Under the worst-case, the maximum channel capacity of robust algorithm is almost equal to the non-robust algorithm, which shows the superiority of the robust algorithm. In Fig. 2b, we compare total interference of various power allocation algorithms. The straight line is the permissible interference power level. It can be observed that the interference caused by SUs transmitter to PU receiver under robust algorithm is always below the permissible threshold while the interference under non-robust algorithm exceed permissible threshold. The non-robust algorithm is not as successful as the robust algorithm at preventing violations of the permissible

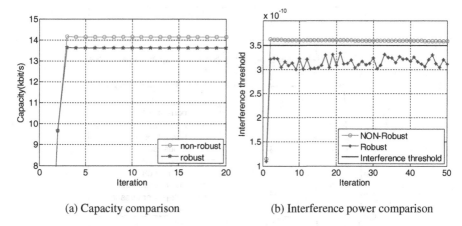

(a) Capacity comparison                    (b) Interference power comparison

**Fig. 2.** Performance comparison for robust scheme and non-robust scheme

interference power level. Therefore, we can summarize that robust algorithm always guarantee the quality of services for PU.

To compare the SINR of SUs receiver, we plot the SUs' SINR for the two power allocation algorithms in Fig. 3. Simulation results show that the SINR of robust algorithm is slightly less than non-robust algorithm because of considering parameter uncertainty under the worst-case. Moreover, the non-robust algorithm violated the permissible interference power level as in Fig. 2b. Therefore, the robust algorithm for cognitive radio wireless ad-hoc networks can attain a good trade-off between uncertainty and capacity.

In Fig. 4, we depict power convergence properties of three users with iteration times for robust algorithm and non-robust algorithm. As seen in Fig. 4, both the proposed scheme and non-robust scheme quickly converge to a certain value which does not exceed the maximum power upper threshold. However, the converge value of

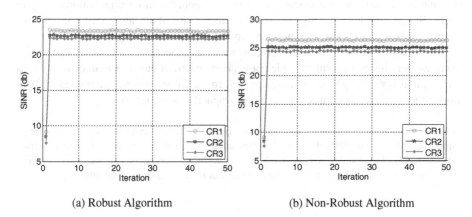

(a) Robust Algorithm                    (b) Non-Robust Algorithm

**Fig. 3.** SU SINR comparison between under robust algorithm and under non-robust algorithm

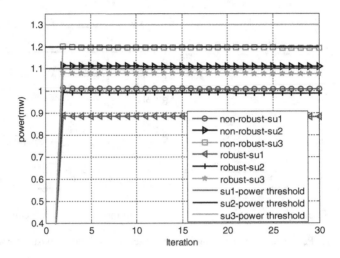

**Fig. 4.** SU power comparison between under robust algorithm and under non-robust algorithm

the proposed scheme is less than that of the non-robust method, it is due to the proposed scheme that considers parameter uncertainty is consider to sacrifice one's own power. These results also demonstrate that the more robustness the system is, the more efficient the robust algorithm is.

## 5  Conclusions

In this paper, we have studied power allocation with parameter uncertainty in underlay CRNs. To maximize the channel capacity under the constraints SU transmit power and interference thresholds, we proposed robust channel capacity maximization algorithm that ensure power threshold and PUs' quality of service requirement. We first describe ellipsoid set model for parameter uncertainty, and formulate it as a standard SOCP problem by considering the worst-case. Then, we apply dual decomposition theory to tackle SOCP problem. Simulation results show that robust algorithm can achieve almost the same maximum channel capacity as the non-robust algorithm.

The study of distributed robust optimization, in general, remains wide open, with many challenging issues and possible applications where robustness to uncertainty is as important as optimality in the nominal model. In the future, we will plan to extend our work to a multiuser system to further study capacity characteristics.

**Acknowledgements.** This work was supported by the Nation Natural Science Foundation of China (Grant No. 61501059) and the Education Department of Jilin Province (Grant No. 2016343). We would like to thank the anonymous reviewers and the editor, whose invaluable comments helped improve the presentation of this paper substantially.

# References

1. Haykin, S.: Cognitive radio: brain-empowered wireless communications. IEEE J. Sel. Areas Commun. **23**, 201–220 (2005)
2. Mitola, J., Maguire, G.Q.: Cognitive radio: making software radios more personal. IEEE Pers. Commun. **6**, 13–18 (1999)
3. Ekin, S., Agarwal, T., Qaraqe, K.A.: Capacity of cognitive radio multiple-access channels in dynamic fading environments. IEEE Sig. Circ. Syst. **9**, 1–4 (2011)
4. Hanif, M.F., Tran, L.N., Jumtti, M., Glisic, S.: On linear precoding strategies for secrecy rate maximization in multiuser multiantenna wireless networks. IEEE Trans. Sig. Process. **62**, 3536–3551 (2014)
5. Hasan, Z., Bansal, G., Hossain, E., Bhargava, V.: Energy-efficient power allocation in OFDM-based cognitive radio systems: a risk-return model. IEEE Trans. Wirel. Commun. **8**, 6078–6088 (2009)
6. Ishihara, S.J.: Robust Kalman filtering for nonlinear systems with parameter uncertainties. In: SICE Annual Conference, pp. 1986–1991. IEEE Press, Sapporo (2014)
7. Xiao, H., Yang, K., Wang, X.D.: Robust power control under channel uncertainty for cognitive radios with sensing delays. IEEE Commun. Soc. **12**, 646–655 (2013)
8. Zhang, L., Liang, Y.C., Xin, Y., Poor, H.V.: Robust cognitive beamforming with partial channel state information. IEEE Trans. Wirel. Commun. **8**, 4143–4153 (2009)
9. Grandhi, S.A., Vijayan, R., Goodman, D.J., Zander, J.: Centralized power control in cellular radio systems. IEEE Trans. Veh. Technol. **42**, 466–468 (1993)
10. Zhou, M.Y., Zhao, X.H., Pan, S., Chen, L.L.: A robust power allocation algorithm in cognitive radio networks. J. Inf. Comput. Sci. **10**, 69–77 (2013)
11. Zheng, Y., Dong, Z.Y., Xu, Y., Meng, K., Zhao, J.H., Qiu, J.: Electric vehicle battery charging/swap stations in distribution systems: comparison study and optimal planning. IEEE Trans. Power Syst. **29**, 221–229 (2014)
12. Boyd, S., Vandenberghe, L.: Convex Optimization. Cambridge University Press, Cambridge (2004)
13. Gao, S., Qian, L., Vaman, D.: Distributed energy efficient spectrum access in cognitive radio wireless ad hoc networks. IEEE Trans. Wirel. Commun. **8**, 5202–5213 (2009)
14. Schreck, J., Wunder, G., Jung, P.: Robust iterative interference alignment for cellular networks with limited feedback. IEEE Trans. Wirel. Commun. **14**, 882–894 (2015)
15. Sanchez, S., Souza, R., Fernandez, E., Reguera, V.: Rate and energy efficient power control in a cognitive radio ad hoc network. IEEE Sig. Process. Lett. **20**, 451–454 (2013)
16. Dong, A., Zhang, H.X., Yuan, D.F.: Probabilistic constraint robust transceiver design for MIMO interference channel networks. J. Commun. **11**, 340–348 (2016)

# Author Index

Printed in the United States
By Bookmasters